Professional dBASE IV™ 1.1 and SQL Programming

PHILIP STEELE

ROBERT HEYDT

John Wiley & Sons, Inc.

New York • Chichester • Brisbane • Toronto • Singapore

Library of Congress Cataloging-in-Publication Data

Steele, Philip. 1941–
Professional dBASE IV 1.1 and SQL programming / Philip Steele. Robert Heydt.
p. cm.
Includes bibliographical references.
ISBN 0-471-50985-X
1. Data base management. 2. dBase IV (Computer program) 3. SQL (Computer program lanaguage I. Heydt, Robert. II. Title.
QA76.9.D3S75 1990
005.75'65—dc20 89-48994
CIP

Printed in the United States of America

90 91 10 9 8 7 6 5 4 3 2 1

To my loving wife Dorothy and daughter Denise who have provided me with the support and time needed to write this book.

P. Steele

To my usually patient wife, Diane; without her encouragement, this book would have been impossible.

R. Heydt

Related Titles of Interest from Wiley

ADVANCED EXCEL FOR THE IBM PC, PS/2, AND COMPATIBLES, Ashley and Fernandez
ADVANCED WORDPERFECT: A POWER USER'S GUIDE, Farrell
WORDSTAR PROFESSIONAL RELEASE 5: AN ADVANCED BOOK, Ashley and Fernandez
R:BASE FOR DOS: A BUSINESS USER'S GUIDE, Condliffe
PARADOX 3.0: A BUSINESS USER'S GUIDE, Condliffe
USING dBASE IV: BASICS FOR BUSINESS, Brownstein
THE PC UPGRADER'S MANUAL: HOW TO BUILD AND EXTEND YOUR SYSTEM, Held
IBM PS/2 USER'S REFERENCE MANUAL, Held
OS/2: FEATURES, FUNCTIONS, AND APPLICATIONS, Krantz, Mizell, and Williams
OS/2: A BUSINESS PERSPECTIVE, Conklin
OS/2 PRESENTATION MANAGER PROGRAMMING, Cheatham, Reich, and Robinson
VENTURA PUBLISHER FOR THE IBM PC: MASTERING DESKTOP PUBLISHING, Jantz
DESKTOP PUBLISHING WITH WORDPERFECT 5.0, Tevis
DESKTOP PUBLISHING WITH PAGEMAKER 3.0: IBM PC AT, PS/2, AND COMPATIBLES, Bove and Rhodes
DESKTOP PUBLISHING WITH PAGEMAKER 3.02: MACINTOSH, Bove and Rhodes
THE POWER OF QUATTRO: A BUSINESS USER'S GUIDE, Salkind
USING LOTUS AGENDA, Goodman and Wolf
MACROS, MENUS, AND MIRACLES FOR LOTUS 1-2-3, Lunsford
LOTUS 1-2-3 RELEASE 2.2, Williams
LOTUS 1-2-3 RELEASE 3, Williams
MASTERING ENABLE OA: OFFICE AUTOMATION SOFTWARE, Spezzano
HARD DISK SMARTS: EVERYTHING YOU NEED TO KNOW TO CHOOSE AND USE YOUR HARD DISK, Bosshardt
INSIDE ALLWAYS: THE SPREADSHEET PUBLISHER, Sandler and Badgett
ADVANCED LOTUS 1-2-3 RELEASE 3, Yu and Harrison
THE NEW DOS 4.0, Christopher, Feigenbaum, and Saliga
DOS 4.0 REFERENCE, Christopher, Feigenbaum, and Saliga
EXCEL: A BUSINESS USER'S GUIDE—IBM AND MACINTOSH, Salkind
DESIGNING INTELLIGENT FRONT ENDS FOR BUSINESS SOFTWARE, Shafer

Preface

This publication is intended for people who already have written many lines of dBASE III™ code, and who wish to upgrade their skills to dBASE IV™.

This publication will:

- Explain each and every command in dBASE IV
- Provide you with examples for each command
- Present a commercial application
- Explain in great detail how the commercial application operates
- Explain SQL
- Explain each and every SQL command
- Present an example of a commercial SQL application
- Explain SQL command and utility functions
- Explain the new security features for both SQL and dBASE IV

How to Use This Publication

This publication is divided into three major sections:

I. dBASE IV commands
II. SQL commands
III. Major Applications

Symbols and conventions are used throughout this publication. Most are the same as those in dBASE manuals, and others reflect programming styles from other languages and manuals. The following typographical conventions are used:

Symbol	Name	Use
*	Asterisk	A comment line in dBASE code
. . .	Ellipsis	Missing related items or lines of code
;	Semicolon	Code continued on the next line
{ }	Braces	Use to show a character that cannot be printed such as a CHR(27) which is the Escape character and cannot be printer on a LASER printer {Esc}
^	Circumflex	Indicates the Control key.^C would mean press and hold down the control key and the press the "C" key simultaneously
[ ]	Brackets square	Indicates that an item is optional
< >	Brackets angle	Indicates that you must supply a specific value of the type required in the brackets
/	Slash	Indicates an either/or choice
K	Kilobyte	1,024 bytes

Versions of the software products used in the code for this publication are always being upgraded. The code in this book is written in dBASE IV release 1.1.

The programs, subroutines, and longer sections of code contained in this publication are available in source code on diskettes (IBM, 5 one-fourth inch, PC-DOS 9 sector double-sided) from the authors. These disks are NOT copy protected in any way and are offered only as a convenience for programmers who do not wish to key these routines themselves. To order, use the form provided at the end of the book.

Acknowledgments

We wish to thank all our friends, colleagues, and clients for their encouragement, ideas, and suggestions.

Contents

Introduction

You probably have been using dBASE II and dBASE III for several years. You know how to add a record to a data base, and you can change the contents of fields, compute fields, and manipulate dates. Now you have read about dBASE IV and you wish to upgrade your skills to include it. This book is intended for all dBase programmers—from beginner to advanced. It is assumed that you, the reader, have written *at least* two medium to large (2,000 to 10,000 lines) dBASE III or dBASE III Plus programs.

You should be familiar with the dBASE IV Control Center. You should know how to build screen forms, reports, queries, and labels. You should be able to create a data base file and be familiar with the dot prompt. This book will *not* cover these elementary techniques.

You do not have to know every new or old dBASE command, as each *programming* command will be covered in detail, but you should be able to accomplish routine file management tasks at the dot prompt, such as listing and indexing data.

This book contains the techniques used by the pros who write in dBASE IV for a living. The examples presented were culled from professional systems that cost thousands of dollars to develop.

In the mid-1970s, George Tate immersed himself in computers after having assembled an Altair 8800. When he had mastered the intricacies of the Altair, Tate set up his own computer repair business, called "The Computer Doctor." He also helped found the Southern California Computer Society, where he met Hal Lashlee.

In 1980, at about the same time that IBM announced the IBM PC®, George Tate and his friend Hal Lashlee were organizing a software distribution company. In the summer of that year, Tate was western sales manager for a computer hardware manufacturer and Lashlee was working as a controller for a southern California banking firm. Inspired by their mutual interest in computers, the two men pooled $7500 and set up the company they called Discount Software. Since there were few software distributors at the time, Discount Software was a success—but it wasn't until six months later, when the two entrepreneurs discovered an obscure software program called Vulcan®, that their company blossomed.

Vulcan was designed by Wayne Ratliff, an engineer who worked for NASA's Jet Propulsion Lab (JPL) in Pasadena, California. The product was a microcomputer data base management program that stored, organized, sorted, and retrieved large amounts of data. Although similar programs were actually available for microcomputers, none were as effective as Vulcan. Ratliff, however, had little time to market his creation, so Vulcan wallowed in near obscurity for almost a year.

Fortunately for Tate and Lashlee, they were able to arrange an exclusive distribution agreement with Ratliff. Because of legal problems, the name Vulcan was dropped and replaced by dBASE II, a catchy, high-tech-sounding moniker suggested by an early marketing consultant to Discount Software. Although the "II" subtly implied an improvement on a previous product, there never was a dBASE I, and to this day that is a source of confusion.

Armed with its new name and an extensive marketing campaign, Vulcan was reintroduced as dBASE II in January 1981. Entering a business software market primed by the likes of VisiCalc and WordStar, the CP/M-based dBASE II was an instant success. When the IBM PC was introduced, Ratliff converted dBASE II to MS-DOS and the product assumed its position as an industry standard. Ashton-Tate extended its leading position in the relational data base market with the introduction of its next data base program, called dBASE III. Designed to take full advantage of the new 16-bit microprocessor, dBASE III was an instant success and provided Ashton-Tate with an effective bridge between the 8-bit and 16-bit environments. dBASE II was improved and upgraded to run on the newest IBM operating systems and dBASE III PLUS was shipped in December 1985. Soon the clone makers attacked the huge installed base of dBASE (over one million copies of dBASE by mid-1986). Ashton-Tate countered with its biggest and best version of dBASE yet, dBASE IV, which was finally shipped in November 1988. This is the product on which we will concentrate in this book.

SECTION I

dBASE IV Commands and Functions

CHAPTER 1

Overview

Even though you have used dBASE III Plus and know most of the commands, the dBASE IV commands are reviewed in this section. Commands and functions that have not changed, have changed very little from dBASE III Plus, are not used for programming, or are elementary will just be listed with an example. Commands and functions that are new or have changed considerably from dBASE III Plus or commands that are complex will be explained in detail, accompanied by an example or two.

Before we start, let us review some general information. If you are an experienced dBASE programmer, you may skip the rest of this section.

dBASE IV has 10 work areas, numbered 1–10 and named A–J, which are available for using data bases concurrently (one data base per work area). Since dBASE IV will attempt to open a data base in the currently selected work area, if more than one data base is to be used at a time, you must explicitly request a particular work area by its number or its name. Once a data base is open, its work area may also be selected by its alias, which is assigned by the USE or ALIAS command or, by default, is the file name itself. To access fields from a data base that is not in the currently selected work area, the field name may be prefixed by the alias name or the work area name using the operator "->", such as "A->LastName".

dBASE IV automatically saves as many commands entered in the interactive command mode as possible. These are stored in order, from most recent to oldest, in memory. The size of the memory area, and, consequently, the maximum number of commands that can be stored, depends on the setting of the HISTORY option in CONFIG.DB. Commands thus saved may be recalled individually for editing and execution using the cursor keys.

The operators available in dBASE IV are grouped into 4 major categories: logical, arithmetic, relational, and string.

LOGICAL (order of precedence)

() to group expressions
.NOT., ! logical negative
.AND. logical AND
.OR. logical OR

ARITHMETIC (order of precedence)

() to group expressions
**, ^ exponentiation
*, / multiplication, division
+, – addition, subtraction

RELATIONAL

< less than
> greater than
<>, # not equal to
<= less than or equal to
>= greater than or equal to

STRING

+ string concatenation
– string concatenation (trailing blanks are moved from the first string to the end of the second string)
$ substring comparison
== character string comparison (trailing blanks are significant when EXACT is ON)

Through the use of SET DEFAULT and SET PATH, dBASE IV enables the user to specify a set of directories (other than the current working directory) to search for files. SET DEFAULT may be used to change the default drive to a drive name that is different from the operating system's default drive. It is important to remember that even though all dBASE IV operations take place on the drive specified by SET DEFAULT, the operating system's default drive remains the same unless it is changed through the DOS CD command.

SET PATH may be used to specify a set of directories to use for file searches once the current directory has been searched. The directories may be specified by either a relative or a fully qualified path name. When dBASE IV attempts to locate a file, it first searches the working directory on the default drive as specified by SET DEFAULT. If the search is unsuccessful, then the path names are used in the order in which they appear in the SET PATH command. If the file name does not specifically include a drive name, the default drive is assumed. These path support rules apply to searches for existing files with only one exception. The DIR command always searches the working directory of the default drive unless a skeleton is supplied with a path name. When files are created by dBASE IV, they are also placed in the working directory of the default drive, unless the file name is qualified with a path name.

In many commands, you will see the phrase "scope" in the command definition. This is used to indicate which records will take place in the operation to be performed. Scope can be defined using one of the following formats:

ALL	Indicates that the operation is to take place for all records in the data base.
NEXT <n>	Indicates that the operation is to be carried out for the next <n> records in the data base.
RECORD <n>	Indicates that record number <n> is to be the subject of the current operation.
REST	Indicates that the operation is to be carried out for a range of records beginning with the current record and ending with the last record in the file.

The scope for a data base operation can be determined by the use of a conditional clause in many dBASE IV commands.

FOR <expression> and WHILE <expression> both indicate which records will be affected during a data base operation.

The WHILE clause causes records to be read only as long as the condition is true. The first time the condition is false, the data base operation ceases.

When the FOR clause is used, all records that meet the condition are affected by the data base operation, however, the entire data base is always searched. FOR and WHILE clauses may appear together in the same dBASE IV statement and may also be used in conjunction with other scope indicators (ALL, NEXT, RECORD, or REST). When FOR and WHILE are both used, the WHILE condition takes precedence.

In Chapter 2, we will look at each dBASE IV command and function.

CHAPTER 2

Commands

! or RUN

Syntax:

```
! <DOS command>
```

or

```
RUN <DOS command>
```

RUN executes a specified DOS command or executable program, from within dBASE IV.

Warnings:

1. The DOS file COMMAND.COM must be in the current directory or be detectable via the DOS COMSPEC parameter.
2. Do not RUN disk reorganization programs like CHKDSK from within dBASE IV. They modify the contents of your disk in a manner that can confuse dBASE IV.

EXAMPLE: To place the current drive and subdirectory into a file, issue the command:

```
RUN CD > DriveFile
```

EXAMPLE: To show the current directory on the screen from inside a dBASE IV program, issue the commands:

```
CLEAR
! DIR/P
```

&&

Syntax:

```
&& ....
```

&& indicates that what follows is the start of a comment. You can use && at the beginning of a line or after a command.

EXAMPLE:

```
memvar  = 14        && initialize numeric memory variable.
memDate = DATE()    && initialize memdate to today.
&& This part of the system is used to . . .
```

???

Syntax:

```
??? [<expC>]
```

??? evaluates <expC> and sends the results to the printer, bypassing printer drivers. This command is used to send characters to the printer that will not change the printer's current row and column position, such as printer control characters. You can use this command to change fonts, turn underline on, and set other printer functions.

EXAMPLE: To reset all the Hewlett-Packard LaserJet settings, use the command:

```
??? "{Esc}E"
```

To set the Hewlett-Packard LaserJet to landscape mode, use

```
???"{Esc}&l1O"
```

or

```
??? "{27}{38}{108}{49}{79}"
```

?/??

Syntax:

```
?/?? [<expression 1>] [PICTURE <expC>]
[FUNCTION <function list>] [AT <expN>]
[STYLE <font number>] [,<expression 2>...][,]
```

?/?? displays an expression or list of expressions separated by commas. This command is used to display strings, variables, and results of calculations. The expressions are evaluated, and their values are displayed on the screen or printer. The difference between "?" and "??" is that "?" displays the value(s) at the beginning of a new line whereas "??" displays the value(s) starting from the last cursor position.

If SET PRINTER is on, the output of the "?/??" command is sent to the printer. If SET CONSOLE is on, the output of the "?/??" command is sent to the console. If SET ALTERNATE is ON and an alternate file is set with SET ALTERNATE TO

<filename>, the output of the "?/??" command is also sent to the alternate file. Any or all of the console, printer, and alternate file devices may be SET ON at any time.

Up to 1024 characters may be displayed or printed.

See the PICTURE / FUNCTION for specifics regarding this option.

AT specifies the column at which the expression displays.

STYLE prints in a specified font or style such as bold or italic, depending on your monitor or printer, using the following codes.

B bold
I Italic
U Underline
R Raised (superscript)
L Lowered (subscript)

The numbers 1 through 5 may be used instead of the five letters. In addition, you may combine codes such as STYLE "BI" for bold italic.

@ CLEAR

Syntax:

```
@ <row1>, <col1> [CLEAR [TO <row2>, <col2>]]
```

@ CLEAR clears the screen within the specified area.

<row1>, <col1> are the coordinates of the upper left corner and <row2>, <col2> are the coordinates of the lower right corner of the area to be cleared, on the screen.

If you omit the CLEAR TO portion of the command @ <row>, <col> will clear the entire line just as if you wrote @ 12,0 CLEAR TO 12,79.

If you omit the TO <row2>, <col2> part of the command @ <row>, <col> CLEAR will clear from <row>, <col> to the bottom of the screen.

EXAMPLE:

```
@ 5,5 CLEAR TO 20,70   && Clears the area from 5,5 to 20,70
@ 5,5                  && Clears the area from 5,5 to 5,79
@ 5,5 CLEAR            && Clears the area from 5,5 to 24,79
```

@. . .SAY. . .GET

Syntax:

```
    @ <row>, <col>
[SAY <expression>
   [PICTURE <expC>] [FUNCTION <function list>]]
[GET <variable>
   [[OPEN] WINDOW <window name>]
   [PICTURE <expC>] [FUNCTION <function list>]
   [RANGE <low>,<high>]] [VALID <condition>]
```

```
[ERROR] <expC>]] [WHEN <condition>]
[DEFAULT <expression>] [MESSAGE <expC>]]
[COLOR [<standard>] [,<enhanced>]]
```

@ . . . SAY/GET creates custom screens and reports for data input and output. SAY displays information in a specified format at <row>, <col>, and GET accepts information at <row>, <col> and permits editing. GET is activated by the READ command.

<row> and <col> are numeric and are used to position the expression. The permitted value for Row is from 0 to 32,767 when using a printer, and from 0 to the maximum line number of the screen display being used. The permitted value for Col is from 0 to 255 on a printer, and 0 to the maximum width of a screen display. When using the window option, <row> and <col> are relative to the upper left corner of the active window.

PICTURE restricts data entry and formats output (see PICTURES/FUNCTIONS for various pictures and functions).

OPEN uses an editing window for memo fields. You do not have to open and close this window if you include the open option in the window option.

^Home is pressed to start entering information in the memo field and ^End is pressed to leave the memo field.

WINDOW uses a separate editing window for memo fields. If this option is omitted, the entire screen is used for memo field editing.

RANGE defines upper and lower GET boundaries. The <low> and <high> expressions must be the same data type. If you skip the field by pressing enter, range checking is ignored.

EXAMPLE:

```
@ 12,12 GET AcctNum PICTURE "999" RANGE 100, 499
```

Values less than 100 and greater than 499 will not be accepted for input in this example.

VALID tests for a valid logical expression. If the condition is not met, the message "*Editing condition not satisfied*" will appear.

EXAMPLE:

```
 @ 12,12 GET AcctNum PICTURE "999";
VALID (AcctNum > PrevAcctN)
```

In this example, if the entered account number is less than the previous account number (defined prior to this statement), the message "*Editing condition not satisfied*" will appear.

ERROR displays a message if VALID is not met. Use this option to replace the standard dBASE IV error message "*Editing condition not satisfied*" with your own custom message.

EXAMPLE:

```
@ 12,12 GET Acctnum PICTURE "9999";
        VALID(Acctnum > PrevAcctN);
        ERROR "Account number must be greater than " +;
              ALLTRIM(STR(PrevAcctN,4,0))
```

This example checks to see if the entered account number is less than the previous account number (defined prior to this statement), and if the result is true, the message "*Account number must be greater than 1234*" will appear.

The WHEN condition is evaluated when the cursor is moved to a GET field. This option is used to skip a field, depending on conditions occurring before this field is reached.

EXAMPLE:
```
@ 12,12 GET AcctNum PICTURE "9999";
                   WHEN Division = 12
```

In this example, the field AcctNum will be skipped unless the previously defined variable "*Division*" contains the value of 12.

DEFAULT supplies a default value for GET. It must match the type of the GET variable and is evaluated only when *adding* records to the data base. This means that an existing value is not overlaid with the default.

EXAMPLE:
```
@ 12,12 GET AcctNum PICTURE "9999" DEFAULT 5555
```

In this example, 5555 will appear in the account number field if a new record is being added to the data base. If there was an existing record with a value of 6666 as the account number, 6666 will appear on the screen.

MESSAGE displays a message at screen bottom when set status is on.

EXAMPLE:
```
@ 12,12 GET AcctNum PICTURE "9999";
MESSAGE "Enter the next account number in sequence"
```

The message "*Enter the next account number in sequence*" will appear centered on the bottom line of the screen when the cursor is on the field account number and a "*READ*" statement has been issued.

COLOR sets the colors for SAY and GET. The standard color is used for SAY and the enhanced color is used for GETs.

EXAMPLES:
```
@ 12,12 GET AcctNum PICTURE "9999";
   COLOR RG+/B,W+/N

@ 12,12 SAY AcctNum PICTURE "9999";
   COLOR RG+/B,W+/N
```

In the first example, the AcctNum field will be bright white on black when it is reached by the cursor. In the second example, the AcctNum field will be bright yellow on blue when it is reached by the cursor.

All of the appropiate previous options may be combined in one SAY or GET statement.

EXAMPLE:
```
@ 12,12 GET AcctNum PICTURE "9999" WHEN Division = 12;
                    VALID(AcctNum > PrevAcctN);
                    DEFAULT PrevAcctN + 1;
                    ERROR "Account number must be " +;
                    "greater than" +;
                    ALLTRIM(STR(PrevAcctN,4,0));
                    MESSAGE "Enter the next number " +;
                            "in sequence";
                    COLOR RG+/B,W+/N
```

@. . .FILL

Syntax:

```
@ <row1>,<col1> FILL TO <row2>,<col2>
[COLOR <color attribute>]
```

@ . . . FILL changes the color of a specified area of the screen. Row1, Col1 are the coordinates of the upper left corner of the area to be filled, while Row2, Col2 indicate the lower right corner. <color attribute> is the color with which the area will be filled. Only the foreground/background colors are affected and the information currently on the screen is changed to these colors. Subsequent commands will revert to the original colors, *not* the fill colors. If you omit the color option, the area specified is cleared, just as if you had used the @. . .CLEAR command.

EXAMPLE:

```
@ 12,12 FILL to 15,60 COLOR W+/R
```

This example will change the data as well as the background in the area from 12,12 to 15,60 to bright white on red. If you want to change only the color or the data, set the background color to the existing color.

EXAMPLE:

```
SET COLOR TO RG+/B
Code = 0
@ 12,12 SAY "Enter code: " GET Code PICTURE "9"
READ
IF Code = 0
    @ 12,11 FILL TO 12,25 COLOR W+/B
ENDIF
```

@. . .TO

Syntax:

```
    @ <row1>,<col1> TO <row2>,<col2>
[DOUBLE/PANEL/<border definition string>]
[COLOR <color attribute>]
```

@ . . . TO draws a box or a line with a default or specified border.

The default border is a single line, unless the default has been changed with the SET BORDER command.

The coordinates row and col refer to the upper left and lower right of the box to be drawn. If the row coordinates are the same, a horizontal line will be drawn. If the col coordinates are the same, a vertical line will be drawn.

[DOUBLE/PANEL/ <border definition string>] Double draws a double-line box rather than a single-line box. Panel draws a solid highlighted border in inverse video. A border definition string is used to draw an unusual box. The characters that define the box are specified by including them in the command. This string may consist of up to eight different characters—four for each of the corners and sides. The characters are written starting from the upper-left-hand corner and continuing clockwise, as shown in the example.

EXAMPLE:

BoxString=' "–", "–", " | ", " ‖ ", "┌", " ╖ ", "└", "╜" '

The variable BoxString would be used to generate the box shown using the command:

```
@ 12,12 TO 16,19 &BoxString
```

Note that the entire variable "Boxstring" is enclosed in single quotes.

ACCEPT

Syntax:

```
ACCEPT [<prompt>] TO <memvar>
```

ACCEPT issues a prompt for keyboard entry. Prompt may be a character memory variable or character string.

Entered data can be up to 254 characters long, and must be terminated by Carriage Return. It is always stored as character data. If <memvar> is used, its contents are displayed on the screen. If <memvar> is a character string literal, it must be delimited.

EXAMPLE:

```
ACCEPT "Enter your first name:" TO FirstName
```

In this example, the message *"Enter your first name:"* will appear on the screen and wait for you to reply. After you enter your first name, you terminate the entry by pressing the enter key.

ACTIVATE MENU

Syntax:

```
ACTIVATE MENU <menu name> [PAD <pad name>]
```

ACTIVATE MENU activates a previously defined menu and displays it over the existing display.

If you use the prompt <pad name>, the highlight bar appears at that prompt.

The last ACTIVATEd menu is always the only active menu. To move between menu prompt pads, use the left and right arrow keys. The pads are always accessed in the order in which they were defined.

EXAMPLES:

```
ACTIVATE MENU MainMenu PAD Return
ACTIVATE MENU UtilMenu
```

In the first example, the *"MainMenu"* will pop up over any existing information on the screen and the highlight bar will be at the *"Return"* prompt. In the second example, the *"UtilMenu"* will pop up over any existing information on the screen and the highlight bar will be at the first pad.

ACTIVATE POPUP

Syntax: `ACTIVATE POPUP <popup name>`

ACTIVATE POPUP activates a previously defined pop up menu.

Only one pop-up menu can be active at a time. The ACTIVATE POPUP command cannot be issued if a pop-up menu is already active. To deactivate a pop-up menu, press Esc, or use the DEACTIVATE POPUP, then use the ACTIVATE POPUP <popup name> command. The new pop up will replace the active pop up.

When one pop-up menu activates another, the first pop up is suspended until the second is deactivated.

EXAMPLE:

```
ACTIVATE POPUP Add
```

This example activates the previously defined pop-up menu add.

ACTIVATE SCREEN

Syntax: `ACTIVATE SCREEN`

ACTIVATE SCREEN restores access to the entire CRT screen. The most recently active window still remains on the screen, but it is no longer used. It can be overprinted, scrolled up, or cleared.

Use the ACTIVATE SCREEN command to place text outside a window. However, make sure that you ACTIVATE WINDOW, if necessary, when you are finished with the full screen display.

To remove the window, deactivate it.

EXAMPLE:

```
ACTIVATE SCREEN
CLEAR
```

This example removes the active window from the screen by using the ACTIVATE SCREEN command followed by the CLEAR command to erase the entire screen.

ACTIVATE WINDOW

Syntax: `ACTIVATE WINDOW <window name list>/ALL`

ACTIVATE WINDOW displays the named window list and activates a specified window. All screen output is then directed to the active window. Remember that only one window can be active at a time.

When the ALL option is invoked, all defined windows currently in memory are displayed, and the window defined last becomes the active window.

EXAMPLES:

```
ACTIVATE WINDOW StartUp

ACTIVATE WINDOW ALL
```

The first example activates the StartUp window; the second example displays all the defined windows and activates the window that was defined last.

APPEND

Syntax:

```
APPEND [BLANK]
```

APPEND adds a record to the end of the active data base file and starts full screen data entry if the BLANK option is omitted.

BLANK adds a blank record to the end of the data base and does not start full screen data entry.

EXAMPLE:

```
USE Clients     && activates the Clients file
APPEND BLANK    && adds a blank record to the end
                && of the file
```

APPEND FROM

Syntax:

```
APPEND FROM
<file name> / ? / ARRAY <array name>
[[TYPE] <file type>]
[FOR <condition>]
```

APPEND FROM adds records to the end of the selected data base from the specified source file. All data contained in matching field names will be copied from the FROM file into the active data base.

The ARRAY option causes the contents of each row in the named array to be added to the data base.

TYPE SDF/DELIMITED [WITH <delimiter>/BLANK]. If the FROM <file name> is not a data base, the TYPE clause is used to specify the physical design of the file.

The SDF (System Data Format ASCII) file looks exactly like the description in the data base. There are no separators between fields and all the defined characters must be present. All records are the same length and end with a carriage return and line feed.

EXAMPLE: DBF definition:

```
Field1 is Character 12
Field2 is Numeric 5
Field3 is Character 4
```

```
SDF data:   abcdef......00123abcd
            Test data   10000 new

   SELECT A  && Use a previously opened database
   APPEND FROM NewFile SDF
```

In the DELIMITED (delimited format) ASCII file, data is appended character by character, starting on the left. Each field is separated from the next by a comma or the optionally specified character. In addition, double quotation marks (") enclose character data. All records do not have to be the same length. However, they all must end with a carriage return and line feed.

EXAMPLE: Use the previous DBF definition.

```
DELIMITED data: "abcdef......",123,"abcd"
                "Test data",10000," new"

   SELECT A  && Use a previously opened database
   APPEND FROM NewFile DELIMITED
```

The array option provides a convenient way to add data to a data base quickly. Data is added element by element from the array to the data base.

EXAMPLE: Use the previous DBF definition.

```
ARRAY data:
    DECLARE InArray[3,2]
    InArray [1,1] = "abcdef......"
    InArray [2,1] = 123
    InArray [3,1] = "abcd"
    InArray [1,2] = "Test data"
    InArray [2,2] = 10000
    InArray [3,2] = "new"
    SELECT A  && Use a previously opened data base
    APPEND FROM ARRAY InArray
```

APPEND MEMO FROM

Syntax:

```
APPEND MEMO <memo field name>
FROM <file name>
[OVERWRITE]
```

APPEND MEMO appends the contents of any text file into a memo field. If the field name is not specified, the first memo field in the data base file structure is used. New text is appended to existing text unless the OVERWRITE option is chosen.

OVERWRITE erases existing text before appending new text.

EXAMPLE:

```
APPEND MEMO FormLetter FROM InputForm.TXT;
OVERWRITE
```

In this example, a text input document "InputForm" is read into the memo field name "FormLetter" in the active data base. Existing information is deleted because the OVERWRITE option is specified.

ASSIST

Syntax:

```
ASSIST
```

This command activates the dBASE IV Control Center, which gives you access to your data, reports, etc., through a menu interface. It is very helpful to beginners because they do not have to remember the commands to be entered at the dot prompt.

Good programming practices prohibit the use of this command in a program.

EXAMPLE:

```
ASSIST
```

AVERAGE

Syntax:

```
AVERAGE [<expN list>]
[<scope>]
[FOR <condition>]
[WHILE <condition>]
[TO <memvar list>/TO ARRAY <array name>]
```

AVERAGE computes the arithmetic mean of numeric expressions and stores the results to variables or arrays. All records, even those not containing data, are included unless otherwise specified by the <scope>, WHILE, or FOR clauses.

Since zero and blank do not exist for numeric data (a blank record is defined as zero by dBASE), you need another method to distinguish them during an AVERAGE operation or an incorrect result will occur. See the third example.

EXAMPLES:

```
AVERAGE Age TO AvgAge

AVERAGE Age, Salary FOR Age > 21 TO ARRAY Two

AVERAGE Age, Salary FOR Age > 21 .AND. Salary > 0;
  TO ARRAY Two
```

The first example computes the average of all the values contained in the field "Age". If there is missing data, the result will be in error. For example, there are 10 records in the data base and only five of them have data in the age field. The values are 25, 23, 21, 21, 30. The average is 24; however, the first example would produce an average of 12. In the second example, the age and salary for people in the data base who are older than 21 would be stored in the array Two, and the results to the command would be correct for the age but may be incorrect for the salary. The third example would produce correct results for both fields.

BEGIN TRANSACTION

Syntax:

```
BEGIN TRANSACTION [<path name>]
   <transaction commands>
END TRANSACTION
```

BEGIN TRANSACTION creates a transaction log file. This file records changes to data base files that occur before the END TRANSACTION command is reached. These changes may be undone by using the ROLLBACK command before the END TRANSACTION is executed.

END TRANSACTION commits the changes to the data base and removes the option of using the ROLLBACK command.

EXAMPLE:

```
ON ERROR DO FixIt WITH "Master"
BEGIN TRANSACTION
   ...
   ...
END TRANSACTION
PROCEDURE FIXIT
PARAMETERS FileInUse
   ROLLBACK FileInUse
   RETURN
*END:FIXIT
```

BROWSE

Syntax:

```
BROWSE [NOINIT] [NOFOLLOW] [NOAPPEND]
[NOMENU] [NOEDIT] [NODELETE] [NOCLEAR]
[COMPRESS] [FORMAT] [LOCK <expN>]
[WIDTH <expN>] [FREEZE <field name>]
[WINDOW <window name>]
[FIELDS <field name1> [/R]
   [/<column width>] /<calculated   field name1>
             = <expression1>]
   [,<field name2> [/R]
   [/<column width>] /<calculated   field name2>
             = <expression2>]  ...]
```

BROWSE provides a view of your data base in which up to 17 records are displayed vertically and as many fields as will fit on the screen are displayed horizontally. You can move the data from record to record or from field to field, examining, modifying, adding, or deleting records. To toggle help on or off, press F1. Help shows which control keys to use for scrolling, editing memo fields, and exiting BROWSE with and without saving your changes. A menu is provided to assist you. The menu selections and options include:

Top	Move the record pointer to the first logical record.
Bottom	Move the record pointer to the last logical record.
Record	Move the record pointer to a specified record number.
Find	Move the record pointer to the record corresponding to the specified key field in an indexed data base.
Skip	Move the record pointer forward or backward a specified number of records.
LOCK	Sets the number of contiguous columns to remain fixed on the screen during the browse operation.
FREEZE	Confines cursor to the one field to be edited.
NOINIT	Uses a previously defined BROWSE table.
FIELDS	Specifies a subset of fields to be browsed.
NOFOLLOW	Does not redisplay a record according to the new key value when a key field is changed—the data base must be indexed for this operation to apply.
NOMENU	Prevents the use and display of the menu.
NOAPPEND	Prevents the user from adding new records.
WIDTH	Limits the column width for character fields.
NOMODIFY	Prevents all modifications of the data base(s).
NOEDIT	Prevents editing of records.
NODELETE	Prevents deletion of records.
NOCLEAR	Causes the display to remain unchanged after the user exits browse.
COMPRESS	Allows for two additional lines of data by removing unnecessary displayed characters.
FORMAT	Activates a predefined .fmt file for use with the browse command.
WINDOW	Uses a predefined window to contain the browse data.
/R	Makes a field read only.

An excellent use for the BROWSE command in a program is for displaying key fields of data so that the user can view a formatted screen based on the record selected in the command.

EXAMPLE:

```
SELECT A
GOTO TOP
BROWSE FIELDS FirstName, LastName, City, State;
        NOAPPEND NOMENU NOEDIT;
        NODELETE NOMODIFY
DO ShowRec   && Custom edit procedure
```

CALCULATE

Syntax:

```
CALCULATE [<scope>] <option list>
[FOR <condition>]
```

```
[WHILE <condition>]
[TO <memvar list>/TO ARRAY <array name>]
```

CALCULATE processes specified records using one or more financial and aggregate functions from the <option list> until the <scope> is exhausted or the FOR or WHILE clause ceases to be true.

Only the following functions <option list> can be used with the CALCULATE command. Note that MAX() and MIN() are also stand-alone functions.

```
AVG(<expN>)
CNT()
MAX(<exp>)
MIN(<exp>)
NPV(<rate>,<flows>,<initial>)
STD(<expN>)
SUM(<expN>)
VAR(<expN>)
```

EXAMPLES:

```
USE MyData
CALCULATE FOR Salary > 50000 AVG(Salary);
   TO HighRollers
? The average salary for high rollers is:
   LTRIM(STR(HighRollers, 7,0))
```

The average salary for high rollers is $123,512.

```
USE TestData
CALCULATE AVG(Grades), STD(Grades) TO;
   AGrades, SDGrades
? "The average grade is " + STR(AGrades,5,2) $" +;
 " and the standard deviation is " + ;
 LTRIM(STR(SDGrades,10,5))
```

The average grade is 74.25 and the standard deviation is 5.33333.

CALL

Syntax:

```
CALL <module name>
[WITH <expression list>]
```

CALL executes a binary file <module name> previously placed in memory using the LOAD command.

<expression list> is a character expression, a memory variable, or an array element containing the parameters being passed to the binary file.

The CALL command executes a binary file that has been previously LOADed into memory. The WITH option is used to pass a parameter to the binary subroutine. It is not necessary to specify an extension on the CALLed file since the extension is stripped from the file when it is LOADed. On entry into the CALLed module, the Code Segment(CS) points to the beginning of the module. The Data Segment(DS) and BX register pair points to the first byte of the parameter passed using the WITH option. If no parameter is passed, BX contains 0.

EXAMPLES:

```
CALL Cursor WITH "OFF"
  && Calls Cursor.Bin to turn the cursor off.

CALL NewTest WITH "ABC"
  && Calls NewTest.Bin with the string "ABC".
```

CANCEL

Syntax:

```
CANCEL
```

The CANCEL command stops the execution of a dBASE IV program file, closes all open program files, and returns to the dot prompt. Procedure files are not closed. Control is returned to either the normal interactive keyboard mode or the host operating system. If a program is executing under the Runtime version, dBASE IV will terminate and return control to the host operating system. If a program is executing under the Development version of dBASE IV, then control is returned to the normal interactive keyboard command mode. When the CANCEL command is executed, all private memory variables are released.

EXAMPLES:

```
IF Password < > "JellyFish"
   CANCEL
ELSE
   DO SecretCode
ENDIF

ON ERROR CANCEL
&& returns control to the dot prompt when an error is
encountered.
```

CASE

Part of the DO CASE programming construct.

Syntax:

```
DO CASE
   CASE <condition>
     <commands>
   CASE <condition>
     <commands>
[OTHERWISE
     <commands>]
ENDCASE
```

When the DO CASE command is executed, CASE <condition> sets up a logical statement (such as A = B) for evaluation. Successive CASE statements are examined sequentially and their <condition> expressions evaluated. The first CASE <condition> that evaluates as ".T." causes the <commands> following it to be executed and no further CASE statements are evaluated. If no <condition> is ".T.", the OTHERWISE <commands> are executed (if present). If no CASE statements are true, and there is no OTHERWISE, dBASE IV goes to the first command following ENDCASE. One, and only one, CASE will be executed—the first one whose <condition> is true, no matter how many other CASE statements have a true <condition>.

EXAMPLE:

```
DO WHILE .T.
   DO CASE
      CASE MenuChoice = "ADD"
        DO AddProc
      CASE MenuChoice = "DELETE"
        DO DelProc
      CASE MenuChoice = "EDIT"
        DO EditProc
      CASE MenuChoice = "RETURN"
        EXIT
      OTHERWISE
        DO MainMenu
   ENDCASE
   SET COLOR TO &ColStandard
ENDDO    && .T.
RETURN
```

This example is a typical use of the CASE statement; namely, to control actions depending on a menu choice.

CHANGE

Syntax:

```
CHANGE [NOINIT] [NOFOLLOW] [NOAPPEND]
[NOMENU] [NOEDIT] [NODELETE] [NOCLEAR]
[<record number>] [FIELDS <field list>]
[<scope>] [FOR <condition>]
[WHILE <condition>]
```

CHANGE and EDIT are identical.

CHANGE allows full screen editing of specified fields and records in the active data base file. All records are available for editing unless a <scope>, FOR, or WHILE clause is specified. If a SET FORMAT TO file is active, the @ . . . SAY/GET commands in the format file control the screen layout used for CHANGing; otherwise, a default, built-in screen layout is used.

<record number> starts the edit on specified record, but lets you move to other records.

The <scope> keyword RECORD limits the edit to a single record.

NOINIT causes the CHANGE table not to be initialized but to use the CHANGE table from the most recent CHANGE session.

NOFOLLOW applies only to an indexed file. It prevents the reordering of the records if the new current record is changed so that it would normally be repositioned.

NOAPPEND prevents the addition of new records.

NOMENU prevents access to the menu bar.

NOEDIT prevents editing of records.

NODELETE prevents the deletion of records.

NOCLEAR causes the table to remain on screen after the user exits CHANGE.

EXAMPLE:

```
CHANGE NOAPPEND NOFOLLOW FIELDS;
LastName, FirstName,  SSN, Address
```

CHDIR

Syntax:

```
CHDIR<[drive:]path>
```

This command changes the current directory on a disk drive. If you omit the [drive:], CHDIR changes the directory on the current drive. *Note:* You can use the DOS defaults "." for the current directory and ".." for the parent directory.

EXAMPLE:

```
SET COLOR TO W+/B
CHDIR H:.              && Current directory is dBASE.
CHDIR H:SAMPLES        && Change the directory to
                       && dBASE\SAMPLES.
```

CLEAR

Syntax:

```
CLEAR [ALL / FIELDS / GETS / MEMORY /
   TYPEAHEAD / MENUS / POPUPS / WINDOWS]
```

This command erases the screen, repositions the cursor to the lower left-hand corner of the screen, and releases all pending GETs created with the @ command.

ALL closes files, releases memory variables, and selects work area 1.

FIELDS releases the SET FIELDS list.

GETS releases the current @. . .GET variables from READ access.

MEMORY releases all memory variables.

TYPEAHEAD clears the type-ahead buffer.

MENUS erases menus from screen and memory.

POPUPS erases pop-up menus.

WINDOWS releases window definitions from memory.

EXAMPLES:

```
CLEAR            && Clears the screen.
CLEAR WINDOWS    && Releases window definitions.
```

CLOSE

Syntax:

```
CLOSE ALL / ALTERNATE / DATABASES /
        FORMAT / INDEX / PROCEDURE
```

ALL closes all files of all types.
ALTERNATE closes alternate file.
DATABASES closes data base files.
FORMAT closes format files.
INDEX closes index files.
PROCEDURE closes procedure files.

EXAMPLES:

```
CLOSE ALL      && Closes all open files.
CLOSE INDEX    && Closes all the indexes.
```

COMPILE

Syntax:

```
COMPILE <file name exp> [RUNTIME]
```

COMPILE reads a file containing dBASE IV commands and creates executable code file (.DBO). Compile does not *really* compile a .PRG file. It creates a pseudo object file that can be executed by dBASE IV. A true compiler generates an .OBJ file that can be linked, producing an .EXE file. An .EXE file is a stand-alone file that can be executed without the presence of either the dBASE IV system or the RUNTIME system. A true compiler is an option available with the developer's edition. The .DBO concept provides faster execution and complete source code error checking, but still requires a copy of dBASE IV or RUNTIME to execute.

If you use MODIFY COMMAND or an external editor specified in Config.db, any prior .dbo of the same name will be written over. If you use an outside editor to create program files and do not SET DEVELOPMENT ON, you must recompile the source code files after modifying them.

RUNTIME causes dBASE IV to print errors if it encounters a command that is illegal in RUNTIME.

EXAMPLE:

```
COMPILE MAIN    && Compiles the MAIN.PRG file.
```

CONTINUE

Syntax:

```
CONTINUE
```

CONTINUE searches for the next record in the active data base file that meets the condition specified by the most recent LOCATE command issued in the current work area.

CONTINUE works only if the last LOCATE was successful and the record pointer has not been moved in the work area.

EXAMPLE:

```
USE MyFile
LOCATE FOR Salary > 50000  &&  Found record = 12
CONTINUE       &&  Found record = 23
CONTINUE       &&  Found record = 42
CONTINUE       &&  EOF() .T.
```

CONVERT

Syntax:

```
CONVERT [TO <expN>]
```

CONVERT adds a field (_dbaselock) to a data base structure that in multiuser user systems, contains information pursuant to change detection and identification of users' locking records.

This command is used in conjunction with the CHANGE() and LKSYS() functions.

The _dbaselock field contains the following.

COUNT A two-byte hexadecimal number used by the CHANGE() function.

TIME A three-byte hexadecimal number containing the time a lock was placed.

DATE A three-byte hexadecimal number containing the date a lock was placed.

NAME A zero- to 16-character containing the log-in name that placed the lock, if a lock is active.

EXAMPLE:

```
CONVERT          &&  The default form, an 8 character
                 &&  log-in name will be saved.
CONVERT TO 24    &&  A 16 character log-in name;
                 &&  will be saved.
CONVERT TO 8     &&  No log-in name will be saved.
```

COPY

Syntax:

```
COPY TO <file name> [[TYPE] <filetype>]
[FIELDS <field list>]
[<scope>]
[FOR <condition>]
[WHILE <condition>]
```

Command duplicates all or part of an active data base file, creating a new file. Records marked for deletion *are* copied unless explicitly excluded or SET DELETED is ON.

```
<filetype> = DBASEII / DELIMITED / DIF / FW2 / RPD / SDF /
                SYLK / WKS
```

EXAMPLES:

```
COPY TO MyFile FIELDS LastName FOR State = "NY"
* Creates a dBASE IV .DBF file containing records.
* from NY state and consisting of one field (LastName).
COPY TO NEW123 FOR .NOT. DELETED() WKS
* Creates a Lotus 1-2-3 WKS file for all nondeleted records.
* Each .DBF record becomes a row and each field becomes a
* column.
```

COPY FILE

Syntax:

```
COPY FILE <file name>  TO <file name>
```

COPY FILE creates a duplicate of any closed file.

If you copy a data base file that has memo fields, the associated memo (.dbt) file must be copied separately. The associated production (.mdx) file must also be copied separately. You *must* specify both file extensions. You can also specify the drive and subdirectories.

EXAMPLES:

```
COPY FILE Main.Prg TO MyMain.Prg
* Makes a copy of Main.Prg.
COPY FILE E:TESTMain.DBT TO NewMemo.DBT
* Copies a Memo file from another drive and directory.
```

COPY INDEXES

Syntax:

```
COPY INDEXES <.ndx file list>
[TO <.mdx file name>]
```

Command converts a list of up to 47 .ndx index files to one .mdx index file. If you do not specify a .mdx file with the TO clause, the tag is written to the production .mdx file. If the production .mdx does not exist, it is created with the same name as the active data base file, and the header of the .dbf is updated to indicate the presence of a production .mdx file.

EXAMPLE:

```
USE MyFile INDEX LastName, SSN, Vendor
COPY INDEXES LastName, Vendor TO MASTER
```

```
* The index files LastName.NDX and Vendor.NDX
* have been added (as tags) to the index MASTER.MDX.
```

COPY MEMO

Syntax:

```
COPY MEMO <memo field name>
TO <file name> [ADDITIVE]
```

Command copies the contents of the memo field in the current record to the named file. If you do not provide an extension for the TO file, a .txt extension is used. If the field name is not specified, the first memo field in the data base file structure is used.

ADDITIVE causes the contents of the memo field to be appended to the end of the file.

EXAMPLE:

```
USE MyFile
SEEK "STEELE"
COPY MEMO Resume TO ResSum ADDITIVE

* The contents of RESUME (a memo field) are appended
* to the end of the ResSum file.
```

COPY STRUCTURE

Syntax:

```
COPY STRUCTURE TO <file name expression>
[FIELDS <field list>]
```

COPY STRUCTURE creates a duplicate data base file with the structure of the file in USE. No records are copied.

The FIELDS option causes only specified fields to be copied to the new structure. If no fields are specified, dBASE IV copies the entire structure.

EXAMPLES:

```
USE MyFile
COPY STRUCTURE TO YourFile

* An empty copy of MyFile called YourFile was created.
* Equivalent to the following commands:

* COPY FILE MyFile.DBF TO YourFile.DBF
* USE YourFile
* ZAP
* USE MyFile

USE MyFile
COPY STRUCTURE TO YourFile FIELDS;
      LastName, FirstName, Address
```

```
* Creates an empty new file called YourFile
* containing three fields: LastName, FirstName, Address.
```

COPY STRUCTURE EXTENDED

Syntax: COPY TO <file name> STRUCTURE EXTENDED

Command creates a new database file with five fields for each field in the currently active database file.

```
FIELD_NAME  && Field name.
FIELD_TYPE  && Data type.
FIELD_LEN   && Field width.
FIELD_DEC   && Number of decimal places (in a numeric field).
FIELD_IDX   && Index flag.
```

The main use of this command is in an application program to create or modify a data base file without using an interactive process.

EXAMPLE:

```
USE MyFile
COPY TO NewStru STRUCTURE EXTENDED
USE NewFile
ZAP
APPEND BLANK
REPLACE;
   FIELD_NAME WITH "Vendor";
   FIELD_TYPE WITH "C";
   FIELD_LEN  WITH 15;
   FIELD_DEC  WITH 0;
   FIELD_IDX  WITH .T.
APPEND BLANK
REPLACE;
   FIELD_NAME WITH "Address";
   FIELD_TYPE WITH "C";
   FIELD_LEN  WITH 25;
   FIELD_DEC  WITH 0;
   FIELD_IDX  WITH .F.
...
CREATE NewFile FROM NewStru
```

This code fragment will create a .DBF file called NewFile by first creating a STRUCTURE EXTENDED file, then zapping it and creating new records containing the structure desired in the new file.

COPY TAG

Syntax:

```
COPY TAG <tag name> [OF <.mdx file name>]
TO <.ndx file name>
```

COPYTAG copies the tag from a .mdx index file to a .ndx index file. The tag must come from an open .mdx file, and the data base file must be in use. It is used to export a dBASE IV index file to a dBASE III application.

EXAMPLE:

```
USE MyFile
COPY TAG Name OF Master TO LastName

* Creates the index file LastName.NDX from MASTER.MDX.

COPY TAG Vendor OF Master TO Vendor

* Create the index file Vendor.NDX from MASTER.MDX.
```

COPY TO ARRAY

Syntax:

```
COPY TO ARRAY <array name>
[FIELDS <fields list>]
[<scope>]
[FOR <condition>]
[WHILE <condition>]
```

COPY TO ARRAY fills an existing ARRAY structure with one or more records from the active data base file. Each row in the array holds a data base record and each column in the array holds a data base field.

EXAMPLE:

```
USE MyFile
COUNT FOR Salary > 50000 TO BigDeals

* Determines the number of array elements needed.

DECLARE BigShots[BigDeals,8]

* Declares the array large enough to hold the data base.

COPY TO ARRAY BigShots FOR Salary > 50000

* Put the data base into the array.
```

COUNT

Syntax:

```
COUNT [TO <memvar>] [<scope>]
[FOR <condition>]
[WHILE <condition>]
```

COUNT tallies the number of records in the active data base that match specified conditions. The "TO" option stores the tally in a memory variable. Records marked for deletion are counted only if DELETE is SET to OFF.

EXAMPLE:

```
USE MyFile
COUNT FOR Salary > 50000 TO BigDeals
* Counts the number of records where the contents of
* the Salary field is greater than 50,000 and stores the
* result in the memory variable BigDeals.
```

CREATE FROM

Syntax:

```
CREATE <file name>
[FROM <structure extended file>]
```

CREATE FROM creates the structure for a new data base file and adds the file to the directory. The new file becomes the active data base file in the currently selected work area.

FROM forms a new file from one created with the COPY STRUCTURE EXTENDED command.

The main use of this command is in an application program to create or modify a data base file without using an interactive process.

EXAMPLE:

```
USE MyFile
COPY TO NewStru STRUCTURE EXTENDED
USE NewFile
ZAP
APPEND BLANK
REPLACE;
   FIELD_NAME WITH "Vendor";
   FIELD_TYPE WITH "C";
   FIELD_LEN  WITH 15;
   FIELD_DEC  WITH 0;
   FIELD_IDX  WITH .T.
APPEND BLANK
REPLACE;
   FIELD_NAME WITH "Address";
   FIELD_TYPE WITH "C";
   FIELD_LEN  WITH 25;
   FIELD_DEC  WITH 0;
   FIELD_IDX  WITH .F.
...
CREATE NewFile FROM NewStru
APPEND BLANK
DO GetNewData
```

This code fragment will create a .DBF file called NewFile by first creating a STRUCTURE EXTENDED file, then zapping it and creating new records containing the structure desired in the new file. NewFile is automatically added as active when it is created. A blank record is added and filled with data.

CREATE/MODIFY LABEL

Syntax: `CREATE/MODIFY LABEL <file name>/?`

This command is a full screen, menu-driven command that is used to create or modify the layout and design of labels that can be printed from data base files.

? allows you to select a file from a list of existing label form files. Unless otherwise specified, dBASE IV creates the file with a .lbl extension and generates a file with a .lbg file extension. LABEL FORM uses .lbg to create the .lbo file for printing labels. If a catalog is opened and SET CATALOG is ON, the label file is added to the catalog.

EXAMPLE: Since this a full screen, menu-driven command, no example can be provided.

CREATE/MODIFY REPORT

Syntax: `CREATE/MODIFY REPORT <file name> /?`

This command is a full screen, menu-driven command used to create or modify the layout and design of reports that will be based on your data base files.

? allows you to select a file from a list of existing report form files.

Report form files have a .frm extension. CREATE / MODIFY creates a .frg file with the same name. REPORT FORM compiles the .frg file into .fro file. If a catalog is opened and SET CATALOG is ON, the report form file is added to the catalog.

EXAMPLE: Since this a full screen, menu-driven command, no example can be provided.

CREATE/MODIFY QUERY

Syntax: `CREATE/MODIFY QUERY <file name>/?`

This command creates or edits query design screens. A query file has a .qbe extension. The extension .upd is an update query file. Earlier versions of dBASE .vue files can be read by dBASE IV.

? allows you to select a file from a list of existing query files. If a catalog is opened and SET CATALOG is ON, the query file is added to the catalog.

EXAMPLE: Since this a full screen, menu-driven command, no example can be provided.

CREATE/MODIFY APPLICATION

Syntax: `CREATE/MODIFY APPLICATION <file name>/?`

This command starts the Applications Generator, which is used to create or modify an application (.app) file and related files. Related file extensions are as follows:

`.bar`	horizontal bar menu
`.str`	structure list
`.pop`	pop-up menu
`.val`	values list
`.fil`	files list
`.bch`	batch process

? allows you to select a file from a list of existing .app files. If a catalog is opened and SET CATALOG is ON, only the application (.app) that you create is added to the catalog. Any other object that you create (.bar, .pop, .fil., .str, .val, or .bch) is added to the current subdirectory.

EXAMPLE: Since this a full screen, menu-driven command, no example can be provided.

CREATE/MODIFY SCREEN

Syntax: `CREATE/MODIFY SCREEN <file name>/?`

This command is a full screen, menu-driven command that is used to create or modify custom screen forms (.scr). When you save a screen form, a .fmt file is created. The SET FORMAT command compiles .fmt into .fmo files.

? allows you to select a file from a list of existing screen format files. If a catalog is opened and SET CATALOG is ON, the query and format files are added to the catalog.

EXAMPLE: Since this a full screen, menu-driven command, no example can be provided.

CREATE/MODIFY VIEW

Syntax:

```
CREATE/MODIFY VIEW <file name>/?
[FROM ENVIRONMENT]
```

This command is a full screen, menu-driven command that is used to create or change files that link one or more related data base files and their ancillary files. This command is identical to CREATE/MODIFY QUERY.

? allows you to select a file from a list of existing view files in the open catalog. FROM ENVIRONMENT builds a view file (.vue) that is compatible with dBASE III

PLUS. If a catalog is opened and SET CATALOG is ON, the query file is added to the catalog.

EXAMPLE: Since this a full screen, menu-driven command, no example can be provided.

DBLINK

Syntax:

```
DBLINK <input file name>/[L]
```

This is a stand-alone utility run from the DOS prompt. It causes the specified file and all format files, command files, and procedures that it references to be linked together into a single object file.

`/L` generates a report of the programs and object files that were linked.

EXAMPLE: Since this a stand-alone utility run from the DOS prompt, no example can be provided.

DEACTIVATE MENU

Syntax:

```
DEACTIVATE MENU
```

Command deactivates the active bar menu and erases it from the screen while leaving it intact in memory.

Control is returned to the program line immediately following the one that activated the menu. If this command is executed from a called procedure, any command following DEACTIVATE is *not* executed. This command has no effect when executed from the dot prompt. Pressing Esc produces the same result.

EXAMPLE:

```
DEFINE MENU Test MESSAGE "This is a test"
DEFINE PAD X1 OF TEST PROMPT "Test 1" AT 0,0
DEFINE PAD X2 OF TEST PROMPT "Test 2" AT 0,20
DEFINE PAD X3 OF TEST PROMPT "Test 3" AT 0,50
ON SELECTION PAD X1 OF Test DO Proc1
ON SELECTION PAD X2 OF Test DO Proc1
ON SELECTION PAD X3 OF Test DEACTIVE MENU
ACTIVATE MENU Test
```

DEACTIVATE POPUP

Syntax:

```
DEACTIVATE POPUP
```

This command deactivates an active pop-up menu and erases it from the screen while leaving it intact in memory. Any text that was covered by the pop-up menu is redisplayed. Pressing Esc produces the same result.

EXAMPLE:

```
DEFINE POPUP Test FROM 5,20
DEFINE BAR 1 OF TEST  PROMPT "Test 1"
DEFINE BAR 2 OF TEST  PROMPT "Test 2"
DEFINE BAR 3 OF TEST  PROMPT "Exit"
ON SELECTION POPUP Test DO Proc
ACTIVATE POPUP Test
PROCEDURE PROC
DO CASE
   CASE BAR() = 1
     DO ProcX1
   CASE BAR() = 2
     DO ProcX2
   CASE BAR() = 3
     DEACTIVATE POPUP
ENDCASE
```

DEACTIVATE WINDOW

Syntax: DEACTIVATE WINDOW <window name list>/ALL

This command deactivates specified windows and erases them from the screen while leaving them intact in memory. When a window is DEACTIVATEd, the previously active window (if any) becomes active again.

Use the ALL option to restore full screen mode.

EXAMPLE:

```
DEFINE WINDOW WinOne FROM 2,20 TO 8,50
ACTIVATE WINDOW WinOne
@ 2,2 SAY "This is window one"
WAIT
DEACTIVATE WINDOW WinOne
```

DEBUG

Syntax: DEBUG <filename>/<procedure name> [WITH <parameter list>]

This command executes a program or procedure and calls the debugger, displaying the contents of the named file in the EDIT window.

The parameter list can accept a maximum of eight constants, including the file name. The number of variables is not limited.

The debugger screen contains four windows that:

Permit you to see the executing commands.
Edit the program or procedure.

Set breakpoints.
Display results of expressions during execution.

Pressing Esc or Ctrl-End will return you to the **ACTION** prompt at the bottom of the screen. The following responses to the **ACTION** prompt are permitted.

KEYSTROKE	RESULTS
B	Activates the **B**reakpoint window.
D	Activates the **D**isplay window.
E	Activates the **E**dit window.
L	Begins execution at a specified **L**ine number.
N	Executes the **N**ext command.
P	Displays **P**rogram trace information.
Q	**Q**uits the program or procedure and debugger.
R	**R**uns the program or procedure.
S	**S**teps through the program or procedure.
X	e**X**its the program to the dot prompt. Resume restarts the debugger.
F1	Displays or removes the help panel.
F9	Removes the debugger screen to show underlying data.

EXAMPLE:

```
DEBUG MyStuff
```

DECLARE

Syntax:

```
DECLARE <array name 1>
[{<number of rows>,} {<number of columns>}]
{,<array name 2>
[{<number of rows>,} {<number of columns>}]...}
```

The square brackets are a required part of the command. The curly braces indicate optional items.

Command names and defines an array of memory variables. One array may contain elements of different data types.

One- or two-dimensional arrays of memory variables can be created by using the DECLARE statement. Subscripts in a memory variable array start with 1. Array elements are automatically initialized as logical variables with a ".F." value when an array is created. STORE is used to assign values to individual elements or to the entire array.

EXAMPLE:

```
DECLARE X(2,3)
STORE 99        TO X(1,3)
STORE .T.       TO X(2,1)
STORE "Hello"   TO X(2,2)
? X(2,2)        && HELLO
```

EXAMPLE:

```
DECLARE States[51]  &&  a one-dimensional array named
                    &&  States containing 51 elements.
```

DEFINE BAR

Syntax:

```
DEFINE BAR <line number> OF <popup name>
 PROMPT <expC> [MESSAGE <expC>]
 [SKIP [FOR <condition>]]
```

This command defines a single option in the named pop-up menu. <line number> is the line in the pop-up menu where the prompt appears. SKIP displays the bar but does not allow its selection.

The MESSAGE appears centered at the bottom of the screen when the PROMPT is active. Do not use PROMPT FIELD, PROMPT FILES, or PROMPT STRUCTURE with DEFINE POPUP if using this command.

If a BAR value is missing, that row is left blank and skipped by the selection bar.

EXAMPLE:

```
DEFINE POPUP Test FROM 5,20
DEFINE BAR 1 OF TEST PROMPT "Add a Record"
DEFINE BAR 3 OF TEST PROMPT "Edit a Record"
DEFINE BAR 5 OF TEST PROMPT "Exit Menu"
ACTIVATE POPUP Test
```

DEFINE BOX

Syntax:

```
DEFINE BOX FROM <column> TO <column>
 HEIGHT <exp> [AT LINE <print line>]
 [SINGLE/DOUBLE/<border definition string>]
```

Command prints a box in a defined area of a report. The system memory variable _box must be set to true for the box to print.

FROM	Is the starting column on the left.
TO	Is the ending column on the right.
HEIGHT	Is the size of the box.
AT LINE	Defines the starting line for the box.
SINGLE	Draws a single-line border.
DOUBLE	Draws a double-line border.

The border definition string follows the same rules as the SET BORDER command, as shown in the following diagram:

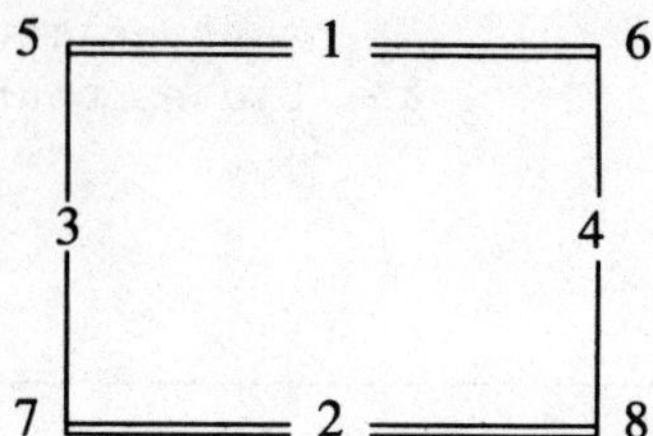

or

```
[<1>],[<2>],[<3>],[<4>],[<5>],[<6>],[<7>],[<8>]]]]]]]]
```

EXAMPLE:

```
DEFINE BOX FROM 1 TO 12 HEIGHT 5 DOUBLE
```

or

```
DEFINE BOX FROM 1 TO 12 HEIGHT 5;
   205,205,179,179,213,184,212,190
* String for the previous box.
```

EXAMPLE:

```
SET TALK OFF        &&  Draw a box around a
SET ECHO OFF        &&  centered heading.
SET COLOR TO W+/B
CLEAR
Heading       = "Phillipps Computer Systems Inc."
 _wrap        = .T.
 _lmargin     = 5
 _rmargin     = 74
 _box         = .T.
SET PRINTER ON
?
?
DEFINE BOX FROM 20 TO 60 HEIGHT 5 DOUBLE
?
 _alignment = "center"
? Heading                    &&  Center heading on page
?
?
?
EJECT
SET PRINTER OFF
```

DEFINE MENU

Syntax:

```
DEFINE MENU <menu name> [MESSAGE <expC>]
```

Command defines a menu bar. You must use DEFINE PAD to individually define the menu prompt pads.

The MESSAGE text field (limited to 79 characters) appears centered at the bottom of the screen, (default).

Each menu bar may have its own message, or one message may be used with all menu options.

EXAMPLE:

```
DEFINE MENU Test MESSAGE "This is a test"
DEFINE PAD X1 OF TEST PROMPT "Test 1" AT 0,0
DEFINE PAD X2 OF TEST PROMPT "Test 2" AT 0,20
DEFINE PAD X3 OF TEST PROMPT "Test 3" AT 0,50
ON SELECTION PAD X1 OF Test DO Proc1
ON SELECTION PAD X2 OF Test DO Proc1
ON SELECTION PAD X3 OF Test DEACTIVE MENU
ACTIVATE MENU Test
```

DEFINE PAD

Syntax:

```
DEFINE PAD <pad name> OF <menu name>
 PROMPT <expC> [AT <row>,<col>]
 [MESSAGE <expC>]
```

Command defines one prompt pad of a defined bar menu.

The <menu name> was defined with DEFINE MENU. PROMPT <expC> is displayed inside the menu option at the optional screen coordinates <row>,<col>. A blank space is added to each side of <expC>.

The MESSAGE <expC>, limited to 79 characters, appears centered at the bottom of the screen, (default).

EXAMPLE:

```
DEFINE MENU Test MESSAGE "This is a test"
DEFINE PAD X1 OF TEST PROMPT "Test 1" AT 0,0
DEFINE PAD X2 OF TEST PROMPT "Test 2" AT 0,20
DEFINE PAD X3 OF TEST PROMPT "Test 3" AT 0,50
ON SELECTION PAD X1 OF Test DO Proc1
ON SELECTION PAD X2 OF Test DO Proc1
ON SELECTION PAD X3 OF Test DEACTIVE MENU
ACTIVATE MENU Test
```

DEFINE POPUP

Syntax:

```
DEFINE POPUP <popup name> FROM <row1>,<col1>
 [TO <row2>,<col2>]
 [PROMPT FIELD <field name>
 /PROMPT FILES [LIKE <skeleton>]
 /PROMPT STRUCTURE]
 [PROMPT MESSAGE <expC>]
```

This command defines the name, location, border, prompts, and message line of a pop-up menu. The PROMPT option displays one of three different lists: FIELD, FILES, or STRUCTURE.

FIELD displays contents of the named field for each record of the data base file in the pop-up menu.

FILES displays the catalog file names. Use the LIKE <skeleton> to restrict the files displayed.

STRUCTURE displays the defined fields of the active data base file.

EXAMPLE:

```
DEFINE POPUP Test FROM 5,20
DEFINE BAR 1 OF TEST  PROMPT "Add a Record"
DEFINE BAR 3 OF TEST  PROMPT "Edit a Record"
DEFINE BAR 5 OF TEST  PROMPT "Exit Menu"
ACTIVATE POPUP Test
```

DEFINE WINDOW

Syntax:

```
DEFINE WINDOW <window name>
 FROM <row1>,<col1> TO <row2>,<col2>
 [DOUBLE/PANEL/NONE/<border definition string>]
 [COLOR [<standard>] [,<enhanced>] [,<frame>]]
```

Command defines the name, location, and display attributes of a window and its border.

The border default is a single-line box. You can define a DOUBLE-line box, a highlighted PANEL, or NONE, or use a border definition string for a custom border. You may specify the color of the window by using the COLOR option.

EXAMPLE:

```
DEFINE WINDOW WinOne FROM 2,20 TO 8,50;
```

or

```
DEFINE WINDOW WinTwo FROM 2,20 TO 8,50;
  CHR(205),CHR(205),CHR(179),CHR(179),;
  CHR(213),CHR(184),CHR(212),CHR(190);
  COLOR W+/B,RG+/B,W+/R
```

DELETE

Syntax:

```
DELETE [<scope>]
 [FOR <condition>] [WHILE <condition>]
```

Command marks records for removal from the active data base file. Unless specified by the <scope>, WHILE, or FOR clauses, only the current record or the record specified by the RECORD phrase is marked for deletion. Records are not physically removed from the file until the PACK command is issued. Records marked for deletion can be unmarked with the RECALL command.

EXAMPLE:
```
DELETE RECORD 8
```
or
```
DELETE FOR Salary > 50000
```

DELETE TAG

Syntax:
```
DELETE TAG <tag name 1>
 [OF <.mdx filename>]/<.ndx filename 1>
 [,<tag name 2>
 [OF <.mdx filename>]/<.ndx filename 2>...]
```

Command removes the specified index tags from the active .mdx file or closes the specified .ndx files. The active catalog is updated. If all .mdx tags are deleted, the .mdx file is also deleted.

In multiuser situations, the associated data base file must be in exclusive use.

EXAMPLE:
```
DELETE TAG Names of Master

* Deletes the Names tag from the Master production
* .mdx file.
```

DELETE FILE or ERASE

Syntax:
```
DELETE FILE <filename>/?
```
or
```
ERASE <filename>
```

Command removes the specified file from the directory and from the catalog. Open files of any type cannot be deleted.

? allows you to select a file from a list of existing files in the open catalog.

The file extension must be included, and if the file is not in the current working directory, <filename> must be a fully qualified path name.

EXAMPLE:
```
DELETE FILE D:\MYSTUFF\TEMP.DBF

* Deletes the file TEMP.DBF located on drive D:
* in subdirectory mystuff.
```

DIR/DIRECTORY

Syntax:
```
DIR/DIRECTORY
 [[ON] <drive>:] [[LIKE] [<path>] <skeleton>]
```

Command displays the file name, number of records, date of last update, and file size (in bytes) for each data base file in the current or indicated disk drive and path. The number of files displayed, the sum of the number of bytes they contain, and the total number of bytes remaining on the disk are also displayed. The file information on the default drive is displayed unless otherwise specified using the <drive:> and/or <path> argument.

Skeleton: By specifying <skeleton>, other file types may also be displayed. The number of files displayed, the sum of the number of bytes they contain, and the total number of bytes remaining on the disk are also displayed when a file <skeleton> is specified.

EXAMPLE:

```
DIR
```

or

```
DIR *.PRG
```

DISPLAY

Syntax:

```
DISPLAY [[FIELDS] <expression list>] [OFF]
 [<scope>] [FOR <condition>] [WHILE <condition>]
 [TO PRINTER/TO FILE <filename>]
```

DISPLAY, with no modifiers, shows only the current record. DISPLAY, when used with <scope>, WHILE, or FOR, stops at each screenful of information. Memo files are not displayed unless explicitly named in the FIELDS list.

OFF	Suppresses record numbers.
TO PRINTER	Prints a hard copy of the contents.
TO FILE	Sends contents to a disk file.

EXAMPLE:

```
USE Master
SET HEADING OFF
DISPLAY FIELDS TRIM(Name) + " " +;
        STR(Salary,10,2) + TRIM(JobTitle) OFF

* Produces a list of employees with their salaries
* and titles.
```

DISPLAY FILES

Syntax:

```
DISPLAY FILES [LIKE] <skeleton>]
 [TO PRINTER/TO FILE <filename> ]
```

Command sends files that match the <skeleton> to the screen or to the printer. DISPLAY stops at each screenful of information.

This variant of DISPLAY is used to list files residing on the disk. You may view all files on a specified disk drive, partition, or directory, or only files that match a <skeleton> pattern containing file "wild cards" characters. The meaning of the characters in <skeleton> depends on your operating system.

DISPLAY FILES without arguments displays the vital statistics of data base files stored in the default directory or disk. The items of data displayed are:

Data base name
Number of records
Last time updated
Size

Also displayed are the total number of bytes contained in all the files, as well as the bytes remaining on the disk.

TO PRINT directs screen display to the printer.

TO FILE sends the files to a disk file.

EXAMPLE:

```
DISPLAY FILES
```

or

```
DISPLAY FILES LIKE PCS*.DBF TO PRINTER
```

DISPLAY HISTORY

Syntax:

```
DISPLAY HISTORY [LAST <expN>]
 [TO PRINTER/TO FILE <filename>]
```

Command produces a list, in chronological order, of the last 20 commands executed. A larger number of commands can be listed if SET HISTORY is set higher.

LAST allows you to specify a number of commands to display other than 20.

TO PRINTER prints a hard copy of the list.

TO FILE sends the list to a disk file.

EXAMPLE:

```
DISPLAY HISTORY
```

or

```
DISPLAY HISTORY LAST 8 TO FILE Last8.Txt
```

DISPLAY MEMORY

Syntax:

```
DISPLAY MEMORY
 [TO PRINTER] [TO FILE<filename>]
```

DISPLAY MEMORY shows the name, type, contents, and status of all memory variables currently defined. It also displays the number of memory variables defined, the number of bytes used for string data, the number of additional memory variables possible, and the number of bytes available for additional string data.

TO PRINTER creates a hard copy of the information.

TO FILE sends the information to a disk file.

EXAMPLE:

```
DISPLAY MEMORY
```

or

```
DISPLAY MEMORY TO PRINTER
```

DISPLAY STATUS

Syntax:

```
DISPLAY STATUS [TO PRINTER/TO FILE <filename>]
```

Command displays information about the current session. It stops at each screenful of information.

The following information is displayed:

Current work area number
Fully qualified data base name
Read-only status
Open index file names
Index file keys including UNIQUE and DESCENDING
Database relations
Currently active memo files
Format files
File search path
Default disk drive
Print destination
Margin setting
Current work area
Reprocess count
Refresh count
DEVICE (SCREEN, PRINT, or FILE) settings
Currency symbol
Delimiter symbols
Number of opened files
ON command settings
SET command switch settings
Function key assignments
Modules currently loaded
Procedure file in use

TO PRINTER prints a hard copy of the list.

TO FILE sends the information to a disk file.

EXAMPLE: `DISPLAY STATUS`

or

```
DISPLAY STATUS TO FILE NewStat.Txt
```

DISPLAY STRUCTURE

Syntax:
```
DISPLAY STRUCTURE [IN <alias>]
 [TO PRINTER/TO FILE <filename>]
```

Command displays information about the structure of the active data base file. Display stops at each screenful of information. If SET FIELDS is ON, the > symbol appears beside each field specified with SET FIELDS TO.

The following data is displayed:

Name of field
Type of field
Size of field, including the number of decimal places

Also displayed is the current number of records in the data base and the date it was last updated.

TO PRINTER prints a hard copy of the list.

TO FILE sends information to a disk file.

EXAMPLE: `DISPLAY STATUS`

or

```
DISPLAY STATUS TO PRINTER
```

DISPLAY USERS

Syntax:
```
DISPLAY USERS
```

Command displays a list of log-in names of all the current system users in a multiuser environment.

EXAMPLE: `DISPLAY USERS`

DO

Syntax:
```
DO <program file>/<procedure name>
 [WITH <parameter list>]
```

DO causes a command file or procedure file containing dBASE IV commands to be executed. The program/procedure file may itself contain additional DO commands; however, such nesting of DOs is limited to a default depth of 20, but can be set from 1 to 256 by changing the value of the "DO = " in the CONFIG.DB file. Commands in the program/procedure file are executed in the order in which they are encountered until a RETURN, CANCEL, or QUIT command is executed, or until execution falls through to a PROCEDURE statement or the end of file. When the program/procedure file's execution is completed, control is returned to the calling program, the dot prompt, or DOS.

The WITH clause allows you to pass parameters to the called program. Parameters may be any valid expression. Up to 50 parameters may be passed. Field names take precedence over memory variables, and so to specify a memory variable, an alias (M->) must be used if you wish to specify a memory variable that has the same name as a data base field.

EXAMPLE:

```
SELECT B    && Master data base
DO WHILE .NOT. EOF()
  M->Salary = B->Salary
  NewSalary = 0.0
  DO Process WITH M->Salary, NewSalary
  Replace B->Salary WITH NewSalary
  SKIP
ENDDO
RETURN

PROCEDURE PROCESS
PARAMETERS OldSalary, NewSalary
* NOTE: "OldSalary" in this procedure is equal to the passed
* parameter "M->Salary."

* Compute new salary
...
...
RETURN
```

DO CASE

Syntax:

```
DO CASE
 CASE <condition>
    <commands>
 [CASE <condition>
    <commands>]
 [OTHERWISE
    <commands>]
ENDCASE
```

This structured programming command selects only one course of action from a set of alternatives. When the DO CASE command is executed, successive CASE statements are examined and their <condition> expressions evaluated. The first CASE <condition> that evaluates as ".T." causes the <commands> following it to be executed until another CASE, OTHERWISE, or ENDCASE is encountered, at which point execution continues after the matching ENDCASE. If no <condition> is ".T.", the OTHERWISE <commands> are executed (if present) and execution continues after the matching ENDCASE.

One, and only one, CASE will be executed—the first one whose <condition> is true, no matter how many other CASE statements have a true <condition>.

EXAMPLE:

```
 Code = 5
 DO CASE
  CASE Code = 1
     Prefix = "Mr."
  CASE Code = 2
     Prefix = "Mrs."
  CASE Code = 3
     Prefix = "Ms."
  CASE Code = 4
     Prefix = "Master."
  CASE Code = 5
     Prefix = "Dr."
  OTHERWISE
     Prefix = SPACE(3)
ENDCASE
```

DO WHILE

Syntax:

```
 DO WHILE <condition>
  <commands>
  [LOOP]
  [EXIT]
ENDDO
```

In this structured programming command, <condition> is evaluated. Command statements between DO WHILE and ENDDO are repeated while the specified condition is true. EXIT and LOOP commands may be placed anywhere between the DO WHILE and ENDDO statements.

EXIT transfers control from within a DO WHILE loop to the first command following the ENDDO.

LOOP causes control to return directly to the DO WHILE command.

EXAMPLE:

```
SELECT B    &&  Master data base
DO WHILE.NOT.EOF()
   M->Salary = B->Salary
   NewSalary = 0.0
   * ... Process
   Replace B->Salary WITH NewSalary
   SKIP
ENDDO
RETURN
```

EXAMPLE:

```
SELECT B                        &&  Master data base
SET ORDER TO TAG Branch
SEEK "NEW YORK"                 &&  Start with NY office.
DO WHILE.NOT.EOF()
   M->Salary = B->Salary
   NewSalary = 0.0
   IF Salary < 2500             &&  Skip Processing if
      LOOP                      &&  Salary is less than
   ENDIF                        &&  $25,000.
   * ... Process
   Replace B->Salary WITH NewSalary
   SKIP
   IF B->Branch < > "NEW YORK"
      EXIT
   ENDIF
ENDDO
* ...                           &&  Processing continues here after
* ...                           &&  EOF() or B->Branch < > NY.
* Note: This condition could have been included in the
* DO WHILE construct Eg. DO WHILE .NOT. EOF();
* .AND.B->Branch = "NEW YORK"
RETURN
```

EDIT

Syntax:

```
EDIT [NOINIT] [NOFOLLOW] [NOAPPEND] [NOMENU]
 [NOEDIT] [NODELETE] [NOCLEAR]
 [<record number>] [FIELDS <field list>]
 [<scope>] [FOR <condition>] [WHILE <condition>]
```

EDIT is a full screen command used to display or alter the contents of a record in the active data base file or view. The current record is edited if no parameters are given.

All fields are available for editing unless a FIELDS <field list> is specified. All records are available for editing unless a <scope>, FOR, or WHILE clause is specified.

A navigation bar showing applicable cursor control keys can be displayed by toggling the F1 function key.

NOFOLLOW	If an indexed file is reordered, the current record is the replacement for the repositioned record.
NOINIT	Calls a previously defined EDIT session.
NOMENU	Prevents access to the menu bar.
NOAPPEND	Prevents addition of new records.
NODELETE	Prevents deletion of records.
NOEDIT	Prevents editing of records.
NOCLEAR	Causes the table to remain on screen after the user exits.

EXAMPLE:

```
USE Master
EDIT RECORD 31  && Edits the 31st record.
```

or

```
USE Master
EDIT FOR Salary >= 50000 FIELDS Salary, Name, Title;
      NOAPPEND NOMENU

* Edits the salary, name, and title fields for employees
* earning $50,000 or more.
```

EJECT

Syntax: EJECT

EJECT causes the printer to advance the paper to the top of the next page (form feed). It only affects the printer. PROW() and PCOL() are reset to zero.

EXAMPLE:

```
SELECT B                                        && Use Master.
GOTO TOP
PageNumber = 0
LineNumber = 99
SET DEVICE TO PRINT
DO WHILE.NOT.EOF()
  IF LineNumber > 60
      EJECT
      LineNumber = 1
      @ LineNumber,0 SAY "Page: " +;
          ALLTRIM(STR(PageNumber,5,0))
      * ...                                     && Heading commands
      PageNumber = PageNumber + 1
  ENDIF
  * ...                                         && Process
  SKIP
ENDDO
SET DEVICE TO SCREEN
```

EJECT PAGE

Syntax:

```
EJECT PAGE
```

Command advances the streaming output to the defined ON PAGE handler on the current page, or to the beginning of the next page.

EJECT PAGE increments _pageno, and resets _plineno to zero. If you defined an ON PAGE handler, EJECT PAGE determines if the current line number (_plineno) is before or after the ON PAGE line. If you did not define an ON PAGE handler and SET PRINTER is ON, EJECT PAGE sends either a form feed or a computed number of line feeds (_plength - _plineno) to the printer depending on whether _padvance = "FORMFEED" or "LINEFEEDS". If SET PRINTER is not ON, a computed number of line feeds (_plength–_plineno) is sent to the output device.

EXAMPLE:

```
USE Master
_peject = "AFTER"
SET PRINT ON
PRINTJOB                              &&  A new dBASE IV command
ON PAGE AT LINE _plength-1 DO NewPage
   * ...                              &&  Process
ENDPRINTJOB
SET PRINT OFF
RETURN

PROCEDURE NEWPAGE
EJECT PAGE
?? DATE() AT 1, "Page:" AT 124, _pageno;
                 PICTURE "999" AT 130
?
?
RETURN
```

ELSE

Syntax:

```
ELSE
```

ELSE is used in the following programming structure:

```
IF <condition>
   <commands>
ELSE
   <commands>
ENDIF
```

If <condition> is true, <commands> are executed.

If <condition> is false, the ELSE commands are processed. This continues until ENDIF is reached.

EXAMPLE:

```
USE Master
NewSalary = 0
IF Salary > 50000
    DO UpDate WITH Salary, NewSalary, 10
ELSE
    NewSalary = 10
    DO UpDate WITH Salary, NewSalary, 25
ENDIF
REPLACE Salary WITH NewSalary
```

ENDCASE

Syntax: `ENDCASE`

ENDCASE terminates the DO CASE programming structure:

```
DO CASE
   CASE <condition>
      <commands>
   [CASE <condition>
      <commands>]
   [OTHERWISE
      <commands>]
ENDCASE
```

EXAMPLE:

```
Code = 5
DO CASE
   CASE Code = 1
      Prefix = "Mr."
   CASE Code = 2
      Prefix = "Mrs."
   CASE Code = 3
      Prefix = "Ms."
   CASE Code = 4
      Prefix = "Master."
   CASE Code = 5
      Prefix = "Dr."
   OTHERWISE
      Prefix = SPACE(3)
ENDCASE
```

ENDDO

Syntax: `ENDDO`

ENDDO terminates the DO WHILE programming structure:

```
DO WHILE <condition>
   <commands>
ENDDO
```

EXAMPLE:

```
SELECT B        &&  USE Master
DO WHILE.NOT.EOF()
   M->Salary = B->Salary
   NewSalary = 0.0
   * ... Process
   Replace B->Salary WITH NewSalary
   SKIP
ENDDO
```

ENDSCAN

Syntax:

```
ENDSCAN
```

ENDSCAN terminates the SCAN programming structure.

```
SCAN [<scope>] [FOR <condition>] [WHILE <condition>]
   [<commands>]
ENDSCAN
```

EXAMPLE:

```
SELECT B        &&  USE Master
SCAN WHILE B->Salary > 50000
   M->Salary = B->Salary
   NewSalary = 0.0
   * ... Process
   Replace B->Salary WITH NewSalary
ENDSCAN
```

ENDIF

Syntax:

```
ENDIF
```

ENDIF terminates the IF programming structure.

```
IF <condition>
    <commands>
[ELSE
    <commands>]
ENDIF
```

EXAMPLE:

```
USE Master
NewSalary = 0
IF Salary > 50000
    DO UpDate WITH Salary, NewSalary, 10
ELSE
    NewSalary = 10
    DO UpDate WITH Salary, NewSalary, 25
ENDIF
REPLACE Salary WITH NewSalary
```

END TRANSACTION

Syntax: END TRANSACTION

Command terminates the active transaction, deletes the transaction .log file, and releases all locks.

The transaction flag in each data base file involved in the transaction is removed to indicate that those files are now in a consistent state.

END TRANSACTION commits all changes made in the data base files.

EXAMPLE:

```
ON ERROR DO FixIt WITH "Master"
BEGIN TRANSACTION
   * ...
   * ...
END TRANSACTION

PROCEDURE FIXIT
PARAMETERS FileInUse
   ROLLBACK FileInUse
   RETURN
*END:FIXIT
```

ENDTEXT

Syntax: ENDTEXT

ENDTEXT terminates the TEXT programming structure.

```
TEXT
   <text characters>
ENDTEXT
```

EXAMPLE:

```
SET COLOR TO W+/B
CLEAR
TEXT
  * ...      &&  Full screen text information
ENDTEXT
```

ERASE / DELETE FILE

Syntax:

```
ERASE <filename>/?
```

or

```
DELETE FILE <filename>/?
```

Command removes the specified file from the directory and from the catalog. Open files of any type cannot be ERASED.

? allows you to select a file from a list of existing files in the open catalog.

The file extension must be included, and if the file is not in the current working directory, <filename> must be a fully qualified path name.

EXAMPLE:

```
ERASE D:\MYSTUFF\TEMP.DBF

* Erases the file TEMP.DBF located on drive D: in
* subdirectory mystuff.
```

EXIT

Syntax:

```
EXIT
```

EXIT allows you to terminate a DO WHILE or SCAN structure before LOOP criteria are satisfied and passes control to the command following ENDDO or ENDSCAN.

EXAMPLE:

```
SELECT B                               &&  Master data base
SET ORDER TO TAG Branch
SEEK "NEW YORK"                        &&  Start with NY office.
DO WHILE .NOT. EOF()
   M->Salary = B->Salary
   NewSalary = 0.0
   DO MakeSal                          &&  Process
   SKIP
   IF B->Branch < > "NEW YORK"
      EXIT                             &&  GOTO the statement
   ENDIF                               &&  after the ENDDO
ENDDO
```

```
* Processing continues here after EXIT is encountered
* or the DO WHILE condition is satisfied.
```

EXAMPLE:

```
SELECT B                                  &&  USE Master
SET ORDER TO TAG Branch
SCAN WHILE B->Branch = "NEW YORK"
  M->Salary = B->Salary
  NewSalary = 0.0
  IF B->Salary > 50000
      EXIT                                &&  GOTO the statement
  ENDIF                                   &&  after the ENDSCAN
  DO MakeSal                              &&  Process
ENDSCAN

* Processing continues here after EXIT is encountered
* or the SCAN condition is satisfied.
```

EXPORT TO

Syntax:

```
EXPORT TO <filename>
[TYPE] PFS/FW2/RPD/dBASEII
[FIELDS <field list>] [<scope>]
[FOR <condition>] [WHILE <condition>]
```

Command copies the data base file in USE to a foreign format. Files resulting from the EXPORT TO command can only be used by PFS:FILE, Framework II, dBASE II, or RapidFile. The COPY command can be used to create files for other systems.

dBASE IV permits you to create files with fields larger than permitted for these systems—so be careful.

EXAMPLE:

```
EXPORT TO NewMast TYPE FW2
```

or

```
EXPORT TO NewMast TYPE FW2 FOR Salary > 50000
```

FIND

Syntax:

```
FIND <literal key>
```

Command searches an indexed data base file for the first record with an index key matching the specified character string or number.

The FIND command requires that an index file be enabled for the currently USEd data base. FIND moves the record pointer to the first record whose index key matches the character string or numeric value. The match must be an exact match unless SET NEAR has been set to ON. If the index key has leading blanks, the character string must be enclosed by quotation marks. If you wish to search for the contents of a character memory variable, the macro function "&" must precede the memory variable as FIND does not evaluate expressions.

EXAMPLE:

```
USE Master
SET ORDER TO TAG Branch
FIND FLORIDA
```

or

```
USE Master
SET ORDER TO TAG Branch
State = "FLORIDA"
FIND                     & State
```

FUNCTION

Syntax:

```
FUNCTION <procedure name>
```

Command identifies a user-defined function in a procedure. FUNCTION procedures must begin with the FUNCTION command and end with a RETURN <exp> command. The PARAMETERS command must be used within the function to receive passed variables.

In release 1.0 of dBASE IV, restrictions have been placed on commands that cannot be used in FUNCTION procedures. These restrictions will be eased or removed entirely in future releases of dBASE IV, and probably will not exist when you are using this book.

EXAMPLE:

```
SET COLOR TO & ColStand
CLEAR
X = {12/7/41}
@ 11,12 SAY DTOC(X) + " is" +;
IIF(.NOT. ISWKEND(X), " not ", " ") + "a weekend."
RETURN

FUNCTION ISWKEND
PARAMETERS WKDate
RETURN(IIF(DOW(WKDate)=1 .OR.;
     DOW(WKDate)=7, .T., .F.))
```

The date 12/7/41 is passed to the FUNCTION ISWKEND as a character string in the "ISWKEND(X)" portion of the "IIF" statement. The FUNCTION ISWKEND then uses the dBASE IV function DOW() to determine whether the passed date falls on a Saturday or Sunday (7 or 1). Notice that a dBASE IV function and a user-defined function (UDF) are used in exactly the same manner. If DOW() did not exist, it too could be written as a UDF and used in the same manner as shown since UDFs can call other UDFs.

GO/GOTO

Syntax:

```
GO/GOTO BOTTOM/TOP [IN <alias>]
```

or

```
GO/GOTO [RECORD] <record number> [IN <alias>]
```

or

```
<record number>
```

The GO/GOTO command positions the record pointer to a specified record in the selected or <alias> data base. GO <record number> positions the record pointer to the physical record number <record number>. GO BOTTOM/TOP positions the record pointer to the last and first record, respectively. If the data base has an enabled index, then "first" means "with the lowest key value" and "last" means "with the highest key value."

TOP moves the pointer to the first record.
BOTTOM moves the pointer to the last record.

EXAMPLE:

```
USE Master
GOTO TOP
```

or

```
SELECT A
USE MASTER
SELECT B
USE DETAIL
GOTO TOP IN A
```

HELP

Syntax:

```
HELP [<dBASE IV keyword>]
```

HELP is a full screen command that displays information about dBASE IV functions and commands. If a <dBASE IV keyword> is specified, the information on that dBASE IV keyword is displayed directly. If a <dBASE IV keyword> is omitted, HELP displays a light bar menu that allows you to select a dBASE IV keyword. The light bar may be positioned by using cursor control keys or by typing as much of the dBASE IV keyword name as necessary. Once the light bar is positioned correctly, a selection is made by pressing carriage return. If additional information is available for a <dBASE IV keyword>, HELP displays a list of subtopics in light bar menu format and allows you to select a subtopic in the same manner. Subtopics may themselves have subtopics that provide even more detail. To return from a subtopic to the next highest level of subject matter, simply press the PgUp key. To exit HELP, continue pressing PgUp until the "dot prompt" is displayed. To exit HELP without erasing the HELP display, press the Esc key.

EXAMPLE:
```
HELP BROWSE
```

or

```
HELP
```

IF

Syntax:
```
IF <condition>
   <commands>
[ELSE
   <commands>]
ENDIF
```

If the <condition> following IF is true, the subsequent commands are executed. If <condition> is false, the commands in the ELSE clause are carried out. This continues until ENDIF is encountered. If <condition> is false and no ELSE has been specified, all statements between the IF statement and the matching ENDIF statement are ignored. IF statements may be nested within one another provided that each IF has a matching ENDIF, although this is not good programming practice.

EXAMPLE:
```
USE Master
NewSalary = 0
IF Salary > 50000
    DO UpDate WITH Salary, NewSalary, 10
ELSE
    NewSalary = 10
    DO UpDate WITH Salary, NewSalary, 25
ENDIF
REPLACE Salary WITH NewSalary
```

IMPORT FROM

Syntax:
```
IMPORT FROM <filename>
[[TYPE] PFS/FW2/RPD/WK1/dBASEII]
```

Command creates a dBASE IV from a foreign format. Permissible formats are PFS:FILE forms, Framework II data base and spreadsheet frames, dBASE II data bases, RapidFile data files, and Lotus .WK1 spreadsheets. The COPY command can be used to create files for other systems.

The <filename> must include the file extension if it is different from the default extension for that file.

EXAMPLE:
```
IMPORT FROM Agents TYPE WK1
```

INDEX ON

Syntax:

```
INDEX ON <key expression>
[TO <.ndx filename>]/[TAG <tag name>]
[OF <.mdx filename>][FOR <condition>]
[UNIQUE] [DESCENDING]
```

INDEX ON creates an index file from the active data base file. The key fields are ordered alphabetically, chronologically, or numerically.

The INDEX command creates an index file for the currently selected data base keyed by <key expression>. The <key expression> must be a numeric, character, or date expression; logical expressions, memo fields, and UDFs are not allowed. The index created is given a default extension of "MDX" or "NDX". Standard DOS rules for naming files must be observed when naming <. . . filename>. The UNIQUE option specifies that the occurrence of records with duplicate keys will cause only the first record encountered with a particular key value to be included in the index file. The FOR clause acts as a filter and produces a smaller index.

TAG names the tag that is put into the .mdx file by this command.
UNIQUE ignores duplicate key fields.
DESCENDING builds the index in descending order (default is ascending).

A multiple index (.mdx) file may contain up to 47 tags. Tag names follow the same naming conventions as variable names.

EXAMPLE:

```
USE MASTER
INDEX ON LastName TO Name                     && Create .NDX index.
```

or

```
USE MASTER
INDEX ON LastName TAG Name OF MINDEX
                                              && Create .MDX index.
```

or

```
USE MASTER
INDEX ON LastName TAG Name OF MINDEX UNIQUE
```

or

```
USE MASTER
INDEX ON LastName TAG Name OF MINDEX FOR Salary > 50000
```

INPUT

Syntax:

```
INPUT [<prompt>] TO <memvar>
```

INPUT permits data to be input from the keyboard into a <memvar>. The optional <prompt> serves as a prompt for the requested input. The data entered may be any valid dBASE IV expression terminated by a Carriage Return. The type of input determines the data type of <memvar>.

EXAMPLE:

```
INPUT "Enter your last name:" TO LastName
```

INSERT

Syntax:

```
INSERT [BLANK] [BEFORE]
```

INSERT adds a new record to the current data base either immediately BEFORE or after the current record. The new record is displayed for full screen editing unless a BLANK record is inserted. If the new record is displayed for full screen editing, data may be only entered into the new record. If CARRY is SET ON, data contained in the previous record is automatically entered into the new record. In the full screen mode, you may press the F1 key to display information for editing an inserted record. If the file is indexed, INSERT works like APPEND. INSERT is not recommended for use with large, unindexed data bases since an insertion near the front of the data base forces the rewriting of nearly every record in the data base.

BLANK adds a blank record without entering the full screen editor.
BEFORE adds a record before the current record.

EXAMPLE:

```
SET CARRY ON
USE Master
LOCATE FOR Salary = 47500
INSERT BLANK
REPLACE Salary WITH 50000
```

or

```
SET CARRY ON
USE Master
LOCATE FOR Salary = 47500
INSERT BLANK BEFORE
REPLACE Salary WITH 46000
```

JOIN WITH

Syntax:

```
JOIN WITH <alias> TO <filename> FOR <condition>
[FIELDS <field list>]
```

Command creates a new data base file by merging specified records and fields from two open data base files.

The JOIN command creates a new data base, <filename>, from two other data bases. One data base is the currently active data base and the second data base is identified by <alias>. JOIN sets the record pointer to the first record in the active data base and searches through the records in the <alias> data base. JOIN evaluates the FOR <condition>, and if it is true, a new record is written to <filename>. JOIN then moves to the second record in the active data base and repeats the procedure. If no FIELDS <field list> is present, all fields in the active data base, plus all fields from the <alias> data base that will fit within the field number limit of dBASE IV, are included in the new <file>. If a FIELDS <field list> is present, only those fields contained in <field list> will be included in <filename>. The field list may consist of any type of field from both files except memo fields.

Make sure you have enough disk space available when joining two files as the resulting file can be quite large if you do not choose your <condition> carefully. The worst case would cause the number of records in <filename> to be equal to the number of records in the active file times the number of records in the <alias>. If the active file contained 2,000 records and the alias file also contained 2,000 records, the resulting file would contain 4,000,000 records. That's *FOUR MILLION* records.

EXAMPLE:

```
USE Master
USE Detail in 2
JOIN WITH Detail TO MasDet FOR;
Branch = B->Branch .AND. Salary > 50000;
FIELDS Branch, B->Title, Salary, B->Grade
```

KEYBOARD

Syntax:

```
KEYBOARD <expC>
```

KEYBOARD places a series of characters into the type-ahead buffer. dBASE IV then reads these characters as if they were keyed by the user. The type-ahead buffer is cleared by the KEYBOARD command before entering any new characters.

EXAMPLE:

```
SET COLOR TO W+/B
CLEAR
USE Master
KEYBOARD CHR(24) + CHR(24)

* Place two-cursor down key into the type-ahead buffer.

BROWSE              &&  Cursor is on the third record.
```

LABEL FORM

Syntax:

```
LABEL FORM <label file name>/?
[<scope>][FOR <condition>] [WHILE <condition>]
```

```
[SAMPLE] [TO PRINTER/TO FILE <filename>]
```

LABEL FORM uses a specified label format file designed with CREATE/MODIFY LABEL to print or display labels. The default extension is ".LBL" for a label <file>. Labels are printed for all records in the data base unless a <scope>, WHILE, or FOR clause is specified. The TO PRINT option sends the label output to the printer. The TO FILE option causes labels to be written to a text file with a default extension of ".TXT". The SAMPLE option allows any number of sample labels to be printed in order to test label alignment on the printer.

SAMPLE prints test labels to check for printer alignment.
TO PRINTER sends labels to the printer.
TO FILE sends labels to an ASCII file.

EXAMPLE:

```
USE Master
LABEL FORM MastLab SAMPLE TO PRINTER
```

or

```
USE Master
LABEL FORM MastLab FOR Salary > 50000;
TO FILE HighRoll
```

LIST

Syntax:

```
LIST [FIELDS] [<expression list>] [OFF]
[<scope>][FOR <condition>] [WHILE <condition>]
[TO PRINTER/TO FILE <filename>]
```

Command lists the contents of a data base file, starting at the specified record and continuing without pause to the end. LIST, with no modifiers, shows only the current record. Memo files are not listed unless explicitly named in the FIELDS list.

FIELDS limits list to specified fields.
OFF suppresses record numbers.
TO PRINTER creates a hard copy of the list.
TO FILE sends the list to a disk file.

EXAMPLE:

```
USE Master
SET HEADING OFF
LIST OFF TRIM(Name) + " " + STR(Salary,10,2) +;
   TRIM(JobTitle)

* Produces a list of employees with their salaries
* and titles.
```

LIST FILES

Syntax:

```
LIST FILES [LIKE <skeleton>]
[TO PRINTER/FILE <filename>]
```

This variant of LIST is used to list files residing on the disk. You may view all files on a specified disk drive, partition, or directory, or only files that match a <skeleton> pattern containing file "wild cards" characters. The meaning of the characters in <skeleton> depends on your operating system. LIST FILES without arguments displays the vital statistics of database files stored in the default directory or disk. The items listed are:

Data base name
Number of records
Last time updated
Size

It also includes total number of bytes contained in all the files, as well as the bytes remaining on the disk.

LIKE compares files to <skeleton> for list.
TO PRINT directs screen display to the printer.
TO FILE sends the files to a disk file.

EXAMPLE:

```
LIST FILES
```

or

```
LIST FILES LIKE PCS*.DBF TO PRINTER
```

LIST HISTORY

Syntax:

```
LIST HISTORY [LAST <expN>]
[TO PRINTER/TO FILE <filename>]
```

Command produces a list in chronological order of the last 20 commands executed. A larger number of commands can be listed if SET HISTORY is set higher.

LAST allows you to specify a number of commands to display other than 20.
TO PRINTER prints a hard copy of the list.
TO FILE sends the list to a disk file.

EXAMPLE:

```
LIST HISTORY
```

or

```
LIST HISTORY LAST 8 TO FILE Last8.Txt
```

LIST MEMORY

Syntax: `LIST MEMORY [TO PRINTER/TO FILE <filename>]`

LIST MEMORY shows the name, type, contents, and status of all memory variables currently defined. It also displays the number of memory variables defined, the number of bytes used for string data, the number of additional memory variables possible, and the number of bytes available for additional string data.

TO PRINTER creates a hard copy of the information.
TO FILE sends the information to a disk file.

EXAMPLE:

```
LIST MEMORY
```

or

```
LIST MEMORY TO PRINTER
```

LIST STATUS

Syntax: `LIST STATUS [TO PRINTER/TO FILE <filename>]`

LIST STATUS lists information about the current session. It stops at each screenful of information.

The following information is displayed:

Current work area number
Fully qualified data base name
Read-only status
Open index file names
Index file keys, including UNIQUE and DESCENDING
Data base relations
Currently active memo files
Format files
File search path
Default disk drive
Print destination
Margin setting
Current work area
Reprocess count
Refresh count
DEVICE (SCREEN, PRINT, or FILE) settings
Currency symbol
Delimiter symbols
Number of opened files
ON command settings

SET command switch settings
Function key assignments
Modules currently loaded
Procedure file in use

TO PRINTER prints a hard copy of the list.
TO FILE sends the information to a disk file.

EXAMPLE: `LIST STATUS`

or

`LIST STATUS TO FILE NewStat.Txt`

LIST STRUCTURE

Syntax:

```
LIST STRUCTURE [IN <alias>]
[TO PRINTER/TO FILE <filename>]
```

Command lists information about the structure of the active data base file. If SET FIELDS is ON, the > symbol appears beside each field specified with SET FIELDS TO. The following data are listed:

Name of field
Type of field
Size of field, including the number of decimal places

Also listed are the current number of records in the data base and the date it was last updated.

TO PRINTER prints a hard copy of the list.
TO FILE sends information to a disk file.

EXAMPLE: `LIST STATUS`

or

`LIST STATUS TO PRINTER`

LIST USERS

Syntax: `LIST USERS`

LIST USERS lists log-in names of all the current system users in a multiuser environment.

EXAMPLE: `LIST USERS`

LOAD

Syntax:

```
LOAD <binary filename>
```

Command loads binary program (.bin) files into memory, where they can be run with the CALL command or CALL() function. Sixteen files (of 32,000 bytes each) may be loaded into memory at one time. Each loaded module must have a unique name. When you CALL an assembler module, the extension should be omitted. Also, if the <binary filename> loaded has the same file name but a different extension than one previously loaded, the new <binary filename> will overwrite the previously loaded <binary filename>.

Use LIST STATUS or DISPLAY STATUS to see the names of LOADed modules.

EXAMPLE:

```
LOAD CURSOROF          &&  Load cursor off module.
LOAD CURSORON          &&  Load cursor on  module.
SET COLOR TO W+/B
CLEAR
DO StartUp
CALL CURSOROF          &&  Turn the cursor off
```

LOCATE FOR

Syntax:

```
LOCATE FOR <condition> [<scope>]
[WHILE <condition>]
```

Command searches the active data base file, sequentially, for the first record that meets the specified criteria. The function FOUND() returns true (.T.) if LOCATE is successful. If no criteria are specified, LOCATE searches the entire data base. If another work area is selected, the iterative search process is suspended until that work area is reselected, and then it may be continued.

EXAMPLE:

```
USE Master
LOCATE FOR Salary = 47500
REPLACE Salary WITH 50000
```

LOGOUT

Syntax:

```
LOGOUT
```

This multiuser system command causes the current user to exit dBASE IV. The command enables you to control user sign-in and sign-out procedures. LOGOUT forces a log-out, clears the screen, closes all open data bases and their associated files, closes program files, and then prompts for a log-in.

EXAMPLE:

```
SET COLOR TO W+/B
CLEAR
INPUT "Enter your Code Number: " TO ID PICTURE "!!"
USE Codes
SEEK ID
IF .NOT. FOUND()
   LOGOUT
ENDIF
*...   &&  Continue to process
```

LOOP

Syntax: `LOOP`

LOOP returns control to the beginning of a DO WHILE . . . ENDDO program structure. It is an optional command that may be added anywhere in a DO WHILE . . . ENDDO command sequence. Execution of this command causes all statements occurring between the LOOP command and the ENDDO command to be bypassed and execution to be continued at the DO WHILE statement.

EXAMPLE:

```
SELECT B                          &&  Master data base
DO WHILE .NOT. EOF()
   M->Salary = B->Salary
   NewSalary = 0.0
   IF Salary < 2500               &&  Skip Processing if
      LOOP                        &&  Salary is less than
   ENDIF                          &&  $25,000
   *... Process
   Replace B->Salary WITH NewSalary
   SKIP
ENDDO
```

MODIFY COMMAND/FILE

Syntax:

```
MODIFY COMMAND/FILE <filename>
[WINDOW <window name>]
```

This command starts the dBASE IV full screen text editor. This editor is most commonly used to create and edit dBASE program and format files, but it can also be used to create or edit any standard ASCII text file. MODIFY COMMAND assumes the default .prg extension. If you do not specify an extension when you create a file with MODIFY FILE, none is provided. WINDOW edits the file in a previously DEFINEd window that is not the currently active window. The modifications made to the file are achieved through the use of control keys specific to the type of editing being performed. For quick reference, this information can be displayed by toggling the F1 function key to display a navigation bar. When modifications to the file are complete, the updated file is written to disk, the corresponding ".dbo" file (if any) is automatically deleted, and the old version of the program (if any) is automatically removed from dBASE IV's internal program storage cache. The dBASE IV editor also creates a backup ".BAK" file. If you are editing a procedure in a procedure program file, it is necessary to issue a CLEAR PROGRAM command in order to clear the procedure from memory.

The maximum file size is 32,000 lines containing up to 1,024 characters each, for a maximum file size of 32,768,000 bytes. If you only use 80 character lines, then the maximum file size is 2,560,000 bytes.

EXAMPLE:

```
MODIFY COMMAND MyCode.Prg
```

or

```
MODI COMM MyCode.Prg
```

MODIFY STRUCTURE

Syntax:

```
MODIFY STRUCTURE
```

Command modifies the structure of an existing data base file. When the MODIFY STRUCTURE is issued, a full screen edit mode is entered that permits the modification of fields, including adding fields, deleting fields, or changing field names, data types, or widths. dBASE IV makes an automatic backup copy of the current data base prior to structural modifications. When changes are complete, the data in the backup ".BAK" file are appended to the newly modified record structure. A memo backup file with a ".TBK" extension is also created if the number of memo fields is changed. *Caution:* Records in the backup file will not be appended if both field names and lengths (or overall record length) are modified in the same session. Therefore, field names should be modified during an initial execution of MODIFY STRUCTURE, and field lengths changed and/or new fields added on a second pass.

EXAMPLE:

```
USE Master
MODIFY STRUCTURE
```

or

```
USE Master
MODI STRU
```

MOVE WINDOW

Syntax:

```
MOVE WINDOW <window name>
TO <row>,<column>/BY<delta row>,<delta col>
```

There are two ways to move a window—absolute and relative. MOVE WINDOW TO moves the active window to an absolute location on the screen specified by <row>,<col>. MOVE WINDOW BY moves the active window to a relative location by shifting the top left corner of the active window by the specified number of rows and columns (<delta row> and <delta col>).

If the window does not fit on the screen at the new location, an error message appears and the MOVE WINDOW command does not take effect.

EXAMPLE:

```
DEFINE WINDOW WinOne FROM 2,20 TO 8,50
ACTIVATE WINDOW WinOne
@ 2,2 SAY "This is window one"
MOVE WINDOW TO 10,40

* Moves the window from 2,20-8,50 to 10,40-16,70.
```

or

```
DEFINE WINDOW WinOne FROM 2,20 TO 8,50
ACTIVATE WINDOW WinOne
@ 2,2 SAY "This is window one"
MOVE WINDOW BY 8,20

* Moves the window from 2,20-8,50 to 10,40-16,70.
```

NOTE

Syntax: `NOTE <text>`

NOTE, an asterisk "*", or double ampersands "&&" are used to indicate comment lines in a dBASE program. If the line containing the && comment ends with a semicolon, dBASE IV treats the next line as part of the comment line. However, if the comment line starts with an asterisk or "NOTE", a semicolon is treated as part of the comment and the next line is *not* a comment line.

&& allows you to place a comment on the same line as a command.

An asterisk "*" in the first space on a line indicates a comment.

EXAMPLE:

```
Salary = Salary * 1.10                && Add 10% to Salary
```

or

```
* Add 10% to Salary
Salary = Salary * 1.10
```

or

```
NOTE  Add 10% to Salary
Salary = Salary * 1.10
```

ON ERROR

Syntax: ON ERROR <command>

The ON ERROR <command> sets a trap and waits for an error condition to occur. Upon encountering an error, ON ERROR executes the <command>. If the ON ERROR is triggered from inside an ON ERROR <command>, the trap is disabled until the procedure or command finishes executing. However, you may set another ON ERROR trap inside an ON ERROR <condition>. ON ERROR does not respond to operating system errors, such as drive not ready or file not found. It only responds to dBASE IV errors, such as a syntax or evaluation error.

EXAMPLE:

```
ON ERROR DO IfError
&& causes dBASE IV to branch to the IfError procedure; upon
encountering an error
PROCEDURE IFERROR
...
...
ON ERROR        &&  Turn off error checking
RETURN
```

ON ESCAPE

Syntax: ON ESCAPE [<command>]

The ON ESCAPE <command> sets a trap and waits for the escape key to be pressed. Upon encountering an escape key , ON ESCAPE executes the <command>.

EXAMPLE:

```
SET COLOR TO W+/B
CLEAR
@ 12,20 SAY "Press the Esc key to stop printing"
ON ESCAPE DO Stoprint
SET DEVICE TO PRINT
USE Master
DO WHILE .NOT. EOF()
  ...                      &&  Print routine
ENDDO
SET DEVICE TO SCREEN
...
PROCEDURE STOPRINT
Key = INKEY()             && Remove Esc from buffer
SET DEVICE TO SCREEN
INPUT PROMPT "Press Y to stop printing " +;
  "N to continue" TO YN PICTURE "Y"
```

```
IF YN = "Y"
   RETURN TO MASTER
ELSE
   SET DEVICE TO PRINT
ENDIF
RETURN
```

ON KEY

Syntax: `ON KEY [LABEL <key label name>] [<command>]`

The ON KEY designates a specific key as a "hot key" so that pressing that key causes <command> to execute. If no <key label name> is specified, ON KEY branches to the specified command or procedure when any key is pressed. A printable character key may be designated as a hot key by making <key label name> equal to the value in this table.

KEY CAP IDENTIFICATION	<key label name>
F1 to F10	F1, F2, F3, . . .
Ctrl-F1 to Ctrl-F10	Ctrl-F1, Ctrl-F2, . . .
Shift-F1 to Shift-F10	Shift-F1, Shift-F2, . . .
Alt-0 to Alt-9	Alt-0, Alt-1, Alt-3, . . .
Alt-A to Alt-Z	Alt-A, Alt-B, Alt-C, . . .
←	LEFTARROW
→	RIGHTARROW
↑	UPARROW
↓	DOWNARROW
Home	Home
End	End
PgUp	PgUp
PgDn	PgDn
Del	Del
Backspace	BACKSPACE
Ctrl-←	Ctrl-leftarrow
Ctrl-→	Ctrl-rightarrow
Ctrl-Home	Ctrl-Home
Ctrl-End	Ctrl-End
Ctrl-PgUp	Ctrl-PgUp
Ctrl-PgDn	Ctrl-PgDn
Ins	INS
Tab	TAB
Back Tab	BACKTAB
Ctrl-A to Ctrl-Z	Ctrl-A, Ctrl-B, Ctrl-C, . . .

EXAMPLE:

```
ON KEY DO Stop

* Branches to the Stop procedure if any key is pressed
```

or

```
ON KEY Ctrl-A DO Stop

* Branches to the Stop procedure if Ctrl-A is pressed
```

ON PAD

Syntax:

```
ON PAD <pad name> OF <menu name>
[ACTIVATE POPUP<popup name>]
```

ON PAD defines which popup menu will be activated when the selection bar is positioned on the prompt pad of the specified menu. ON PAD is triggered simply by navigating to the prompt pad, not by pressing RETURN.

ACTIVATE POPUP allows a menu bar and a popup menu to be active at the same time.

EXAMPLE:

```
DEFINE MENU Main
DEFINE PAD View OF Main PROMPT "View" AT 2,4
DEFINE PAD GoTo OF Main PROMPT "Find" AT 2,16
DEFINE PAD Exit OF Main PROMPT "Exit" AT 2,30

* Assign popup to pads

ON PAD View OF Main ACTIVATE POPUP ViewPop
ON PAD GoTo OF Main ACTIVATE POPUP GoToPop
ON PAD Exit OF Main ACTIVATE POPUP ExitPop

* Define the View pad's first popup and first bar

DEFINE POPUP ViewPop FROM 3,4;
                     MESSAGE "Select View"
DEFINE BAR 1 OF ViewPop PROMPT "Choose View"
...
...
ACTIVATE MENU Main
```

ON PAGE

Syntax:

```
ON PAGE [AT LINE <expN> <command>]
```

ON PAGE causes dBASE to execute specified commands when the streaming output reaches a specified line number on the current page during a ?/?? or EJECT PAGE command. This command is used to handle page breaks with footers and headers on a report.

EXAMPLE:

```
ON PAGE AT LINE 60 FO PageBrk
SET PRINT ON
DO Heading          &&  Print page 1 heading
SCAN ALL
  ...               &&  Process
ENDSCAN
EJECT PAGE
DO Footing          &&  Print last page footer
SET PRINT OFF
ON PAGE             &&  Turn off the page handler
RETURN

PROCEDURE HEADING
EJECT PAGE
?
? "Heading line"
?
RETURN

PROCEDURE FOOTING
?
? "Footing Line"
?
RETURN

PROCEDURE PAGEBRK
DO Footing
DO Heading
RETURN
```

ON READERROR

Syntax: ON READERROR [<command>]

ON READERROR executes the specified command when an error condition is encountered, or when the RANGE or VALID criteria are not met.

Specifying ON READERROR without a command disables the program's ability to trap read errors.

EXAMPLE:

```
SET COLOR TO W+/B,W+/N
CLEAR
ON READERROR DO BadAge
@ 9,7 SAY "Enter your age: " GET AGE PICTURE "99";
       RANGE 21,65
...
READ
...
```

```
PROCEDURE BADAGE
SET COLOR TO W+/R
@ 12,23 TO 15,56 DOUBLE
@ 13,25 SAY "Age must be between 21 and 65"
@ 14,34 SAY "Please Reenter"
Key = INKEY(5)
RETURN
```

ON SELECTION PAD

Syntax:

```
ON SELECTION PAD <pad name>
OF <menu name>[<command>]
```

ON SELECTION PAD specifies the action taken when a bar menu selection is made.

When you select any pad from the active menu, ON SELECTION PAD executes the command specified by <command>. All menus are deactivated, but are not erased from the screen.

If ON SELECTION PAD is used without a command, the named menu and prompt pad are deactivated.

EXAMPLE:

```
DEFINE MENU Test MESSAGE "This is a test"
DEFINE PAD X1 OF TEST PROMPT "Test 1" AT 0,0
DEFINE PAD X2 OF TEST PROMPT "Test 2" AT 0,20
DEFINE PAD X3 OF TEST PROMPT "Test 3" AT 0,50
ON SELECTION PAD X1 OF Test DO Proc1
ON SELECTION PAD X2 OF Test DO Proc1
ON SELECTION PAD X3 OF Test DEACTIVE MENU
ACTIVATE MENU Test
```

ON SELECTION POPUP

Syntax:

```
ON SELECTION POPUP <popup name>/ALL
[<command>]
```

ON SELECTION POPUP specifies the action taken when a popup menu selection is made.

If ON SELECTION POPUP is used with the ALL keyword instead of a popup menu name, the ON SELECTION command applies to any popup menu selection.

If ON SELECTION POPUP is used without a command, the named popup menu (or all popup menus if ALL is specified) are deactivated.

EXAMPLE:

```
DEFINE POPUP Test FROM 5,20
DEFINE BAR 1 OF TEST PROMPT "Test 1"
DEFINE BAR 2 OF TEST PROMPT "Test 2"
```

```
DEFINE BAR 3 OF TEST PROMPT "Exit"
ON SELECTION POPUP Test DO Proc
ACTIVATE POPUP Test

PROCEDURE PROC
DO CASE
   CASE BAR() = 1
     DO ProcX1
   CASE BAR() = 2
     DO ProcX2
   CASE BAR() = 3
     DEACTIVATE POPUP
ENDCASE
```

OTHERWISE

Syntax: `OTHERWISE`

OTHERWISE is part of the DO CASE programming structure:

```
DO CASE
   CASE <condition>
     <commands>
  [CASE <condition>
     <commands>]
  [OTHERWISE
     <commands>]
ENDCASE
```

When the DO CASE command is executed, successive CASE statements are examined and their <condition> expressions evaluated. The first CASE <condition> that evaluates as ".T." causes the <commands> following it to be executed until another CASE, OTHERWISE, or ENDCASE is encountered, at which point execution continues after the matching ENDCASE. If no <condition> is ".T.", the OTHERWISE <commands> are executed. OTHERWISE causes the program to take an alternative path of action when all CASE statements evaluate to False (.F.).

EXAMPLE:

```
Code = 3
DO CASE
   CASE Code = 1
     Prefix = "Mr."
   CASE Code = 2
     Prefix = "Mrs."
   CASE Code = 3
     Prefix = "Ms."
   OTHERWISE
     Prefix = SPACE(3)
ENDCASE
```

PACK

Syntax:

```
PACK
```

The PACK command permanently removes all records marked for deletion from the data base in USE. If the data base in USE is being used with one or more indexes enabled, PACK will rebuild the index files. The disk space released by packing records is reclaimed when the data base is closed, and DIR, LIST, and DISPLAY FILES do not reflect changes until the data base is closed.

Warning: There is no way to retrieve DELETEd records once the PACK command has been issued.

EXAMPLE:

```
USE MASTER
DELETE RECORD 8
PACK
```

PARAMETERS

Syntax:

```
PARAMETERS <parameter list>
```

The PARAMETERS command allows local variable names to be assigned to data passed from a calling program and must appear as the first statement in the "called program." Parameters in the <parameter list> are valid memory variable names separated by commas (,) and they must correspond exactly to the number of items in the calling program's list. If the value of a memory variable is changed in the called program, the new value is passed back to the calling program. See the DO <file> WITH <parameter list> command for more information.

EXAMPLE:

```
PROCEDURE TAX                 &&  PROCEDURE TAX
PARAMETERS Amt,Tax,Ans        &&  Amount to be taxed
                              &&  Tax amount
                              &&  Results of Proc
Ans = Amt + (Tax * Amt)       &&  Compute Answer
RETURN                        &&  Return
*END:TAX
```

PICTURE / FUNCTION

Syntax:

```
PICTURE
```

PICTURE, FUNCTION, AT, and STYLE options permit the formatting of the output.

Picture functions are special format options for each field. They are not available for date and logical fields. Function codes may be used with the FUNCTION clause or combined with template codes in a PICTURE clause by using the sequence:

```
"@ <code> <space> <format>"
```

EXAMPLE:

```
PICTURE "@( $****.**"
```

Some of the available codes are as follows:

FUNCTIONS

A	Allows alphabetic characters only and disallows number entry.
B	Left-justifies alphabetic string.
C	Displays CR after a positive number. SAY clause only.
D	The current SET DATE format for dates.
E	Edits data as a European date.
I	Displays a centered alphabetic string.
J	Displays a right-justified alphabetic string.
L	Displays leading zeros for numbers.
N	Allows a choice for GET values.
N	Allows letters and digits only.
R	Causes nontemplate characters to be displayed, but not stored.
S	Limits display width and permits horizontal scrolling to view data.
T	Displays a field with leading and trailing blanks removed.
X	Displays DB after negative numbers. SAY clause only.
Z	Displays field as blanks if its numeric value is 0.
^	Displays numbers in scientific notation.

PICTURES

(	Negative numbers enclosed in parentheses. SAY clause only.
!	Alphabetic characters will be converted to uppercase.
#	Digits, blanks, and signs, disallows alphabetic entry.
$	Displays the current "set currency" string in place of leading zeros.
*	Displays asterisks in place of leading zeros.
,	Displays commas if there are digits to the left of the comma.
.	Displays a decimal point for a numeric field.
9	Allows digits for character data and digits and signs for numeric data.
A	Allows alphabetic characters only.
L	Allows logic values only.
N	Allows numeric and alphabetic characters only.
X	Allows any character.
Y	Allows Y, y, N, n only. Converts input to uppercase automatically.

EXAMPLES:

```
Payment = -1,234.56
FirstName = "Phil"
? "Do you wish to print the results? " GET Answer PICTURE "Y"
      &&  Answer must equal a "Y" or "N" after this command.
? -Payment PICTURE "@C"                  && Displays 1234.56 CR
? Payment PICTURE "@("                   && Displays (   1234.56)
? ALLTRIM(FirstName) PICTURE "R  !!!!!!!!!!"      && ‖Phil‖
? Payment PICTURE "*999,999.99"          && **-1,234.56
? Payment PICTURE "99,999.99"            && -1,234.56
? Payment PICTURE "$ 999,999.99"         && $$-1,234.56
? Payment PICTURE "@^ 9999999"           && -.12345600E+4
? Payment PICTURE "@L 9999999.99"        && -001234.56
? Payment PICTURE "@Z 9999999999.99" && 1234.56
```

Often you may want to display a dollar amount with a single dollar sign, commas, and a decimal point. The following PICTURE clause is what you need. If DollarAmt = -1,234.56, it will be displayed properly using:

```
? DollarAmt PICTURE "@$Z 9,999,999.99"          && $-1,234.56
```

PLAY MACRO

Syntax:

```
PLAY MACRO <macro name>
```

This command plays macros created through the dBASE IV Control Center. Macros may be identified with a macro key or a macro name. The macro key may be Alt-F1 through Alt-F9. Additional macro keys can be Alt-F10 followed by a letter from A to Z. Therefore, you can assign up to 35 unique macros at one time.

A macro is nothing more than a series of keystrokes that you saved in a macro library.

This command plays the keystrokes stored in the macro definition as if you were currently entering them. Macros are played in LIFO (Last In, First Out order); thus, if you place four PLAY MACRO commands in a row, macro four will play first and macro one will play last.

EXAMPLE:

1. From the dot prompt press SHIFT and F10 together.
2. The message "dBASE IV Macro Processing" with two choices—"Begin recording" and "Cancel"—will appear. Select "Begin recording."
3. The message "Press the key that will call this macro" will appear. Press "A" through "Z".
4. The message "Record macro" will appear. Enter your macro.
5. Press SHIFT and F10 together again. The choices "End recording," "Insert user breakpoint," and "Continue processing" will be displayed. Select "End recording".

6. The macro will be recorded. To save the macro, enter the command SAVE MACROS TO <filename>.
7. Your responses needed to record and save a macro are as follows:

```
SHIFT-F10
↵
U
↑↑↑↵
SHIFT-F10
↵
SAVE MACROS TO UP3
```

The preceding instructions were used to create and save a macro to produce three up arrows and to enter a keystroke sequence. This macro (U) was saved in the file UP3. The code to use this macro in a program is as follows:

```
...          &&  Previous program instructions
RESTORE MACROS FROM UP3
PLAY MACRO U
```

PRINTJOB

Syntax:

```
PRINTJOB
   <commands>
ENDPRINTJOB
```

This command is a structured programming construct for defining and implementing print settings, such as starting and ending print codes, starting and ending print pages, print eject, and number of copies.

The command PRINTJOB defines the beginning of a print job and sends the starting print codes defined by _pscodes, ejects the page if _peject is set to either "BEFORE" or "BOTH," and initializes _pcolno to 0.

ENDPRINTJOB defines the end of a print job, sends the ending print codes defined by _pecodes, ejects the page if _peject is set to either "AFTER" or "BOTH," and loops back to PRINTJOB the number of times defined by _pcopies.

EXAMPLE:

```
USE Master
_peject  = "AFTER"
_pcopies = 2
SET PRINT ON
PRINTJOB
SCAN
  *...                    &&  Process.
ENDSCAN
ENDPRINTJOB
SET PRINT OFF
RETURN
```

PRIVATE

Syntax: `PRIVATE ALL [LIKE/EXCEPT <skeleton>]]`

The PRIVATE command allows you to create new memory variables in a lower-level program with the same names as memory variables that were created in a calling program or were previously declared as PUBLIC. These memory variables may be reused without destroying the previous values. During execution of the program containing the PRIVATE memory variables, any variables that share the same name will be "hidden" from the user until this program has completed execution. Once the program containing the PRIVATE command has completed execution, all memory variables that shared the same name as those in the PRIVATE command will be reinstated. A specific list of PRIVATE memory variables may be declared or a template may be used to specify PRIVATE memory variables.

Changes made to a PRIVATE memory variable do not overwrite the values on memory variables with the same name in other programs. Previous values of PRIVATE memory variables are retained in memory with the names of the programs that created them.

EXAMPLE:

```
LastName  = "Simnett"
FirstName = "Richard"
? LastName              &&  Simnett
DO PROC1
? LastName              &&  Simnett
PROC1
?LastName               &&  Simnett
PRIVATE LastName
LastName = "Chabak"
?LastName               &&  Chabak
RETURN
```

PROCEDURE

Syntax: `PROCEDURE <procedure name>`

A PROCEDURE statement identifies the beginning of a subroutine and must be the first statement in each procedure module. Procedure names may be a maximum of ten characters long. They must begin with a letter and may contain any combination of letters, numbers, and underscores thereafter. Every procedure must end with a RETURN

EXAMPLE:

```
PROCEDURE Error1
@ 22,0 CLEAR
@ 22,0 SAY "Password error - Please reenter."
RETURN
```

PROTECT

Syntax:

```
PROTECT
```

PROTECT provides a system for setting up data security by assigning privilege levels to users and files.

It provides file security and access control to a single computer or to many nodes on a local area network. This is a full screen, menu-driven command, and is issued with dBASE IV by the security administrator.

PROTECT is optional and works in single- or multiuser systems. It includes three types of data base protection:

1. Log-in security, which prevents unauthorized access to dBASE IV.
2. File and field access security, which permits you to define what files, and fields within these files, each user can access.
3. Data encryption, which encrypts dBASE files.

If you do not wish to do so, it is not necessary to implement all three levels of security; however you must implement security in the preceding order.

EXAMPLE:

```
PROTECT  &&  Follow the directions provided by the full;
             screen commands.
```

PUBLIC

Syntax:

```
PUBLIC <memory variable list>
 /[ARRAY<array definition list>]
```

PUBLIC defines memory variables or arrays as global. Such variables can be accessed and modified *by* any dBASE program or subprogram in the current dBASE IV session. Memory variables that are created with the PUBLIC statement are, by default, initialized to ".F.". You may redeclare any PUBLIC memory variable to be PUBLIC; however, assigning a value to a PRIVATE memory variable and then declaring it to be PUBLIC will result in a syntax error. A one- or two-dimensional array may also be created with the PUBLIC command.

EXAMPLE:

```
? LastName                 &&  Undefined
FirstName = "Phil"
? FirstName                &&  Phil
DO PROC1
? FirstName                &&  Phil
? LastName                 &&  Chabak

PROC1
?LastName                  &&  Undefined
PUBLIC LastName
```

```
FirstName = "Andy"
LastName  = "Chabak"
?FirstName                 &&  Andy
?LastName                  &&  Chabak
RETURN
```

QUIT

Syntax:

```
QUIT
```

QUIT closes all open files (including data, indexes, program, and other files), terminates the dBASE IV session, and returns control to the operating system.

Warning: A QUIT should always be performed to terminate the dBASE IV session. Turning the machine off without quitting dBASE IV may result in damage to open files and the loss of data.

EXAMPLE:

```
INPUT 'Enter "Q" to Quit or "C" to continue' TO GoOn
IF UPPER(GoOn) = "Q"
   QUIT
ENDIF
...
```

READ

Syntax:

```
READ [SAVE]
```

READ activates all @. . .GETs issued since the last CLEAR, CLEAR ALL, CLEAR GETS, or READ. It is most commonly used in dBASE program files for full screen entry or editing of data. The cursor can be positioned to each of the @ GET locations, allowing data to be entered or edited. The result is stored in the field or memory variable designated in the @ GET statement. If READ is issued when no GETs are pending, dBASE IV waits for the next keystroke and then continues. All GET statements are automatically cleared following a READ command unless the SAVE option is specified. SAVE does not clear GETs, so the same set of GETs appears for editing the next time the READ is issued. If GETs are being SAVEd, be sure to issue a CLEAR GETS command before the memory pool allocated for the storage of GET information becomes full.

EXAMPLE:

```
USE MASTER
@ 10,5  GET LastName
@ 10,50 GET FirstName
@ 12,5  GET Address
...                         && Additional GETs
READ
```

RECALL

Syntax:

```
RECALL [<scope>]
       [FOR <condition>][WHILE <condition>]
```

RECALL reinstates records that are marked for deletion in the active data base. Any DELETE command can be undone by a matching RECALL command, provided a PACK or ZAP command has not been performed on the file.

If SET DELETED is ON, you must specify which records to RECALL with RECALL RECORD <n>>.

EXAMPLE:

```
USE MASTER
RECALL RECORD 8
```

or

```
USE MASTER
RECALL ALL
```

REINDEX

Syntax:

```
REINDEX
```

REINDEX rebuilds all active index (.ndx) and multiple index (.mdx) files in the current work area

Index files may be obsolete because they were not active when key fields in the corresponding data base were altered. By using the REINDEX command the currently active index files will be updated.

REINDEX retains the original UNIQUE status of the index file when it is rebuilt, in spite of the current state of the SET UNIQUE command.

EXAMPLE:

```
USE MASTER INDEX Master
REINDEX
```

RELEASE

Syntax:

```
RELEASE <memvar list>/
 [ALL [LIKE/EXCEPT<skeleton>]]
 /[MODULE <module name>]
```

RELEASE deletes memory variables and opens memory space for other uses.

MODULE removes specified LOADed assembly modules from memory.
ALL used within a program only deletes memory variables created in the current program.
LIKE removes those that match a criterion.
EXCEPT limits the scope of deletion.

EXAMPLE:

```
RELEASE ALL LIKE Col*
```

or

```
RELEASE ColHelp, LastName, Address
```

or

```
RELEASE MODULE CursorOn
```

RELEASE MENUS

Syntax:

```
RELEASE MENUS [<menu name list>]
```

Command erases menus from the screen and clears them from memory.

It DEACTIVATEs menus, if necessary, and clears all ON SELECTION and ON PAD commands associated with them. A menu cannot be released if it is currently in use but it can be released once it is deactivated.

If <menu name list> is not specified, all menus are released.

EXAMPLE:

```
DEFINE MENU Test MESSAGE "This is a test"
DEFINE PAD X1 OF TEST PROMPT "Test 1" AT 0,0
DEFINE PAD X2 OF TEST PROMPT "Test 2" AT 0,20
DEFINE PAD X3 OF TEST PROMPT "Exit  " AT 0,50
ON SELECTION PAD X1 OF Test DO Procl
ON SELECTION PAD X2 OF Test DO Procl
ON SELECTION PAD X3 OF Test DO Exit
ACTIVATE MENU Test
PROCEDURE TEST
DEACTIVATE MENU
RELEASE MENU Test
RETURN
```

RELEASE POPUPS

Syntax: RELEASE POPUPS [<popup name list>]

Command erases popup menus from the screen, deactivates popup menus (if necessary), and clears all ON SELECTION commands associated with them.

If <popup name list> is not specified, all popup menus are released.

EXAMPLE:

```
DEFINE POPUP Test FROM 5,20
DEFINE BAR 1 OF TEST PROMPT "Test 1"
DEFINE BAR 2 OF TEST PROMPT "Test 2"
DEFINE BAR 3 OF TEST PROMPT "Exit"
ON SELECTION POPUP Test DO Proc
ACTIVATE POPUP Test
RETURN

PROCEDURE PROC
DO CASE
   CASE BAR() = 1
     DO ProcX1
   CASE BAR() = 2
     DO ProcX2
   CASE BAR() = 3
     RELEASE POPUP Test
ENDCASE
```

RELEASE SCREENS

Syntax: RELEASE SCREENS [<screens name list>]

Command erases saved screen images from memory. The <screens name list> contains names of previous defined screens, separated by commas. If no screens are listed, all saved screens are released.

EXAMPLE:

```
SET COLOR TO W+/B
CLEAR
DO DispSay                        && Displays a .fmt Screen
DO Part1Get                       && Get a portion of all the GETs
SAVE SCREEN TO Part1
...                               && Additional processing
RESTORE SCREEN FROM Part1
...                               && Additional processing
RELEASE SCREENS Part1
```

RELEASE WINDOWS

Syntax:

```
RELEASE WINDOWS [<window name list>]
```

Command erases windows from the screen and clears them from memory. The <window name list> contains names of previous defined windows, separated by commas.

Any text that was covered by the released windows is restored. Windows can be selectively removed.

EXAMPLE:

```
DEFINE WINDOW WinOne FROM 10,20 TO 16,50
DEFINE WINDOW WinTwo FROM 12,30 TO 18,60
...
DEFINE WINDOW WinSix FROM 20,60 TO 23,75
ACTIVATE WINDOW WinOne
@ 2,2 SAY "This is window one"
WAIT
RELEASE WINDOWS WinOne, WinSix
```

RENAME

Syntax:

```
RENAME <old filename> TO <new filename>
```

RENAME changes the name of a disk file from its present name (<old filename>) TO a new name (<new filename>). File extensions must be supplied for both <old filename> and <new filename> names. Drive specifiers may be used if the files are not on the default drive. Successful execution of the RENAME command requires that the <new filename> must not already exist and that the <old filename> must exist and not be open.

EXAMPLE:

```
USE    &&  Close Active Database (OldMastr)
RENAME OldMastr.DBF TO Master.DBF
```

REPLACE

Syntax:

```
REPLACE [<scope>]
 [FOR <condition>][WHILE <condition>]
 <field> WITH <exp>[ADDITIVE]
 [,<field> WITH <exp>[ADDITIVE]]
```

REPLACE overwrites the contents of specified fields <field> in the active data base file with the <exp> value. Unless a <scope>, FOR, or WHILE clause is specified, only the current record is affected by the REPLACE command.

Warning: Because the REPLACE command updates activated indexes with each execution, replacements should never be performed on the key field of an indexed file with a <scope>, FOR, or WHILE clause. Otherwise, only part of the intended replacements may actually occur.

ADDITIVE adds the new contents to the ends of memo fields without deleting the old contents.

EXAMPLE:

```
USE Master                          &&  10% across the board raise
REPLACE ALL Salary WITH Salary * 1.1
```

REPLACE FROM ARRAY

Syntax:

```
REPLACE FROM ARRAY <array name> [<scope>]
 [FILEDS <field list>] [FOR <condition>]
 [WHILE <condition>]
```

Command overwrites the contents of specified fields <field> in the active data base file with the <array name> values. Unless a <scope>, FOR, or WHILE clause is specified, only the current record is affected by the REPLACE command.

Warning: Because the REPLACE command updates activated indexes with each execution of the command, replacements should never be performed on the key field of an indexed file with a <scope>, FOR, or WHILE clause. Otherwise, only part of the intended replacements may actually occur.

Data is copied from the first row of the specified array into fields of the active data base. The first array element is copied to the first field, the second element to the second field, and so on. The process stops when there are no more fields to replace or there are no more elements in the first row of the array.

EXAMPLE:

```
USE Master
MaxAmt = RECCOUNT()
DECLARE Amount[MaxAmt]
J = 1
DO WHILE J < MaxAmt + 1
   Amount[J] = MastFix(J)

* MastFix is a UDF to compute amount.

   J = J + 1
ENDDO
REPLACE FROM ARRAY Amount ALL Salary

* Put the new amounts into the data base.
```

REPORT FORM

Syntax:

```
REPORT FORM <report form file name>/? [PLAIN]
  [HEADING <expC>] [NOEJECT] [SUMMARY]
  [<scope>] [FOR <condition>] [WHILE<condition>]
  [TO PRINTER/TO FILE <filename>]
```

REPORT FORM prints information from the active data base using the report form file created by CREATE or MODIFY REPORT. A report may be directed to the screen, the printer, or an ASCII text file. The default extension is .FRM for report form <files>. A detail line for each record in the active data base will be printed unless a <scope>, FOR, or WHILE clause is specified.

PLAIN	Page number and date are suppressed and page headings appear only on the first page of the report.
HEADING	An additional heading is printed on each page.
NOEJECT	The initial form feed to the printer is suppressed.
TO PRINT	Report is routed to both screen and printer.
TO FILE	Report is routed to screen and an ASCII text <file>.
SUMMARY	Only totals and subtotals (no details) are printed.

EXAMPLE:

```
USE Master
SET FILTER TO Salary > 50000
GOTO TOP
REPORT FORM MastRpt Heading "High Rollers";
     NOEJECT TO FILE SaveMstr
```

RESET

Syntax:

```
RESET [IN <alias>]
```

RESET removes the integrity check tag set by the BEGIN TRANSACTION command in the specified work area, thus allowing the data base file to be used. This tag normally stays on a file until the transaction has been completed or a successful ROLLBACK has occurred.

RESET is used when you do not want to, or cannot, ROLLBACK a data base file. Normally, this command is not used in a program, but only at the dot prompt. Alias is the alias name of a data base file opened in the nonactive work area.

EXAMPLE:

```
ON ERROR DO FixIt WITH "Master"
BEGIN TRANSACTION
...
...
END TRANSACTION

PROCEDURE FIXIT
```

```
PARAMETERS FileInUse
ON ERROR DO CantFix
ROLLBACK FileInUse
RETURN
*END:FIXIT

PROCEDURE CANTFIX
ON ERROR
RESET Master
*END:CANTFIX
```

RESTORE FROM

Syntax: `RESTORE FROM <filename> [ADDITIVE]`

Command retrieves and activates memory variables previously saved in a ".MEM" file and places them in memory. Memory variables currently in memory are erased unless ADDITIVE is specified. If the number of memory variables to be added exceeds dBASE IV's memory variable limit, then as many memory variables as possible are retrieved. From a command file, memory variables are restored as private variables; from the interactive command mode, memory variables are restored as public variables.

ADDITIVE causes RESTOREd memory variables to be added to the current list instead of overwriting it.

Up to 25,000 memory variables are available if you so specify in Config.DB. The default value is 500; however, memory constraints may limit this value to less than 500.

EXAMPLE:

```
RESTORE FROM ColChoice ADDITIVE
```

or

```
* Restore colors as PUBLIC variables.

PUBLIC ColWarning, ColEntry, ColStand,;
      ColHelp, ColData, ColMenu
RESTORE FROM ColChoice ADDITIVE
```

RESTORE MACROS FROM

Syntax: `RESTORE MACROS FROM <macro file>`

Command reads a macro file from disk and activates the macro definitions it contains.

Macros can be created through the dBASE IV Control Center. They may be identified with a macro key or a macro name. The macro key may be Alt-F1 through Alt-F9. Additional macro keys can be Alt-F10 followed by a letter from A to Z. Therefore, you can assign up to 35 unique macros at one time.

A macro is nothing more than a series of keystrokes that you saved in a macro library.

EXAMPLE:

1. From the dot prompt, press SHIFT and F10 together.
2. The message "dBASE IV Macro Processing" with two choices—"Begin recording" and "Cancel"—will appear. Select "Begin recording."
3. The message "Press the key that will call this macro" will appear. Press "A" through "Z".
4. The message "Record macro" will appear. Enter your macro.
5. Press Shift and F10 together again. The choices "End recording," "Insert user breakpoint," and "Continue processing" will be displayed. Select "End recording".
6. The macro will be recorded. To save the macro, enter the command SAVE MACROS TO <filename>.
7. Your responses needed to record and save a macro are as follows:

```
SHIFT-F10
←
U
↑↑↑←
SHIFT-F10
←
SAVE MACROS TO UP3
```

The preceding instructions were used to create and save a macro to produce three up arrows and to enter a keystroke sequence. This macro (U) was saved in the file UP3. The code to use this macro in a program is as follows:

```
...             &&  Previous program instructions
RESTORE MACROS FROM UP3
PLAY MACRO U
```

RESTORE SCREEN

Syntax: `RESTORE SCREEN FROM <buffer variable>`

This restores a previously saved screen image from a buffer. The screen image must have been stored in memory with a SAVE SCREEN TO <screen name>. Images can be restored many times from a single saved image.

EXAMPLE:

```
USE Master
DO Special      &&  A Special routine which creates a;
                    complex screen display
SAVE SCREEN TO Complex
CLEAR
BROWSE
```

```
CLEAR
@ 12,12 SAY "Press 'A' to review complex display"
Key = INKEY()
IF Key = ASC("A")
    RESTORE SCREEN FROM Complex
ENDIF
```

RESTORE WINDOW

Syntax:

```
RESTORE WINDOW <window name list>/ALL
 FROM<filename>
```

Command restores windows from a .win disk file.
The file must have been created with the SAVE WINDOW command.
If ALL is specified, all the defined windows in the .win file are restored.

EXAMPLE:

```
DEFINE WINDOW WinOne FROM 10,20 TO 16,50
DEFINE WINDOW WinTwo FROM 12,30 TO 18,60
...
DEFINE WINDOW WinSix FROM 20,60 TO 23,75
...
SAVE WINDOW ALL TO NewWin
CLEAR ALL
...
...
RESTORE WINDOW WinOne, WinSix FROM NewWin
* If you wish to restore all the windows, issue the next
* command.
&&  RESTORE WINDOW ALL FROM NewWin
```

RESUME

Syntax: RESUME

RESUME causes a SUSPENDed program to continue execution at the line on which execution was suspended. Use of the SUSPEND and RESUME commands is a valuable debugging aid for developers. While program execution is suspended, the current status of the dBASE IV environment may be examined to determine why problems are occurring. It is helpful to either CLEAR or SAVE and RESTORE the screen before to resuming so that any commands entered during command suspension will not interfere with future screen I/O.

EXAMPLE:

```
DO MyCode
...    &&  The escape key was pressed.
* From the dot prompt.
CLEAR
DISPLAY MEMORY
Salary = 51000
RESUME
```

or

```
DO MyCode
...
DISPLAY MEMORY
RESUME
```

RETRY

Syntax: RETRY

Used mainly in error recovery, RETRY returns control to the calling program, causing the last line executed in that program to be reexecuted. The RETRY command is similar to the RETURN command except that the RETURN command causes the next line in the calling program to be executed rather than reexecuting the last line. RETRY is especially useful when a set of commands should be repeated until a certain condition is true, or in error-handling routines. Control is returned to the calling program and the command that called the ON ERROR DO <program> is retried. IF and DO WHILE commands are not reevaluated. RETRY clears the value returned by ERROR().

EXAMPLE:

```
ON ERROR DO FixIt WITH ERROR()
USE Master
...
RETURN

PROCEDURE FIXIT
PARAMETERS ErrorNum
DO CASE
   CASE ErrorNum = 3
     CLOSE DATABASES
     RETRY     &&  Causes the USE command to be repeated.
   CASE ErrorNum = ...
     ...
ENDCASE
RETURN
*END:FIXIT
```

RETURN

Syntax: `RETURN [TO MASTER/<procedure name>]/[expression]`

RETURN terminates execution of a command file and returns control to one of the following:

The calling file
Interactive mode
The host operating system

Use of a RETURN command at the end of a program is optional, since an implicit RETURN is added by dBASE IV following the last statement of a program file. In either case, all PRIVATE memory variables are released at this time. If the TO MASTER option is specified with this command, control is returned to the highest-level calling program. If the program is to be referenced as a user-defined function, RETURN must be followed by <expr>.

RETURN executes the line following the line that called the second program whereas RETRY reexecutes the calling line in the program.

EXAMPLE:

```
USE Master
DO CutSalry
RETURN TO MASTER
PROCEDURE CUTSALRY
REPLACE ALL Salary WITH Salary * .95
RETURN
```

ROLLBACK

Syntax: `ROLLBACK [<database filename>]`

ROLLBACK restores the data base and index files that were part of a transaction to their condition before the start of the transaction. It closes and deletes all index and data base files that may have been created during the transaction and terminates the transaction.

This command is usually used when more than one record in a data base is to be changed at a time.

EXAMPLE:

```
USE Master
DO CutSalry
RETURN TO MASTER
PROCEDURE CUTSALRY
ON ERROR ROLLBACK
```

```
BEGIN TRANSACTION
   REPLACE ALL Salary WITH Salary * .95
END TRANSACTION
RETURN
*END:CUTSALRY
```

RUN/!

Syntax:

```
RUN <DOS command>
```

or

```
! <DOS command>
```

RUN executes a specified DOS command, or any program executable by DOS, from within dBASE IV, and then returns to dBASE IV.

Some DOS commands, such as ASSIGN and PRINT, remain in memory after being RUN.

Warnings:

1. The DOS file COMMAND.COM must be in the current directory, or otherwise be locatable via the DOS COMSPEC parameter.
2. Do not RUN disk reorganization programs like CHKDSK from within dBASE IV. They modify the contents of your disk in a manner that can confuse dBASE IV.

EXAMPLE:

```
USE MASTER
...
SET DEVICE TO PRINT
* Download a soft font to the printer.
RUN DOWNLOAD TR12R.SFP,20,P
...
```

SAVE TO

Syntax:

```
SAVE TO <filename> [ALL LIKE/EXCEPT <skeleton>]
```

SAVE TO stores all or part of the current set of memory variables to a disk file. The default extension is ".MEM" for <filename>. If the ALL LIKE <skeleton> option is included, only those memory variables that are "LIKE" the skeleton are saved. If the ALL EXCEPT <skeleton> option is included, all memory variables except those that match the skeleton are saved.

EXAMPLE:

```
SAVE ALL LIKE Col* TO OldColor
```

SAVE MACROS TO

Syntax: `SAVE MACROS TO <macro file>`

Command saves a defined macro to a macro file. A macro file contains a library of macros. The default file extension for macro files is .key.

Macros can be created through the dBASE IV Control Center. They may be identified with a macro key or a macro name. The macro key may be Alt-F1 through Alt-F9. Additional macro keys can be Alt-F10 followed by a letter from A to Z. Therefore, you can assign up to 35 unique macros at one time.

A macro is nothing more than a series of keystrokes that you saved in a macro library.

EXAMPLE:

1. From the dot prompt, press SHIFT and F10 together.
2. The message "dBASE IV Macro Processing" with two choices—"Begin recording" and "Cancel"—will appear. Select "Begin recording".
3. The message "Press the key that will call this macro"will appear. Press "A" through "Z".
4. The message "Record macro" will appear. Enter your macro.
5. Press Shift and F10 together again. The choices "End recording," "Insert user breakpoint," and "Continue processing" will be displayed. Select "End recording".
6. The macro will be recorded. To save the macro, enter the command SAVE MACROS TO <filename>.
7. Your responses needed to record and save a macro are as follows:

```
SHIFT-F10
↵
U
↑ ↑ ↑↵
SHIFT-F10
↵
SAVE MACROS TO UP3
```

The preceding instructions were used to create and save a macro to produce three up arrows and to enter a keystroke sequence. This macro (U) was saved in the file UP3.

SAVE SCREEN

Syntax: `SAVE SCREEN TO <screen name>`

SAVE SCREEN saves the current screen image to memory so that it may later be restored. Multiple screens may be saved to different <screen names>. The <screen name> can be any name that is valid for a memory variable. Although they are named and stored in memory like memory variables, screen images are *not* memory variables.

EXAMPLE:

```
USE Master
DO Special                 && A special routine that creates a;
                              complex screen display.
SAVE SCREEN TO Complex
CLEAR
BROWSE
CLEAR
@ 12,12 SAY "Press 'A' to review complex display"
Key = INKEY()
IF Key = ASC("A")
   RESTORE SCREEN FROM Complex
ENDIF
```

SAVE WINDOW

Syntax:

```
SAVE WINDOW <window name list>/ALL
 TO <filename>
```

Command saves window definitions to a disk file. It automatically assigns a .win extension unless another is specified. Saved window definitions can be used again with the RESTORE WINDOW command.

If ALL is specified, all the defined windows in the .win file are saved.

EXAMPLE:

```
DEFINE WINDOW WinOne FROM 10,20 TO 16,50
DEFINE WINDOW WinTwo FROM 12,30 TO 18,60
...
DEFINE WINDOW WinSix FROM 20,60 TO 23,75
...
SAVE WINDOW ALL TO NewWin
```

SCAN/ENDSCAN

Syntax:

```
SCAN [<scope>]
   [FOR <condition>] [WHILE <condition>]
      [<commands>]
      [LOOP] [EXIT]
ENDSCAN
```

SCAN . . . ENDSCAN is a simplified programming construct and an alternative to the DO . . . ENDDO construct for processing selected records or all records in a data base file. SCAN finds the first record that meets the <scope>, FOR, and WHILE criteria; processes the record using the commands between SCAN and ENDSCAN; and then goes on to find the next record to process. EXIT and LOOP commands may be placed anywhere between the SCAN and ENDSCAN statements.

The <scope> default is ALL, starting from the beginning of the file.

EXIT transfers control from within a SCAN loop to the first command following the ENDSCAN.

LOOP causes control to return directly back to the SCAN command.

EXAMPLE:

```
SELECT B          &&  Master database
SCAN
  * ... Process
  REPLACE B->Salary WITH NewSalary
ENDSCAN
RETURN
```

or

```
SELECT B       &&  Master data base.
SCAN FOR Salary < 50000
  * ... Process
  REPLACE B->Salary WITH NewSalary
ENDSCAN
RETURN
```

SEEK

Syntax:

```
SEEK <exp>
```

SEEK evaluates a specified expression and attempts to find the first occurrence of a record whose index key expression matches the specified <expr> in the master index of the data base file. It returns a logical true (.T.) if the index key is found, and a logical false (.F.) if it is not found. Single quotes (' '), double quotes (" "), or square brackets ([ ]) must be used to enclose a character string literal. SEEK is similar to the FIND command; however, SEEK can be used to search for matches on general expressions.

EXAMPLE:

```
USE Master ORDER LastRaise OF Master
SEEK {11/03/87}
```

SELECT

Syntax:

```
SELECT <work area name/alias>
```

SELECT chooses a work area from the ten that are available to open a data base file or selects a work area in which a data base file is already open. The valid work areas are 1 through 10, or A through J. Work area 10 is reserved for an open catalog. A work area may be selected by specifying the work area number (1 through 10) or letter (A through J). Once a data base is opened in a work area, the work area may also be selected by the alias name.

EXAMPLE:

```
SELECT 1
USE MASTER ALIAS Old
SELECT B
USE TRANS
SELECT Old
```

SET

Syntax: SET

SET is a full screen, menu-driven command for displaying and editing the value of many SET commands.

Select a command setting to alter from one of the seven submenus. Exit by pressing the Esc key.

Warning: All SET commands revert to the default setting when you leave dBASE IV.

Individual SET commands and their syntaxes are discussed fully in the SET COMMANDS section of this book.

SHOW MENU

Syntax: SHOW MENU <menu name> [PAD <pad name>]

SHOW MENU displays a menu without activating it. The cursor cannot be moved in nor can options be selected from a menu displayed with this command.

PAD highlights a specified menu pad instead of the default first menu pad.

This command is used during program development to check the appearance of the screen being designed.

EXAMPLE:

```
DEFINE MENU Main
DEFINE PAD View OF Main PROMPT "View" AT 2,4
DEFINE PAD GoTo OF Main PROMPT "Find" AT 2,16
DEFINE PAD Exit OF Main PROMPT "Exit" AT 2,30
SHOW MENU Main
```

or

```
DEFINE MENU Main
DEFINE PAD View OF Main PROMPT "View" AT 2,4
DEFINE PAD GoTo OF Main PROMPT "Find" AT 2,16
DEFINE PAD Exit OF Main PROMPT "Exit" AT 2,30
SHOW MENU Main PAD GoTo
```

SHOW POPUP

Syntax: `SHOW POPUP <popup name>`

SHOW POPUP displays a popup menu without activating it. The cursor cannot be moved in the displayed popup menu. Messages associated with the popup menu are not displayed and the cursor remains at the dot prompt.

This command is used during program development to check the appearance of the screen being designed.

EXAMPLE:

```
DEFINE POPUP Test FROM 5,20
DEFINE BAR 1 OF TEST PROMPT "Test 1"
DEFINE BAR 2 OF TEST PROMPT "Test 2"
DEFINE BAR 3 OF TEST PROMPT "Exit"
SHOW POPUP Test
```

SKIP

Syntax: `SKIP [<expN>] [IN <alias>]`

SKIP moves the record pointer forward or backward in the active data base file. If an index file is in use with the data base file, SKIP follows index record order. If the file is not indexed, SKIP moves sequentially by record number. SKIP without <expN> advances the record pointer to the next record. If <expN> is positive, the record pointer moves forward <expN> records; if <expN> is negative, the record pointer moves backward <expN> records. If the record pointer is positioned on the last record and a SKIP is executed, RECNO( ) evaluates to one greater than the last record and EOF( ) is ".T.". If the record pointer is positioned on the first record and SKIP -1 is executed, RECNO( ) evaluates to 1 and BOF( ) is ".T.". If an index is in use, the sequence of the records is the same as the key sequence in the controlling index file. The SKIP operation does not count records that are marked for deletion if DELETE is ON or records that do not match an active filter.

IN <alias name> causes SKIP to select the designated work area before processing, move the record pointer, and then reselect the original work area.

EXAMPLE:

```
USE MASTER
SKIP 12
```

or

```
USE MASTER INDEX Salary
SEEK 50000
SKIP -1
```

SORT TO

Syntax:

```
SORT TO <filename> ON <field1>
  [/A] [/C] [/D] [,<field2> [/A] [/C] [/D] ...]
  [ASCENDING/DESCENDING] [<scope>]
  [FOR <condition>] [WHILE <condition>]
```

SORT TO creates a new data base file in which the records of the active data base file are reordered alphabetically, chronologically, or numerically by the specified key fields, and outputs the result to <filename>. The SORT is performed in ASCENDING (/A) order, unless DESCENDING (/D) is specified.

/A sorts in ASCENDING order.
/C sorts by upper- and lowerCASE, and therefore, not in strict ASCII order.
/D sorts in DESCENDING order.
ASCENDING and DESCENDING affect all fields that do not have an /A or /D.

You may combine /C with either /A or /D (for example, /DC).
Logical and memo fields cannot be SORTed.
A maximum of ten fields can be SORTed.

EXAMPLE:

```
USE Master
SORT TO Biggies ON STR(Salary,8,2) + LastName +;
        FirstName FOR Salary >= 50000;
        DESCENDING
```

STORE

Syntax:

```
STORE <expression>
 TO <memvar list>/<array element list>
```

STORE creates and initializes one or more memory variables, and initializes array elements previously created with the DECLARE command.

If a memory variable of the same name already exists, it is overwritten.

You can use STORE instead of "=" when you want to initialize many variables to the same value.

EXAMPLE:

```
STORE 0 TO N, NewAnswer, OldAnswer, M->Salary
STORE SPACE(5) TO Names[10], Names[11], Names[12]
```

SUM

Syntax:

```
SUM  [<expN list>]
    [TO <memvar list>/TO ARRAY<array name>]
    [<scope>] [FOR <condition>][WHILE <condition>]
```

SUM totals numeric expressions within the active data base to memory variables or arrays. Unless otherwise specified by a <scope> or a WHILE or FOR clause, all data base records are summed. If no expression list is provided, all numeric fields are summed.

EXAMPLE:

```
USE Master
SUM Salary TO TotalSal
```

or

```
USE Master
SUM Salary * 1.1, IIF(Sex="M", Factor1 * Salary,;
     Factor2 * Salary TO TotNewSal, AdjSalary
```

SUSPEND

Syntax:

```
SUSPEND
```

SUSPEND provides a debugging tool that lets you stop a program while it is executing and enter commands from the keyboard or the history buffer. At the dot prompt, intervening commands may be issued until program execution is either resumed or canceled. The ability to suspend program execution and execute commands interactively is particularly useful for debugging applications. Memory variables that are created while program execution is suspended are created as private memory variables.

EXAMPLE:

```
DO MyCode
...    &&  Process.
SUSPEND
* From the dot prompt.
CLEAR
DISPLAY MEMORY
Salary = 51000
RESUME
```

TEXT/ENDTEXT

Syntax:

```
TEXT
    <text characters>
ENDTEXT
```

Used in programs to output blocks of text to the screen or printer, This command provides a simple, convenient way to write to the output device. The TEXT command signals dBASE IV to begin copying all lines of text, exactly as they appear, to the current output device(s). This process continues until either an ENDTEXT statement is encountered or the end of the current command file is reached, whichever occurs first.

EXAMPLE:

```
TEXT
This is text to be displayed on the screen.
So is this:
...
ENDTEXT
```

TOTAL ON

Syntax:

```
TOTAL ON <key field>
 TO <filename> [FIELDS <field list>]
 [<scope>] [FOR <condition>] [WHILE <condition>]
```

TOTAL ON sums the numeric fields of the active data base file and creates a second data base file to hold the results. The numeric fields in the TO data base file contain the totals for all records that have the same key value in the original data base file. The TOTAL command computes numeric field totals for records with matching <key fields> expression values in the data base in USE and places them in the corresponding fields of records in a second data base. One record is created in the TO <filename> for each <key field> encountered. The numeric fields from the active data base are totaled and placed in the record. The value of the field from the first record encountered with <key field> will be placed in the record for all other data types.

The data base in USE must either be sorted on the <key field> or have an INDEX enabled on the <key field>. All records will be totaled unless a <scope> or FOR/WHILE <condition> clause is issued. All numeric fields are totaled unless the FIELDS <field list> clause is specified.

This command is very useful for computing the totals of an unknown number of possibilities. One of the authors had a data base containing the source of the security price listed for each security in the data base and needed a report containing the total number of prices supplied by each of the pricing services. Using traditional methods of indexing the data base on the pricing source and counting the number of occurrences would take many hours to produce a report. A field called "One" was added to the data base and given a length of 5. Filling the field with the number one and totaling the "Ones" provided the desired results—in less than three minutes.

EXAMPLE:

```
USE Security INDEX PSource
REPLACE ALL One WITH 1
TOTAL ON PSource TO Answers FIELDS One
USE Answers
SET DEVICE TO PRINT
LNum = 1
DO WHILE .NOT. EOF()
   @ LNum,2  SAY PSource
   @ LNum,15 SAY One
   SKIP
ENDDO
```

TYPE

Syntax: `TYPE <filename> [NUMBER] [TO PRINTER]`

TYPE displays the contents of an ASCII text or procedure file. Data base, index, and other non-ASCII files cannot be easily read because they contain other than alphanumeric characters. An extension must be specified for <filename>.

NUMBER displays line numbers in both the printed output and the displayed file.

TO PRINTER sends the output to a printer.

EXAMPLE:

```
TYPE Master.Prg NUMBER TO PRINTER
```

UNLOCK

Syntax: `UNLOCK [ALL/IN <alias>]`

UNLOCK releases record and file locks on the active data base file. The current record lock is the last LOCK( ), FLOCK( ), or RLOCK( ) issued on the data base file in the currently selected work area. UNLOCK ALL releases all record and file locks in all work areas.

IN <alias name> releases locks in specified work areas only.

EXAMPLE:

```
USE Master
? FLOCK()        &&  .T.
REPLACE Salary WITH 25000, TITLE WITH "Clerk"
UNLOCK
```

UPDATE ON

Syntax:

```
UPDATE ON <key field> FROM <alias>
 REPLACE <field name 1> WITH <expression>
 [,<field name 2> WITH <expression 2>...] [RANDOM]
```

Command uses data from another data base file to replace fields in the current data base file. The FROM <alias> file must be in USE in one of the unselected work areas. The UPDATEs are controlled by the value in the <key field> field. The <key field> field name must be the same in both data bases. The active data base must always be indexed on the <key field> field. If the FROM <alias> file is not sorted on the <key field> field, then the RANDOM clause must be supplied. The changes are made by matching records in the two data base files based on a single key field.

EXAMPLE:

```
USE Master ORDER Salary
REPLACE ALL Salary WITH 0
```

```
USE NewSal ORDER Salary IN 2
UPDATE ON Salary FROM NewSal REPLACE Salary;
       WITH B->Salary
```

USE

Syntax:

```
USE [<database filename>/?] [IN <work area number>]
 [[INDEX <.ndx or .mdx file list>]
 [ORDER <.ndx filename>/<.mdx tag>
 [OF <.mdx filename>]] [ALIAS <alias>]
 [EXCLUSIVE] [NOUPDATE]]
```

USE opens the existing data base file, and may open .mdx and .ndx index files in the selected work area. If the data base contains index fields, the associated OF specifies the .MDX if a tag is not in the production .mdx. If USE is issued without the <filename> expression, or if another <filename> is used, then the currently active data base is closed. All indexes will be updated automatically if their key fields are altered, even if they are not the active index.

IN	opens files in another work area.
INDEX	opens index files.
ORDER	determines the controlling index.
OF	specifies the .mdx if a tag is not in the production .mdx.
ALIAS	allows you to provide an alias name for the data base file.
EXCLUSIVE	prevents other users from working with the file until you close it with CLOSE, CLEAR ALL, or USE.
NOUPDATE	makes file read-only.

EXAMPLE:

```
USE Master INDEX Salary, Names ALIAS Employees
```

WAIT

Syntax:

```
WAIT <prompt> [TO <memvar>]
```

WAIT causes all processing to pause until any key is pressed. The key value is saved if the TO <memvar> clause is supplied; otherwise, it is discarded. If the <memvar> has not already been defined when the WAIT statement is executed, it is created. If the key pressed is a nonprintable character, <memvar> is assigned a NULL character. If the optional <prompt> is not specified, the default message "Press any key to continue. . ." is displayed on the screen.

EXAMPLE:

```
WAIT
```

or

```
WAIT "Press C to Continue, S to Stop" TO Cont
```

ZAP

Syntax: `ZAP`

ZAP removes all records from the active data base file. It is equivalent to issuing a DELETE ALL command followed by a PACK. Records zapped from the currently active data base may not be recalled.

Any open index files in the current work area are automatically reindexed to reflect the empty data base file.

EXAMPLE:

```
USE MASTER
ZAP
```

CHAPTER 3

SET Commands

SET ALTERNATE

Syntax: `SET ALTERNATE on/OFF`

Command records all output other than that of full screen commands (@ commands) to a text file. ON/OFF is used to enable or disable screen output to the output file created by the SET ALTERNATE TO [filename] command.

ON enables output.
OFF disables output.

EXAMPLE:

```
SET ALTERNATE TO SaveIt
SET ALTERNATE ON
? LIST STRUCTURE
? SET ALTERNATE OFF
```

SET ALTERNATE TO

Syntax: `SET ALTERNATE TO [<filename>] [ADDITIVE]`

Command names a text file in which to save commands and output, or closes the file. The default file extension is .txt. If [filename] is omitted, this format closes the current alternate file.

ADDITIVE adds the information to the end of the last alternate file without erasing it first.

EXAMPLE:
```
SET ALTERNATE TO SaveIt ADDITIVE
SET ALTERNATE ON
USE MASTER
? LIST
? SET ALTERNATE OFF
```

SET AUTOSAVE

Syntax: SET AUTOSAVE on/OFF

Command saves any changes made to data base files as they are made. Each record is written at once rather than being held in a buffer and written when the buffer is filled. This safeguards against loss of files as a result of a power or hardware failure.

When SET AUTOSAVE is OFF, changes are stored in a memory buffer until the file is closed or the buffer is full.

Note: When performing an I/O intensive operation, such as appending many records from another file, AUTOSAVE should be turned off to improve performance.

EXAMPLE:
```
USE MASTER
SET AUTOSAVE OFF
APPEND FROM NewData
SET AUTOSAVE ON
```

SET BELL ON/off

Syntax: SET BELL ON/off

This enables (ON) or disables (OFF) the sounding of the computer bell (tone) upon entry of invalid data in a field, or when a field is completely filled. The default frequency is 512 hertz, and the duration is 0.1 second.

Most users find the sounding of the bell irritating and good programming practice calls for setting the bell OFF, except under extreme conditions.

Note: You can "ring" the bell even when it is set OFF by using the command ? CHR(7).

EXAMPLE:
```
SET BELL OFF
DO GetData
...
```

SET BELL TO

Syntax:

```
SET BELL TO [<frequency>,<duration>]
```

This command sets the frequency and duration of the computer bell. The default frequency is 512 hertz, and the duration is 2 ticks or 0.1 second. The available frequency range is between 19 and 10,000 hertz and the duration is between 2 and 19 ticks or 0.1 to 1.1 seconds. If you want to use your settings as the default bell settings, place them in the Config.DB file. SET BELL TO without a <frequency> and <duration> resets the default values. ? CHR(7) can be used to test the bell setting.

EXAMPLE:

```
* Start up attention tones
SET BELL TO 300,2
?CHR(7)
SET BELL TO 499,10
?CHR(7)
SET BELL TO 700,10
?CHR(7)
WAIT
* Serious error tones
SET BELL TO 150,16
?CHR(7)
SET BELL TO 130,19
?CHR(7)
```

SET BLOCKSIZE TO

Syntax:

```
SET BLOCKSIZE TO <expN>
```

Command changes the default block size of memo and multiple index (.mdx) files. <expN> is a number between 1 and 32. This is multiplied by 64 to get the actual number of bytes. The default is 1, for compatibility with dBASE III PLUS. Large blocks provide faster string manipulation and slow down I/O processing, while small blocks provide slower string manipulation and faster I/O processing. You will need a block size of 7 or 8 for large memo fields.

EXAMPLE:

```
SET BLOCKSIZE TO 7
USE Master
EDIT
```

SET BORDER TO

Syntax:

```
SET BORDER TO [SINGLE / DOUBLE / PANEL /
 NONE / <border definition string>]
```

This command changes the default border from a single-line box to one of several border types. The <border definition string> is entered using the ASCII values for the line-drawing characters of the IBM extended character set.

SINGLE draws a single-line border.
DOUBLE draws a double-line border.
PANEL draws an inverse video border (CHR(219)).
NONE does not draw a border.

The border definition string follows the same rules as shown in the following diagram:

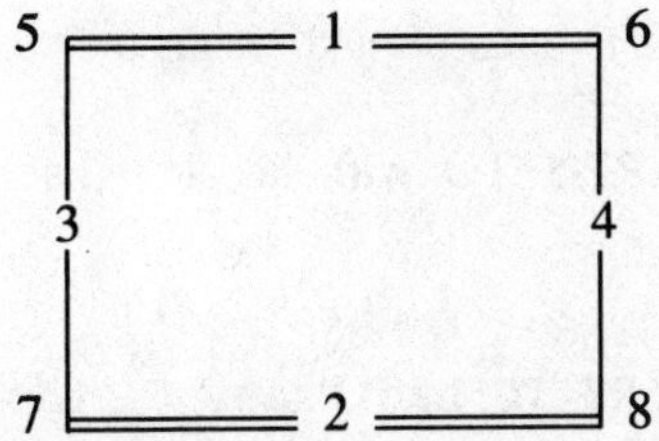

or

```
[<1>],[<2>],[<3>],[<4>],[<5>],[<6>],[<7>],[<8>]]]]]]]]
```

which would translate to the following command

```
SET BORDER TO 205,205,179,179,213,184,212,190
```

EXAMPLE:

```
SET BORDER TO DOUBLE
```

or

```
SET BORDER TO NONE
```

Note: Borders defined explicitly in a DEFINE WINDOW command override the SET BORDER settings.

SET CARRY

Syntax:

```
SET CARRY ON/OFF
```

When ON, this command enables, or when OFF, it disables the ability to CARRY data forward from the previously entered record to the new (present) record when using the full screen APPEND or INSERT facility.

Note: An inserted record that has been carried forward will not be saved unless it is modified in some way.

EXAMPLE:

```
USE MASTER
SET CARRY ON
APPEND
```

```
REPLACE Salary WITH 25000
SET CARRY OFF
...
```

SET CARRY TO

Syntax:

```
SET CARRY TO [<field list>] [ADDITIVE]
```

This command brings the specified fields from the previous to the new record with APPEND, BROWSE, or INSERT.

ADDITIVE adds copied fields to the end of the file, saving previously existing fields.

SET CARRY TO with no field list returns to the default condition (all fields carried).

EXAMPLE:

```
USE MASTER
SET CARRY TO LastName, FirstName, Address, Title
APPEND
REPLACE Salary WITH 25000
SET CARRY TO     &&  Carry all fields forward.
...
```

SET CATALOG

Syntax:

```
SET CATALOG ON/OFF
```

This command is use to create or open a catalog. When ON, new files are added to the currently open catalog. When OFF, no new files are added.

dBASE IV searches for a catalog in the home directory, followed by the current drive and directory. When you create or select a catalog it is placed in work area 10 (J); therefore, area 10 is not available for a data base. All data base and associated files, such as index, query, format, report, and label, are added to the catalog. To stop adding files to the catalog, set it off. Even though the catalog is set off, if you use the "?" along with a MODIFY command, a menu list of available files from the catalog will be presented.

When the catalog is set on, a new entry is automatically added to the active catalog when any of the following commands are used.

COPY STRUCTURE
COPY STRUCTURE EXTENDED
CREATE
CREATE FROM
CREATE/MODIFY LABEL
CREATE/MODIFY QUERY
CREATE/MODIFY REPORT
IMPORT FROM
INDEX
JOIN
SET FILTER TO FILE
SET FORMAT
SET VIEW
SORT

CREATE/MODIFY SCREEN	TOTAL
CREATE/MODIFY VIEW	USE

EXAMPLE:

```
SET CATALOG TO Phils
USE ?                          &&  Select file from the catalog
                                   list
SET CATALOG OFF
COPY TO TEMP
SET CATALOG ON                 &&  Reuse Catalog
INDEX ON Salary TO Salary      &&  Add index to catalog
SET CATALOG TO                 &&  Close Catalog
```

SET CATALOG TO

Syntax: `SET CATALOG TO [<filename>/?]`

Command opens an existing catalog or, if one does not exist, creates a new catalog. ? lists available catalogs from which to select.

dBASE IV searches for a catalog in the home directory followed by the current drive and directory. When you create or select a catalog, it is placed in work area 10 (J); therefore, area 10 is not available for a data base. All data base and associated files, such as index, query, format, report, and label, are added to the catalog. To stop adding files to the catalog, set it off. Even though the catalog is set off, if you use the "?" along with a MODIFY command, a menu list of available files from the catalog will be presented. The command SET CATALOG TO with no <filename> closes the catalog.

If <filename> exists, it is opened; if it does not, it is created. Catalog names are limited to eight characters. dBASE IV appends the .CAT extension to the file name. The master catalog allows you to use the SET CATALOG TO ? command, since it stores the catalog file names and descriptions.

Catalogs are nothing more than data base files with a predefined structure as follows:

Structure for a catalog

Field	Field Name	Type	Width
1	PATH	Character	70
2	FILE_NAME	Character	12
3	ALIAS	Character	8
4	TYPE	Character	3
5	TITLE	Character	80
6	CODE	Numeric	3
7	TAG	Character	4

EXAMPLE:

```
SET CATALOG TO Phils
USE ?      &&  Select file from the catalog list
```

```
SET CATALOG OFF
COPY TO TEMP
SET CATALOG ON                  && Reuse Catalog
INDEX ON Salary TO Salary       && Add index to catalog
SET CATALOG TO                  && Close Catalog
```

SET CENTURY

Syntax: `SET CENTURY ON/OFF`

Command toggles data input and display of century prefixes in the year portion of dates. It allows you to determine how the year is to be formatted when dates are displayed. If CENTURY is SET ON, the year is displayed with 4 digits. If CENTURY is OFF, a 2-digit year is shown (which assumes the 20th century in date calculations). When CENTURY is SET ON, the date display is 10 characters long; when it is OFF, the display is 8 characters.

EXAMPLE:

```
? DATE()        &&  12/07/41 default is off.
SET CENTURY ON
? DATE()        &&  12/07/1941
```

SET CLOCK

Syntax: `SET CLOCK on/OFF`

Command toggles display of the system clock in the default location on the screen, unless a new position is specified with SET CLOCK TO. The clock display is not suppressed with full screen menu commands, regardless of its setting.

EXAMPLE:

```
SET COLOR TO W+/B,W+/N
CLEAR           &&  Clear the screen
SET CLOCK ON    &&  Turn on the clock
DO GetData
```

SET CLOCK TO

Syntax: `SET CLOCK TO [<row>,<column>]`

This command determines the position of the system clock on the screen when the clock is set on. The default position is 0,69. If the command SET CLOCK TO is issued without the <row>,<column> entries, it defaults to the default position.

EXAMPLE:

```
SET COLOR TO W+/B,W+/N
CLEAR              && Clear the screen
SET CLOCK TO 0,0   && Put the clock on the left side.
SET CLOCK ON       && Turn on the clock
DO GetData
```

SET COLOR

Syntax:

```
SET COLOR ON/OFF
```

This command switches between color and monochrome monitors on systems equipped with two monitors, one color and one monochrome. The default is whatever the system is using when you start dBASE IV.

EXAMPLE:

```
* Make the monochrome monitor active.
SET COLOR OFF
@ 12, 12 SAY "This is on the monochrome screen"
...
* Make the color monitor active.
SET COLOR ON
@ 12, 12 SAY "This is on the color screen"
...
```

SET COLOR TO

Syntax:

```
SET COLOR TO [[<standard>] [,[<enhanced>]
  [,[<perimeter>][,[<background>]]]]]
```

This command sets the colors that display the background, borders, and highlighted areas of the screen. Colors are designated by alpha codes. Standard and enhanced displays are determined by pairs of color codes separated by a slash (/). The perimeter attribute (color monitors only) is represented by a single color code. You can selectively change one of the color settings by using a "," to skip those areas you wish to skip. For example, SET COLOR TO ,,B, sets the perimeter color to blue.

The color codes are:

Black	N	Green	G	Blank	X		
Magenta	RB	Blue	B	Red	R		
Brown	GR	White	W	Cyan	BG		
Yellow	GR+	Blank	X	Blink	*	High intensity	+
On monochrome monitors				Underlining	U	Inverse video	I

SET COLOR TO resets the screen to the default colors of black and white.

EXAMPLE:

```
&&  Set colors to bright white on blue.
SET COLOR TO W+/B
CLEAR SCREEN
```

or

```
&&  Set colors to bright white on blue for the standard;
    colors and bright white on black for data entry.
SET COLOR TO W+/B,W+/N
CLEAR SCREEN
```

SET COLOR OF

Syntax:

```
SET COLOR OF NORMAL/MESSAGES/TITLES/BOX/
 HIGHLIGHT/INFORMATION/FIELDS TO
 [< color attribute>]
```

Comman selects the colors to display various screen elements. Colors are designated with alpha codes as follows:

Black	N	Green	G	Blank	X		
Magenta	RB	Blue	B	Red	R		
Brown	GR	White	W	Cyan	BG		
Yellow	GR+	Blank	X	Blink	*	High intensity	+
On monochrome monitors				Underlining	U	Inverse video	I

EXAMPLE:

```
SET COLOR OF NORMAL TO W+/B
SET COLOR OF FIELDS TO W+/N
SET COLOR OF MESSAGES TO W+/R
SET COLOR OF BOX TO RG+/B
```

SET CONFIRM

Syntax:

```
SET CONFIRM on/OFF
```

SET CONFIRM determines whether a carriage return is required at the end of each data entry item or before moving to the next input field. Normally, when the last character in a full screen input field is entered, the input operation is automatically terminated. The cursor then skips to the next field, sounding the bell if BELL ON has been selected. This is convenient for fields in which the data entered is always the same length; for example, Zip codes, Social Security numbers, or telephone numbers. If CONFIRM is turned ON, then the user is required to press a terminating key (CR, PgUp, etc.) to indicate explicitly that input into the field is complete. When data items of varying lengths are to be entered into a field, this mode helps to ensure the accuracy of the data being entered, and avoids operator confusion. SET CONFIRM requires the enter key to be pressed for all fields, instead of some fields requiring enter and others automatically skipping to the next field.

EXAMPLE:

```
USE MASTER
SET CONFIRM ON
DO GetData
```

SET CONSOLE

Syntax: `SET CONSOLE on/OFF`

SET CONSOLE only works from within a program and suppresses output to the screen. Output from the @ . . . SAY command is controlled by the DEVICE setting. The command is primarily used to prevent the display of reports and programs routed to the printer.

The SET CONSOLE command does not affect @ . . . SAY or @ . . . GET commands or full screen commands.

ON sends all output to the screen.
OFF inhibits output to the screen.

EXAMPLE:

```
USE Master
SET CONSOLE OFF
REPORT FORM Salary TO PRINTER
SET CONSOLE ON
```

SET CURRENCY

Syntax: `SET CURRENCY LEFT/right`

SET CURRENCY designates whether the currency symbol will appear to the left or the right of the currency amount. The default is for the currency symbol to be on the left of the currency amount, as in the United States ($20,000). If you are reporting currency in a country that places the currency symbol on the right, such as with French francs, use this command.

EXAMPLE:

```
SET CURRENCY RIGHT
SET CURRENCY TO "¥"
SET POINT TO ","
SET SEPARATOR TO "."
Salary = 20000
@ 12,12 SAY Salary PICTURE "@$"  &&  20000,00¥
```

SET CURRENCY TO

Syntax:

```
SET CURRENCY TO <expC>
```

SET CURRENCY TO changes the symbol associated with the currency unit used in data and calculations. A maximum of nine characters may be used for this symbol. As no standard symbols are supplied, you must enter them yourself.

EXAMPLE:

```
SET CURRENCY RIGHT
SET CURRENCY TO "¥"
SET POINT TO ","
SET SEPARATOR TO "."
Salary = 20000
@ 12,12 SAY Salary PICTURE "$$$,$$$,$$$.99"
                                          && 20.000,00¥
```

SET CURSOR

Syntax:

```
SET CURSOR ON/off
```

When SET CURSOR is OFF, the cursor is hidden. SET CURSOR ON redisplays the cursor.

EXAMPLE:

```
SET COLOR TO &ColStand
CLEAR
Speed = 0
@ 0,0 GET Speed PICTURE "999"
READ
A = LOGO(Speed)

FUNCTION LOGO
*
*   Program...: LOGO
*   Author....: Phil Steele -- President
*               Phillipps Computer Systems Inc.
*   Address...: 52 Hook Mountain Road,
*               Montville, NJ 07045
*   Phone.....: (201) 575-8575
*   Date......: 01/02/89
*   Notice....: Copyright 1989  Philip Steele,
*               All Rights Reserved.
*   Notes.....: This function moves a logo across the
*               screen from left to right and right to
*               left stopping at the middle of the
*               screen.
```

```
*|| Parameters: Speed -- A number used to control the
*||                      movement of the display.
*||
PARAMETERS Speed
PRIVATE  Speed, N, J, X, Y
X = SPACE(14)
Y = SPACE(18)
DECLARE LOGO[8]
STORE "██████████████    " TO P1
STORE "██████    ██████  " TO P2
STORE "  ████       ████ " TO P3
STORE "  ████    ██████  " TO P4
STORE "  ████████████    " TO P5
STORE "  ████            " TO P6
STORE " █████            " TO P7
STORE "█████████         " TO P8
STORE "     ██████████   " TO C1
STORE "    ████████████  " TO C2
STORE "   ███         ███" TO C3
STORE "  ███             " TO C4
STORE "  ███             " TO C5
STORE "   ███         ███" TO C6
STORE "    ████████████  " TO C7
STORE "     █████████    " TO C8
STORE "     ████████████  " TO S1
STORE "   █████████   ███ " TO S2
STORE "   ██████        ██" TO S3
STORE "     ██████████    " TO S4
STORE "       ██████████  " TO S5
STORE "   ██          ████" TO S6
STORE "    ████     ██████" TO S7
STORE "     █████████████ " TO S8
STORE X + P1 + C1 + S1 + Y TO LOGO[1]
STORE X + P2 + C2 + S2 + Y TO LOGO[2]
STORE X + P3 + C3 + S3 + Y TO LOGO[3]
STORE X + P4 + C4 + S4 + Y TO LOGO[4]
STORE X + P5 + C5 + S5 + Y TO LOGO[5]
STORE X + P6 + C6 + S6 + Y TO LOGO[6]
STORE X + P7 + C7 + S7 + Y TO LOGO[7]
STORE X + P8 + C8 + S8 + Y TO LOGO[8]
N = 0
SET CURSOR OFF
DO WHILE N <= 80
 J = 1
```

```
  DO WHILE J <= 8
    IF J = 1 .OR. J = 3 .OR. J = 5 .OR. J = 7
      @ J+2,0 SAY SUBSTR(LOGO[J], 80 - N) +;
           REPLICATE(" ", 80 - N)
    ELSE
     @ J+2,0 SAY REPLICATE(" ", 80 - N) +;
          SUBSTR(LOGO[J], 1, N)
    ENDIF
   J = J + 1
  ENDDO
  N = N + Speed
ENDDO
@ 3,0 SAY LOGO[1]
@ 5,0 SAY LOGO[3]
@ 7,0 SAY LOGO[5]
@ 9,0 SAY LOGO[7]
RETURN(.T.)
*END:LOGO
```

SET DATE

Syntax:

```
SET DATE [TO] AMERICAN/ansi/british/french/
german/italian/japan/usa/mdy/dmy/ymd
```

SET DATE determines the format of the date display, as follows:

AMERICAN	mm/dd/yy
ANSI	yy.mm.dd
BRITISH	dd/mm/yy
ITALIAN	dd-mm-yy
FRENCH	dd/mm/yy
GERMAN	dd.mm.yy
JAPAN	yy/mm/dd
USA	mm-dd-yy
MDY	mm/dd/yy
DMY	dd/mm/yy
YMD	yy/mm/dd

If century is set on the yy portion of the date, it becomes yyyy.

EXAMPLE:

```
?DATE()              &&  12/07/41
SET DATE TO GERMAN
?DATE()              &&  07.12.41
SET DATE TO JAPAN
?DATE()              &&  41/12/07
```

SET DEBUG

Syntax: `SET DEBUG on/OFF`

SET DEBUG determines whether output from SET ECHO is sent to the screen or to the printer. It is used to locate errors in programs. OFF sends output to the screen. ON sends output to the printer. Setting both DEBUG and ECHO ON provides a valuable tool for debugging applications by capturing a trace of the program execution in print without interfering with the normal screen output.

EXAMPLE:

```
SET STEP ON
SET ECHO ON
SET DEBUG ON
DO NewCode
SET STEP OFF
SET ECHO OFF
SET DEBUG OFF
```

SET DECIMALS TO

Syntax: `SET DECIMALS TO <expN>`

Command determines the minimum number of decimal places that are to be displayed as the result of numeric functions and calculations. SET DECIMALS affects division, multiplication, trigonometric, financial, and EXP( ), LOG( ), and SQRT( ) calculations. The decimal display default is 2 places. Other decimal displays are determined according to the nature of the constants and calculations involved.

<expN> can be any number between 0 and 18.

EXAMPLE:

```
SET DECIMALS TO 5
? 3/8                  &&  0.37500
SET DECIMALS TO 3
? 3/8                  &&  0.375
```

SET DEFAULT TO

Syntax: `SET DEFAULT TO <drive>[:]`

Command sets drive where all operations take place and all files are stored, unless otherwise directed. dBASE IV uses the specified drive as the default disk drive for future I/O operations. When you return to the previous drive, you will still be in the subdirectory you left. SET DEFAULT does not check to see if the drive you specified exists, and does not return to the previous drive if you quit dBASE IV while the alternate drive is set.

Warning: dBASE IV retains command files in memory for subsequent execution; therefore, the command file currently stored in memory will be executed regardless of a change in the default drive specification. To clear a command file currently stored in memory, the CLEAR PROGRAM command should be executed. The default drive specification will be respected upon the execution of this command.

EXAMPLE:

```
USE Master          && Error file does not exist
SET DEFAULT TO D
USE Master          && OK
```

SET DELETED

Syntax:

```
SET DELETED on/OFF
```

SET DELETED determines whether records marked for deletion are included or ignored by other commands. When the ON option is selected, all commands that select records using a scope will ignore records that have been marked for deletion. Commands that operate on the current record or that have a scope of RECORD <n> disregard the DELETED setting. The OFF option permits such commands to access all records, whether or not they are marked for deletion. INDEX and REINDEX both include all records in the data base file regardless of SET DELETED status.

Note: RECALL ALL will not recall any records if SET DELETED is ON.

EXAMPLE:

```
USE Master
SET DELETED ON
RECALL ALL          &&  0 records recalled
SET DELETED OFF
RECALL ALL          &&  22 records recalled
```

SET DELIMITERS

Syntax:

```
SET DELIMITERS on/OFF
```

Command separates fields with a colon (:) character unless otherwise specified with SET DELIMITERS TO in the full screen editing mode. SET DELIMITERS OFF is the default display mode in which only reverse video or highlighting is used to emphasize fields when SET INTENSITY is ON rather than delimiter characters. SET DELIMITERS ON brackets fields with colons (:) or any other delimiter that may have been selected with the SET DELIMITERS TO command.

EXAMPLE:

```
USE MASTER
SET DELIMITERS TO "[]"
SET DELIMITERS ON
DO GetData  &&  All entry fields are surrounded with "[]"
```

SET DELIMITERS TO

Syntax: `SET DELIMITERS TO <expC>/DEFAULT`

Command sets the characters used as delimiters for fields. SET DELIMITERS TO <expC> allows an alternative set of delimiters to be designated for field display. <expC> may contain 1 or 2 characters. If one character is specified, this character is used for both the beginning and ending delimiters. If two characters are specified, the first character is the beginning delimiter and the second character is the ending delimiter. The SET DELIMITERS must be ON for the symbols defined by the SET DELIMITERS TO to be in effect.

SET DELIMITERS TO DEFAULT resets the field delimiters to colons.

EXAMPLE:

```
USE MASTER
SET DELIMITERS TO "[]"
SET DELIMITERS ON
DO GetData   &&  All entry fields are surrounded with "[]"
```

SET DESIGN

Syntax: `SET DESIGN ON/off`

When OFF, SET DESIGN prevents a user from transferring to a design surface from BROWSE or EDIT, or from the Control Center or the Dot Prompt. When OFF, it deactivates the "Shift-F2" key combination, and prevents going to the dot prompt or QBE from the EDIT/BROWSE mode. This command allows the developer to use the Control Center menu system as an interface for limited applications and still keep the user out of dBASE IV functionality.

EXAMPLE:

```
USE Master
SET DESIGN OFF
SEEK "STEELE"
EDIT
```

SET DEVELOPMENT

Syntax: `SET DEVELOPMENT ON/off`

This command activates a checking program in dBASE IV that compares the creation date of the compiled object file (.dbo) with its program source file (.prg) to prevent use of an outdated object file. If you use an external editor, this command is needed.

Add DEVELOPMENT = ON to the config.db file if you prefer to use an external editor.

EXAMPLE:

```
SET DEVELOPMENT ON
RUN SPFPC /E MyProc.prg   &&  An external editor
```

SET DEVICE TO

Syntax:

```
SET DEVICE TO SCREEN/printer/file <filename>
```

Command sends the results of @. . .SAY commands to the screen, printer, or a specified disk file. When the <row> <column> values in an @ . . . SAY command are lower than those of the previous @ . . . SAY command, a page eject results if the device is set to the printer. On some printers you may have to issue an EJECT command to release the last page from the printer buffer and get it to print.

EXAMPLE:

```
* Print the report to a file for modifications.
USE Master
SET DEVICE TO FILE Modify
DO PrintIt
SET DEVICE TO SCREEN
```

SET DISPLAY

Syntax:

```
SET DISPLAY TO MONO / COLOR / EGA25 / EGA43 /
 MONO43
```

SET DISPLAY allows you to change the display settings for the type of monitor you are using and determines the number of lines displayed by most graphic cards. On some monitor/display card combinations, EGA43 does not completely fill the screen. If your hardware does not support settings available in this command, there is no effect in the display mode and an error message is displayed.

EXAMPLE:

```
SET DISPLAY TO EGA43
SET CLOCK TO 40,0
```

SET DOHISTORY

Syntax:

```
SET DOHISTORY on/OFF
```

This command is not used in dBASE IV and is retained for compatibility with dBASE III PLUS.

SET ECHO

Syntax: `SET ECHO on/OFF`

When SET ECHO is ON, command lines from programs are displayed on the screen, or on the printer if SET DEBUG is on, as they are executed.

SET ECHO ON is one of the four dBASE IV commands that are useful with DEBUG in debugging dBASE IV programs. The other commands are:

SET DEBUG
SET STEP
SET TALK

EXAMPLE:

```
SET ECHO ON
SET STEP ON
SET DEBUG ON
DO NewCode
SET STEP OFF
SET ECHO OFF
SET DEBUG OFF
```

SET ENCRYPTION

Syntax: `SET ENCRYPTION on/OFF`

This command determines whether copied files (created through COPY, JOIN, and TOTAL) are created as encrypted files. Files created after ENCRYPTION is set OFF will not be encrypted as specified when using PROTECT. To access an encrypted file, you must enter a valid user name, password, and group name after the log-in screen prompts. Your access levels and authorization determine whether you can copy an encrypted file.

You must set encryption off before you can copy or export the file.

EXAMPLE:

```
SET ENCRYPTION OFF
USE Master
COPY TO Temp FOR Salary >= 50000
SET ENCRYPTION ON
```

SET ESCAPE

Syntax: `SET ESCAPE ON/off`

SET ESCAPE determines whether pressing the Esc key will halt processing of a program or pressing the left arrow or Ctrl-S will halt scrolling. It also affects whether INKEY() is able to record these keys.

OFF disables use of the Escape key to interrupt command execution. ON allows command execution to be interrupted with the Escape key. If you press escape during the execution of a command while in an interactive mode, the following message will appear: "*** INTERRUPTED ***." If you press Escape during program execution, dBASE IV prompts Called from <file> xxxxxxxx — Cancel, Ignore, Suspend? The user may choose one of these options by pressing C, I, or S.

EXAMPLE:

```
Esc = CHR(27)
USE Master
SET ESCAPE ON
@ 12, 10 GET Salary
...                         &&  Additional Gets
READ
IF LASTKEY() = Escape
   RETURN
ELSE
   ...                      &&  Process
ENDIF
```

SET EXACT

Syntax: SET EXACT on/OFF

SET EXACT determines whether string comparisons will return true (.T.) when comparing strings of different lengths. If EXACT is OFF, then two strings can be compared even if they have different lengths. That is, if the strings match up to the point where one or the other is exhausted, then they are considered equal. If EXACT is ON, strings must match character for character and be of the same length to be considered equal.

EXAMPLE:

```
Long  = "Philip"
Short = "Phil"
SET EXACT ON
? Long = Short    &&  .F.
SET EXACT OFF
? Long = Short    &&  .T.
```

SET EXCLUSIVE

Syntax: SET EXCLUSIVE on/OFF

This network command determines the shared attribute status of subsequently opened data base files. When SET EXCLUSIVE is ON, no other user may access subsequently used data base files. When SET EXCLUSIVE is OFF, all data base files that are later opened may be shared among multiple users (as long as the EXCLUSIVE option on the USE command is omitted). Changing the setting of EXCLUSIVE does not change the status of previously opened data bases.

Both the CREATE and SAVE commands automatically SET EXCLUSIVE ON when they are executed.

EXAMPLE:

```
SET EXCLUSIVE ON
USE Master   &&  Only you can use the Master data base.
REPLACE ALL Salary WITH Salary * 1.1
SET EXCLUSIVE OFF
```

SET FIELDS

Syntax:

```
SET FIELDS on/OFF
```

When SET FIELDS is ON, only fields designated with SET FIELDS TO can be accessed or displayed. If SET FIELDS is OFF, then all the fields in the currently USEd data bases are accessible to the user. Do not use SET FIELDS ON without first specifying a fields list.

When SET FIELDS is ON , the LIST and DISPLAY STRUCTURE commands indicate, with the ">" symbol, the fields that are in the currently defined fields list.

EXAMPLE:

```
USE Master
SET FIELDS TO LastName, FirstName, Title, Salary
SET FIELDS ON
BROWSE        &&  Only the four fields are displayed.
SET FIELDS OFF
BROWSE        &&  All the fields in the file are displayed.
```

SET FIELDS TO

Syntax:

```
SET FIELDS TO <field> [/R]/<calculated field id>...]
[,<field> [/R]/<calculated field id>...]
/ ALL [LIKE/EXCEPT <skeleton>]
```

Command defines a list of fields that may be accessed in one or more files. The <field> specified is activated when SET FIELDS is ON. SET FIELDS TO (without <field> or ALL) removes all fields from <field>. SET FIELDS TO ALL adds all the fields to the <field>. Consecutive SET FIELDS TO <field> commands may be executed to add fields to those that are currently accessible. SET FIELDS TO <field> does not automatically SET FIELDS ON. By using a file alias, you can specify fields in other than the active data base.

/R is the optional read-only flag.

EXAMPLE:

```
USE Master
SET FIELDS TO Name, Cost, Quantity,;
          Total = "$" + STR(Cost * Quantity,8,2) /R
SET FIELDS ON
BROWSE     &&  Only the four fields are displayed.
```

SET FILTER TO

Syntax: `SET FILTER TO [FILE <filename>/?] [<condition>]`

Command limits access to those data base records that meet the filter condition. Once this SET command is executed, only those records that meet the condition will appear to be present in the data base. All dBASE IV commands that access the used data base respect the SET FILTER condition. SET FILTER TO (without optional <condition>) turns off the conditional restrictions on the active data base. A separate FILTER may be set for each data base file in use. Filters are not activated until the record pointer in a file is moved. If you are on a record in which the Salary field is equal to 23000 and you issue the command "SET FILTER TO Salary >= 50000", you will still be pointing to the record where the Salary is equal to 23000. You should issue the command GOTO TOP after every SET FILTER TO command.

The SET FILTER TO FILE <filename>/? adds a filter (query) file to a catalog if a catalog is opened and SET CATALOG is ON.

EXAMPLE:

```
USE MASTER
SET FILTER TO Salary >= 50000
GOTO TOP
COPY TO HighRoll
SET FILTER TO       && Turn off the filter
GOTO TOP
```

SET FIXED

Syntax: `SET FIXED on/OFF`

This command is included for compatibility with dBASE III PLUS only. It has no effect on the number of decimals displayed.

SET FORMAT TO

Syntax: `SET FORMAT TO [<format filename>/?]`

Command allows the user to select custom forms stored as format (.fmo) files. These formats are used in READ, EDIT, APPEND, INSERT, CHANGE, or BROWSE, and are created with the MODIFY SCREEN command. If <filename> is omitted, the currently active format file is deactivated. The default extension for <filename> is .FMO. Multipage-format files may be created by placing a READ command at the end of each page. PgUp and PgDn keys may then be used to move from screen to screen within the format file. When using READ with a format file, it is possible to edit MEMO fields. (Normally, READ cannot access MEMO fields.)

If a catalog is opened and SET CATALOG is ON, the SET FORMAT TO command updates the catalog.

EXAMPLE:

```
USE Master
SET FORMAT TO MastIn
EDIT
```

SET FULLPATH

Syntax:

```
SET FULLPATH on/OFF
```

This command is used with dBASE III PLUS programs that use the functions MDX(), NDX(), and DBF() to suppress the return of the full file specification.

In dBASE III PLUS, the functions NDX() and DBF() return the drive and file name only (?DBF() && C:Master.dbf).

In dBASE IV, the drive, path, and file name are returned (?DBF() && C:\dbase\Master.dbf) by MDX(), NDX(), and DBF().

By setting the FULLPATH OFF, compatibility with dBASE III PLUS is retained.

EXAMPLE:

```
USE Master
?DBF()          &&  C:Master.dbf &&  Default is OFF
SET FULLPATH ON
?DBF()          &&  C:dbaseMaster.dbf
```

SET FUNCTION

Syntax:

```
SET FUNCTION <expN> TO <expC>
```

SET FUNCTION reprograms a function key with a character string expression of up to 238 characters. dBASE IV translates semicolons (;) occurring in the string into carriage returns. The value of <exp> may range from F2 to F10, Shift-F1 through Shift-F9, and Ctrl-F1 through Ctrl-F10 inclusive. The F1 function key is assigned to the Help function and cannot be reprogrammed. Shift-F10 and the Alt key combinations are macro keys and cannot be reprogrammed. The function keys F11 and F12 are also not reprogrammable.

The current function key assignments can be displayed with the DISPLAY STATUS command. Unless function keys' values are assigned with SET FUNCTION, they have the following default values:

F1	help;	F6	display status;
F2	assist;	F7	display memory;
F3	list;	F8	display;
F4	dir;	F9	append;
F5	display structure;	F10	edit;

EXAMPLE:

```
SET FUNCTION F9 TO "CLEAR;USE Master;BROWSE"
@ 12,12 SAY "Press F9 to BROWSE the file"
```

SET HEADING

Syntax:

```
SET HEADING ON/off
```

This command determines whether column titles are shown above DISPLAY, LIST, SUM, and AVERAGE fields when these commands are issued. The column width is the larger of the field length or the title length.

EXAMPLE:

```
USE Master
DISPLAY FIELDS LastName, FirstName, Title, Salary
* Lists these fields with headings
SET HEADING OFF
DISPLAY FIELDS LastName, FirstName, Title, Salary
* Lists these fields without headings
```

SET HELP

Syntax:

```
SET HELP ON/off
```

Command determines whether a prompt popup window offering help appears when a command is incorrectly entered at the dot prompt.

If SET HELP is ON and you enter an incorrect command at the dot prompt, a window will popup on the screen that will offer you three choices: CANCEL, EDIT, or HELP. By moving the light bar or pressing the letter C, E, or H, the appropriate action will be taken. If you select HELP, the system will try to provide help on the topic in the command producing the error.

EXAMPLE:

```
* All these commands are from the dot prompt.

SET FILTERS TO Salary >= 50000

* The help box will appear because "FILTER" has an "S" on
* the end of it.

SET HELP OFF

* If the previous incorrect command was entered, no help
* box will appear.
```

SET HISTORY

Syntax: SET HISTORY ON/off

Command determines whether previously executed commands are stored in a history buffer. SET HISTORY OFF inhibits the storage of commands for history recall. However, commands that are executed before turning history off may still be recalled for editing and reexecution. The ↑ and ↓ keys are used to redisplay previously entered command when SET HISTORY is ON. A LIFO buffer is used so that the last command entered is the first one recalled. You can use the LIST/DISPLAY HISTORY command to view all the commands in the buffer.

EXAMPLE:

```
USE Master
...                 &&  Additional commands
? Salary            &&  53000
↑                   &&  Displays the last command issued from the;
                        dot prompt.     (? Salary)
SET HISTORY TO 0
SET HISTORY OFF
↑                   &&  No Commands are in the buffer to display.
```

SET HISTORY TO

Syntax: SET HISTORY TO <expn>

Command specifies the desired number of executed commands to be stored in the history buffer. The default number is 20 commands; however, you may change it to any value between 0 and 16,000, depending on the amount of available memory in your system. SET HISTORY TO 0 clears all commands from the history buffer.

EXAMPLE:

```
USE Master
...                 &&  Additional commands
? Salary            &&  53000
↑                   &&  Displays the last command issued from the;
                        dot prompt.     (? Salary)
SET HISTORY TO 0
SET HISTORY OFF
↑                   &&  No Commands are in the buffer to
                        display.
SET HISTORY TO 40   &&  Set the buffer to hold 40;
                        commands.
```

SET HOURS TO

Syntax:

```
SET HOURS TO [12/24]
```

SET HOURS TO toggles the clock display between a 12-hour display and a 24-hour display. The default setting is 12 hours. This command affects all the screens that show the clock. You may enter this command in the Config.db file to have the clock always displayed in the way you wish.

12-hour display — 3:51:25 p.m.
24-hour display — 15:51:25

EXAMPLE:

```
SET HOURS TO 24    &&  13:45:00
SET HOURS TO 12    &&  1:45:00 pm
SET HOURS TO       &&  Reverts to Config.db; value or 12
                       if it is not set in Config.db
```

SET INDEX TO

Syntax:

```
SET INDEX TO [?/[<filename list>
 [ORDER [TAG] <ndx filename>/<TAGNAME>
 [OF <mdx filename>]]]]
```

Command opens a specified list of index or mdx files and specifies the controlling order ndx or mdx tag. All tag names are automatically updated as records are added to or deleted from the data base. The index given using the ORDER option is the primary index that controls the order in which records are accessed. The SET ORDER TO command may be executed to change the order of index files in <filename list>. A maximum of 47 .mdx tag names or 10 .ndx files and .mdx files plus the production .mdx file may be enabled for a data base at one time. If <filename list> is omitted, all active indexes are deactivated for the data base in USE in the current work area. The record pointer is positioned at the beginning of the file as determined by the controlling index file.

EXAMPLE:

```
USE Master
SET INDEX TO Salary OF Main
USE Detail
SET INDEX TO Title ORDER PartName
```

SET INSTRUCT

Syntax:

```
SET INSTRUCT ON/off
```

This command enables the display of dBASE code as forms, reports, or labels are generated. If SET INSTRUCT is ON, the prompt box of actions is displayed in the

Control Center when a file is selected. If SET INSTRUCT is OFF and SET TALK is ON, generated dBASE code is displayed on the screen as it is generated during the CREATE/MODIFY LABEL, CREATE/MODIFY REPORT, or CREATE/MODIFY SCREEN operations.

EXAMPLE:

```
USE Master
SET INSTRUCT ON   && The instructions are on the top
...               &&  of the screen
SET INSTRUCT OFF
MODIFY SCREEN     &&  The generated dBASE IV
                  &&  code is displayed on the screen
```

SET INTENSITY

Syntax:

```
SET INTENSITY ON/off
```

Command determines whether the enhanced fields screen attribute is used for full screen operations such as EDIT. If SET INTENSITY is OFF, the standard attribute is used for both @. . .GET and @. . .SAY commands. When INTENSITY is ON, the enhanced screen attribute is used to highlight input fields; @ . . . SAY commands are displayed using the *standard* screen attributes and @ . . . GET commands are displayed using the *enhanced* screen attributes. When INTENSITY is OFF, the normal screen attribute is used. Input fields may also be delimited using the SET DELIMITER TO command. The status line display is also affected by SET INTENSITY.

EXAMPLE:

```
USE Master
SDate = DATE()
SET COLOR TO W+/B, RG+/N
SET INTENSITY OFF
@ 12,12 SAY "Enter the date to start: " GET SDate

* Both the prompt and SDate field are displayed in
* bright white on blue.
SET INTENSITY OFF
@ 12,12 SAY "Enter the date to start: " GET SDate

* The prompt is displayed in bright white on blue while
* SDate is displayed in yellow on black.
```

SET LOCK

Syntax:

```
SET LOCK ON/off
```

SET LOCK determines whether a lock is applied to records in a multiuser system to prevent records from being updated by more than one user at a time. Files and records in use are automatically locked when you use any update or edit command. Locks permit read-only access by any user, even when records are in the process of being updated. SET LOCK does not automatically release locks when multiple records are locked using the RLOCK() function. You must use the UNLOCK command to unlock these.

EXAMPLE:

```
SET EXCLUSIVE OFF      && If ON, automatic locking is in force.
USE Master INDEX Name
SEEK "Steele"
IF FOUND()
    SET LOCK ON
    SET REPROCESS TO 10

* dBASE IV will attempt to lock the record 10 times.
* If the record is not locked after 10 attempts, an error
* message appears.

    IF RLOCK()
        ...                 &&  Process the record
        UNLOCK
        SET LOCK OFF
    ENDIF
ENDIF
```

SET MARGIN TO

Syntax: SET MARGIN TO <expN>

Command adjusts the printer offset for the left margin for all printed output. The video display is not affected. The default is 0.

The SET MARGIN value is the same as _ploffset. Both of these commands move the left margin. They are not additive and the last one issued sets the margin. When _wrap is true, the value of the system variable _lmargin is added to the SET MARGIN value to determine the true left margin.

EXAMPLE:

```
_wrap = .T.
_lmargin = 5       &&  Printing starts at column 5
SET MARGIN TO 5
* Printing now starts at column 10
_wrap = .F.
* Printing starts at column 5 again.
```

SET MARK TO

Syntax: SET MARK TO [<expC>]

SET MARK TO changes the delimiter between the month, day, and year in the date display. The default delimiter for the United States is /, as in: 4/9/87. To restore the default delimiter, use just SET MARK TO.

EXAMPLE:

```
?DATE()          &&  12/07/41
SET MARK TO "."
?DATE()          &&  12.07.41
SET MARK TO
?DATE()          &&  12/07/41
```

SET MEMOWIDTH TO

Syntax:

```
SET MEMOWIDTH TO <expN>
```

Command adjusts the width of memo field output for LIST and DISPLAY. The default is 50 characters. The minimum width is 8 and the maximum width is 255. If _wrap is true, the system variables _lmargin and _rmargin determine the memo width.

EXAMPLE:

```
USE Master
SET MEMOWIDTH TO 25
```

SET MENU

Syntax:

```
SET MENU ON/off
```

Command determines whether a menu of cursor movement keys appears with the full screen commands. Applies to dBASE III PLUS only and has no effect in dBASE IV.

SET MESSAGE TO

Syntax:

```
SET MESSAGE TO [<expC> [LINE <expN>]]
```

SET MESSAGE TO displays a specified character string on the default bottom line of the screen when SET STATUS is ON unless the LINE <expN> option is specified. The character string may be a maximum of 79 characters long. The string must be delimited with single quotes (' '), double quotes (" "), or square brackets ([ ]). The message is displayed when STATUS is ON in interactive mode or during the execution of full screen editing commands. SET MESSAGE TO resets the character message to the null string.

EXAMPLE:

```
USE Master
SET COLOR TO W+/B, RG+/N
CLEAR
SET MESSAGE TO "Select record to change using " +;
               "the ↑ ↓ keys"

* The message is displayed on the bottom line of the screen.
```

```
BROWSE
SET MESSAGE TO "Select record to change using " +;
        "the ↑ ↓ keys" LINE 0

* The message is displayed on line 0 of the screen.
```

SET NEAR

Syntax: SET NEAR on/OFF

SET NEAR positions the record pointer to the record nearest a key expression for which a search made with SEEK or FIND was unsuccessful.

This command is very useful when you need to find a record near the record you want. For example, you present a light-bar-actuated list of all possible vendors. This permits you to start a selection by entering a letter to find the appropriate vendor. If a "Q" is entered and there are no vendors starting with "Q", you would normally be positioned at the end of the file. However, if you SET NEAR ON, you would be positioned at the first vendor's name starting after a "Q". See the following programming example.

EXAMPLE:

```
USE Master INDEX LastName
SEEK "White"                 &&  White is not in the data base
?EOF()                       &&  .T.
SET NEAR ON
SEEK "White"                 &&  White is not in the data base
?EOF()                       &&  .F.
?LastName                    &&  Wythe
```

SET ODOMETER TO

Syntax: SET ODOMETER TO [<expN>]

SET ODOMETER is used to change the reporting interval used by TALK. It determines the interval at which the record counter is updated on the screen for commands such as COPY and RECALL. The default interval is one and the maximum is 200.

The record counter can be removed from the screen entirely by issuing the SET TALK OFF command.

EXAMPLE:

```
USE Master
SET ODOMETER TO 100
COPY TO TEMP

* The display will be updated every 100 records.
SET ODOMETER TO 20
COPY TO TEMP1

* The display will be updated every 20 records.
```

SET ORDER TO

Syntax:

```
SET ORDER TO [<expN>]/[TAG <mdxtag>
             [OF <mdxname>]]
```

SET ORDER TO sets up any open index file or .mdx tag as the master index, or removes control from all open index files or .mdx tags without closing any .mdx or .ndx files. It determines which index is to be the controlling index for the data base in the current work area. The <expN> may range from 0 to 47, depending on how many indexes are currently enabled. If <expN> is set to 0, then the index control is turned off without disabling the .ndx index files. The data base is then accessed in its natural order (record number sequence). SET ORDER TO (without <expN>) will also turn all index controls off.

EXAMPLE:

```
USE Master INDEX LastName ORDER LastName
SEEK "Chan"
?RECNO()                    && 55
SET ORDER TO TAG Salary
SEEK "Chan"
?RECNO()                    && EOF()
SEEK 50000
?RECNO()                    && 25
SET ORDER TO
SKIP
?RECNO()                    && 26
```

SET PATH TO

Syntax:

```
SET PATH TO [<path list>]
```

SET PATH TO specifies the route to follow to find files not found in the current directory. dBASE IV does not use the path established by the DOS PATH command, nor does DOS use the path the dBASE IV establishes with the SET PATH command. The Control Center does *not* use the path set by the SET PATH command.

SET PATH applies only to commands that search for existing files. If you create a file and the file is to be placed in a directory other than the current directory, you must explicitly specify the path name with the file name.

A path list is a series of directory names separated by commas or semicolons and may be up to 60 characters long.

EXAMPLE:

```
USE Master INDEX LastName ORDER LastName

* Message: FILE NOT FOUND
SET PATH TO D:\DBASE\DATA
USE Master INDEX LastName ORDER LastName

* The file is now available for processing.
```

SET POINT TO

Syntax: SET POINT TO [<expC>]

SET POINT TO changes the character used for the decimal point in numeric output. The default character is a period (.) which is the standard for American systems.

EXAMPLE:

```
USE Master INDEX LastName ORDER LastName
? Salary                 &&  51234.56
SET POINT TO ","         &&  51234.56
? Salary                 &&  51234,56
```

SET PRECISION TO

Syntax: SET PRECISION TO [<expN>]

Command sets a precision of decimal places while doing decimal arithmetic with numbers of type N.

The default is 16. The range is from 10 to 20.

EXAMPLE:

```
SET DECIMALS TO 18
? 87 / 5.1             &&  17.058823529411760000
SET PRECISION TO 10
? 87 / 5.1             &&  17.058823530000000000
SET PRECISION TO 20
? 87 / 5.1             &&  17.058823529411764706
```

SET PRINTER

Syntax: SET PRINTER on/OFF

SET PRINTER directs all output not formatted with the @. . .SAY command to the printer as well as to the screen. The ON option enables output to the printer, including TALK, LIST, and ? . OFF disables printer output. To direct @. . .SAY commands to the printer, the SET DEVICE TO PRINT command must be used.

EXAMPLE:

```
USE Master
LIST                 &&  Sends list to the screen.
SET PRINTER ON
LIST                 &&  Sends list to the printer
```

SET PRINTER TO

Syntax:

```
SET PRINTER TO <DOS device>
SET PRINTER TO \\<computer name>
               \<printer name> = <destination>
SET PRINTER TO \\SPOOLER
SET PRINTER TO \\CAPTURE
SET PRINTER TO FILE <filename>
```

dBASE IV allows PRINTER to be SET TO either a device or a file. If PRINTER is SET TO a file, then the file must be identified by a fully qualified path name. If PRINTER is SET TO a printer device, then all output is directed to <device>. The default printer device is PRN: for MS/PC-DOS. Use SET DEVICE TO PRINTER to direct @. . .SAY commands. SET PRINTER ON has no effect on @. . .SAY commands.

EXAMPLE:

```
USE Master
SET PRINTER ON
LIST                     &&  Sends list to the printer
SET PRINTER TO Master.TXT
LIST                     &&  Sends list to the file
                         &&  Master.TXT
SET PRINTER TO
LIST                     &&  Sends list to the printer again
```

SET PROCEDURE TO

Syntax:

```
SET PROCEDURE TO [<procedure filename>]
```

Command opens a procedure file and gives any executing command file access to the procedures within it. A .DBO extension is assumed if one is not specified in <filename>. If a DBO extension is not found but a PRG extension is found, the PRG source file will be compiled.

Only one procedure file may be open at a time. A procedure file may contain up to 1,170 procedures (which, it is hoped, will be is enough); however, available RAM now becomes the restraining factor.

SET PROCEDURE TO (without <filename>) closes any currently open procedure file.

EXAMPLE:

```
SET PROCEDURE TO PhilTest   &&  Open Procedure
DO Phill                    &&  Execute Procedure Phill
DO Phil2                    &&  Execute Procedure Phil2
CLOSE PROCEDURE             &&  Close PhilTest
```

SET REFRESH TO

Syntax:

```
SET REFRESH TO <expN>
```

This command specifies the length of time between file checking to determine whether a record has changed in a file that is being BROWSEd or EDITed on a network. It only works on files that have been CONVERTed. The range of <expN> is between 1 second and 3,600 seconds (one hour) and the default is 0. If changes have been made to the file by another user on the network, the browse or edit screen is updated if the refresh count reaches zero.

If the refresh interval is 0, the system will not refresh browse or edit screens.

EXAMPLE:

```
USE Master
SET REFRESH TO 15        &&  Set a 15 Second interval.
BROWSE NOEDIT            &&  Browse the data
```

SET RELATION TO

Syntax:

```
SET RELATION TO <exp>/<expN>
 INTO <alias>[,<expN> INTO <alias>]...
```

Command links two or more open data base files according to a key expression common to all related files. One data base is the currently active data base and the other is an open data base in another work area. The second data base is identified by the INTO <alias> clause. Each time the record pointer in the SELECTed data base is moved, the record pointer in the related file is moved to the corresponding record. If a matching record cannot be found in the related data base, the record pointer for that data base is positioned to the end of the file and EOF() is true (.T.).

EXAMPLE:

```
SELECT 1
USE Master ORDER CustNumb          &&  Open parent
USE Customer IN 2                  &&  Open Childl
USE Invoice ORDER CodeNumb IN 3    &&  Child2
SET RELATION     TO CustNumb INTO Customer,;
                 TO CodeNumb INTO Invoice

* Relate the three files

GOTO TOP
LIST NEXT 3 Customer->Name, Invoice->Item, Rating
```

Record#	Customer->Name	Invoice->Item	Rating
1	Joyce, James	Ink	AAA
2	Fletcher, JB	Typewriter Ribbon	AA
3	Steele, Phil	Laser Cartridge	A

SET REPROCESS TO

Syntax:

```
SET REPROCESS TO <expN>
```

Command sets the number of times dBASE IV attempts a command or function that results in a NET error (network file or record lock). It is used in a network environment to attempt to lock files or records.

The default is zero and the range is from –1 to 32,000. If –1 is specified from within a program, an infinite number of retrys will occur. This may prevent you from ever getting past the code requesting the lock.

If 0 is specified without an "ON ERROR" command, the message *"Please Wait, another user has locked this record or file"* will appear while it tries to lock the record or file.

EXAMPLE:

```
USE Master ORDER CustName
SET REPROCESS TO 20
SEEK "WhiteRobert"
IF FOUND()
    RLOCK(RECNO(),"Master")
ENDIF
...
```

In this example, dBASE IV will attempt to lock the record twenty times. If the record is not locked after twenty attempts, an error message will appear.

SET SAFETY

Syntax:

```
SET SAFETY ON/off
```

SET SAFETY provides a level of protection against overwriting or otherwise destroying files. The default is ON.

If a file with the same name as the one you are creating already exists, or you issue the "ZAP" command and SET SAFETY ON is in effect, dBASE IV prompts *"<filename> already exists, overwrite it? (Y/N)"* or requests verification that you really want to delete the data.

EXAMPLE:

```
USE Master ORDER CustName
SET REPROCESS ON
COPY TO NewMast"        &&  NewMast Exists
"NEWMAST already exists, overwrite it? (Y/N)"
```

SET SCOREBOARD

Syntax:

```
SET SCOREBOARD ON/off
```

This command, in conjunction with SET STATUS, determines where dBASE IV messages appear on the screen. Scoreboard information is displayed on line 0 if SCOREBOARD is ON and STATUS is OFF. However, if STATUS is ON, scoreboard information will be displayed on line 22 regardless of how SCOREBOARD is SET. If both STATUS and SCOREBOARD are OFF, the scoreboard information is not displayed. Scoreboard information includes current environment indicators (e.g., keyboard), Del to indicate that a record is marked for deletion in full screen editing, record statuses, and dBASE IV messages (e.g., @ . . . GET RANGE errors). The default is ON.

EXAMPLE:

```
SET SCOREBOARD OFF  &&  Turn off all indicators
SET STATUS OFF      &&  ...
SET TALK OFF
SET ECHO OFF
...
```

SET SEPARATOR TO

Syntax:

```
SET SEPARATOR TO [<expC>]
```

Command changes the comma used for the numeric separator to the specified character.

EXAMPLE:

```
SET SEPARATOR TO "."
SET POINT TO ","
Number = 123987.12
@ 10,0 SAY Number GET Number PICTURE "999,999"
READ

* The screen shows: 123.987,12 instead of 123,987.12
```

SET SKIP TO

Syntax:

```
SET SKIP TO [<alias> [,<alias>]...]
```

SET SKIP and SET RELATION together allow access to multiple records of the same key across related data base files.

EXAMPLE:

```
SELECT 1
USE Master ORDER CustNumb                   &&  Open parent
USE Customer IN 2                           &&  Open Child1
USE Invoice ORDER CodeNumb IN 3             &&  Child2
SET RELATION    TO CustNumb INTO Customer,;
                TO CodeNumb INTO Invoice
GOTO TOP
SET SKIP TO Customer, Invoice
LIST NEXT 3 Customer->Name, Invoice->Item, Rating
```

Record#	Customer->Name	Invoice->Item	Rating
1	Joyce, James	Ink	AAA
1	Joyce, James	Paper	AAA

1	Joyce, James	Erasers	AAA
1	Joyce, James	Erasers	C
2	Fletcher, JB	Typewriter Ribbon	AA
3	Steele, Phil	Laser Cartridge	A
3	Steele, Phil	Laser Cartridge	B

SET SPACE

Syntax: `SET SPACE ON/off`

SET SPACE ON causes an extra space to print between fields when the ? and ?? commands are used. Use commas between the printed expressions you want to separate with SET SPACE as in the example. The default is ON.

EXAMPLE:

```
SELECT 1
USE Master ORDER CustNumb
? City, State                  &&  Montville New Jersey
SET SPACE OFF
? City, State                  &&  MontvilleNew Jersey
```

SET SQL

Syntax: `SET SQL on/OFF`

Command activates and deactivates SQL commands in dBASE IV. When SQL is set ON, SQL commands are used to access data bases. When SQL is set OFF, dBASE language commands are used to access data bases.

Note that while SQL is ON, some dBASE IV commands are disabled.

See the SQL section of this book for additional information.

SET STATUS

Syntax: `SET STATUS ON/off`

SET STATUS determines whether the status bar appears at the bottom of the screen when working from the dot prompt, and in full screen editing commands such as EDIT. The default is ON.

With STATUS set ON, a status line is displayed at the bottom of the screen. The information displayed on the status line includes the current command being executed, the working directory, the active data base file, the record pointer position, the number of records in the file, and scoreboard information (CAPS—Caps Lock is ON, etc.). The status line is updated each time a command is executed that changes the status information. If STATUS is set OFF and SCOREBOARD is set ON, the scoreboard information is displayed on line 0. If both STATUS and SCOREBOARD are set OFF, the status information will not be displayed on the screen.

EXAMPLE:

```
SET SCOREBOARD OFF   &&  Turn off all indicators
SET STATUS OFF       &&  ...
SET TALK OFF
SET ECHO OFF
...
```

SET STEP

Syntax: `SET STEP on/OFF`

SET STEP halts the execution of a program after each instruction and allows you to step through a program one line at a time.

This SET command is one of the tools available for debugging application programs. SET STEP ON pauses program execution after each statement and prompts the user with the following message: "Press SPACE to step, S to suspend, or Esc to cancel . . ." At this point, you may press S to suspend program execution and check any memory variable values or execute intervening commands. Simply execute the RESUME command when you wish to continue program execution.

EXAMPLE:

```
SET SCOREBOARD ON   &&  Set up environment for
SET STATUS OFF      &&  the correction of a bug.
SET TALK ON
SET ECHO ON
SET STEP ON
...
```

SET TALK

Syntax: `SET TALK ON/off`

SET TALK displays record numbers and memory variables as commands are processed, and displays the results of commands such as APPEND FROM, COPY, PACK, STORE, and SUM. When TALK is OFF, these progress reports are not displayed.

Execution speed can be substantially degraded when SET TALK is ON because of the potentially large amount of screen output. This SET command is one of the tools available for debugging application programs.

EXAMPLE:

```
SET SCOREBOARD ON   &&  Set up environment for
SET STATUS OFF      &&  the correction of a bug.
```

```
SET TALK ON
SET ECHO ON
SET STEP ON
...
```

SET TITLE

Syntax: SET TITLE ON/off

The SET TITLE turns the catalog file title prompt on and off. dBASE IV prompts you for a catalog file title when you add a new file to a catalog. If SET TITLE is set to OFF, dBASE IV does not prompt you for the catalog title. The default is ON.

EXAMPLE:

```
SET TITLE OFF              &&  Turn off Catalog prompt
SELECT 1
USE Master ORDER CustNumb
SET TITLE ON               &&  Turn on Catalog prompt
COPY TO NewFile
USE NewFile IN 2           &&  System prompts for catalog
```

SET TRAP

Syntax: SET TRAP on/OFF

SET TRAP calls the debugger after an error occurs in a program, or if you press the Esc key during program execution. The default is OFF.

SET TRAP does not do anything if ON ERROR is activated.

EXAMPLE:

```
SET SCOREBOARD ON   &&  Set up environment for
SET STATUS OFF      &&  the correction of a bug.
SET TALK ON
SET ECHO ON
SET STEP ON
SET TRAP ON
...
```

SET TYPEAHEAD TO

Syntax: SET TYPEAHEAD TO <expN>

Command specifies the size of the type-ahead buffer. The default size is 20 characters. The allowable range is from 0 to 32,000.

If TYPEAHEAD is SET TO 0, no characters are held in the type-ahead buffer and the ON KEY command and INKEY() function are disabled. In full screen EDIT or APPEND operations, the type-ahead buffer will only hold 20 characters. If you try to enter more characters than the type-ahead buffer will hold, all extra characters will be lost and the BELL will sound if it has not been turned off.

EXAMPLE:

```
SET STEP OFF                && Standard Preamble
SET ECHO OFF
SET TALK OFF
SET BELL OFF
SET PRINT  OFF
SET DELETE ON
SET STATUS OFF
SET SAFETY OFF
SET ESCAPE OFF
SET CONFIRM ON
SET HEADING OFF
SET TYPEAHEAD TO 20
SET SCOREBOARD OFF
SET DEVICE TO SCREEN
CLEAR WINDOWS
...
```

SET UNIQUE

Syntax: `SET UNIQUE on/OFF`

SET UNIQUE determines whether all records with the same key value are included in the index file. The default is off.

If set OFF, all records are included in an index.

If set ON, only the first occurrence of the indexed value is included in the index and any records encountered with duplicate keys will not be included in the index file. The file retains its UNIQUE status when you REINDEX.

EXAMPLE:

```
SELECT 1
USE Master
SET UNIQUE ON
INDEX ON Name TO LastName
SEEK "SMITH"
LIST NEXT 3 Name
Record#   Name
   1      SMITH
   2      SMYTH
   3      SMYTHY
SET UNIQUE OFF
INDEX ON Name TO LastName
```

```
SEEK "SMITH"
LIST NEXT 3 Name
Record#    Name
   1       SMITH
   2       SMITH
   3       SMITH
```

SET VIEW TO

Syntax: `SET VIEW TO <query filename>/?`

Command opens a view file, setting up the data base files and a SET RELATION previously established using CREATE/MODIFY VIEW/QUERY or CREATE VIEW FROM ENVIRONMENT.

A dBASE IV view consists of:

- The active filter, if any.
- The active field list, if any.
- The opened format (.FMT) file, if any.
- The currently selected work area number.
- All relations between the data base files, if any.
- All open data base files, index files, and work area numbers.

SET WINDOW

Syntax: `SET WINDOW OF MEMO TO <window name>`

SET WINDOW causes editing of memo fields to take place within a specified window, instead of the default, full screen editing window when you are in APPEND, EDIT, BROWSE, CHANGE, or READ.

The <window name> is a previously DEFINEd window. The WINDOW clause specified with an @. . .GET command overrides the window specified by the SET WINDOW command.

EXAMPLE:

```
SELECT 1
USE Master
DEFINE WINDOW Letter FROM 1,40 TO 10,78
SET WINDOW OF MEMO TO Letter
@ 1,1  GET LastName
@ 1,30 GET FirstName
@ 2,10 GET Letter
READ
...
```

CHAPTER 4

Functions

&

Syntax:

```
& <character variable> [.]
```

The & function signals that dBASE IV is to perform macro substitution. It must precede the name of a <character variable>. dBASE IV substitutes the contents of a memory variable for its name in cases where dBASE IV would otherwise take the variable name literally. It is like indirect addressing in other languages. When a macro is used as a prefix to a literal string, use the period (.) to delimit the end of the macro. The character string substituted by the & function may itself contain &s. If a memory variable exists whose name follows such a nested &, that variable's content is also substituted in the command. Macros (& functions) can be nested, as desired, in this manner.

You cannot use structured programming commands in macros as dBASE IV cannot compile them at run time. These include DO WHILE loops, DO CASE and IF constructs, SCAN . . . ENDSCAN, TEXT . . . ENDTEXT, and PRINTJOB . . . ENDPRINTJOB. However, you can use macros in the condition portion of an IF, CASE, DO WHILE, or SCAN command.

It is not legal to have a variable reference itself recursively in a macro. Also, the complete expansion of any macro may not exceed the maximum statement length permitted in dBASE IV.

EXAMPLE:

```
ColStand = "W+/B,N/W,B"
DO StartUp
...
PROCEDURE STARTUP
SET COLOR TO &ColStand
CLEAR
```

Normally, the "SET COLOR TO" command requires a literal such as "W+/R". The command "SET COLOR TO ColStand" would give you a syntax error, even if preceded by the statement: "ColStand = "W+/B,N/W,B". However, if you place the "&" (macro) character in front of the expression "ColStand" the color will be set to the value pointed to by the variable ColStand.

Another popular use of macros is shown in the next example.

EXAMPLE:

```
Temp = "LastName='STEELE' .AND. FName='PHIL'"
SET FILTER TO &Temp
```

In this example, the FILTER is set to the string pointed to by the variable Temp rather than being set to the condition Temp = .T., which the statement "SET FILTER TO Temp" would do.

ABS

Syntax: ABS(<expN>)

This function returns the absolute value of a numeric expression.

EXAMPLE:

```
? ABS(-48)                           &&  48
? ABS({12/25/89} - {04/01/89})       &&  268
? ABS(35-10)                         &&  25
Num1 = 37
Num2 = 2
? ABS(Num2-Num1)                     &&  35
```

ACCESS

Syntax: ACCESS()

ACCESS returns the access level of the last user to log in on the network. It is commonly used to test file access privileges assigned with PROTECT.

EXAMPLE:

```
DO LogIn          &&  Perform log-in procedure.
IF ACCESS() > 3
   DO UnAuthor    &&  Perform Unauthorized routine.
ELSE
   DO ReadData    &&  Perform Read routine.
ENDIF
```

ACOS

Syntax: ACOS(<expN>)

ACOS is the "arccosine" function. It returns the angle, in radians, whose cosine is <expN>.

The variable <expN> is a number representing the cosine of an angle and must be between –1.0 and +1.0 inclusive.

The SET DECIMALS and SET PRECISION commands determine the number of decimals and accuracy displayed.

EXAMPLE:

```
SET PRECISION TO 15
SET DECIMALS TO 10
? ACOS(1)        &&  0
? ACOS(.5)       &&  1.0471975512
? ACOS(-.5)      &&  2.0943951024
```

ALIAS

Syntax: ALIAS([<expN>])

Alias returns the alias name of the data base file in the specified work area in all uppercase letters. If no work area is specified, the current one is assumed. The valid range for <expN> is between 1 and 10.

EXAMPLE:

```
SELECT A
USE Master ALIAS Main
USE Invoice IN 2
USE Details IN 3 ALIAS Amount
? ALIAS()           &&  Main
? ALIAS(2)          &&  Invoice
? ALIAS(3)          &&  Amount
```

ASC

Syntax: ASC(<expC>)

ASC returns the ASCII decimal code (value) of the first character in a character expression <expC>.

EXAMPLE:

```
? ASC("1")          &&  Returns 49
? ASC("Phil")       &&  Returns 80
```

ASIN

Syntax: `ASIN(<expN>)`

ASIN is the "arcsine" function. It returns the angle, in radians, whose sine is <expN>.

The variable <expN> is a number representing the sine of an angle and must be between –1.0 and +1.0 inclusive.

The SET DECIMALS and SET PRECISION commands determine the number of decimals and accuracy displayed.

EXAMPLE:

```
SET PRECISION TO 15
SET DECIMALS TO 10
? ASIN(1)       &&  1.57079632680
? ASIN(.5)      &&  0.5235987756
? ASIN(-.5)     &&  -0.5235987756
```

AT

Syntax: `AT(<expC1>,<expC2>/<memofield name>)`

The AT function has two character strings or character string expressions or a memo field name and a character string or character string expression as its arguments. It searches <expC2> for the first occurrence of <expC1>, and returns the position where it was found as an integer. If <expC1> does not occur in <expC2>, zero is returned.

EXAMPLE:

```
USE Master
? LastName                 &&  Smith
Code = "i"
? AT("it", LastName)       &&  Returns 3
? AT("ih", LastName)       &&  Returns 0
? AT(Code, LastName)       &&  Returns 3
```

ATAN

Syntax: `ATAN(<expN>)`

ATAN is the "arctangent" function. It returns the angle, in radians, whose tangent is <expN>.

The variable <expN> is a number representing the tangent of an angle.

The SET DECIMALS and SET PRECISION commands determine the number of decimals and accuracy displayed.

EXAMPLE:

```
SET PRECISION TO 15
SET DECIMALS TO 10
? ATAN(1)      &&  0.7853981634
? ATAN(.5)     &&  0.4636476090
? ATAN(-.5)    &&  -0.4636476090
```

ATN2

Syntax:

```
ATN2(<expN1>, <expN2>)
```

Function returns the arctangent in radians when the sine (<expN1>) and the cosine (<expN2>) of an angle are provided. The sine and cosine must be of the same angle. The SET DECIMALS and SET PRECISION commands determine the number of decimals and accuracy displayed.

EXAMPLE:

```
SET PRECISION TO 15
SET DECIMALS TO 10
? RTOD(ATN2(SIN(DTOR(30)), COS(DTOR(30))))
&& 30.0000000000
```

In this example, we also used the DTOR() and RTOD() functions. DTOR()m converts from degrees to radians, while RTOD() converts from radians to degrees. As you can see, we can use functions inside of other functions. In this example, we are using five functions in RTOD().

BAR

Syntax:

```
BAR()
```

BAR returns the number of the most recently selected popup menu option. If there is no active popup menu, the *Esc* key was pressed, or if no popup menu has been defined, BAR returns 0.

EXAMPLE:

```
DEFINE POPUP Test FROM 5,20
DEFINE BAR 1 OF TEST PROMPT "Test 1"
DEFINE BAR 2 OF TEST PROMPT "Test 2"
DEFINE BAR 3 OF TEST PROMPT "Exit"
ON SELECTION POPUP Test DO Proc
ACTIVATE POPUP Test

PROCEDURE PROC
```

```
DO CASE
   CASE BAR() = 1
     DO ProcX1
   CASE BAR() = 2
     DO ProcX2
   CASE BAR() = 3
     DEACTIVATE POPUP
ENDCASE
```

BOF

Syntax: `BOF([<alias>])`

The BOF function tests for the beginning of file condition for a data base file. ".T." is returned when you have attempted to move the record pointer before the first logical record in the file. BOF returns information for the data base in the current work area unless the optional argument <alias> is supplied that specifies a different work area. If no data base is open in the indicated work area, ".F." is returned. It is usually used when the data base is processed in reverse order.

EXAMPLE:

```
CursorUp = 5
CursorDn = 24
USE Master             &&  Data base with 10 Records.
SET COLOR TO N/W
J = 0
DO WHILE J < 10
   @ J,10 SAY LastName
   SET COLOR TO W+/B
   SKIP
   J = J + 1
ENDDO

J = 1
@ 24,25 SAY "Use the cursor keys to select name"

DO WHILE Key < > CursorUp .AND. Key < > CursorDn
   Key = INKEY(0)
ENDDO
SET COLOR TO W+/B
@ J,10 SAY LastName
IF Key = CursorDn
   J = J + 1
   SKIP
```

```
    IF EOF()
       GOTO TOP
       J = 1
    ENDIF
ELSE
    J = J - 1
    SKIP -1
    IF BOF()
       GOTO BOTTOM
       J = 10
    ENDIF
ENDIF
SET COLOR TO N/W
@ J,10 SAY LastName
```

CALL

Syntax: CALL(<expC>,<expC>/<memvar>)

The CALL command executes binary programs written in other languages, such as C or assembler, that have been previously LOADed into memory. The <memvar> option is used to pass a parameter to the binary subroutine which may be either an array element or a memory variable of any data type. An extension is not specified for the CALLed file since the extension is stripped from the file when it is LOADed. dBASE IV may then use the returned value of a LOADed binary program module as input to standard dBASE IV commands.

EXAMPLE:

```
LOAD MyCode                                 &&  Returns an inverted
                                                String.
InString  = "Phil Steele"
OutString = CALL("MyCode",InString)
? OutString                                 &&  eleetS lihP
```

CDOW

Syntax: CDOW(<expD>)

CDOW returns the name of the day of the week from a date expression.

EXAMPLE:

```
SET COLOR TO W+/B
CLEAR
PearlH = {12/07/41}
? CDOW(PearlH)           &&  Returns "Sunday"
? CDOW({12/07/41})       &&  Returns "Sunday"
```

CEILING

Syntax: `CEILING(<expN>)`

CEILING returns the smallest integer greater than or equal to the value of <expN>. CEILING(), unlike ROUND(), always returns an integer closer to zero.

EXAMPLE:

```
SET COLOR TO W+/B
CLEAR
? CEILING(-2.5)    &&  Returns -2
? CEILING(2.5)     &&  Returns 3
```

CHANGE

Syntax: `CHANGE()`

This is a network environment function that determines whether a record has been changed by another user. A true (.T.) is returned if the record has been changed since you opened it. This command only works with a data base created using the CONVERT command.

EXAMPLE:

```
SET COLOR TO W+/B
CLEAR
USE Master
SEEK "Steele"
...                &&  Display data
IF CHANGE()        &&  Returns .T. if changed.
   DO ReDisplay    &&  Redisplay record.
ELSE
   REPLACE;        &&  Update the data base.
...
ENDIF
```

CHR

Syntax: `CHR(<expN>)`

CHR converts an ASCII number to a character. Used to display "*odd*" characters, graphics, or foreign letters.

EXAMPLE:

```
SET COLOR TO W+/B
CLEAR
?CHR(65)   &&  Returns "A"
```

```
?CHR(200)  &&  Returns "╚"
?CHR(24)   &&  Returns "↑"
?CHR(137)  &&  Returns "ë"
```

CMONTH

Syntax:

```
CMONTH(<expD>)
```

CMONTH returns the name of the month from a date expression.

EXAMPLE:

```
SET COLOR TO W+/B
CLEAR
PearlH = {12/07/41}
? CMONTH(PearlH)        &&  Returns "December"
? CMONTH({12/07/41})    &&  Returns "December"
```

COL

Syntax:

```
COL()
```

COL returns the current column position of the cursor on the screen. This is useful in continuing a sentence as in the example.

EXAMPLE:

```
SET COLOR TO W+/B
CLEAR
USE Master
SCAN
   @ 12, 1 SAY TRIM(FirstName) + " " + TRIM(LastName)
   @ 12, COL() +1 SAY " lives at " + Address1
ENDSCAN
```

COMPLETED

Syntax:

```
COMPLETED()
```

Function determines whether a transaction has been completed; that is, a BEGIN TRANSACTION command has been terminated with an END TRANSACTION command or a successful ROLLBACK has occurred.

When a BEGIN TRANSACTION command is issued, COMPLETED() is made false (.F.). When the END TRANSACTION command is reached, COMPLETED() is made true (.T.).

EXAMPLE:

```
BEGIN TRANSACTION
...
END TRANSACTION
IF .NOT. COMPLETED()
     ROLLBACK
     IF .NOT. ROLLBACK()
          IF ISMARKED()
               RESET
          ENDIF
          ? "The transaction was not completed and "
          ? "could not be restoreD"
          RETURN
     ENDIF
ENDIF
```

COS

Syntax: COS(<expN>)

COS returns the cosine of an angle expressed in radians. The result is always between –1 and +1 inclusive.

The variable <expN> is a number representing the size of an angle measured in radians. There are no limits on its range.

The SET DECIMALS and SET PRECISION commands determine the number of decimals and accuracy displayed.

EXAMPLE:

```
SET PRECISION TO 15
SET DECIMALS TO 10
? COS(Pi())          &&  -1
? COS(.5)            &&  0.8775825619
? COS(DTOR(60))      &&  0.5
```

CTOD

Syntax: CTOD(<expC>)/{expC}

CTOD converts a date that has been entered or stored as a character string to a date type variable. The format of <expC> is "mm/dd/yy" unless the SET DATE and SET CENTURY commands are used to change this default format. If the century is not specified when entering a date, then the twentieth century is assumed. <expC> must contain a valid date from "1/1/0100" to "12/31/9999." You can also use the curly braces to create a date from a literal, as shown in the example.

EXAMPLE:

```
PearlH = CTOD("12/07/41")    &&  TYPE = Date
PearlH = {12/07/41}          &&  TYPE = Date
```

DATE

Syntax: `DATE()`

DATE returns the system date in the form mm/dd/yy unless the format is changed with SET CENTURY, SET DATE, or SET MARK.

EXAMPLE:

```
? DATE()          &&  Returns the system date, 03/12/90.
SET CENTURY ON
? DATE()          &&  03/12/1990
```

DAY

Syntax: `DAY(<expD>)`

DAY this is the day of month function. It returns the numeric day of the month (1 to 31) corresponding to <expD>. The date expression may be the system date function, a memory variable, or a data base field.

EXAMPLE:

```
PearlH = {12/07/41}
? DAY(PearlH)          &&  Returns 7.
```

DBF

Syntax: `DBF([<alias>])`

DBF returns the name of the data base in the current work area, unless the optional argument is supplied specifying a different work area. In any case, if no data base is open in the indicated work area, a null string is returned.

EXAMPLE:

```
USE Master
USE Detail IN 2
USE Invoice IN 3
? DBF()              &&  Returns Master
? DBF(2)             &&  Returns Detail
? DBF("C")           &&  Returns Invoice
```

DELETED

Syntax: DELETED([<alias>])

DELETED returns a logical true (.T.) if the current record in the specified work area is marked for deletion, and ".F." if it is not. Information is returned for the data base in the current work area, unless the optional argument is supplied specifying a different work area. In any case, if no data base is open in the indicated work area, ".F." is returned.

EXAMPLE:

```
USE Master
SET DELETE OFF
USE Detail IN 2
SEEK "Steele"
? DELETED()         &&  Returns .T.
SKIP
? DELETED()         &&  Returns .F.
? DELETED(2)        &&  Returns .F.
```

DIFFERENCE

Syntax: DIFFERENCE(<expC>, <expC>)

DIFFERENCE returns the difference between two SOUNDEX codes. It returns an integer between 0 and 4. Two closely matched <expC> codes return a difference of 4, and two <expC> codes that have no letters in common return a difference of 0. One common letter in each <expC> returns a 1.

EXAMPLE:

```
USE Master
SET NEAR ON
LookFor = "SMITH"
SEEK LookFor
DIFFERENCE(LookFor,LastName)  &&  Returns 4
? LastName                    &&  "SMYTH"
SKIP
DIFFERENCE(LookFor,LastName)  &&  Returns 0
? LastName                    &&  "TARE"
```

DISKSPACE

Syntax: DISKSPACE()

DISKSPACE returns an integer representing the number of bytes available on the default drive. The DISKSPACE function is extremely useful when determining whether sufficient space is available for backups or to execute commands, such as SORT, that require substantial work files.

EXAMPLE:

```
USE Master
RoomNeeded = (RECCOUNT() * RECSIZE()) + 5000
IF DISKSPACE() > RoomNeeded
   DO Backup          && Perform a file backup
ELSE
   @ 12,20 SAY "Insufficient diskspace. Backup Aborted."
ENDIF
```

DMY

Syntax:

```
DMY(<expD>)
```

DMY converts a date to a DD Month YY format. The day is shown without a leading zero as one or two digits. The month is spelled out in full, and the year is shown with the last two digits, unless CENTURY is set ON, in which case the year is shown using four digits. This is extremely useful for report headings.

EXAMPLE:

```
PearlH = {12/07/41}
? DMY(PearlH)      &&  7 December 41
SET CENTURY ON
? DMY(PearlH)      &&  7 December 1941
```

DOW

Syntax:

```
DOW(<expD>)
```

DOW returns a number that represents the day of the week from a date expression. Sunday is day 1, and Saturday is day 7.

EXAMPLE:

```
PearlH = {12/07/41}
? "Pearl harbor day did" +;
   IIF(WeekEnd(PearlH), " ", " not")+;
   " occur on a weekend"

FUNCTION WEEKEND
PARAMETERS CheckDate
RETURN IIF(DOW(CheckDate) = 1 .OR.;
          DOW(CheckDate) = 7), .T., .F.)
*END:WEEKEND

* Pearl Harbor Day did occur on a weekend.
```

DTOC

Syntax: DTOC(<expD>)

DTOC converts a date to a character string. The format is controlled by the SET DATE and SET CENTURY options currently in effect.

EXAMPLE:

```
USE History
SEEK "Pearl"
IF FOUND()
     PearlH = MajorDate
     ? SAY "On " + DTOC(PearlH) + " the events leading"
     ...
ENDIF
```

DTOR

Syntax: DTOR(<expN>)

DTOR converts angles from degrees to radians.

EXAMPLE:

```
SET PRECISION TO 15
SET DECIMALS TO 10
? RTOD(ATN2(SIN(DTOR(30)), COS(DTOR(30))))
&&  30.0000000000
```

DTOS

Syntax: DTOS(<expD>)

DTOS converts a date variable to a character string for indexing purposes. The date is returned in the format: CCYYMMDD (Century, Year, Month, Day).

DTOS always returns the century, regardless of what SET CENTURY has been set to. This function returns the date in a format suitable for use in INDEXing.

EXAMPLE:

```
USE History
INDEX ON DTOS(HistDate) + Event TO History
PearlH = "19410712PEARL HARBOR"
SEEK PearlH
IF FOUND()
     DO Report
     ...
ENDIF
```

EOF

Syntax:

```
EOF([<alias name>])
```

EOF returns a logical true (.T.) when the last logical record of the data base file in the selected work area is passed (RECNO() = RECOUNT() + 1). EOF returns the value ".F." if end of file has not been reached. EOF returns information for the data base in the current work area, unless the optional argument <alias name> is supplied specifying a different work area. In any case, if no data base is open in the indicated work area, ".F." is returned.

EXAMPLE:

```
USE Master
USE Detail IN 2
SEEK "Steele"
IF EOF()
    @ 23,0 SAY "Master record not found"
    INKEY(5)
ELSE
    X = LOOKUP(A->LastName,"Steele",B->LastName)
    IF EOF(2)
       @ 23,0 SAY "Detail record not found"
    ENDIF
ENDIF
```

ERROR

Syntax:

```
ERROR()
```

ERROR returns the number corresponding to the error that caused an ON ERROR condition. An ON ERROR command must be active. RETRY and RETURN clear the value returned by ERROR().

EXAMPLE:

```
PROCEDURE MAIN
ON ERROR DO ItsAnErr
...        &&  Main Procedure
*END:MAIN

PROCEDURE ITSANERR
ON ERROR
DO CASE
   CASE ERROR() = 106
     ? "File" "&(FileName) has an " + MESSAGE()
   ...
ENDCASE
*END:ITSANERROR
```

EXP

Syntax: `EXP(<expN>)`

EXP returns the value of exponent X in the equation (e to the xth power). The returned value is a "*real*" number, and the SET DECIMALS determines the accuracy of the answer. *Note:* Any number raised to the power of 1 equals the number; therefore, raising e to 1 returns the value of e.

EXAMPLE:

```
SET DECIMALS TO 10
? EXP(1.0)      &&  Returns 2.7182818285
? EXP(PI())     &&  Returns 23.1406926328
? EXP(0.5)      &&  Returns 1.6487212707
? EXP(-0.5)     &&  Returns 0.6065306597
```

FIELD

Syntax: `FIELD(<expC>[,<alias>])`

FIELD returns the field name in the specified numeric position in the file structure of the specified data base file. If the optional <alias> name is specified, FIELD() will return the field name from the alias file.

The field name returned is in uppercase letters. If the field number exceeds 255 or is less than 1, or the numeric expression refers to an unused field, a null string is returned. This function may be used to handle fields as array elements.

EXAMPLE:

```
USE MASTER

* Contains three fields: LastName, FirstName, IdCode.

USE Salary IN 2

* Contains two fields: IdCode, Salary.

? FIELD(3)              &&  IDCODE
? FIELD(1,2)            &&  IDCODE
```

FILE

Syntax: `FILE(<expC>)`

FILE returns a logical true (.T.) if the character expression <expC> is the name of an existing file. It returns ".F." if no such file exists. Any extensions in <file> must be explicitly specified. If a simple file name is specified, only the current working directory is searched for <file>. Alternately, a fully qualified DOS path name may be specified to search for a file in a directory other than the current working directory.

Note: FILE() attempts to open the file briefly to determine if it exists.

EXAMPLE:

```
USE MASTER
IF FILE("MTEMP.DBF")
   USE MTemp IN 2
ELSE
   COPY TO MTemp FOR Salary > 50000
   USE MTemp IN 2
ENDIF
```

FIXED

Syntax:

```
FIXED(<expN>)
```

FIXED converts type F (IEEE, long, real floating point) numeric data to type N (binary coded decimal) numbers. Some levels of precision may be lost in the conversion. If an expression uses both number types, all numbers are automatically converted to type F. The range is between 10^{308} and 10^{-308}.

EXAMPLE:

```
USE MASTER
NewSalary = FIXED(Salary * 1.098885132)
```

FKLABEL

Syntax:

```
FKLABEL(<expN>)
```

FKLABEL returns a character string containing the name of the function key corresponding to the specified numeric expression <expN>. The value of <expN> should be between 1 and FKMAX(); otherwise, the null string is returned. You may program a total of 28 function keys:

Function keys 2–10.
Shift function keys 1–9.
Ctrl function keys 1–10.

Note: Function key 1 is the help key and Shift function key 10 is the Macro key.

EXAMPLE:

```
? FKLABEL(1)    && Returns F2
? FKLABEL(10)   && Returns F9
```

FKMAX

Syntax: FKMAX()

FKMAX returns an integer representing the number of programmable function keys on the keyboard. The following function keys are *not* programmable:

F1 Help
Shift-F10 Macro
F11
Shift-F11
Ctrl-F11
F12
Shift-F12
Ctrl-F12

EXAMPLE:

```
? FKMAX()        &&  Returns 28 on a standard PC
```

FLOAT

Syntax: FLOAT(<expN>)

FLOAT converts type N (binary coded decimal) numeric data to type F (IEEE, long, real floating point) numeric data. Some levels of precision may be lost in the conversion. If an expression uses both number types, all numbers are automatically converted to type F.

EXAMPLE:

```
USE MASTER
NewSalary = FLOAT(Salary * 1.098885132)
```

FLOCK

Syntax: FLOCK([alias])

FLOCK is a multiple-user environment function. When the FLOCK() function is encountered, dBASE IV attempts to lock the entire data base file selected, returning ".T." if successful or ".F." if not. If the lock is successful, both read and exclusive write access are granted for all records contained in the data base file. The lock attempt is unsuccessful when either the entire data base file or at least one record has been locked by another user.

EXAMPLE:

```
USE Master
IF FLOCK()         &&  Lock was successful.
   COPY TO NewMaster
   UNLOCK
```

```
ELSE                    && Lock was unsuccessful.
   ? "Database is not available"
ENDIF
```

FLOOR

Syntax: FLOOR(<expN>)

Returns the largest integer less than or equal to <expN>.

EXAMPLE:

```
FLOOR(87.43)               && Returns 87
Numbr = 396
Denom = 13
? FLOOR(Numbr / Denom)     && Returns 30
```

FOUND

Syntax: FOUND([<alias>])

FOUND returns a logical true (.T.) if the previous FIND, SEEK, LOCATE, or CONTINUE command was successful in the specified work area. ".F." is returned if the last search command was unsuccessful or the record pointer was moved by a nonsearch command (e.g., GOTO command). FOUND supports an optional argument <alias> that indicates the work area to which the function is to be applied. If no data base is open in the indicated work area, ".F." is returned. If the argument is omitted, the value for the currently selected work area is returned.

EXAMPLE:

```
USE Master ORDER LName
SEEK "Steele"
IF FOUND()
   DO DispData
ELSE
   ? "Record NOT found"
ENDIF
```

FV

Syntax: FV(<payment>,<rate>,<periods>)

This function calculates the future (compounded) value of equal regular deposits earning a fixed interest rate per compounding period for a given length of time.

<payment> is a numeric expression that can be negative or positive.
<rate> is a decimal number representing the interest rate (0.08 is 8%).

<periods> is the total number of payments in equal intervals of time, such as weeks, months, or years.

In this example, we will compute the amount that a periodic investment of the same amount, at the same interest rate, would be worth at the end of a fixed period of time. For example, let us assume that you put $2000 per year into your IRA account and earn 10% per year. How much would you have in your account at the end of 20 years?

EXAMPLE:

```
SET COLOR TO W+/B
CLEAR
Int = 0.10                 && Rate     = 10.0%
Dep = 2000                 && Payment  = $2000
Yrs = 20                   && Period   = 20 years
NFV = FV(Dep, Int, Yrs)
? NFV                      && Returns $114,550
```

GETENV

Syntax: `GETENV(<expC>)`

GETENV returns the contents of an environmental system variable such as PATH or COMSPEC. The name of the system variable must be entered as a character string.

If the character expression is not found, dBASE IV returns a null string.

In this example, we set the dBASE IV path to the DOS path by obtaining the DOS path using the GETENV function.

EXAMPLE:

```
DOSPath = GETENV("PATH")
SET PATH TO &DOSPath
```

IIF

Syntax: `IIF(<expL>,<expr1>,<expr2>)`

IIF returns the value of <expr1> or <expr2>, depending on the logical value of <expL>. If the logical expression <expL> is ".T.", then <expr1> is returned; otherwise, <expr2> is returned.

A typical use is for converting numbers to strings, as shown in the following example.

EXAMPLE:

```
Num = 10
Char = IIF(Num>9, STR(Num,2), STR(Num,1))
? Char                                          && 10
Num = 9
Char = IIF(Num>9, STR(Num,2), STR(Num,1))
? Char                                          && 9
```

INKEY

Syntax: INKEY([n])

INKEY returns an integer representing the most recent key pressed by the operator.

This value corresponds to the ASCII code value of the input key pressed by the user. The integer returned will be between 0 and 255. If there are several keys in the type-ahead buffer, the value of the first key entered in the buffer will be returned and the buffer will be cleared.

The INKEY function also takes an optional numeric argument that specifies how many seconds the program will wait for a keystroke before reporting that no key has been struck. If INKEY is called with no argument, it immediately returns either a pending keystroke or 0, if no key has been pressed. If called with an argument of 0, INKEY will wait indefinitely for a keystroke.

This example displays the INKEY() value of any key pressed.

EXAMPLE:

```
SET COLOR TO &ColStand
CLEAR
@22,13 SAY  "Press any key to see its INKEY() " +;
            "value - Esc to quit".
A = FindKey

FUNCTION FINDKEY
ViewChoice = 0
DO WHILE ViewChoice < > 27    &&  Escape key
   ViewChoice = INKEY(0)
   IF ViewChoice < > 0
      @12,18 SAY    "THE CONTROL CODE OF " +;
                    "THE KEY YOU PRESSED IS "
      @12,61 SAY "  "
      @12,61 SAY ViewChoice PICTURE "9999"
   ENDIF
ENDDO
RETURN(.T.)
*END:FINDKEY
```

Note: A functional value (0.5) is permitted as the option number in Release 1.1.

INT

Syntax: INT(<expN>)

INT converts any numeric expression to an integer by discarding all digits to the right of the decimal point in converting the numeric expression.

EXAMPLE:

```
? INT(84.875)      &&  Returns 84
? INT(397 / 13)    &&  Returns 30
```

ISALPHA

Syntax: ISALPHA(<expC>)

ISALPHA returns a logical true (.T.) if the specified character string begins with an alpha character. ".F." is returned if <expC> begins with any nonalphabetic character.

EXAMPLE:

```
USE Master
? ISALPHA(LastName)      &&  Returns .T.
? LastName               &&  Returns Steele
? ISALPHA(Zip)           &&  Returns .F.
? Zip                    &&  Returns 07045
```

ISCOLOR

Syntax: ISCOLOR()

ISCOLOR returns a logical true (.T.) if a color graphics card is installed in the computer. This function checks the setting of the hardware address for the graphics adapter card. On monochrome monitors that emulate color screens, this function is not reliable as it reports on the graphic *CARD*, not the monitor attached to the card.

EXAMPLE:

```
ColStand = IIF(ISCOLOR(),  "W+/B,N/W,B", "W+/N, N/W")

SET COLOR TO &ColStand
CLEAR
```

ISLOWER

Syntax: ISLOWER(<expC>)

Function returns a logical true (.T.) if the specified character string begins with a lowercase alpha. ".F." is returned if the first character is any character other than a lowercase alpha character.

EXAMPLE:

```
USE Master
? ISLOWER(LastName)                &&  Returns .T.
? LastName                         &&  Returns steele
REPLACE LastName WITH "Steele"
? ISLOWER(LastName)                &&  Returns .F.
? ISLOWER(ZipCode)                 &&  Returns .F.
```

ISMARKED

Syntax: `ISMARKED([<alias>])`

Function returns true (.T.) if the file in the current work area (or alias area, if supplied), is in a state of change, such as records being added. This command is useful when trying to ROLLBACK transactions in a BEGIN TRANSACTION . . . END TRANSACTION construct.

EXAMPLE:

```
BEGIN TRANSACTION
...
END TRANSACTION
IF .NOT. COMPLETED()
    ROLLBACK
    IF .NOT. ROLLBACK()
        IF ISMARKED()
            RESET
        ENDIF
        ? "The transaction was not completed and "
        ? "could not be restored"
        RETURN
  ENDIF
ENDIF
```

ISUPPER

Syntax: `ISUPPER(<expC>)`

ISUPPER returns a logical true (.T.) if the specified character string begins with an uppercase alpha. ".F." is returned if the first character is any character other than an uppercase alphabetic character.

EXAMPLE:

```
USE Master
? ISUPPER(LastName)    &&  Returns .T.
? LastName             &&  Returns Steele
? ISUPPER(ZipCode)     &&  Returns .F.
? ZipCode              &&  Returns 07045
```

KEY

Syntax: `KEY([<.mdx filename>,] <expN> [,<alias>])`

KEY returns the key expression for the index file specified by <expN> in the current work area, or the alias area if it is specified. If an .mdx file is not used, dBASE IV considers all open index files, including .NDX files. If the file does not exist, a null string is returned. KEY() operates in the current work area unless you use the <alias> parameter.

EXAMPLE:

```
USE Master INDEX MASTER
USE Detail INDEX Detail IN 2
? KEY(1)
* Returns TRIM(LastName) + TRIM(FirstName)
? KEY(1, Detail)
* Returns TRIM(LastName) + TRIM(FirstName) + DTOS(InDate)
```

LASTKEY

Syntax: `LASTKEY()`

LASTKEY returns the decimal ASCII value of the last character entered that exited a command such as BROWSE, EDIT, or READ.

EXAMPLE:

```
USE MASTER
mSalary = Salary
@ 10,10    SAY "Enter new salary ";
           GET mSalary PICTURE "9,999,999.99"
READ
IF LASTKEY() < > 27          &&  Escape
   REPLACE Salary WITH mSalary
ENDIF
```

LEFT

Syntax: `LEFT(<expC>/<memofield name>,<expN>)`

LEFT returns a specified number of characters from a specified character string or a memo field starting with the first character on the left. If <expN> is greater than the length of <expC>, the entire string is returned by the LEFT function. If <expN> is less than or equal to zero, the null string is returned.

EXAMPLE:

```
USE MASTER
? Name                                 &&  Returns Steele Phil
LName = LEFT(Name, AT(" ", Name)-1)
? LName                                &&  Returns Steele
```

Note: The AT() function returns the value 7 (the location of the blank); thus the LEFT() function degenerates to LEFT(Name, 6).

LEN

Syntax: `LEN(<expC>)/<memofield name>`

LEN returns the number of characters in a data base field, specified character string, or memo field.

EXAMPLE:

```
USE MASTER
? Name                                  &&  Returns Steele Phil
LName = LEFT(Name, AT(" ", Name)-1)
? LEN(LName)                            &&  Returns 6
LName = LEFT(Name, AT(" ", Name))
? LEN(LName)                            &&  Returns 7
```

LIKE

Syntax: `LIKE(<pattern>, <expC>)`

LIKE returns true (.T.) if the string in the <pattern> matches the character expression. Wild card symbols ? and * can be used in the <pattern> string. This function *is* case sensitive.

When used with wild card symbols, * represents any number of characters and ? represents a single character.

EXAMPLE:

```
USE Master
? LastName                         &&  Returns Steele
? LIKE("*ee", LastName)            &&  Returns .T.
? LIKE("*e?e", LastName)           &&  Returns .T.
? LIKE("?Ee", LastName)            &&  Returns .F.
```

LINENO

Syntax: `LINENO()`

LINENO returns the relative line number of the current command (the line that is about to be executed) in a command or procedure file. This function can be used in the debugger's breakpoint window or with an ON ERROR() routine.

EXAMPLE:

```
PROCEDURE MAIN
ON ERROR DO ItsAnErr
...          &&  Main Procedure
*END:MAIN

PROCEDURE ITSANERR
ON ERROR
```

```
? "The error occurred at " +;
STR(LINENO(),4,0)
INKEY(0)
RETURN
*END:ITSANERR
```

LKSYS

Syntax: `LKSYS(n)`

LKSYS returns the log-in name of the user who has locked a record or a file, and the date and time the file or record was locked, for files that you have tried unsuccessfully to access.

n = 0 returns the time when the lock was placed.
n = 1 returns the date when the lock was placed.
n = 3 returns the log-in name of the user who placed the lock.

This function will return a null string, unless the person who locked the file used the CONVERT command to create an invisible field of 8 to 24 characters in the active data base file.

EXAMPLE:

```
USE Master
SEEK "Steele"
IsLocked = RLOCK(RECNO())
IF IsLocked
    SET COLOR TO W+/R
    CLEAR
    * Display Name of lock holder
    ? LKSYS(3) +;
    " is using the record."
ENDIF
```

LOG

Syntax: `LOG(<expN>)`

LOG returns the natural logarithm of a specified number. $Y = e^x$, where x is equal to <expN>. <expN> is a number greater than zero. If you use a number less than or equal to zero, numeric overflow will occur. LOG() returns the value of X, which is a type F (long, real) number.

EXAMPLE:

```
SET DECIMALS TO 5
? LOG(10)           &&  Returns 2.30259
? LOG(10 * 2)       &&  Returns 2.99573
? LOG(2.71828)      &&  Returns 1.00000
```

LOG10

Syntax: `LOG10(<expN>)`

LOG10 returns the base 10 logarithm of <expN>. Y = LOG10(x), where x is equal to <expN>. <expN> is a number greater than zero. If you use a number less than or equal to zero, numeric overflow will occur. LOG() returns the value of Y, which is a type F (long, real) number.

EXAMPLE:

```
SET DECIMALS TO 5
? LOG10(10)            &&  Returns 1
? LOG10(10 * 2)        &&  Returns 1.30103
? LOG10(2.71828)       &&  Returns 0.43429
```

LOOKUP

Syntax:

```
LOOKUP(<active database field>, <look-for exp>,
       <look in field>)
```

LOOKUP searches for a record based on a value from the active data base file and returns a value from a data base file other than the active file. This function is very handy for checking secondary files to see if there are records that correspond to those in the master data base.

EXAMPLE:

```
USE Master
?FName                  &&  Phillipps Computer Systems Inc.
USE Detail ORDER FirmName IN 2
? FName                 &&  Phil Steele Inc.
NewFirm = "dBase Services"
Answer = LOOKUP(A->FName,NewFirm,B->FName)
? A->FName              &&  Phillipps Computer Systems Inc.
? B->FName              &&  dBase Services.
? Answer                &&  Phillipps Computer Systems Inc.
? FName                 &&  Phil Steele Inc.
```

Notice:

1. The record pointer in the active data base does not move.
2. The answer is set to the record in the active data base.
3. The <look-for exp> determines the record in area "B".
4. The record pointer in the nonactive data base moves.

LOWER

Syntax: LOWER(<expC>)

LOWER converts uppercase letters to lowercase. LOWER() returns alphabetic characters in the <expC> converted to lowercase. All other characters are ignored.

EXAMPLE:

```
SET COLOR TO W+/B
USE Master
? LastName                                  && Returns STEELE
mLastName = LOWER(SUBSTR(LastName,2))
? mLastName                                 && Returns Steele
```

LTRIM

Syntax: LTRIM(<expC>)

LTRIM removes leading blanks from a character expression. <expC> is the character string to be returned with leading spaces removed.

EXAMPLE:

```
Number = 18
? STR(Number)                   && Returns 18
? LEN(STR(Number))              && Returns 10
? LTRIM(STR(Number))            && Returns 18
? LEN(LTRIM(STR(Number)))       && Returns 2
```

LUPDATE

Syntax: LUPDATE([<alias>])

LUPDATE returns the date of the last update of the specified data base file in a date format. This function is useful when verifying that a particular update procedure is run on a daily basis.

EXAMPLE:

```
USE Master
IF LUPDATE() < DATE() - 5
   SET COLOR TO W+/R
   CLEAR
   @ 12,0 SAY "The update procedure has not been " +;
                 "run in a week--Please run it!"
   ? CHR(7)
   DUMMY = INKEY(10)
ENDIF
```

MAX

Syntax: MAX(<expression1>, <expression2>)

MAX returns the largest value of two numeric, date, or character expressions.

EXAMPLE:

```
Number1     = 143.345
Number2     = 141.111
Biggest     = MAX(Number1, Number2)
? Biggest                              && Returns 143.345
PearlH      = {12/07/41}
LongAgo     = DATE() - 365.25 * 45
Oldest      = MAX(LongAgo, PearlH)
? Oldest                               && Returns LongAgo
```

MDX

Syntax: MDX(<expN> [,<alias>])

MDX returns the file name for the open active .mdx directory in the .mdx file list for the current work area. <expN> is numeric and specifies the .mdx file position in the index file list specified by the SET INDEX TO command. If <alias> is specified, the .mdx file associated with it is used.

EXAMPLE:

```
USE Master INDEX Master
USE Detail INDEX Detail IN 2
? MDX(1)                          &&  Returns H:DBASE\Master.MDX
? MDX(1,2)                        &&  Returns H:DBASE\Detail.MDX
? MDX(2)                          &&  Returns ""--null string.
```

MDY

Syntax: MDY(<expD>)

MDY converts the date to the month/dd/yy format, which is very useful in report headers. If SET CENTURY is ON, four digits are displayed for the year.

EXAMPLE:

```
PearlH = {12/07/41}
? MDY(PearlH)           &&  Returns December 7, 41
SET CENTURY ON
? MDY(PearlH)           &&  Returns December 7, 1941
```

MEMLINES

Syntax: MEMLINES(memo field name)

MEMLINES returns the number of lines that are contained in a memo field when it is word wrapped at the current SET MEMOWIDTH value.

EXAMPLE:

```
USE Master
SET MEMO WIDTH TO 10
? Letter
This is to
inform you
that your
December
payment
has not
yet been
received.
? MEMLINES(Letter)    &&  Returns 8
SET MEMO WIDTH TO 20
? Letter
This is to inform
your that your
December payment has
not yet been
received.
? MEMLINES(Letter)    &&  Returns 5
```

MEMORY

Syntax: MEMORY([0])

MEMORY returns the amount of unused RAM in kilobytes (1024 bytes). The parameter "0" is optional and the function works in the same way with and without the "0".

EXAMPLE:

```
SET COLOR TO W+/B
...
CLEAR
? MEMORY()    &&  Returns 12
? MEMORY(0)   &&  Returns 12, which is 12,228 bytes.
```

MENU

Syntax: MENU()

MENU returns the name (alphanumeric string) of the most recently activated menu. If there is no active menu, a null string is returned.

EXAMPLE:

```
DEFINE MENU Test MESSAGE "This is a test"
DEFINE PAD X1 OF TEST PROMPT "Test 1" AT 0,0
DEFINE PAD X2 OF TEST PROMPT "Test 2" AT 0,20
DEFINE PAD X3 OF TEST PROMPT "Test 3" AT 0,50
ON SELECTION PAD X1 OF Test DO Procl
ON SELECTION PAD X2 OF Test DO Procl
ON SELECTION PAD X3 OF Test DEACTIVE MENU
ACTIVATE MENU Test
...
? MENU()        &&  Returns test
```

MESSAGE

Syntax: MESSAGE()

MESSAGE returns the message corresponding to the last error that caused an ON ERROR condition.

EXAMPLE:

```
PROCEDURE MAIN
ON ERROR DO ItsAnErr
...          &&  Main Procedure
*END:MAIN

PROCEDURE ITSANERR
ON ERROR
DO CASE
   CASE ERROR() = 106
     ? "File" "&(FileName) has an " + MESSAGE()
    ...
ENDCASE
*END:ITSANERROR
```

MIN

Syntax: MIN(<expN1>/<expD1>,<expN2>/<expD2>)

MIN returns the smaller of two numeric, date, or character expressions.

EXAMPLE:

```
Number1      = 143.345
Number2      = 141.111
Smallest     = MIN(Number1, Number2)
? Smallest                                 && Returns 141.111
PearlH       = {12/07/41}
LongAgo      = DATE() - 365.25 * 75
Newest       = MIN(LongAgo, PearlH)
? Newest                                   && Returns LongAgo
```

MLINE

Syntax: MLINE(<memo field name>,<expN>)

MLINE extracts the specified numbered line of text from a memo field, when it is word wrapped at the current SET MEMOWIDTH value.

EXAMPLE:

```
USE Master
SET MEMO WIDTH TO 10
? Letter
This is to
inform you
that your
December
payment
has not
yet been
received.
? MLINE(Letter,4)     &&  Returns  December
SET MEMO WIDTH TO 20
? Letter
This is to inform
your that your
December payment has
not yet been
received.
? MLINE(Letter,4)     &&  Returns  not yet been
```

MOD

Syntax: MOD(<expN1>,<expN2>)

MOD returns the remainder from a division of <expN1>, <expN2> (numeric expressions). A positive number is returned if <expN2> is positive and a negative number if <expN2> is negative.

EXAMPLE:

```
? MOD(1026,16)     && Returns 2
? MOD(1026,-16)    && Returns -2
? MOD(0,16)        && Returns 0
```

MONTH

Syntax: `MONTH(<expD>)`

MONTH returns a number representing the month from a date expression.

EXAMPLE:

```
PearlH = {12/07/41}
? MONTH(PearlH)           && Returns 12
```

NDX

Syntax: `NDX(<expN> [,<alias>])`

NDX returns the names of active index files in the specified work area.

It returns the file name for the open active .ndx file in the current work area. <expN> is numeric and specifies the order of the index If <alias> is specified, the .ndx file associated with it is used.

EXAMPLE:

```
USE Master INDEX Master
USE Detail INDEX Detail IN 2
? NDX(1)                        && Returns H:dBASEMaster.NDX
? NDX(1,2)                      && Returns H:dBASEDetail.NDX
? NDX(1,5)                      && Returns error--ALIAS
                                   not found.
```

NETWORK

Syntax: `NETWORK()`

NETWORK returns a True (.T.) if dBASE IV is running on a network.

EXAMPLE:

```
? NETWORK()          && Returns .F.
```

ORDER

Syntax: `ORDER([<alias>])`

ORDER returns the name of the primary index controlling the order of records in any open data base file using .mdx. For .ndx files, the root portion of the file name is returned in uppercase. If there is no .ndx file and just a .mdx file the .mdx tagname is returned, also in uppercase.

EXAMPLE:

```
USE Master ORDER LastName
USE Detail ORDER DetNum IN 2
? ORDER()                        &&  Returns LASTNAME
SET ORDER TO AcctNum
? ORDER()                        &&  Returns ACCTNUM
? ORDER("Detail")                &&  Returns DETNUM
```

OS

Syntax: `OS()`

OS returns the name of the current operating system.

EXAMPLE:

```
? OS()        &&  Returns DOS 3.30
```

PAD

Syntax: `PAD()`

PAD returns the prompt pad name of the most recent selected PAD from the active menu. If no menu is active, or none have been defined, PAD returns a null string.

EXAMPLE:

```
DEFINE MENU Test MESSAGE "This is a test"
DEFINE PAD X1 OF TEST PROMPT "Test 1" AT 0,0
DEFINE PAD X2 OF TEST PROMPT "Test 2" AT 0,20
DEFINE PAD X3 OF TEST PROMPT "Test 3" AT 0,50
ON SELECTION PAD X1 OF Test DO Proc1
ON SELECTION PAD X2 OF Test DO Proc2
ON SELECTION PAD X3 OF Test DEACTIVE MENU
ACTIVATE MENU Test
...
PROCEDURE PROC1
? PAD()       &&  Returns X1
...
*END:PROC1
```

PAYMENT

Syntax: `PAYMENT(<principal>,<rate>,<periods>)`

PAYMENT calculates the constant, regular payments required to amortize (pay off) a loan (principal and interest) with constant interest over a given number of payment periods.

<principal> is a numeric expression representing the principal balance of the loan. It can be positive or negative.

<rate> is a numeric expression representing the interest rate, expressed as a decimal (0.105 is 10.5%). It must be positive.

<periods> is a numeric expression representing the total number of payments made at regular intervals, such as weeks or months. Fractional numbers are rounded.

An example of the use of this function is for determining how much a loan will cost you per time period—the amount of a loan. You know that you can obtain $250,000 for 30 years at 11.5%; how much do you have to pay back per month? In other words, what is the amount of your loan payment? This calculation is usually performed when computing a fixed-rate mortgage. A fixed-rate mortgage is nothing more than a loan with an interest rate that does not vary over the life of the loan. The previous example could be considered a 30-year fixed-rate mortgage if a lien on specific property was given by the borrower as security for the loan.

For this example, we will assume that you plan to take a $250,000 30-year fixed-rate mortgage at 11.5% per year. How much will you pay a month on the mortgage?

EXAMPLE:

```
CLEAR
Prin = 250000
Int  = 0.115
Yrs  = 30
MPay = PAYMENT(Prin, Int, Yrs) / 12
? MPay          &&  Returns 2490.92
```

PCOL

Syntax: PCOL()

PCOL returns the current column position on the printer and keeps track of its position in programs. PCOL() only works with the printer.

EXAMPLE:

```
SET COLOR TO W+/B
CLEAR
USE Master
SET DEVICE TO PRINT
SCAN
   @ 12, 1 SAY TRIM(FirstName) + " " + TRIM(LastName)
   @ 12, PCOL( ) +1 SAY " lives at " + Address1
   ...
ENDSCAN
```

PI

Syntax: `PI()`

PI returns the value of pi (3.1415926535897. . .), which is the ratio of the circumference of a circle to its diameter. SET DECIMALS and SET PRECISION determine the accuracy of the displayed number.

EXAMPLE:

```
SET COLOR TO W+/B,N/W
CLEAR
SET DECIMALS TO 5
SET PRECISION TO 18
Radius = 0
@ 12,5 SAY "Enter the radius of the circle you need the " +;
           "area of: " GET Radius PICTURE "999.999"
READ
Area = PI() * Radius * Radius
@ 14,5 SAY "The area of the circle is: " + ;
               ALLTRIM(STR(Area, 14,5))
```

POPUP

Syntax: `POPUP()`

POPUP returns the name of the most recently activated popup menu. If no popup menu has been defined, the error message "POPUP has not been defined" is displayed.

EXAMPLE:

```
DEFINE POPUP Test FROM 5,20
DEFINE BAR 1 OF TEST  PROMPT "Test 1"
DEFINE BAR 2 OF TEST  PROMPT "Test 2"
DEFINE BAR 3 OF TEST  PROMPT "Exit"
ON SELECTION POPUP Test DO Proc
ACTIVATE POPUP Test

PROCEDURE PROC
DO CASE
   CASE BAR() = 1
     DO ProcX1
   CASE BAR() = 2
     DO ProcX2
   CASE BAR() = 3
     DEACTIVATE POPUP
ENDCASE
*END:PROC
```

```
PROCEDURE PROCX1
? POPUP()    &&  Returns Test
...
*END:PROCX1
```

PRINTSTATUS

Syntax: PRINTSTATUS()

Function returns a logical true (.T.) if the print device is ready to accept output.

EXAMPLE:

```
FUNCTION TESTPRNT             &&  Checks to see if
Key      = 0                  &&  the printer is on
PrntOK   = .F.                &&  line and waits
PrntOK   = PRINTSTATUS()      &&  after displaying a
SET DEVICE TO SCREEN          &&  message to the
IF .NOT. PrntOK               &&  user.
    CLEAR
    @ 10,24 TO 14,57 DOUBLE
    @ 11,26 SAY "Please make the printer ready"
    @ 12,38 SAY "or"
    @ 13,31 SAY "press Esc to return"
ENDIF
DO WHILE .NOT. PrntOK
   Key         = INKEY(0.5)
   PrntOK      = PRINTSTATUS()
   IF Key = 27                &&  Escape
      PrntOK   = .T.
   ENDIF
ENDDO
IF Key = 27                   &&  Escape
   SET DEVICE TO SCREEN
OKToPrnt = .F.
ELSE
   SET DEVICE TO PRINT
   OKToPrnt = .T.
ENDIF
RETURN(OKToPrnt)
*END:TESTPRNT
```

PROGRAM

Syntax: PROGRAM()

PROGRAM returns the name (in a character string) of the program or procedure that was executing when an error occurred. The program name does not include an extension.

EXAMPLE:

```
PROCEDURE MAIN
ON ERROR DO ItsAnErr
...          &&  Main Procedure
*END:MAIN

PROCEDURE ITSANERR
?  "The error occurred in program: " + PROGRAM() +;
   "at line number " + LTRIM(STR(LINENO()))
INKEY(5)
*END:ITSANERROR
```

PROMPT

Syntax: `PROMPT()`

PROMPT returns the prompt of the most recently selected popup menu option.

EXAMPLE:

```
DEFINE POPUP Test FROM 5,20 TO 15,50
DEFINE BAR 1 OF TEST  PROMPT "Execute Test 1"
DEFINE BAR 2 OF TEST  PROMPT "Execute Test 2"
...
DEFINE BAR 9 OF TEST  PROMPT "Exit dBASE IV"
ON SELECTION POPUP Test SET MESSAGE TO PROMPT()
SET STATUS ON
ACTIVATE POPUP Test
```

PROW

Syntax: `PROW()`

PROW returns the current row on the printer. PROW() is set to zero after a page eject. PROW is especially useful for relative addressing of output to the printer.

EXAMPLE:

```
SET COLOR TO W+/B
CLEAR
USE Master
SET DEVICE TO PRINT
EJECT
```

```
SCAN
   @ PROW(), 1 SAY TRIM(FirstName) + " "
   @ PROW( ), PCOL( ) +1 SAY TRIM(LastName)
   @ PROW( ), PCOL( ) +1 SAY " lives at " + Address1
    ...
ENDSCAN
```

PV

Syntax: `PV(<payment>,<rate>,<periods>)`

PV calculates the present value of equal, regular payments invested at a constant interest rate for a given number of periods.

<payment> is a numeric expression that can be negative or positive.

<rate> is a decimal number representing the interest rate (0.08 is 8%).

<periods> is the total number of payments at equal intervals of time, such as weeks, months, or years.

In this example, we will compute the amount the present value of an investment based on the same amount of money being paid and invested at a fixed interest rate. Let us assume that you hit the lottery for a million dollars paid over 20 years ($50,000 a year for 20 years). You can take either the $50,000 a year, or take a lump-sum payment of $400,000. What do you do? If you take the $50,000 a year, you can invest it at 9.5%.

EXAMPLE:

```
SET COLOR TO W+/B
CLEAR
Int = .095
Pay = 50000
Yrs = 20
NPV = PV(Pay, Int, Yrs)
? NPV

* NPV Should be $440,619.11
```

RAND

Syntax: `RAND([<expN>])`

RAND generates a random number between 0 and 0.999999 inclusive.

<expN> is an optional numeric expression whose value is used as the seed to generate a new random number. If <expN> is a negative number, RAND() uses the system clock to generate a new random number. To reset the seed to the default value, use RAND(100001).

EXAMPLE:

```
SET COLOR TO W+/B
CLEAR
```

```
SET DECIMALS TO 10
? RAND(100001)     &&  Returns 0.7990660907
? RAND()           &&  Returns 0.8832613369
? RAND(100001)     &&  Returns 0.7990660907
? RAND(-1)         &&  Returns 0.3399824691
? RAND(-1)         &&  Returns 0.4703925287
```

READKEY

Syntax: `READKEY()`

READKEY returns an integer for the key pressed to exit from a full screen command, such as APPEND, BROWSE, CHANGE, CREATE, EDIT, INSERT, MODIFY, or READ. The integer changes if any data is changed during the full screen commands.

Key Pressed	Data Unchanged	Data Updated	READKEY Value
Ctrl-S	0	256	Backward one character
←	0	256	Backward one character
Ctrl-H	0	256	Backward one character
Backspace	-	256	Backward one characterr
Ctrl-D	1	257	Forward one character
→	1	257	Forward one character
Ctrl-L	1	257	Forward one character
Ctrl-E	4	260	Backward one field
Ctrl-K	4	260	Backward one field
↑	4	260	Backward one field
Ctrl-J	5	261	Forward one field
Ctrl-X	5	261	Forward one field
↓	5	261	Forward one field
Ctrl-R	6	262	Backward one screen
PgUp	6	262	Backward one screen
Ctrl-C	7	263	Forward one screen
PgDn	7	263	Forward one screen
Ctrl-Q	12	–	Terminate without save
Esc	12	–	Terminate without save
Ctrl-W	–	270	Terminate with save
Ctrl-End	–	270	Terminate with save
Ctrl-M	15	271	Fill last record—RETURN
↵	15	271	Fill last record—RETURN
Ctrl-M	16	–	Start of record—APPEND
↵	16	–	start of record—APPEND

Ctrl-Home	33	289	Menu display toggle
Ctrl-PgUp	34	290	Zoom out
Ctrl-PgDn	35	291	Zoom in
F1	36	292	HELP function key

EXAMPLE: READKEY() gives 270 if CTRL-END or CTRL-W was pressed.

EXAMPLE:

```
SaveKey = 270
SET COLOR TO W+/B,N/W
CLEAR
USE Master
DO WHILE .T.
   BROWSE
   YN = "Y"
   IF READKEY() <> SaveKey
      YN = "N"
      @12,10      SAY "Data will not be saved! OK (Y/N) ";
                  GET YN PICTURE "Y"
   READ
   ENDIF
   IF YN = "Y"
      EXIT
   ENDIF
ENDDO
```

RECCOUNT

Syntax: `RECCOUNT([<alias>])`

Function returns the number of records in a data base, counting *all* records regardless of the status of SET DELETED and SET FILTER. RECCOUNT returns information for the data base in the current work area, unless <alias> is supplied specifying a different work area.

If no file is active, RECCOUNT() returns a zero.

Old Code	New Code
SELECT B GOTO BOTTOM LastRec = RECNO() GOTO TOP	LastRec = RECCOUNT(B)

EXAMPLE:

```
SET COLOR TO W+/B
USE MASTER
LastRec = RECCOUNT()
SEEK 50000
? "The salary record equal to $50,000.00 is " +;
    LTRIM(STR(RECNO()*100/LastRec)) +;
    " Percent into the database"
```

RECNO

Syntax: `RECNO([<alias>])`

RECNO returns the current record number of the specified file. The record number is the physical position of a record in the selected data base. RECNO will return one greater than the number of records in the file if the record pointer is moved past the last record. RECNO will return a one if the record pointer is moved to one before the first record in the file. RECNO supports the optional argument <alias>, which indicates the work area in which to apply the function. If the argument is omitted, the value for the currently selected work area is returned.

If there is an empty data base file, RECNO() returns 1.

If there is no data base file in use, RECNO() returns 0.

EXAMPLE:

```
SET COLOR TO W+/B
USE MASTER
LastRec = RECCOUNT()
SEEK 50000
? "The salary record equal to $50,000.00 is " +;
    LTRIM(STR(RECNO()*100/LastRec)) +;
    "Percent into the database"
```

RECSIZE

Syntax: `RECSIZE([<alias>])`

RECSIZE returns the size of a record in the specified file. If no file is in use, RECSIZE returns zero. RECSIZE supports the optional argument <alias>, which indicates the work area in which to apply the function. If no data base is open in the indicated work area, 0 is returned. If the argument is omitted, the value for the currently selected work area is returned.

EXAMPLE:

```
SET COLOR TO W+/B
USE MASTER
USE Detail IN 2
SizeA = RECSIZE()
SizeB = RECSIZE(B)
? "The " + IIF(SizeA>SizeB, "Master ", "Detail ") +;
    "record size is greater then the " +;
    IIF(SizeA>SizeB, "Detail ", "Master ") +;
    "record size"
```

REPLICATE

Syntax: `REPLICATE(<expC>,<expN>)`

REPLICATE repeats a character expression <expC> a specified number of times <expN>. The resulting character expression must not exceed 254 characters.

EXAMPLE:

```
*-----------------------
* Calling Code BARGRAPH
*-----------------------
SET COLOR TO W+/B,R+/B,B,B
CLEAR
@ 12, 30 SAY "P R O C E S S I N G"
@ 18,10 TO 23,69 DOUBLE
@ 21,11 TO 21,68 DOUBLE
@ 21,10 SAY " "
@ 21,69 SAY " "
@ 19,24 SAY "P E R C E N T   C O M P L E T E"
@ 20,14 SAY "0    10    20    30    40    50"
@ 20,44 SAY "60   70    80    90    100"
USE Employee
TotalRec = RECCOUNT()
SET COLOR TO R+/B,W+/B,B
GOTO TOP
SCAN
   DUMMY=BarGraph(RELNO( )*100/Total Rec
   * ...     &&  Processing steps
   INKEY(1)
   SKIP
ENDSCAN
SET COLOR TO &ColStand
```

```
FUNCTION BARGRAPH
*
*   Program...:  BARGRAPH
*   Author....:  Phil Steele--President
*                Phillipps Computer Systems Inc.
*   Address...:  52 Hook Mountain Road,
*                Montville NJ 07045
*   Phone.....:  (201) 575-8575
*   Date......:  01/02/90
*   Notice....:  Copyright 1989  Philip Steele,
*                All Rights Reserved.
*   Notes.....:  This function displays a bar graph
*                depicting the progress of a DO WHILE
*                or other sequential operation.
*   Parameters:  Tot--Total number of records in the
*                     data base.
*
PARAMETERS Tot
PRIVATE    Tot, Pct
IF RECNO() < Tot + 1
  Pct = RECNO() * 100 / Tot
  @ 22,14 SAY REPLICATE("■",(Pct/2)+1)     && CHR(219)
ENDIF
RETURN(.T.)
*END:BARGRAPH
```

RIGHT

Syntax: RIGHT(<expC>/<variable>,<expN>)

RIGHT returns a specified number of characters from a string or memo field, counting from the last character. If <variable>, <expN> is less than or equal to zero, the null string will be returned. If <variable>, <expN> is greater than the length of <expC>, the entire character string will be returned.

EXAMPLE:

```
SET COLOR TO W+/B
TestStr = "Phil Steele"
? RIGHT(TestStr, 6)          &&  Returns Steele
? SUBSTR(TestStr, 6, 6)      &&  Returns Steele
```

RLOCK

Syntax: RLOCK([<expC list>, <alias>]/[<alias>])

BLOCK locks data base records to prevent multiuser access. RLOCK remains in effect until the UNLOCK function is encountered. RLOCK() returns a value of either ".T." or ".F.". If the RLOCK() function returns ".T.", you have gained both read and write access to the record. If the RLOCK() function returns ".F.", the record (or data base) has already been locked by another user, and the requested record is available to you for read access only.

EXAMPLE:

```
USE Master
SEEK "Steele"
IsLocked = RLOCK(RECNO())
IF IsLocked
    SET COLOR TO W+/R
    CLEAR
* Display Name of lock holder
    ? LKSYS(3) +;
    " is using the record."
```

ROLLBACK

Syntax: `ROLLBACK()`

ROLLBACK Returns true (.T.) if the most recent attempt to execute the ROLLBACK command was successful.

EXAMPLE:

```
BEGIN TRANSACTION
...
END TRANSACTION
IF .NOT. COMPLETED()
    ROLLBACK
    IF .NOT. ROLLBACK()
        IF ISMARKED()
            RESET
        ENDIF
        ? "The transaction was not completed and "
        ? "could not be restored"
        RETURN
    ENDIF
ENDIF
```

ROUND

Syntax: `ROUND(<expN1>, <expN2>)`

ROUND rounds the numeric expression <expN1> by the number of decimal places specified in <expN2>. If <expN2> is negative, the rounded number returned will be a whole number containing <expN2> trailing zeros. For instance, if <expN2> is –2, the result is rounded to even hundreds.

EXAMPLE:

```
SET COLOR TO W+/B
Salary1 = 50000.1234
Salary2 = 50000.1289
? ROUND(Salary1, -1)      && Returns 50000
? ROUND(Salary1, 2)       && Returns 50000.12
? ROUND(Salary2, 2)       && Returns 50000.13
```

ROW

Syntax: `ROW()`

ROW returns the row number of the cursor position on the screen. This function is useful for relative screen addressing within .PRG files.

EXAMPLE:

```
SET COLOR TO W+/B
CLEAR
USE Master
SCAN
   @ 12, 1 SAY TRIM(FirstName) + " "
   @ ROW( ), COL( ) +1 SAY TRIM(LastName)
   @ ROW( ), COL( ) +1 SAY " lives at " + Address1
ENDSCAN
```

RTOD

Syntax: `RTOD(<expN>)`

RTOD Converts angles from radians to degrees.

EXAMPLE:

```
SET PRECISION TO 15
SET DECIMALS TO 10
? RTOD(ATN2(SIN(DTOR(30)), COS(DTOR(30))))

* Displays 30.0000000000
```

RTRIM

Syntax: `RTRIM(<expC>)`

RTRIM removes trailing blanks from a character string. If <expC> is composed entirely of blanks, RTRIM returns the null string. The RTRIM function is identical to the TRIM function.

EXAMPLE:

```
SET COLOR TO W+/B
CLEAR
USE Master
SCAN
   @ 12, 1 SAY RTRIM(FirstName) + " "
   @ ROW( ), COL( )  + 1 SAY TRIM(LastName)
   @ ROW( ), COL( )  + 1 SAY " lives at " + Addressl
ENDSCAN
```

SEEK

Syntax: SEEK(<expC> [,<alias>])

SEEK performs lookups in indexed data base files. SEEK searches an indexed data base for the first occurrence of a record whose index key expression matches the specified <expC> and returns a .T. if a match is found or .F. if a match is not found. Single quotes (' '), double quotes (" "), or square brackets ([ ]) must be used to enclose a character string literal. Because SEEK() both moves the record pointer and returns a logical result, SEEK() can be used instead of a FIND/SEEK and FOUND() combination.

EXAMPLE:

```
USE Master ORDER LName
IF SEEK("Steele")
   DO DispData
ELSE
   ? "Record NOT found"
ENDIF
```

instead of:

```
USE Master ORDER LName
SEEK "Steele"
IF FOUND()
   DO DispData
ELSE
   ? "Record NOT found"
ENDIF
```

SELECT

Syntax: SELECT()

SELECT returns a number from 1 to 10 representing the highest unused work area available. If all ten work areas are in use, SELECT() returns 0.

EXAMPLE:

```
SET COLOR TO W+/B
CLEAR
```

```
USE Master
USE Detail IN 2
USE Invoice IN 3
? SELECT()            &&  Returns 4
USE Salary IN SELECT()
```

SET()

Syntax: SET(<ExpC>)

The SET() function returns the status of SET TO and SET ON commands. The argument of the function SET(<ExpC>) must be a valid SET command. Valid SET commands include those whose set values are ON or OFF, an integer value, or a path name or file name. The following table lists the supported SET commands and the possible values returned when they are used as the argument of the function SET().

Set Keyword	Value Returned by SET()
ALTERNATE	"ON" or "OFF"
AUTOSAVE	"ON" or "OFF"
BELL	"ON" or "OFF"
BLOCKSIZE	<ExpN>
CARRY	"ON" or "OFF"
CATALOG	"ON" or "OFF"
CENTURY	"ON" or "OFF"
CLOCK	"ON" or "OFF"
COLOR	"ON" or "OFF"
CONFIRM	"ON" or "OFF"
CONSOLE	"ON" or "OFF"
CURSOR	"ON" or "OFF"
DEBUG	"ON" or "OFF"
DECIMALS	<ExpN>
DEFAULT	Path name
DELETED	"ON" or "OFF"
DELIMITERS	"ON" or "OFF"
DESIGN	"ON" or "OFF"
DEVELOPMENT	"ON" or "OFF"
DIRECTORY	Path name
ECHO	"ON" or "OFF"
ENCRYPTION	"ON" or "OFF"
ESCAPE	"ON" or "OFF"
EXACT	"ON" or "OFF"
EXCLUSIVE	"ON" or "OFF"
FIELDS	"ON" or "OFF"
FULLPATH	"ON" or "OFF"
HEADINGS	"ON" or "OFF"

Set Keyword	Value Returned by SET()
HELP	"ON" or "OFF"
HISTORY	"ON" or "OFF"
HOURS	12 or 24
INSTRUCT	"ON" or "OFF"
INTENSITY	"ON" or "OFF"
LOCK	"ON" or "OFF"
MARGIN	<ExpN>
NEAR	"ON" or "OFF"
ODOMETER	<ExpN>
PATH	Path name
PAUSE	"ON" or "OFF"
PRECISION	<ExpN>
PRINTER	"ON" or "OFF"
PROCEDURE	File name
REFRESH	<ExpN>
REPROCESS	<ExpN>
SAFETY	"ON" or "OFF"
SCOREBOARD	"ON" or "OFF"
SPACE	"ON" or "OFF"
SQL	"ON" or "OFF"
STATUS	"ON" or "OFF"
STEP	"ON" or "OFF"
TALK	"ON" or "OFF"
TITLE	"ON" or "OFF"
TRAP	"ON" or "OFF"
TYPEAHEAD	<ExpN>
UNIQUE	"ON" or "OFF"
VIEW	File name

The SET() function returns a character string or an integer. The character string result is ON, OFF, path name, or file name. The result depends on the type and status of the named SET command when the SET() function is invoked.

If the SET command controls both ON/OFF and an integer, SET() returns only ON or OFF.

If the SET command controls both ON/OFF and a file name, SET() returns only ON or OFF.

EXAMPLE:

```
* Determine if SET CARRY is ON or OFF

? SET("CARRY")    &&  Returns OFF

* Change the dBASE path, and restore the path without
* knowing the original dBASE path.

SavePath = SET("PATH")
SET PATH TO NewPath
```

SIGN

Syntax: SIGN(<expN>)

SIGN determines whether <expN> is positive, negative, or zero and returns 1 for a positive number, –1 for a negative number, or 0 for zero.

EXAMPLE:

```
SET COLOR TO W+/B
CLEAR
USE Grades
Pass = IIF(SIGN(TestScore)>=0, .T., .F.)

* Assign true if grade is zero or positive.
```

SIN

Syntax: SIN(<expN>)

SIN calculates the trigonometric sine of an angle in radians.

EXAMPLE:

```
SET COLOR TO W+/B
CLEAR
? SIN(PI()/2)  &&  Returns 1
SET PRECISION TO 15
SET DECIMALS TO 10
? RTOD(ATN2(SIN(DTOR(30)), COS(DTOR(30))))
&&  30.0000000000
```

SOUNDEX

Syntax: SOUNDEX(<expC>)

Function provides a phonetic or "sounds like" match or a sound-alike code from the specified character string. It may be used to select near matches of a character string. The SOUNDEX() function returns a four-character string code using the following rules:

A. It retains the first letter of <expC>.
B. It drops all other occurrences of the letters a, e, h, i, o u, w, y.
C. It assigns the following numbers to the remaining letters:
1 = b, f, p, v
2 = c, g, j, k, q, s, x, z
3 = d, t
4 = l
5 = m, n
6 = r

D. If two or more adjacent letters have the same code, it drops all but the first letter.

E. It provides a code in the form of letter, digit, digit, digit.
   1. It adds trailing zeros if there are less than three digits.
   2. It drops all digits after the third one on the right.

F. It stops at the first nonalpha character.

G. It skips leading blanks.

H. It returns "0000" if the first nonblank character is nonalpha.

EXAMPLE:

```
SET COLOR TO W+/B
CLEAR
USE Master
INDEX ON SOUNDEX(Salesman) TO Salesman
ACCEPT "Enter the name to find: " TO FindName
LookFor = SOUNDEX(FindName)
SEEK LookFor
? FirstName

* Entered        Found
-----------     ----------
Allen           Alan
Jimmy           John
Jammy           John
Jonsey          James
Lenny           Leon
```

SPACE

Syntax: SPACE (<expN>)

The SPACE function returns a character string comprised of <expN> blanks. The maximum number of spaces that may be specified is 254.

EXAMPLE:

```
SET COLOR TO W+/B,N/W
CLEAR
*...           &&  Additional code
LastName = SPACE(20)
@ 12,12    SAY "Enter your last name: " +;
           GET LastName;
           PICTURE "!XXXXXXXXXXXXXXXXXXX"
IF .NOT. SET("CURSOR")
    SET CURSOR ON
ENDIF
READ
```

SQRT

Syntax:

```
SQRT(<expN>)
```

SQRT returns the square root of a positive numeric expression (<expN>).

Warning: The SQRT function accepts only nonnegative arguments and always returns a type F number.

EXAMPLE:

```
SQRT(100)       &&  Returns 10
SQRT(2*2)       &&  Returns 2
```

STR

Syntax:

```
STR(<expN> [,<length>] [, <decimal>])
```

STR converts a number <expN> to a character string. This function may have one, two, or three arguments.

<expN> is the number to be evaluated.

<length> is the width of the returned character string.

[decimals] is the width of the digits to the right of the decimal point.

The <length> of the value is assumed to include both the decimal point and the digits to the right of the decimal point.

EXAMPLE:

```
SET COLOR TO W+/B
CLEAR
Number = 123.456
? STR(Number)             &&  Returns "123" LENGTH 10
? STR(Number, 3)          &&  Returns "123" LENGTH 3
? STR(Number, 6, 2)       &&  Returns "123.45" LENGTH 6
```

STUFF

Syntax:

```
STUFF(<expC1>,<start>,<num_char>,<expC2>)
```

STUFF inserts or replaces a portion of a character string with another character string.

<expC1> is the string worked on.

<start> is the position in <exp1> to begin working.

<numb of characters> is the number of characters in <exp1> to delete starting at <start>.

<expC2> is the replacement string.

If <numb of characters> is equal to 0, the replacement string will be inserted but no characters will be removed from the current character string. If <expC2> is the null string, the number of characters specified by <numb of characters> will be removed from the current string without adding any additional characters.

EXAMPLE:

```
? STUFF("ABCDEF", 2, 0, "xyz")      && Returns AxyzBCDEFs
? STUFF("ABCDEF", 2, 3, "xyz")      && Returns AxyzEF
? STUFF("ABCDEF", 2, 2, "")         && Returns ADEF
? STUFF("ABCDEF", 2, 1, "xyz")      && Returns AxyzCDEF
? STUFF("ABCDEF", 2, 4, "xyz")      && Returns AxyzF
? STUFF("ABCDEF", 2, 10, "xyz")     && Returns Axyz
```

SUBSTR

Syntax:

```
SUBSTR(<expC>/<memo field name>,
       <start> [,<number of characters>])
```

SUBSTR extracts a specified number of characters from a character string or memo field. This function may have two or three arguments. It extracts characters from <expC> starting at position <start> and continuing for <number of characters> characters. If <number of characters> is omitted, characters are extracted until the end of the expression is reached.

EXAMPLE:

```
SET COLOR TO W+/B
  TestStr = "Phil Steele"
  ? SUBSTR(TestStr, 6, 6)        && Returns Steele
  ? SUBSTR(TestStr, 6)           && Returns Steele
  ? RIGHT(TestStr, 6)            && Returns Steele
```

TAG

Syntax:

```
TAG([<MDXfile>,] <expN> [,<alias>])
```

TAG returns the TAG name (character string) in the specified MDX or NDX file, or a null string if there is no index.

<expN> represents the index file.

<alias name> is the ALIAS name of an open data base file.

EXAMPLE:

```
SET COLOR TO W+/B
CLEAR
USE Master
? TAG(2)        && Returns the 2nd index--LastName
```

TAN

Syntax: `TAN(<expN>)`

TAN calculates the trigonometric tangent of an angle given in radians. The variable <expN> in a number representing an angle in radians.

The SET DECIMALS and SET PRECISION commands determine the number of decimals and accuracy displayed.

EXAMPLE:

```
SET PRECISION TO 15
SET DECIMALS TO 10
? TAN(0.7853981634)      &&  1.0
? TAN(0.463647609)       &&  0.50
```

TIME

Syntax: `TIME()`

TIME returns the system time as a an eight-character string in the 24-hour time format hh:mm:ss.

EXAMPLE:

```
SET COLOR TO &ColStand
CLEAR
X = TIME()                 &&  Time1 "14:32:21"
Y = "17:18:06"             &&  Time2
Z = ElapTime(X,Y)
? Z

* Elap Time = 2:45:45

FUNCTION ELAPTIME
*
*   Program...:  ELAPTIME
*   Author....:  Phil Steele - President
*                Phillipps Computer Systems Inc.
*   Address...:  52 Hook Mountain Road,
*                Montville NJ 07045
*   Phone.....:  (201) 575-8575
*   Date......:  01/02/90
*   Notice....:  Copyright 1989  Philip Steele,
*                All Rights Reserved.
*   Notes.....:  This function computes the difference
*                between time one and time two.
*   Parameters:  X--String containing time one.
*                Y--String containing time two.
*
```

```
PARAMETERS X, Y
PRIVATE  Timel, Time2, Z, Hrs, Min, Sec
Timel = (VAL(SUBSTR(X,1,2)) * 3600) +;
   (VAL(SUBSTR(X,4,2)) * 60) + (VAL(SUBSTR(X,7)))
Time2 = (VAL(SUBSTR(Y,1,2)) * 3600) +;
   (VAL(SUBSTR(Y,4,2)) * 60) + (VAL(SUBSTR(Y,7)))
Z   = ABS(Timel - Time2)
Hrs = INT(Z / 3600)
Min = INT((Z - Hrs * 3600) / 60)
Sec = Z - (Hrs * 3600) - (Min * 60)
RETURN (LTRIM(STR(Hrs,4,0) + ":" + STR(Min,2,0) +;
  ":" + Str(Sec,2,0)))
*END:ELAPTIME
```

TRANSFORM

Syntax: TRANSFORM(<exp>,<expC>)

Function allows PICTURE formatting of character logical, date, and numeric data without using the @. . .SAY command. <expr> is the variable you wish to format. <expC> is the format expression to be used with the variable. See the @ command for additional information on the picture formats.

EXAMPLE:

```
SET COLOR TO W+/B
CLEAR
USE Master
? TRANSFORM(LastName), "@R X X X X X X")

* Displays "S T E E L E"

? TRANSFORM(LastName), "@R X*X*X*X*X*X")

* Displays "S*T*E*E*L*E"
```

TRIM

Syntax: TRIM(<expC>)

TRIM removes trailing blanks from a character string. If <expC> is composed entirely of blanks, RTRIM returns the null string. The RTRIM function is identical to the TRIM function.

EXAMPLE:

```
SET COLOR TO W+/B
CLEAR
USE Master
```

```
SCAN
    @ 12, 1 SAY TRIM(FirstName) + " "
    @ ROW( ), COL( ) +1 SAY TRIM(LastName)
    @ ROW( ), COL( ) +1 SAY " lives at " + Address1
ENDSCAN
```

TYPE

Syntax: `TYPE(<expC>)`

TYPE evaluates the expression <expC> and returns a single uppercase character that indicates the expression type as follows:

C Character
N Numeric
D Date
F Float
L Logical
M Memo
U Undefined.

EXAMPLE:

```
SET COLOR TO W+/B
CLEAR
USE Master
? TYPE(LastName)       &&  Returns C
? TYPE(Salary)         &&  Returns N
? TYPE(LastUpDate)     &&  Returns D
```

UPPER

Syntax: `UPPER(<expC>)`

UPPER converts all lowercase letters to uppercase letters in a specified character string expression.

EXAMPLE:

```
SET COLOR TO W+/B
CLEAR
USE Master
? LastName          &&  Returns Chan
? UPPER(LastName)   &&  Returns CHAN
```

USER

Syntax: `USER()`

USER returns the name of the user logged in to a PROTECTed system. On a system that does not use PROTECT, USER() returns a null string.

EXAMPLE:

```
SET COLOR TO W+/B
CLEAR
USE Master     &&  A PROTECTed system
? USER()       &&  Returns Andy Chabak
```

VAL

Syntax: `VAL(<expC>)`

The VAL() function converts <expC> to a numeric value. The string <expC> must contain the ASCII representation of a valid number.

EXAMPLE:

```
SET COLOR TO W+/B
CLEAR
ACCEPT "Enter your age : " TO sAge
nAge = VAL(sAge)
```

Note: ACCEPT only obtains *character* expressions.

VARREAD

Syntax: `VARREAD()`

Function returns the name of the field or memory variable currently being edited. This information is very important in creating a context-sensitive help subsystem.

EXAMPLE:

```
SET COLOR TO W+/B
CLEAR
ON KEY F1 DO HelpMe
@ 3,5 SAY "First Name: " GET FirstName
@ 4,5 SAY "Last Name : " GET LastName
...

PROCEDURE HELPME
CLEAR TYPEAHEAD                    &&  Clear the keyboard buffer
ACTIVATE WINDOW HelpWindow
```

```
DO CASE
   CASE VARREAD() = "LastName"  &&  Display the Last Name
                                &&  help text
  CASE VARREAD() = "FirstName"  &&  Display the First Name
                                &&  help text
  ...
ENDCASE
INKEY(0)                        &&  Pause to permit message
                                &&  to be read.
DEACTIVATE WINDOW HelpWindow
RETURN
*END:HELPME
```

VERSION

Syntax: `VERSION()`

VERSION returns a character string containing the number of the dBASE IV version in use. This function could be used conditionally to execute portions of code that are version specific in your applications.

EXAMPLE:

```
SET COLOR TO W+/B
CLEAR
IF VERSION() = "dBASE IV  1.1"
   SET CURSOR OFF
ELSE
  LOAD CurOff
  CALL CurOff
ENDIF
```

YEAR

Syntax: `YEAR(<expD>)`

YEAR returns the numeric value of the year from a date expression. The result is always a four-digit number.

EXAMPLE:

```
PearlH = {12/07/41}
? YEAR(PearlH)          &&  Returns 1941
```

CHAPTER 5

System Memory Variables

dBASE IV uses system memory variables to control the overall appearance of data that is displayed or printed sequentially (streaming output). Some system memory variables also affect the dBASE IV word-wrap editors.

This section contains information to help you tailor your streaming output needs by utilizing these system memory variables.

_alignment

Syntax:

```
_alignment = "LEFT"/"RIGHT"/"CENTER"
```

_alignment specifies the alignment of output from the ? and ?? commands between the margins when _wrap is true. By default, output is aligned to the left margin.

Note: The PICTURE functions (B, I, and J) control alignment of text *within* field templates, whereas _alignment controls alignment of text between margins.

EXAMPLE:

```
SET TALK OFF
SET COLOR TO W+/B
CLEAR
Heading      = "Phillipps Computer Systems Inc."
_wrap        = .T.
_lmargin     = 5
_rmargin     = 130
_alignment   = "center"
```

```
SET PRINTER ON
? Heading          &&  Center heading on page
...
```

_box

Syntax: `_box = <condition>`

_box controls the display of boxes specified with the DEFINE BOX command. If the default condition is true, boxes print. You may also draw boxes using the @ . . . TO construct, which will draw a box regardless of the condition of the _box variable.

EXAMPLE:

```
SET TALK OFF                          &&  Draw a box around a
SET ECHO OFF                          &&  centered heading
SET COLOR TO W+/B
CLEAR
Heading    = "Phillipps Computer Systems Inc."
_wrap      = .T.
_lmargin   = 5
_rmargin   = 74
_box       = .T.
SET PRINTER ON
?
?
DEFINE BOX FROM 20 TO 60 HEIGHT 5 DOUBLE
?
_alignment = "center"
? Heading         &&  Center heading on page
?
?
?
EJECT
SET PRINTER OFF
```

_indent

Syntax: `_indent = <expN>`

_indent is used to indent the first line of a new paragraph that is printed with the ? command. _wrap must be true and <expN> must be between -(_lmargin) and (_rmargin - _lmargin - 1).

Note: dBASE IV starts a new paragraph at each ? command.

EXAMPLE:

```
SET TALK OFF
SET ECHO OFF
SET COLOR TO W+/B
CLEAR
_wrap      = .T.
_lmargin   = 5
_rmargin   = 74
_indent    = 10
USE MASTER
SET PRINTER ON
SCAN
   ? MemoStart
   ...
   ? ...
ENDSCAN
EJECT
SET PRINTER OFF
```

_lmargin

Syntax: _lmargin = <expN>

_lmargin defines the left margin on a page for output produced by the ? command when _wrap is true. <expN> must be between 0 and 254

EXAMPLE:

```
SET TALK OFF
SET ECHO OFF
SET COLOR TO W+/B
CLEAR
_wrap       = .T.
_lmargin    = 5
_rmargin    = 74
_indent     = 10
USE MASTER
SET PRINTER ON
SCAN
   ? MemoStart
   ...
   ? ...
ENDSCAN
EJECT
SET PRINTER OFF
```

_padvance

Syntax: `_padvance = "FORMFEED"/"LINEFEEDS"`

_padvance determines the type of page advance that will be used for streaming output. "FORMFEED" issues a top of form character to advance the paper to the next page. "LINEFEEDS" issues a computed number of line-feed characters to advance the paper to the next page.

EXAMPLE:

```
SET TALK OFF
SET ECHO OFF
SET COLOR TO W+/B
CLEAR
_wrap      = .T.
_lmargin   = 5
_rmargin   = 74
_indent    = 10
_padvance  = "FORMFEED"
USE MASTER
SET PRINTER ON
SCAN
   ? MemoStart
   ...
   ? ...
   EJECT              &&  Eject using a formfeed
ENDSCAN
SET PRINTER OFF
```

_pageno

Syntax: `_pageno = <expN>`

_pageno determines or sets the current page number. <expN> must be between 1 and 32,767

EXAMPLE:

```
SET TALK OFF
SET ECHO OFF
SET COLOR TO W+/B
CLEAR
_wrap        = .T.
_lmargin     = 5
_rmargin     = 74
_indent      = 10
```

```
_padvance     = "FORMFEED"
_alignment    = "RIGHT"
_pageno       = 1
USE MASTER
SET PRINTER ON
SCAN
   ? "Page: " + ALLTRIM(STR(_pageno))
   _alignment = "LEFT"
   ...
   EJECT                  && Eject using a formfeed
ENDSCAN
SET PRINTER OFF
```

_pbpage

Syntax: `_pbpage = <expN>`

_pbpage is used to specify the beginning page of a print job. <expN> must be between 1 and 32,767. Pages that are less than _pbpage are not printed. A common use of this feature is to restart a failed job.

EXAMPLE:

```
SET TALK OFF
SET ECHO OFF
SET COLOR TO W+/B
CLEAR
pStart  = 1
RName   = "Master Report"
...
@ 12,10      SAY "Enter the page number to start at: ";
             GET pStart PICTURE "99999"
READ
_pbpage = pStart
DO ReStrt WITH RName
```

_pcolno

Syntax: `_pcolno = <expN>`

_pcolno is used in the same manner as the PCOL() function. It moves the output to begin at a given column on the current line or returns the current column number. <expN> must be between 0 and 255.

If _wrap is false and the printer is on, _pcolno enables you to overstrike characters by using a value less than the current one. If _wrap is true, the output buffer will be overwritten and previous output will be lost.

_pcolno always changes when the streaming output changes regardless of the SET PRINTER setting.

EXAMPLE:

```
SET TALK OFF
SET ECHO OFF
SET COLOR TO W+/B
SET PRINTER ON
_wrap     = .F.
_lmargin  = 5
_rmargin  = 74
_padvance = "FORMFEED"
? "This is a test"
_pcolno   = _pcolno - 4
? "____"
?? " TEST"

* The output looks like the next line
* This is a TEST
```

_pcopies

Syntax:

```
_pcopies = <expN>
```

_pcopies sets the number of copies to be printed. <expN> must be between 1 and 32,767. This command can only be used in a program because it requires the PRINTJOB . . . ENDPRINTJOB construct.

EXAMPLE:

```
SET TALK OFF
SET ECHO OFF
SET COLOR TO W+/B
CLEAR
NumCopies = 1
@ 12,10   SAY "Enter the number of copies you desire: ";
          GET NumCopies PICTURE "99999"
READ
_pcopies = NumCopies
PRINTJOB
  ...
ENDPRINTJOB
```

_pdriver

Syntax:

```
_pdriver = "<printer driver filename>"
```

_pdriver activates the desired printer driver or returns the name of the current driver. <printer driver filename> must be a valid DOS file name and may include a DOS path. You may omit the .PR2 file extension.

EXAMPLE:

```
SET TALK OFF
SET ECHO OFF
SET COLOR TO W+/B
CLEAR
WantP = SPACE 17
@ 12,10   SAY "Select the printer you desire: ";
          GET WantP
          PICTURE "@M Epson, HP Laser, Other" ;
          MESSAGE "Space to view. - Enter to select."
READ
DO CASE
   CASE WantP   = "Epson"
    _pdriver    = "FX80_1.PR2"
   CASE WantP   = "HP Laser"
    _pdriver    = "HPLAS100.PR2"
   CASE WantP   = "Other"
    _pdriver    = "GENERIC.PR2"
ENDCASE
```

_pecode

Syntax: `_pecode = <expC>`

_pecode is used to reset the printer and the end of a PRINTJOB, and, therefore, it can only be used in a program because it requires the PRINTJOB . . . ENDPRINTJOB construct. <expC> is a string of less than 255 char. A typical use for this command would be to remove memory resident overlays from a Hewlett-Packard LaserJet printer.

EXAMPLE:

```
SET TALK OFF
SET ECHO OFF
SET COLOR TO W+/B
CLEAR

* Download a form

RUN TYPE Macro.TXT>LPT1

* Make the form macro temporary

_pscode = "(27)(38)(102)(57)(88)"

* Remove all temporary macros at the end of printing.

_pecode = "(27)(38)(102)(55)(88)"
```

```
PRINTJOB
   ...
ENDPRINTJOB
```

_peject

Syntax: `_peject = "BEFORE"/"AFTER"/"BOTH"/"NONE"`

_peject controls the ejecting of paper before and/or after a PRINTJOB. Although you can set the _peject at the dot prompt, it can only be used in a program because it requires the PRINTJOB . . . ENDPRINTJOB construct.

"BEFORE"	ejects a page before printing the first page.
"AFTER"	ejects a page after printing the last page.
"BOTH"	ejects a page before the first and after the last page.
"NONE"	ejects no page before the first or after the last page.

EXAMPLE:

```
SET TALK OFF
SET ECHO OFF
SET COLOR TO W+/B
CLEAR
&&  Download a form
RUN TYPE Macro.TXT>LPT1

* Make the form macro temporary

_pscode = "(27)(38)(102)(57)(88)"

* Remove all temporary macros at the end of printing.

_pecode = "(27)(38)(102)(55)(88)"
_peject = "AFTER"          &&  Eject page after printing.
PRINTJOB
   ...
ENDPRINTJOB
```

_pepage

Syntax: `_pepage = <expN>`

_pepage is used to specify the ending page of a print job. <expN> must be between 1 and 32,767. Pages that are greater than _pepage are not printed. A common use of this feature is to print part of a job and to test the ENDPRINTJOB logic.

EXAMPLE:

```
SET TALK OFF
SET ECHO OFF
```

```
SET COLOR TO W+/B
CLEAR
pEnd  = 500
RName = "Master Report"
...
@ 12,10   SAY "Enter the page number to end at: ";
          GET pEnd PICTURE "99999"
READ
_pepage = pEnd
DO Rpt WITH RName
```

_pform

Syntax:

```
_pform = "<printer form filename>"
```

_pform either returns the name of the current print form file or activates a print form file. "<printer form filename>" must be a valid DOS filename. A print form (.PRF) is a binary file containing data regarding the following print settings:

_padvance	_pecode	_ppitch
_pageno	_peject	_pquality
_pbpage	_pepage	_pscode
_pcopies	_plength	_pspacing
_pdriver	_ploffset	_pwait

A .PRF file is created from the report and label generators when the object (report of label) is saved. This file is loaded and modified whenever you modify or print the object from the design screen or the control center. When you have a _pform you like, you can use the DOS COPY command to copy it to a file, which you can then load and use in subsequent print jobs.

EXAMPLE:

```
SET TALK OFF
SET ECHO OFF

* Use desired default print variables in RptlForm

_pform = "RptlForm"
PRINTJOB
   ...
ENDPRINTJOB
```

_plength

Syntax:

```
_plength = <expN>
```

_plength is used to set the page length of the output page. <expN> is an integer between 1 and 32,767. The page length is defined as the number of lines from the top of the page to the bottom of the page. Note that if you change the height of a letter, the _plength will change. The default value is 66 lines for a $\frac{1}{6}$-inch-high letter.

EXAMPLE:

```
SET TALK OFF
SET ECHO OFF
SET COLOR TO W+/B
CLEAR
_wrap       = .T.
_lmargin    = 3.5
_plength    = 24
_padvance   = "FORMFEED"
USE MASTER
SET PRINTER ON
SCAN
   ? FirstName + " " + LastName
   ? Address1
   ? Address2
   ? City + " " + State + " " + Zip
   EJECT                    &&  Eject using a formfeed
ENDSCAN
```

_plineno

Syntax:

```
_plineno = <expN>
```

_plineno is used in the same manner as the PROW() function. It moves the output to begin at a given line number or returns the current line number. <expN> must be between 0 and (_plength - 1).

_plineno always changes when the streaming output changes regardless of the SET PRINTER setting, even if it is off. Unlike PROW(), _plineno cannot exceed _plength.

EXAMPLE:

```
SET TALK OFF
SET ECHO OFF
SET COLOR TO W+/B
CLEAR
SET PRINTER ON
_lmargin  = 5
_rmargin  = 74
_padvance = "FORMFEED"
? "This is a test"
_plineno  = _plineno + 3     &&  Triple space
? "This is a test too"
```

_ploffset

Syntax:

```
_ploffset = <expN>
```

_ploffset sets the left offset for printed output only. The page left offset is measured from the left edge of the page, _lmargin begins at the the end of _ploffset. <expN> is an integer between 0 and 254 with a default of 0. The SET MARGIN command is equivalent to the _ploffset system variable—not _lmargin. SET MARGIN is automatically adjusted to match the value of _ploffset. This variable is used to adjust for paper that is slightly off center in the printer without changing margins.

EXAMPLE:

```
SET TALK OFF
SET ECHO OFF
SET COLOR TO W+/B
CLEAR
SET PRINTER ON
_lmargin  = 5
_ploffset = 10
DO WHILE .T.
   SET PRINTER ON
   ? "XXXXXXXXXXXXXXXXXXXXXXXXX"
   ? " "
   ? " "
   SET PRINTER OFF
   SET DEVICE TO SCREEN
   Adjust = 1
   @ 12,12 SAY "Enter an adjustment factor (-9 to +9)or";
     " 0 if correct: "  GET Adjust PICTURE "99"
   IF Adjust = 0
      EXIT
   ENDIF
   _ploffset = _ploffset + Adjust
ENDDO
```

_ppitch

Syntax:

```
_ppitch = "PICA"/"ELITE"/"CONDENSED"/"DEFAULT"
```

_ppitch either returns the a string showing the current pitch or sets the printer pitch. The default pitch is "DEFAULT" or the pitch defined by your printer's DIP switches or setup code.

"PICA"	10 characters per inch.
"ELITE"	12 characters per inch.
"CONDENSED"	cbout 17.16 characters per inch.
"DEFAULT"	unmodified printer pitch setting.

EXAMPLE:

```
SET TALK OFF
SET ECHO OFF
SET COLOR TO W+/B
SET PRINTER ON
_lmargin  = 5
_rmargin  = 132
_padvance = "FORMFEED"
_ppitch = "PICA"            &&  Big letters for header
? "H E A D E R"
_ppitch = "CONDENSED"       &&  Condensed for details
SCAN
  ? LastName
  ...
ENDSCAN
```

_pquality

Syntax: `_pquality = <condition>`

_pquality selects letter quality or near letter quality (.T.) if it is supported by your printer, or draft mode (.F.) on the printer, or returns a logical TRUE or FALSE showing the currently defined print mode. The default is .F. (false) or draft mode.

EXAMPLE:

```
SET TALK OFF
SET ECHO OFF
SET COLOR TO W+/B
CLEAR
_lmargin  = 5
_rmargin  = 132
_padvance = "FORMFEED"
_pquality = .T.
YN    = "Y"
? ACCEPT "Do you want letter quality?" TO YN
IF YN = "N"
  _pquality   = .F.
ENDIF
SET PRINTER ON
SCAN
  ? LastName
  ...
ENDSCAN
```

_pscode

Syntax: `_pscode = <expC>`

_pscode is used to set the printer and the beginning of a PRINTJOB, and, therefore it can only be used in a program because it requires the PRINTJOB . . . ENDPRINTJOB construct. <expC> is a string of fewer than 255 characters. A typical use for this command would be to place a temporary memory resident overlay in a Hewlett-Packard LaserJet printer.

EXAMPLE:

```
SET TALK OFF
SET ECHO OFF
SET COLOR TO W+/B
CLEAR

* Download a form

RUN TYPE Macro.TXT>LPT1

* Make the form macro temporary

_pscode = "(27)(38)(102)(57)(88)"

* Remove all temporary macros at the end of printing.

_pecode = "(27)(38)(102)(55)(88)"
PRINTJOB
  ...
ENDPRINTJOB
```

_pspacing

Syntax:

```
_pspacing = 1/2/3
```

_pspacing selects single, double, or triple spacing. The default is 1—single spacing.

EXAMPLE:

```
SET TALK OFF
SET ECHO OFF
SET COLOR TO W+/B
CLEAR
_lmargin  = 5
_rmargin  = 132
_padvance = "FORMFEED"
_pspacing = 1
Spacing   = 1
? 12,12 SAY "Enter 1 for single spacing, 2 for double ";
            "or 3 for triple: " GET Spacing PICTURE "9";
            RANGE 1,3
_pspacing = Spacing
SET PRINTER ON
SCAN
  ? LastName
  ...
ENDSCAN
```

_pwait

Syntax:

```
_pwait = <condition>
```

_pwait determines whether the printer will wait after printing each page. The default is .F.—do not wait. This variable is useful when using a cut sheet printer such as a daisy wheel.

EXAMPLE:

```
SET TALK OFF
SET ECHO OFF
SET COLOR TO W+/B
CLEAR
_lmargin  = 5
_rmargin  = 74
_padvance = "FORMFEED"
_pwait    = .T.
Spacing   = 1
? 12,12 SAY "Place the 1040 form into the printer and ";
                    "press any key when ready"
INKEY(0)
SET PRINTER ON
SCAN
  ? LastName
  ...
ENDSCAN
```

_rmargin

Syntax:

```
_rmargin = <expN>
```

_rmargin defines the right margin on a page for output produced by the ? command when _wrap is true. <expN> must be between 0 and 254. _rmargin is useful for changing the printing width of memo fields.

EXAMPLE:

```
SET TALK OFF
SET ECHO OFF
SET COLOR TO W+/B
CLEAR
_wrap    = .T.
_lmargin = 5
_rmargin = 74
_indent  = 10
USE MASTER
SET PRINTER ON
SCAN
  ? ...
```

```
  ? ...
  _rmargin = 30
  ? MemoStart
  _rmargin = 74
ENDSCAN
EJECT
SET PRINTER OFF
```

_tabs

Syntax: `_tabs = <expC>`

_tabs sets one or more tab stops for screen, printer, or file output printed with the ?/?? command, as well as the tab stops for the word-wrap editor. <expC> is a character string of numbers separated by commas in ascending order. When a tab character CHR(9) is printed, it is expanded to the number of spaces needed to reach the next tab stop.

EXAMPLE:

```
SET TALK OFF
SET ECHO OFF
SET COLOR TO W+/B
CLEAR
_wrap    = .T.
_lmargin = 5
_rmargin = 74
_tabs    = "5, 15, 25, 35, 45, 70"
USE MASTER
SET PRINTER ON
SCAN
  ? Name + CHR(9) + Address + CHR(9) + Salary
ENDSCAN
EJECT
SET PRINTER OFF
```

_wrap

Syntax: `_wrap = <condition>`

_wrap sets word wrapping between the margins on and off. It also affects the memory variables _alignment, _indent, _lmargin, and _rmargin.

EXAMPLE:

```
SET TALK OFF
SET ECHO OFF
SET COLOR TO W+/B
CLEAR
```

```
_wrap    = .T.
_lmargin = 10
_rmargin = 30
_indent = 3
Test     = "This is a test showing the effects of _wrap"
? Test

* The output look like this:
* "This is a test showing the effects of _wrap"
```

CHAPTER 6

New Features

dBASE IV has more than 250 new commands and functions, a new user interface, an SQL (Structured Query Language) interface, a template language, menus, UDFs (user defined functions), arrays, windows, and an application generator. This abundance of new features makes moving from dBASE III PLUS to dBASE IV a big step, almost as big as going from dBASE II to dBASE III. This section will cover the most important of these new features in detail.

Menus

Among all the new features, menus and UDFs are the most important. Remember how you had to write a light-bar menu using dBASE III?

```
*
*  Program.: MENU.PRG
*  Author..: Phil Steele - President
*            Phillipps Computer Systems Inc.
*  Address.: 52 Hook Mountain Road, Montville NJ 07045
*  Phone...: (201) 575-8575
*  Date....: 11/01/89
*  Notice..: Copyright 1989, Phil Steele
*            All Rights Reserved
*  Version.: dBASE III PLUS
*  Notes...: GENERAL PURPOSE LIGHT BAR MENU
*
PARAMETERS Selection
*_______________
* STANDARD PREAMBLE
```

```
*____________________
SET STEP OFF
SET ECHO OFF
SET TALK OFF
SET MENU OFF
SET BELL OFF
SET PRINT OFF
SET STATUS OFF
SET SAFETY OFF
SET ESCAPE OFF
SET CONFIRM ON
SET HEADING OFF
SET SCOREBOARD OFF
SET DEVICE TO  SCREEN
SET COLOR TO W+/B,N/W,B,B

Enter  = 13
Up     = 5
Down   = 24

A1     = "   1. Choice A    "    && MENU CHOICES A1-A5
A2     = "   2. Choice B    "
A3     = "   3. Choice C    "
A4     = "   4. Choice D    "
A5     = "   5. Choice E    "
CLEAR
@ 5,0 SAY " "
TEXT
                ┌──────────────┐
                │LIGHT BAR MENU│
                ├──────────────┤
                │              │
                │              │
                │              │
                │              │
                └──────────────┘

                ↑↓-scroll  ←┘-select
ENDTEXT
N         = 1
Selection = 1
Macro     = " "
DO WHILE N <= 5                              && INITIALIZE CHOICES
   Macro = "A" + STR(N,1,0)
   @ N+8,17 SAY &Macro
   N = N + 1
ENDDO
DO WHILE .T.                                 && MAIN MENU LOOP
```

```
    Macro = "A" + STR(Selection,1,0)
    @ Selection+8,17 GET &Macro        && REVERSE COLORS
    CLEAR GETS
    Key = 0
    DO WHILE Key <> Up .AND. Key <> Down;
                .AND. Key <> Enter
      Key = INKEY()
    ENDDO
    DO CASE
       CASE Key = Up                   && GO UP AND WRAPAROUND
          @ Selection+8,17 SAY &Macro
          Selection = IIF(Selection>1, Selection-1, 5)
       CASE Key = Down                 && GO DOWN AND WRAPAROUND
          @ Selection+8,17 SAY &Macro
          Selection = IIF(Selection<5, Selection+1, 1)
       CASE Key = Enter                && SELECT CHOICE AND EXIT
          EXIT
    ENDCASE
ENDDO
RETURN
```

A macro is used to access the proper line of the menu as follows:

1. Place the elements of the "array" into numbered variables.

   A1 = " 1. Choice A "
   A2 = " 2. Choice B "
   A3 = " 3. Choice C "
   A4 = " 4. Choice D "
   A5 = " 5. Choice E "

2. Create a second variable in a Do loop to access the first variable using the STR command.

```
N = 1
DO WHILE .T.
   Select = "A" + STR(N,1,0)
   @ N+5,10 SAY Select
   ...
   ...
ENDDO
...
```

3. Reverse the color of the current selection by GETting the line instead of SAYing the line. To avoid queuing up multiple GETs, we then clear the gets and wait for a valid key stroke, up arrow, down arrow, or enter.
4. If the key is down arrow, add one to the row counter.
   If it is up arrow, we subtract one from the row counter.
   If we go beyond the limits of the box, we substitute the highest or lowest value, as applicable.
5. Enter takes us out of our infinite loop.

With dBASE IV we have the "MENU" commands. To produce the same menu we can use the following code:

```
*
*  Program.: MENU.PRG
*  Author..: Phil Steele - President
*            Phillipps Computer Systems Inc.
*  Address.: 52 Hook Mountain Road, Montville NJ 07045
*  Phone...: (201) 575-8575
*  Date....: 11/01/89
*  Notice..: Copyright 1989, Phil Steele
*            All Rights Reserved
*  Version.: dBASE IV
*  Notes...: GENERAL PURPOSE LIGHT BAR MENU
*

*__________________
* STANDARD PREAMBLE
*__________________

SET PATH TO \DBASE;\DBASE\STEP;\DBASE\PRGS
SET STEP OFF
SET ECHO OFF
SET TALK OFF
SET BELL OFF
SET CURSOR  OFF
SET PRINT   OFF
SET DELETE  ON
SET STATUS  OFF
SET SAFETY  OFF
SET ESCAPE  OFF
SET CONFIRM ON
SET HEADING OFF
SET SCOREBOARD OFF
SET DISPLAY TO EGA25
SET DEVICE  TO SCREEN
SET COLOR TO W+/B,N/W,B,B

CLEAR
@ 5,0 SAY " "
TEXT
              ┌──────────────────┐
              │  LIGHT BAR MENU  │
              ├──────────────────┤
              │                  │
              │                  │
              │                  │
              │                  │
              └──────────────────┘

              ↑↓-scroll  ←┘-select
ENDTEXT
SET BORDER TO NONE
```

```
DEFINE POPUP Main FROM 8,16
DEFINE BAR 1 OF Main PROMPT "   1. Choice A    " MESSAGE "Select choice A."
DEFINE BAR 2 OF Main PROMPT "   2. Choice B    " MESSAGE "Select choice B."
DEFINE BAR 3 OF Main PROMPT "   3. Choice C    " MESSAGE "Select choice C."
DEFINE BAR 4 OF Main PROMPT "   4. Choice D    " MESSAGE "Select choice D."
DEFINE BAR 5 OF Main PROMPT "   5. Choice E    " MESSAGE "Select choice E."
ON SELECTION POPUP Main DO MainCode WITH BAR()
SET BORDER TO SINGLE
ACTIVATE POPUP Main
* ...
RETURN


*________________
PROCEDURE MAINCODE
*________________
PARAMETER Choice
@ 20,40 SAY Choice
* ...
RETURN
```

The MENU portion of our code is almost automatic. Let us look at it.

1. Turn off the borders since we are using a TEXT . . . ENDTEXT construct to produce the box for our menu to reside in. We also could have used a "WINDOW" or the @ X,Y TO X1,Y1 command to produce the box for the menu.
2. Define where the first bar of the menu will appear on the screen and assign a name (MAIN) to the menu.
3. Define the "BARs" for the menu and supply an optional message for each bar.
4. Tell dBASE what to do when a selection is made from the menu, "ON SELECTION POPUP Main DO MainCode WITH BAR()."
5. Reset the BORDER.
6. Activate the menu.

This is much easier, faster, and cleaner than using dBASE III PLUS.

We can also produce "Pull-Down" menus using the menu commands available in dBASE IV, as the next example shows:

```
*
* Program.: MENU.PRG
* Author..: Phil Steele - President
*           Phillipps Computer Systems Inc.
* Address.: 52 Hook Mountain Road, Montville NJ 07045
* Phone...: (201) 575-8575
* Date....: 11/01/89
* Notice..: Copyright 1989, Phil Steele
*           All Rights Reserved
* Version.: dBASE IV
* Notes...: GENERAL PURPOSE LIGHT BAR MENU
*
```

```
*__________
* PREAMBLE
*__________
SET STEP OFF
SET ECHO OFF
SET TALK OFF
SET BELL OFF
SET PRINT   OFF
SET DELETE  ON
SET STATUS  OFF
SET SAFETY  OFF
SET ESCAPE  OFF
SET CONFIRM ON
SET HEADING OFF
SET SCOREBOARD OFF
SET DISPLAY TO EGA25
SET DEVICE  TO SCREEN

DoubleBox  = CHR(201)+CHR(205)+CHR(187)+CHR(186)+;
             CHR(188)+CHR(205)+CHR(200)+CHR(186)+CHR(32)
SingleBox  = CHR(218)+CHR(196)+CHR(191)+CHR(179)+;
             CHR(217)+CHR(196)+CHR(192)+CHR(179)+CHR(32)
Laser = .T.

SET COLOR TO W+/B,N/W,B
CLEAR
SET COLOR TO W+/R,N/W,B

*________________
* Menu Definitions
*________________


*___________________
* Horizontal Bar Menu
*___________________
DEFINE MENU Main MESSAGE "Cursor keys scroll, Enter selects, Esc quits."

DEFINE PAD Inquiry OF Main PROMPT  " Inquiry and Update ";
                   AT 3,2  MESSAGE "View and Update Information."

DEFINE PAD Rpts    OF Main PROMPT  " Reports ";
                   AT 3,31 MESSAGE "Select and Print Reports."

DEFINE PAD Util    OF Main PROMPT  " Utility ";
                   AT 3,52 MESSAGE "Perform Utility Operations."

DEFINE PAD Done   OF Main  PROMPT  " Exit ";
                   AT 3,70 MESSAGE "Return to the Operating System."


*______________
* Menu Actions
```

```
*_______________
* Main horizontal menu actions.
ON SELECTION PAD Inquiry OF Main ACTIVATE POPUP PInqy
ON SELECTION PAD Rpts    OF Main ACTIVATE POPUP PRpts
ON SELECTION PAD Util    OF Main ACTIVATE POPUP PUtil
ON SELECTION PAD Done    OF Main DO Fini


SET BORDER TO 205,196,179,179,209,209,192,217
*_____________________
* Pull-down for Inquiry
*_____________________
DEFINE POPUP PInqy FROM 4,2 TO 9,15
DEFINE BAR 1 OF PInqy PROMPT "    View    ";
                      MESSAGE "View the databases."
DEFINE BAR 2 OF PInqy PROMPT "    Add     ";
                      MESSAGE "Add records to the databases."
DEFINE BAR 3 OF PInqy PROMPT "   Change   ";
                      MESSAGE "Change existing records."
DEFINE BAR 4 OF PInqy PROMPT "   Delete   ";
                      MESSAGE "Delete an existing record."
*_____________________
* Pull-down for Reports
*_____________________
DEFINE POPUP PRpts FROM 4,20 TO 14,50
DEFINE BAR 1 OF PRpts PROMPT " 1. Vendor Reports          ";
                      MESSAGE  "Select Vendor Reports."
DEFINE BAR 2 OF PRpts PROMPT " 2. Confidentiality Reports ";
                      MESSAGE  "Select Confidentiality Reports."
DEFINE BAR 3 OF PRpts PROMPT " 3. Summary Reports         ";
                      MESSAGE  "Select Summary Reports."
DEFINE BAR 4 OF PRpts PROMPT " 4. Control Reports         ";
                      MESSAGE  "Select Control Reports."
DEFINE BAR 5 OF PRpts PROMPT " 5. Form Letters            ";
                      MESSAGE  "Select Form Letter Reports."
DEFINE BAR 6 OF PRpts PROMPT IIF(Laser, " 6. Use Laser Printer       ",;
                                        " 6. Use Dot Matrix Printer  ");
                    MESSAGE  "Select Printer to Use - Press Enter to Change Printer Type."
DEFINE BAR 7 OF PRpts PROMPT " 7. Create a Filter         ";
                      MESSAGE  "Create a Filter to use in producing Reports Containing
Subsets of the Data."
DEFINE BAR 8 OF PRpts PROMPT " 8. Use a Filter for Reports ";
                      MESSAGE  "Select a Filter to use in producing Reports."
DEFINE BAR 9 OF PRpts PROMPT " 9. Remove Active Filter    ";
                      MESSAGE  "Remove the Current Filter used in producing Reports."
ON SELECTION POPUP PRpts DO NextRpt


*_______________________
* Pull-down for Utilities
*_______________________
DEFINE POPUP PUtil FROM 4,42 TO 12,72
```

```
DEFINE BAR 1 OF PUtil PROMPT " 1. Download Data              ";
                      MESSAGE  "Add or Replace Vendor Information on the System."
DEFINE BAR 2 OF PUtil PROMPT " 2. Utilities D.O.S.           ";
                      MESSAGE  "Perform DOS Functions"
DEFINE BAR 3 OF PUtil PROMPT " 3. Change System Colors       ";
                      MESSAGE  "Change the Default Colors."
DEFINE BAR 4 OF PUtil PROMPT " 4. Change Codes for Choices ";
                      MESSAGE  "Change the Choices that Popup for Data Entry."
DEFINE BAR 5 OF PUtil PROMPT " 5. Make Distribution Copies ";
                      MESSAGE  "Create Diskettes to be Used on Other Computers."
DEFINE BAR 6 OF PUtil PROMPT " 6. Letter Changes             ";
                      MESSAGE  "Change the Exp. Cert. and Terms Letters."
DEFINE BAR 7 OF PUtil PROMPT " 7. Display Available Memory ";
                      MESSAGE  "Show the amount of memory left when the system is running."
ON SELECTION POPUP PUtil DO NextUtl
*___________________________
* Pull-down for Vendor Rpts
*___________________________
SET BORDER TO 196,196,179,179,017,191,192,217
DEFINE POPUP PVend FROM 5,50 TO 14,78
DEFINE BAR 1 OF PVend PROMPT " 1. 31 - 60 Day Expiration "
DEFINE BAR 2 OF PVend PROMPT " 2.  1 - 30 Day Expiration "
DEFINE BAR 3 OF PVend PROMPT " 3. Past Due Expiration    "
DEFINE BAR 4 OF PVend PROMPT " 4. Vendor Termination     "
DEFINE BAR 5 OF PVend PROMPT " 5. Insurance Deficiency   "
DEFINE BAR 6 OF PVend PROMPT " 6. Contract Noncompliance "
DEFINE BAR 7 OF PVend PROMPT " 7. Cancel Term Deficiency "
DEFINE BAR 8 OF PVend PROMPT " 8. Orig. Cert. Exceptions "
*
*___________________________________
* Pull-down for Confidentiality Rpts
*___________________________________
DEFINE POPUP PConf FROM 6,50 TO 11,78
DEFINE BAR 1 OF PConf PROMPT " 1. Vendor Non-compliance  "
DEFINE BAR 2 OF PConf PROMPT " 2. Ven/Emp Non-compliance "
DEFINE BAR 3 OF PConf PROMPT " 3. Expiration  1 - 30     "
DEFINE BAR 4 OF PConf PROMPT " 4. Expiration  Past Due   "
*
*____________________________
* Pull-down for Summary Rpts
*____________________________
DEFINE POPUP PSumm FROM 7,50 TO 13,76
DEFINE BAR 1 OF PSumm PROMPT "  1. Summary Compliance  "
DEFINE BAR 2 OF PSumm PROMPT "  2. Summary Vendor Type "
DEFINE BAR 3 OF PSumm PROMPT "  3. Detail Profile      "
DEFINE BAR 4 OF PSumm PROMPT "  4. Vendor Contact      "
DEFINE BAR 5 OF PSumm PROMPT "  5. Contract Detail     "
*
*____________________________
* Pull-down for Control Rpts
*____________________________
DEFINE POPUP PCont FROM 8,50 TO 14,78
```

```
DEFINE BAR 1 OF PCont PROMPT " 1. Input Control          "
DEFINE BAR 2 OF PCont PROMPT " 2. Outstanding Insurance  "
DEFINE BAR 3 OF PCont PROMPT " 3. Outstanding Confident. "
DEFINE BAR 4 OF PCont PROMPT " 4. No Insurance Coverage  "
DEFINE BAR 5 OF PCont PROMPT " 5. Vendor Identification  "
*
*________________________________
* Pull-down for Form Letters Rpts
*________________________________
DEFINE POPUP PLett FROM 9,50 TO 18,79
DEFINE BAR 1 OF PLett PROMPT " 1. Expiration Letter One   "
DEFINE BAR 2 OF PLett PROMPT " 2. Expiration Letter Two   "
DEFINE BAR 3 OF PLett PROMPT " 3. Expiration Letter Three "
DEFINE BAR 4 OF PLett PROMPT " 4. Certification Letter    "
DEFINE BAR 5 OF PLett PROMPT " 5. Terms Letter            "
DEFINE BAR 6 OF PLett PROMPT " 6. No Insurance Letter     "
DEFINE BAR 7 OF PLett PROMPT " 7. Sign-Off Letter         "
DEFINE BAR 8 OF PLett PROMPT " 8. Free Form Letter        "
*
*________________________________
* Pull-down for D.O.S. Utilities
*________________________________
SET BORDER TO 196,196,179,179,218,016,192,217
DEFINE POPUP PDOS FROM 6,27 TO 16,42
DEFINE BAR 1 OF PDOS  PROMPT " 1. Use DOS   " MESSAGE "Access DOS - Type EXIT to Return."
DEFINE BAR 2 OF PDOS  PROMPT " 2. Copy File " MESSAGE "Copy one File to Another."
DEFINE BAR 3 OF PDOS  PROMPT " 3. Disk Copy " MESSAGE "Copy a Disk on A: to Disk on B:"
DEFINE BAR 4 OF PDOS  PROMPT " 4. Format A: " MESSAGE "Format a Disk on Drive A:"
DEFINE BAR 5 OF PDOS  PROMPT " 5. Format B: " MESSAGE "Format a Disk on Drive B: (360K)"
DEFINE BAR 6 OF PDOS  PROMPT " 6. Directory " MESSAGE "View the Directory on the Screen."
DEFINE BAR 7 OF PDOS  PROMPT " 7. Print Dir " MESSAGE "Print a Listing of the Directory."
DEFINE BAR 8 OF PDOS  PROMPT " 8. Backup    " MESSAGE "Backup the databases and Indexs."
DEFINE BAR 9 OF PDOS  PROMPT " 9. Restore   " MESSAGE "Restore the databases and Indexs."
*
*____________________________
* Pull-down for Change Codes
*____________________________
DEFINE POPUP PChng FROM 8,23 TO 15,42
DEFINE BAR 1 OF PChng PROMPT " 1. Vendor        " MESSAGE  "Change the Vendors."
DEFINE BAR 2 OF PChng PROMPT " 2. Arrangement   " MESSAGE  "Change the Arrangements."
DEFINE BAR 3 OF PChng PROMPT " 3. COS Unit      " MESSAGE  "Change the Expenses."
DEFINE BAR 4 OF PChng PROMPT " 4. Insurance     " MESSAGE  "Change the Insurance."
DEFINE BAR 5 OF PChng PROMPT " 5. BTCo Standard " MESSAGE  "Change the Bank Limits."
DEFINE BAR 6 OF PChng PROMPT " 6. Contract Type " MESSAGE  "Change the Confidentiality."
*
*__________________________________
* Pull-down for Form Letters Change
*__________________________________
DEFINE POPUP PLetC FROM 10,13 TO 19,42
DEFINE BAR 1 OF PLetC PROMPT " 1. Expiration Letter One   "
DEFINE BAR 2 OF PLetC PROMPT " 2. Expiration Letter Two   "
DEFINE BAR 3 OF PLetC PROMPT " 3. Expiration Letter Three "
```

```
DEFINE BAR 4 OF PLetC PROMPT " 4. Certification Letter    "
DEFINE BAR 5 OF PLetC PROMPT " 5. Terms Letter            "
DEFINE BAR 6 OF PLetC PROMPT " 6. No-Insurance Letter     "
DEFINE BAR 7 OF PLetC PROMPT " 7. Sign-Off Letter         "
DEFINE BAR 8 OF PLetC PROMPT " 8. Free Form Letter        "
*___________________
* Begin Menu Program
*___________________
SET COLOR TO RG+/B,N/W,B
A = CENT(0,80,"I N S U R A N C E   C O M P L I A N C E   S Y S T E M")
@ 1,12 SAY REPLICATE("—",55)
Dummy =  BOXES(2, 0, 4, 79, .F., "D", "W+/R,N/W,B")
DO WHILE .T.
   ACTIVATE MENU Main PAD Inquiry
   IF LASTKEY() = Escape
      EXIT
   ENDIF
ENDDO
RETURN
*END:MENUS


*_____________
PROCEDURE FINI
*_____________
CLEAR
QUIT
*END:FINI


*________________
PROCEDURE NEXTRPT
*________________
DO CASE
   CASE BAR() = 1
      ACTIVATE POPUP PVend
   CASE BAR() = 2
      ACTIVATE POPUP PConf
   CASE BAR() = 3
      ACTIVATE POPUP PSumm
   CASE BAR() = 4
      ACTIVATE POPUP PCont
   CASE BAR() = 5
      ACTIVATE POPUP PLett
   CASE BAR() = 6
      Laser = IIF(Laser, .F., .T.)
   CASE BAR() = 7
      DUMMY = NotYet()
   CASE BAR() = 8
      DUMMY = NotYet()
   CASE BAR() = 9
      DUMMY = NotYet()
```

```
ENDCASE
RETURN
*END:NEXTRPT
*________________
PROCEDURE NEXTUTL
*________________
DO CASE
   CASE BAR() = 1
      DUMMY = NotYet()
   CASE BAR() = 2
      ACTIVATE POPUP PDOS
   CASE BAR() = 3
      DUMMY = NotYet()
   CASE BAR() = 4
      ACTIVATE POPUP PChng
   CASE BAR() = 5
      DUMMY = NotYet()
   CASE BAR() = 6
      ACTIVATE POPUP PLetC
   CASE BAR() = 7
      @ 20,35 SAY MEMORY()
      A = INKEY(5)
      @ 20,35
ENDCASE
RETURN
*END:NEXTUTL


* ____________
FUNCTION NOTYET
* ____________
SAVE SCREEN TO TempScrn
Dummy = BOXES(11, 21, 13, 59, .T., "D", "N/BG")
Key = CENT(12, 80, "This function is NOT available yet")
Key = INKEY(5)
RESTORE SCREEN FROM TempScrn
SET COLOR TO W+/R,N/W,B
RETURN(.T.)
*END:NOTYET


* ____________
FUNCTION BOXES
* ____________
PARAMETERS T, L, B, R, Shadow, SD, BC
PRIVATE    T, L, B, R, Shadow, SD, BC, Kind
DO CASE
   CASE SD = "D"
      Kind = "DOUBLE"
   CASE SD = "S"
      Kind = " "
```

```
   CASE SD = "N"
      Kind = "NONE"
ENDCASE

IF Shadow
   SET COLOR TO N/N,N/N                  && With or without a drop shadow
   @ T+1,L+1 CLEAR TO B+1,R+2            && T,L,B,R = Corners of the box
ENDIF                                    && Shadow = .T. or .F.
SET COLOR TO &BC                         && SD = SIngle or Double line box.
@ T,L CLEAR TO B,R                       && BC = Color of the box.
@ T,L     TO B,R &Kind
RETURN(.T.)
*END:BOXES


* __________
FUNCTION CENT                            && Center a line of text based
* __________                             && upon the max width of page.
PARAMETERS XRow, MLen, Message           && XRow = row to place message on.
PRIVATE XCol                             && MLen = Maximum page width.
XCol = (MLen - LEN(Message)) / 2         && Message = Message to be centered.
@ XRow, XCol SAY Message
RETURN (.T.)
*END:CENT
```

The menu will look something like Figure 6-1 if REPORTS, FORM LETTERS, and SIGN OFF LETTER are selected from the pull-down menus.

Although there is a great deal of code here, it is quite simple.

1. Start with our standard preamble for all dBASE IV programs.
2. Set some colors and clear the screen.
3. Define the menus starting with the horizontal bar menu.
   a. DEFINE "MENU" Main instead of DEFINE "POPUP" Main.
   b. You must specify where each horizontal element (PAD) will go in a horizontal menu. *Note:* All elements do not have to go on the same line—but they usually do.
   c. Tell dBASE IV what to do for each PAD selection. (ON SELECTION PAD OF Main . . .).
4. Set the border for the pull-down box.
5. Define the Inquiry, Reports, Utility, and Exit POPUP menus.
6. Define the POPUP menus the Main POPUP menus will use.
7. Write the main procedure to place the heading on the screen and activate the main menu inside a DO WHILE LOOP. Do not forget to provide a method of exiting from the loop if desired.
8. Write the procedures called by the pull-down menus.
9. Write the general-purpose UDFs needed for the menus. These will be discussed in the UDF portion of this section.
10. That is it. You now have code to produce pull-down menus.

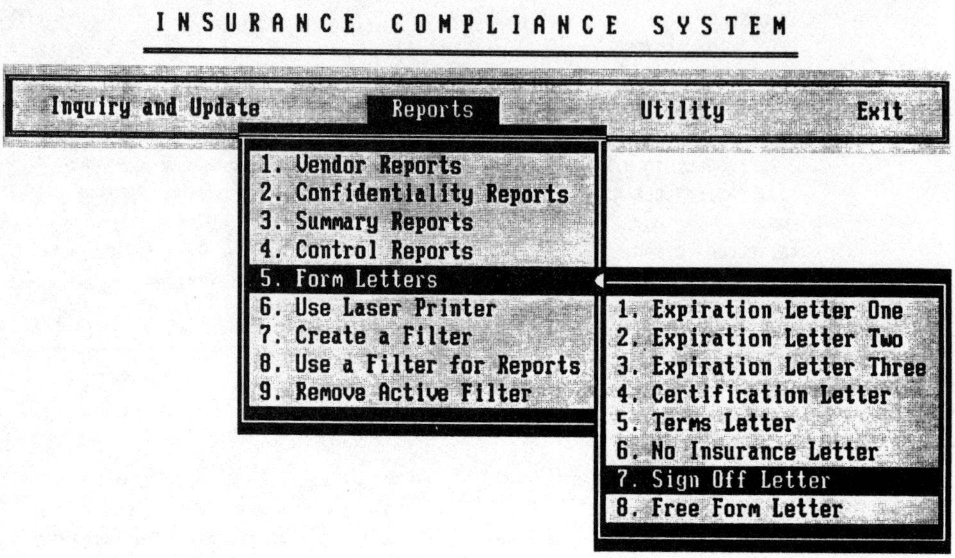

```
I N S U R A N C E   C O M P L I A N C E   S Y S T E M

Inquiry and Update      Reports          Utility        Exit

      1. Vendor Reports
      2. Confidentiality Reports
      3. Summary Reports
      4. Control Reports
      5. Form Letters
      6. Use Laser Printer          1. Expiration Letter One
      7. Create a Filter            2. Expiration Letter Two
      8. Use a Filter for Reports   3. Expiration Letter Three
      9. Remove Active Filter       4. Certification Letter
                                    5. Terms Letter
                                    6. No Insurance Letter
                                    7. Sign Off Letter
                                    8. Free Form Letter
```

Figure 6-1. Select form letter reports.

User-Defined Functions

As pointed out, among all the new features of dBASE IV, menus and UDFs are the most important.

What Is a User-Defined Function?

A UDF is nothing more than a method to enable dBASE IV programmers to write their own functions using dBASE IV as the source language. It can be used to create functions not provided by dBASE IV, such as changing all proper names to start with an uppercase letter. Why was this functionality provided? What good is it?

Why Use a User Defined Function?

By using a UDF, as a programmer, you can add any feature you like to dBASE IV—you can: verify data entry fields, add mathematical features that are not present in the language such as factorials, enhance screen displays, and make your code easier to read and debug.

UDF written in dBASE IV are almost the same as dBASE IV procedures. You can write as many as you need, compile them, and incorporate them in any and all your applications. Your applications can use your UDF just as if they were native dBASE IV functions such as EOF().

In dBASE IV a UDF starts with the keyword FUNCTION followed by a function name, such as PHIL. A UDF returns a value (any valid dBASE IV data type is permitted), whereas a procedure does not. A UDF is called by assigning a variable to it, such as: A =

PHIL(X,Y,Z). A procedure is called using the DO command DO PHIL WITH X,Y,Z. Sometimes you must write a UDF as a procedure because of dBASE language restrictions.

A major advantage to UDF is that once they are written and tested, they can be used in any appropriate situation without any additional debugging problems. Thus a library of useful, tested functions can be written and incorporated into new code without repeating the debugging process.

Let us look at the UDF we wrote in the menu part of this section.

We wrote three UDFs

BOXES
NOTYET
CENTER

BOXES draws a box on the screen with a single-line border, with a double-line border, or without a border. The box can have an optional drop shadow, and will be in the colors passed in the parameter list. The function accepts the **T**op, **L**eft and **B**ottom, **R**ight coordinates to position the box; a .T. or .F. for a drop shadow; a "S", "D", or "N" for the border; and a string containing the colors to be used. The UDF sets Kind to " ," "DOUBLE," or "NONE," depending on the value of SD. If a drop shadow is called for, it adds one to the **T**op, **L**eft, and **B**ottom coordinates and two to the **R**ight coordinate and draws a black box. It then sets the color to the passed color and clears the area for the box, and, if a border is requested, draws it. It then returns a .T. as it must return a value. The .T. is arbitrary; a zero, 1492, "PHIL", or any other value could have been returned since the returned value is not used. You can change this UDF to use an additional parameter indicating where the shadow should be placed (top left, top right, bottom left, or bottom right). You could also include other borders, as well as sound. Just remember to start with the declaration "FUNCTION" and to return something.

NOTYET is a simple UDF that can be used to develop any application. Write all the procedures and execute the command "Dummy = NotYet()" until you get around to coding the procedure. NOTYET calls two other UDFs, BOXES and CENTER. It saves the screen, places a box on the screen using the UDF BOXES, and then places a centered message in the box using the UDF CENT. It displays the message for five seconds, or until a key is pressed (whichever interval is shorter), restores the saved screen, and resets the color to the menu color (this could be a passed color), and returns a .T. again.

CENT is used to center a message on any size area on the screen or on a printer. It accepts the row in which the message will be written to, the length of the line on which the message is to be centered (80 for a screen; 80, 132, 240, or some other value for a report), and the message to be centered. It computes the starting position for the message by subtracting the length of the message from the length of the area where it is to appear and dividing the result by two. It writes the message and returns our .T. once again.

As you can see, UDFs can be used for many purposes, and are easy to write. Just remember to start with "FUNCTION" and end with RETURN(<something>).

New Indexing System

In dBASE III PLUS, the indexing scheme created a file (.NDX) containing a record for each entry in the .DBF file consisting of the index key and the physical record number of the entry in the data base associated with the key. These entries are maintained in ascending alphabetic order and enabled dBASE III PLUS to provide a "*sorted*" view of the data base.

By supporting index files, the enormous overhead associated with maintaining a physically sorted data base is eliminated. Index files are easily created and the "*sort order*" can be changed instantly by switching to another index. As long as an index is active, any newly added records will automatically be inserted into the index and will appear in the "*correct place*" in the data base.

Under dBASE III PLUS, each index required its own .NDX file (and a DOS file handle), and a maximum of ten index files were the most you could use at any one time. Therefore, you were limited to ten index keys for any file.

dBASE IV uses a multiple index file (.MDX) that lets you create and store up to 47 (a strange number—why not 48 or 64?) different index keys in a single file using a single DOS file handle. You can include UNIQUE indexes, compound index expressions, and descending as well as ascending indexes in the same .MDX file.

The first time you create a .MDX file, you do *not* supply a name. dBASE IV will give it the same name as the .DBF file. This .MDX file becomes the production index file and dBASE IV will automatically open and update the indexes in this file whenever the underlying .DBF is opened. For example, if you have a vendor file called VENDOR.DBF and you created an index for vendor numbers, dBASE IV would create a file called VENDOR.MDX that would contain your index. To add other indexes to this file, an associated *tag* would be created to identify each index in the .MDX file. The following code could be used to created these indexes.

```
USE Vendor
INDEX ON VendorID TAG ID
INDEX ON VendName TAG VName
INDEX ON VendAdd TAG VAddress
```

In this example, the .MDX file VENDOR.MDX is automatically created. Three indexes are created and each is given its own name (tag). The index currently in use is referred to as the primary key; all other indexes are called secondary keys. dBASE IV does not automatically assign the primary key, but that must be done by the user.

Multiple File Relations

In previous releases of dBASE, the ability to express and control multiple relationships between many files was severely limited. In effect, you could not relate a file to more than one other file. If you wanted to relate one main (parent) file to two or more secondary (children) files, you had to relate the parent to child one and child one to child two, etc. If child two did not exist and child three did, you had problems. Most programmers did not use more than one relationship and programmed around it as follows:

```
SELECT A
USE Master
INDEX ON AcctNumb TO Master
SELECT B
USE Child1
INDEX ON AcctNumb TO Child1
SELECT C
USE Child2
INDEX ON AcctNumb TO Child2
SELECT A
mAcctNumb = 0
DO GetFindIt WITH mAcctNumb
SEEK mAcctNumb
?? A->VendName + " "
IF B->AcctNumb = A->AcctNumb
   ?? B->PartName + " "
ELSE
   ?? SPACE(12)
ENDIF
SELECT C
SEEK mAcctNumb
IF C->AcctNumb = A->AcctNumb
   ?? C->CustName + " "
ELSE
   ?? SPACE(25)
ENDIF
```

In dBASE IV you can relate a number of files together, including many child files for one parent. In addition, you can use the new command "SET SKIP" to display all matching records in multiple child relationships, as shown in the following code:

```
SELECT 1
USE Master
INDEX ON AcctNumb TAG Master
USE Child1 IN 2
INDEX ON AcctNumb TAG Child1
USE Child2 IN 3
INDEX ON AcctNumb TAG Child2
SET RELATION TO AcctNumb INTO B, AcctNumb INTO C
SET SKIP TO B, C
GOTO TOP
LIST A->VendName, B->PartName, C->CustName
```

The output would look something like this:

Record #	A->VendName	B->PartNumb	C->CustName
1	ABC Inc.	Keyboard	Alanso
1	ABC Inc.	Keyboard	Chaback
1	ABC Inc.	Keyboard	Chan
1	ABC Inc.	Monitor	Chaback
1	ABC Inc.	Monitor	White
2	IBM Comp.	CPU	Chaback
2	IBM Comp.	CPU	White
. . .			

You may have noticed another new feature of dBASE IV; namely, the ability to open a file in a different area ("USE Child2 IN 3"). This permits more compact and easier reading code.

Windows

A window is an area on the screen that can be overlaid on an existing area and then removed or moved without changing the underlying screen. For example, if you had a data entry form on the screen and an error was committed in entering the data, you could popup a window over the form to point out the error. After reading the message, the user could remove it with a single keystroke and the underlying form would reappear unchanged.

In languages without "*REAL*" windows, you have to save and restore the screen, or portions thereof, to simulate a window. If there is no method to save a screen, you have a considerable programming challenge facing you.

To set up a window, you must define it, activate it to use it, then deactivate it, and finally remove it from memory. In addition, if you are going to be using the window in different applications, or do not want to build it into the application, you can save it, or a series of windows, to a file and restore them as necessary, just as if they were memory variables.

To define a window, you must give it a name and the coordinates of the upper left and lower right corners, which must fit on the screen. You may also specify the border characters and colors. Up to 20 windows can be defined at one time. After the window is defined, it is activated using the **"ACTIVATE WINDOW <window name>"** command. When a window is activated, it appears on the screen over the area defined by the window corners. All screen output is mapped to the window. The upper left cursor position in the window becomes the reference point 0,0. Therefore, if you are using windows, it makes no difference where the window is on the screen as all output is relative to position 0,0 in the window that you are using. Let us look at the following example to clarify this point.

```
*  ┌──────────────────────────────────────────────────────────────────────┐
*  | Program.: Window Demonstration Program                               |
*  | Author..: Phil Steele - President Phillipps Computer Systems Inc.    |
*  | Address.: 52 Hook Mountain Road,  Montville NJ 07045                 |
*  | Phone...: (201) 575-8575                                             |
*  | Date....: January 15, 1990                                           |
*  |                                                                      |
*  | Notice..: Copyright 1990  Philip Steele  -  All Rights Reserved.     |
*  |                                                                      |
*  | Version.: dBASE IV Release 1.1                                       |
*  └──────────────────────────────────────────────────────────────────────┘
*
*__________________
* STANDARD PREAMBLE
*__________________
CLEAR ALL
SET STEP OFF
SET ECHO OFF
SET TALK OFF
SET BELL OFF
SET PRINT   OFF
SET DELETE  ON
SET STATUS  OFF
SET SAFETY  OFF
SET ESCAPE  OFF
SET CONFIRM ON
SET HEADING OFF
SET SCOREBOARD OFF
SET DISPLAY TO EGA25
SET DEVICE  TO SCREEN
SET CURSOR  OFF

DO WinDemo WITH 20,35        && Maximum number of windows = 20
RETURN
*_________________
PROCEDURE WINDEMO
*_________________
PARAMETERS NumberWins, Cycles

DECLARE ColStand[8]
ColStand[1]="N/W"
ColStand[2]="N/B"
ColStand[3]="W+/G"
ColStand[4]="N/R"
ColStand[5]="W+/RG"
```

```
ColStand[6]="N/RB"
ColStand[7]="W+/BG"
ColStand[8]="W+/N"

Dummy = RAND(-1)              && Set random number from clock
J     = 0
DO WHILE J < NumberWins
   J         = J + 1
   Top       = GetRand(18)
   Lft       = GetRand(64)
   ColBorder = GetRand(8)
   ColWin    = GetRand(8)
   WinName   = "TempWin" + IIF(J<10, STR(J,1,0), STR(J,2,0))
   DEFINE WINDOW &WinName FROM Top,Lft TO Top+6,Lft+15;
          COLOR &ColStand[ColWin],,&ColStand[ColBorder]
   ACTIVATE WINDOW &WinName
   @ 1,1 SAY J PICTURE "99"  && Inside window relative row, col
ENDDO
K = 0
DO WHILE K < Cycles
   K       = K + 1
   WN      = GetRand(NumberWins)
   WinName = "TempWin" + IIF(WN<10, STR(WN,1,0), STR(WN,2,0))
   ACTIVATE WINDOW &WinName
   MOVE WINDOW &WinName TO GetRand(18),GetRand(64)
ENDDO
RETURN
*END:WINDEMO

*______________
FUNCTION GETRAND
*______________
PARAMETERS Num
PRIVATE Num, Answer
Answer = INT(Num * RAND())
RETURN IIF(Answer=0, 1, Answer)
*END:GETRAND
```

Thanks are due dLAB member R. Freeland for the idea of using random popup windows.

This example begins with a standard dBASE IV preamble for setting the dBASE IV environment. Next the routines that will do the work are called. Twenty different-colored windows (the maximum) are requested, together with 35 cycles of moving the windows.

In the main procedure, eight different colors are defined. Next, the random number generator is set based on the system clock "RAND(-1)" and the variables defined. A random top left corner must be obtained for the windows. Since all the windows will be made the same size by adding 6 to the row and 15 to the column, choosing 18 and 64 for the row and column maximum will ensure that the limits of the screen will not be exceeded. *Note:* The maximum value for the row is 24 (18 + 6) and for the column is 79 (64 + 15). Now, a random color is obtained for the border and body of the windows. The windows are assigned the names TEMPWIN1 through TEMPWIN20. Now the twenty windows are "DEFINEd" and "ACTIVATEd". Since all screen I/O is relative to the window, not the screen, you can "SAY" the window number at 1,1 regardless of where the window is on the screen.

Now that all the windows are defined and activated, use the "MOVE WINDOW" command to move the windows about at random, employing the techniques discussed in the previous paragraph.

The GETRAND function obtains a random number between zero and one. This is converted to an integer with a maximum value equal to the passed number "Num" by multiplying Num by the random number. If a zero is produced, it is changed to one as zero is an invalid subscript for the color array.

DBASE IV has many useful features, but the following section focuses on SQL and the other five most important of these features.

Miscellaneous Commands and Functions

SET AUTOSAVE ON/OFF

Many users became alarmed when an operation appears to take a long time with nothing happening, such as during an INDEX or SUM operation. The tendency is either to shut the system off or to give it the three finger salute (Ctrl, Alt, Del). Either action will cause the contents of data buffers to be lost. For example, one user turned the system off when he finished entering the data assigned to him. Most of the data he keyed was lost until the command "SET AUTOSAVE ON" was added to the program. This command forces dBASE IV to save each record to disk as soon as it is entered or modified, rather than just updating it in its buffer.

LOOKUP()

The "LOOKUP()" function permits you to find records in a data base located in a different work area than the one in which you are currently working. You specify an expression to evaluate, the field to be used as input, and a place to put the answer as follows:

```
LOOKUP(<Any Field, Expression to Evaluate, Look in field>)
```

If the Look in field is in an unselected data base, the lookup is performed in that work area. If the expression to evaluate is a valid index key in the master index for the Look in Field file, dBASE IV uses a fast index key search, rather than a slow sequential search.

Old Method	**New Method**
`SELECT A`	`SELECT A`
`USE Master INDEX MNumber`	`USE Master ORDER MNumber`
`SELECT B`	`USE Detail ORDER Account IN 2`
`USE Detail INDEX Account`	`? Account`
`SELECT A`	`. "Phillipps"`
`? Account`	`Z = LOOKUP(Item, Account,;`
`. "Phillipps"`	`B->DNumber)`
`SELECT B`	`? B->Item`
`SEEK A->Account`	`. "DP services"`
`? Item`	
`. "DP services"`	

SCAN

The SCAN command combines elements of DO WHILE, LOCATE, FIND, and SEEK in one construct. SEEK with no parameters is the same as a GOTO TOP and DO WHILE .NOT. EOF() as shown:

Old Method

```
SELECT A
GOTO TOP
DO WHILE .NOT. EOF()
   ...
   SKIP
ENDDO
```

New Method

```
SELECT A
SCAN
   ...
ENDSCAN
```

or

Old Method

```
SELECT A
GOTO TOP
DO WHILE AcctNum > 50000;
   .AND. .NOT. EOF()
   ...
   SKIP
ENDDO
```

New Method

```
SELECT A
SCAN FOR AcctNumb > 50000
   ...
ENDSCAN
```

ARRAYS

Arrays were needed in dBASE III and III PLUS. Now they have finally appeared in dBASE IV. The array function provides both one- and two-dimensional arrays. The array elements are referred to by row–column coordinates. For example, the following commands sets up a 4-by-17 array called Master. Element 3,13 is initialized to zero and element 1,17 is initialized to a character string containing "Heydt". Other elements are initialized to date and logical values.

```
DECLARE Master[4,17]
        Master[3,13] = 0
        Master[1,16] = 12/07/41
        Master[1,15] = .T.
        Master[1,17] = "Heydt"
```

As you see, data types can be mixed for various elements in an array; therefore, the commands "COPY TO ARRAY" and "APPEND FROM ARRAY" can be used to move records to an array for editing and then back to the data base if they are acceptable as shown:

```
    USE MASTER  &&  A database containing 20 fields and 75 records
DECLARE MastArray[75,20]
    COPY ALL TO MastArray
    * ... Process the data in the array
    IF OK       &&  If user tells you to,  accept the changes
       ZAP
       APPEND FROM ARRAY MastArray
    ENDIF
```

INDEX FOR

Not only is there a new index type (MDX), which was discussed previously, but release 1.1 of dBASE IV now permits partial indexing. In the past, if you needed a portion of the data base, you would use the "SET FILTER TO" command to narrow your search. If the data base was large and the filtered portion small, you had to copy it to a temporary data base to speed up processing. With the new INDEX command, you can combine all of these operations and also have the speed and pseudosorting ability of an index beside.

Old Method	**New Method**
`SELECT A`	`SELECT A`
`SET FILTER TO State = "NJ"`	`INDEX ON State TAG State;`
`GOTO TOP`	`   FOR State = "NJ"`
`COPY TO TEMP`	`* ... Process`
`USE Temp`	`* END`
`* ... Process`	

```
* If updated, write an update procedure
```

Although there are many additional commands that can be expanded, we have covered the major ones, and most of the rest will be explained using our real-life application.

SECTION II

dBASE IV SQL Commands, Statements, and Functions

CHAPTER 7

SQL Introduction

Introduction

Structured Query Language (SQL) is more than a query or retrieval language. It is a data base management language that allows for data modification, definition, and control of user access.

The subset of SQL that is implemented under dBASE IV is very similar to IBM's Relational Data Base Management Systems mainframe computer products, DATABASE 2 (DB2) and SQL/DS. The authors of this book have had extensive experience with dBASE, as well as with both IBM relational products. SQL features that are likely to be added to dBASE in the near future will be presented and indicated as being future enhancements. Therefore, this book should serve as a reference for several years to come.

SQL as a data base management system (DBMS) was born of the concepts, formulated by Dr. Edgar Codd, that resulted in the relational data model. Relational technology is derived from the application of mathematical principles to data base management, as first published by Codd in 1970. His work remains the foundation of all relational development.

A dBASE IV SQL relational data base is composed of a collection of *tables*. All information is stored in these tables. Every table is a two-dimensional data structure consisting of zero or more *rows* and one or more *columns*. A row may be thought of as a record and a column as analogous to a field. The value at the intersection of a row and a column is atomic: repeating values are not allowed. Figure 7-1 depicts a SQL table that contains employee information. When a table is first created, its definition consists of column headings and their related data attributes (e.g., numeric, character, date). The sequence in which these columns are defined will be the actual physical sequence of the column values when a row is stored. As this table is populated, one row of data will be

EMP_TABLE

C O L U M N S

	EMPL_NO	F_NAME	M_INIT	L_NAME
	10023	JOE	S.	SMITH
	99991	WILLIAM	------	DAY
R	78567	ALLAN	MARTIN	O'DEY
O	39457	GEORGE	SAM	SCOTT
W	58295	DIANE	MAY	STEEL
S	29456	MARY	ANN	LONGO
	09567	WILLIAM	------	SMITH
	000001	ROBERT	A	BROWN

Figure 7-1. SQL table example

inserted for each employee. When dealing with SQL tables throughout the remainder of this book, the terms row(s) and column(s) will be used.

Relational theory draws most of its strength from its distinction between user views of data and the actual physical storage representation of the same data. Whereas most nonrelational DBMSs require some knowledge and manipulation of data based on physical storage concepts, relational theory presents data for manipulation in the form of tables that are comprised of rows and columns. At a minimum, a person retrieving data from a table need only know that table's name. SQL will determine how to access the table, and the sequence in which to return the rows and deal with the different data types for each column.

This data independence and consistency of table handling mean that access strategies will be transparent to the user and, therefore, insulated from many physical storage modifications.

Figure 7-2 illustrates row retrieval using two different formats of a DATA MANIPULATION LANGUAGE SELECT statement. Both will return the same number of rows—one for every row that exists in the EMP_TABLE. The first example utilizes an

```
1.      SELECT*
           FROM EMP_TABLE;
2.      SELECT F_NAME,L_NAME
           FROM EMP_TABLE;
```

Figure 7-2. SQL table retrieval

asterisk to represent a request that all columns are to be retrieved in the sequence in which the columns were originally defined. The second example will return only the columns F_NAME and L_LAME, and the returned columns will be in the sequence specified after the select statement. Both examples will return their respective rows in the sequence in which they are physically stored. Note that the user executing either of these statements only need know what data is required and not how to access it.

As previously stated, SQL as implemented under dBASE IV represents data to the user in table form. Data definition, manipulation, access, and control are managed by SQL through one of its three component languages: Data Definition Language (DDL), Data Manipulation Language (DML), and Data Control Language (DCL). The chart in Figure 7-3 illustrates the SQL dependencies and components.

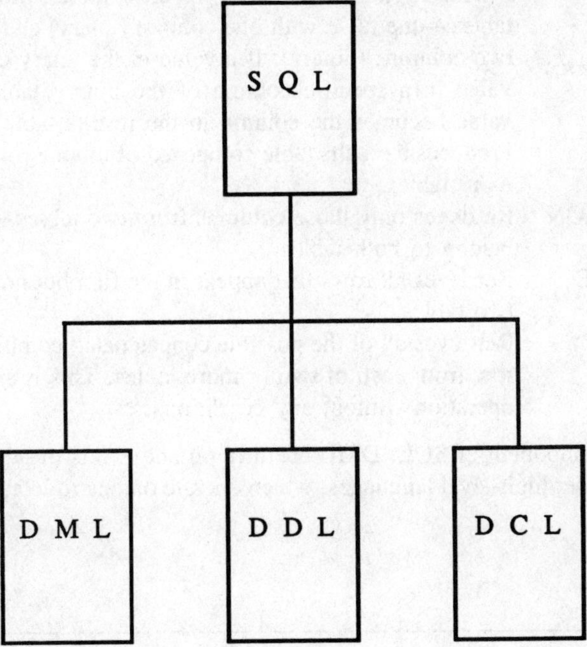

Figure 7-3. SQL components

Data Definition Language (DDL) defines all DB2 objects. An object is defined as anything that can be manipulated by SQL.

Data Control Language (DCL) *explicitly* extends privileges to potential users of SQL objects through the two primary statements GRANT and REVOKE. This is in contrast to *implicit* privileges obtained by users without the use of DCL, most commonly in cases where ownership of a SQL object has been established during its creation or overall administrative authority applies.

Data Manipulation Language (DML), as its name implies, is used to retrieve, update, insert, and delete any data stored in SQL tables with a somewhat free-form language that may be executed interactively or as embedded code within a program. A set of relational operators (either explicit or implicit) used in the relational model forms the basis of relational algebra. Derived from mathematical set theory, these operators dictate that the application of DML operator(s) will always generate a new results table. Examples of each operator will be illustrated in Chapter 9. They are defined in the relational model as follows:

SELECTION	Retrieves a horizontal subset (rows) of a given table based on a scalar comparison.
PROJECTION	Produces a vertical subset (columns) of a given relation such that all duplicate rows are excluded.
JOIN:	Retrieves data (concatenated rows) from two or more tables based on a successful comparison of one or more of the related row's columns.
DIVISION	Produces a one-column results table built from two tables—one table with one column (unary) and the other with two columns (binary). If a value in the unary table matches a value in a specific column of the binary table, the parallel value becomes the column in the results table.
UNION	Produces a results table composed of unique rows from two or more tables.
INTERSECTION	Retrieves only those columns from two tables where the rows belong to both tables.
DIFFERENCE	Retrieves all rows that appear in the first but not the second of two tables.
PRODUCT	Retrieves all of the possible concatenated combinations of one row from each of two or more tables. This is similar to a join operation without any conditions.

A powerful component of SQL, DML operates on entire sets of table rows at one time, unlike most other high-level languages, which operate on one row (e.g., record) at a time.

History

Distinguished from other DBMSs, SQL (and its predecessors) did not evolve until the data model upon which it was based (i.e., the relational data model) had matured and been precisely defined.

The translation of Codd's relational theory into a functional data model has progressively developed from research and prototyping of relational languages and data base systems in a way that embodies the principles of Codd's model.

Significant among language prototypes, Structured English Query Language (SEQUEL) was introduced by IBM in 1974 and revised in 1976. With the definition of a relational language prototype known as SQL, IBM research produced a compatible data base prototype that became operational in 1977. This prototype, dubbed **System R,** was so well accepted that it spawned several efforts at IBM aimed at incorporating SQL into a line of relational products. Thus, SQL/DS for VM operating systems, in 1982, and DB2 for MVS environments, in 1983, remain the most popular mainframe applications of relational DBMS theory.

The introduction of Codd's relational theory (and DB2, in particular) was in total harmony with the economic and technical shifts in the data processing environment. Once the primary focus of cost control measures, hardware expenses were rapidly being exceeded by the costs of employing computer personnel trained to utilize the hardware.

User groups were downgrading software requests to levels thought to be achievable by technical staff within a reasonable time, rather than to levels that addressed true user requirements.

Demand was strong for a DBMS that would raise programmer productivity to levels that would satisfy real user needs, as well as allow users to interact directly with the system, in terms of both application development and real-time information requests.

Consequently, a RELATIONAL DBMS architecture had to incorporate access to data in several forms, across several environments, by a number of users. This implied a simplicity in a design model that could be employed by programmers and users alike, reduce lead time for application development, and handle high-volume data processing with security and integrity, as well as acceptable performance—performance that encompassed the entire time frame from the origin of the system to the realization of its growth potential. The DBMS also had to offer the user increased participation in the development phases, as well as provide the capability for formatted report generation and problem analysis of existing applications.

In addition to dBASE IV SQL, there are currently several SQL-based DBMSs available for personal computers. Among other leading products are Professional Oracle, Oracle Corp.; XDB-SQL, XDB Systems; Ingress, Relational Technologies; Informix's SQL/4GL; and IBM's PS/2 SQL data base manager included with OS/2 Extended Edition.

The Twelve Commandments

In order for a data base product to be considered truly relational, it must adhere to the following twelve rules (also known as "The Twelve Commandments") of E. F. Codd's relational theory.

RULE 1 All information in a relational data base is represented explicitly at the logical level and in exactly one way—by values in R-tables.

RULE 2 Each and every datum (atomic value) in a relational data base is guaranteed to be logically accessible by resorting to a combination of R-table name, primary key value, and column name.

RULE 3 Indicators (distinct from the empty character string or a string of blank characters, and distinct from zero or any other number) are supported in a fully relational DBMS for representing, at the logical level, the fact that *the information is missing* (applicable and inapplicable information) in a systematic way, independent of data type. Besides the logical representation, the DBMS must support manipulative functions for these indicators, and these must be independent of the data type of the missing information.

RULE 4 The data base description is represented at the logical level just like ordinary data, so that authorized users can apply the same relational language to its interrogation as they apply to the regular data.

RULE 5 A relational DBMS (no matter how many languages and what modes of terminal use it supports—for example, the fill-in-the-blanks mode) *must* support at least one language whose statements are expressible according to some well-defined syntax as character strings, and which is *comprehensive* in supporting *all* of the following items:

1. data definition
2. view definition
3. data manipulation (interactive and by program)
4. authorization
6. transaction boundaries (begin, commit, roll back)

RULE 6 The DBMS includes an algorithm for determining (at view definition time) whether that view is tuple-insertible and tuple-deletable, and whether each of its columns is updatable. It records the result of this investigation in the catalog.

RULE 7 The capability of handling a base relation or a derived relation as a single operand applies not only to the retrieval of data, but also to the insertion, updating, and deletion of data.

RULE 8 Application programs and terminal activities remain logically unimpaired whenever any changes are made in either storage representations or access methods.

RULE 9 Application programs and terminal activities remain logically unimpaired when information-preserving changes of any kind that theoretically permit unimpairment are made to the base tables.

RULE 10 Integrity constraints specific to a particular relational data base must be definable in the relational data sublanguage and storable in the catalog (not in application programs).

RULE 11 A relational system has distribution independence.

RULE 12 If a relational system has a low-level (single-record-at-a-time) language, that low level cannot be used to subvert the integrity rules and constraints expressed in the higher-level relational language (multiple-records-at-a-time).

The relational approach was itself a response to the need for data independence, integration of flat files into data bases, simultaneous access by multiple user types in multiple on-line sessions, and the ability to share data and to satisfy requirements for networks of remote data bases. The resulting relational model provides simplicity, uniformity, completeness, data independence, and data integrity and security.

It is obvious that there exists a strong compatibility between the objectives demanded in a new RELATIONAL DBMS based on the changing technical and economic environment and those designed into the relational data model and, thus, SQL.

Future of SQL

At this point, there is absolutely no doubt that SQL is a very strategic product for Ashton-Tate and the data processing community. Therefore, its future will have far-reaching ramifications at all user levels, from PCs to mainframes.

SQL is a very young product that is experiencing an evolution of design and performance. Other nonrelational DBMS products have been available since the early 1970s, leaving data processing professionals with preconceived notions relating to mature data base structures and processing.

SQL and other RELATIONAL DBMS products show great promise for promoting Codd's relational model, a model that itself has grown to accommodate new data types and access path selection criteria. Because SQL data models are so predictable and readily modified, further prototyping of applications is sure to occur, increasing the interaction of users and reducing development times.

The area of most concern with regard to SQL at this writing is the excessive amounts and types of resources that will be necessary to support all 12 rules of the relational model. SQL relieves the user and/or application of having to navigate through a data base and its related data definitions. This data independence may result in excessive resource consumption. Other requirements, such as entity integrity (i.e., unique key fields) and *referential integrity*, may also require extensive resources.

Further, there are various discrepancies between Codd's relational data model and its representation by SQL, which need to be rectified. According to Dr. Codd, except for IBM's DB2 and SQL/DS, very few SQL products on the market come close to satisfying even half of the twelve rules of the relational model. Moreover, some relational data base systems augment their products with features that actually produce nonrelational results. These inconsistencies and/or incompatibilities may result in serious portability problems for SQL products.

Until relational DBMSs became a reality, data base products had only to be concerned with the rapid retrieval of small pieces of detail information. In contrast, relational built-in functions return results information that may consist of many rows of detail. Consequently, considerably more data is being manipulated, which also adds to resource requirements.

An interesting phenomenon has been taking place in the PC world. Let us call it the "faster and smaller" syndrome. A person may have a PC that has the processing speed of some currently used mainframes (4 to 5 MIPS). These PCs support such applications as word processing and spread sheets that have an insatiable need for data. The people who need this data cannot understand why it takes so long for it to be transferred to their PCs from a mainframe or another PC that is only a few hundred feet away. Because of economy of scale, this requirement will be satisfied very quickly. Until a few years ago, distributed processing was considered nothing more than a mainframe-to-mainframe environment with a daily download to some other computer. With this endless appetite for data at the PC level, distributed processing is being redefined.

Distributed processing is expected to enable table joins across SQL systems and, possibly, to tie PC tables into multiple SQL systems. System architecture to facilitate such processing would require a universal language (such as the PC "C" Language) for use by both mainframes and PCs. The potential for distributed processing with such capabilities is tremendous.

With data stored within SQL-type tables, it will become advantageous to JOIN data from tables located at different nodes (i.e., mainframes) as well as those on mini- and microcomputer systems. The demand for high-speed telecommunications will be unrelenting. SQL distributed processing will finally become a reality.

SQL must become portable across the spectrum of computers, ranging from mainframes through PC systems, and must include an application language (that should also be portable) to interface with SQL. As just discussed, that language will probably be "C Language." Currently, C Language compilers are available for mainframes and for micro and minicomputers.

SQL Objects

An item is classified as a **SQL object** if it is defined in the **SQL Catalog Tables** and can be manipulated by a SQL statement.

The most encompassing object of dBASE IV SQL is the **data base**; all components related to the data base pertain to it exclusively. At the same time, a data base is established within a distinct DOS path that will contain a separate DOS data set for each table and related indexes that are defined within that data base. Except for the master catalog table, SYSDBS, every data base will also contain its own set of SQL Catalog Tables. When a data base is created, an entry is made in SYSDBS.

A **table** is a physical DOS data set (suffix must be **DBF**) that contains the actual rows and columns of data. When a table is created, its definition is recorded within the SQL Catalog Tables of the current active data base. A later enhancement will allow the table creator to specify a data base, thus removing the active data base restriction. The present implementation of dBASE IV SQL allows access to and creation of tables in the active data base. Only one data base may be active at one time.

An **index** is also a physical data set (suffix MDX) that contains a separate set of tags for each index that is created on a table. An index may be either unique or nonunique. A unique index on the primary key columns of a table will enforce entity integrity (Rule 10).

A **view** is an alternative method of presenting data to a user without actually requiring storage space. It may contain subsets of tables or joins between them and, as such, may encompass more than one table. Later enhancements will allow views to join tables that are defined in different data bases. A view may also act as a filter to restrict access to rows and/or columns of a table. In this way, a view may act as a security mechanism.

A **synonym** defines an alias or synonym for a table or a view. The only current use for this type of object is to allow for abbreviations. Since table and view names may not exceed ten characters in length, abbreviating already abbreviated names may cause more harm than good. When later enhancements allow tables and views to be active that are defined within different data bases, these objects will require qualification with their respective data base names. Then synonyms may be employed to circumvent fully qualified object names.

Comprehensive storage of data definitions and access authorization for all SQL objects is maintained in special SQL tables collectively called the **SQL Catalog Tables**. The catalog is controlled by SQL and contains information that may be accessed by any authorized user, as though it were any common SQL table. As such, its potential as a resource, or even as a quasi-data dictionary, is unlimited.

SQL Language Syntax

SQL is a high-level, *nonprocedural* language consisting of statements, keywords, and parameters. SQL uses semicolons, left and right parentheses, commas, and periods as standard operators. Semicolons are SQL statement delimiters. Periods are used to delimit qualification of column names. Commas must be coded to delimit entries of a list. Parentheses are used to enclose item lists or to change the evaluation sequence of operators.

Statements must be entered first and may be considered an action to be accomplished. One of the statement's parameters must be an SQL object on which the action is to be performed. Therefore, every SQL statement will have an action and an object, as demonstrated in Figure 7-4. Because SQL is structured in a format consistent with the English language, it provides a framework within which both end users

```
                  DML
ACTION: SELECT  <column-list>
OBJECT:  FROM   <table-list>
   [WHERE <search condition-1> ]
   [ORDER BY <seq-parm> ] ;

                  DDL
ACTION: CREATE
OBJECT:  TABLE <object-name>
   (<col_nam> <data-type> ,....);
                  DCL
ACTION: GRANT  <privilege-list>
OBJECT:  ON  <object-list>    ;
```

Figure 7-4. SQL action and object associations

and programmers may develop a narrow specification of data requirements. SQL applies strictly to data base management without regard to elements of program control. As such, it delivers its strongest impact—application development languages are freed from the burden of navigating data base structures.

Every SQL statement must end with a semicolon (;) delimiter. This is in contrast to dBASE IV statements, where the semicolon indicates a continuation.

In the DATA MANIPULATION LANGUAGE example in Figure 7-4, the statement or action is a SELECT statement and the object is a table name clause of the FROM keyword. In the DDL example, the action is the CREATE statement and the object is a table as specified by the TABLE keyword. The DCL action is GRANT and its object follows the ON keyword.

In this book, the authors opted to use the conventions utilized in Ashton-Tate's dBASE IV manuals to describe the syntax of statements as follows:

1. Statements and keywords are shown in uppercase letters. Statements and keywords may be entered in any combination of either upper- or lowercase letters.
2. Left and right parentheses are used to delimit a list of parameters or to override precedence rules of operators (i.e., AND, OR) and must be entered as shown. Parentheses, as shown, are required even when only one parameter is entered.
3. Ellipses, several dots (. . . .), indicate that additional optional clauses may follow. The DDL CREATE TABLE statement uses ellipses

   ```
   ( <col_nam> <data-type> ,....)
   ```

   to indicate that additional column specifications may be entered after the comma. Table creation will be further discussed in Chapter 8.
4. The angle brackets (<>) indicate parameters that must be entered. Within the CREATE TABLE statement,

   ```
   <col_nam> <data-type>
   ```

   a column name and corresponding data type, must be entered.
5. The square brackets [ ] indicate that optional keywords may be entered. The WHERE parameter search condition

   ```
   [WHERE  <search condition-1> ]
   ```

   within the SELECT statement is indicated as optional with the square brackets. If coded, a search condition (angle brackets) is required.

The coding of dBASE IV SQL statements and keywords must adhere to specific guidelines. In addition to SQL format conventions, data base and table names will be affected by DOS subdirectory (i.e., pathname) and file-naming conventions. The format of SQL object names is as follows:

SQL Object	**Description**
DATABASE name	In addition to following the DOS directory naming convention of a maximum of eight characters, the first character must be alphabetic. A separate directory will be established for each data base.

TABLE name	Follows the DOS file naming convention of eight characters or less and dBASE IV SQL requires the first character to be alphabetic. A table is created within a data base. Therefore, a DOS file will be created within its data base's directory.
VIEW name	Same requirements as table name, but no DOS file is created.
SYNONYM name	Same requirements as table name; again no DOS file is created.
INDEX name	Same requirements as table name. However, only one DOS file is allocated, in which a maximum of 47 indexes per table may be established.

Table, view, synonym, and index names must be unique within a data base. You cannot have a table and a view with the same names (e.g., EMPLOYEE) in the same data base. For this reason, the authors strongly recommend that the first character of an object name reflect the object type (e.g., T for table, V for view, etc.). More comprehensive object naming conventions will be presented in Chapter 8.

The parameters entered in dBASE IV SQL statements must also follow guidelines. These parameters/items are not affected by any DOS conventions.

Item	**Description**
correlation-name	Also known as an alias. Used within queries to correlate column names to their respective table. A correlation-name is temporary and only exists for the duration of a query (DML) statement. Correlation-names are normally used within correlated queries. (Other relational products require that correlation-names be used in correlated queries.) Its format follows the same rules as table names.
column-name	A column-name of a table or view may be up to ten alphabetic or numeric characters in length. The first character must be alphabetic and underscore delimiters are permitted. A column name may be qualified in the form: `qualifier.column-name` where the *qualifier* may be a table, view, synonym, or correlation-name.
expression	May be a character string up to 254 characters (enclosed in quotes), a numeric literal, or a derived (calculated) column. (If a column named SALARY contains the annual salary, the expression SALARY/12 can be used to derive the monthly salary.) An expression could be the result of two or more columns added together.
data-type	A value is the smallest unit of data that can be manipulated by dBASE IV SQL. The basic data types of a value may be integer (small or large), decimal, floating point, character, date, or logical.
search-condition	The result of an operation that results in either a true or false status. Search conditions will control row-selection criteria.
table-list	One or more table names. If more than one table is specified, they must be delimited with commas. A table-list is utilized when joining tables.

Item	Description
column-list	A list of one or more column names to be retrieved from one or more tables. If more than one table is specified, they must be delimited with commas. An asterisk (*) may be entered to request the retrieval of all columns as they were defined when the table was created. The sequence of the column names in the list determines the *column-retrieval* sequence.
relational operator	An implicit keyword or an implied operator that supports DML relational requirements. An implicit relational operator is the UNION keyword. An implied operator is JOIN.

Interactive SQL

The fastest and easiest way to learn dBASE IV SQL is to execute statements interactively. In addition to the feedback obtained from immediate results, dBASE IV provides extensive help facilities to assist with syntax, protocol, and other relevant information.

Experienced dBASE IV SQL users will find interactive SQL an invaluable tool for use during development life cycles. SQL statements may be coded and tested outside of programs, access strategies (i.e., number of indices) refined, performance objectives confirmed, and test data (i.e., tables) maintained. Data base administrators may query the SQL catalogs to monitor system use, create utility statements, and control authorization privileges.

All examples in this section and Chapter 9 will utilize tables that are part of the data base installed with dBASE IV. The data base is coincidentally named SAMPLES and contains the following tables: CUSTOMER, STAFF, INVENTRY, ASSEMBLY, SALES, and ITEMS. Figure 7-5 shows the relationships between these tables.

To execute SQL statements interactively you must be at the SQL dot prompt as illustrated in Figures 7-6 and 7-7. Normally, dBASE IV starts up with the Control Center. You must exit the Control Center by depressing either function key **F10 (MENU)** and selecting EXIT to dot prompt (not to DOS), or by depressing the escape (ESC) key. Either method will bring up your default dot prompt screen. Your default dot prompt (dBASE command or SQL) is determined by the CONFIG.DB file. If your default is the dBASE dot prompt, you must enter

```
SET SQL ON
```

to activate the SQL dot prompt screen. To return to the Control Center, you must enter ASSIST or function key F2 from the dBASE dot prompt. ASSIST may not be entered from the SQL dot prompt, so you must enter

```
SET SQL OFF
```

to enter this dBASE command. Figure 7-6 (dBASE dot prompt) and Figure 7-7 (SQL dot prompt) illustrate the differences between the two prompt screens. The lower left-hand corner of the screen will display either Command or SQL. The lowercase "x" characters indicate where commands or statements are entered. Commands and SQL statements at

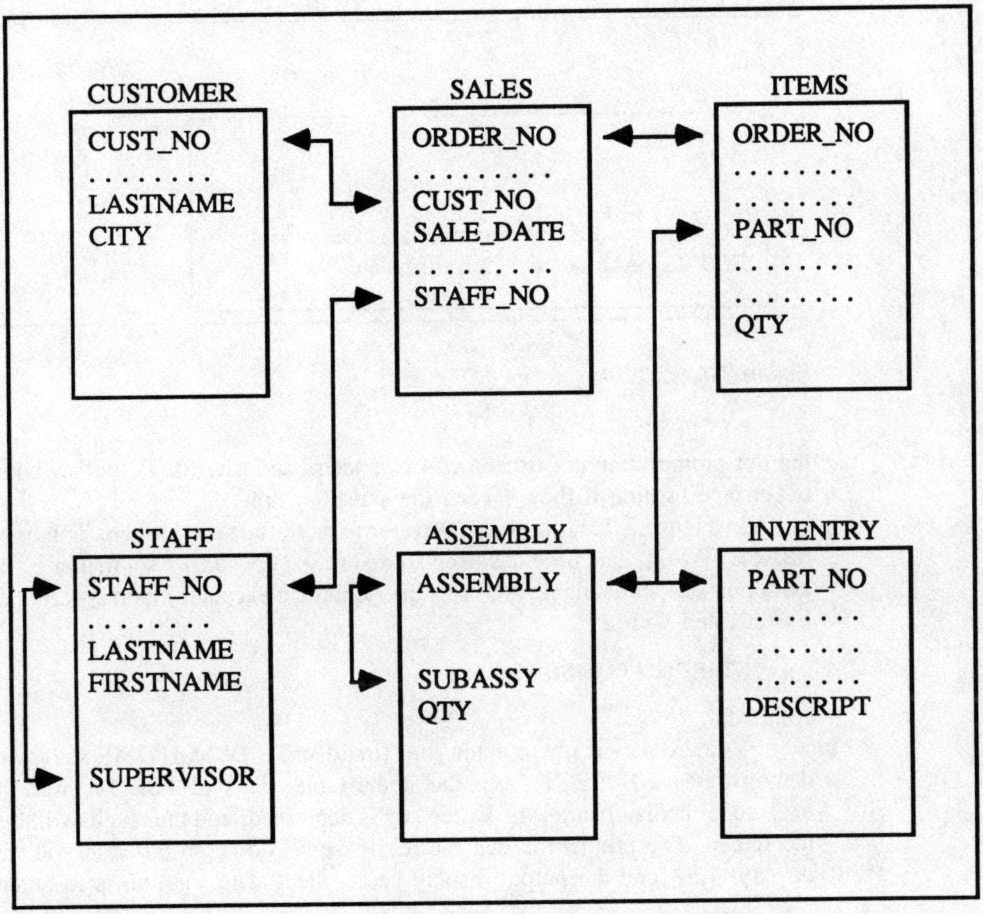

CUSTOMER
CUST_NO
LASTNAME
CITY
SALES
ORDER_NO
CUST_NO
SALE_DATE
STAFF_NO
ITEMS
ORDER_NO
PART_NO
QTY
STAFF
STAFF_NO
LASTNAME
FIRSTNAME
SUPERVISOR
ASSEMBLY
ASSEMBLY
SUBASSY
QTY
INVENTRY
PART_NO
DESCRIPT

Figure 7-5. Sample table relationships

```
.xxxxxxxxxxxxxxxxxxxxxxxxxxxxxxxxxx
Command |          |      |
```

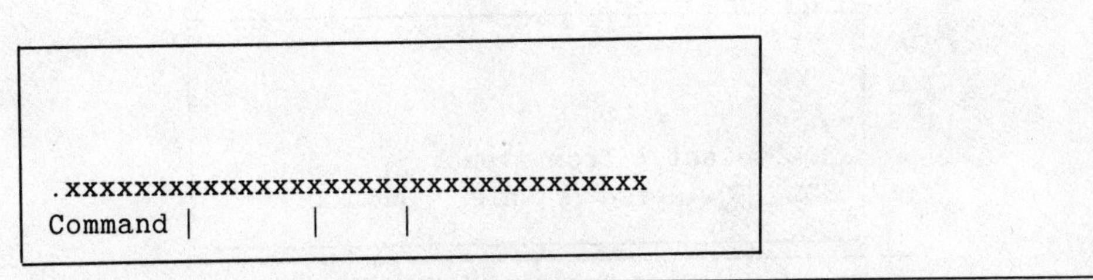

Figure 7-6. BASE dot prompt

```
SQL.xxxxxxxxxxxxxxxxxxxxxxxxxxxxxx;
SQL    |pathname    |DB:dbname
```

Figure 7-7. SQL dot prompt

the dot prompt may not exceed 254 characters and dBASE IV will window entries in a ticker-tape fashion if they exceed the screen width.

In Figure 7-7, no specific **pathname** or **dbname** is shown. This is so because no dBASE IV SQL data base has been started (e.g., opened). As a matter of fact, pathname and dbname will be blank. Before a query may be executed, its respective data base must be activated with a

```
START DATABASE dbname;
```

command.

You are now ready to enter your first dBASE IV SQL DML statement. Figure 7-8 demonstrates a SELECT from the items table. This dBASE IV SQL statement will execute immediately after the **Enter** key is depressed, and the results will be displayed on the screen. The problem is that the results scroll down so fast that you cannot read the display! How can the output display be scrolled? The solution is to enter

```
SET PAUSE ON
```

before running a query to ensure a pause after every screen of data. You may also simultaneously enter the **Ctrl-S** keys to halt a display at any time.

```
SQL.select * from items;
SQL   |C:\dbase\samples\ |DB:xxx
```

Figure 7-8. SQL dot prompt with statement

```
ORDER_NO       PART_NO        QTY       SHIPPED
020002         001032         2         .F.
020002         001025         1         .F.
020002         001013         9         .F.
020003         001021         4         .F.

   .       .       .          .          .
   .       .       .          .          .
   .       .       .          .          .
   .       .       .          .          .
   .       .       .          .          .
   .       .       .          .          .
   .       .       .          .          .
020011         001031         7         .F.
Press any key to continue...
SQL      |pathname spec     |   |DB:xxxxxx
```

Figure 7-9. Query results

Figure 7-9 is an example of the output from an interactive query. The table's column names that were specified in the query will form a heading for this first screen. Successive output screens will not display any column headings. Since the query used a **SELECT *** to get back all columns of the ITEM table, their names appear across the top of the screen in the sequence in which they were originally defined when the table was created. The actual column values for each row fall under their respective column names. The "Press any key to continue" message is displayed at the second line from the bottom because PAUSE has been set.

When a query executes successfully, output is displayed on your screen. What happens if no rows are returned as a result of an empty table or a restrictive WHERE clause search condition? No positive indication is given during interactive processing. The SQL dot screen will be redisplayed and the SQL statement area will be blanked out. Some clear indication that no rows were returned would be helpful.

If a query uses qualified column names in its column-list like Figure 7-10, then the screen output display will also use the same qualified names. Neither of the IBM relational products support this qualification feature and the authors have found this IBM DB2 shortcoming to be quite confusing.

Eventually, you will need to enter a SQL statement that is greater than 254 characters or you can no longer tolerate the ticker-tape effect. A full screen editor then is in order. Fortunately, dBASE IV supports full screen editing that allows both dBASE IV commands and SQL statements to be a maximum of 1024 characters long. To invoke the full screen editing window, simultaneously depress the **Ctrl-Home** keys. Now, the entire screen may be used to receive SQL statements. Figure 7-11 is an example of a multiline query that requires full screen editing.

```
SELECT IT.ORDER_NO,SA.ORDER_NO
     FROM ITEMS IT ,SALES SA
     ...

     query results

IT->ORDER_NO       SA->ORDER_NO
020002             020002
     ...
     ...

090007             010093
```

Figure 7-10. Qualified column-names

```
...|...|...|...|...|...|
SELECT
         ST.LASTNAME                 ,ST.FIRSTNAME
        ,CST.LASTNAME                ,CITY
        ,SA.ORDER_NO                 ,SALE_DATE
        ,ITM.PART_NO
        ,INV.DESCRIPT

FROM STAFF                           ST
        ,CUSTOMER                    CST
        ,SALES                       SA
        ,ITEMS                       ITM
        ,INVENTRY                    INV

WHERE   ST.STAFF_NO       =          SA.STAFF_NO
 AND    SA.CUST_NO        =          CST.CUST_NO
 AND    SA.ORDER_NO       =          ITM.ORDER_NO
 AND    ITM.PART_NO       =          INV.PART_NO

 AND    ST.LASTNAME       =          'SMITH'

 ORDER BY SALE_DATE DESC
      ;
```

Figure 7-11. Full screen query

The query in Figure 7-11 answers the question, "What orders and items where sold to what customers in what cities by staff member SMITH?" The

```
ORDER BY SALE_DATE DESC
```

clause will list the latest orders first. This query joins five tables (STAFF, CUSTOMER, SALES, ITEMS, and INVENTRY) using the common columns specified in the WHERE parameter. The correlation names (ST, CST, SA, ITM, and INV) are required to qualify the column-names that are defined in more than one table. In this case, the actual table names could have been used as qualifiers. The columns that are not qualified are unique to one table.

To leave the full screen editor and run the query, depress **Ctrl-End**. If errors are detected, a beep will sound and a short message will be displayed. When first learning SQL, these short message may be inadequate. For more information, strike (not too hard) the **F1** function key for additional help from the dBASE IV full screen help facility. The help facility in dBASE IV is excellent and will greatly reduce the time spent thumbing through countless pages of documentation.

In addition to being executed, the query is added to the history buffer. The purpose of the history buffer is to allow for the display and recall of previously entered commands (default 20) and SQL statements. Use the up arrow key to go backward in the buffer and the down arrow key to go forward. The following commands control the history buffer:

SET HISTORY ON/OFF	Enables or disables command capture.
SET HISTORY TO nn	Controls the number of commands/statements that may be captured where "nn" is the maximum number.
DISPLAY HISTORY	Lists all commands/statements stored in the history buffer with a pause at each screen.
LIST HISTORY	Lists all commands/statements without pausing.

A considerable amount of time was just spent coding a fairly sophisticated SQL DML statement. Since it resides in the history buffer, which is only memory, the statement will be lost when dBASE IV is terminated. Fortunately, a facility is available to save queries as ASCII files. Moreover, ASCII files containing SQL statements may be created and maintained outside of dBASE IV. This is accomplished through the use of the dBASE MODIFY COMMAND/FILE command.

Before entering any SQL statements, type

```
MODIFY COMMAND d:\pathname\xxxxxxxx.PRS
```
(This data-set name must be appended with 'PRS'.)

at the SQL dot prompt. Upon depressing the ENTER key, you will be presented with a dBASE IV full screen text editor that is the same as the above **Ctrl-Home** full screen editor. The difference is that this screen allows data to be saved to a DOS file (default is the name specified in the MODIFY COMMAND/FILE command) and more than one statement (SQL or dBASE IV commands) may be entered. To execute this file (program) and all its statement(s), either save, exit, and use the DO command to invoke this file or pick the RUN PROGRAM option from the EXIT drop-down menu.

Security

The spirit of security within the IBM relational (SQL) products is that everyone is guilty until proven innocent. Security is an intrinsic part of DB2 and SQL/DS; therefore, no one may access anything unless authorized. However, security within dBASE IV SQL is not active until a **PROTECT** command is executed by someone using the **log-in** name of **SQLDBA**. Before this occurs, all data bases and tables are open to access by all users.

```
dBASE IV Password Security System
  Enter Password ________
```

Figure 7-12. dBASE IV Password Security System log-in screen

The first invoker (SQLDBA or any other log-in name) of the PROTECT command establishes the password that will allow access to the **dBASE IV Security System** (see Figure 7-12). Knowledge of this password, *not the log-in name,* allows any user to perform security administration functions, such as defining **log-in names** and **passwords**, assigning **group names** and relating them to log-in names, and defining **file privilege schemes** on dBASE IV data bases. During this inaugural processing, the system will verify this password by prompting the user with

```
Please reenter password to confirm.
```

From this point on, all users will only be prompted once for their respective passwords. It is essential that this security administrator's password be remembered and be retained in a secure place. There is no facility to retrieve it! The security administrator will not be able to gain subsequent access to the security system without this password. See Chapter 13 for a discussion of how to reinstate dBASE IV security.

Once the Security System has been activated, all users of dBASE IV will be prompted for a **group name, log-in name,** and **password** (Fig. 7-13). Theses names and password (e.g., user profile) must be preassigned using the facilities provided by the PROTECT command. Once PROTECT is invoked by a log-in name of SQLDBA, dBASE IV SQL security is activated, which requires that explicit or grouped privileges be

```
dBASE IV Login
Enter group name: ______
Enter your name: ______
Enter Password: ______
```

Figure 7-13. dBASE IV log-on screen

granted to allow creation and/or manipulation of SQL objects. Since the Security Administrator must provide for log-in security, **file privilege schemes,** and **user** and **grouped** security capabilities, the authors recommend that the Security Administrator also be the Data Base Administrator by having the log-in name of SQLDBA.

Briefly, dBASE IV SQL privileges are extended by means of the **GRANT** command and taken away by the **REVOKE** statement. GRANT enables one user to provide a privilege to another user; thus, the Data Base Administrator (SQLDBA) is the ultimate point of origin of all privileges. REVOKE disables the privileges previously extended to a user via a GRANT statement. However, REVOKE acts with a **cascading effect** to revoke any privileges that were extended to another user exclusively by the user whose authorization is being revoked. Therefore, it is important that users be aware of the origin of their particular authority. Any revoked privilege may be reinstated by issuance of another GRANT statement by an authorized user. This topic is extensively covered in Chapter 13.

Why Use SQL?

Perhaps the dominant feature of dBASE IV SQL, which makes it preferable to a multitude of other DBMSs, is its appeal to end users, whose business requirements have become progressively compromised in recent history. A nonprocedural language, SQL code states the problem—not the procedure required to resolve it. Moreover, it operates in terms of sets that are specifically defined for the data relation in question. There are no hidden relationships built into the structure to intimidate the user. Therefore, SQL is adaptable to a wide range of skill levels and since projections are for more rapid growth in the number of casual on-line users than in all other categories, this appeal to a broad range of skill levels is even more significant. This, in turn, promises further education and productivity in its use.

SQL operates in a table structure that is the same data model for both users and technical developers. Since tables most closely exhibit the qualities of flat files, logical data structure is simpler. As such, this data model brings users closer to development sooner than would be the case with other data models. Application understanding during development is increased as well as monitored *throughout the design process,* rather than at the end when design errors brought on by misinterpretation of user requests represent the necessity for costly, if not formidable, modifications. Further, the data model built around a table concept is more easily reduced for distribution to all levels involved in the application development than might otherwise be the case. Design can be done in phases and modified for additional requirements or error detection through normalization techniques. Finally, third normal form lends more stability to the design model by reducing redundancy. All these considerations taken together will stimulate the utilization of *system prototyping*—the development of high-level models in a small time frame to bring the user immediate feedback as to the progress of the application under development. Such prototyping is significant in that it introduces feedback at a point where corrections make more sense and are simpler to implement.

The independence of logical data representation from physical data representation enables modification to data base structure without a corresponding change to the program accessing it. Access strategies such as index utilization are automatically incorporated as appropriate into the execution of a program through a feature called **SQL optimization.** This feature is capable of evaluating the access data available to it and modifying the **access path strategy** (determined during the dBASE IV compile process) of the program in question. This type of automatic access adjustment is possible owing to the noninterpretive nature of SQL. That is, SQL uses a compilation approach to data requests; requests are converted from SQL statements and parameters to executable code for utilization within the application program. Performance is enhanced since the interpretation of statements is not left until actual execution time.

An extension of this independence of physical data from logical design can be seen in the addition of a new table to an existing data base (or column to an existing table) without interfering with the work of current users of the system. This is especially appropriate for applications involving a large number of relationships, or where several relationships may initially be unidentified or subject to change.

The high-level nature of the relational language permits it to incorporate semantics to tell the system what the user is trying to accomplish. This is in direct contrast to a nonrelational system, which cannot always detect when the user is in error. After compilation, a tailored code is produced that captures the user's intent.

The pathlength of instruction execution is likely to be shorter for a compilation-approach relational DBMS such as dBASE IV SQL than for an interpretive one. This is so because the access strategy is chosen, execution authorization checked, and machine code generated from most SQL instructions before execution takes place. This reduction in runtime is not accomplished at the expense of flexibility; remember that a change of access strategy prompted by a change of physical data representation requires that all related programs be recompiled.

Beyond pathlength, the actual number of I/O operations may be reduced by being rendered more effective by the access strategy choices of the system. Access optimization may be greater when performed by the system rather than by the programmer, because the system generally has more information available to it. The system optimizer is aware of how the data is actually sequenced, the table size, index selectivity, and the complexity of the requested access, among many other items. Because SQL is constantly reviewing this information, up-to-date strategies are reflected before any execution takes place. The process of adjusting these access strategies within SQL is itself a trivial matter, as already discussed in the compile process. Hierarchic structures, in contrast, force the programmer to choose an access path by anticipating factors, usually when initially coding a program. Furthermore, every SQL join or union request is itself a relationship; this cannot be extended to hierarchic linkage of relationships. This is not to say that nonrelational systems will not have tailored code that succeeds in more impressive performance. There is ample evidence to demonstrate that data that forms a natural hierarchy anticipated to be stable for all applications is much better served, to date, by a hierarchic data structure.

This is particularly true if a given application needs access to only one data record, or at least to one record at a time. Further, in an environment where resource constraints and performance tuning are more significant than flexibility of design, hierarchic data structures are, again, the appropriate choice at this writing. However, with the addition of new applications, especially those that change the logical structure of the data model, performance is generally substantially degraded by lack of flexibility.

Flexibility is significantly reduced in a hierarchic structure because of the use of parent–child links to represent the user's view of data. To a significant degree, logical relationships are represented by the physical structure itself. Nonrelational links, insofar as they are both physical and logical, are rendered more static than relational foreign key usage. Relational data structures represent all relationships between data values strictly by the values of the data themselves—it is that simple. All equivalent data values for the same column represent the same relationship. Further, relational data values are not directional as are parent–child links; the relationship is consistent when taken from either direction. Each operation performed on a relational table takes place in terms of table rows and columns identified by the values they contain, not of implicit relationships and dependencies as in hierarchic systems. For each new link that must be added to a hierarchic structure to represent a user view, a new access path will be created. Again, given the physical nature of links, such design modification becomes extremely complex. Links add complexity but not power to hierarchic structures; there is nothing that may be represented in a hierarchic structure that cannot be paralleled by relational representation. In fact, a hierarchic link is capable of representing only a one-to-many relationship, whereas relational design may represent many-to-many relationships.

All this flexibility is certainly not without cost, at least at the moment. There is currently a lack of support in dBASE IV SQL for foreign key constraints. That is, there is no mechanism to guarantee that all occurrences of a foreign key column reference will be modified (or deleted) to correspond to a modification in the key itself, or vice versa. However, it is expected that a future release of dBASE IV SQL will incorporate corrections for this shortcoming. In any case, flexibility may be well worth the price of monitoring foreign keys within the application.

A foreign key is defined as one or more columns whose composite value matches the primary key value of one row in the same or in different tables. The STAFF_NO in the Sample SALES table is a foreign key of STAFF_NO in the Sample STAFF table. Primary and foreign key columns are not required to be spelled the same.

The level at which data manipulation occurs between hierarchic and relational data models also contributes to the relative complexity of each. Relational models—and SQL models, in particular—provide only one way to express most data manipulation requests. A manipulative expression is actually a definition of the **set** of data values requested—direct support for relational theory that states that all data values are acted on in sets. As previously discussed, relational model relationships are always represented by the values of the data in the table structures. Because all relationships are represented in a similar manner (i.e., field data values), data manipulation requests of the relationships are similar in format. Since there is only subtle latitude in the way in which data requests may be formed, communication is more effective (one request per set rather than one request per element) and there is a lower incidence of decision error regarding the request. Further, the result of each table set operation is itself a table, which may, in turn, be used as input to another set level operation. The functionality of the SQL Data Manipulation Language (DML) is maximized since it accomplishes retrieval without branching. Hierarchic data manipulation occurs on an element-by-element basis, thereby making direct representation of a relationship too complex to support in most instances. Retrieval occurs within a procedure rather than simply through a statement.

The fact that dBASE IV SQL DML uses nonembedded statements and parameters makes its intent obvious to the SQL optimizer, which, in turn, may dynamically determine access strategy using information it has available to it at all times. Data sequencing may be achieved through judicious use of the UNLOAD/LOAD utilities.

SQL, in its user orientation, dramatically reduces the amount of development and maintenance time required to achieve functionality. Clearly, the trade-off between performance of hierarchic structures and usability of relational models becomes the issue.

SQL provides sophisticated security capabilities that effectively limit table access to the row and column level, and provide both a basis for transaction recovery or concurrent execution and authorization specific to an individual user. A major feature offered in the security framework is the concept of a view. The SQL view provides a simple presentation to multiple users based on variable sets of criteria without use of actual storage.

CHAPTER 8

Data Definition Language

When presenting the Data Definition Language (DDL) and Data Manipulation Language (DML) components of SQL, it is very difficult to discuss one without referencing the other. To add to the confusion, which component should be presented first? This is very similar to the enigma of the chicken or the egg. In this book, the authors have decided to present the basics of DDL first, followed by DML, and then a more detailed dialogue of DDL and DML in Chapter 10. In the DDL/DML paradox, DDL came first.

dBASE IV SQL acts upon objects that range in significance hierarchically from data bases to tables, indices, and views. A dBASE IV SQL object is classified as something that is defined in the dBASE IV SQL catalog and can be manipulated by an SQL statement. It is precisely this manipulation of dBASE IV SQL objects with respect to creation and performance considerations that will be presented in this chapter.

Object Dependencies

Within dBASE IV SQL, a hierarchy of object dependencies exists. A VIEW is subordinate to a table, and a TABLE is dependent on a DATABASE. A SYNONYM may be defined on either a TABLE or a VIEW. Figure 8-1 illustrates these object dependencies.

In addition to the dependencies discussed, Figure 8-1 shows that a VIEW may be established on an existing TABLE or any existing VIEW, including itself or even on two tables. Also note that indices depend on tables and may only be created on tables. Dependencies also exist for object deletion. If a table is removed, all its dependent objects

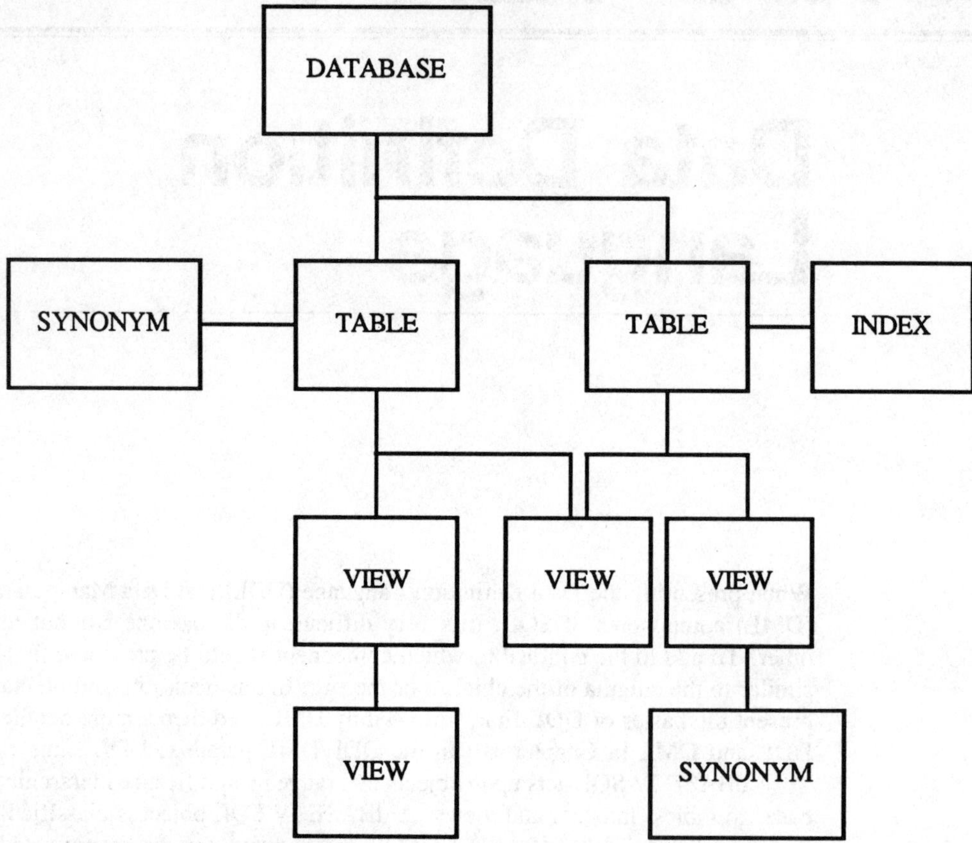

Figure 8-1. Object dependencies

will automatically be deleted. Worse still, if a data base is deleted, all tables and their dependencies are also deleted!

Objects are defined/allocated with the dBASE IV SQL CREATE statement and may be deleted or removed with the DROP statement. The following sections discuss each object.

Data Bases

A dBASE IV SQL **DATABASE** is a means of referencing sets of tables and indexes for operational and security purposes. A dBASE IV SQL data base may be the unit of access to tables and indices, thereby minimizing the impact on applications that do not require use of the data base and its related objects. dBASE IV SQL security mechanisms may also grant authorization at the data base level.

dBASE IV SQL data base creation is simple because there are only two options that dBASE IV SQL will accept in a data base create request. These options establish the DOS

```
CREATE DATABASE [ path ] data-base-name
;
```

Figure 8-2. Data base create syntax

path and directory under which all tables and indexes will be defined for that data base. The syntax for the creation of a data base is shown in Figure 8-2.

path	This optional parameter allows an *explicit* path of up to 64 characters to be specified. The path up to the data-base-name directory must exist before execution of this statement. The explicit path must be specified as dBASE IV SQL will not access a relative path when creating a new data base. If path is omitted, then the data-base-name becomes a directory of the current path.
data-base-name	This must be unique among all data bases in a dBASE IV SQL system and must begin with an alphabetic character. A separate DOS directory will be established for each data base. If the DOS directory does not exist, dBASE IV SQL will make the directory. If the directory exists, dBASE IV SQL will establish a new data base.

dBASE IV SQL will store information pertinent to a data base, such as the path name, the creator, the date created, and the actual data base name in the master catalog table SYSDBS. The master catalog is established when dBASE IV SQL is installed and resides in the SQL home directory (default is: drive-spec:\DBASE\SQLHOME\ ).

Every dBASE IV SQL data base will have its own set of dBASE IV SQL catalog tables. As of the current release, only one data base may be opened at a time. Therefore, only tables and other objects in the active data base may be accessed. *Note:* One reason for this restriction, which may be removed from later releases, is to limit the size of the dBASE IV SQL catalog tables. Since they do not utilize indices, catalog access could be severely degraded

To remove a data base, a DROP statement must be executed. If password protection is active, only the data base creator or the SQLDBA user can execute this command. The syntax of the DROP DATABASE is shown in Figure 8-3.

```
DROP DATABASE data-base-name
;
```

Figure 8-3. DROP DATABASE statement syntax

data-base-name This must be an existing data base name and cannot be active. If you are in doubt as to the status of the data base, use the STOP DATABASE command to ensure that it is deactivated.

If a data base is dropped (deleted), all its dependent objects are also dropped or deleted—including tables, views, synonyms, indices, and all .dbf and .mdx data sets in that data base's directory. All programs that referenced tables within this data base would be inoperative. Moreover, all authorities for access would also be lost and would have to be reestablished if the related tables were created. Consequently, dropping a data base may have a wide and cascading effect. Fortunately, a warning message will give the invoker of this statement a second chance to reconsider the action.

Tables

A dBASE IV SQL TABLE is a named set of *unordered* rows, each composed of the same sequence of columns. The column sequence itself is not critical, and the values within the columns are variable. Before a table can be created, a data base must be activated with the START DATABASE command. If no data base is active, an error message will be generated. Recall that a data base is tied to a DOS directory and that each data base has its own set of dBASE IV SQL catalog tables. Therefore, a START DATABASE command relates a DOS directory to a specific collection of tables and their dBASE IV SQL catalog definitions. Only tables in the current active data base may be created, accessed, or dropped.

Tables are the single form of external data presentation in the dBASE IV SQL environment. Even dBASE IV SQL catalog information is presented to the user in the form of tables, and can be manipulated (accessed) on the same basis as any other dBASE IV SQL table. Additionally, table structure is often the primary point of control and contact for the average user. Security is often administered at the table level by the granting of authorization or denial of access to a table. It follows that logical and physical table design and administration have wide-sweeping consequences for dBASE IV SQL performance and integrity.

Logical design falls victim to a trade-off between the practical issues involved in application requirements and design issues of good normalization techniques. In proper normalization methodology, increasing levels of normalization are sought to achieve declining levels of redundancy and table maintenance (i.e., update overhead). This design progression almost certainly will yield the highest number of dBASE IV SQL tables for physical implementation. The proliferation of tables, however, is in direct conflict with performance considerations that would arise in an application known to require multiple table accesses if the normalized data model were used. Performance may suffer in situations where multiple tables must be joined (in fact, denormalized) to accomplish application objectives. Therefore, a delicate balance must be attained between *update overhead* of less than ultimate normalization data models and the *performance reduction* of fully normalized data models.

One method of reducing the number of tables with minimal effect on normalization is to eliminate the use of tables that act as indicators to other tables for the actual retrieval of data. This situation typically results in frequent table joins in order to obtain the entire data picture. For example, consider a situation in which state abbreviations and little else are stored in one table which must be frequently joined with at least one other table to obtain Zip code, area code, and sales tax information. In this case, the designer, having realized the potential for performance degradation, should merge the two tables and permit minor redundancy to prevent unnecessary table joins. The issue comes down to the fact that while normalization seeks to minimize redundancy, it may do so without qualifying information about application requirements. The designer must realize that, on a practical level, *not all redundancy is bad*. This attitude will best approach the proper balance of normalization and performance considerations.

Consider the definition of views to "store" data derived from two or more other columns that make up the view when the data does not require its own physical existence. A view is particularly desirable if these derived columns are not needed consistently and its use would not degrade performance.

Each table should be designed with at least a primary key, defined as unique to ensure that each row of a table is "fingerprinted" and can be distinguished from all others in the table. Foreign keys may also be utilized to associate the table with one or more others, based on columns that are analogous between them. The keys, in turn, may be employed to assign indexing or to enable join functions that otherwise would have been difficult. *Note:* The integrity of foreign keys or referential integrity is not currently supported under dBASE IV SQL.

The actual composition of the rows (i.e., the column data structures) must accord with the specified design. In order to obtain the most efficient data definitions, all columns that may be compared with each other should have the same lengths wherever possible. For numeric items, this means that both the precision (total number of digits) and scale (number of positions to the right of the decimal point) should be equal. Failure to implement this can result in a full scan of the table associated with the columns under comparison—dBASE IV SQL may not elect to use any indices defined for the tables. Where a number of tables are present in a data base, the ramifications of such a seemingly small point are much more severe. Moreover, in many installations, design will be the last area responsible for such evaluations. Inefficiencies introduced at this point are likely to remain in the system indefinitely.

Figure 8-4 outlines the syntax of the CREATE TABLE statement. Note that the definition as presented may be executed interactively or as embedded code in an application program. If security is active, the user must be in the same group as the creator of the data base to be able to define new tables in the data base.

```
CREATE TABLE <table-name>
    (<column-name>      <data-type>
  [,.<column-name>      <data-type>]
                .
                .
    )
;
```

Figure 8-4. Basic CREATE TABLE syntax

table-name — A user-supplied name of the table being defined. The name must be unique from any other table, view, or synonym name currently residing in the dBASE IV SQL catalog of the active data base.

column-name — A unique name for a column in this table. Note that unique in one table does not preclude its use as a name for corresponding columns in other tables. This is especially useful in demonstrating relationships between tables for the purposes of joins, unions, foreign key definition, and the like. A maximum of 255 columns may be defined for a table and total row length or table width may not exceed 4000 bytes.

data-type — Specifies the storage representation of the column in the table.

As previously discussed, make certain to create compatible definitions for columns that will be the participants in comparisons. The choices are as follows:

SMALLINT — May contain an integer value up to 6 digits. This column type maps to a NUMERIC(6,0) field in a xxxxxxxx.dbf file. Values may range from –99,999 through 999,999. If a plus sign is specified, the maximum value is +99,999.

INTEGER — May contain an integer value up to 11 digits. This column type maps to a NUMERIC(11,0) field in a xxxxxxxx.dbf file. Values may range from –9,999,999,999 through 99,999,999,999. If a plus sign is specified, the maximum value is +9,999,999,999.

DECIMAL (x,y) — May hold a signed fixed decimal point number with a precision of "x" (including the sign) and a scale of "y." The precision may range from 1 through 19 digits, including a sign. The scale may range from 0 through 18 digits. This column type maps to a NUMERIC(x+1,y) field in a xxxxxxxx.dbf file.

NUMERIC (x,y) — May hold a signed fixed decimal point number with a precision of "x" (including a sign and decimal point) and a scale of "y." The precision may range from 1 through 20 digits, including a sign. The scale may range from 0 through 18 digits. This column type maps to a NUMERIC(x,y) field in a xxxxxxxx.dbf file.

FLOAT (x,y) — May hold a floating-point signed decimal number with "x" total digits (including a sign and decimal point) and "y" decimal places. The precision may range from 1 through 20, including a sign. The decimal positions may range from 0 through 18 digits. A number may be specified using exponential notation in the range of 0.1 10^{-307} through 0.9 10^{+308}. This column data type maps to a FLOAT(x,y) field in a xxxxxxxx.dbf file.

DATE — Holds a date and returns it in the format specified by the SET DATE and SET CENTURY commands. The possible date formats are:

	ANSI YYYY.MM.DD USA MM-DD-YYYY AMERICAN MM/DD/YYYY BRITISH DD/MM/YYYY FRENCH DD/MM/YYYY GERMAN DD.MM.YYYY ITALIAN DD-MM-YYYY JAPANESE YYYY/MM/DD MDY MM/DD/YYYY DMY DD/MM/YYYY YMD YYYY/MM/DD where YYYY will be either a two- or four-digit century, depending on the SET CENTURY command. This column type maps to a date field in a xxxxxxxx.dbf file.
CHAR(integer)	Up to 254 characters, fixed length. This column type maps to a CHAR(integer) field in a xxxxxxxx.dbf file.
LOGICAL	Used to contain logical true or false values. Values represented are either (.T.) for true or (.F.) for false. The actual constant is in the three characters period-letter-period, where the letter must be either a "T" or "F" in upper- or lowercase. This column type maps to a logical field in a xxxxxxxx.dbf file.

Care should be taken when determining numeric field sizes. When performing calculations in an SQL query statement, it is possible to cause an overflow. One application the authors developed required the calculation of daily interest. Columns in question were defined thus:

```
ACCT_BAL    DECIMAL(15,2)
ANNL_INT    DECIMAL(10,9)
```

When the expression

```
ACCT_BAL * ANNL_INT / 365
```

was processed, an overflow condition occurred. Ensure that your column definitions can accommodate the maximum size of any calculations. If in doubt, define columns at their maximum sizes.

When a table is populated or additional rows are inserted, it may not be possible to provide a value for every column in a row. In dBASE IV SQL, all columns will default to values that are dependent on their respective data types. Numeric columns will default to zero and character columns will default to spaces. *Note:* A DATE data-type is considered character and will default to spaces.

Recall that the width of a table or row length may not exceed 4000 characters or bytes. To dBASE IV SQL these 4000 characters are a unit of control, or what in SQL terms is known as a *PAGE*. If the row length is less than 4000 characters, then as many rows as can fit into 4000 bytes will be placed into one page. If a table's row size is 127 characters, one page will only be able to contain thirty-one rows and sixty-three bytes will be wasted per page. Table PAGE information may be found in the SYSTABLS SQL Catalog table columns CARD and NPAGES.

```
DROP TABLE table-name
;
```

Figure 8-5. DROP TABLE statement

To delete or remove a table and its related objects, a DROP TABLE statement may be utilized, as depicted in Figure 8-5.

table-name Must be the name of a table in the currently active data base. This name may not refer to a view or a synonym. Take care to ensure that the proper data base is active or you will drop the wrong table.

When a table is dropped, all dependent indices, views, and synonyms are automatically dropped. No warning message is issued and there will be no second chance to reconsider your action!

Indices

An index is an *ordered* set of tags or pointers to rows in a dBASE IV SQL data table; its name is the same as the table on which it is defined. However, SQL indices are maintained in dBASE .mdx files. One .mdx file is utilized to contain all the indices for one table. Therefore, the actual DOS data set name will be the related table name suffixed with **.MDX** (e.g., CUSTOMER.MDX). SQL indices exist for internal use by dBASE IV SQL only, and thus are never explicitly referenced by the user or SQL statements.

There are likely to be three primary objectives in establishing indices over data tables:

1. To ensure uniqueness of column values used as the indexing column(s). This is a referential integrity requirement for a primary key.
2. To guarantee the *clustering* (or physical) sequence of data in the table when particular access paths are known to be required.
3. To avoid a situation where an entire table scan will be performed where no index is otherwise to be considered.

Clustering, or rather CLUSTERED, is used by other SQL products to identify which index will control the actual physical sequence of a table. Although not supported under the first release of dBASE IV SQL, the necessary columns to control this feature exist in the SQL catalog tables and the authors were able to create a clustered index using the dBASE IV SQL CREATE INDEX statement. The authors are sure that this facility will be available in a later release.

An index defined as unique (a unique index on a primary key supports the Entity Integrity requirement of the relational integrity rule) will guarantee that no duplicate values will be allowed to exist within the column(s) specified as the indexing columns.

```
CREATE [UNIQUE] INDEX index-name
        ON table-name

    (column_name_1 ASC | DESC ...
    ,column_name_n ASC | DESC
    )
    [ CLUSTER ]
;
```

Figure 8-6. CREATE INDEX syntax

This also applies to defaulted values. Duplicate values of key columns encountered during the table loads will cause the load to fail and the index not to be populated. Columns that are designated, after table population has occurred, to make up a unique key should be screened prior to index definition and reorganization to prevent load or index creation failure.

A dBASE IV SQL table may have a maximum of 47 indices, and one or more may be unique. However, the more indices a table has, the more processing will be required for data modification (i.e., SELECT, UPDATE, INSERT). The syntax for creating either a unique or nonunique index is shown in Figure 8-6. Note that the CLUSTER optional is not yet documented in the dBASE IV SQL manuals.

UNIQUE — Optional keyword that specifies that the key column(s) in this index must be unique (i.e., contain a unique value for each row). As previously mentioned, any key column with a high degree of cardinality should be considered for definition as unique to ensure that no duplicate values of the key column(s) will exist at any time. Uniqueness of key column values will promote the use of the index by dBASE IV SQL, all other things being equal. More than one unique index per table may be created.

index-name — A user-defined name for the index being created. The actual name cannot contain more than ten characters and the first character must be alphabetic.

table-name — Must be an existing table name as described in the CREATE TABLE statement and the table being indexed must be in the currently active data base. An index may not be created on a VIEW or SYNONYM.

column_name_1 ASC|DESC — Identifies the column(s) for the index and whether each will be in ascending or descending sequence. Ascending is the default. The following is a valid column list for an index:

```
(CUST_NO  ASC
,CITY     ASC
,STATE    ASC
)
```

The columns must all be in either ascending or descending sequence. This presents a design consideration in that dates are more useful in descending (i.e., earliest dates first) sequence.

CLUSTER — Although not yet totally supported, this parameter is intended to identify an index that will control the physical sequence of its related table. An error should occur if CLUSTER is specified on more than one index for a table. However, the authors were able to create two indices on the same table that specified CLUSTER. The first chronologically defined index retained the clustering attribute and the second did not. Note that in other relational DBMS products, if CLUSTER is not defined on any of a tables indices, the first chronologically defined index defaults to a clustering attribute. See Chapter 10 for a detailed explanation of CLUSTER use.

To remove or delete an index, a DROP INDEX must be executed, as shown in Figure 8-7.

index-name — Must be the name of an index in the currently active data base. As with the DROP TABLE statement, take care to ensure that the proper data base is active or you will drop the wrong index.

When an index is dropped, its related table is still accessible, although response time may be degraded. No warning message is issued and there will be no second chance to reconsider your action.

```
DROP INDEX index-name
;
```

Figure 8-7. DROP INDEX statement

Views

A dBASE IV SQL view is a logical representation of data that exists in one or more underlying dBASE IV SQL tables. This data may be composed of all or a subset of the columns and/or rows defined for one or many tables. Note that the term "underlying" does not exclude the possibility of data being extracted from another view representation, although the physical basis will always be a table at some point. Figure 8-8 depicts a possible implementation of multilevel views.

For most purposes, the definition and access of a view are transparent to the user (i.e., identical to the definition and access of a table). Physically, however, a table is distinct from a view in that a table has a physical storage representation, whereas the view relating to that table does not. dBASE IV SQL accomplishes this condition by storing the view definition in a dBASE IV SQL catalog table, SYSVIEWS, where it will reside awaiting an access request for the view. When a view is requested, the definition of the view will be retrieved by dBASE IV SQL and executed against the physical table(s) in the definition. This execution will produce, in most cases, a temporary "results" data table

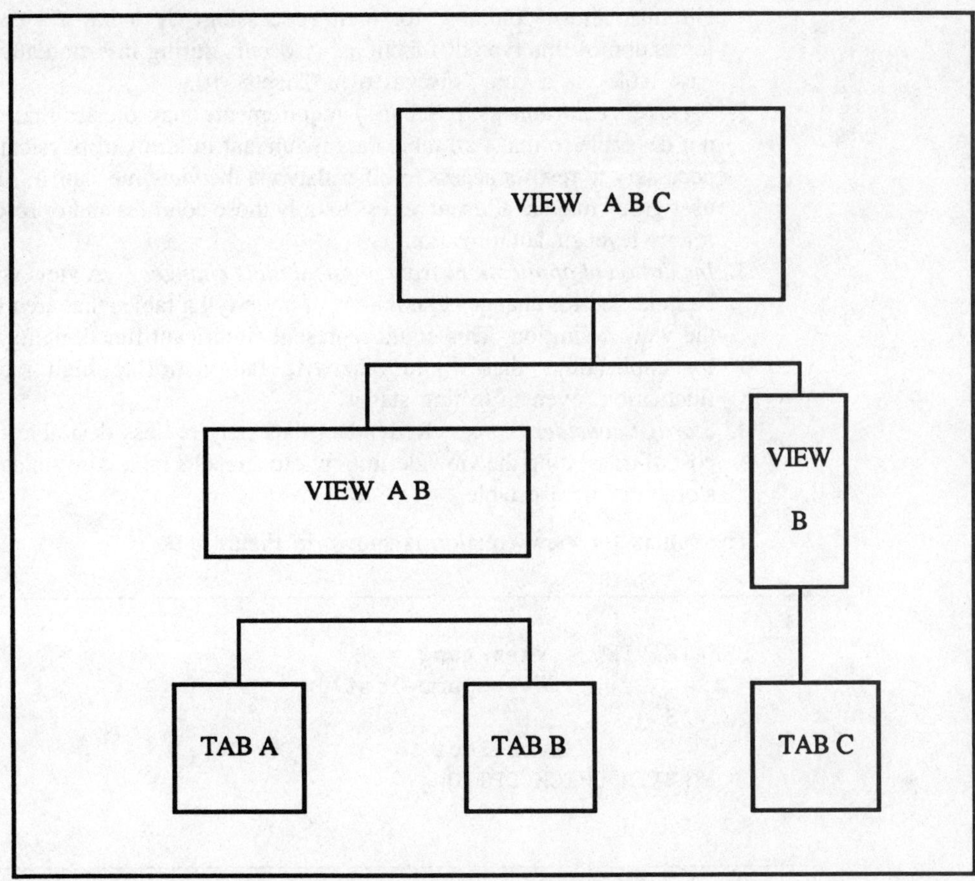

Figure 8-8. Table and view relationships

similar to the physical table that would have existed in the absence of an available view. In this manner, dBASE IV SQL succeeds in eliminating redundant data storage until actual access of the data is required.

There is no specific authorization required to create a view; rather, it is implied with other privileges or authorizations. If password protection is in effect, any user may create a view over any tables for which the user holds the SELECT privilege. The creator of a table implicitly holds all privileges (including SELECT) over his table. Also, views may be created on any tables by the SQLDBA user.

Given that all views have a physical basis as a table at some point, questions may arise as to the significance of the view mechanism:

1. *Reduction and/or combination of table columns specific to a user group.* A view definition allows actual SQL commands to join multiple tables to be avoided for nontechnical users; the view by definition does the joining. Since dBASE IV SQL will execute the definitional requirements upon request for the view, most differences are undetectable to the average user. Users who do not desire access to all columns and/or rows within a table set may effectively eliminate those columns, for their processing, by using a view. The major restriction of this type of functionality occurs during insertion attempts into the base table via a view, discussed in Chapter 10.
2. *Security requirements.* Security requirements may dictate that although it is not desirable to make all table data redundant in terms of physical storage, it is necessary to restrict access to other data via the view mechanism. In this way, a user group may be allowed access to only those columns and/or rows appropriate for its level of authorization.
3. *Insulation of applications from physical table changes.* A view will not have to be modified for changes to columns of underlying tables that are not included in the view definition. This could represent significant functionality enhancement for applications that would otherwise fall victim to high rates of design fluctuation, even in testing stages.
4. *Storage considerations.* Redundant data may be less desirable than the CPU cost of translating the view definition into a results table to simulate the physical storage of a base table.

The syntax for view creation is shown in Figure 8-9.

```
CREATE VIEW < view-name >
         [(view-column-list)]
    AS
         < subselect >
    [WITH CHECK OPTION]
    ;
```

Figure 8-9. CREATE VIEW syntax

```
DROP VIEW view-name
;
```

Figure 8-10. DROP VIEW statement

The column names in the view-column-list, if utilized, must correspond on a one-to-one basis to the columns in the subselect. See Chapter 10 for examples of VIEWs using subselects and restrictions on subselects in a VIEW.

view-name	A user-defined name for the view being created. This name may not be the same as any other table, synonym, or view in the currently active data base. The actual name may not be longer than ten characters and must begin with an alphabetic character.
view-column-list	A list of names for columns in this view. This list corresponds positionally on a one-to-one basis to the columns in the subselect. It is not required unless the results of the subselect contain duplicate names or have derived columns from an arithmetic expression, function, or constant.
subselect	Consists of a SELECT statement to retrieve columns and rows from one or more tables.
WITH CHECK OPTION	When specified for an *updatable view,* will prevent modification or insertion of a row whose columns' values do not conform to all of the conditions specified in the subselect. Modification (INSERT or UPDATE) through a VIEW is restricted. See Chapter 10 for more information.

To delete or remove a view and its related objects, a DROP VIEW statement may be utilized, as illustrated in Figure 8-10.

view-name	Must be the name of a view in the currently active data base. Take care to ensure that the proper data base is active or you will drop the wrong view.

When a view is dropped, all dependent views and synonyms are also automatically dropped. No warning message is issued.

Synonyms

The CREATE SYNONYM statement will define an alias or synonym for a table or view. Under the current implementation of dBASE IV SQL, synonyms may only be used to

```
CREATE SYNONYM < synonym-name >
    FOR  < table-name | view-name >
;
```

Figure 8-11. CREATE SYNONYM statement

create another name or abbreviation for a table or view in the currently active data base. Furthermore, when a synonym is established in one data base, it may only be referenced while that data base is active. The authors find little value in the use of synonyms under such limitations.

A synonym may be created by any user who may LOGIN to dBASE IV. No special dBASE IV SQL privileges are required. However, to utilize a synonym in a SQL query requires that the invoker of the statement hold that proper table privileges to access the actual table.

A CREATE SYNONYM is shown in Figure 8-11.

synonym-name	May be up to ten characters long and the first character must be alphabetic. A synonym name may not be the same as any other table, view, or synonym in the currently active data base.
table-name | view-name	Must specify a table or view in the currently active data base.

To remove a synonym, explicitly execute a DROP SYNONYM statement. Recall that a synonym is implicitly dropped when its respective table or view is dropped or any object on which it is dependent is dropped. A DROP SYNONYM statement is illustrated in Figure 8-12.

synonym-name	Must be the name of a synonym in the currently active data base. Take care to ensure that the proper data base is active or you will drop the wrong synonym.

Recall that views cannot be created on a synonym. Therefore, when a synonym is dropped, no other dBASE IV SQL objects are affected. Also, no warning message is issued.

```
DROP SYNONYM synonym-name
;
```

Figure 8-12. DROP SYNONYM statement

Alter Table

The ALTER TABLE statement allows additional columns to be appended to the end of every row in a table. To execute this statement, you must, at minimum, hold the ALTER privilege for the table being modified. If you were the creator of the table, you implicitly hold the ALTER privilege. Of course, the SQLDBA user may alter any table. The syntax of the ALTER TABLE statement is shown in Figure 8-13.

table-name — A required parameter that identifies the table to be altered. This cannot be a view or synonym. Synonyms and views cannot be altered.

column-name — A unique name (maximum of 10 characters) for the column in the table. A maximum of 255 columns may be defined for a table and total row length or table width may not exceed 4000 bytes. See the CREATE TABLE statement for additional considerations.

data-type — Specifies the storage representation of the column in the table. As previously discussed, make certain to create compatible definitions for columns that will be the participants in comparisons. The column's data type may be one of the following:

`CHAR(n)`	Character string data
`DATE`	Dates
`INTEGER`	Integer values up to 11 digits
`SMALLINT`	Integer values up to 6 digits
`NUMERIC(x,y)`	Fixed decimal point numbers
`DECIMAL(x,y)`	Fixed decimal point numbers
`FLOAT(x,y)`	Floating-point numbers
`LOGICAL`	Logical (true or false) values

Memo fields are not permitted in dBASE IV SQL tables. Therefore, there is no data type for memo fields in either a CREATE TABLE statement or an ALTER TABLE statement.

The syntax of this statement allows multiple columns to be added during one execution. The authors attempted to alter a table by adding two columns with one ALTER TABLE statement. The alter completed successfully. Unfortunately, later attempts to retrieve rows with a SELECT statement generated an error message and no rows were returned.

```
ALTER TABLE < table-name >
     ADD
          (column_name 1    data-type, ..
.)
;
```

Figure 8-13. ALTER TABLE syntax

```
INSERT INTO new-table
      (new_coll, new_col2,.....)
      SELECT old_coll, old_col2, ....
            FROM old_table
;
```

Figure 8-14. Table copy example

There is no dBASE IV SQL statement that allows columns to be removed from a table. Also, column widths (i.e., field sizes) cannot be changed. If a column must be removed or a column width modified, create a different table with the required attributes (i.e., number of columns and column widths) and copy your data with an INSERT statement, as shown in Figure 8-14.

The trick is to copy only the required columns to the new table. The column width changes and decimal alignment will be managed by dBASE IV SQL during the actual column movement.

Transaction Restrictions

Data Definition Language statements are more global in nature and, therefore, have a greater effect when executed. On the other hand, transaction processing is intended to back out or *roll back* table data modifications, such as insert, update, and delete rows. The table definition remains intact. However, dropping a table removes that table's definition from the SQL catalogs and deletes its DOS data set. For this reason, the CREATE and DROP Data Definition Language statements may not be executed in a transaction. They are not recoverable!

CHAPTER 9

Data Manipulation Language

Getting Started

As discussed in Chapter 7, Structured Query Language (SQL) consists of three components that may create, manipulate, or control the access and use of dBASE IV SQL objects. The Data Manipulation Language (DML) component of SQL allows users to query tables (retrieve rows), insert new rows, update existing data, and delete rows from dBASE IV SQL tables. Most people in the data processing community who have not utilized relational data base management systems have a record-at-a-time mentality that originates from the typical report generation program logic of read-a-record, write-a-report-line, and break processing. Think **RELATIONAL**! DBASE IV SQL deals with sets of rows and the resulting rows from those sets. This is not to say that your application will not have to process single rows, but rather that you should not perpetuate the preconceived notion that your application must process one row at a time. When designing or coding an application, first think how to process your functions using SQL, and then resort to application code. One SQL statement may accomplish what would normally require several pages of conventional code! An example that appears later in this chapter will utilize one query to produce a detailed report with two levels of breaks.

Recall that an SQL table may consist of zero or more *unordered* rows, each row consisting of one or more columns. The physical sequence of table rows is never guaranteed unless a specific sequence is requested during row retrieval.

Should you as a designer and/or programmer be concerned with the physical sequence of tables? The answer is, "Maybe." Remember, the user can only specify what data to retrieve: dBASE IV SQL will determine how to access it! However, you still should be cognizant of what columns are indexed, what indices are available, and the size or scale/precision of columns. These are some of the factors that will affect how the SQL optimizer will access tables referenced in DML queries. Therefore, how a query is coded will have a definite impact on performance. The last section of this chapter will present more detailed DML performance guidelines.

All examples in this chapter will use the dBASE IV SQL sample tables that were described in Chapter 7.

Query Syntax

The purpose of a dBASE IV SQL query is to retrieve data from tables. This retrieval is accomplished with a DML SELECT statement. Table modification is performed by DELETE, INSERT, and UPDATE statements.

A SELECT statement must specify what columns to return and the tables from which these columns are to be retrieved. Optionally, the SELECT statement can specify which rows to select and what the sequence of the results should be. Figure 9-1 illustrates the format for a basic SELECT statement.

column-list | * — A required parameter that specifies which columns are requested. Either a list of column names or an asterisk (*) may be entered. The sequence of the columns in the column-list will be the sequence of the columns in the output results. An asterisk designates that all columns of a table are requested and that these columns will be in the same sequence in which the table was defined. A column-list may consist of any combination of column names, constants, expressions, aggregate functions, and dBASE IV functions and/or variables. Commas must separate column names if more than one entry is coded.

table-list — This required parameter specifies which table(s), view(s), or synonym(s) contain the columns entered in the column-list. If more than one entry is coded, rows from multiple tables *may* be joined to derive the results. Commas must separate table names

```
SELECT       <column-list> | *

FROM         <table-list>

[WHERE       search conditions]

[ORDER BY    sequence-list]

     ;       delimiter
```

Figure 9-1. Basic SELECT statement syntax

if more than one entry is specified. A table-list may be composed of any combination of tables, views, or synonyms. Note that views or synonyms of views may have restrictions on their use. See Chapter 10 for more information on view restrictions.

search conditions — This optional clause acts as a filter for row selection and/or governs the matching of rows for table joins. In order for a row to be retrieved, it must meet all the search conditions of this clause. One search condition is composed of two expressions or predicates and a *comparison operator* such as an equal sign:

```
LASTNAME = 'Vidoni'
```

Entire search conditions may be negated through use of the NOT keyword. This is accomplished by prefixing the search condition with NOT:

```
WHERE NOT LASTNAME = 'Vidoni'
AND NOT FIRSTNAME = 'Cheryl'
```

The NOT keyword, if used, must precede each search condition that it is to be negated.

Values within parentheses are processed as entered. They will not be folded to upper- or lowercase. Since the character string 'Vidoni' was inserted into the table with a capital 'V' and the remaining letters in lowercase, it must always be coded as it was originally entered. However, column names, as well as other expressions, will be folded to uppercase.

sequence-list — This optional clause controls the sequence of the results. If no ORDER BY clause is specified, the rows will be returned in the physical sequence in which they are stored within the table.

delimiter — A semicolon delimiter is required after every dBASE IV SQL statement.

The coding of search conditions and associated predicates of a WHERE clause will directly affect processing time. If the entire clause is omitted, all rows will be returned or a *cartesian product* of all tables being joined will result. (A cartesian product is defined as a set that is constructed from two given sets and comprises all pairs of elements such that one element of the pair is from the first set and the other element is from the second set.) If index columns are not referenced in predicates, then a full table scan will be chosen by the SQL optimizer. See the performance guidelines section at the end of this chapter for more information.

The allowable comparison operators that are used in expressions are shown in Figure 9-2.

When two characters are used in a comparison operators, they must be coded in the sequence shown. The greater-than symbol (>) must precede the equal sign (=), the not symbol (!) must precede the greater-than symbol (>), etc. And operators may never be longer than two characters (i.e., the combination !<= may not be coded).

OPERATOR	DESCRIPTION
=	Equal
>	Greater than
<	Less than
>=	Greater than or equal to
<=	Less than or equal to
< >	Not equal
!=	Not equal
!>	Not greater than
!<	Not less than

Figure 9-2. SQL comparison operators

Basic Queries

The easiest way to learn DML is to work with actual examples. These examples will be divided into two sections. The first section will present basic queries with different types of WHERE clause search conditions. The second section will consist of more complex real-life problems. One possible solution per problem will be illustrated, and the processing of the query will be explained. As the problems progress, they will become more and more difficult. No solution should take longer than thirty minutes to code and test. If thirty minutes seems exorbitant, consider how long it would take to design, code, and debug a program to achieve the same results.

As you read each example, test it with interactive SQL, if possible. (Interactive SQL will facilitate this testing.) The sample tables are very small; none of them contain more than fifty rows. For this reason, no indices were created for any of these tables. As each solution is discussed, the effect of index availability will be contrasted.

WHERE Clause Search Conditions

A simple SELECT to retrieve all rows and all columns from the staff table is shown in Figure 9-3.

To limit the rows to staff members located in Chicago, modify the query to include a search condition within the WHERE clause, as in Figure 9-4.

```
SELECT * FROM STAFF;
```

Figure 9-3. Simple SELECT

```
SELECT * FROM STAFF
 WHERE LOCATION = 'CHICAGO';
```

Figure 9-4. Simple SELECT with WHERE clause

The first two queries are very straightforward. If all applications had data requirements as simple as these, dBASE IV SQL and most other data base products would not be necessary. As is usually the way, applications demand ever-more-sophisticated data retrieval scenarios.

Normally, not all columns are required. To select only the names for staff members located in Chicago, enter the query shown in Figure 9-5.

```
SELECT firstname, lastname
 FROM STAFF
 WHERE LOCATION = 'CHICAGO';
```

Figure 9-5. SELECT with column list

Of interest is that the result rows consisting of first name and last name are determined by the LOCATION column, which is not part of the results.

Columns within search conditions are not required to be part of the output. Recall that column names are folded to uppercase and, therefore, may be coded in any combination of upper- and lowercase letters. However, the character string 'CHICAGO' must be entered as it was originally inserted into the table. If 'CHICAGO' were entered in any other combination of lowercase and uppercase letters, the search condition could never be true and no rows would be returned. However, the dBASE IV UPPER function could be able to resolve this problem, as depicted in Figure 9-6.

```
SELECT firstname, lastname
    FROM STAFF
    WHERE
     UPPER(LOCATION) = 'CHICAGO';
```

Figure 9-6. SELECT with dBASE IV UPPER function

This blending of dBASE IV functions and SQL statements enables the best of both worlds. Most other relational products do not support this level of compatibility.

Compound Search Conditions (AND, OR)

If a query is to return information based on more than one search condition, then the search conditions can be combined by using **AND** and **OR** keyword operators. The AND operator specifies that all search conditions must be true to return a row. The OR operator specifies that either search condition must be true to return a row. The query in Figure 9-7 illustrates a compound search condition to list the manager's name in the Chicago location. Both the location and the supervisor search conditions must be true for a row to be selected.

```
SELECT FIRSTNAME, LASTNAME
    FROM STAFF
    WHERE LOCATION = 'CHICAGO'
    AND SUPERVISOR = STAFF_NO;
```

Figure 9-7. SELECT with compound AND predicate

In the staff table, a supervisor is identified when the STAFF_NO and SUPERVISOR columns are equal.

In the next example, Figure 9-8, we need to list the names and locations of all staff members who either are managers or have salaries greater than or equal to $5000. If either search condition is true, a row must be returned.

```
SELECT FIRSTNAME ,LASTNAME ,location
     FROM STAFF
     WHERE SALARY >= 5000
     OR   SUPERVISOR = STAFF_NO;
```

Figure 9-8. SELECT with compound OR predicate

If a prospective row satisfies either search condition, it is returned. A row is never returned more than once per SELECT statement, no matter how many additional search conditions it satisfies.

Recall that dBASE IV SQL establishes its precedence rules for combining search conditions with AND and OR operators utilizing Boolean logic. The AND operator connects search conditions where each selected row must satisfy *all* search conditions. Use OR to connect search conditions where each selected row must satisfy *any* search condition. When it is necessary to override these precedence rules, parentheses must be used.

In the query in Figure 9-9, we want a list of names, locations, and *annual* salaries of all employees who are located in either Chicago or New York. Their respective salaries must be greater than $60,000 per year.

```
SELECT FIRSTNAME ,LASTNAME
     ,LOCATION,SALARY * 12
     FROM STAFF
     WHERE     SALARY * 12 > 60000
     AND (LOCATION = 'NEW YORK'
     OR   LOCATION = 'CHICAGO');
```

Figure 9-9. SELECT with precedence override

If parentheses were not used, the search condition

```
LOCATION = 'CHICAGO'
```

would act independently of the salary requirement. All employees located in Chicago would be selected regardless of salary. The AND operator between the search conditions

```
WHERE     SALARY * 12 > 60000
AND LOCATION = 'NEW YORK'
```

would require both tests to be true before returning any employees located in New York. The expression

```
SALARY * 12
```

multiplies every salary column by 12 to calculate the annual value. The salary search condition test would be more efficient if no calculations were performed. The search condition

```
SALARY > 5000
```

would achieve the same results and not require a computation to test each row.

In addition to multiplication, other arithmetic operators may be utilized in DML statements. Figure 9-10 lists the arithmetic operators and their descriptions.

OPERATOR	DESCRIPTION
** and ^	Exponentiation
+ and -	Addition or subtraction (plus sign is the default)
* and \	Multiplication or division
+ and -	Unary operator (plus sign is the default)

Figure 9-10. Arithmetic operators

The sequence in which arithmetic operators will be processed is multiply, divide, add, and then subtract (M. D. A. S.). To remember this sequence use the phrase "My Dear Aunt Sally" as a mnemonic. Exponentiation is performed before all other calculations.

IN, BETWEEN, LIKE Keywords (Shortcuts for Search Conditions)

If one column in a WHERE clause may equal several different values, it is necessary to repeat this column in several expressions. Figure 9-11 illustrates one method to retrieve all customers who have addresses in the states of California (CA), Wisconsin (WI), or New York (NY).

```
SELECT * FROM CUSTOMER
     WHERE        STATE = 'CA'
     OR           STATE = 'WI'
     OR           STATE = 'NY';
```

Figure 9-11. Compound SELECT

Fortunately, dBASE IV SQL provides the IN keyword predicate that allows a field to be compared with a list of values. The SELECT for customers could be shortened, as shown in Figure 9-12.

```
SELECT * FROM CUSTOMER
     WHERE        STAT IN ('CA','WI','NY');
```

Figure 9-12. SELECT with IN keyword

In some instances, the IN predicate may simplify compound search conditions. The query to retrieve employee names, locations, and annual salaries could have been coded utilizing an IN predicate, which would have removed the requirement to override the precedence operators with parentheses (Figure 9-13).

```
SELECT FIRSTNAME ,LASTNAME
           ,LOCATION ,SALARY * 12
     FROM STAFF
     WHERE      SALARY * 12 > 60000
     AND        LOCATION  IN
         ('NEW YORK', 'CHICAGO');
```

Figure 9-13. Compound SELECT with IN keyword

Another shortcut is the BETWEEN keyword. A BETWEEN predicate will return all rows that are between and inclusive of two values. The SELECT statement in Figure 9-14 would return all staff members who have salaries that are equal to or greater than $5000 and less than or equal to $6000.

```
SELECT*FROM STAFF
     WHERE SALARY
          BETWEEN 5000 AND 6000;
```

Figure 9-14. SELECT with BETWEEN keyword

The same results could be produced with the compound search condition in Figure 9-15.

```
SELECT*FROM STAFF
     WHERE SALARY >= 5000
     AND SALARY <= 6000;
```

Figure 9-15. SELECT with BETWEEN equivalent

The LIKE predicate allows searches for character string data that partially matches a specific string, a character type memory variable, or the USER keyword. The pattern may use the percent symbol (%) to represent zero or more characters and an underscore (_) to represent exactly one character. Multiple underscores may be utilized to indicate that additional characters must be present. A classic example for the use of the LIKE predicate would be the retrieval of all staff members with the last name of Smith. Unfortunately, in this example, one or more persons had their names incorrectly entered as Smyth. Fortunately, we can still retrieve all staff members with one search condition, as in Figure 9-16.

```
SELECT*FROM STAFF
     WHERE LASTNAME LIKE 'Sm_th';
```

Figure 9-16. SELECT with LIKE keyword

The underscore allows the third character of the last name to be any character, including a blank. In this example, LASTNAME was defined to contain a maximum of fifteen positions. Will Smith, Smyth, or Sm?th still be returned? SQL under dBASE IV will right-pad character strings with blanks so that the character string and the actual column are the same length. Therefore, trailing blanks are assumed and any LASTNAME column that matches the pattern in the above LIKE predicate will be returned.

Recall that lowercase letters are not folded to uppercase when they are within parentheses. Note that the dBASE IV UPPER function does not work with the SQL LIKE predicate in dBASE IV SQL release 1.0 . It is hoped that this oversight will be corrected in the next release. The UPPER function will work with the comparison operators, such as equal "=" and greater than ">". For this reason, the authors strongly recommend that all character data be stored in uppercase in all dBASE IV SQL data bases. Also, note that most mainframe products fold lowercase to uppercase during data entry at their respective terminals. To maintain compatibility with other vendors' data base products during data transfers or data manipulation, use uppercase.

To assist the company's sales force with the NEW sales campaign that stresses NEW, we have been asked to provide a list of all customers in cities with names that begin with "N," "e," "w," blank (Figure 9-17).

```
SELECT*FROM CUSTOMERS
     WHERE CITY LIKE'New %';
```

Figure 9-17. SELECT with LIKE keyword

Thus, all cities that begin with "New," no matter how long the name, will satisfy this search condition. In this example, we are only concerned with the leading characters.

In the next example, a list of customers must be created in which company name ends in either Inc. or Incorporated. Again, the LIKE predicate is utilized, but this time we are looking for trailing characters. The character string is prefixed with a percent symbol (Figure 9-18).

```
SELECT*FROM CUSTOMERS
     WHERE    COMPANY LIKE '%Inc.';
     OR       COMPANY LIKE
                   '%Incorporated';
```

Figure 9-18. SELECT with LIKE keyword

If necessary, we can look for imbedded characters only. To search for customers whose company names contain the word "Furniture," leading and trailing percent symbols are utilized, as in Figure 9-19.

```
SELECT*FROM CUSTOMERS
    WHERE COMPANY LIKE '%Furniture%';
```

Figure 9-19. SELECT with LIKE keyword

The question that usually follows is: "Can the percent symbol (%) and an underscore (_) be combined?" The answer is, "Absolutely, and in most combinations!" As a matter of fact, the authors tried combinations of underscores with leading, trailing, and imbedded percent symbols. In all cases, the anticipated results were received. Following are some common and uncommon examples of possible combinations used with a LIKE predicate.

1. The first character in CITY is an "S," trailed by at least two characters in which the second character is a lowercase "o." To satisfy this search condition, CITY must consist of at least three characters, the first character must be an "S," and the third through last character must be an "o."

   `WHERE CITY LIKE 'S%_o%'`

2. The characters "th" appear anywhere in LASTNAME, *including* the first or last characters.

   `WHERE LASTNAME LIKE '%th%'`

3. The trailing three characters in CITY are "ton," as in Washington or Stockton.

   `WHERE CITY LIKE '%ton'`

4. The following search condition works. We have used search conditions like this when performing audits.

   `WHERE COMPANY LIKE 'To%_Des__%_ure%'`

The authors strongly suggest experimenting with the LIKE clause to fully appreciate its potential.

Negating Search Conditions

Coding a query might be simplified if a reverse search condition could be entered. For instance, it would be easier to produce a list of customers with addresses other than New York or California if the negative were used, as in Figure 9-20.

```
SELECT*FROM CUSTOMERS
WHERE    STATE != 'NY'
AND      STATE != 'CA'
```

Figure 9-20. SELECT with not equal

Or it can be coded as in Figure 9-21.

```
SELECT*FROM CUSTOMERS
    WHERE STATE NOT IN ('NY', 'CA');
```

Figure 9-21. SELECT with not IN keyword

Other possibilities for the WHERE clause include

```
WHERE NOT STATE IN ('NY', 'CA');
```

and

```
WHERE NOT STATE = 'NY'
AND   NOT STATE = 'CA';
```

These examples illustrate how an entire search condition may be negated through the use of the NOT keyword or how the not-operator "!" may be used to reverse a comparison.

What would be the results if a NOT keyword and a not-operator were used in the same search condition as follows?

```
WHERE NOT STATE != 'NY'
```

The answer is that only rows where the state is *equal* to "NY" would be returned. The following WHERE clause would yield the same results as the previous double-negative clause.

```
WHERE     STATE  = 'NY'
```

Aggregate Functions

In addition to the functions available with dBASE IV, built-in or aggregate functions may be utilized specifically with the SQL SELECT command. The argument of an aggregate function may be a column name or an expression. An expression is a combination of column names and/or constants (e.g., SALARY * 12). These functions are:

AVG(. . .) Calculates the average of the values in a numeric column or expression. The column may only be defined as numeric.

COUNT(*) Counts the number of selected rows regardless of their column contents. The results will be integer.

COUNT(DISTINCT col_name_1 [,. . . . ,col_name_n]) Counts the distinct values for the column(s) specified in the selected rows.

MAX(. . .) Returns the largest value of the specified column for all the *selected rows*. The column may be defined as character, date, or numeric.

MIN(. . .) Returns the smallest value of the specified column for all the *selected rows*. The column may be defined as character, date, or numeric.

SUM(. . .) Sums the value of a column or expression for all the *selected rows*. The column(s) in the expression must be defined as numeric.

Recall that SQL Data Manipulation Language operates on sets of rows. Nowhere is this more apparent than when retrieving rows that are being processed by aggregate functions. The query in Figure 9-22 implies a set or group that is composed of an entire table.

```
SELECT AVG(SALARY*12)
          ,MAX(SALARY)
          ,MIN(SALARY)
          ,MAX LASTNAME)
          FROM STAFF,
```

Figure 9-22. Aggregate function example

Since there is no WHERE clause, every row will be examined to return one results row. This results row will consist of four columns—the average annual salary, the lowest salary, the highest salary, and highest (value) lastname among all staff members in the company. The actual returned column values may come from any combination of rows in the STAFF table. Your only concern is the results, not which row had the highest or lowest values.

If a WHERE clause is added to limit the calculation to staff members located in Los Angeles, the set or group of rows will be limited to one location. Figure 9-23 depicts a query that will return the average salary for all staff members located in Los Angeles.

```
SELECT AVG(SALARY)
          FROM STAFF
          WHERE
          LOCATION = 'LOS ANGELES';
```

Figure 9-23. Average salary of Los Angeles staff members

Ordering Results

Earlier the authors stated that a dBASE IV SQL table consists of zero or more unordered rows. Clearly, there will be occasions when a process requires that rows be in a specific sequence. Use of the ORDER BY clause will control the sequence in which the results table must be presented. This statement overrides the otherwise unpredictable sequence generated by the system.

Ordering can be requested in an ascending (the default) or descending sequence of one or more columns or expressions (derived columns) in the SELECT column-list. Since the results table will be in the sequence specified by the ORDER BY clause, it is impossible to sort on columns or expressions that are not in the selected column-list. The ORDER BY clause may refer to actual column names or an integer value. The integer value refers to a corresponding column position in the select list. Integer(s) must be used when sequencing on expressions. Expressions are not defined when a table is created and so may never have a column name.

The following problems will require a specific sequence on both columns and/or expressions. Their related solutions will clarify how returned row sequence is controlled.

SELECT Sales Data

Provide a list for an individual customer showing all order numbers and dates of sale. The list should be in date and order number sequence, with the latest dates first. Customer '000016' will be the first customer to be reported. The solution appears in Figure 9-24.

```
SELECT     ORDER_NO ,SALE_DATE
           ,CUST_NO

FROM SALES

WHERE      CUST_NO = '000016'

ORDER BY   SALE_DATE DESC
           ,ORDER_NO ASC

;
```

Figure 9-24. SELECT sales data

The column-list consists of three columns (ORDER_NO, SALE_DATE, CUST_NO) that are being retrieved from the SALES table. The clause

```
WHERE      CUST_NO = '000016'
```

limits the row(s) being returned to those that have a customer number of '000016'. After the rows have been selected, the results will be sorted in the sequence specified in the ORDER BY clause. If an index were available on the CUST_NO column, the SQL optimizer would be able randomly to select only rows that meet the criteria of the WHERE search condition. Since no index is available, a full table scan and results table sort are required.

SELECT Sales/Customer Data

The foregoing Sales Data list is very useful, but we also need the customer's company name. The first thought that comes to mind is to add a separate SELECT to retrieve the company name from the customer table:

```
SELECT COMPANY
    FROM CUSTOMER
    WHERE CUST_NO = '000016';
```

What the user really wants is the company name to appear on each row of the results list, which will require that all data items be returned with one query. In relational terms, we need to JOIN data items from more than one table. The resulting rows will be composed of columns from two different tables. The solution appears in Figure 9-25.

```
SELECT      ORDER_NO,SALE_DATE
            ,CST.CUST_NO
            ,COMPANY

FROM SALES SA
            ,CUSTOMER CST

WHERE    SA.CUST_NO = '000016'

    AND CST.CUST_NO = '000016'
    AND CST.CUST_NO = SA.CUST_NO

ORDER BY  SALE_DATE DESC
          ,ORDER_NO ASC

;
```

Figure 9-25. SELECT sales/customer data

In the solution, modifications to the initial Sales Data query are indicated with italic letters. An additional column (COMPANY) has been added to the SELECT column-list. Since this column is defined on the CUSTOMER table, that table must also be added to the table-list. Recall that in SQL there is no specific parameter for a JOIN operator. The fact that more than one table is coded in a table-list indicates that tables are to be joined.

However, another consideration arises in that the column CUST_NO exists in both the SALES and CUSTOMER tables. Therefore, to obviate any ambiguity, the CUST_NO column must be qualified within this query. The *alias* or *correlation name*, SA, will be used to qualify columns in the SALES table and CST will qualify columns of the CUSTOMER table. (dBASE IV SQL uses the term "alias" whereas IBM DB2 utilizes "correlation name." Since the reason for a correlation name is to qualify column names, that term will be used throughout this text.)

The correlation names are established in the FROM parameter

```
FROM SALES SA   ,CUSTOMER CS
```

by the fact that there is *no comma between the table and its correlation name*. Correlation names may be composed of from one to ten characters in dBASE IV SQL. The question that usually follows is, "What happens if I forget the required comma between two names in a table-list and correlation names are not used?" The answer is, "The second name after a comma becomes a correlation name." If the FROM clause were coded

```
FROM SALES   CUSTOMER
```

the second name, CUSTOMER, would become the correlation name for SALES. This situation is not as unlikely as one might think. One of the authors made the same error when first learning DML several years ago.

SELECT Inventory Items and Total Value

Calculate the total unit value of each part currently held in inventory. Present the total values, preceded by their respective part descriptions, in descending order by dollar amount. The solution appears in Figure 9-26.

```
SELECT DESCRIPT
     ,ON_HAND * UNITCOST
FROM INVENTRY
     ORDER BY 2    DESC
;
```

Figure 9-26. ORDER BY expression

The SELECT in Figure 9-26 will present two columns for each part currently residing in the inventory table. The first column, DESCRIPT, was defined when the table was created. The second column is an expression and is derived by multiplying ON_HAND by UNITCOST. Therefore, the ORDER BY clause must refer to its corresponding integer value to sort the dollar amount in descending sequence. If a secondary sequence is required on part description, DESCRIPT, the ORDER BY clause could be modified in either of two ways:

```
ORDER BY 2 DESC, 1 ASC
```

or:

```
ORDER BY 2 DESC, DESCRIPT ASC
```

Column names and integer values may be mixed in a sequence list and any combination of ASC and DESC may be specified. Commas are required to delineate specifications in a list. Recall that ascending is the default and need not be coded.

SELECT Using a Five-Table JOIN

The data model in Figure 9-27 shows the relationships among the five tables that are accessed in the five-table JOIN example.

There are two salespersons with the last name SMITH, and to complicate matters further, their first names are Robert and Roger. This similarity in names has caused their sales information to be incorrectly entered. A query is required that will list the staff members' (e.g., salespersons') last and first names, related customer names and cities, associated order numbers and dates of sale, and all items/descriptions for each order. The list must be in descending sequence by sale date. The solution appears in Figure 9-28.

The required information exists as columns in the STAFF, CUSTOMER, SALES, ITEMS, and INVENTRY tables. The resulting rows will consist of all columns from the different tables in the SELECT column-list. In order to retrieve all particulars with one query, a JOIN must be performed. Recall that there is no specific dBASE IV SQL relational operator or keyword to signal a JOIN; rather, the number of entries in the table-list of the FROM clause indicates that tables are to be joined. To limit the number of rows being returned, the WHERE clause must specify some relationships (i.e., common columns) among the different rows to be combined. The search conditions

```
AND  ST.LASTNAME = 'Smith'
AND  ST.FIRSTNAME LIKE 'Ro%'
```

establish the starting point for this query by retrieving all rows from the STAFF table that satisfy the LASTNAME and FIRSTNAME requirements. Then the applicable

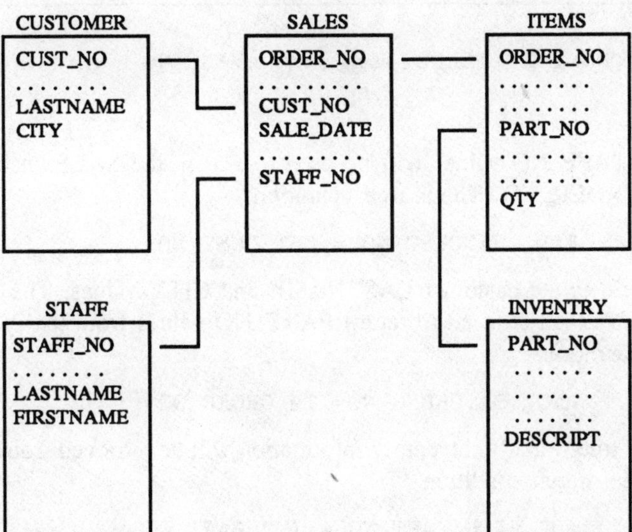

Figure 9-27. Five-table JOIN relationships

```
SELECT
ST.LASTNAME,ST.FIRSTNAME
,CST.LASTNAME,CITY
,SA.ORDER_NO,SALE_DATE
,ITM.PART_NO
,INV.DESCRIPT

FROM
STAFF          ST
,CUSTOMER      CST
,SALES         SA
,ITEMS         ITM
,INVENTRY      INV

WHERE
    ST.STAFF_NO=SA.STAFF_NO
AND SA.CUST_NO=CST.CUST_NO
AND SA.ORDER_NO=ITM.ORDER_NO
AND ITM.PART_NO=INV.PART_NO

AND ST.LASTNAME='Smith'
AND ST.FIRSTNAME LIKE'RO%'

    ORDER BY SALE_DATE DESC
    ;
```

Figure 9-28. SELECT using a five-table JOIN

STAFF_NO values will be used to access the SALES table to obtain CUST_NO and ORDER_NO. The search condition

```
AND  SA.CUST_NO = CST.CUST_NO
```

selects the customer LASTNAME and CITY values. The order number from the sales table will be used to return PART_NO values from the ITEMS table where the search condition

```
AND  SA.ORDER_NO=ITM.ORDER_NO
```

is true. Finally, inventory information will be retrieved from the INVENTRY table where the search condition

```
AND  ITM.PART_NO = INV.PART_NO
```

is true. If no WHERE search conditions were coded, the total number of rows returned would be the *cartesian product* of the total number of rows in each table. Thus, the tables in the examples (CUSTOMER 24, STAFF 12 INVENTRY 33, SALES 25, ITEMS 43) would return 10,216,800 rows if no JOIN search conditions were specified. The authors attempted just such a query, but never received a response from dBASE IV SQL. Needless to say, care must be taken when coding these types of queries.

In the example in Figure 9-28, STAFF and SALES are combined on the common column staff number (STAFF_NO). However, the column name, STAFF_NO, is spelled the same way in both tables. Therefore, it is necessary to qualify this column name with either its table name or a correlation name. The search condition

```
ST.STAFF_NO = SA.STAFF_NO
```

utilizes correlation names ST and SA. In this query, table names may also be utilized uniquely to identify a column:

```
STAFF.STAFF_NO = SALES.STAFF_NO
```

In this example, you have the luxury of choice. However, there is one instance where correlation names must be used. *When a table is joined to itself, correlation names must be used,* because the table name is the same and may not be used to qualify its column names.

Although not required, another strong candidate for correlated name use is within a *correlated subselect*. In this instance, ease of coding and self-documentation justify its use.

Joining a Table to Itself

A list of staff members must be created for each employee and his or her manager. The results must contain the managers' first and last names, the staff members' first and last names, and the employees' staff numbers. Since the STAFF table contains both managers and employees, it must be joined to itself where the supervisor number of an employee is equal to the staff number of a manager. The solution appears in Figure 9-29.

In the example in Figure 9-29, correlation names must be utilized to distinguish between managers and employees. As the table names are the same, they cannot be used

```
SELECT   MGR.LASTNAME
        ,MGR.FIRSTNAME
        ,EMP.LASTNAME
        ,EMP.FIRSTNAME
        ,EMP.STAFF_NO
FROM STAFF MGR
   ,STAFF EMP
 WHERE
   EMP.SUPERVISOR = MGR.STAFF_NO
;
```

Figure 9-29. Table joined to itself

to qualify the duplicate column names. In this example, the correlation names also assist in documenting which columns are managers and which are employees. Even though correlation names may be from one to ten characters long, they serve more utility when more meaningful.

GROUP BY Clause

The SELECT statements in Figures 9-22 and 9-23 only returned one row. The implied set or group of rows is either the entire table or just those rows with a location of Los Angeles. To obtain an average salary for each location, dBASE IV SQL allows multiple groupings to be broken out based on matching values in one or more columns. In Figure 9-30, one results row will be returned for every set of rows that have the same location.

```
SELECT AVG(SALARY),LOCATION
     FROM STAFF
     GROUP BY LOCATION;
```

Figure 9-30. Average salary grouped by location

A column must be specified in a GROUP BY clause if it is not part of an aggregate function in the column-list of the SELECT statement. The query in Figure 9-31 would cause an error because the GROUP BY clause does not reference the DESCRIPT column. You may know that PART_NO and DESCRIPT are functionally dependent (i.e., if description changes, so must the part number and conversely), but dBASE IV SQL does not. Therefore, the query is ambiguous. You must specify which columns control the groupings.

```
SELECT AVG(UNITCOST)
     ,PART_NO
     ,DESCRIPT
     FROM STAFF
     GROUP BY PART_NO;
```

Figure 9-31. GROUP BY error

Figure 9-32 corrects the grouping error by adding column DESCRIPT to the GROUP BY clause.

In summary, the GROUP BY clause breaks up the large group (entire table or all rows based on a WHERE clause) into smaller groups based on matching column values.

```
SELECT AVG(UNITCOST)
      ,PART_NO
      ,DESCRIPT
      FROM STAFF
      GROUP BY PART_NO;
                ,DESCRIPT;
```

Figure 9-32. Corrected GROUP BY query

HAVING Clause

Grouped results may be made more selective through use of the HAVING clause, which adds search conditions to the final selection criteria. The search conditions in a HAVING clause are applied to a group or groups and not the original selected rows. Multiple search conditions may be specified in a HAVING clause, which must be combined by AND and/or OR keywords. Recall that aggregate functions may be utilized without a GROUP BY clause. In this case, the HAVING clause criteria will be exercised against the results of the implied group or the one results row.

To illustrate, produce a total unit cost for all inventory items where parts are located in more than one geographic location. *Hint:* The INVENTRY table has one entry for each item/part at each location. The solution appears in Figure 9-33.

```
SELECT DESCRIPT
        ,SUM (ON_HAND*UNITCOST)
 FROM INVENTRY
GROUP BY DESCRIPT
HAVING COUNT (*) > 1
;
```

Figure 9-33. GROUP BY with a HAVING clause

Except for the HAVING clause, the query in Figure 9-33 is a basic SELECT and GROUP BY. Since there is no WHERE clause, all rows in the INVENTRY table will be accessed to form the initial groups. Once the groups are established, the HAVING clause will be applied. The clause

```
HAVING COUNT (*) > 1
```

refers to an aggregate function that is not in the SELECT column-list. This is no cause for concern, as each group will have an implied count for the number of rows that were used to derive it. As a matter of fact, any aggregate function may be used within a HAVING clause as long as the column names were defined in one or more of the tables in the FROM table-list.

Subselect

Subselect in a Query

A subselect may be used to derive a value or a set of values for use in a SELECT statement. Similarly, a subselect may also refer to a subselect. The number of subselects is limited by system constraints and performance considerations.

Subselects are used in WHERE and HAVING clauses to return one or more values for a search condition. Note that a subselect that returns *only* one value may be coded immediately to the right of the comparison operator in the search condition of a WHERE or HAVING search condition. A subselect that returns more than one value must be preceded by the IN, ALL, or ANY keyword in the search condition. ANY and ALL, although not documented for dBASE IV SQL, are part of the SQL language. The authors found that ANY and ALL did not cause syntax errors in dBASE IV SQL.

The ALL keyword indicates that the comparison must evaluate as true for every value returned by the subselect. The ANY keyword, in contrast, indicates that the comparison must evaluate as true for at least one value returned by the subselect. The SQL language standard specifies that ALL is also true *if the subselect returns no values*. This is not currently supported by dBASE IV SQL. The IN keyword indicates that the search condition must be satisfied for one of a set of values returned by the subselect. The ANY and IN keywords are functionally identical in the number of rows that will be returned, but internal processing differs. ANY is part of the SQL language standard.

To illustrate the use of a subselect, provide a list of part numbers, part descriptions, quantity on hand, and location of inventory for parts where the quantity ordered is greater than the quantity in inventory. The solution appears in Figure 9-34.

```
SELECT INVENTRY.PART_NO,DESCRIPT
        ,ON_HAND,LOCATION
FROM INVENTRY
WHERE INVENTRY.PART_NO
 IN (
    SELECT ITEMS.PART_NO
       FROM ITEMS
    WHERE
     ITEMS.QTY > INVENTRY.ON_HAND
    )
;
```

Figure 9-34. Query with subselect

The subselect in the example in Figure 9-34 is executed only once to build the list of values for the IN clause. When the subselect completes, the "outer" query will retrieve rows from the INVENTRY table based in the values generated from the "inner" query. In this example, the authors used the table names to qualify column names that existed in both tables. Optionally, correlation names could have been utilized.

Because the subselect could return more than one value for PART_NO, the IN keyword must be specified.

Testing for Existence

Sometimes it is necessary to check for the existence of a certain search condition or value. In a very active business, customers are constantly placing orders. To process and ship an order usually requires three to five days. If multiple orders to the same customer are combined, processing and shipping costs can be reduced. When an order is received, we need to know whether additional orders for the same customer exist. The solution appears in Figure 9-35.

```
SELECT COMPANY,CUST_NO
 FROM CUSTOMER
 WHERE CUST_NO = '??????'
    AND EXISTS
    (SELECT*
      FROM SALES
      WHERE = CUST_NO = '??????')
;
```

Figure 9-35. EXISTS subselect

Question marks are used in Figure 9-35 to indicate that values must be supplied. Of interest is the asterisk in the EXISTS subselect:

```
AND EXISTS
(SELECT *
  FROM SALES
  WHERE = CUST_NO = '??????')
```

Actually, *no values will be returned, but a true or false condition will be set*. Therefore, the column-list in the subselect may specify an asterisk or one or more column names of the SALES table. Processing begins with the outer query to COMPANY and then accesses the inner table (SALES). Only when both search conditions are satisfied will COMPANY and CUST_NO be returned.

Nonexistence may also be checked. For example, as a result of "keypunch errors" (the catch-all term for design and coding errors), some orders may exist on the SALES table that do not have valid customers in the CUSTOMER table. Or, in other terms, there are CUST_NO values in the CUSTOMER table that do not have matching CUST_NO values in the SALES table. The solution is to create a query that returns rows where a search condition is not true (NOT EXISTS) in another table. The solution appears in Figure 9-36.

```
SELECT ORDER_NO ,SALE_DATE
     ,STAFF_NO, COST_NO,INVOICED
 FROM SALES SA
 WHERE NOT EXISTS
 (SELECT * FROM CUSTOMER CS
  WHERE CS.CUST_NO = SA.CUST_NO)
;
```

Figure 9-36. NOT EXISTS subselect

Processing begins with the retrieval of the first customer number value from the SALES table. Then the CUSTOMER table is accessed for a matching customer number. The inner table is scanned until a match is found or the end of the CUSTOMER table is encountered. If a corresponding customer is *not* found, one row is listed from the SALES table. This process is repeated for each row of the SALES table. *Note:* The NOT EXISTS subselect is the only method to report on *referential integrity* violations. Referential Integrity has become the generally accepted locution to encompass two basic relational integrity rules: Entity Integrity and Integrity of Reference. Entity Integrity states that a primary key must be unique and may never be NULL. Integrity of Reference states that foreign keys of a dependent table must exactly match the primary key of a related parent table or the foreign key must be NULL.

Correlated Subselect

The authors made reference to correlated subselects while discussing joins in the example in Figure 9-28 (SELECT using a five table JOIN). We said that correlation names are recommended when coding a correlated subselect. Other SQL language processors, such as IBM's DB2, halt execution if column names are not qualified; dBASE IV SQL does not. Instead, *dBASE IV SQL returns no rows if correlation/qualified names are not used with a correlated subselect*. This oversight should be corrected in the next release of dBASE IV SQL. Let us state a problem and then clarify this situation in the explanation of the solution.

A report is required that will show which orders require a greater number of any one item than is on hand in inventory at any location. The solution appears in Figure 9-37.

In this example, lowercase letters are used to identify the outer table correlation names and uppercase letters for the inner table correlation names. Recall that dBASE IV

```
SELECT itm.*
 FROM ITEMS itm
WHERE
     QTY >
    (
    SELECT MAX (ON_HAND)
     FROM INVENTRY INV
    WHERE INV.PART_NO = itm.PART_NO
    )
;
```

Figure 9-37. CORRELATED subselect

SQL will fold lowercase letters to uppercase as long as the characters are not part of a literal.

At first glance, the thought that comes to mind is, "How do you know if this query works?" As queries become more and more complex, you really cannot be sure if too few or too many rows are being returned. The best way to verify your results is to disassemble the query into single SELECT statements. Since the inner query will return a value for the outer query, let us begin there:

```
SELECT MAX (ON_HAND)
  FROM INVENTRY INV
WHERE INV.PART_NO = itm.PART_NO
```

As shown, this query will not run unless a value is substituted for the part number of the ITEMS table (i.e., itm.PART_NO). After the correct substitution,

```
SELECT MAX (ON_HAND)
  FROM INVENTRY INV
WHERE INV.PART_NO = '000120'
```

one maximum numeric value for ON_HAND will be returned. This value may manually replace the subselect:

```
SELECT itm.*
  FROM ITEMS itm
WHERE
      QTY > your-max-value
```

However, we still need to *correlate* to the same part number that was used to retrieve the maximum value from the INVENTRY table.

```
SELECT itm.*
  FROM ITEMS itm
```

```
WHERE
     QTY > your-max-value
 AND itm.PART_NO = '000120'
```

Now, the outer query will simulate one iteration of the original correlated subselect. The steps taken to test this query are the same that dBASE IV SQL would utilize to process the query in the solution. The correlated subselect in the inner query will be executed once for every row of the outer query. This is necessary because a maximum value for ON_HAND in the INVENTRY table must be derived for each PART_NO in the ITEMS table. The qualified column names in the WHERE clause

```
WHERE INV.PART_NO = itm.PART_NO
```

are necessary to correlate the inner and outer values. Even if the column names were spelled differently, correlation names would still be required.

Correlated Subselect with JOINs

After being presented with the output of the correlated subselect, the typical user responds with, "I'm sorry, I wanted to see the company name also!" The good news is that the company name is in the CUSTOMER table. The bad news is that there is no direct link between the ITEMS and CUSTOMER tables. The SALES table will have to be used as a junction relationship to tie ITEMS order numbers to CUSTOMER customer numbers.

To accomplish the retrieval of company name, it will be necessary to JOIN CUSTOMER, SALES, and ITEMS tables (Fig 9-38). NO SALES data must be in the output; therefore, SALES column names are not referenced in the SELECT column-list. Note that

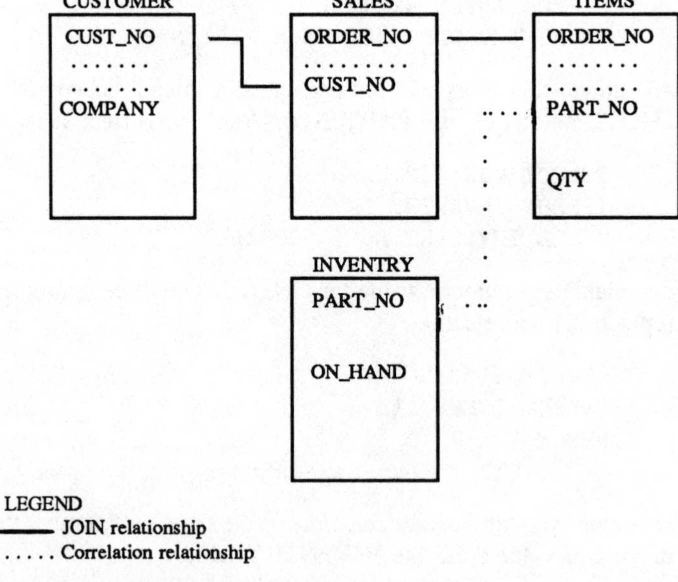

Figure 9-38. JOIN and correlation relationships

the order number and customer number columns of the SALES table are part of search conditions in the WHERE clause. The solution appears in Figure 9-39.

```
SELECT itm.*
|   ,COMPANY
 FROM ITEMS itm
|         ,CUSTOMER CS ,SALES SA
WHERE
|   itm.ORDER_NO = SA.ORDER_NO
|  AND    SA.CUST_NO = CS.CUST_NO
|  AND
    QTY >
   (
   SELECT MAX (ON_HAND)
    FROM INVENTRY INV
   WHERE INV.PART_NO = itm.PART_NO
   )
;
```

Figure 9-39. Correlated subselect with JOIN

All the new coding for this query is indicated with vertical bars at the left of each new line. The COMPANY column has been added to the SELECT column-list, CUSTOMER and SALES have been added to the FROM table-list, and additional search conditions have been added to the WHERE clause to control the JOIN process. Correlation names are still utilized in the subselect.

Four tables are accessed in this query. The correlated subselect on INVENTRY determines which ITEMS table rows will be joined to rows of the SALES and CUSTOMER tables. The relationship of customers to orders and items is controlled in the WHERE predicate by the following search conditions:

```
 itm.ORDER_NO = SA.ORDER_NO
AND  SA.CUST_NO = CS.CUST_NO
```

In this example, correlation names are not required, but they facilitate coding and ease comprehension of what appears to be a complicated query.

UNION Operator

The UNION operator is used to concatenate the *results* from two or more queries and remove all duplicates. Unlike a JOIN (no specific relational operator) where columns are added to rows, a UNION adds rows from two or more outer queries to the final results table. A JOIN processes columns of rows horizontally and a UNION processes rows vertically. The JOIN query in Figure 9-40 would produce the results illustrated in Figure 9-41.

```
SELECT TA.COL_A,TA.COL_B
      ,TB.COL_1,TB.COL_2
FROM TABLE_A TA ,TABLE_B TB
      WHERE TA.COL_A = TB.COL_1
;
```

Figure 9-40. JOIN query

TA.COL_A	TA.COL_B	TB.COL_1	TB.COL_2
AAAAA	more data	AAAAA	unknown
CCCCC	a name	CCCCC	a name
DDDD	a number	DDDD	data

Figure 9-41. JOIN query results

In Figure 9-41, columns from two tables are part of *each* results row. Each results row consists of four columns. The UNION illustrated in Figure 9-42 will demonstrate the differences between a JOIN and a UNION.

```
      SELECT COL_A,COL_B
            FROM TABLE_A
      UNION
      SELECT COL_1,COL_2
            FROM TABLE_B
;
```

Figure 9-42. UNION query

The results rows from the two tables will be concatenated to produce the results shown in Figure 9-43.

Table	COL_1	COL_2
TABLE_A	AAAAA	more data
TABLE_B	AAAAA	unknown
TABLE_A	CCCCC	a name
TABLE_A	DDDD	a number
TABLE_B	DDDD	data

Figure 9-43. UNION query results

The results consist of two columns and five rows. Each SELECT column-list specified only two columns. Since duplicates are removed, there is only one entry for:

```
| CCCCC    | a name
```

Both TABLE_A and TABLE_B had a row where COL_1 and COL_2 contained the same values. Did this row come from TABLE_A or TABLE_B? Does it matter? Could this cause concern (i.e., a problem)? If required, can duplicates be retrieved? If an ORDER BY is not specified, what is the sequence of the results? Each of these questions is a design consideration and must be addressed separately.

- Did this row come from TABLE_A or TABLE_B?
  Recall that dBASE IV SQL is navigation-free. However, internal processing will usually present the first row received. This is due to sort criteria.
- Does it matter?
  It should not. Since both rows consisting of only two columns must contain the identical data before duplicates (two or more) are removed, the correct value is always returned.
- Could this cause concern (i.e., a problem)?
  Absolutely! One of the authors experienced an occasion where two transaction files were being combined with a UNION. Even though uniqueness was guaranteed by date and time columns, the actual queries only specified account number and money fields in their respective column-lists. Since several accounts had identical transaction amounts, transactions were lost.
- If required, can duplicates be retrieved?
  By definition of a UNION, all duplicates are removed. Therefore, it is the responsibility of application developers to code queries in such a way that the applicable column-list cannot return duplicates. Additionally, tables must be designed to provide columns (e.g., date, time) that will allow for unique rows.
- If an ORDER BY is not specified, what is the sequence of the results?

A sort will always be performed to remove duplicates. Currently, the default sort criterion for the results is ascending sequence on the fields specified in the column-list. This is not documented. The authors strongly recommend that an ORDER BY clause always be specified to protect applications from future dBASE IV SQL enhancements.

To be combined, *the data types of the corresponding columns must be compatible*. Each SELECT column-list must have the same number of columns and the data types in the corresponding columns must be of the same type and length. If ordering is required, the ORDER BY clause must be entered after the last query in the UNION. The ORDER BY clause must specify integers (e.g., corresponding column positions) to identify the column sort criteria. Therefore, it is not possible to sort the results on a column that is not part of the SELECT column-list.

Basic SELECT with a UNION

Due to some entry errors, staff and company data have been incorrectly entered. It seems that some staff members' names have been entered into the customer table. A list of both customers' and staff members' names must be created. The solution appears in Figure 9-44.

```
SELECT FIRSTNAME,LASTNAME,'STAFF'
     FROM STAFF
UNION
SELECT FIRSTNAME,LASTNAME,'CUST-'
     FROM CUSTOMER
ORDER BY 2,3
;
```

Figure 9-44. Basic UNION SELECT

Effectively, there are two distinct outer queries in the example in Figure 9-44. The UNION relational operator will combine each query's output into one results table. An ORDER BY clause is utilized to sort the output by LASTNAME and literal constant. The literal constant serves two purposes. First, it identifies which table (CUSTOMER, STAFF) input the row. Second, in the event that the same first and last names exist in both tables, the literal constant ensures that rows from the different tables cannot be duplicated and, therefore, will not be removed. Recall that corresponding column data types and lengths must be identical. FIRSTNAME and LASTNAME in either table are character data and are the same length. However, *the literal constants (character data) must also be the same length*. It was necessary to pad 'CUST-' with one extra character (in this case, a dash) so that it would be the same length as 'STAFF'. Padding of literals may utilize any character. A dash was used in the example for clarity.

UNION with Aggregate Values

The Human Resources department requires a list of managers and their respective salaries, plus the total salary of all who report directly to them. The list should be sorted so that the managers' information prints before the total salary information. *Hint:* The supervisor's column in a supervisor's row will contain zeroes. The solution appears in Figure 9-45.

```
SELECT STAFF NO ,SALARY + 0,'1'
      FROM STAFF
      WHERE SUPERVISOR = '000000'
UNION
SELECT SUPERVISOR,SUM(SALARY),'2'
      FROM STAFF
      WHERE SUPERVISOR != '000000'
      GROUP BY SUPERVISOR
ORDER BY 1,3
;
```

Figure 9-45. UNION with aggregate functions

The first SELECT returns the salaries of supervisors. The expression SALARY + 0 in the first SELECT is necessary to match up with the data type and length of the aggregate expression SUM(SALARY) in the second query. The literal constants (i.e., '1', '2') will force the supervisor rows to be listed before the respective salary summary rows. Note that the sort criterion

```
ORDER BY 1,3
```

specifies the literal constant second. A GROUP BY clause is required in the second query because of the aggregate expression SUM(SALARY).

Report with Two Breaks Utilizing One Query

At the beginning of this chapter, the authors said they would demonstrate how to generate a report with two levels of breaks from one SQL query. The following query will list the sales for each staff member by customer and order. One detail will be created for each order and summaries will be shown by customer and staff member. The solution appears in Figure 9-46.

DML does not provide a method to summarize detail lines. Therefore, it is necessary to provide a separate GROUP BY for each report break. Each of the three queries must process all the related tables as if they were executing alone. The final ORDER BY sorts the results into the correct report sequence. The literal constants (i. e.,

```
SELECT LASTNAME,SA.CUST_NO
      ,SA.ORDER_NO,SUM (QTY*UNITCOST)
 FROM STAFF ST,SALES SA
    ,ITEMS  ITM,INVENTRY IV
  WHERE ITM.PART_NO = IV.PART_NO
  AND ITM.ORDER_NO = SA.ORDER_NO
  AND SA.STAFF_NO = ST.STAFF_NO
 GROUP BY LASTNAME,SA.CUTS_NO
                  ,SA.ORDER_NO
UNION
SELECT LASTNAME ,SA.CUST_NO,'999999'
      ,SUM (QTY*UNITCOST)
 FROM STAFF ST ,SALES SA
    ,ITEMS  ITM ,INVENTRY IV
  WHERE ITM.PART_NO = IV.PART_NO
  AND ITM.ORDER_NO = SA.ORDER_NO
  AND SA.STAFF_NO = ST.STAFF_NO
 GROUP BY LASTNAME,SA.CUST_NO
UNION
SELECT LASTNAME ,'999999', '999999'
     ,SUM (QTY*UNITCOST)
FROM STAFF ST ,SALES SA
     ,ITEMS ITM ,INVENTRY IV
  WHERE ITM.PART_NO = IV.PART_NO
  AND ITM.ORDER_NO = SA.ORDER_NO
  AND SA.STAFF_NO = ST.STAFF_NO
 GROUP BY LASTNAME
ORDER BY 1 ,2 ,3;
```

Figure 9-46. Query for a report with two breaks

'999999') are necessary to support the GROUP BY clauses and to ensure the sort sequence.

Additional Data Manipulation

SQL, or rather its DML subset, is heavily biased toward retrieval. As a matter of fact, over eighty-five percent of DML is retrieval in nature. Recall that SQL is based on a relational model that was developed to support relationships between entities. To traverse these relationships requires sophisticated access techniques or retrieval. That is why all the previous examples were SELECT statements. Since dBASE IV SQL is, in its own right, a data base management system, there must be additional facilities for insertion, deletion, and modification.

DML provides for additional manipulation with the INSERT, DELETE, and UPDATE statements. These statements allow for search conditions that, fortunately, utilize the same search conditions (i.e., WHERE clauses) as SELECT statements.

INSERT Statement

The purpose of the INSERT statement is to add one or more rows to a table. Values must be provided for every column of each row. These values can be specifically coded in the INSERT statement or data can be retrieved from one or more tables in the form of a subselect statement. Figures 9-47 and 9-48, respectively, illustrate a basic INSERT statement and an INSERT statement with a subselect. The columns to receive values may be explicitly entered in a column-list; if the list is omitted, an implied list is assumed. An implied column-list consists of the column names and sequence as they were defined when the table was created. Also, data types and lengths must match. This matching of data types and lengths is very similar to what was required when processing SELECTs with the UNION operator. An exception to the data lengths requirement exists when numeric or character literal constants in the value-list may be shorter than their receiving columns.

```
        INSERT INTO <table-name>
               [(column-list)]
        VALUES
              < (value-list) >
  ;
```

Figure 9-47. Basic INSERT statement

The items of data in the value-list must sequentially correspond, one to one, to the names in the column-list. If a column-list consisted of

```
(COLUMN_1, COLUMN_2, COLUMN_3)
```

and its corresponding value-list was

```
('VALUE-1', 'VALUE-2', 'VALUE-3')
```

then 'VALUE-1' would be moved into COLUMN_1, 'VALUE-2' would be moved into COLUMN_2, and 'VALUE-3' would be moved into COLUMN_3. Note that the column-list in Figure 9-47 is optional. If the column-list is not coded, the data in the value-list must match the sequence of columns at table creation. Also note that one or more table column names may be absent from the column-list. If the table consisted of six columns and the column-list contained three columns,

```
(COLUMN_1, COLUMN_5, COLUMN_6)
```

its corresponding value-list

```
('VALUE-1', 'VALUE-2', 'VALUE-3')
```

could not provide data for columns that are not in the column-list. All unnamed columns would default to blanks. At present, dBASE IV SQL has no mechanism to tag a column's value as unknown.

The INSERT with a subselect is similar to the basic INSERT statement except that the input values come from another table or tables via a subselect. A message indicating the number of rows inserted will be generated after the INSERT statement completes.

```
INSERT INTO <table-name>
     [(column-list)]
SELECT * | <column-list>
     FROM table-list
     [WHERE clause(s)]
;
```

Figure 9-48. INSERT statement with subselect

The INSERT column-list must implicitly or explicitly sequentially correspond to the SELECT column-list. Data types and lengths must match. Again, the columns in the INSERT column-list may be same length as or longer than the columns in the SELECT column-list. Let us look at some examples.

Copying Tables

In order to test a new customer application where the CUST_NO must be increased to seven characters from six, it is necessary to copy the production customer table to a test customer table. To facilitate testing, we only want to copy twenty percent of the production CUSTOMER table. The solution appears in Figure 9-49.

```
INSERT INTO TCUST
     SELECT*
          FROM CUSTOMER
          WHERE CUST_NO LIKE'%1'
          OR  CUST_NO LIKE'%2'
;
```

Figure 9-49. Copying a table

In the example in Figure 9-49, both tables have the same *physical* attributes, except that the CUST_NO column in the CUSTOMER (production) table is only six characters long. They have the same number of columns, and their remaining corresponding columns have the same data types and lengths. Note that their respective column names *do not* have to be spelled the same, because dBASE IV SQL will move the first column, second column, etc., of table CUSTOMER to the first column, second column, etc., of TCUST regardless of column names.

In order to restrict the selection to twenty percent, two LIKE clauses are utilized to restrict selection to customers with a customer number ending with '1' or '2'. The assumption is that CUST_NO is equally distributed on its last digit.

ADDING NEW ROWS

To fully test the new customer application, it is necessary to add a row with a seven-character customer number. The solution appears in Figure 9-50.

```
INSERT INTO TCUST
      (cust_no7 ,address ,lastname
      ,firstname ,company ,state)
VALUES
      ('9999999','123 Main','Williams'
      ,'Joseph','comp X','Pa'
;
```

Figure 9-50. Basic INSERT statement

The values specified in the value-list must correspond to the column names in the column-list. The value '999999' will be moved to the CUST_NO7 column, the value '123 Main' will be moved to the ADDRESS column, etc. One row will be inserted.

When the table TCUST was created, its columns were sequenced: CUST_NO7, COMPANY, LASTNAME, FIRSTNAME, ADDRESS, CITY, STATE, and ZIP. The column-list in Figure 9-50 references the columns in a different sequence and two columns are absent. Will this INSERT complete? What values will be in the unreferenced columns?

This INSERT will complete correctly because no data types and lengths were incompatible. The value in each column will depend on corresponding locations of values and column names in their respective lists, and not the table's physical definition. The unreferenced *columns* will not contain data and will appear to contain blanks when referenced in other SQL statements.

OTHER INSERT STATEMENTS

When developing an application or converting data for dBASE IV SQL tables, it may be necessary to extract information from several temporary tables. The example in Figure 9-51 shows how to populate one table from a JOIN of two other tables.

```
INSERT INTO t_table
     (col_1,col_2....,col_12)
SELECT col_a,col_e,....col_m
     FROM in_tab_1,in_tab_2
     WHERE col_a = col_m
;
```

Figure 9-51. INSERT statement with JOIN

To speed up a long-running application, it may be necessary to create a temporary summary table. Figure 9-52 illustrates one method of providing summary data for an INSERT statement.

```
INSERT INTO s_table
     (col_1,sum_info)
SELECT col_a,SUM(num_detail)
     FROM d_table
     GROUP by col_a
;
```

Figure 9-52. INSERT statement with GROUP BY

UPDATE Statement

The purpose of the dBASE IV SQL UPDATE statement is to modify the values of one or more columns in one or more rows of one table. The rows to be updated are determined by WHERE clause search conditions. If no WHERE clause is present, all rows of a specified table will be updated. During interactive SQL, dBASE IV SQL will prompt for a confirmation before executing this type of UPDATE. Depressing the Escape key will cancel the UPDATE action. The format of the UPDATE statement is shown in Figure 9-53.

```
UPDATE <table name>
     SET <column name = expression>
     [,column name = expression] ....
     [WHERE clause]
;
```

Figure 9-53. UPDATE statement format

```
UPDATE STAFF
     SET SALARY = SALARY * 1.1
     WHERE LOCATION = 'NEW YORK
     AND COMMISION < 8.0
;
```

Figure 9-54. Simple UPDATE

At a minimum, a table name and one column name expression set are required. An expression may consist of literal constants, program variables, or column names of the table being updated. The components of an expression may not reference columns of another table. The WHERE clause may specify one or more search conditions for related columns of the table to be modified or may be more complex and include subselects. As in a SELECT statement, the number of rows to be affected is controlled with the search condition(s).

A good example of an UPDATE statement would be a ten percent salary increase for all employees located in New York who do not receive a commission that is greater than eight percent. Figure 9-54 demonstrates this increase.

The STAFF table is searched until a row is located that matches the WHERE clause. That one row's SALARY column is updated and the search continues to update all subsequent rows that match the search condition until the end of the table is detected.

In another example, we need to indicate that an order is invoiced when all the items of a given order are shipped. Figure 9-55 illustrates the several levels of subselects necessary to meet such a requirement.

The nested subselects actually represent a correlated subselect. The purpose of the correlated subselect is to return item ORDER_NO values that have all their items flagged as shipped. These order numbers become the values for the IN clause of the first search condition in the UPDATE statement.

It would not be possible to utilize one UPDATE statement to set salary to total a compensation that would include salary and commission. Additional commission data for unit cost and quantity sold is located in two separate tables. Recall that *expressions in a SET clause may not reference columns from other tables*.

DELETE Statement

The purpose of a dBASE IV SQL DELETE statement is to delete one or more rows from a table. Note that columns may be updated, but not deleted. Therefore, when a row is deleted, the respective data values for its columns no longer exist.

The rows to be deleted are determined by WHERE clause search condition(s). If no WHERE clause is present, all rows of a specified table will be deleted. During interactive SQL, dBASE IV SQL will prompt for a confirmation before executing this type of DELETE. Depressing the Escape (ESC) key will cancel the DELETE action. The format of a DELETE statement is shown in Figure 9-56.

```
UPDATE SALES SA
 SET INVOICED = .T.
WHERE SA.ORDER_NO IN
(
SELECT ITM1.ORDER_NO
 FROM ITEMS ITM1
 WHERE ITM1.SHIPPED = .T.
 AND ITM1.SHIPPED = ALL
 (
     SELECT ITM2.SHIPPED
      FROM ITEMS ITM2
      WHERE
      ITM2.ORDER_NO = ITM1.ORDER_NO
    )
)
;
```

Figure 9-55. UPDATE with nested subselects

```
DELETE FROM < table name>
     [WHERE clause]
;
```

Figure 9-56. DELETE statement format

An example of a DELETE statement would be the need to remove all orders that have ship dates that are older than one year (Figure 9-57).

```
DELETE FROM SALES
     WHERE INVOICED = .T.
     AND SALE_DATE < DATE() - 365
;
```

Figure 9-57. Basic DELETE statement

The DELETE in Figure 9-57 utilizes a compound search condition to test for an invoiced search condition and check for SALE_DATEs that are less than the current date minus 365 days. The dBASE IV DATE() function is used to return the current system

```
DELETE FROM SALES SA
WHERE SALE_DATE < DATE() - 365
AND SA.ORDER_NO IN
(
SELECT ITM1.ORDER_NO
 FROM ITEMS ITM1
 WHERE ITM1.SHIPPED = .T.
 AND ITM1.SHIPPED = ALL
 (
    SELECT ITM2.SHIPPED
     FROM ITEMS ITM2
     WHERE
     ITM2.ORDER_NO = ITM1.ORDER_NO
    )
)
;
```

Figure 9-58. DELETE with subselects

date. The use of dBASE IV functions in SQL statements greatly simplifies application development.

Search conditions in DELETE statements may also include subselects. The UPDATE example in Figure 9-55 may be modified to delete SALES rows that have had all their related items shipped and have a SALE_DATE that is over one year old (Figure 9-58).

Figure 9-58 illustrates the DELETE statement necessary to purge SALES rows that are more than one year old. Again, the dBASE IV DATE() function is utilized to determine the date and subselects are employed to verify that all the related items have been shipped.

If logging is in effect as a result of BEGIN TRANSACTION/END TRANSACTION processing, rows will not be physically deleted from a dBASE IV SQL table until an END TRANSACTION is processed.

Saving Query Results

The foregoing queries were somewhat sophisticated. Isn't it a pity that when execution completed all results data was lost? A query like SELECT using a five-table JOIN example could create results that, if processed by dBASE IV commands, would facilitate report and/or label creation. Another reason to save query results is to simplify DML coding. Large complicated queries could be broken down into smaller, less complex SELECT statements. Then each query's results could be examined and used as input to subsequent SELECT statements. Fortunately, dBASE IV SQL provides a DML clause to accomplish this.

```
SELECT s-column-list | *
     FROM ....
     [WHERE ......]
      [subquery]
     [GROUP BY .....]
         [HAVING .....]
 [UNION .............]

  SELECT .....

[ORDER BY .....]

    SAVE TO TEMP <table-name>
         [(t-column-list)]
         [KEEP]
;
```

Figure 9-59. SAVE TO TEMP clause

SAVE TO TEMP Clause

The SAVE TO TEMP clause allows the results data of a SELECT statement to be permanently or temporarily saved to a dBASE IV SQL table. Temporary tables will exist as long as the current data base remains active. The SAVE TO TEMP clause may only be utilized in SELECT statements, and when coded, must be the last clause of the statement. Figure 9-59 illustrates the SAVE TO TEMP clause.

s-column-list | * Either an explicit list of column names or an asterisk to create an implicit list of all the columns of a table. The sequence of the column names is significant in that it must correspond to the subsequent t-column-list.

table-name A standard eight character (maximum) table name that must be unique in the currently active data base. You cannot save to an existing table or you cannot save to the same temporary table. If the "TEMP" table must be in a specific order, use an ORDER BY clause to sequence the corresponding results table. Be creative. Let SQL summarize your data with a GROUP BY clause, join several tables, or even concatenate like rows from different tables with a UNION. It is difficult to combine two or more data bases when using the dBASE IV report writer. Utilize DML SELECT statements to combine data bases and then

```
SAVE TO TEMP ..... KEEP
```

to create and populate one .dbf data base for the report writer.

t-column-list — Optional list of names for columns in this "temp" table. This list corresponds positionally on a one-to-one basis to the columns in the s-column-list. Even though this parameter is optional, it is required when the results of the SELECT will contain fewer columns than the original table, a different column sequence, duplicate names, columns derived from an arithmetic expression, aggregate functions, constants, joined columns, etc. Unless the results data was generated by a

```
SELECT    *
```

or the s-column-list consists of only column names from one table, a t-column-list is required. If this parameter is omitted, the "temp" table's columns will have the same names and be in the same sequence as the columns in the s-column-list parameter.

KEEP — Allows the "TEMP" table to be permanently saved. To process this permanent table, it will be necessary to execute the DBDEFINE utility command.

Relational Operators and DML

Relational operators were discussed in Chapter 7. These relational operators are formally known as *Relational Algebra*. In this section, the operators will be discussed in more detail and DML examples will be demonstrated for each relational operator. A UNION is the only explicit relational operator; all other operators are supported (implied) with DML.

The operators break down into two groups. The first group is called the Traditional Set Operators and consists of UNION, DIFFERENCE, INTERSECTION, and PRODUCT (modified cartesian). The second group is known as the Special Relational Operators and consists of SELECT, PROJECT, JOIN, and DIVIDE.

A majority of the relational operators are supported by DML through subselects. A few points on subselects:

- Subselects can be nested. The number of nested subselects is limited by system resources.
- Subselects can retrieve data from other tables.
- If a match is found for the subselect, the result is then used for the next highest subselect (SELECT if highest-level) statement.
- When evaluating statements that contain subselects, DML evaluates the innermost SELECT first.

Traditional Set Operators

UNION

A UNION operation produces a results table composed of unique rows from two or more tables (Figure 9-60).

All rows consisting of the columns LASTNAME and FIRSTNAME are returned from the STAFF and CUSTOMER tables. Duplicates, if any, are removed.

```
SELECT LASTNAME,FIRSTNAME
    FROM STAFF
UNION
SELECT LASTNAME,FIRSTNAME
    FROM CUSTOMER
;
```

Figure 9-60. UNION operation

INTERSECTION

An INTERSECTION retrieves only those columns from two tables where the rows belong to both tables. The INTERSECTION operation is implemented with the WHERE EXISTS clause (Figure 9-61).

```
SELECT ORDER_NO
    FROM SALES
    WHERE EXISTS
  (SELECT ORDER_NO FROM ITEMS
   WHERE
   ITEMS.ORDER_NO = SALES.ORDER_NO
);
```

Figure 9-61. INTERSECTION operation

DIFFERENCE

The DIFFERENCE operator retrieves all rows that appear in the first but not the second of two tables. The DIFFERENCE operation is implemented with the WHERE NOT EXISTS clause (Figure 9-62).

PRODUCT

A PRODUCT operation retrieves all of the possible concatenated combinations of one row from each of two or more tables. This is similar to a JOIN operation without any search conditions (WHERE clause). Note that the data returned will be what you requested; however, it may not be usable owing to the exorbitant number of rows (Figure 9-63).

The column-list in Figure 9-63 requests all columns from both tables. The table name qualification is required to control the sequence of columns in the output.

```
SELECT ORDER_NO
    FROM SALES
    WHERE NOT EXISTS
 (SELECT ORDER_NO FROM ITEMS
  WHERE
  ITEMS.ORDER_NO = SALES.ORDER_NO
);
```

Figure 9-62. DIFFERENCE operation

```
SELECT ITEMS.*,INVENTRY.*
    FROM ITEMS,INVENTRY
;
```

Figure 9-63. PRODUCT operation

Special Relational Operators

SELECTION

The SELECTION operator retrieves a horizontal subset (rows) of a given table based on a scalar comparison. The subset of rows is controlled by search conditions in the form of WHERE clauses (Figure 9-64).

```
SELECT*
    FROM CUSTOMERS
    WHERE STATE = 'NV'
;
```

Figure 9-64. SELECTION operation

PROJECTION

A PROJECTION operation produces a vertical subset (columns) of a given relation (one table) such that all duplicate rows are excluded. This is in contrast to the UNION operator where two or more tables are manipulated. Duplicate rows are removed from one SELECT statement through use of the DISTINCT keyword (Figure 9-65).

The results table produced by the query in Figure 9-65 will consist of a distinct list of inventory items no matter how many locations stock the same item.

```
SELECT DISTINCT PART NO,DESCRIPT
    FROM INVENTRY
;
```

Figure 9-65. PROJECTION Operation

JOIN

The JOIN operator retrieves data (concatenated rows) from two or more tables based on a successful comparison of one or more of the related rows' columns (Figure 9-66). This is in contrast to the PRODUCT operation that utilizes no search conditions.

```
SELECT ST.LASTNAME,COMPANY
           ORDER_NO
    FROM       STAFF ST
              ,CUSTOMER CS
              ,SALES SA
  WHERE ST.STAFF_NO = SA.STAFF_NO
  AND    SA.CUST_NO = CS.CUST_NO
;
```

Figure 9-66. JOIN operation

DIVISION

The DIVISION operator produces a one-column results table built from two tables—one table having one column (unary) and the other table having two columns (binary). If a value in the unary table matches a value in a specific column of the binary table, the parallel value becomes the column in the results table (Figure 9-67).

Performance Considerations

When designing applications that will utilize dBASE IV SQL tables, access requirements must be identified at the earliest possible time. Frequently accessed table columns will mandate that indices be available for DML processing. Recall that you cannot tell dBASE IV SQL how to retrieve data, but that you request what columns (i.e., column-list) and what rows (i.e., search conditions) to return. The SQL optimizer determines how to access the data for your request. *In order for the SQL optimizer to evaluate the most*

```
SELECT DISTINCT PART_NO
  FROM INVENTRY   IV1
WHERE NOT EXISTS
 (SELECT ORDER_NO
   FROM ITEMS IT
  WHERE NOT EXISTS
   (SELECT *
     FROM INVENTRY IV2
    WHERE IV2.PART_NO = IV1.PART_NO
    AND IV2.PART_NO = IT.PARTNO
    )
  )
;
```

Figure 9-67. DIVISION operation

efficient access strategy, the physical characteristics of all related tables must be available. These characteristics or statistics consist of the number of rows in each table, the number of pages in each table, available indices, table sequence, and distribution of column values within each index.

Needless to say, how an SQL query is coded will affect the method chosen by the SQL optimizer to access the tables related to a query. If an ORDER BY or a GROUP BY clause is utilized, all I/O is completed before the first results row is presented. If a search condition is improperly coded, the entire table may be accessed. If tables are not joined on common columns, a cartesian product may result. Some of the more important query coding considerations are as follows:

- All SELECT statements must use a column-list. No "SELECT *" statements should be used. Do not retrieve more columns than needed.

  Reason: Performance and ease of change. Results tables will be smaller, which will decrease sort time and reduce data transfer overhead.
- All WHERE clauses should include search conditions for indexed columns.

  Reason: Allows dBASE IV SQL to use indexes and decrease I/O.
- Even for indexed columns, avoid the use of leading '%' or '_' characters in a "LIKE" predicate:

  `WHERE COL_1 LIKE '%some value'`

  Reason: dBASE IV SQL will have to scan the entire index, which will result in more I/O.
- Avoid the use of subselects in an "IN" predicate.

  Reason: dBASE IV SQL will access the subselect table with a full table or index scan.
- Avoid the use of "NOT LIKE," "NOT IN," "NOT BETWEEN," and "NOT EXISTS" predicates.

Reason: Performance dBASE IV SQL will not use the index structure, but an index or table scan will be chosen.

- When a results table will be generated, do not retrieve more rows than necessary. Within the WHERE search condition, establish beginning and ending values. Use a LIKE predicate with trailing wild card characters or use a compound search condition:

```
WHERE  COL_1 >= beginning value
AND  COL-1 <= ending value
```

Reason: Locking and resource utilization will be minimized. The fewer rows retrieved, the less I/O there will be and the less memory and CPU time will be consumed.

- Use "ORDER BY" when retrieving rows in a specific sequence (cluster or otherwise).

Reason: Tables are in clustering sequence only after an initial load or a reorganization. Subsequent row inserts may be stored in any page. To guarantee the query sequence, you must use an "ORDER BY" clause.

- When using a single SELECT statement to check for the existence of a value, use:

```
SELECT COUNT(DISTINCT COL_1)
FROM table_1
WHERE COL_1 = :search-arg
```

Reason: Performance. dBASE IV SQL will stop the processing when it encounters the first row whose COL_1 equals the value in "SEARCH-ARG" of the WHERE search condition.

- Avoid use of the OR keyword on the same index column. A UNION will be more efficient. In the following two examples, assume that COL_1 is indexed.

Index is not considered:

```
SELECT COL_1 ,COL_2 FROM SOME_TAB
    WHERE COL_1 = 'SMITH'
    OR  COL_1 = 'JONES' ;
```

Index is considered:

```
SELECT COL_1 ,COL_2 FROM SOME_TAB
    WHERE COL_1 = 'SMITH'
UNION
SELECT COL_1 ,COL_2 FROM SOME_TAB
     WHERE COL_1 = 'JONES'
```

Reason: Performance. dBASE IV SQL will not consider use of an index when an OR keyword is encountered for a search condition on the same indexed column.

- If an index is composed of more than one column, be sure to include the first column in at least one search condition. Assume that an index exists on COL_1, COL_2, and COL_3.

Index is considered:

```
WHERE COL_1 = 'SMITH'
AND   COL_2 = 'ROBERT'
```

Index is also considered:

```
WHERE COL_1 = 'SMITH'
AND   COL_3 = 'other data'
```

Index is not considered:

```
WHERE COL_2 = 'ROBERT'
AND   COL_3 = 'other data'
```

Reason: dBASE IV SQL will have to scan the entire index, which will result in more I/O. This is similar to what occurs when a LIKE predicate utilizes leading wild card characters.

- Avoid derived or calculated expressions in search conditions. Do calculations prior to the actual DML execution. The expression

```
WHERE SALARY / 12 > 2000.00
```

will run slower than a search condition without an expression.

```
WHERE SALARY > 24000.00
```

Reason: Performance and tuning. The calculation will be performed for every row. Although PCs are fast, adding another 0.002 second to process one row will add 2 seconds for each 1000 rows of a table. In addition to increasing the response time for the current transaction, other transactions will queue up behind it.

Performance Summary

The current release of dBASE IV SQL provides no tools or facilities to aid in the tuning of SQL queries. Other relational data base products provide mechanisms for their respective access path selection mechanisms to explain their access strategies. As of this writing, no relational DBMS product allows users to override or determine the access selection. If a user or program could override SQL access selection, one of the principles of SQL would be defeated.

The only recourse a developer may explore is to provide indices for the most common access requirements and experiment (e.g., model) using interactive SQL to obtain the most efficient retrieval. In short, the three considerations for efficient data retrieval are: I/O, I/O, and I/O! If queries are coded according to the preceding guidelines, the number of table rows being manipulated will be minimized, memory requirements will be limited, and CPU time will be reduced.

CHAPTER 10

SQL Performance and Tuning

Now that you have been exposed to Data Manipulation Language and understand what the capabilities of that SQL component are, it is time to comprehend how and why DML accesses tables. Will an index be used? If more than one index is created on a table, which index will be chosen? How will an index be used? Does table size affect access path selection? These and other questions will be addressed in this chapter. Remember, you may only request data; dBASE IV SQL will determine how to retrieve it.

Index Utilization

A clustering index will cause rows in the table to be physically positioned during insert and update processing as closely as possible to the sequence specified for the clustering index. Also, the table physically will be in clustering sequence after an UNLOAD/RELOAD (i.e., reorganization) execution. A clustering index should be specified when columns are frequently used in a certain order. SQL statements such as ORDER BY, GROUP BY, and WHERE clauses, where large groupings of data are required, are indicative of this type of situation. By accessing data in clustered sequence, dBASE IV SQL may be able to avoid a sort prior to satisfaction of the SQL request.

Note that judgment should be used in designating clustering criteria. It may be preferable to assign the column that is the object of a WHERE clause rather than one that is the object of an ORDER BY or GROUP BY clause. It may be more efficient to retrieve the data first via the index based on the WHERE criteria and then sort it into proper groupings than to select the data via an ordering criterion to fulfill the WHERE criteria. The resulting sort may be insignificant because of the small number of rows retrieved.

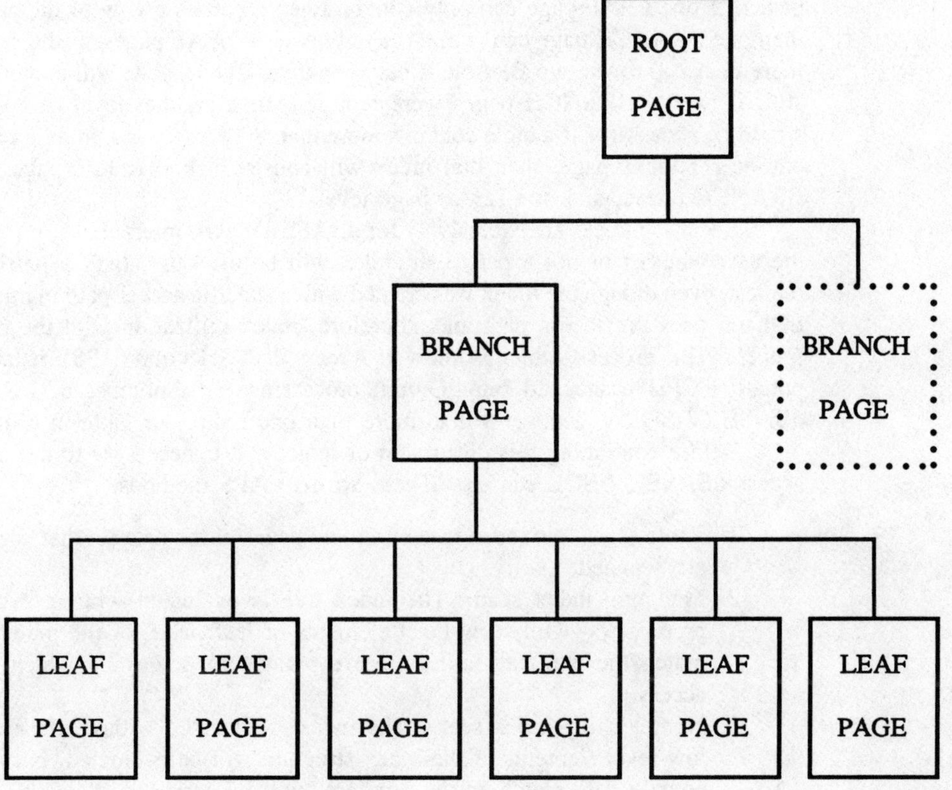

Figure 10-1. Index "tree" structure

The following discussion and Figure 10-1 will describe how indices are structured in a true Relational Data Base Management System. The current SQL catalog table (e.g., SYSIDXS) provides the necessary statistical and control columns to support a "tree" type of index structure. See the RUNSTATS command in the Chapter 12 for additional information on statistical data that is maintained in the SQL catalogs for access strategy selection.

An index may be thought of as a tree. Like a tree, it will have a trunk or root that has several branches. The branches, in turn, terminate at leaves. The larger a tree, the more branches or levels it will have. As such, an index may consist of several types of pages. A LEAF page is composed of *one entry for every row* in the related table. These entries are composed of the actual key column(s) and a relative record address. ROOT and BRANCH pages contain *one entry for the highest key value in each of their subordinate pages* (LEAF or BRANCH). The number of entries that may fit on one page depends on the size of the actual key. A key consisting of a thirty-byte character column (e.g., LASTNAME) will allow fewer entries in a page than a five-byte numeric column (e.g., STAFF NO). If your table is small and all of its entries will fit in one page, no BRANCH or ROOT pages will be necessary. On the other hand, a large table may require several levels of BRANCH pages. If one LEAF page can only contain twenty entries owing to the size of its keys, then one BRANCH page can "point" to only twenty LEAF pages. If the related table has more than 200 rows, two BRANCH pages and one ROOT page will be necessary. Worse still, if twenty BRANCH pages were required, then another level of BRANCH pages would be necessary. If a table contains more than 8000 rows and an index allows only 20 entries per index page, then that index will consist of one ROOT page, two levels of BRANCH pages, and one LEAF page level.

Because indices are exclusively for dBASE IV SQL internal use, it is not obvious to the user whether or not a particular index will be used to satisfy a particular retrieval request, even though the index was created with a specific access path in mind. dBASE IV SQL chooses the access path and, therefore, index utilization with the SQL optimizer process. This process, which is know as Access Path Selection (APS), is largely based on potential CPU usage and Input/Output processing (i.e., number of I/Os). Moreover, dBASE IV SQL will never utilize more than one index per table in a query.

Before continuing this discussion of indices, it is necessary to define the types of access dBASE IV SQL can use. There are five APS methods:

1. Table scan No index is used and all pages of the data set that contains the table are scanned.
2. Matching index scan The index tree is evaluated with respect to the SQL predicate(s). Only low-level elements or leaf pages of the index structure that match the predicate criteria are evaluated to determine which table rows to access.
3. Nonmatching index scan The index is accessed without the tree search. All low-level elements of the index structure will be evaluated, but only rows that contain data matching the predicate will be accessed.
4. Matching index without data reference Similar to the matching index scan, except that the index alone is sufficient to satisfy the SQL predicate. No data pages or table rows are accessed (e.g., counting rows or testing for existence of a specific value in a column of a table).
5. Nonmatching index scan without data reference Similar to the nonmatching index scan with the exception that the index alone is sufficient to satisfy the SQL predicate. No data pages or table rows are accessed.

To completely understand the five APS methods, an example will be presented that will include the DDL to create a table with two indices as well as five DML examples to access the table by the five methods. Figure 10-2 illustrates the DDL to create the table and indices.

The CUSTOMER table being created is one of the dBASE IV SQL sample tables. The CUST_NO_IX index specifies one column and is defined as unique and clustered. Therefore, the CUST_NO values must be unique within this table. Recall that cluster is an undocumented feature at this time.

The second index, CUST_LOCIX, specifies three columns. Unique is not specified, so duplicates will be allowed. All columns specified in this index will be in ascending sequence because you may not mix ASC and DESC within the same index.

```
CREATE TABLE CUSTOMER
      (CUST_NO    CHAR(06)
      ,COMPANY    CHAR(25)
      ,LASTNAME   CHAR(15)
      ,FIRSTNAME  CHAR(10)
      ,CITY       CHAR(15)
      ,STATE      CHAR(02)
      ,ZIP        CHAR(05)
      )
      ;

CREATE UNIQUE INDEX CUST_NO_IX
      ON CUSTOMER
      (CUST_NO    ASC
      )
      cluster
      ;

CREATE INDEX CUST_LOCIX
      ON CUSTOMER
      (CITY       ASC
      ,STATE      ASC
      ,ZIP        ASC
      )
      ;
```

Figure 10-2. Create table and index

Examples of Access Methods

TABLE SCAN

```
SELECT CITY ,STATE,
      FROM CUSTOMER
      WHERE COMPANY = 'Brand X Inc.'
;
```

Figure 10-3. Table scan

A full table scan is chosen in Figure 10-3 because the predicate in the WHERE clause specified a nonindexed column. Even though CITY and STATE are part of the CUST_LOCIX index, the actual rows to be returned depend on the values of the COMPANY column. Therefore, an index cannot be utilized. In this example, the entire table will be scanned to retrieve what the user knows is one row This table scan is necessary because dBASE IV SQL does not know how many rows contain a COMPANY column with the value of "Brand X Inc.".

MATCHING INDEX SCAN

```
SELECT COMPANY ,CITY, STATE, ZIP
      FROM CUSTOMER
      WHERE CUST_NO = '111000'
;
```

Figure 10-4. Matching index scan.

The most important point of the matching index scan example (Figure 10-4) is that enough information is provided in the WHERE predicate so that the entire "tree" structure (ROOT, BRANCH, and LEAF pages) may be utilized. Since the column-list specifies columns that are not part of the index, row retrieval is necessary to return the actual data.

NONMATCHING INDEX SCAN

```
SELECT COMPANY ,CITY, STATE, ZIP
      FROM CUSTOMER
      WHERE CUST_NO LIKE '%000'
;

SELECT COMPANY ,CITY ,STATE, ZIP
      FROM CUSTOMER
      WHERE STATE       = 'CA'
       AND ZIP          = '93003'
;
```

Figure 10-5. Nonmatching index scan

The key point for both SELECT statements in the nonmatching index scan example (Figure 10-5) is that *index columns are specified* in the WHERE clause predicates, but *insufficient data is provided to fully utilize the "tree" structure*. APS will elect to access only the LEAF pages. ROOT and BRANCH pages cannot be utilized because *leading index values are not provided*. In the first WHERE clause,

```
WHERE CUST_NO LIKE '%000'
```

the trailing zeroes of the LIKE predicate disallow use of the ROOT and BRANCH pages of the CUST_NO_IX index. APS does not know where to start in the index and most scan all LEAF pages.

In the second example, in Figure 10-5, the CUST_LOCIX will be chosen and a LEAF page scan will be utilized. Since CITY was omitted from the WHERE clause and the index is composed of CITY, STATE, and ZIP, leading values are not provided. Suppose the second example in Figure 10-5 were modified and only the first and third columns of the CUST_LOCIX index were specified:

```
WHERE CITY      = 'VENTURA'
AND ZIP         = '93003'
```

Now imbedded values are missing. In this case, the ROOT must be utilized to locate the first LEAF page and only LEAF pages where the CITY and ZIP conditions are true will be scanned.

In both examples of the nonmatching index scan, table rows may be retrieved because the column-list specified columns that were not part of an index.

MATCHING INDEX WITHOUT DATA REFERENCE

```
SELECT CITY ,STATE, ZIP
    FROM CUSTOMER
    WHERE CITY        = 'Wasau'
    AND ZIP           = '93003'
;
```

Figure 10-6. Matching index without data reference

In the matching index without data reference example in Figure 10-6, the column-list consists of indexed columns only, and all of the clauses in the WHERE predicate specify index columns. No table rows must be accessed or retrieved. Leading index values are also provided, which allows use of the "tree" structure.

NONMATCHING INDEX WITHOUT DATA REFERENCE

```
SELECT CITY ,STATE, ZIP
     FROM CUSTOMER
     WHERE STATE        = 'MO'
;
```

Figure 10-7. Nonmatching index without data reference

In Figure 10-7, a nonmatching index without data reference query is shown. Again, the column-list consists of indexed columns only. However, the WHERE predicate does not provide any leading index values. An index LEAF page scan will be required.

Index Utilization Conclusion

From the examples, you can develop a robust respect for the considerations necessary when coding an SQL query. Although you may not dictate how to retrieve data, how you code a query will strongly influence access path selection.

With respect to performance, a matching index access strategy is preferable because of the minimization of input/output processing and the degree of data transfer necessary to satisfy the predicate. Where data requests are limited to index columns, a scan will be attempted without data reference, maximizing efficiency by reducing all cost factors. This is particularly true for large tables where I/O, data transfer, and CPU costs are most dramatically reflected. When a matching index strategy is not possible, a non-matching index scan without data reference is the next best alternative. Table scans are normally the least effective access strategy, unless one row or more per page will be retrieved.

In addition to index page types, table rows may also be considered to be stored in DATA pages. Although not physically stored in this fashion in dBASE IV SQL release 1.0, support for this process may be found in the CARD and NPAGES columns of the SQL catalog table SYSTABLS. The authors created a CUSTOMER table with the attributes depicted in Figure 10-8.

The table width or row length was 132 bytes and the total number of rows was 7684. A unique cluster index was created on CUSTID and a nonunique secondary index was created on SERVNAME and NLINES. To update the statistical columns in the SYS-TABLS, SYSCOLS, and SYSIDXS SQL catalog tables, the RUNSTATS command/utility was invoked. Upon completion of the RUNSTATS command, the following values were set in the indicated SQL catalog table columns.

SQL Catalog Table	*Column*	*Value*
SYSTABLS	NPAGES	0991
SYSTABLS	CARD	7684
SYSIDXS	NLEAF	0125 (CUSTID index)
SYSIDXS	NLEAF	0257
SYSIDXS	NLEVELS	0003 (CUSTID index)
SYSIDXS	NLEVELS	0003

The column named CARD in the SYSTABLS catalog table refers to the number of rows in a specific table. The authors have no idea why record or row was not used as a column name. Back in ancient history (twenty years ago), data was inputted on stiff paper that was know as keypunch cards. Perhaps this is a touch of nostalgia. In any event, a similar but more sophisticated process is utilized by IBM's relational product DB2 to determine APS. The fact that these values are maintained by dBASE IV SQL indicates that Ashton-Tate is headed in the same direction.

If an average data page contains 25 rows and a query is anticipated to return 4 percent or more rows of the table, then APS assumes that a random distribution of rows will be processed and scans every page in the table! This is not as terrible as it sounds; on the average, you are processing every page in the table. Consider that 4 percent of a 25-row page is one row for each page. Therefore, it can be anticipated that every page will be retrieved. Moreover, useless index I/O and processing time will be avoided.

```
CREATE TABLE CUSTOMER
    (
    SERVNAME       CHAR(20),
    CUSTID         CHAR(11),
    NLINES         NUMERIC(5)
    WEIGHT         NUMERIC(15,7),
    USE1           NUMERIC(8),
    USE2           NUMERIC(8),
    USE3           NUMERIC(8),
    USE4           NUMERIC(8),
    USE5           NUMERIC(8),
    REV1           NUMERIC(8),
    REV2           NUMERIC(8),
    REV3           NUMERIC(8),
    REV4           NUMERIC(8),
    REV5           NUMERIC(8),
    );
```

Figure 10-8. CUSTOMER table for page example

The performance effects of indices vary according to table size, cardinality (or proportion of distinct key values) of the index, the number of insert, update, and delete processing requests, and the frequency of index use. The following instances do not necessarily justify the creation of an index:

1. A small table (less than 5 data pages) that is frequently accessed but is predominantly read-only when accessed.
2. A small table (less than 10 data pages) that is not frequently accessed but is predominantly read-only when accessed.
3. A small table (less than 15 data pages) that is frequently accessed for insert, update, or delete activity.
4. A table in which more than 5 percent of the rows have key columns containing nonunique data and for which no clustered index exists. (This case would require more I/O with an index than for a table scan.)

On the other hand, a large table should almost always have at least one index as an alternative to a table scan. Additionally, smaller tables that do not meet the previous criteria should also be considered candidates for index definition.

Consideration should be given to the temporary availability of indices where permanent support cannot be justified. A good example would be tables that are processed in one sequence except for a single month-end process. Should two indices be maintained throughout the month to support both access requirements? Whenever table rows are updated, inserted, or deleted, both indices will have to be updated. In such a situation, an index conceivably could be created before to month-end processing and dropped immediately thereafter.

Views

This section presents several advanced uses for views. In Chapter 8, reference was made to updatable views. Now updatable views will be clarified. Figure 10-9 illustrates an extended view creation statement with all possible subselect parameters.

```
CREATE VIEW view_name
[(view-column-list)]
AS
     SELECT < select-column-list | * >
          FROM table_1, [..,table_n]
           [WHERE predicate(s)]
          [GROUP BY group_list]
           [HAVING predicate(s)]
[WITH CHECK OPTION]
     ;
```

Figure 10-9. Extended view syntax

A subselect in a view may not contain a UNION or an ORDER BY. If both the view definition and a query utilizing the same view specify an ORDER BY, which sequence should the results table be in? Should two sorts be performed when only one is needed? The restriction on UNIONs is due to process limitations. Even IBM's DB2 does not allow UNIONs or ORDER BY parameters in a view definition.

The most important administrative consideration when using views is the adherence to naming standards. Pay special attention to the "*view-column-list*" and the "*select-column-list*" parameters. If the view column names are not carefully chosen, application development will become a nightmare. Recall that table, view, and synonym names must be unique in a dBASE IV SQL data base. Care must be taken to avoid a plethora of useless rubble. The parameters were originally presented in Chapter 8, and are repeated here for review and clarification only.

view-name	May be up to ten characters long and must be unique within a dBASE IV SQL data base. This name should reflect the major meaning or purpose of the view being created.
view-column-list	A list of names for columns in this view. This list corresponds positionally on a one-to-one to with the columns in the subselect. It is not required unless the result of the subselect contains duplicate names or has derived columns from an arithmetic expression, a function, or a constant.
select-column-list | *	A standard column list for a SELECT statement. The order of the names will correspond positionally on a one-to-one basis to the columns named in the view-column-list. In the example in Figure 10-9, CU_ACCT_NO will be known as CB_ACCT_NO when processing through view VDDA_CB. If an asterisk were specified and the view-column-list omitted, then the view would use the column names as they were originally defined in the CREATE definition of the table.
WITH CHECK OPTION	When specified for an updatable view, will prevent modification or insertion of a row whose columns' values do not conform to all of the conditions in the WHERE predicate.

A comprehensive example of a view definition is shown in Figure 10-10. Note that the names in the view-column-list are prefixed with the view acronym CB. The rest of each name is derived from the column names in the table.

The example in Figure 10-10 illustrates a condition where a view, VDDA_CB, has been defined to join two tables, TDDA_CUST (customer data) and TDDA_BAL (account balance information), on the basis of common columns named CU_ACCT_NO and BAL_ACCT_NO respectively. Only rows whose account numbers begin with the characters "01" may be accessed by the user of this view. Further, only information pertaining to the account, name, address, and outstanding balance will be available from the rows returned. The columns returned have been renamed with a prefix of "CB", although

```
CREATE VIEW   VDDA_CB

     (CB_ACCT_NO, CB_NAME,
      CB_ADDR, CB_BAL_AMT)

AS

SELECT CU_ACCT_NO, CU_NAME,
       CU_ADDR, BAL_OS_AMT
  FROM TDDA_CUST, TDDA_BAL
   WHERE CU_ACCT_NO = BAL_ ACCT_NO
     AND CU_ACCT_NO LIKE '01%'
;
```

Figure 10-10. View defined with JOIN

dBASE IV SQL catalog information will still supply the physical characteristics of the columns.

As previously stated, access to this view by the average user is identical to access to the actual physical tables themselves. However, restrictions on view access, if pertinent, may require that the user have more familiarity with the view definition and tables underlying it.

1. A view that is defined as the join of multiple tables may not participate in any update, delete, or insert processing requests through that view.
2. A view that uses aggregate functions such as SUM, AVG, MIN, or MAX in its definition may not participate in any insert, delete, or update processing requests through the view.
3. A view that is defined as the grouping of data or elimination of duplicate data using GROUP BY, HAVING, or DISTINCT clauses also may not participate in any update, insert, or delete processing requests through the view.
4. A view that contains a column where information has been derived through constants or arithmetic and scalar functions is restricted from participation in an update request for that column. An example would be the column CB_BAL_AMT in our previous view definition if it had been derived as BAL_OS_AMT/100 to present the cents position.

In summary, if the physical sequence of a table is modified, short of excluding rows, or a column does not reflect its original attributes or value, then that view is strictly available for "READ ONLY" access.

The preceding restrictions on processing through the view mechanism may appear more reasonable when you consider that most of the conditions would have produced data, in the views, that was not consistent with column definitions in the original base tables, or the view changed the composition of rows and/or columns that were in the original tables (e.g., AVG, GROUP BY, and DISTINCT).

To update or delete a row via a view, it is not necessary for a view to contain the same number of columns or rows as its base table. However, the view should relate to the base table through its primary key (i.e., the view should contain the primary key of the table) in order to prevent the update from corrupting the base table's relationships.

By using a view, the user is capable of performing functions against the base table that would violate the access to the tables authorized in the view definition. dBASE IV SQL does not verify that the actual values of the columns being inserted or updated through a view are consistent with the definition of the view itself.

In the definition for the view VDDA_CB, illustrated in our example, the user was clearly prohibited from access to any accounts that did not begin with the digits "01". However, the user would have been capable of inserting an account number beginning with "22" into table TDDA_CUST if it had not been joined to table TDDA_BAL and did not conflict with any of the other restrictions indicated previously.

The only way to provide integrity for the base table against such update and insert violations is through the use of the WITH CHECK OPTION feature of the view definition. Note that this check will be performed for every update and insert request through the view, and could represent significant performance costs for views heavily utilized in this manner.

An adaptation of the original definition for view VDDA_CB illustrates the inclusion of the WITH CHECK OPTION clause (Figure 10-11).

```
CREATE VIEW    VDDA_CB

     (CB_ACCT_NO, CB_NAME, CB_ADDR)
 AS

SELECT CU_ACCT_NO, CU-NAME,CU_ADDR
 FROM TDDA_CUST
  WHERE CU_ACCT_NO LIKE'01%'

WITH CHECK OPTION
;
```

Figure 10-11. Updatable view WITH CHECK OPTION

This view will allow updates on table TDDA_CUST as long as the first two characters of column CU_ACCT_NO are "01."

Using Views in Place of Small Tables

Every system will need a few small tables. The usual requirement is reference data such as STATE CODES, ACCOUNT TYPE CODES, INTEREST RATE CODES, and the like.

The authors have worked on one system where one table consisted of four rows Since most site standards require every table to have a unique index, those four rows would have utilized two data sets. Would it not be more efficient to keep all small tables together and not incur the additional overhead of multiple indices? Every table must have a separate index data set.

The examples in Figures 10-12 through 10-18 will show how to utilize views to, in effect, support multiple row definitions in one table. The reference data table, TDDA_

```
--
CREATE TABLE    TDDA_REF
( R_CD           CHAR(02)
 ,R_ROW_CD       CHAR(01)
 ,R_TXT          CHAR(30)
 ,R_CO_DC_CD     LOGICAL
 ,R_CA_DC_CD     LOGICAL
 ,R_GL_BK_CD     LOGICAL
 ,R_MAN_CD       LOGICAL
 ,R_FUNC1_NM     CHAR(08)
 ,R_STAT1_CD     CHAR(01)
 ,R_FUNC2_NM     CHAR(08)
 ,R_STAT2_CD     CHAR(01)
 ,R_FUNC3_NM     CHAR(08)
 ,R_STAT3_CD     CHAR(01)
 ,R_FUNC4_NM     CHAR(08)
 ,R_STAT4_CD     CHAR(01)
 ,R_FUNC5_NM     CHAR(08)
 ,R_STAT5_CD     CHAR(01)
 ,R_FUNC6_NM     CHAR(08)
 ,R_STAT6_CD     CHAR(01)
 ,R_FUNC7_NM     CHAR(08)
 ,R_STAT7_CD     CHAR(01)
 ,R_FUNC8_NM     CHAR(08)
 ,R_STAT8_CD     CHAR(01)
 ,R_LAST_USR     CHAR(08)
 ,R_PRV_DT       DATE
 ,R_CUR_DT       DATE
 ,R_NXT_DT       DATE
 ,R_PRV_MDT      DATE
 ,R_CUR_MDT      DATE
 ,R_NXT_MDT      DATE
 )
;
```

Figure 10-12. Common reference data table example

REF (Figure 10-12), consists of 30 columns and is the base for six views. The total number of rows will not exceed 200. The system date view, VDDA_SYDT (Figure 10-17), requires only one row. None of the views need all the columns defined in the base table, but every column will be utilized by at least one of the six different views.

The most important benefit of this design is that there is only one table and, more important, only one index. The index will be unique, which will heavily influence its use by APS.

Figure 10-12 creates the only base table. The first two columns, R_CD and R_ROW_CD, will be common to all views. They represent the unique sequence for this table and its dependent views and will, therefore, be the indexed columns for this table. The R_ROW_CD will be used in conjunction with the "WITH CHECK OPTION" to ensure view integrity. If the R_ROW_CD does not meet the criteria of the WHERE clause for a specific view, rows cannot be manipulated through that view.

```
CREATE VIEW      VDDA_ANAM   (
   ANAM_CD ,ANAM_ROW_CD ,ANAM_TXT
  ,ANAM_RPT_SEQ_CD
  ,NAM_SHRT_NAM
  ,ANAM_LAST_USR
)    AS
  SELECT   R_CD,  R_ROW_CD,  R_TXT
  ,R_FUNC1_NM
  ,R_FUNC2_NM
  ,R_LAST_USR
       FROM TDDA_REF
  WHERE R_ROW_CD = 'A'
    AND R_CD              LIKE 'X%'
WITH CHECK OPTION;
```

Figure 10-13. Account type name view example

The VDDA_SYDT view (Figure 10-17) will allow only one row to exist in the base table. Its WHERE clause tests the index columns for one specific value. Therefore, a SELECT from this view will not require a WHERE predicate.

Multiple Row Definition Summary

This use of views in our example eliminates the necessity for multiple tables and indices and their related overhead. One table and one index replace six tables and six indices. Extra DISK space is required due to the number of columns in the base table, but this is offset by decreasing the number of open files that would have to have been kept open.

```
CREATE VIEW     VDDA_ATYP    (
   ATYP_CD ,ATYP_ROW_CD ,ATYP_TXT
  ,ATYP_FUNC1_NM ,ATYP_STAT1_CD
  ,ATYP_FUNC2_   ,ATYP_STAT2_CD
  ,ATYP_FUNC3_NM ,ATYP_STAT3_CD
  ,ATYP_FUNC4_   ,ATYP_STAT4_CD
  ,ATYP_FUNC5_NM ,ATYP_STAT5_CD
  ,ATYP_FUNC6_NM ,ATYP_STAT6_CD
  ,ATYP_FUNC7_NM ,ATYP_STAT7_CD
  ,ATYP_FUNC8_NM ,ATYP_STAT8_CD
  ,ATYP_LAST_USR
)   AS
  SELECT   R_CD,  R_ROW_CD,  R_TXT
  ,R_FUNC1_NM ,R_STAT1_CD
  ,R_FUNC2_NM ,R_STAT2_CD
  ,R_FUNC3_NM ,R_STAT3_CD
  ,R_FUNC4_NM ,R_STAT4_CD
  ,R_FUNC5_NM ,R_STAT5_CD
  ,R_FUNC6_NM ,R_STAT6_CD
  ,R_FUNC7_NM ,R_STAT7_CD
  ,R_FUNC8_NM ,R_STAT8_CD
  ,R_LAST_USR
        FROM TDDA_REF
  WHERE R_ROW_CD = 'A'
    AND R_CD        NOT LIKE 'X%'
             WITH CHECK OPTION;
```

Figure 10-14. Account type codes view example

```
CREATE VIEW     VDDA_IDXN (
   IDXN_CD ,IDXN_ROW_CD ,IDXN_NAM
  ,IDXN_LAST_USR
)  AS
  SELECT   R_CD, R_ROW_CD,  R_TXT
  ,R_LAST_USR
        FROM TDDA_REF
  WHERE R_ROW_CD = 'I'
WITH CHECK OPTION;
```

Figure 10-15. Rate index name view example

```
CREATE VIEW     VDDA_ST (
   ST_CD ,ST_ROW_CD ,ST_NAM
  ,ST_LAST_USR
)    AS
  SELECT   R_CD,  R_ROW_CD,  R_TXT
  ,R_LAST_USR
        FROM TDDA_REF
  WHERE R_ROW_CD = 'S'
WITH CHECK OPTION;
```

Figure 10-16. State code view example

```
CREATE VIEW     VDDA_SYDT    (
   SYDT_CD ,SYDT_ROW_CD ,SYDT_TXT
  ,SYDT_PRV_DT ,SYDT_CUR_DT
  ,SYDT_NXT_DT ,SYDT_PRV_MDT
  ,SYDT_CUR_MDT ,SYDT_NXT_MO_SYS_
)     AS
  SELECT   R_CD,  R_ROW_CD,  R_TXT
  ,R_PRV_DT ,R_CUR_DT
  ,R_NXT_DT ,R_PRV_MDT
  ,R_CUR_MDT ,R_NXT_MO_SYS_D
        FROM TDDA_REF


WHERE R_ROW_CD = '['
    AND R_CD      = '[['
    AND R_PRV_DT         != '        '
    AND R_CUR_DT         != '        '
    AND R_NXT_DT         != '        '
    AND R_PRV_MDT      != '      '
    AND R_CUR_MDT      != '      '
    AND R_NXT_MDT      != '      '


WITH CHECK OPTION;
```

Figure 10-17. Current system date view example

```
CREATE VIEW    VDDA_TC     (

   TC_CD    ,TC_ROW_CD    ,TC_TXT
  ,TC_CO_DC_CD ,TC_CA_DC_CD
  ,TC_GL_BK_CD ,TC_MAN_CD
  ,TC_LAST_USR
)   AS
  SELECT   R_CD,  R_ROW_CD,  R_TXT
     ,R_CO_DC_CD ,R_CA_DC_CD
     ,R_GL_BK_CD ,R_MAN_CD
     ,R_LAST_USR
        FROM TDDA_REF
  WHERE R_ROW_CD = 'T'
WITH CHECK OPTION;
```

Figure 10-18. Transaction code description verify view example

CHAPTER 11

SQL Application Code

SQL application code, or embedded SQL refers to the commands, functions, and statements that may be used in a host language program. DB2 and SQL/DS, IBM's relational data base mainframe products, allow their SQL statements to be embedded in programs written in COBOL, PL/1, FORTRAN, APL, BASIC, and, as of DB2's latest release, C language.

Programs in dBASE IV may be written in either SQL mode (*.prs* suffix) or native dBASE (*.prg* suffix). SQL mode allows SQL table access (i.e., SQL statements) only and native mode allows dBASE data base access only. In addition to the table and data base restriction, not all dBASE IV commands and functions can be utilized in *.prs* programs.

One other difference between the two types of programs is the use of the semicolon. SQL statements utilize a semicolon as a delimiter (end of statement), whereas dBASE programs use the semicolon as a continuation character. dBASE commands that are permitted in SQL mode programs may still use the semicolon as a continuation character. In any event, dBASE commands and SQL statements may be a maximum of 1024 characters in length.

With a few changes, all the statements presented in the discussion of the Data Manipulation Language (Chapter 9) may be coded in *.prs* programs. These changes will allow memory variables to receive, modify, or input column values or to be used in WHERE predicates. The biggest adjustment for an application programmer when working with SQL statements in a program is the extra instructions required to retrieve one row at a time. This single-record/row mentality is the result of the limited vocabulary of most programming languages.

Program Creation and Structure

SQL programs may be created with any text editor or with the MODIFY COMMAND editor as long as their DOS file names are suffixed with *.prs*. An SQL program may call (e.g., DO program) a dBASE program and a dBASE program may call a SQL program. dBASE IV will switch to the SQL mode or native dBASE depending on the file suffix. Note that the *.prs* suffix is not required if you are in an SQL program and wish to call another SQL program. The current mode is always the default mode.

Some applications may require more than one data base. Recall that dBASE IV SQL allows only one data base to be active at a time and that a subsequent START DATABASE command will also stop the active data base and release all current SQL work files. Therefore, the work file limitation and data base restriction can be more easily managed if each SQL program begins with a START DATABASE command and all related DML statements in the program are constrained to the current data base.

The dBASE IV compiler requires that all dBASE IV SQL objects physically exist prior to any references in a program. You may still place DDL statements such as CREATE TABLE in a program. But they must be located before any respective DML statements (i.e., SELECT, INSERT, etc.) or the Data Control Language statements GRANT and REVOKE.

Duplicate Object Name Creation

Another idiosyncrasy of the dBASE IV compiler is its inability to distinguish between application program flow and physical placement of object definition statements. A program may require a table to be created with different column attributes where the actual attributes are dependent on a condition. Figure 11-1 represents one possible coding routine that would cause an error.

```
if some-condition
        CREATE TABLE TEMP1
             (COL_A    DECIMAL(5,1)
             ,COL_B    CHAR(5) );
else
        CREATE TABLE TEMP1
             (COL_A    DECIMAL(7,1)
             ,COL_B    CHAR(9) );
```

Figure 11-1. Compile object create error example

Even though the application would never create more than one table per execution, the compiler will still flag this as a duplicate creation error. This error will occur for any duplicate object creation, such as views, synonyms, or indices. Moreover, the same duplicate object error will arise when different SAVE TO TEMP clauses utilize the same temporary table name as in Figure 11-2.

```
if some-condition
        SELECT COL_A, COL_B, COL_C
              FROM YOUR_TAB
              WHERE condition-1
        SAVE TO TEMP T_TAB KEEP;
else
        SELECT COL_A, COL_B, COL_C
              FROM YOUR_TAB
              WHERE condition-2
        SAVE TO TEMP T_TAB KEEP;
```

Figure 11-2. TEMP table error example

The two queries in Figure 11-2 are identical except for their WHERE predicates. The results columns will have the same attributes but their output rows will be composed of different values. The dBASE IV compiler will still flag this as an error. At this point, one becomes a bit frustrated. This conditional SAVE TO TEMP might be very useful. With a few not too negligible changes, as shown if Figure 11-3, a conditional SAVE TO TEMP may be processed.

```
if some-condition
        SELECT COL_A, COL_B, COL_C
              FROM YOUR_TAB
              WHERE condition-1
              SAVE TO TEMP T_TAB KEEP;
        DO some-pgm
        DROP T_TAB;
else
        SELECT COL_A, COL_B, COL_C
              FROM YOUR_TAB
              WHERE condition-2
              SAVE TO TEMP T_TAB KEEP;
        DO some-pgm
        DROP T_TAB;
```

Figure 11-3. TEMP table error example

The compiler will allow duplicate object creation as long as any subsequent CREATE statements are preceded by a DROP statement. Note that similar changes may be applied to the conditional table create example in Figure 11-1.

The authors were not too excited about the potential resource consumption of a SAVE TO TEMP and successive DROP statements. Since the only difference between the two SAVE TO TEMP examples was their respective WHERE predicates, why not utilize the IF command to set the memory variables in the conditions rather then execute the SELECT statement? The query then would be unconditional. Figure 11-4 shows a reworked SAVE TO TEMP example.

```
if some-condition
        set condition-x
else
        set condition-x
endif

SELECT COL_A, COL_B, COL_C
      FROM YOUR_TAB
      WHERE condition-x
SAVE TO TEMP T_TAB;
```

Figure 11-4. Correct TEMP table example

Single Row Processing

Single row processing is intended to retrieve zero or one row. The first thing that comes to mind is, "Why be concerned with the retrieval of zero rows?" The answer is, "A not-found condition may be more important than the data returned for a found condition!" When a potential customer walks into a bank to withdraw funds, is it more important to verify his or her account balance or to verify that the person does indeed have an account there?

The return of one or fewer rows will normally be utilized to retrieve a specific row when the key column(s) are known or to verify row existence. Figure 11-5 shows a single row SELECT statement.

column-list | * A required parameter that specifies which columns are requested. Either a list of column names or an asterisk (*) may be entered. The sequence of the columns in the column-list will be the sequence of the columns that will be transferred to the corresponding memory variables. An asterisk designates that all columns of a table are requested and that these columns will be in the same sequence in which the table was defined. A

```
SELECT <column-list> | *

    INTO ( < mem-var-list > )
FROM < table-list >
     [WHERE ......
        other clauses]
;
```

Figure 11-5. Single row SELECT

	column-list may consist of any combination of column names, constants, expressions, aggregate functions, and dBASE IV functions and/or variables. Commas must separate column names if more than one entry is coded.
mem-var-list	A list of memory variables that will receive data from this SELECT statement. This list corresponds positionally on a one-to-one basis to the column-list. Too few or too many variables in this list will result in errors. If a SELECT * is utilized, this list must correspond to the table creation column sequence. If the table is ever changed, all programs that coded SELECT * must be modified. However, if an explicit column-list and mem-var-list are utilized, no program changes will be required. Select only the data you need.
table-list	This required parameter specifies which table(s), view(s), or synonym(s) contain the columns entered in the column-list. If more than one entry is coded, rows from multiple tables may be joined to derive the results. (A table-list may be composed of any combination of tables, views, or synonyms. Note that views or synonyms of views may have restrictions on their use.) Commas must separate table names if more than one entry is specified.
other clauses	Any other valid combination of SELECT clauses may be entered.

Application Table Modification

With one exception, the UPDATE, INSERT, and DELETE statements in application programs function in the same fashion as their interactive counterparts. This exception for application code allows the WHERE clause of an UPDATE or DELETE statement to utilize a clause that specifies the current row in a table. The only difference, or rather addition, is that values in list entries or expression in conditions may use memory variables.

The number of rows processed will be contained in SQLCNT after an UPDATE, INSERT, or DELETE has completed.

UPDATE Statement

The purpose of the UPDATE statement is to modify the values of one or more columns in one or more rows of a table. The columns to be updated are identified by the SET clause and the rows to be modified are determined with a WHERE clause search condition. If no WHERE clause is present, all rows of the specified table will be updated. An UPDATE statement is shown in Figure 11-6.

```
UPDATE <table-name>
    SET <column-name = expression>
    [,column-name-n = expression] ....
    [WHERE clause]
;
```

Figure 11-6. UPDATE statement format

expression — An expression may consist of literal constants, memory variables, or column names of the table being updated.

At a minimum, a table name and one column name expression set are required. The components of an expression may not reference columns of another table. The WHERE clause may specify one or more search conditions for related columns of the table to be modified or may be more complex and include subselects. As in a SELECT statement, the number of rows to be affected is controlled with the search condition(s).

INSERT Statement

The purpose of the INSERT statement is to add one or more rows to a table. Values should be provided for every column of each row. These values may be coded in the INSERT statement or data may be retrieved from one or more tables in the form of a subselect statement. Figure 11-7 depicts a basic INSERT statement.

```
INSERT INTO <table-name>
     [(column-list)]
VALUES
     < (value-list) >
;
```

Figure 11-7. Basic INSERT statement

value-list The data items in the value-list must sequentially correspond, one-to-one, to the names in the column-list. The columns to receive values may be explicitly entered in a column-list; if the list is omitted, an implied list is assumed. An implied column-list consists of the column names and sequence as they were defined when the table was created. Also, data types and lengths must match. An exception to the data lengths requirement exists when numeric or character data in the value-list is shorter than their respective receiving columns. Note that the column-list in Figure 11-7 is optional. All unnamed columns will default to blanks. At present, dBASE IV SQL has no mechanism to tag a column's value as unknown.

The INSERT with a subselect is similar to the basic INSERT statement, except that the input values come from another table or tables via a subselect. The number of rows inserted will be found in SQLCNT after the INSERT statement completes. An INSERT with a subselect is shown in Figure 11-8.

```
        INSERT INTO <table-name>
            [ (column-list) ]
        SELECT * | <column-list>
            FROM table-list
            [ WHERE clause(s) ]
    ;
```

Figure 11-8. INSERT statement with subselect

The INSERT column-list must implicitly or explicitly sequentially correspond to the SELECT column-list. Data types and lengths must match. Again, the columns in the INSERT column-list may be same length or longer than the columns in the SELECT column-list.

An insert operation will fail when duplicate keyed rows are inserted into a table that has any unique indices defined. No rows will be inserted

DELETE Statement

The purpose of a dBASE IV SQL DELETE statement is to delete one or more rows from a table. The rows to be deleted are determined by a WHERE clause. If no WHERE clause is present, all rows of the specified table will be deleted. The syntax of a DELETE statement is shown in Figure 11-9.

```
    DELETE FROM < table name >
        [WHERE clause]
    ;
```

Figure 11-9. DELETE statement format

Caution: If transaction processing is in effect (i. e., BEGIN TRANSACTION . . . . END TRANSACTION), rows will not be deleted until the transaction ends. The *deleted rows will be accessible* until the END TRANSACTION command executes. Use the SET DELETE ON command to ignore logically deleted rows in succeeding SQL statements.

Multiple Row Processing

SQL is designed to manipulate sets of rows at one execution. The actual rows that are returned may consist of summary information or a subset of columns and rows. On the other hand, programs are usually designed to process one record at a time. A protocol is required to pass one row on request from the results to the program. Moreover, the same protocol must provide the ability to return rows from concurrent results tables and maintain the positioning or sequence of each results work table. As with other relational products, dBASE IV SQL utilizes *cursors* to point to the current row of a results table.

The topic of cursor processing is difficult to present in a sequential manner. To fully understand the effect and dependencies of processing with cursors, scan the next few paragraphs very quickly, and then reread them more slowly.

DECLARE CURSOR Statement

This one-row-at-a-time protocol is established with the DECLARE cursor-name CURSOR statement, as illustrated in Figure 11-10.

```
DECLARE < cursor-name > CURSOR FOR
     < SELECT column-list | *
          FROM table-list >
          [WHERE .....]
          [GROUP BY .....]
          [HAVING .....]
     [UNION .....]

[ORDER BY .. | FOR UPDATE OF updt-list]
;
```

Figure 11-10. DECLARE CURSOR statement

The DECLARE CURSOR statement relates a SELECT statement to a cursor-name. Other statements will reference this cursor-name to activate (OPEN) its SELECT statement, retrieve (FETCH) rows, and terminate (CLOSE) and/or release the cursor's resources. Also, a DECLARE CURSOR establishes a program's intentions. If the program may update a row of a table that was retrieved using this cursor, a

```
OR UPDATE OF updt-list
```

parameter must be specified.

A DECLARE CURSOR statement defines a cursor and is not required to be executed. However, *it must be physically located before any other statements that refer to its cursor name*.

cursor-name	A required entry that may be up to ten characters long and must be unique in a program and/or transaction. The cursor is similar to a record pointer in that it points to rows of a results table rather than data base records. Other statements (i.e., OPEN, FETCH, CLOSE) will refer to this name.
column-list | *	An explicit list of columns that this query, and hence cursor name, will return in its results rows. An asterisk may be coded to specify an implicit list of all the columns in a table. An implicit or explicit list must be entered.
table-list	A required parameter that specifies which table or tables contain the columns in the column-list.
ORDER BY | FOR UPDATE OF	As in a normal query, the results may be in the specific sequence coded after an ORDER BY parameter. If a program intends to update one or more columns of this cursor's results table, FOR UPDATE OF must be coded and an ORDER BY parameter *cannot be specified*. These parameters are mutually exclusive.
updt-list	A list of one or more columns that may be updated with this cursor. Although the columns in an updt-list must be in the SELECT column-list, not all columns in the column-list need be in the updt-list.

In effect, a DECLARE CURSOR statement is similar to a view in many ways. Like a view, different cursors can be defined in the same program for the same table. Each cursor can specify a different column-list and sequence. Their respective results tables will exist for the duration of each individual cursor.

Like read-only views, cursors may be READ ONLY. The restrictions are the same. A cursor is read-only when its related DECLARE CURSOR query:

1. Is a join of two or more tables.
2. Contains aggregate functions such as SUM, AVG, MIN, or MAX in its column-list.
3. Utilizes the GROUP BY, HAVING, or DISTINCT clause.
4. Specifies constants, arithmetic, or scalar functions in its column-list.

In summary, if the physical sequence of the base table is modified, short of excluding rows, or a column does not reflect its original attributes or values, then that cursor is available for "READ ONLY" access.

OPEN CURSOR Statement

The purpose of the OPEN CURSOR statement is to execute the query defined in a DECLARE CURSOR statement with the same cursor-name. The corresponding results table will be established during open processing. Therefore, all variables in WHERE clause predicates must be set before execution of the respective OPEN statement. A cursor must be closed before it is subsequently opened for other processing, because the same cursor-name cannot process two work files either concurrently or sequencely. (Figure 11-11).

```
OPEN < cursor-name > ;
```

Figure 11-11. OPEN CURSOR statement

The current release of dBASE IV SQL sets SQLCNT to the number of rows retrieved by the applicable cursor's query. *Caution:* Later releases of dBASE IV SQL may not always create a results table, which means that SQLCNT cannot be set.

cursor-name This cursor-name may be up to ten characters long and must be unique in a program. The cursor is similar to a record pointer in that it points to rows of a results table rather than data base records. This is a required entry and only one name may be entered.

The number of different open cursors in a program is limited to system storage and the dBASE IV ten file limit. One work file is required per open cursor. If a DECLARE CURSOR represents a join, the associated OPEN will process *all* base tables and one cursor work file. All base tables and intermediate files will be released at the completion of the OPEN statement and the cursor work file will remain open until closed.

FETCH CURSOR Statement

The purpose of the FETCH statement is to retrieve one results row for a program. Figure 11-12 depicts a FETCH statement.

```
FETCH < cursor-name > INTO
      < mem-var-list >
;
```

Figure 11-12. FETCH CURSOR statement

cursor-name Must be a name that was previously defined in a DECLARE CURSOR statement, and prior to first FETCH, this cursor must have been processed with an OPEN statement.

mem-var-list A list of one or more memory variables that will receive data from the results table of the cursor-name. This list corresponds positionally on a one-to-one basis to the column-list in the respective DECLARE CURSOR statement. Too few or too many variables in this list will result in errors. If a SELECT * is utilized, this list must correspond to the table creation column sequence. If the table is ever changed, all programs that coded SELECT * must be modified. However, if an explicit column-list and mem-var-list are utilized, no program changes will be required as long as no columns are removed. As with the single row SELECT, *return only the rows and columns you need*.

When the SQLCODE equals a +100, a FETCH is attempted past the end of the results table. No more rows are available. Therefore, it is necessary to test the SQLCODE after each FETCH statement. A value of zero indicates that a row was returned.

CLOSE CURSOR Statement

The function of a CLOSE statement (Figure 11-13) is to release the resources of a results table that was being processed via a cursor. Before a cursor and subsequent results table can be reused, the table must be closed and then opened. If different rows are to be returned, different values must be substituted in the variables of the associated DECLARE CURSOR WHERE predicate conditions.

```
CLOSE < cursor-name > ;
```

Figure 11-13. CLOSE CURSOR statement

cursor-name This required parameter must be the same name as its related DECLARE CURSOR statement. Only one cursor name may be specified.

An application may close a cursor at any time. It is not necessary to process an entire cursor work file. To release resources and free work files, close all cursors as soon as possible.

WHERE CURRENT OF Clause

The purpose of the WHERE CURRENT OF clause in an UPDATE or DELETE statement is to modify the *current* row that is pointed to by some cursor-name. This is the only way to delete or update only one nonunique row in a table. This clause restricts processing to the *current* row. Moreover, when processing with cursors, an UPDATE or DELETE statement without a CURRENT OF clause may be utilized concurrently.

Noncursor updates and deletes must be utilized when the query in a DECLARE CURSOR statement contains an ORDER BY clause or is READ ONLY. (Recall that FOR UPDATE OF and ORDER BY are mutually exclusive.) When using noncursor updates and deletes, be sure to include a WHERE condition to control the number of rows that will be updated or deleted. An UPDATE WHERE CURRENT OF statement is shown in Figure 11-14.

```
UPDATE <table-name>
     SET <column-name = expression>
     [,column-name-n = expression] ....
     WHERE CURRENT OF <cursor-name>
;
```

Figure 11-14. UPDATE statement with CURRENT OF clause

table-name	A required parameter that must reference the table-name entered in the previous DECLARE CURSOR statement.
column-name	Must refer to a column-name that was in an updt-list of a FOR UPDATE OF clause in a *previous* DECLARE CURSOR statement.
cursor-name	This parameter must refer to a cursor that was opened and had at least one row fetched. Position must be established with a previous *successful* FETCH statement prior to executing an UPDATE WHERE CURRENT OF statement.

When a SQLCODE +100 is returned, your application is past the end of the table. No rows, including the last row, may be processed.

At a minimum, a table name and one SET column name expression are required. An expression may consist of literal constants, program variables, or column names of the table being updated. The components of an expression may not reference columns in another table.

A DELETE WHERE CURRENT OF statement is shown in Figure 11-15.

```
DELETE FROM <table-name>
     WHERE CURRENT OF <cursor-name>
;
```

Figure 11-15. DELETE statement with CURRENT OF clause

table-name Again, a table-name is required that was part of a previous DECLARE CURSOR statement.

cursor-name As with an update, must refer to an open cursor that is current/positioned on a row.

A DELETE WHERE CURRENT OF does not require a FOR UPDATE OF clause in its corresponding DECLARE CURSOR statement. Unfortunately, you still may not utilize an ORDER BY clause.

Error Conditions and SQL Status

Programs executing in SQL mode may utilize the ON ERROR command and ERROR( ) function for error handling. The ON ERROR command may execute a command (e.g. DO) or execute a user defined function.

A partial list of error function values follow:

2000 Duplicate value in unique index (row not inserted).
2002 Database does not exist (Database may have been dropped).
2006 Keys not unique, index not created.
2005 Row violates view definition (WITH CHECK OPTION).
2007 Memory variable or column not defined or memory variable is an invalid type.
2008 Too many work areas open (more than ten tables open or other .dbf files not closed).

Prior to executing an application SQL statement, it may be best to set a memory variable to a character string that identifies the actual SQL statement that originated the error. The error routine could then display the memory variable (literal) to facilitate debugging and application design. In this fashion it will be easier to identify which SQL statement caused the error.

Two memory variables are provided by dBASE IV SQL to indicate the status of a request. SQLCODE is used to signal errors, flag warnings, and indicate successful completion of a SQL statement. SQLCNT will contain the number of rows that were affected by the last executed SQL statement. SQLCODE is set as follows:

+ 100 Warning to indicate that no rows were retrieved for:
1. OPEN CURSOR,
2. INSERT INTO . . . . SELECT FROM or no rows were deleted or updated for a DELETE or UPDATE statement.

0 SQL statement completed successfully. One or more rows affected.

– 1 Error condition occurred. If ON ERROR condition is not set, the program should test SQLCODE first and then utilize the ERROR() function to check for a specific error condition.

Maximum Number of Work Areas

The current release of dBASE IV allows for a maximum of ten work areas. Depending on how a DML query is coded, more work areas may be utilized than anticipated. The following guidelines may be used to count the number of work areas employed in SQL queries:

Open cursors	One work area (results file) is required for every open cursor. The work area is released when the cursor is closed.
One work area per table in a query	One work area is required for every table in a table-list or subquery.
SAVE TO TEMP	Each SAVE TO TEMP clause will require one work area for each TEMP table.
Intermediate work areas	One intermediate work area is required for each GROUP BY *and/or* ORDER BY. If each subquery in a UNION utilizes a GROUP BY, each GROUP BY will require a separate work area.
Transaction processing	When a transaction is established (i.e., BEGIN TRANSACTION . . . . . . END TRANSACTION), an additional work area is required for each open SQL catalog table.

When attempting to execute a complicated query that makes extensive use of joins , subqueries, and/or unions, the ten-work-file limit may prove to be somewhat restrictive. Your only recourse may be to break up a large query into several small ones and utilize the SAVE TO TEMP clause to pass work files between the queries. Take heart, even IBM's DB2 allows a maximum of fifteen tables or intermediate work tables per query.

Conclusion

A cursor may be serially opened and closed several times during one execution of a program. Every time a cursor is opened, a different set of rows may be returned by changing the values in the WHERE predicate conditions of the associated cursor's DECLARE CURSOR query.

Under no condition can a program "back up" in a results table. If concurrent forward and backward processing are required, use two separate cursors—one to utilize an ORDER BY ASC and the other an ORDER BY DESC. The trick is to open the descending process cursor only when it is necessary to "back up." As soon as the required rows are retrieved, close the descending cursor.

Make extensive use of the ON ERROR command, ERROR () function, SQLCODE, and SQLCNT in development and production. If a common SQL error program/routine is employed, provide a means to identify which SQL statement originated the error.

Avoid DDL CREATE statements in application code. They confuse the compiler, complicate code, and consume more resources.

CHAPTER 12

Utilities and Data Base Commands

In dBASE IV SQL, there are several statements that function as utilities and data base level commands. The utility statements may be used to populate or load data into a dBASE IV SQL table from non-SQL files, export or unload an SQL table to a non-SQL file, initialize or reset statistics for the SQL optimizer, allow a dBASE IV .dbf to be processed by SQL statements, or verify the consistency between SQL catalog tables and their respective application tables. The data base commands are necessary to activate (open) or deactivate (close) any one data base. Recall that SQL tables may not be accessed until their corresponding data base is activated. Moreover, a subsequent data base may not be opened until the current active data base is closed.

These utilities and data base commands are considered dBASE IV SQL statements and may be invoked interactively or imbedded within a *.prs* program. Programs containing SQL statements must be suffixed with *.prs*.

Data Base Commands

There are three SQL statements that function as data base commands. At this writing, there are no commands that are specific to dependents of a data base. Recall that tables depend on data bases, indices depend on tables, views depend on tables or views, etc. Large applications may require the ability to disable one or two tables for maintenance purposes while the remainder of the tables in the current data base remain available to other applications. Some maintenance functions, such as ALTER, utilities execution, or adding an index, may cause SQL catalog contention. The only recourse available in a large application with several huge tables is to schedule maintenance during off-peak hours.

SHOW DATABASE Command

One embarrassing question that you may find yourself asking is: "What was the name of that data base I created last month?" Fortunately, dBASE IV SQL provides the SHOW DATABASE command to answer your question. The syntax for this command is shown in Figure 12-1.

```
SHOW DATABASE;
```

Figure 12-1. SHOW DATABASE command syntax

The SHOW DATABASE command may be executed at any time and no data base is required to be active. Its output will list the name of each data base, the user ID of the data base's creator, the date it was created, and the DOS path of each data base directory. This information is stored in the *master* catalog table, SYSDBS. Unlike the SQL catalog tables where a separate set is created for each data base, only one SYSDBS master catalog is maintained in the SQL home directory. The SQL home directory is established by the SQLHOME specification in the config.db file as follows:

```
SQLHOME = drive-spec:\DOS-path1\DOS-pathN
```

The default DOS path directory for SQL home is:

```
C:\DBASE\SQLHOME
```

The SQLHOME DOS path may specify any valid DOS path directory.

START DATABASE Command

To access dBASE IV SQL tables, the data base in which they were created must be activated with the START DATABASE command (Figure 12-2). Only one data base may be active at a time. All subsequent references to tables, views, or other objects will be to objects only in the active data base. All object creation will also occur in the current data base. *Be sure the correct data base is active before doing anything!* There is no command or statement that shows which data base in a dBASE IV SQL system is active. Therefore, if you are in doubt, issue a STOP DATABASE command followed by a START DATABASE command for the correct data base.

```
START DATABASE [database-name];
```

Figure 12-2. START DATABASE command syntax

database-name An optional parameter that specifies the data base to be started. *Note;* This parameter is optional only if one data base was created in your dBASE IV SQL system. If your system has more than one data base defined, you must specify a data base name. A data base is automatically activated at the completion of its creation.

A START DATABASE command may be imbedded in a program or executed interactively.

STOP DATABASE Command

A STOP DATABASE command deactivates or closes the currently active data base (Figure 12-3). The current data base must be closed before any other data base can be activated. Fortunately, a START DATABASE command for a subsequent data base or a CREATE DATABASE statement will close the current data base and then open the specified data base.

```
STOP DATABASE no-spec;
```

Figure 12-3. STOP DATABASE command syntax

no-spec. No data base name can be coded in this command or an error will result. The current release does not allow multiple data bases to be active. Therefore, no data base name is required or allowed. When a later release allows more than one open data base, a data base name may be required.

There is one instance when a data base must not be active or open. This occurs when a data base is to be dropped with a

```
DROP DATABASE database-name
```

statement. Then it is necessary specifically to stop a data base or an error message will be generated.

Utilities

At this time, there are five utility functions that may be used to load, unload, create dBASE IV SQL catalog entries for a dBASE IV .dbf data base, verify SQL catalog entries, and update SQL catalog statistics to optimize access path selection. There is no reorganization utility per se, but a table may be unloaded and then reloaded from the unload output to accomplish a reorganization. When cluster indices are fully implemented, tables will be unloaded in the sequence specified in the cluster index. Chapter 10 contains a detailed account of clustered indices.

DBCHECK Command

The DBCHECK command verifies that dBASE IV SQL catalog tables are consistent with one or all application tables and indexes in the active data base (Figure 12-4).

```
DBCHECK [table-name];
```

Figure 12-4. DBCHECK command syntax

tablc-name This optional parameter allows only one table and its related indices to be verified. Only the .dbf and .mdx file for the named table will be checked. If no table-name is entered, all tables and indices in the current data base will be examined for inconsistencies.

Note that DBCHECK cannot check files that were encrypted using the PROTECT dBASE IV command.

Error messages will be produced for every table and/or index that is not consistent with its SQL catalog description. Errors in application tables may be corrected as follows:

- Copy the applicable .dbf and .mdx dBASE IV files to a backup copy in a different directory or disk.
- Using the SQL DROP TABLE statement, delete the table(s) in error.
- Copy the backup files into the data base directory.
- Use the *DBDEFINE* command to create correct catalog entries for the germane tables and indices.

DBCHECK will also flag blunders in the SQL catalogs. The authors encountered a problem when running the RUNSTATS utility against a 1-million-byte table that caused (through this author's stupidity) some of the SQL catalog tables to be deleted. A subsequent execution of DBCHECK produced several screens of incomprehensible error messages. We had to reinstall the entire dBASE IV package to remedy the problem.

Note: DBCHECK may not be executed when transaction processing is in effect. It may not be run while dBASE IV is logging because of BEGIN TRANSACTION/END TRANSACTION processing.

DBDEFINE Command

This command creates SQL catalog entries for dBASE IV .dbf and .mdx files. The .dbf and related .mdx files must be moved into the data base directory of the data base that will be active when DBDEFINE is invoked (Figure 12-5).

```
DBDEFINE [ ????????.dbf ];
```

Figure 12-5. DBDEFINE command syntax

????????.dbf	Allows the person executing this command to specify a .dbf file for which SQL catalog entries are to be created. The question marks are replaced with the file name. If no .dbf file name is specified, SQL catalog entries will be generated for all .dbf and .mdx files in the DOS directory of the current data base *that are not registered* in the SQL catalog.

dBASE IV SQL tables do not allow memo fields. Any memo field in a .dbf file will not be processed (i.e., will be ignored) during DBDEFINE processing. *Caution:* A dBASE index file (.mdx) that was defined with the UNIQUE option cannot be processed by a DBDEFINE command.

In order to convert dBASE IV data base files to SQL tables, perform the following steps:

- Create a data base with the CREATE DATABASE statement that will contain the converted tables. This command creates all the necessary SQL catalogs and the DOS directory for the data base.
- Using the DOS COPY command, migrate the .mdf and related .mdx dBASE IV files to the new directory.
- Execute the DBDEFINE command.

DBDEFINE will display error messages for files that it cannot process. To recover from these errors, use the same procedure as described for DBCHECK file rehabilitation.

Note: DBDEFINE may not be executed when transaction processing is in effect. It may not be run while dBASE IV is logging because of BEGIN TRANSACTION/END TRANSACTION processing.

LOAD DATA Command

The purpose of the LOAD DATA utility command is initially to populate or append additional rows to an existing dBASE IV SQL table. The table must exist before execution of this utility. If password protection is active (see dBASE IV PROTECT command), you must hold the INSERT privilege or be the creator of the table. Recall that the creator of a dBASE IV SQL object implicitly holds all privileges with regard to that object. Of course, the SQLDBA user may do anything in a dBASE IV SQL system, including loading any table.

The two formats for the LOAD DATA command are illustrated in Figure 12-6.

The keyword TYPE is optional and is provided to make this command more legible. The keywords DATA, FROM, and TABLE are required.

file-name	A required parameter that identifies the input file to be loaded. See the type-spec parameter for the types of files that may be processed by the LOAD DATA command.
table-name	Indicates the SQL table that is to receive the input data. This parameter is also required.
path	An optional parameter that allows the input file to be located on any drive and/or DOS path. The default is the current path.

```
LOAD DATA FROM
    [ path ] < file-name >
INTO TABLE < table-name >
    [ TYPE ] < type-spec >
;
```

```
LOAD DATA FROM
         [ path ] < file-name >
INTO TABLE < table-name >
      [[ TYPE ]
       [ DELIMITED [ WITH BLANK | delimiter ]
      ]
;
```

Figure 12-6. LOAD DATA command utility syntax

type-spec — An optional parameter that specifies the type, and hence the format, of the input file. The default is a .dbf file if no type-spec is coded. The following values may be substituted for type-spec to migrate data from these formats:

dBASE II	dBASE II through dBASE IV files
RPD	RapidFile data base file
FW2	Framework II data base and spreadsheet file
SDF	ASCII System Data Format
DIF	VisiCalc format files
SYLK	MultiPlan spreadsheet format files
WKS	Lotus 1-2-3 format files

DELIMITED *no-specification* — Indicates that input is from an ASCII file with default delimiters. The default field delimiter is a comma. Character fields are enclosed in double quotes as well as being delimited with commas. This is the default if no type-spec or DELIMITED WITH spec is entered.

WITH BLANK | *delimiter* — An optional parameter that allows for optional field/column delimiters specification when reading standard ASCII (.txt) files. This option must be used in conjunction with the DELIMITED parameter. When

`DELIMITED WITH BLANK`

is coded, each input field is separated with a blank and character fields are *not enclosed* in double quotes. Character fields will be padded to their full size. When

`DELIMITED WITH` *`delimiter`*

is specified, each input field is separated with commas and character fields are enclosed with whatever single ASCII character was used to substitute for *delimiter*. No matter which delimiter is utilized, all ASCII input records must be suffixed with a carriage return and a line feed character.

The LOAD DATA command utility is similar to the APPEND FROM dBASE IV command. Blank rows in any spreadsheet are converted to blank rows in the applicable table. Also, fields in the spreadsheet must be in the same sequence and format as the receiving table. Be sure that applicable spreadsheet is stored in *row major* order and not *column major* order.

The table being loaded must already exist and be in the active data base. As with spreadsheets, the receiving table must have its columns in the same sequence and format as the input data fields. The input fields must be of the same data type and length as the respective table columns.

UNLOAD DATA Command

The UNLOAD DATA command utility copies data from an SQL table to an external file. If dBASE IV SQL is password protected, you must hold, at a minimum, the SELECT privilege for the table being unloaded. If you were the table creator of the table or are the SQLDBA dBASE IV SQL user, you may also unload the respective table. The syntax of the UNLOAD DATA command is shown in Figure 12-7.

As with the LOAD DATA command utility, the keyword TYPE is optional and is provided to make this command more legible. The keywords DATA, TO, and TABLE are also required.

file-name — A required parameter that identifies the output file to receive the output data. See the type-spec parameter for the types of files that may be processed by the UNLOAD DATA command.

table-name — Indicates the SQL table that is to be the source of the output data. This is a required parameter .

path — An optional parameter that allows the output file to be located on any drive and/or DOS path. The default is the current path.

```
UNLOAD DATA TO
    [ path ] < file-name >
FROM TABLE < table-name >
    [ TYPE ] < type-spec >
;
```

```
UNLOAD DATA TO
            [ path ] < file-name >
FROM TABLE < table-name >
    [[ TYPE ]
     [ DELIMITED [ WITH BLANK | delimiter ]
    ]
;
```

Figure 12-7. UNLOAD DATA command utility syntax

type-spec — An optional parameter that specifies the type of file that will receive the exported data. If no type-spec is coded, the default is a .dbf file. Type-spec may be substituted with one of the following values to indicate the receiving file format:

dBase II	dBASE II through dBASE IV files
RPD	RapidFile data base file
FW2	Framework II data base and spreadsheet file
SDF	ASCII System Data Format
DIF	VisiCalc format files
SYLK	MultiPlan spreadsheet format files
WKS	Lotus 1-2-3 format files

DELIMITED *no-specification* — Indicates that output is to an ASCII file with default delimiters. The default field delimiter is a comma. Character fields are enclosed in double quotes as well as being delimited with commas. This is the default if no type-spec or DELIMITED WITH spec is entered.

WITH BLANK | *delimiter* — An optional parameter that allows for optional field/column delimiter specification when writing standard ASCII (.txt) files. This option must be used in conjunction with the DELIMITED parameter. When

```
DELIMITED WITH BLANK
```

is coded, each output field is separated with a blank and character fields are not enclosed with double quotes. When

```
DELIMITED WITH delimiter
```

is specified, each output field is separated with commas and character fields are enclosed with whatever single ASCII character was declared for delimiter.

No matter which delimiter is utilized, all ASCII output records must be suffixed with a carriage return and a line feed character.

RUNSTATS Command

This command utility is intended to update statistics in the SQL catalog tables for one or more application tables in the current data base. This utility only processes tables in the active data base. The syntax for the RUNSTATS command utility is illustrated in Figure 12-8.

```
RUNSTATS [ table-name ] ;
```

Figure 12-8. RUNSTATS command utility syntax

table-name An optional parameter to specify one table for which statistics are to be generated. If this parameter is omitted, all application tables in the current data base will be processed. No SQL catalog tables will be processed.

The full effect of this utility will be felt when **SQL** is fully implemented in dBASE IV SQL. Essentially, this utility scans a table and records the number of rows, the number of PAGES, and information pertinent to index structure. These statistics are later used to determine Access Path Selection. If RUNSTATS is not used to update statistics, performance may be degraded.

RUNSTATS should be executed after a table is loaded, after a number of its rows (approximately ten percent) have been either inserted or deleted, or after ten percent of its key columns have been modified.

At present, no specific authorization is required to execute the RUNSTATS command utility.

Command Generation

One benefit of the SQL catalog tables is the ability to generate utility commands from them. For instance, the LOAD DATA and UNLOAD DATA utility commands require a specific table name for their execution. The SQL catalogs could be used to generate, via a query, a LOAD DATA command for each table in the active data base. Figure 12-9 illustrates one possible query.

```
select
        'UNLOAD DATA TO G:\'
,tbname,
        '.TXT FROM TABLE'
,tbname
        ,.,
       ,' ;'
from systabls

        where tbname not like 'SYS%'
;
```

Figure 12-9. Utility command generation example

The key to utility command generation in Figure 12-9 is the use of literals in the select-list to generate the required keywords for the utility commands. The column TBNAME of the SQL catalog table is referenced twice—once for the actual table name and once as part of the output DOS data set name. The resulting output, complete with trailing semicolons, may be utilized as either interactive SQL or a .prs program to unload every table in the current data base. The predicate

```
tbname not like 'SYS%'
```

was added to prevent the SQL catalog tables from being included in the output listing.

Figure 12-10 shows the actual output from the query in Figure 12-9.

```
EXP1               TBNAME     EXP2            TBNAME     EXP3
UNLOAD DATA TO G:\ ASSEMBLY   .TXT FROM TABLE ASSEMBLY   ;
UNLOAD DATA TO G:\ CUSTOMER   .TXT FROM TABLE CUSTOMER   ;
UNLOAD DATA TO G:\ INVENTRY   .TXT FROM TABLE INVENTRY   ;
UNLOAD DATA TO G:\ ITEMS      .TXT FROM TABLE ITEMS      ;
UNLOAD DATA TO G:\ SALES      .TXT FROM TABLE SALES      ;
UNLOAD DATA TO G:\ STAFF      .TXT FROM TABLE STAFF      ;
```

Figure 12-10. Output result of query in Figure 12-9

To generate modifiable and executable statements from interactive SQL, utilize the dBASE IV SET ALTERNATE command and SQL statements at the SQL prompt as follows:

SET ALTERNATE file-spec .prs
SET ALTERNATE ON
Enter and execute your SQL query
CLOSE ALTERNATE
MODIFY COMMAND
Execute the new .prs program

The file-spec for the first SET ALTERNATE must specify a DOS file that is suffixed with .prs to later identify it as a program that contains SQL statements. You cannot execute a program that contains SQL statements that is not suffixed with .prs. In this fashion, the output from your query will be written to a DOS data set specified by file-spec. The MODIFY command allows you to edit and then execute these statements.

Unfortunately, before these utility commands can be utilized, it will be necessary to remove the blanks from the DOS data set name and delete the "column names" heading. The primary benefit of this process is that *no* tables will be missed. Additionally, no errors will be made while coding utility command statements because they are generated for you.

CHAPTER 13

dBASE IV and dBASE IV SQL Security Environment

The security structure in other data base products ranges from nonexistent to "guilty until proved innocent." Security is an intrinsic part of of relational theory and was part of rule 5 in The Twelve Commandments (see Chapter 7). However, security in dBASE IV SQL is not operational until an outer layer of security is activated by execution of the menu-driven **PROTECT** command. Once the PROTECT command is executed, all users of dBASE IV must utilize a log-in identifier. Moreover, dBASE IV SQL security is not activated until someone using the **log-in** name of **SQLDBA** enters SQL mode. Before execution of the PROTECT command, all dBASE IV data bases and tables are open to any access by all users, and prior to the SQLDBA user's invoking SQL mode, all dBASE IV SQL tables are available for any access by any user. Loosely speaking, PROTECT is an "optional" command that, when issued, invokes security system control over data. Figure 13-1 illustrates the dependencies of the PROTECT command when a user is in either dBASE mode (dot prompt) or SQL mode.

The PROTECT command of the dBASE IV security system may be invoked in one of two ways in dBASE IV:

1. Select the "Protect data" option of the **Tools** menu in the Control Center.
2. Type "PROTECT" at the dot (dBASE mode) prompt or SQL prompt and depress the enter key.

The *first invoker* (SQLDBA or any other log-in name) of the PROTECT command establishes the password that will allow access to the **dBASE IV Security System** (Figure 13-2). The password will not be displayed during screen entry. The password should incorporate the maximum of 16 characters (alpha/uppercase or lowercase, and numerics) to secure log-in most effectively. Knowledge of this password, *not of the log-in name,* allows any user to perform security administration functions, such as defining **log-in**

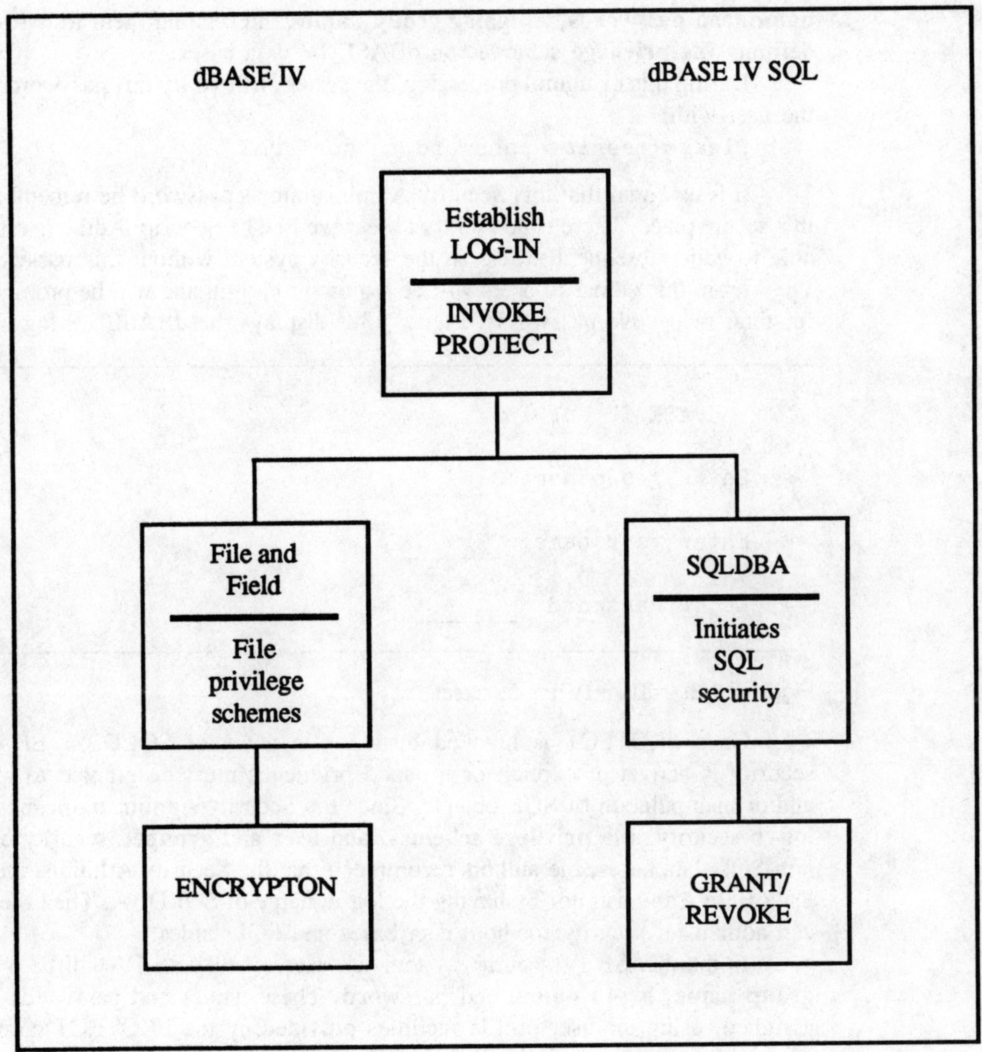

Figure 13-1. PROTECT command dependencies

```
dBASE IV Password Security System

Enter Password ________
```

Figure 13-2. dBASE IV password security system log-in screen

names and **passwords,** assigning **group names** and relating them to log-in names, and defining **file privilege schemes** on dBASE IV data bases.

During this inaugural processing, the system will verify this password by prompting the user with:

```
Please reenter password to confirm.
```

It is essential that this Security Administrator's password be remembered and kept in a secure place. There is no facility to retrieve it! The Security Administrator will not be able to gain subsequent access to the security system without this password.

From this point, all users will be required to log-in and will be prompted only once for their respective passwords. Figure 13-3 displays the dBASE IV log-in screen.

```
  dBASE IV Log-in

Enter group name: ______

Enter your name: _______

Enter Password: _______
```

Figure 13-3. dBase IV log-in screen

Once PROTECT is invoked by a log-in name of SQLDBA, dBASE IV SQL security is activated: explicit or grouped privileges must be granted to allow creation and/or manipulation of SQL objects. Since the Security Administrator must provide for log-in security, **file privilege schemes,** and **user** and **grouped** security capabilities of non-SQL data bases, the authors recommend that the Security Administrator also be the Data Base Administrator by having the log-in name of SQLDBA. Then the same person can administer security for both data bases and SQL tables.

In the dBASE IV security system, all users of dBASE IV will be prompted for a **group name, log-in name,** and **password.** These names and passwords must be pre-assigned, using the user profile facilities provided by the PROTECT command.

User profiles are established via the *user's* menu, which appears following successful access to the security system via the PROTECT command. The user's menu provides facilities for the creation, modification, or deletion of user profiles, as well as the specification of access levels for each user.

To create a user profile after PROTECT log-in, serial entry of several fields must occur, as illustrated by Figure 13-4. The log-in name, password, and group name are required for successful user profile creation.

An *application* is normally the most logical basis for the grouping of users and files. For file access to take place, user and file group names will be matched.

The user is assigned an *access level* within each group of which the user is a member. For each data base, its files, and fields within files, the group access levels will be matched to access levels defined by **Files** menu processing.

Full name, the optional entry in user profile creation, may be used as documentation of the user log-in name since it is not considered in log-in evaluation.

User Log-in Name	1-8 alphanumerics	Req.
Password	1-16 alphanumerics	Req.
Group Name	1-8 alphanumerics	Req.
Full Name	1-24 alphanumerics	Opt.
Access Level	Values 1-8	Req.
Store	enter	Req.

Figure 13-4. dBASE IV user profile fields

Failure to store user profile entry will abort its processing.

Modification and deletion of user profiles require entry of the log-in name, password, and group name. Once PROTECT confirms the existence of a user profile for the combination entered (and the user responds to the edit prompt), all other associated entries are presented. Once presented, any entry may be changed. Of course, all changes must be saved to become effective.

Do not change or delete the group name. Files associated with the former group name will no longer be accessible.

Delete processing is initiated in a fashion similar to a modification request. The selection for "delete user from group" is chosen rather than responding "*y*" to the edit prompt.

File Privilege Establishment

File and field privileges must be established to correspond to user access levels. These privilege schemes are stored as part of the data base file structure.

The **Files** menu may be accessed to associate a file with a group, add or change access levels for file privilege schemes, or associate specific field access privileges with file access privileges.

Within the **Files** menu, default access levels are set to the most restrictive level (level 8), and field privileges are set at FULL. Failure to set file privilege schemes subjects files to controls by the network operating system.

To create a file privilege scheme, select a data base file via the **New file** option of the Files menu. Assign the file to only *one* group—a group name to be matched to the user group name before access. Obviously, segregating applications into functional groupings will greatly facilitate security administration. Figure 13-5 illustrates file access levels.

```
File Access Levels

READ          8

Update        8

Extend        8

Delete        8
```

Figure 13-5. dBASE IV file privilege fields

Select the **File access privileges** option of the Files menu to define the privilege level of access to the file. Access levels range from 1 to 8, with 1 specifying maximum privilege level. Typically, users defined for maximum access authorization are limited in number in order to maintain some data security. Access privileges include DELETE, EXTEND, READ, and UPDATE. For each access type, the most restrictive level is specified. Any user authorized for at least the level of privilege assigned to the file will obtain file access. Conversely, users defined with access privileges below the level defined for the access request will be denied file privileges.

Note that a file designated as "read-only" at the operating system level cannot have its access superseded by file privilege selection.

The maximum number of data base file privilege schemes is nine. Failure to save the schemes or to exit from the menu option will produce an error message of "too many files are open."

Field access may be specified in the file access definition via the **Establish field privileges** option. A menu of fields will be presented, for which FULL, R/O (read-only), or NONE access choices are possible.

While specifiying field access privileges, consider that they are subordinate to the access level defined for the file containing the field. For instance, a field within a read-only file may not be specified for update access. Furthermore, specification of field restriction will not prevent file corruption from DELETE or ZAP actions when file privileges are concurrently specified.

The SQLDBA user is required to be added in order to enable SQL usage. This requirement exists because SQLDBA possesses privileges for all SQL operations. Two of these commands, GRANT and REVOKE, are used to associate file and field access levels with the log-in names assigned by PROTECT. You do not need PROTECT file and field level security to utilize dBASE IV SQL table and column security

Briefly, dBASE IV SQL privileges are extended by means of the **GRANT** command and taken away by the **REVOKE** statement. GRANT enables one user to provide a privilege to another user; thus, the data base administrator (SQLDBA) is the ultimate point of origin of all privileges. REVOKE disables the privileges previously extended to a user via a GRANT statement. However, REVOKE acts with a **cascading**

effect to revoke any privileges that were extended to another user exclusively by the user whose authorization is being revoked. Therefore, it is important that a user be aware of the origin of his particular authority. A REVOKE from PUBLIC only disables authority exclusively obtained by a GRANT to PUBLIC. Authorities granted to users by other specifically authorized users will remain active. Any revoked privilege may be reinstated by issuance of another GRANT statement by an authorized user.

GRANT and REVOKE Examples

The results of a REVOKE statement depend on either the AUTHID of the issuer of the GRANT request or the time when it was executed. Additionally, all GRANT requests would have to include the "WITH GRANT OPTION." To illustrate the preceding points, a few examples follow.

TIME		ACTION
11:00	usr1	GRANT SELECT ON TABLE T_PROJ TO usra
11:08	usr1	GRANT SELECT ON TABLE T_PROJ TO usra
11:15	usr1	REVOKE SELECT ON TABLE T_PROJ FROM usra

Figure 13-6. Multiple GRANTs by same user

- Example 1 "usra" receives the same privilege from "usr1" twice. At a later time, the privilege is REVOKED by "usr1" (Figure 13-6).

Result: The privilege is revoked because the last chronological action was a REVOKE.

TIME		ACTION
12:00	usr1	GRANT SELECT ON TABLE T_PROJ TO usra
12:05	usr2	GRANT SELECT ON TABLE T_PROJ TO usra
13:10	usr1	REVOKE SELECT ON TABLE T_PROJ FROM usra

Figure 13-7. Mutiple GRANTs by different users

- Example 2 "usra" receives the same privilege from "usr1" and "usr2." At a later time, the privilege is REVOKED by "usr1." Both "usr1" and "usr2" obtained the privilege from another log-in ID (creator?) (Figure 13-7).

Result: The privilege is not revoked because the privilege is still in effect from "usr2."

TIME	ACTION		
12:00	usrl	GRANT SELECT ON TABLE T_PROJ TO	usra
12:05	usra	GRANT SELECT ON TABLE T_PROJ TO	usrx
13:10	usrl	REVOKE SELECT ON TABLE T_PROJ FROM	usra

Figure 13-8. Cascading REVOKE dependency

- Example 3 "usra" receives the SELECT privilege from "usrl" and then "usra" grants the identical privilege to "usrx." Later, "usrl" revokes the privilege that was originally given to "usra" (Figure 13-8).

Result: The privilege is revoked from both "usra" and "usrx" because the principle of a REVOKE is to reset authorities to the state prior to the related GRANT.

TIME	ACTION		
10:00	usrl	GRANT SELECT ON TABLE T_PROJ TO	usra
10:20	usra	GRANT SELECT ON TABLE T_PROJ.TO	usrb
11:00	usrx	GRANT SELECT ON TABLE T_PROJ TO	usra
13:10	usrx	REVOKE SELECT ON TABLE T_PROJ FROM	usra

Figure 13-9. GRANT and REVOKE time dependency without loss

- Example 4: "usra" receives a privilege from "usrl." Then "usra" gives the same privilege to "usrb." Later, "usrx" grants the same SELECT privilege to "usra." Finally, "usrx" revokes the SELECT privilege (Figure 13-9).

Result: The privilege is not revoked from either "usra" or "usrb" because "usra" received the SELECT from "usrl" prior to the GRANT executed by "usrx". The privilege obtained from usrx by usra is effectively redundant.

- Example 5 "usra" receives a privilege from "usrl." Then "usra" gives the same privilege to "usrb." Later, "usrx" grants the same SELECT privilege to "usra." As for the difference from example 4, **"usrl"** here revokes the SELECT privilege (Figure 13-10).

TIME		ACTION
15:00	usr1	GRANT SELECT ON TABLE T_PROJ TO usra
16:20	usra	GRANT SELECT ON TABLE T_PROJ TO usrb
17:00	usrx	GRANT SELECT ON TABLE T_PROJ TO usra
17:10	usr1	REVOKE SELECT ON TABLE T_PROJ FROM usra

Figure 13-10. GRANT and REVOKE time dependency with loss

Result: The privilege is revoked from **"usrb"** *and not* **"usra"** because "usra" received the SELECT privilege from "usrx" after the initial extension of the privilege from "usr1." The REVOKE removed the path through which "usrb" received the privilege. However, "usra" retains the SELECT privilege through a second path established by "usrx."

By now you have a healthy respect for the potential effect of multiple levels of privileges. The previous examples by no means reflect a "worst case" scenerio, but were intended to give you a flavor of dBASE IV SQL security.

SECTION III

Major Applications

CHAPTER 14

Overview

Before we start our major application, let us review some basics about professional programming in general, and dBASE IV in particular.

When you program for yourself, it does not matter what style you use to write your code. However, when you are a professional programmer, it matters a great deal. The style in which you program can have a direct bearing on whether you obtain another contract with your client or, if you are an employee, whether you will be promoted. Someone will have to maintain the code you write, and so the clearer it is, the easier that job becomes. Thus, make sure that you are consistent in your use of:

Memory variable names
Memory variable capitalization
Memory variable size
Command indentation
Procedure use
Command usage
Comments/internal documentation
General coding techniques

Memory Variable Names

dBASE permits memory variables to be up to ten characters in length. Make use of this ability. If you need a field to compute an average age, for example, use the variable "AverageAge," not "AA," or even "Average." The longer name makes the code easier to read, understand, and debug months later when you have forgotten what a routine was doing or what a variable was used for. Notice that this variable was called

"AverageAge," not "Average_ag," because an underscore really make the code less readable. It adds an extra character that sometimes can make the difference between being able to understand the code and finding it difficult. Do not be afraid of having to type long names. You can either type the full name at the time you are coding the system, or type codes for long variable names and use the global replace function of your editor to change all the codes back to long variable names. Always use meaningful memory variable names.

Capitalization and Procedure Use

Since we are not going to use underscores, we need a way to make long names easy to read. This is accomplished by mixing uppercase and lowercases characters in the memory variable name to differentiate words in memory variables. Use LastName instead of LAST_NAME or Lastname.

Capitalize all dBASE reserved words—for example, PROCEDURE, SET FILTER TO, LOCATE FOR, SET RELATION TO. When calling a procedure using the DO procedure name syntax, use both upper- and lowercase for the procedure name; however, when defining a procedure, use all uppercase. For example:

```
DO FindName
...
...
PROCEDURE FINDNAME
```

This allows you to find the procedure by searching for the name with all uppercase and to find all calls to the procedure by searching with a mix of upper- and lowercase.

Indentation

Indent all IF, DO WHILE, SCAN, BEGIN TRANSACTION, PRINT JOB, and DO CASE statements by three characters. This provides readability and still allows enough characters to be viewed for easy understanding of the code. It also aids in debugging.

```
PROCEDURE TEST
.....
....
DO WHILE .NOT. EOF()
    next line
  ........
  .......
  IF CONDITION
     next line
   .......
   .......
   ENDIF
   .....
  ENDDO
```

DO CASE structures can be indented in many different ways. The author's preferred usage is to indent the individual CASE statements 3 spaces, and then to indent all statements under the CASE statement an additional 3 spaces, as follows:

```
PROCEDURE TEST
...
...
...
DO CASE
   CASE LastName = "Steele"
      ...
      ...
      ...
   CASE LastName = "Klion"
      ...
      ...
      ...
   CASE LastName = "Shapiro"
      ...
      ...
      ...
   OTHERWISE
      ...
ENDCASE
```

Note: When using the CASE statement, the following example will print "A." To print "ABC," you must issue the statement SET EXACT ON before issuing the CASE instruction.

```
Test = "ABC"
DO CASE
   CASE Test = "A"
      @ 12,12 SAY "A"
   CASE Test = "AB"
      @ 12,12 SAY "AB"
   CASE Test = "ABC"
      @ 12,12 SAY "ABC"
ENDCASE
```

Command Usage

Various commands are more efficient and easier to read than others that carry out the same function, such as "STORE vs =". When you wish to set a group of memory variables to the same values, use STORE. For example:

```
STORE 0      TO AccountNum, FoundRecord, MainMenuSel
STORE .T.    TO FirstTime, OK, SkipScreen
STORE "Y"    TO Choice, Continue, GoOn
```

Notice that all the TO words are aligned. This technique allows easier reading and debugging, and usually separates professional code from that of the typical hacker.

The "=" sign is used in place of the STORE . . . TO construct when only one variable is being accessed. For example:

```
Count          = Count   + 1
Yesterday      = DATE() - 1
OK             = .T.
```

Comments/Internal Documentation

When code becomes complex or unclear, use comments. Whenever a procedure is called by many other procedures, document the purpose of the called procedure, the calling sequence, and the returned results of the procedure. For example:

```
PROCEDURE CENTER

PARAMETERS InString, OutLength

*****************************************************************
*                                                               *
* This procedure inserts leading spaces to center a string      *
*                                                               *
* Input:  The string to be centered, Length of output line      *
*                                                               *
* Output: The string with leading blanks                        *
*                                                               *
* Assumptions:  The length of the output line is greater        *
*               than the length of the string to be             *
*               centered.                                       *
*                                                               *
*****************************************************************
```

```
LeadingBlnk = (OutLength - LEN(TRIM(InString))) / 2
InString = REPLICATE(" ",LeadingBlnk) + TRIM(InString)
RETURN
*END:CENTER
```

If your printer can print the full IBM character set, you may wish to replace the "*******" with the double underscore. The preceding code then would look like this:

```
PROCEDURE CENTER

PARAMETERS InString, OutLength

*┌──────────────────────────────────────────────────────┐
*|                                                      |
*|This procedure inserts leading spaces to center a string |
*|                                                      |
*|Input:  The string to be centered, Length of output line |
*|                                                      |
*|Output: The string with leading blanks                |
*|                                                      |
*|Assumptions:  The length of the output line is greater |
*|              than the length of the string to be      |
*|              centered.                                |
*|                                                      |
*└──────────────────────────────────────────────────────┘

LeadingBlnk = (OutLength - LEN(TRIM(InString))) / 2
InString = REPLICATE(" ",LeadingBlnk) + TRIM(InString)
RETURN
*END:CENTER
```

Note: The extended characters can be entered into dBASE code using the Alt key and the numbers on the numeric pad. For example, a double box character 205 (═) can be entered into your code by pressing and holding the Alt key down while you press the numbers 2, 0, and 5 in sequence on the numeric pad.

The following chart shows the "Alt characters" needed to draw various boxes.

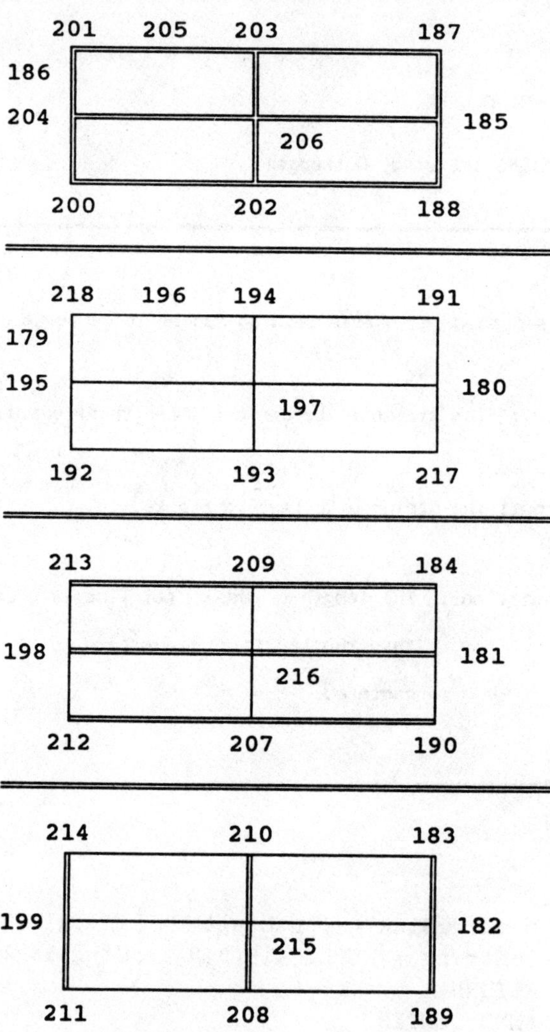

In the corporate environment, a very important use of comments in code is to indicate who wrote the code, what the code does, and the revision level. This is even more important if you are an independent contractor, as it provides a place for your client to find your name and phone number for additional assignments. For example:

```
*
* Program.: XYZ.PRG
* Author..: Phil Steele - President Phillipps Computer Systems Inc.
* Address.: 52 Hook Mountain Road,  Montville NJ 07045
* Phone...: (201) 575-8575
* Date....: 12/26/89
* Notice..: Copyright 1989, Phillipps Computer Systems,
*           All Rights Reserved
* Version.: CLIPPER SUMMER 1989
* Notes...: MAIN Driver for XYZ Release 2.10
*
```

In addition to your general information block, you need to set key parameters before you start to write a line of code. This preamble should be included after the general information block. Here is an example of such a preamble.

```
*________________________
* MAIN PROCEDURE PREAMBLE
*________________________
CLEAR ALL
SET STEP OFF
SET ECHO OFF
SET TALK OFF
SET BELL OFF
SET PRINT OFF
SET DELETE ON
SET STATUS OFF
SET SAFETY OFF
SET ESCAPE OFF
SET CONFIRM ON
SET HEADING OFF
SET SCOREBOARD OFF
SET DISPLAY TO EGA25
SET DEVICE TO SCREEN
SET CURSOR OFF

*________________
* STANDARD COLORS
* ________________
RESTORE FROM COLOR ADDITIVE
*
* IF COLOR.MEM does not not exist, create it using the
* following:
*
*  Cl              = ISCOLOR()
*  ColBlank        = "N/N,N/N,N"
*  ColFunc         = "N/W"
```

```
*  ColOther   = IIF(Cl, "BG+/B"       , "W+/N")
*  ColHelp    = IIF(Cl, "N/G,N/W,B"  , "W+/N,N/W,N")
*  ColData    = IIF(Cl, "RG+/B,N/W,B" , "W+/N,N/W,N")
*  ColError   = IIF(Cl, "W+/R,W+/N,B" , "W/N,N/W,N")
*  ColEntry   = IIF(Cl, "N/W,W+/N,B" , "N/W,W+/N,N")
*  ColStand   = IIF(Cl, "W+/B,N/W,B" , "W+/N,N/W,N")
*  ColMenu    = IIF(Cl, "BG+/R,BG+/N,B", "W+/N,N/W,N")
*  ColWarning = IIF(Cl, "N/BG,W+/N,B" , "W/N,N/W,N")
*  SAVE TO COLOR ALL LIKE COL*


* ______________
* MISC CONSTANTS
* ______________
DoubleBox = CHR(201)+CHR(205)+CHR(187)+CHR(186)+;
            CHR(188)+CHR(205)+CHR(200)+CHR(186)+CHR(32)
SingleBox = CHR(218)+CHR(196)+CHR(191)+CHR(179)+;
            CHR(217)+CHR(196)+CHR(192)+CHR(179)+CHR(32)
Esc       =  CHR(27)

* _____________
* KEY CONSTANTS
* _____________
Key          = 0    &&  General-purpose key variable.
Home         = 1
CtrlPgUp     = 1
PgDn         = 3
CurRight     = 4
CurUp        = 5
EndKey       = 6
Del          = 7
Tab          = 9
Enter        = 13
PgUp         = 18
CurLeft      = 19
CInsert      = 22
CtrlW        = 23
CurDn        = 24
CtrlY        = 25
ESCAPE       = 27
F1Key        = 28
CtrlPgDn     = 30
Space        = 32
BackTab      = 271
F2Key        = -1
F3Key        = -2
```

```
F4Key         = -3
F5Key         = -4
F6Key         = -5
F7Key         = -6
F8Key         = -7
F9Key         = -8
F10Key        = -9
AltF9Key      = -38
AltF10Key     = -39
```

User Interface

Corporate users are unique animals. While we are willing to forgive small errors and work around awkward screens and menus and occasional error messages, corporate users are terrified of computers, and are afraid that an error on their part will "break" the equipment. Anything more complex than making a choice from a menu is intimidating, and having to respond to cryptic messages is beyond the call of duty. Therefore, **Keep your systems simple**. Remember that users are neither programmers nor systems oriented. They may be knowledgeable in their spheres of expertise, but they know **nothing** about computers or computer systems. It is your job as a professional programmer to make the application run itself. All messages to users must be easily understood and consistent and interfaces must be simple to use. Always keep users informed. At no time should there be a blank screen. If the system is indexing, tell the users. If the system is doing complex number crunching, tell the users.

CHAPTER 15

A Commercial Example Written in dBASE IV

For our major dBASE IV application, we will use a real-life example. As they say on television, "The names have been changed to protect the innocent."

This application involved a large hospital, which we will call Phillipps Memorial Hospital. The hospital employs various independent (nonhospital employees) vendors to perform diverse functions in and around the hospital such as: window cleaning, computer programming, insurance investigations, housekeeping, patient care, patient transportation, testing, etc.

These functions require that the independent contractor (vendor) has the proper insurance, ranging from automobile insurance, to workers compensation insurance, to liability insurance, etc. Each of these types of insurance must provide for a minimum amount of insurance coverage that meets hospital limits. In addition some of the functions performed by the vendors require that a confidentiality agreement be signed. At this time there are four different types of confidentiality agreements in effect at Phillipps Memorial Hospital.

USER GENERATED SYSTEM REQUIREMENTS:

1. The system must be very easy to use by nontechnical personnel.
2. The system must be easy to modify.
3. It must provide for the input of information pursuant to:
   Each vendor.
   Each type of insurance coverage (11 maximum).
   Four confidentiality agreements.
4. The system has to produce various reports including:
   Insurance coverage.
   Expiration dates.

Dollar limits.
Compliance/Noncompliance with internal hospital policies.

5. The system has to produce form letters.
   Automatically generated when selected from the menu
6. The data in the system must be able to be:
   Viewed
   Changed
   Downloaded
   Deleted
7. The system must be written in dBASE IV release 1.1 or higher.

DATA BASE

Before any code is written we must define the data base then, using the data base, we can design the screens and reports we need. The first consideration in data base design is the number of data bases and the relations hips among them. In this application, it appears that three related data bases will be required. If we determine, as we go along, that we need additional fields, or that we included fields we are not using, or that the lengths of the fields are wrong, we can change them—even if there is data in them. This is the beauty of using dBASE as compared with other languages. All we have to do is use dBASE in the interactive mode and execute the command MODIFY STRUCTURE. All changes we make will be reflected in the data base and we will not have to write any "conversion" programs. The data bases that we will start with will be called Vendor, Insuranc, and Confidnt, and will look like this:

Structure for Data Base: VENDOR.DBF

Field	Field Name	Type	Width
1	VENDNUM	Character	9
2	VENDNAME	Character	30
3	VENSHORTN	Character	10
4	ADDRESS1	Character	30
5	ADDRESS2	Character	30
6	CITY	Character	20
7	STATE	Character	3
8	ZIP	Character	9
9	TELEPHONE	Character	10
10	STATUS	Character	1
11	ATTNNAME	Character	25
12	TYPECODE	Character	2
13	ONPREMISE	Logical	1
14	PRIMEBU	Character	25
15	ARRANGCOD	Character	2
16	ORIGINAL	Logical	1
17	CONFIDENT	Logical	1

18	CERTIF	Logical	1
19	CANCELTERM	Character	2
20	EXPENSECD	Character	2
21	VENINPUT	Date	8
22	INCERTLET	Date	8
23	CERTLET	Date	8
24	TERMLET	Date	8
25	SIGNLET	Date	8
26	CONINSCOM	Logical	1
27	CONCONFCOM	Logical	1
** Total **			257

Structure for Data Base: INSURANC.DBF

Field	Field Name	Type	Width
1	VENDNUM	Character	9
2	INSURTYPE	Character	2
3	AMOUNT	Numeric	5
4	CONTAMT	Numeric	5
5	INPUT	Date	8
6	EFFECTIVE	Date	8
7	EXPIRATION	Date	8
8	EXPLET1	Date	8
9	EXPLET2	Date	8
10	EXPLET3	Date	8
** Total **			70

Structure for Data Base: CONFIDNT.DBF

Field	Field Name	Type	Width
1	VENDNUM	Character	9
2	CONFCODE	Character	1
3	CONFINPUT	Date	8
4	CONFEFFECT	Date	8
5	CONFEXPIRE	Date	8
6	CONFRECVD	Date	8
7	SIGNOFF	Logical	1
** Total **			44

Note 1: All three data bases contain the field VendNum. This was done so that we can relate the children files (Insuranc and Confidnt) records to the parent file (Vendor).

Note 2: This listing can be obtained in dBASE after creating the data bases by using the following commands:

```
SET ALTERNATE TO DOC.TXT
SET ALTERNATE ON
USE VENDOR
LIST STRUCTURE
USE INSURANC
LIST STRUCTURE
USE CONFIDNT
LIST STRUCTURE
SET ALTERNATE OFF
QUIT
```

Screens

Now that we have the data base defined, we can design the screens the system will need. All systems, no matter how simple, need a starting screen, which enables the users to select the features of the system they wish to use. This screen is the MASTER MENU. In addition, there will usually be a data input screen, a view screen, an edit screen, a report selection screen, and a report run screen. You may be able to combine the input, edit, and view screens into one—as we will do in this application.

Menus

An easy way to create a system that is simple to use (the primary requirement for this application) is to utilize menus. Then all the users have to do is either to enter a number or to point to a menu selection to accomplish the desired action, thus affording little opportunity for error.

By using menus, VALID, and range statements in dBASE IV, user errors can be kept to a minimum. However, even when using a menu, users will make errors. They will select "reports" when they want to choose "edit a record," for instance, and so all menus and the screens following the menus should include a method by which to return to the previous screen.

All menus should look professional; they should be centered and the choices limited, and related where possible. If more than one report is to be printed, use a separate report menu. If more than one data base can be used for similar reports, use a data base selection menu.

Where possible, make the initial menu specific to the company for which you are writing the application. If the corporation has a corporate logo, try to incorporate it in the initial menu. If it has a unique motto, use it. Remember, this is a professional system.

The reports will not be included in this example as you will not learn much from all the code they occupy. Instead, you will be shown how to create reports using both the dBASE IV report generator and SQL. Remember that if you give people a fish, you will feed them for a day, but if you teach them how to fish, you feed them for life. This example will feed your reporting needs for the life of dBASE IV.

Instead of guiding you through all the steps necessary to generate this application (which would make this book at least twice its size), the following lists the entire system with line numbers. The line numbers will be used in the explanations. If you key this example, do not include the line numbers.

Note: All the code examples in this book are available from the authors. See the order blank for additional information.

```
1  *
2  *  Program.: Phillipps Memorial Hospital
3  *           Insurance Compliance System
4  *  Author..: Phil Steele - President Phillipps Computer Systems Inc.
5  *  Address.: 52 Hook Mountain Road,  Montville NJ 07045
6  *  Phone...: (201) 575-8575
7  *  Date....: Started:   December 5, 1989
8  *           Completed: January  4, 1990
9  *
10 *  Notice..: Copyright 1990  Philip Steele  -  All Rights Reserved.
11 *
12 *  Version.: dBASE IV Release 1.1
13 *
14 *
15 *_______________
16 * MAIN PROCEDURE PREAMBLE
17 *_______________
18 CLEAR ALL
19 SET STEP OFF
20 SET ECHO OFF
21 SET TALK OFF
22 SET BELL OFF
23 SET PRINT    OFF
24 SET DELETE   ON
25 SET STATUS   OFF
26 SET SAFETY   OFF
27 SET ESCAPE   OFF
28 SET CONFIRM  ON
29 SET HEADING OFF
30 SET SCOREBOARD OFF
31 SET DISPLAY TO EGA25
32 SET DEVICE   TO SCREEN
33 SET CURSOR   OFF
34
35
36 *_______________
37 * STANDARD COLORS
38 * _______________
39 RESTORE FROM COLOR ADDITIVE
40 *
41 * IF COLOR.MEM Doen not exist create using the following:
42 *
43 *   Cl         = ISCOLOR()
44 *   ColBlank   = "N/N,N/N,N"
45 *   ColFunc    = "N/W"
46 *   ColOther   = IIF(Cl, "BG+/B"        , "W+/N")
47 *   ColHelp    = IIF(Cl, "N/G,N/W,B"    , "W+/N,N/W,N")
48 *   ColData    = IIF(Cl, "RG+/B,N/W,B"  , "W+/N,N/W,N")
49 *   ColError   = IIF(Cl, "W+/R,W+/N,B"  , "W/N,N/W,N")
50 *   ColEntry   = IIF(Cl, "N/W,W+/N,B"   , "N/W,W+/N,N")
51 *   ColStand   = IIF(Cl, "W+/B,N/W,B"   , "W+/N,N/W,N")
52 *   ColMenu    = IIF(Cl, "BG+/R,BG+/N,B", "W+/N,N/W,N")
53 *   ColWarning = IIF(Cl, "N/BG,W+/N,B"  , "W/N,N/W,N")
54 *   SAVE TO COLOR ALL LIKE COL*
```

```
* ______________
* MISC CONSTANTS
* ______________
DoubleBox  = CHR(201)+CHR(205)+CHR(187)+CHR(186)+;
   CHR(188)+CHR(205)+CHR(200)+CHR(186)+CHR(32)
SingleBox  = CHR(218)+CHR(196)+CHR(191)+CHR(179)+;
   CHR(217)+CHR(196)+CHR(192)+CHR(179)+CHR(32)
Esc        = CHR(27)
LP         = CHR(40)
COrder     = "Vendor"
HEAD       = "Insurance Compliance System"
OKToPrnt   = .F.
ByPass     = .F.
PUBLIC ARRAY AMenu[25]

* _____________
* KEY CONSTANTS
* _____________
KEY           =  0   && General purpose key variable
EndKey        =  2
PgDn          =  3
CurRight      =  4
CurUp         =  5
Del           =  7
Tab           =  9
Enter         = 13
PgUp          = 18
CurLeft       = 19
CInsert       = 22
CtrlW         = 23
CurDn         = 24
CtrlY         = 25
Home          = 26
ESCAPE        = 27
F1Key         = 28
CtrlPgDn      = 30
CtrlPgUp      = 31
Space         = 32
F2Key         = -1
F3Key         = -2
F4Key         = -3
F5Key         = -4
F6Key         = -5
F7Key         = -6
F8Key         = -7
F9Key         = -8
F10Key        = -9
BackTab       = -400
AltL          = -424


* ____________
* STARTUP CODE
* ____________
Dummy = Logo()                                  && Put Logos on the screen
Dummy = Intro()
Dummy = CENT( 4, 80, "Insurance Compliance System")
Dummy = CENT( 6, 80, "Phillipps Memorial Hospital")
Dummy = CENT( 8, 80, "DEMO Program - Release 2.01")
Dummy = CENT(10, 80, "Copyright 1990 Philip Steele")
Dummy = CENT(11, 80, "All Rights Reserved")
```

```
SET COLOR TO &ColStand
SET CURSOR OFF
DO OpenData                                  && Open the databases
DO FillArry                                  && Fill the arrays
CLEAR TYPEAHEAD
CurrentDate = DATE()
Dummy       = MESSBOX(17, "Enter today's date:      ",;
              .T., "S", ColWarning)
SET COLOR TO &ColEntry
SET CURSOR ON
@ 17, 46 GET CurrentDate                     && Get Processing Date -
READ                                         && Default is Systems Date
SET CURSOR OFF
SET MESSAGE TO                               && Turn off messages


* ---------
* MAINMENU                                   && Do the Main Menu
* ---------
DO WHILE .T.
   SET COLOR TO &ColStand
   CLEAR
   SET MESSAGE TO " " AT 23,0                && Put all message on line 23
   RELEASE POPUP
   CLEAR TYPEAHEAD
   MainC = 0
   Dummy = START()
   Dummy = FKEYS(2)
   Dummy = MBOX(26, 5, 15, .T., "D", ColMenu, "M A I N   M E N U")
   SET BORDER TO NONE
   DEFINE POPUP Main FROM 7,27
   DEFINE BAR 1 OF Main PROMPT "1. Inquiry & Update Menu";
             MESSAGE MESSCENT( "View and Update Information.")
   DEFINE BAR 3 OF Main PROMPT "2. Report Menu          ";
             MESSAGE MESSCENT( "Select and Print Reports.")
   DEFINE BAR 5 OF Main PROMPT "3. Utility Menu         ";
             MESSAGE MESSCENT("Perform Utility Operations.")
   DEFINE BAR 7 OF Main PROMPT "4. Exit to DOS          ";
             MESSAGE MESSCENT( "Return to the Operating System.")
   ON SELECTION POPUP Main DO PopSel WITH MainC
   SET BORDER TO SINGLE
   ACTIVATE POPUP Main

   DO CASE
      CASE MainC = 1                         && View & Change Data
         DO DVend
      CASE MainC = 3                         && CReports
         DO DRpts
         Dummy = NotYet()
      CASE MainC = 5                         && Utilities
         DO DUtil
      CASE MainC = 7 .OR. MainC = 0          && Return
         DO Fini
   ENDCASE
ENDDO
*END:MAINMENU


* ------------------------------------------------------------------
*U S E R   D E F I N E D   F U N C T I O N S   &   P R O C E D U R E S*
* ------------------------------------------------------------------

* -----------
```

```
PROCEDURE FINI
* ————————————
SET MESSAGE TO
Mess1 = "DO YOU REALLY WISH TO EXIT?"
Mess2 = ""
YN    = .F.
YN    = YesOrN(Mess1, Mess2, ColWarning)
IF .NOT. YN
   RETURN
ENDIF
RELEASE POPUP
SET COLOR TO &ColStand                  && Clean up system before
CLEAR                                   && Returning to DOS
@ 0,0 SAY " "
SET CURSOR ON
CLOSE ALL
IF FILE("TEMP.DBF")
   RUN DEL TEMP.DBF
ENDIF
QUIT
*END:FINI
FUNCTION INTRO
*
*  Notes.....: This function presents an exploding
*              box with a drop shadow to be used at
*              the beginning of a system usually to
*              show the system name, author and
*              release number.
*
*              The final Box Values (Top, Left,
*              Bottom, Right) = 7, 20, 16, 60
*  Parameters: None.
*
PRIVATE J, K
SET COLOR TO RG+/R,N/W,B,B
J = 8
DO WHILE J < 12
   K = INT((J-6) * 5)
   SET COLOR TO W+/R
   @ 15-J, 50-K CLEAR TO 1+J, K+30
   @ 15-J, 50-K TO 1+J, K+30 DOUBLE COLOR W+/R
   J = J +.2
ENDDO
SET COLOR TO N/N
@ 16-J, K+31 CLEAR TO 1+J, K+32
@ 1+J,  52-K CLEAR TO 1+J, K+32
SET COLOR TO RG+/R,N/W,B,B
RETURN(.T.)
*END:INTRO
* ————————————
PROCEDURE OPENDATA                      && Open all files - set relationships
* ————————————                          && and initialize lookup arrays
USE VENDOR
   INDEX ON VendNum  TAG Vendor   OF Vend
   INDEX ON VendName TAG VendName OF Vend
   INDEX ON ExpenseCD + VendName TAG VendDept OF Vend
USE INSURANC
   INDEX ON VendNum + InsurType TAG Insuranc OF Insur
```

```
USE CONFIDNT
   INDEX ON VendNum + ConfCode TAG Confidnt OF CONF
SELECT D
USE Codes
SELECT A
USE Vendor   INDEX Vend  ORDER TAG Vendor   OF Vend
SELECT B
USE Insuranc INDEX Insur ORDER TAG Insuranc OF Insur
SELECT C
USE Confidnt INDEX CONF  ORDER TAG Confidnt OF CONF
SELECT A
SET RELATION TO VendNum INTO B, VendNum INTO C
RETURN
*END:OPENDATA
* ________________
PROCEDURE FILLARRY                          && Fill the POPUP Arrays
* ________________
SELECT D
PUBLIC MaxNum                               && Declare and initialize
MaxNum = 20                                 && lookup arrays
PUBLIC ARRAY Arr[MaxNum], Hos[MaxNum], Con[MaxNum],;
             Exp[MaxNum], Ins[MaxNum], Ven[MaxNum]
DECLARE TEMP[MaxNum,1]
K = 1
DO WHILE K < 7
   DO CASE
      CASE K = 1
         CodeTyp = "Arr"
      CASE K = 2
         CodeTyp = "Hos"
      CASE K = 3
         CodeTyp = "Con"
      CASE K = 4
         CodeTyp = "Exp"
      CASE K = 5
         CodeTyp = "Ins"
      CASE K = 6
         CodeTyp = "Ven"
   ENDCASE
   COPY TO ARRAY Temp FIELDS Code FOR CodeType = CodeTyp
   J = 1
   DO WHILE J <= MaxNum
      &CodeTyp[J] = TEMP[J,1]
      J = J + 1
   ENDDO
   K = K + 1
ENDDO
SELECT A
RETURN
*END:FILLARRY
* ____________
FUNCTION ZEROM
* ____________
J = 0
DO WHILE J <= 25
   AMenu[25] = " "
   J = J + 1
```

```
ENDDO
RETURN(.T.)
*END:ZEROM
* ------------
FUNCTION CENT                           && Center a line of text based
* ------------                          && upon the max width of page
PARAMETERS XRow, MLen, MESSAGE          && XRow = row to place message on
PRIVATE XCol                            && MLen = Maximum page width
XCol = (MLen - LEN(MESSAGE)) / 2        && Message = Message to be centered
@ XRow, XCol SAY MESSAGE
RETURN (.T.)
*END:CENT
* ----------------
FUNCTION MESSCENT                       && Center a menu message
* ----------------
PARAMETERS MESS                         && Mess = Message to be centered
PRIVATE    MESS, LM
MESS = ALLTRIM(MESS)
LM   = INT(LEN(MESS) / 2)
MESS = SPACE(40-LM) + MESS + SPACE(40-LM)
MESS = IIF(LEN(MESS)>80, LEFT(MESS,80), MESS)
RETURN(MESS)
*END:MESSCENT
* ---------------
PROCEDURE ASCAN
* ---------------
*
*  Notes.....: This function scans an array for a
*              specific string value.
*  Parameters: Array -  The name of the array to
*                       scan.
*              Exp   -  The expression to scan for.
*              Strt  -  The number of the element to
*                       start with.
*              Size  -  The number of elements to scan
*              Ret   -  The element position of first
*                       matching value - 0 if no match
*                       is found.
*
PARAMETERS Array, Exp, Strt, Size, Ret
PRIVATE    Array, Exp, Strt, Size, N, Z, K, LExp, LA,;
           MLen, Y
LExp = LEN(Exp)
N    = 1
Ret  = 0
DO WHILE N <= Size
   Z    = &Array[Strt]
   K    = 1
   LA   = LEN(Z)
   MLen = LA - LExp + 1
   DO WHILE K <= MLen
      Y = SUBSTR(Z, K, LExp)
      IF Y = Exp
         Ret = Strt
         EXIT
      ENDIF
      K = K + 1
```

```
   ENDDO
   IF Ret = 0
      Strt = Strt + 1
      N    = N + 1
   ELSE
      EXIT
   ENDIF
ENDDO
RETURN
*END:ASCAN


* ____________
FUNCTION YESORN
* ____________
*
* Notes.....: This function displays a box containing
*             a question. A user can choose either a
*             Y or N response. The Y or N is then
*             returned by the procedure.
* Parameters: Mess1    - The first message line to
*                        be displayed.
*             Mess2    - The second message line to
*                        be displayed.
*             BoxColor - The color for the displayed
*                        box.
*
PARAMETERS Mess1, Mess2, BoxColor
PRIVATE Special, B1, B2, B3
Special = '"-","═","|","║","┌","┐","└","┘"'
*   ┌──┐
*   │  │
*   └──┘
YN = .F.
B2 = 0
B3 = 20
B1 = LEN(Mess1)
B2 = (40-B1)/2
IF .NOT. EMPTY(Mess2)
   B1 = LEN(Mess2)
   B3 = (40-B1)/2
ENDIF
WName  = "Temp"
Shadow = .T.
Dummy  = WBox(WName,7,19,15,62,"D",Shadow,BoxColor)
@ 1,B2 SAY Mess1
@ 2,B3 SAY Mess2
@ 4,8  TO 6,14 &Special
@ 4,28 TO 6,34 &Special
DEFINE MENU YNMenu
DEFINE PAD Yes OF YNMenu PROMPT "Yes" AT 5,9
DEFINE PAD No  OF YNMenu PROMPT " No" AT 5,29
ON SELECTION PAD Yes OF YNMenu DO MAKEYN WITH YN, WName
ON SELECTION PAD No  OF YNMenu DO MAKEYN WITH YN, WName
ACTIVATE MENU YNMenu PAD No
RETURN(YN)
*END:YESORN


* ____________
PROCEDURE MAKEYN
* ____________
PARAMETERS YN, WName
```

```
YN = IIF(PAD()="YES", .T., .F.)
DEACTIVATE WINDOW ALL
RELEASE    WINDOW &WName
DEACTIVATE MENU
RELEASE    MENU
RETURN
*END:MAKEYN
* ___________
FUNCTION WBOX
* ___________
*
*  Notes.....: This function returns a window with
*              optional drop shadow and no, single,
*              or double border.
*  Parameters: WName  - The name of the window.
*  Parameters: T      - The top of the window.
*              L      - The left of the window.
*              B      - The bottom of the window.
*              R      - The right of the window.
*              SD     - Draw a single "S", double "D"
*                       or "N" border.
*              Shadow - Should a shadow be drawn?
*              BColor - Color of the box.
*
PARAMETERS WName,T, L, B, R, SD, Shadow, BColor
DEFINE WINDOW &WName FROM T,L TO B,R NONE COLOR &BColor
BB = B - T
BR = R - L
IF Shadow
   SName = "S" + WName
   DEFINE WINDOW &SName FROM T+1,L+1 TO B+1,R+2;
                 NONE COLOR N,N,N
   ACTIVATE WINDOW &SName
ENDIF
ACTIVATE WINDOW &WName
DO CASE
   CASE SD = "D"
      Kind = "DOUBLE"
   CASE SD = "S"
      Kind = " "
   CASE SD = "N"
      Kind = "NONE"
ENDCASE
SET COLOR TO &BColor
@ 0,0 TO BB,BR &Kind
RETURN(.T.)
*END:WBOX
* ____________
FUNCTION BOXES
* ____________
PARAMETERS T, L, B, R, Shadow, SD, BC
PRIVATE    T, L, B, R, Shadow, SD, BC, Kind
DO CASE
   CASE SD = "D"
      Kind = "DOUBLE"
   CASE SD = "S"
      Kind = " "
   CASE SD = "N"
      Kind = "NONE"
```

```
ENDCASE
IF Shadow
   SET COLOR TO &ColBlank                  && With or without a drop shadow
   @ T+1,L+1 CLEAR TO B+1,R+2              && T,L,B,R = Corners of the box
ENDIF                                      && Shadow = .T. or .F.
SET COLOR TO &BC                           && SD = SIngle or Double line box
@ T,L CLEAR TO B,R                         && BC = Color of the box
@ T,L        TO B,R &Kind
RETURN(.T.)
*END:BOXES


* ____________
FUNCTION MBOX
* ____________
PARAMETERS S, T, B, Shadow, SD, BC, MESS
PRIVATE    S, T, L, B, R, Shadow, SD, BC, MESS
L     = (78 - S) / 2                       &&
R     = L + S + 1                          &&   MESS        MESS
Dummy = BOXES(T,L,B,R,Shadow,SD,BC)        &&
SET COLOR TO &BC                           &&
IF SD = "S"                                &&
   @ T+2,L+1 TO T+2,R-1 DOUBLE             &&
   @ T+2,L SAY "├"                         &&
   @ T+2,R SAY "┤"                         && S = Width of centered box
ELSE                                       && T & B = Top and Bottom lines
   @ T+2,L+1 TO T+2,R-1                    &&         for the box
   @ T+2,L SAY "╞"                         && Shadow = .T. or .F.
   @ T+2,R SAY "╡"                         && SD = Single or Double lines
ENDIF                                      && BC = Color of the box
Dummy = CENT(T+1,80,MESS)                  && Mess = Message for the top of
RETURN(.T.)
*END:MBOX


* ______________
FUNCTION MESSBOX
* ______________
PARAMETERS Line, MESS, Shadow, SD, BC
PRIVATE    Line, MESS, Shadow, SD, BC, Kind,;
   SCol, MLen, T, L, B, R
MLen  = LEN(MESS)                          && Line = Line to put the message
SCol  = (80 - MLen) / 2                    && Mess = Message to display
T     = Line - 1                           && Shadow = .T. or .F. indicating
L     = SCol-2                             &&          if a shadow is needed
B     = Line + 1                           && SD = Single or Double line box
R     = SCol + MLen + 2                    && BC = Box color
Dummy = BOXES(T, L, B, R, Shadow, SD, BC)
SET COLOR TO &BC
@ Line, SCol SAY MESS
RETURN(.T.)
*END:MESSBOX


* ____________
FUNCTION FKEYS
* ____________
PARAMETER BarNumber                        && key choices.
PRIVATE   BarNumber
IF BarNumber = 1 .OR. (BarNumber > 2 .AND. BarNumber < 5)
   SET COLOR TO &ColStand
   @ 23,0 CLEAR TO 24,79
   SET COLOR TO N/G,N/W,B,B
```

```
ELSE
    SET COLOR TO &ColHelp
    @ 24,0 CLEAR
ENDIF
DO CASE
    CASE BarNumber = 1
        @ 24, 4 SAY " insur  "
        @ 24,16 SAY " prev-next "
        @ 24,31 SAY " edit "
        @ 24,41 SAY " numb  name "
        @ 24,57 SAY " return "
        @ 24,69 SAY " conf "
        SET COLOR TO W+/G
        @ 23, 4 SAY "   F3   "
        @ 23,16 SAY "           "
        @ 23,31 SAY "  F9  "
        @ 23,41 SAY " F5 find F6 "
        @ 23,57 SAY "  Esc   "
        @ 23,69 SAY "  F4  "
    CASE BarNumber = 2
        @ 24,9  SAY "-scroll"
        @ 24,22 SAY "-first"
        @ 24,33 SAY "-last"
        @ 24,43 SAY "-return"
        @ 24,66 SAY "-select"
        SET COLOR TO &ColFunc
        @ 24,7  SAY ""
        @ 24,18 SAY "Home"
        @ 24,30 SAY "End"
        @ 24,40 SAY "Esc"
        @ 24,52 SAY "Number or ──┘"
    CASE BarNumber = 3
        @ 24, 7 SAY "insur "
        @ 24,23 SAY "prev-next"
        @ 24,33 SAY "delete record"
        @ 24,48 SAY "numb  name"
        @ 24,61 SAY "return"
        @ 24,72 SAY "conf"
        SET COLOR TO W+/G
        @ 23, 7 SAY "  F3  "
        @ 23,23 SAY "         "
        @ 23,33 SAY "     del      "
        @ 23,48 SAY "F5 find F6"
        @ 23,61 SAY " Esc  "
        @ 23,72 SAY " F4 "
    CASE BarNumber = 4
        @ 24, 7 SAY "insur "
        @ 24,25 SAY "prev-next"
        @ 24,44 SAY "numb  name"
        @ 24,60 SAY "return"
        @ 24,71 SAY "conf"
        SET COLOR TO W+/G
        @ 23, 7 SAY "  F3  "
        @ 23,25 SAY "         "
        @ 23,44 SAY "F5 find F6"
        @ 23,60 SAY " Esc  "
        @ 23,71 SAY " F4 "
    CASE BarNumber = 5
        @ 24,4  SAY "-scroll"
        @ 24,17 SAY "-first"
        @ 24,28 SAY "-last"
        @ 24,44 SAY "-prev/next"
        @ 24,59 SAY "-find"
```

```
         @ 24,70 SAY "-select"
         SET COLOR TO &ColFunc
         @ 24,2  SAY ""
         @ 24,13 SAY "Home"
         @ 24,25 SAY "End"
         @ 24,35 SAY "PgUp/PgDn"
         @ 24,56 SAY "Key"
         @ 24,66 SAY "─┘"
      CASE BarNumber = 6
         @ 24,3  SAY "-scroll"
         @ 24,16 SAY "-first"
         @ 24,27 SAY "-last"
         @ 24,37 SAY "-delete the current selection"
         @ 24,72 SAY "-select"
         SET COLOR TO &ColFunc
         @ 24,1  SAY ""
         @ 24,12 SAY "Home"
         @ 24,24 SAY "End"
         @ 24,34 SAY "Del"
         @ 24,68 SAY "─┘"
      CASE BarNumber = 9
         @ 24,42 SAY "-return"
         SET COLOR TO &ColFunc
         @ 24,33 SAY "Page Down"
ENDCASE
RETURN(.T.)
*END:FKEYS


* ────────────
FUNCTION DELREC
* ────────────
PARAMETERS MESS                            && record from any database
PRIVATE    MESS, OldScreen
OldScreen = SPACE(4000)                    && Mess = Message to display
SAVE SCREEN TO OldScreen
Mess1 = "TO DELETE THIS RECORD SELECT YES"
Mess2 = "This action can NOT be reversed!"
YN    = .F.
YN = YESORN(Mess1, Mess2, ColWarning)
IF YN
   MESS = "Deleting " + MESS
   STORE 0 TO Lft, Rgt
   DO LR WITH Lft, Rgt, MESS
   Dummy = BOXES(11, Lft, 13, Rgt, .T., "D", ColError)
   Dummy = CENT(12, 80, MESS)
   DELETE
   Dummy = INKEY(3)
ENDIF
RESTORE SCREEN FROM OldScreen
RETURN(.T.)
*END:DELREC


* ─────────
PROCEDURE LR                               && Returns the number of spaces
* ─────────                                && to the left and right of a
PARAMETERS Lft ,Rgt, MESS                  && centered message
Lft = ((80 - LEN(MESS)) / 2) - 2
Rgt = Lft + LEN(MESS) + 3
RETURN
*END:LR
```

```

* ____________
FUNCTION XYBAR                                  && Draws a bar on the screen with
* ____________                                  && a length equal to PCT / 2
PARAMETERS Pct                                  && Use in drawing bar charts to
PRIVATE    Pct                                  && indicate progress of events
@ 18,14 SAY REPLICATE("█",(Pct/2)+1)
RETURN(.T.)
*END:XYBAR


* ____________
FUNCTION START
* ____________
SET DEVICE TO SCREEN
SET COLOR TO &ColStand
CLEAR
SET COLOR TO &ColOther
Dummy = CENT(0,80,HEAD)
SET COLOR TO &ColStand
RETURN(.T.)
*END:START


* ______________
FUNCTION MYERROR
* ______________
*
*  Notes.....: This function produces an "exploding"
*              box at the bottom of the screen
*              containing an error message.
*  Parameters: NMess - The error message number.
*              DS    - Double or Single line box.
*
PARAMETERS NMess, DS
PRIVATE    NMess, DS, Kind, Mes
SAVE SCREEN TO ErrScr
SET COLOR TO &ColError
Kind = IIF(DS="D", "Double", " ")
N = 39
DO WHILE N > 0
   @ 22,N CLEAR TO 24,79-N
   @ 22,N       TO 24,79-N &Kind
   N = N - 4
ENDDO
Mes = " "
DO CASE
   CASE NMess = 1
      Mes = "The input file you specified does NOT exist - " +;
            "Please Reenter"
   CASE NMess = 2
      Mes = "The vendor you entered exists - Please Reenter"
   CASE NMess = 3
      Mes = "Data for vendor exists on the insurance database - " +;
            "Please Delete first"
   CASE NMess = 4
      Mes = "Data for vendor exists on the confidentiality database - " +;
            "Please Delete first"
   CASE NMess = 5
      Mes = "Entered code exceeds the maximum - Please Reenter"
   CASE NMess = 6
      Mes = "Entry must be between 1 and 99 or blank - Please Reenter"
   CASE NMess = 7
```

```
         Mes = "The arrangement code you entered does not exists - " +;
               "Please Reenter"
      CASE NMess = 8
         Mes = "The arrangement code you entered exists - Please Reenter"
      CASE NMess = 9
         Mes = "This coverage already exists for this vendor - Please Reenter"
      CASE NMess = 10
         Mes = "You must enter a vendor number - Please Reenter"
      CASE NMess = 11
         Mes = "The selection you chose does not exists - Use F8 to add"
      CASE NMess = 12
         Mes = "Please check contract amount - " +;
               "It may be incorrect for this insurance"
   ENDCASE
   @ 23, (80-LEN(Mes))/2 SAY Mes
   KEY = INKEY(5)
   RESTORE SCREEN FROM ErrScr
   RETURN(.T.)
   *END:MYERROR


   * ______________
   FUNCTION TESTPRNT
   * ______________
   PUBLIC PrntOk
   KEY    = 0                               && displaying a message to the
   PrntOK = .F.                             && user
   PrntOK = PRINTSTATUS()
   SAVE SCREEN TO SavScrn
   SET DEVICE TO SCREEN
   IF .NOT. PrntOK
      Dummy = BOXES(10, 22, 14, 56, .T., "D", ColError)
      @ 11,26 SAY "Please make the printer ready"
      @ 12,38 SAY "or"
      @ 13,24 SAY "press Esc to return to the menu"
   ENDIF
   DO WHILE .NOT. PrntOK
      KEY = INKEY(.51)
      PrntOK = PRINTSTATUS()
      IF KEY = ESCAPE
         PrntOK = .T.
      ENDIF
   ENDDO
   RESTORE SCREEN FROM SavScrn
   SET DEVICE TO PRINT
   IF KEY = ESCAPE
      SET PRINT OFF
      SET DEVICE TO SCREEN
      PrntOK = .F.
   ENDIF
   RETURN(PrntOK)
   *END:TESTPRNT


   * __________
   FUNCTION LOGO
   * __________
   PRIVATE Speed, N, J, X, Y                && bottom to top and then
   SET COLOR TO &ColStand                   && lap disolves ICS on the screen
   CLEAR
   SET CURSOR OFF
   DECLARE LOGOS[12]
   LOGOS[12] = "┌──────────┐       "
   LOGOS[11] = "│          │       "
```

```
LOGOS[10] = "│  P            │      "
LOGOS[ 9] = "│     ┌─────────┼─────┐"
LOGOS[ 8] = "│     │         │     │"
LOGOS[ 7] = "│     │         │     │"
LOGOS[ 6] = "│     │    M    │     │"
LOGOS[ 5] = "│     │         │     │"
LOGOS[ 4] = "└─────┼─────────┘     │"
LOGOS[ 3] = "      │           H   │"
LOGOS[ 2] = "      │               │"
LOGOS[ 1] = "      └───────────────┘"
DEFINE   WINDOW GoUp FROM 13,25 TO 24,55 NONE
ACTIVATE WINDOW GoUp
N = 12
DO WHILE N >= 1
   @ 12-N,0 SAY LOGOS[N]
   N = N - 1
ENDDO
N = 0
DO WHILE N <= 10
   MOVE WINDOW GoUp BY -1,0
   N      = N + 1
   XTemp = 0
   Dummy = KillTime(XTemp)
ENDDO
RELEASE WINDOWS GoUp
N = 1
DO WHILE N <= 12
   @ N,25 SAY LOGOS[13-N]
   N = N + 1
ENDDO
Speed = 5
X      = SPACE(14)
DECLARE LOGO1[8]
STORE   "███████████    " TO P1
STORE   "█████    ████  " TO P2
STORE   "  ███      ███ " TO P3
STORE   "  ███    ████  " TO P4
STORE   "  ██████████   " TO P5
STORE   "  ███          " TO P6
STORE   " ████          " TO P7
STORE   "███████        " TO P8

STORE "  ████      ████ " TO C1
STORE "   ████     ████ " TO C2
STORE "   █████   █████ " TO C3
STORE "   ███ ██ ██ ███ " TO C4
STORE "   ███   █   ███ " TO C5
STORE "   ███       ███ " TO C6
STORE "   ███       ███ " TO C7
STORE "  █████     █████" TO C8

STORE "    █████    █████" TO S1
STORE "     ███       ███" TO S2
STORE "     ███       ███" TO S3
STORE "     █████████████" TO S4
STORE "     █████████████" TO S5
STORE "     ███       ███" TO S6
STORE "     ███       ███" TO S7
STORE "    █████    █████" TO S8
STORE X + P1 + C1 + S1 + X TO LOGO1[1]
STORE X + P2 + C2 + S2 + X TO LOGO1[2]
STORE X + P3 + C3 + S3 + X TO LOGO1[3]
STORE X + P4 + C4 + S4 + X TO LOGO1[4]
STORE X + P5 + C5 + S5 + X TO LOGO1[5]
```

```
STORE X + P6 + C6 + S6 + X TO LOGO1[6]
STORE X + P7 + C7 + S7 + X TO LOGO1[7]
STORE X + P8 + C8 + S8 + X TO LOGO1[8]
N = 0
DO WHILE N <= 80
   J = 15
   DO WHILE J <= 22
      IF J = 15 .OR. J = 17 .OR. J = 19 .OR. J = 21
         @ J+2,0 SAY SUBSTR(LOGO1[J-14],80-N) +;
                     REPLICATE(" ",80-N)
      ELSE
         @ J+2,0 SAY REPLICATE(" ",80-N) +;
                     SUBSTR(LOGO1[J-14],1,N)
      ENDIF
   J = J + 1
   ENDDO
   N = N + Speed
ENDDO
@ 17,0 SAY LOGO1[1]
@ 19,0 SAY LOGO1[3]
@ 21,0 SAY LOGO1[5]
@ 23,0 SAY LOGO1[7]
@ 0,0 CLEAR TO 14,79
RETURN(.T.)
*END:LOGO


* ________________
FUNCTION KILLTIME
* ________________
PARAMETERS XTemp
PRIVATE X, Y
X = RAND() * 1000 + 5
Y = RAND() * 100  + 2
XTemp = X/Y
RETURN(.T.)
*END:KILLTIME


* _____________
FUNCTION EMPTY
* _____________
*
*  Notes.....: This function returns a .T. if a data
*              entry field contains blanks or a null.
*  Parameters: Passed - The variable to check for a
*                       blank or a null.
*
PARAMETERS Passed
PRIVATE    Z
Y = 0
Z = TYPE("Passed")
DO CASE
   CASE Z = "C" .OR. Z = "M"
      Y = LEN(ALLTRIM(Passed))
   CASE Z = "N" .OR. Z = "F"
      Y = Passed
   CASE Z = "D"
      Y = MONTH(Passed)
   CASE Z = "L"
      RETURN(Passed)
ENDCASE
RETURN IIF(Y=0, .T., .F.)
```

```
*END:EMPTY


* ---------------
FUNCTION ALLTRIM
* ---------------
*
*  Notes.....: This function returns the sting with
*              leading and trailing blanks removed.
*  Parameters: String - The string to trim.
*
PARAMETER String
RETURN LTRIM(TRIM(String))
*END:ALLTRIM


* ---------------
PROCEDURE ACHOICE
* ---------------
*
*  Notes.....: This function returns the users choice
*              where the PUBLIC array AMenu acts as
*              individual PROMPT statements in a
*              MENU TO syntax.
*  Parameters: Choice - Contains the number of prompts
*                       in the array and returns the
*                       user's selection.
*              Title  - Displable Title for Box.
*              AMenu  - Must be a PUBLIC array which
*                       contains "menu" choices.
*
*  Note......: All the values must be the same length
*              fill with blanks if necessary.
*
*              MAXIMUM lenght = 78 characters.
*
*              MAXIMUM Entries = 20.
*
PARAMETERS Choice, TITLE, T, L, B, R
PRIVATE X, T, L, B, R, N, TITLE
SET MESSAGE TO
X  = AMenu[1]
LX = LEN(X)
SET BORDER TO NONE
DEFINE POPUP ChooseIt FROM T, L+1 TO B, R-1
N = 1
DO WHILE N <= Choice
   DEFINE BAR N OF ChooseIt PROMPT AMenu[N]
   N = N + 1
ENDDO
ON SELECTION POPUP ChooseIt DO PopSel WITH Choice
SET BORDER TO SINGLE
ACTIVATE POPUP ChooseIt
SET MESSAGE TO " " AT 23,0
RETURN
*END:ACHOICE


* ---------------
PROCEDURE POPSEL
* ---------------
PARAMETERS mVar
mVar = BAR()
```

```
DEACTIVATE POPUP
RETURN
*END:POPSEL


* ______________
PROCEDURE PADSEL
* ______________
YN = VAL(SUBSTR(PAD(), 2))
DEACTIVATE MENU
RETURN
*END:PADSEL


* ______________
FUNCTION NOTYET
* ______________
SAVE SCREEN TO TempScrn
Dummy = BOXES(11, 21, 13, 59, .T., "D", ColWarning)
KEY   = CENT(12, 80, "This function is NOT available yet")
KEY   = INKEY(5)
RESTORE SCREEN FROM TempScrn
RETURN(.T.)
*END:NOTYET


*______________
PROCEDURE DUTIL                                  && Main Utility Menu
*______________
DO WHILE .T.
   Dummy = START()
   Dummy = FKEYS(2)
   Dummy = MBOX(25,5,17,.T., "D", ColMenu, "U T I L I T Y")
   SET BORDER TO NONE
   DEFINE POPUP Util FROM 7, 26
   DEFINE BAR 1 OF Util PROMPT " 1. Download Data         ";
     MESSAGE MESSCENT ("Add or Replace Vendor Information on the System.")
   DEFINE BAR 3 OF Util PROMPT " 2. Utilities D.O.S.      ";
     MESSAGE MESSCENT ("Perform DOS Functions")
   DEFINE BAR 5 OF Util PROMPT " 3. Change System Colors ";
     MESSAGE MESSCENT ("Change the Default Colors.")
   DEFINE BAR 7 OF Util PROMPT " 4. Additional Utilities ";
     MESSAGE MESSCENT ("Execute Additional Utilities - " +;
                       "A Password is Necessary")
   DEFINE BAR 9 OF Util PROMPT " 5. Return to Main Menu  ";
     MESSAGE MESSCENT ("Return to the Main Menu.")
   UtilC = 0
   ON SELECTION POPUP Util DO PopSel WITH UtilC
   SET BORDER TO SINGLE
   ACTIVATE POPUP Util
   DO CASE
      CASE UtilC = 1                             && Download Data
         DO Download
      CASE UtilC = 3                             && DOS
         DO DoDOS
      CASE UtilC = 5                             && Colors
         DO Colors
      CASE UtilC = 7                             && Addition Utilities
         DO Util1
      CASE UtilC = 0 .OR. UtilC = 9              && RETURN
         EXIT
   ENDCASE
ENDDO
```

```
Temp = " "
RETURN
*END:DOUTIL
* ____________
PROCEDURE UTIL1                              && Called by pressing Alt L
* ____________                               && Secret Utility menu
ValidPass = .F.
Dummy = Password(ValidPass)
IF .NOT. ValidPass
    KEYBOARD CHR(ESCAPE)                     && Check to see if user knows
   RETURN                                    && Password - One try only
ENDIF                                        && then By By
DO WHILE .T.
   Dummy = START()
   Dummy = FKEYS(2)
   Dummy = MBOX(29,5,17,.T., "D", ColMenu, "SPECIAL UTILITY MENU")
   SET BORDER TO NONE
   DEFINE POPUP Special FROM 7, 24
   DEFINE BAR 1 OF Special PROMPT " 1. Change Pop Up Choices    ";
     MESSAGE MESSCENT ("Change the Choices that Popup for Data Entry.")
   DEFINE BAR 3 OF Special PROMPT " 2. Make Distribution Copies ";
     MESSAGE MESSCENT ("Create Diskettes to be Used on Other Computers.")
   DEFINE BAR 5 OF Special PROMPT " 3. Letter Changes           ";
     MESSAGE MESSCENT ("Change the Exp. Cert. and Terms Letters.")
   DEFINE BAR 7 OF Special PROMPT " 4. Display Available Memory ";
     MESSAGE MESSCENT ("Show the amount of memory left while running.")
   DEFINE BAR 9 OF Special PROMPT " 5. Return to Utility Menu   ";
     MESSAGE MESSCENT ("Return to the Utility Menu.")
   SChoice = 0
   ON SELECTION POPUP Special DO PopSel WITH SChoice
   SET BORDER TO SINGLE
   ACTIVATE POPUP Special
   DO CASE
      CASE SChoice = 1                       && Change Choices
         DO CCode
      CASE SChoice = 3                       && Create Distribution Copies
         DO Dist
      CASE SChoice = 5                       && Change Letters
         DO Letters
      CASE SChoice = 7                       && Display Available Memory
         SET COLOR TO &ColStand
         CLEAR
         MemStr = ALLTRIM(STR(MEMORY(0),5,0))
         Dummy = MESSBOX(14, "There are " + MemStr +;
                " kbytes of memory available",.T., "D", ColWarning)
         KEY = INKEY(0)
      CASE SChoice = 0 .OR. SChoice = 9                && RETURN
         EXIT
   ENDCASE
ENDDO
RESTORE SCREEN FROM Temp
KEYBOARD CHR(CurDn) + CHR(CurUp)
RETURN
*END:UTIL1
* ____________
PROCEDURE DIST                               && Make a copy of the system
* ____________                               && Including all existing data
SET COLOR TO &ColStand                       && Need enough memory to run COPY
CLEAR
```

```
Mess1 = "You need 2 blank formatted diskettes"
Mess2 = "to make distribution copies - PROCEED?"
YN    = .F.
KEYBOARD CHR(CurRight)
YN = YesOrN(Mess1, Mess2, ColWarning)
SET COLOR TO &ColStand
CLEAR
IF .NOT. YN
   Dummy = MESSBOX(12, "Exit the system or go to DOS and format" +;
            " diskettes you need.",.T., "S", ColHelp)
   KEY = INKEY(7)
   SET COLOR TO &ColStand
   RETURN
ENDIF
Mess1  = 'Do you wish to use drive "A"'
Mess2  = "for the distribution diskettes?"
YN     = .T.
YN     = YesOrN(Mess1, Mess2, ColWarning)
DDrive = IIF(YN, "A:", "B:")
SET COLOR TO &ColStand
CLEAR
Dummy = MESSBOX(12, "Insert the diskette into drive " + ;
        SUBSTR(DDrive,1,1) + " and press any key to proceed",;
        .T., "D", ColHelp)
KEY   = INKEY(0)
SET COLOR TO &ColStand
CLEAR
Dummy = MESSBOX(12, "Creating distribution diskette one",.T., "S",;
        ColWarning)
CLOSE DATA
RUN COPY PMH.EXE &DDrive > NUL
RUN COPY RUN.BAT &DDrive > NUL
RUN COPY   *.MEM &DDrive > NUL
Dummy = MESSBOX(12,"Insert another diskette into drive " +;
        SUBSTR(DDrive,1,1) + " and press any key to proceed",;
        .T., "D", ColHelp)
KEY   = INKEY(0)
SET COLOR TO &ColStand
CLEAR
Dummy = MESSBOX(12, "Creating distribution diskette two",.T., "S",;
        ColWarning)
RUN COPY TR12R.SFP &DDrive > NUL
RUN COPY *.DBF &DDrive > NUL
RUN COPY *.DBT &DDrive > NUL
RUN COPY *.??X &DDrive > NUL
RUN COPY *.COM &DDrive > NUL
SET COLOR TO &ColStand
CLEAR
Dummy = MESSBOX(12, "The copies have been made - " +;
        "Press any key to return to the menu",.T., "D", ColHelp)
DO OpenData
KEY = INKEY(0)
RETURN
*END:DIST


* _______________
PROCEDURE LETTERS                              && Modify Form Letters Menu
* _______________
DO WHILE .T.
   Dummy = START()
   Dummy = FKEYS(2)
   Dummy = MBOX(28,2,20,.T., "D", ColMenu, "CHANGE LETTERS")
```

```
      SET BORDER TO NONE
      DEFINE POPUP Letter FROM 4, 25
      DEFINE BAR 1  OF Letter PROMPT " 1. Expiration Letter One   ";
         MESSAGE MESSCENT ("Change the First expiration Letter.")
      DEFINE BAR 3  OF Letter PROMPT " 2. Expiration Letter Two   ";
         MESSAGE MESSCENT ("Change the Second expiration Letter.")
      DEFINE BAR 5  OF Letter PROMPT " 3. Expiration Letter Three ";
         MESSAGE MESSCENT ("Change the Third expiration Letter.")
      DEFINE BAR 7  OF Letter PROMPT " 4. Certification Letter    ";
         MESSAGE MESSCENT ("Change the Certification Letter.")
      DEFINE BAR 9  OF Letter PROMPT " 5. Terms Letter            ";
         MESSAGE MESSCENT ("Change the Terms Letter.")
      DEFINE BAR 11 OF Letter PROMPT " 6. No Insurance Letter     ";
         MESSAGE MESSCENT ("Change the No Insurance Letter.")
      DEFINE BAR 13 OF Letter PROMPT " 7. Sign Off Letter         ";
         MESSAGE MESSCENT ("Change the Sign Off Letter.")
      DEFINE BAR 15 OF Letter PROMPT " 8. Return to Utility Menu  ";
         MESSAGE MESSCENT ("Return to the Utility Menu.")
      LetChoice = 0
      ON SELECTION POPUP Letter DO PopSel WITH LetChoice
      SET BORDER TO SINGLE
      ACTIVATE POPUP Letter
      IF LetChoice = 0 .OR. LetChoice = 15
         EXIT
      ELSE
         DO LetFix WITH (LetChoice + 1) / 2
      ENDIF
   ENDDO
   RETURN
   *END:LETTERS

   * ____________
   PROCEDURE LETFIX                                && Modify the form letters
   * ____________                                  && LetChoice = Letter number
   PARAMETERS LetChoice                            && and physical position of the
   SELECT J                                        && letter in the file "MLet"
   USE MLet
   GOTO LetChoice                                  && Use standard dBASE IV edit
   SET COLOR TO &ColStand                          && commands and keystrokes
   CLEAR
   SET COLOR TO &ColWarning
   Dummy = CENT(1, 80,;
           "Change the letter but leave the blank lines and the .........")
   Dummy = CENT(2, 80,;
           " Press CONTROL W to save changes or Esc to abandon changes ")
   SET CURSOR ON
   SET ESCAPE ON
   DEFINE WINDOW NewMemo FROM 3,0 TO 20,79 COLOR &ColWarning
   SET MEMOWIDTH TO 78
   KEYBOARD CHR(29)                   && Control Home
   SET WINDOW OF MEMO TO NewMemo
   @ 3,1 GET MLetter
   READ
   SET CURSOR OFF
   SET ESCAPE OFF
   DEACTIVATE WINDOW NewMemo
   RELEASE WINDOWS NewMemo
   RETURN
   *END:LETFIX

   * ____________
```

```
PROCEDURE CCODE                                    && MENU to
* -----------                                      && Change the default MEM files
DO WHILE .T.
   Dummy = START()
   Dummy = FKEYS(2)
   Dummy = MBOX(22,4,14,.T., "D", ColMenu, "CHANGE CODES")
   SET BORDER TO NONE
   DEFINE POPUP ChangeCode FROM 6, 30
   DEFINE BAR 1 OF ChangeCode PROMPT " 1. Vendor          ";
      MESSAGE MESSCENT ("Change the Pop-up Vendor Choices.")
   DEFINE BAR 2 OF ChangeCode PROMPT " 2. Arrangement     ";
      MESSAGE MESSCENT ("Change the Pop-up Arrangement Choices.")
   DEFINE BAR 3 OF ChangeCode PROMPT " 3. COS Unit        ";
      MESSAGE MESSCENT ("Change the Pop-up Expense Choices.")
   DEFINE BAR 4 OF ChangeCode PROMPT " 4. Insurance       ";
      MESSAGE MESSCENT ("Change the Pop-up Insurance Choices.")
   DEFINE BAR 5 OF ChangeCode PROMPT " 5. PMH Standard  ";
      MESSAGE MESSCENT ("Change the Pop-up Hospital Limits.")
   DEFINE BAR 6 OF ChangeCode PROMPT " 6. Contract Type  ";
      MESSAGE MESSCENT ("Change the Pop-up Confidentiality Choices.")
   DEFINE BAR 7 OF ChangeCode PROMPT " 7. Return to Util ";
      MESSAGE MESSCENT ("Return to the Special Utility Menu")
   Util = 0
   ON SELECTION POPUP ChangeCode DO PopSel WITH Util
   SET BORDER TO SINGLE
   ACTIVATE POPUP ChangeCode
   IF Util = 0 .OR. Util = 7
      EXIT
   ELSE
      DO ChngCode WITH Util
   ENDIF
ENDDO
RETURN
*END:CCODE


* ---------------
PROCEDURE CHNGCODE
* ---------------
PARAMETERS Util
* +----------------------------------------------------------------------+
* |                                                                      |
* | This procedure changes the popup choices for the input screen.       |
* | ---------------------------------------------------------------      |
* |                                                                      |
* | These choices are stored in the file CODES which contains           |
* |                                                                      |
* | two fields - CodeType and Code.                                      |
* |                                                                      |
* | CodeType contains: "Ven", "Arr, "Exp", "Ins", "Hos", or "Con"        |
* |                                                                      |
* | Code contains the actual code for upto 20 different choices.        |
* |                                                                      |
* | The CodeType must be stored using both upper and lower characters   |
* |                                                                      |
* | as shown for this code to work.                                      |
```

```
* |                                                                  |
* | The valuse for the choices are stored in arrays with the same    |
* |                                                                  |
* | names as the CodeType in the database CODES.DBF for clarity.     |
* |                                                                  |
* └──────────────────────────────────────────────────────────────────┘
PRIVATE Choice
Choice = 0
SET COLOR TO &ColStand
CLEAR
DO CASE
  CASE Util = 1                                    && Vendor
     Prefix   = "Ven"
     NewTitle = "VENDOR CODES"
  CASE Util = 2                                    && Arrangement
     Prefix   = "Arr"
     NewTitle = "ARRANGEMENT CODES"
  CASE Util = 3                                    && Expense
     Prefix   = "Exp"
     NewTitle = "COS UNIT"
  CASE Util = 4                                    && Insurance
     Prefix   = "Ins"
     NewTitle = "INSURANCE CODES"
  CASE Util = 5                                    && Hospital Limit
     Prefix   = "Hos"
     NewTitle = "Hosptial STANDARD"
  CASE Util = 6                                    && Confidentiality
     Prefix   = "Con"
     NewTitle = "CONTRACT TYPES"
ENDCASE
Dummy = ZeroM()
SELECT D
SET ORDER TO CodeType
SEEK PREFIX
J = 1
SCAN FOR CodeType = Prefix
   AMenu[J] = D->Code
   J        = J + 1
ENDSCAN
 SET ESCAPE ON
NLast  = J - 1
Choice = IIF(NLast=0,  16, NLast)
Choice = IIF(NLast>16, 16, Choice)
LX     = LEN(AMenu[1])
T      = INT(((24 - Choice) / 2) - 1)
B      = T + Choice + 1
L      = INT((80 - LX) / 2)
```

```
R      = L + LX + 3
CLEAR GETS
SET MESSAGE TO
DO WHILE .T.
   Dummy = BOXES(T,L,B,R,.T.,"D",ColMenu)
   SET COLOR TO &ColMenu
   DO ACHOICE WITH Choice, NewTitle, T, L, B, R
   SET COLOR TO &ColStand
   IF LASTKEY() = Escape .OR. Choice = 0
      EXIT
   ENDIF
   Dummy = &Prefix[Choice]
   &Prefix[Choice] = &Prefix[Choice] + SPACE(25-LEN(Dummy))
   SET COLOR TO &ColStand
   @ 23,19 SAY "Change the data: "
   SET COLOR TO &ColEntry
   InField = &Prefix[Choice]
   SET CURSOR ON
   @ 23,36 GET InField PICTURE "@!"    && Get the item to change
   READ                                && Change it
   SET CURSOR OFF
   SET ESCAPE OFF
   IF LASTKEY() = Escape .OR. Choice = 0
      EXIT
   ENDIF
   STORE LTRIM(InField) TO AMenu[Choice], &Prefix[Choice]
   Choice = 16
   J      = 1
   SCAN FOR CodeType = Prefix
      REPLACE D->Code WITH AMenu[J]
      J = J + 1
   ENDSCAN
ENDDO
SET COLOR TO &ColStand
CLEAR
SET MESSAGE TO " " AT 23,0
RETURN
*END:CHNGCODE


* ________________
PROCEDURE DOWNLOAD                          && Download database from disk
* ________________                          && Input must be in SDF format
SET COLOR TO &ColStand
CLEAR
Mess1 = "The data can be on disk or on-line"
Mess2 = "Is the data on disk?"
YN    = .T.
YN    = YesOrN(Mess1, Mess2, ColWarning)
IF .NOT. YN
   SET COLOR TO &ColStand
```

```
   CLEAR
   Dummy = MESSBOX(12, "Exit the system and download the data to disk" +;
           " for import to this system",.T., "S", ColHelp)
   KEY   = INKEY(7)
   SET COLOR TO &ColStand
   RETURN
ENDIF
FromFile = "C:\VendorIn.Ext                    "
SET ESCAPE ON
SET CURSOR ON
Dummy = BOXES(11,19,14,61,.T., "D", ColHelp)
Dummy = CENT(12,80, "Enter the name of the input vendor file")
DO WHILE .T.
   @ 13,25 GET FromFile  PICTURE "@!K" COLOR &ColEntry
   READ
   IF LASTKEY() = ESCAPE
      EXIT
   ENDIF
   IF FILE(FromFile)
      EXIT
   ELSE
      SET CURSOR OFF
      Dummy = MyError(1, "D")
      SET CURSOR ON
   ENDIF
ENDDO
SET CURSOR OFF
SET ESCAPE OFF
IF LASTKEY() = ESCAPE
   RETURN
ENDIF
ByPass = .T.
*DO RptStart
ByPass = .F.
SET COLOR TO &ColStand
Dummy = CENT(6,80, "P a r t O n e")
SET COLOR TO R/B
Dummy    = XYBar(1)
BRCount = 0
GOTO TOP
SELECT A
COPY STRUCTURE TO TEMP
SELECT J
USE TEMP
INDEX ON VendNum TO TEMP
APPEND FROM &FromFile SDF                  && Replace values with defaults
Dummy = XYBar(50)
REPLACE ALL;
   J->Confident  WITH .T.,;
   J->Certif     WITH .T.,;
   J->ConInsCom  WITH .T.,;
   J->ConConfCom WITH .T.,;
   J->OnPremise  WITH .T.,;
   J->VenInput   WITH CurrentDate
Dummy = XYBar(75)
REPLACE ALL J->STATUS     WITH "A" FOR J->STATUS = "N" .OR. J->STATUS = " "
Dummy = XYBar(88)
REPLACE ALL J->AttnName   WITH "Insurance Department" FOR EMPTY(J->AttnName)
Dummy = XYBar(100)
NumRec = RECCOUNT()
GOTO TOP
SELECT A                                   && EXISTING VENDOR DATA
GOTO TOP
```

```
SELECT J                                   && NEW DATA
GOTO TOP
SET COLOR TO &ColStand
Dummy = CENT(6,80, "P a r t T w o")
@ 18,14 CLEAR TO 18,64
SET COLOR TO R/B
Dummy = XYBar(1)
DO WHILE .NOT. EOF()                       && Add new records or update
   BRCount = BRCount + 1                   && existing records
   Dummy = XYBar(BRCount * 75 / NumRec)
   VKey = J->VendNum
   SELECT A
   SEEK VKey
   IF .NOT. FOUND()                        && New record
      APPEND BLANK
      REPLACE;
         A->ConInsCom  WITH .T.,;
         A->ConConfCom WITH .T.,;
         A->OnPremise  WITH .T.,;
         A->Confident  WITH .T.,;
         A->Certif     WITH .T.,;
         A->VenInput   WITH CurrentDate
   ENDIF
   * * * UPDATE FIELDS REGARDLESS IF NEW OR OLD * * *
   REPLACE;
      A->VenShortN WITH IIF(.NOT. EMPTY(J->VenShortn),;
                        J->VenShortn,  A->VenShortn),;
      A->VendName  WITH IIF(.NOT. EMPTY(J->VendName),;
                        J->VendName,   A->VendName),;
      A->Address1  WITH IIF(.NOT. EMPTY(J->Address1),;
                        J->Address1,   A->Address1),;
      A->Address2  WITH IIF(.NOT. EMPTY(J->Address2),;
                        J->Address2,   A->Address2),;
      A->City      WITH IIF(.NOT. EMPTY(J->City),;
                        J->City,       A->City),;
      A->State     WITH IIF(.NOT. EMPTY(J->State),;
                        J->State,      A->State)
   * Second replace statement needed do to dBASE IV limit of 1024 char/line
   REPLACE;
      A->Zip       WITH IIF(.NOT. EMPTY(J->Zip),;
                        J->Zip,        A->Zip),;
      A->STATUS    WITH IIF(.NOT. EMPTY(J->STATUS),;
                        J->STATUS,     A->STATUS),;
      A->STATUS    WITH IIF(A->STATUS= "N" .OR. A->STATUS= " ",;
                        "A",           A->STATUS),;
      A->Telephone WITH IIF(.NOT. EMPTY(J->Telephone),;
                        J->Telephone,  A->Telephone),;
      A->VendNum   WITH IIF(.NOT. EMPTY(J->VendNum),;
                        J->VendNum,    A->VendNum),;
      A->AttnName  WITH IIF(.NOT. EMPTY(J->AttnName),;
                        J->AttnName,   IIF(EMPTY(A->AttnName),;
                        "Insurance Department", A->AttnName)),;
      A->VenInput  WITH IIF(A->STATUS<> "A",;
                        CurrentDate, A->VenInput)
   SELECT J
   SKIP
ENDDO
CLOSE DATA                                 && Delete temporary files
IF FILE("TEMP.DBF")
   RUN DEL TEMP.* >NUL
ENDIF
```

```
DO OpenData
SELECT A
SET ORDER TO 1
NumRec  = RECCOUNT() * .25 + NumRec
BRCount = NumRec * .75
Factor  = (NumRec - BRCount) / RECCOUNT()
GOTO TOP
DO WHILE .NOT. EOF()
   BRCount = BRCount + Factor
   Dummy = XYBar(BRCount * 100 / NumRec)
   IF B->VendNum <> A->VendNum               && No Insurance Record
      IF A->Certif                           && and Certif = .T.
         REPLACE A->ConInsCom WITH .F.
      ENDIF
   ELSE                                      && Insurance Record
      SELECT B
      DO WHILE B->VendNum = A->VendNum .AND. .NOT. EOF()
         IF (B->ContAmt = 0 .OR. B->ContAmt > B->Amount) .AND. A->Certif
            SELECT A
            REPLACE A->ConInsCom WITH .F.
            EXIT
         ENDIF
         SKIP
      ENDDO
   ENDIF
   SELECT A
   IF C->VendNum <> A->VendNum .AND. A->Confident && No Confidentiality Recor
      REPLACE A->ConConfCom WITH .F.
   ENDIF
   IF C->VendNum = A->VendNum .AND. A->Confident
      SELECT C
      DO WHILE C->VendNum = A->VendNum .AND. .NOT. EOF()
         IF EMPTY(C->ConfRecvd) .AND. .NOT. C->SignOff
            SELECT A
            REPLACE A->ConConfCom WITH .F.  && Ooh Ooh - false
            EXIT
         ENDIF
         SKIP
      ENDDO
   ENDIF
   SELECT A
   SKIP
ENDDO
Dummy = XYBar(100)
KEY = INKEY(1)
RETURN
*END:DOWNLOAD


* ______________
PROCEDURE DODOS                                && Invoke DOS commands
* ______________
STemp = SPACE(4000)
SAVE SCREEN TO STemp
DO WHILE .T.
   Dummy = START()
   Dummy = FKEYS(2)
   Dummy = MBOX(14,4,17,.T., "D", ColMenu, "DOS MENU")
   SET BORDER TO NONE
   DEFINE POPUP DOS FROM 6, 32
   DEFINE BAR 1  OF DOS PROMPT " 1. Use DOS   ";
```

```
      MESSAGE MESSCENT ("Access DOS - Type EXIT to Return.")
   DEFINE BAR 2  OF DOS PROMPT " 2. Copy File ";
      MESSAGE MESSCENT ("Copy one File to Another.")
   DEFINE BAR 3  OF DOS PROMPT " 3. Disk Copy ";
      MESSAGE MESSCENT ("Copy a Diskette on A: to Diskette on B:")
   DEFINE BAR 4  OF DOS PROMPT " 4. Format A: ";
      MESSAGE MESSCENT ("Format a Disk on Drive A: (1.2M on ATs - " +;
                       "1.4M on PS2s)")
   DEFINE BAR 5  OF DOS PROMPT " 5. Format B: ";
      MESSAGE MESSCENT ("Format a Disk on Drive B: (360K)")
   DEFINE BAR 6  OF DOS PROMPT " 6. Directory ";
      MESSAGE MESSCENT ("View the Directory on the Screen.")
   DEFINE BAR 7  OF DOS PROMPT " 7. Print Dir ";
      MESSAGE MESSCENT ("Print a Listing of the Directory.")
   DEFINE BAR 8  OF DOS PROMPT " 8. Backup    ";
      MESSAGE MESSCENT ("Backup the Databases and Index Files.")
   DEFINE BAR 9  OF DOS PROMPT " 9. Restore   ";
      MESSAGE MESSCENT ("Restore Previous Backed up Databases " +;
                       "and Index Files.")
   DEFINE BAR 10 OF DOS PROMPT " 0. Return    ";
      MESSAGE MESSCENT ("Return to the Main Menu.")
   DOSChoice = 0
   ON SELECTION POPUP DOS DO PopSel WITH DOSChoice
   SET BORDER TO SINGLE
   SET MESSAGE TO
   ACTIVATE POPUP DOS
   DO CASE
      CASE DOSChoice = 1                     && Use DOS  - Get secondary
         RUN CD >TEMP.TXT                    && command processor
         SELECT J                            && Save drive and current Dir
         USE Drv                             && in file DRV.DBF
         ZAP
         PACK
         APPEND FROM TEMP.TXT SDF
         Drv  = SUBSTR(Drive,1,2)
         SDir = TRIM(SUBSTR(Drive,3))
         SAVE TO Temp                        && SaveStuff
         SAVE SCREEN TO STemp
         SET COLOR TO &ColStand
         CLEAR
         @ 0,0 SAY "Type EXIT to return to B800CSS"
         SET CURSOR ON
         RUN COMMAND                         && Invoke secondary command
         SET CURSOR OFF && processor
         RUN &Drv                            && Go to correct drive
         RUN CD &SDir                        && and subdirectory
         RESTORE SCREEN FROM TEMP
         RESTORE FROM TEMP ADDITIVE          && restore stuff
         IF FILE("TEMP.MEM")
            RUN DEL TEMP.MEM >NUL
         ENDIF
         SELECT A
      CASE DOSChoice = 2                     && Copy File
         FromFile = "C:\FROMFILE.EXT                 "
         ToFile   = "C:\TOFILE.EXT                   "
         SAVE SCREEN TO TEMP
         SET ESCAPE ON
         SET CURSOR ON
         Dummy = BOXES(8,16,13,63,.T., "D", ColHelp)
         Dummy = CENT(9,80, "Enter the name of the file to be copied from")
         Dummy = CENT(11,80, "Enter the name of the file to be copied to")
         @ 10,18 GET FromFile  PICTURE "@!K" COLOR &ColEntry
```

```
      @ 12,18 GET ToFile    PICTURE "@!K" COLOR &ColEntry
      READ
      SET ESCAPE OFF
      IF LASTKEY() <> ESCAPE
         RUN COPY &FromFile &ToFile
      ENDIF
      RESTORE SCREEN FROM TEMP
      SET CURSOR OFF
   CASE DOSChoice = 3                   && DISKCOPY A to B
      RUN DISKCOPY A: B:
   CASE DOSChoice = 4                   && FORMAT A
      RUN FORMAT A:
   CASE DOSChoice = 5                   && FORMAT B
      RUN FORMAT B:
   CASE DOSChoice = 6                   && DIRECTORY
      RUN DIR/P
      WAIT
   CASE DOSChoice = 7                   && Print DIRECTORY
      SAVE SCREEN TO Temp
      PrntOK = .F.
      PrntOK = PRINTSTATUS()
      IF .NOT. PrntOK
         Dummy = BOXES(10,22,14,56,.T., "D", ColError)
         @ 11,26 SAY "Please turn on the printer"
         @ 12,38 SAY "or"
         @ 13,24 SAY "press Esc to return to the menu"
      ENDIF
      DO WHILE .NOT. PrntOK
         KEY     = INKEY(1)
         PrntOK = PRINTSTATUS()
         IF KEY = ESCAPE
            RESTORE SCREEN FROM Temp
            RETURN
         ENDIF
      ENDDO
      Dummy = MESSBOX(12, "Printing the Directory",.T., "D", ColError)
      RUN DIR>LPT1
      SET DEVICE TO PRINT
      EJECT
      SET DEVICE TO SCREEN
      RESTORE SCREEN FROM Temp
   CASE DOSChoice = 8                   && BACKUP
      SAVE SCREEN TO TEMP
      Dummy = MESSBOX(10, "Please Insert a Formated Diskette " +;
              "into Drive A:" + " for the files",.F., "S", ColHelp)
      @ 21,30 SAY ""
      WAIT
      Dummy = MESSBOX(14,"Backing Up the Database Files",.T.,"D",ColWarning)
      @ 21,30 SAY ""
      CLOSE DATA
      RUN COPY *.DBF A: >NUL
      RUN COPY *.??X A: >NUL
      RUN COPY *.MEM A: >NUL
      SELECT A
      RESTORE SCREEN FROM TEMP
   CASE DOSChoice = 9                   && RESTORE
      SAVE SCREEN TO TEMP
      Dummy = MESSBOX(10, "Please Insert the Diskette with the Backed Up" +;
              " files in drive A",.T., "S", ColHelp)
      @ 21,30 SAY ""
      WAIT
      Dummy = MESSBOX(14,"Restoring the Database Files",.T.,"D",ColWarning)
```

```
            @ 21,30 SAY ""
            CLOSE DATA
            RUN COPY A:*.DBF >NUL
            RUN COPY A:*.MEM >NUL
            RUN DEL *.??X >NUL
            DO OpenData
            RESTORE SCREEN FROM TEMP
         CASE DOSChoice = 10 .OR. DOSChoice = 0     && RETURN
            EXIT
      ENDCASE
      SET MESSAGE TO " " AT 23,0
   ENDDO
   RESTORE SCREEN FROM STemp
   Temp = " "
   RETURN
   *END:DODOS


   * ______________
   PROCEDURE COLORS
   * ______________
   *
   *            LISTING OF COLOR.MEM
   *
   *   ColFunc    = "N/W"
   *   ColBlank   = "N/N,N/N,B"
   *   ColHelp    = "N/G,N/W,B"
   *   ColData    = "RG+/B,N/W,B"
   *   ColError   = "W+/R,W+/R,B"
   *   ColEntry   = "N/W,W+/N,B,B"
   *   ColStand   = "W+/B,N/W,B"
   *   ColMenu    = "RG+/R,N/W,B"
   *   ColWarning = "N/BG,W+/N,B"
   *

   DO WHILE .T.
      Dummy = BOXES(14,6,23,21,.F., "S", ColMenu)
      @ 15,12 SAY "MENU"
      @ 16,7  TO 16,20 DOUBLE
      @ 16,6  SAY "╞"
      @ 16,21 SAY "╡"
      SET BORDER  TO NONE
      SET MESSAGE TO
      DEFINE POPUP ColChoice FROM 16, 7
      DEFINE BAR 1 OF ColChoice PROMPT "1. Background"
      DEFINE BAR 2 OF ColChoice PROMPT "2. Data      "
      DEFINE BAR 3 OF ColChoice PROMPT "3. Help      "
      DEFINE BAR 4 OF ColChoice PROMPT "4. Menu      "
      DEFINE BAR 5 OF ColChoice PROMPT "5. Warning "
      DEFINE BAR 6 OF ColChoice PROMPT "6. Return "
      mChoice = 0
      ON SELECTION POPUP ColChoice DO PopSel WITH mChoice
      SET BORDER TO SINGLE
      ACTIVATE POPUP ColChoice
      IF mChoice = 0 .OR. mChoice = 6
         EXIT
      ELSE
         DO CLRS WITH mChoice
      ENDIF
   ENDDO
```

```
SET MESSAGE TO " " AT 23,0
RETURN
*END:COLORS


* ___________
PROCEDURE CLRS
* ___________
PARAMETERS BDHMW
IF BDHMW > 5
   RETURN
ENDIF
Pass = 1
DECLARE mColArray[16]
RESTORE FROM COLOR ADDITIVE
mColArray [ 1] = "W+"
mColArray [ 2] = "W"
mColArray [ 3] = "RG+"
mColArray [ 4] = "RG"
mColArray [ 5] = "RB+"
mColArray [ 6] = "RB"
mColArray [ 7] = "R+"
mColArray [ 8] = "R"
mColArray [ 9] = "GB+"
mColArray [10] = "GB"
mColArray [11] = "G+"
mColArray [12] = "G"
mColArray [13] = "B+"
mColArray [14] = "B"
mColArray [15] = "N+"
mColArray [16] = "N"
STORE 6  TO X1,X2,HoldX,X
STORE 50 TO Y1,Y
STORE 65 TO Y2,HoldY
Forg   = "W+"
Bakg   = "W"
Active = "X"
DO ColDisp WITH Forg,Bakg,Active,X1,X2,Y1,Y2,9,Pass,BDHMW
DO WHILE .T.
   SET CURSOR OFF
   KEY = INKEY(0)
   DO CASE
      CASE KEY = CurDn .OR. KEY = CurUp
         IF Active = "X"
            X = X1
            Y = Y1
         ELSE
            X = X2
            Y = Y2
         ENDIF
         X = IIF(KEY = CurDn,X + 1,X - 1)
         X = IIF(Y = 65 .AND. X = 15,6,X)
         X = IIF(Y = 65 .AND. X = 5,14,X)
         X = IIF(Y = 50 .AND. X = 22,6,X)
         X = IIF(Y = 50 .AND. X = 5,21,X)
      CASE KEY = CurRight
         SET COLOR TO W+/B
         @ X1,Y1 SAY ""
         SET COLOR TO W+*/B
         @ HoldX,HoldY SAY ""
         X = HoldX
         Y = HoldY
```

```
      HoldX = X1
      HoldY = 50
      STORE 65 TO Y2,Y
      Active = "Y"
   CASE KEY = CurLeft
      SET COLOR TO W+/B
      @ X2,Y2 SAY ""
      SET COLOR TO W+*/B
      @ HoldX,HoldY SAY ""
      X = HoldX
      Y = HoldY
      HoldX = X2
      HoldY = 65
      STORE 50 TO Y1,Y
      Active = "X"
   CASE KEY = ESCAPE
      EXIT
ENDCASE
IF Active = "X"
   SET COLOR TO B/B
   @ X1,Y1 SAY " "
   X1 = X
   Y1 = Y
   SET COLOR TO W+*/B
   @ X1,Y1 SAY ""
ENDIF
IF Active = "Y"
   SET COLOR TO B/B
   @ X2,Y2 SAY " "
   X2 = X
   Y2 = Y
   SET COLOR TO W+*/B
   @ X2,Y2 SAY ""
ENDIF
DoIt = .T.
IF Active = "Y" .AND. X2 = 14 .AND. KEY = Enter
   DoIt       = .F.
   ColFunc    = "N/W"
   ColBlank   = "N/N,N/N,B"
   ColHelp    = "N/G,N/W,B"
   ColData    = "RG+/B,N/W,B"
   ColError   = "W+/R,W+/R,B"
   ColEntry   = "N/W,W+/N,B,"
   ColStand   = "W+/B,N/W,B"
   ColMenu    = "RG+/R,N/W,B"
   ColWarning = "N/BG,W+/N,B"
   DO CASE
      CASE BDHMW = 1
         Forg = "W+/"
         Bakg = "B"
      CASE BDHMW = 2
         Forg = "RG+/"
         Bakg = "B"
      CASE BDHMW = 3
         Forg = "N/"
         Bakg = "G"
      CASE BDHMW = 4
         Forg = "RG+/"
         Bakg = "R"
      CASE BDHMW = 5
         Forg = "N/"
         Bakg = "BG"
   ENDCASE
```

```
      DO ColDisp WITH Forg,Bakg,Active,X1,X2,Y1,Y2,BDHMW,Pass,BDHMW
   ENDIF
   IF KEY = Enter
      SET COLOR TO W+*/R
      @ 17,66 SAY "    SAVING    "
      SAVE TO COLOR ALL LIKE COL*
      DoIt        = .F.
      DO CASE
         CASE BDHMW = 1
            ColStand   = Forg + Bakg + ",N/W,B"
         CASE BDHMW = 2
            ColData    = Forg + Bakg + ",N/W,B"
         CASE BDHMW = 3
            ColHelp    = Forg + Bakg + ",N/W,B"
         CASE BDHMW = 4
            ColMenu    = Forg + Bakg + ",N/W,B"
         CASE BDHMW = 5
            ColWarning = Forg + Bakg + ",W+/N,B"
      ENDCASE
      KEY = INKEY(3)
      SET COLOR TO W+/B
      @ 17,66 SAY "              "
      EXIT
   ENDIF
   IF DoIt
      IF KEY <> Enter
         Forg = mColArray[X1-5] + "/"
         IF X2 < 14
            Bakg = mColArray[(X2-5)*2]
         ENDIF
      ENDIF
      DO CASE
         CASE BDHMW = 1
            ColStand   = Forg + Bakg + ",N/W,B"
         CASE BDHMW = 2
            ColData    = Forg + Bakg + ",N/W,B"
         CASE BDHMW = 3
            ColHelp    = Forg + Bakg + ",N/W,B"
         CASE BDHMW = 4
            ColMenu    = Forg + Bakg + ",N/W,B"
         CASE BDHMW = 5
            ColWarning = Forg + Bakg + ",W+/N,B"
      ENDCASE
      DO ColDisp WITH Forg,Bakg,Active,X1,X2,Y1,Y2,BDHMW,Pass,BDHMW
   ENDIF
ENDDO
SET COLOR TO &ColStand
DO NOARROW
RETURN
*END:CLRS.PRG


* ______________
PROCEDURE COLDISP
* ______________
PARAMETERS Forg,Bakg,Active,X1,X2,Y1,Y2,Choice,Pass,BDHMW
NewCol = Forg + Bakg
IF Choice = 1                                  && STANDARD COLOR
   SET COLOR TO &NewCol
ELSE
   SET COLOR TO &ColStand
ENDIF
@  3,0 CLEAR TO 23,47
```

```
@  3,18          TO  5,33
@  3,0 SAY "║ "
@  4,0 SAY "║ │"
@  5,0 SAY "║ │"
@  6,0 SAY "║ │Customer:"
@  7,0 SAY "║ │"
@  8,0 SAY "║ │Address :"
@  9,0 SAY "║ │"
@ 10,0 SAY "║ │City     :                          State:"
@ 11,0 SAY "║ │"
@ 12,0 SAY "║ │Phone    : (   )  -                 Zip  :"
@ 13,0 SAY "╟─┼──────────────────────────────────────────────"
@ 14,0 SAY "║ │  │                      │"
@ 15,0 SAY "║ │  │                      │"
@ 16,0 SAY "║ │  │                      │"
@ 17,0 SAY "║ │  └─                     │"
@ 18,0 SAY "║ │                       ──┘"
@ 19,0 SAY "║ └───                          "
@ 20,0 SAY "║                               │"
@ 21,0 SAY "║                         ──────┘"
@ 22,0 SAY "║"
@ 23,0 SAY "╚"
@ 23,1 TO 23,47 DOUBLE
@ 4,20 SAY "MAIN HEADING"

IF Choice = 2                              && DATA COLOR
   SET COLOR TO &NewCol
ELSE
   SET COLOR TO &ColData
ENDIF
@  6,13 SAY "Phillipps Computer Systems Inc."
@  8,13 SAY "52 Hook Mountain Road"
@ 10,13 SAY "Montville"
@ 10,41 SAY "NJ"
@ 12,14 SAY "201"
@ 12,18 SAY "575"
@ 12,22 SAY "8575"
@ 12,40 SAY " 07045"
SET COLOR TO N/N
@ 16,42 CLEAR TO 19,44
@ 19,30 CLEAR TO 19,44

IF Choice = 3                              && HELP COLOR
   SET COLOR TO &NewCol
ELSE
   SET COLOR TO &ColHelp
ENDIF
@ 0,0 SAY "┌──────────────────────────────────────────────┐"
@ 1,0 SAY "│     These are the help colors.               │"
@ 2,0 SAY "└──────────────────────────────────────────────┘"

IF Choice = 4                              && MENU COLOR
   SET COLOR TO &NewCol
ELSE
   SET COLOR TO &ColMenu
ENDIF
```

```
@ 14,6 SAY "┌──────────────┐"
@ 15,6 SAY "│     MENU     │"
@ 16,6 SAY "╞══════════════╡"
@ 17,6 SAY "├1. Background │"
@ 18,6 SAY "│ 2. Data──────┤"
@ 19,6 SAY "├3. Help       │"
@ 20,6 SAY "│ 4. Menu      │"
@ 21,6 SAY "│ 5. Warning───┤"
@ 22,6 SAY "│ 6. Return    │"
@ 23,6 SAY "└──────────────┘"
SET COLOR TO &ColFunc
DO CASE
   CASE BDHMW = 1
      @ 17,8 SAY "1. Background"
   CASE BDHMW = 2
      @ 18,8 SAY "2. Data──────"
   CASE BDHMW = 3
      @ 19,8 SAY "3. Help      "
   CASE BDHMW = 4
      @ 20,8 SAY "4. Menu      "
   CASE BDHMW = 5
      @ 21,8 SAY "5. Warning───"
ENDCASE

IF Choice = 5                                  && WARNING COLOR
   SET COLOR TO &NewCol
ELSE
   SET COLOR TO &ColWarning
ENDIF
@ 15,28 TO 18,41
@ 16,29 SAY "  Warning   "
@ 17,29 SAY "   Colors   "

IF Pass = 1
   Pass = 2
   SET COLOR TO  &ColHelp
   @ 24,0 CLEAR TO 24,79
   @ 24,7  SAY "-return"
   @ 24,19 SAY "-up/down"
   @ 24,33 SAY "-background"
   @ 24,48 SAY "-foreground"
   @ 24,65 SAY "-reset/save"
   SET COLOR TO  &ColFunc
   @ 24,4 SAY "ESC"
   @ 24,17 SAY ""
   @ 24,32 SAY CHR(26)                         && -
   @ 24,47 SAY CHR(27)                         && -
   @ 24,61 SAY "─┘"
   SET COLOR TO W+/B,W+/B,B,B                  && CHOICES
   @ 0,48 CLEAR TO 23,79
   @ 0,48       TO 23,79
   @  0,48 SAY "╒─────── SCREEN COLOR ───────┐"
   @  2,52 SAY "SELECT COLORS COMBINATIONS"
   @  4,52 SAY "Foreground     Background"
   @  5,52 SAY "──────────     ──────────"
   SET COLOR TO W+/B
```

```
@  6,52 SAY "HI WHITE    "
Forg = "W+"
SET COLOR TO W/B
@  7,52 SAY "WHITE       "
Forg = "W"
SET COLOR TO RG+/B
@  8,52 SAY "HI YELLOW   "
Forg = "RG+"
SET COLOR TO RG/B
@  9,52 SAY "BROWN       "
Forg = "RG"
SET COLOR TO RB+/B
@ 10,52 SAY "HI MAGENTA  "
Forg = "RB+"
SET COLOR TO RB/B
@ 11,52 SAY "MAGENTA     "
Forg = "RB"
SET COLOR TO R+/B
@ 12,52 SAY "HI RED      "
Forg = "R+"
SET COLOR TO R/B
@ 13,52 SAY "RED         "
Forg = "R"
SET COLOR TO GB+/B
@ 14,52 SAY "HI CYAN     "
Forg = "GB+"
SET COLOR TO GB/B
@ 15,52 SAY "CYAN        "
Forg = "GB"
SET COLOR TO G+/B
@ 16,52 SAY "HI GREEN    "
Forg = "G+"
SET COLOR TO G/B
@ 17,52 SAY "GREEN       "
Forg = "G"
SET COLOR TO B+/B
@ 18,52 SAY "HI BLUE     "
Forg = "B+"
SET COLOR TO B/B
@ 19,52 SAY "BLUE        "
Forg = "B"
SET COLOR TO N+/B
@ 20,52 SAY "HI BLACK    "
Forg = "N+"
SET COLOR TO N/B
@ 21,52 SAY "BLACK       "
Forg = "N"
SET COLOR TO  /W
Bakg = "W"
@  6,66 SAY "WHITE      "
SET COLOR TO  /RG
Bakg = "RG"
@  7,66 SAY "BROWN      "
SET COLOR TO  /RB
Bakg = "RB"
@  8,66 SAY "MAGENTA    "
SET COLOR TO  /R
Bakg = "R"
@  9,66 SAY "RED        "
SET COLOR TO  /GB
Bakg = "GB"
@ 10,66 SAY "CYAN       "
```

```
   SET COLOR TO  /G
   Bakg = "G"
   @ 11,66 SAY "GREEN       "
   SET COLOR TO  /B
   Bakg = "B"
   @ 12,66 SAY "BLUE        "
   SET COLOR TO  /N
   Bakg = "N"
   @ 13,66 SAY "BLACK       "
   SET COLOR TO N/W
   @ 14,66 SAY "RESET ORIG."
ENDIF
IF Active = "X"
   SET COLOR TO W+*/B
   @ X1,Y1 SAY ""
   SET COLOR TO W+/B
   @ X2,Y2 SAY ""
ELSE
   SET COLOR TO W+*/B
   @ X2,Y2 SAY ""
   SET COLOR TO W+/B
   @ X1,Y1 SAY ""
ENDIF
SET CURSOR OFF
RETURN
*EOF:COLDISP


* _______________
PROCEDURE NOARROW
* _______________
SET COLOR TO W+/B
X = 5
DO WHILE X < 22
   X = X + 1
   @ X,50 SAY " "
   IF X < 15
      @ X,65 SAY " "
   ENDIF
ENDDO
RETURN
*END:NOARROR


* _______________
FUNCTION PASSWORD
* _______________
PARAMETERS ValidPass
SET COLOR TO &ColStand
CLEAR
SET MESSAGE TO
Pass = SPACE(12)
AB   = "ABCDEFGHIJKLMNOPQRSTUVWXYZabcdefghijklmnopqrstuvwxyz"
SET ESCAPE ON
SET CURSOR ON
Dummy = BOXES(11,22,13,57,.T., "D", ColMenu)
Dummy = CENT(12,80, "Enter the Password: XXXXXXXXXXXX")
SET COLOR TO &ColBlank
DO WHILE .T.
   Ret = .F.
   @ 12,44 GET Pass PICTURE "@!"
   READ
```

```
      IF LASTKEY() = ESCAPE
         EXIT
      ENDIF
      * Written this way to prevent showing password in this listing
      IF SUBSTR(Pass,1, 1) = SUBSTR(AB,09,1) .AND.;
         SUBSTR(Pass,2, 1) = SUBSTR(AB,03,1) .AND.;
         SUBSTR(Pass,3, 1) = SUBSTR(AB,19,1) .AND.;
         SUBSTR(Pass,4, 1) = SUBSTR(AB,03,1) .AND.;
         SUBSTR(Pass,5, 1) = SUBSTR(AB,08,1) .AND.;
         SUBSTR(Pass,6, 1) = SUBSTR(AB,01,1) .AND.;
         SUBSTR(Pass,7, 1) = SUBSTR(AB,14,1) .AND.;
         SUBSTR(Pass,8, 1) = SUBSTR(AB,07,1) .AND.;
         SUBSTR(Pass,9, 1) = SUBSTR(AB,05,1) .AND.;
         SUBSTR(Pass,10,1) = SUBSTR(AB,19,1)
         Ret = .T.
      ENDIF
      EXIT
ENDDO
SET ESCAPE OFF
SET CURSOR OFF
SET COLOR TO &ColData
CLEAR
SET MESSAGE TO " " AT 23,0
ValidPass = (Ret)
RETURN(.T.)
*END:PASSWORD


*______________
PROCEDURE DVEND                                  && Vendor Master Menu
*______________
DO WHILE .T.
   RELEASE POPUP
   CLEAR TYPEAHEAD
   MastC = 0
   Dummy = START()
   Dummy = FKEYS(2)
   Dummy = MBOX(34,5,17,.T., "D", ColMenu, "INQUIRY & UPDATE MENU")
   @ 23,0
   SET BORDER TO NONE
   DEFINE POPUP VendInfo FROM 7, 23
   DEFINE BAR 1 OF VendInfo PROMPT " 1. View Information            ";
      MESSAGE MESSCENT("View the Information in the Database.")
   DEFINE BAR 3 OF VendInfo PROMPT " 2. Change Information          ";
      MESSAGE MESSCENT("Modify the Information in the Database.")
   DEFINE BAR 5 OF VendInfo PROMPT " 3. Add New Information         ";
      MESSAGE MESSCENT("Add a New Vendor and Related Information " +;
                       "to the Database.")
   DEFINE BAR 7 OF VendInfo PROMPT " 4. Delete Existing Information ";
      MESSAGE MESSCENT("Delete Existing Information from the Database.")
   DEFINE BAR 9 OF VendInfo PROMPT " 5. Return to Main Menu         ";
      MESSAGE MESSCENT("Return to the Main Menu.")
   ON SELECTION POPUP VendInfo DO PopSel WITH MastC
   SET BORDER TO SINGLE
   ACTIVATE POPUP VendInfo
   IF MastC = 9 .OR. MastC = 0                  && Return
      EXIT
   ENDIF
   DO MastCont WITH MastC
```

```
ENDDO
RETURN
*END:DVEND
*_______________
PROCEDURE MASTCONT
*_______________
PARAMETERS MastC
SELECT A
GOTO TOP
SET MESSAGE TO
DO CASE
   CASE MastC = 1                              && View Data
      DO VendProf WITH MastC
   CASE MastC = 3                              && Change Data
      DO VendProf WITH MastC
   CASE MastC = 5                              && Add Data
      DO VendProf WITH MastC
   CASE MastC = 7                              && Delete Data
      DO VendProf WITH MastC
ENDCASE
* Reprocess with different screen depending on key press
DO WHILE .T.
   DO CASE
      CASE KEY = F2Key
         DO VendProf WITH MastC
      CASE KEY = F3Key
         DO InsProf WITH MastC
      CASE KEY = F4Key
         DO ConfProf WITH MastC
      CASE KEY = ESCAPE
         EXIT
      OTHERWISE
         EXIT
   ENDCASE
ENDDO
SET MESSAGE TO " " AT 23,0
RETURN
*END:MASTCONT
*_______________
PROCEDURE VENDPROF                             && Main Vendor Processing Code
*_______________
PARAMETERS Action
SELECT A
SET COLOR TO &ColStand
CLEAR
DO CASE                                        && Set bottom of the screen
   CASE Action = 1                             && View
      Dummy = FKEYS(4)
   CASE Action = 3                             && Change
      Dummy = FKEYS(1)
   CASE Action = 5                             && Add
      Dummy = FKEYS(9)
   CASE Action = 7                             && Delete
      Dummy = FKEYS(3)
ENDCASE
SET NEAR ON
DO VendSay                                     && Display the Vendor Screen
```

```
SET COLOR TO &ColStand
KEY = 0
DO WHILE .T.
   DO CASE
      CASE KEY = F3Key .OR. KEY = F4Key
         EXIT
      CASE Action = 1                          && View existing vendor
         DO VendGet                            && Display data
         CLEAR GETS
      CASE Action = 3                          && Change vendor data
         DO VendGet                            && Display data
         CLEAR GETS
      CASE Action = 5                          && Add new vendor
         GOTO BOTTOM
         APPEND BLANK
         DO VendGet                            && Display blank data
         SET ESCAPE ON
         SET CURSOR ON
         READ                                  && Get new data
         IF LASTKEY() = ESCAPE
            DELETE
         ENDIF
         SET CURSOR OFF
         SET ESCAPE OFF
         KEYBOARD CHR(ESCAPE)
         REPLACE A->VenInput WITH CurrentDate
         @ 16,30 SAY A->VenInput
         DO FixFlag WITH "A"
         SET AUTOSAVE ON
         SKIP 0
         SET AUTOSAVE OFF
      CASE Action = 7                          && Delete Vendor
         DO VendGet                            && Display data
         CLEAR GETS
   ENDCASE
   KEY = 0
   DO GetNext WITH KEY                         && Read key
   DO CASE                                     && Branck on key action
      CASE KEY = ESCAPE
         EXIT
      CASE KEY = F9Key .AND. Action = 3 && Key = Change and
         SET COLOR TO &ColStand                && Action = Change
         @ 23,41 CLEAR TO 24,52
         SET COLOR TO W+/G
         @ 23,16 SAY "    Pg Dn    "
         SET COLOR TO N/G
         @ 24,16 SAY "    done     "
         SET COLOR TO &ColStand
         SET CURSOR ON
         DO VendGet                            && Get new data
         READ
         REPLACE A->VenInput WITH CurrentDate
         @ 16,30 SAY A->VenInput         && Process special case
         IF VAL(A->ArrangCod) = 1 .AND. B->VendNum = A->VendNum
            AHold = RECNO()
            SELECT B
            SET NEAR ON
            SEEK B->VendNum + " "
            DO WHILE A->VendNum = B->VendNum
               IF VAL(B->InsurType) <> 0    && Override ContAmt
                  REPLACE B->ContAmt WITH VAL(Hos[VAL(B->InsurType)])
               ENDIF
```

```
               SKIP
            ENDDO
            SET NEAR OFF
            SELECT A
            GOTO AHold
         ENDIF
         IF B->VendNum <> A->VendNum .AND. A->Certif
            REPLACE A->ConInsCom WITH .F.   && No Insurance Record
         ENDIF
         IF C->VendNum <> A->VendNum .AND. A->Confident
            REPLACE A->ConConfCom WITH .F.  && No Confidentiality Record
         ENDIF
         SET CURSOR OFF
         SET COLOR TO W+/G
         @ 23,16 SAY "         "
         @ 23,41 SAY " F5 find F6 "
         SET COLOR TO N/G
         @ 24,16 SAY " prev-next "
         @ 24,41 SAY " numb  name "
         SET COLOR TO &ColStand
         DO FixFlag WITH "A"            && Change flag settings?
         SET AUTOSAVE ON
         SKIP 0
         SET AUTOSAVE OFF
      CASE KEY = Del .AND. Action = 7   && Key = delete and
         mVendNum = A->VendNum          && Action = delete
         SELECT B                       && Can't delete if
         SEEK mVendNum                  && Insurance
         IF FOUND()
            Dummy = MyError(3, "S")
         ELSE
            SELECT C                    && Can't delete if
            SEEK mVendNum               && Confidentiality
            IF FOUND()
               Dummy = MyError(4, "S")
            ELSE                        && OK no other records
               SELECT A
               Dummy = DelRec("Vendor " + VendNum)    && Call delete UDF
            ENDIF
         ENDIF
         SELECT A
         SET COLOR TO &ColStand
   ENDCASE
ENDDO
SET NEAR OFF
RETURN
*END:VENDPROF


*_________________
PROCEDURE INSPROF                       && Process Insurance record(s)
*_________________
PARAMETERS Action
DO Adc WITH Action, "I"                 && Redisplay bottom of screen
SET COLOR TO &ColStand
SELECT A
SET ORDER TO TAG Vendor                 && Set order to relation order
RecKey = A->VendNum
FirstTime = .T.
SELECT B
* * * Action = Display or Delete and NO insurance record
```

```
IF (Action = 1 .OR. Action = 7) .AND. RecKey <> SUBSTR(B->VendNum,1,9)
   SAVE SCREEN TO Temp
   Dummy = MESSBOX(12, "There are no insurance records for this vendor!",;
                 .T., "D", ColHelp)
   Dummy = INKEY(3)
   RESTORE SCREEN FROM Temp              && Restore to conditiond before
   KEY = F2Key                           && this section and return
   SELECT A
   SEEK RecKey
   SET ORDER TO TAG (COrder)
   RETURN
ENDIF
DO WHILE .T.                             && Not previous condition
   DO DoIns                              && Display Insurance screen
   DO CASE
      * * Add - delete second part of statement to remove automatic add
      CASE Action = 5 .OR. KEY = F8Key .OR. ;
         (RecKey <> SUBSTR(B->VendNum,1,9) .AND. FirstTime)
         KEY       = 0
         FirstTime = .F.
         APPEND BLANK                       && Add an insurance record
         REPLACE B->VendNum WITH RecKey     && Update key
         SET CURSOR ON
         CLEAR GETS
         DO DoIns                           && Redisplay screen
         READ                               && Get new data
         REPLACE B->INPUT WITH CurrentDate
         @ 16,64 SAY B->INPUT               && Replace input date
         IF VAL(A->ArrangCod) = 1 .AND. VAL(B->InsurType) <> 0
            REPLACE B->ContAmt WITH VAL(Hos[VAL(B->InsurType)])
            @ 21,30 SAY B->ContAmt PICTURE "$99,999"
         ENDIF                              && Override ContAmt
         SET CURSOR OFF
         * * * If insurance not wanted - remove record
         IF LASTKEY() = ESCAPE .OR. VAL(B->InsurType) = 0
            DELETE
         ELSE
            DO FixFlag WITH "B"             && Fix the flage
         ENDIF
         SET AUTOSAVE ON
         SKIP 0
         SET AUTOSAVE OFF
      CASE Action = 1                       && View only
         CLEAR GETS
      CASE Action = 3 .AND. KEY = F9Key   && Change
         SET COLOR TO W+/G                  && Fix bottom of screen
         @ 23,32 SAY "  Pg Dn "
         SET COLOR TO N/G
         @ 24,32 SAY "  done  "
         SET COLOR TO &ColStand
         KEY = 0
         SET CURSOR ON
         READ                            && Get new data
         OldInsType = VAL(B->InsurType)
         REPLACE B->INPUT WITH CurrentDate
         @ 16,64 SAY B->INPUT
         DO DoIns                        && Redisplay data
         CLEAR GETS
         SET AUTOSAVE ON
         SKIP 0
         SET AUTOSAVE OFF
```

```
      IF VAL(A->ArrangCod) = 1 .AND. VAL(B->InsurType) <> 0
         REPLACE B->ContAmt WITH VAL(Hos[VAL(B->InsurType)])
         @ 21,30 SAY B->ContAmt PICTURE "$99,999"
      ENDIF                          && Override ContAmt
      IF VAL(A->ArrangCod) = 1 .AND. VAL(B->InsurType) <> OldInsType
         Dummy = MyError(12, "D")   && Warning
      ENDIF
      SET CURSOR OFF
      SET COLOR TO &ColStand
      @ 23,32 CLEAR TO 24,39
      DO FixFlag WITH "B"            && Fix flags
   CASE Action = 7 .AND. KEY = Del  && Delete
      SELECT B                       && Call delete UDF
      Dummy = DelRec("Insurance " + VendNum + InsurType)
      SET COLOR TO &ColStand
      @ 16,6  CLEAR TO 21,73
      @ 16,39 TO 21,39
      SELECT A
      IF A->VendNum <> B->VendNum   && Reset ConInsCom flag
         REPLACE ConInsCom WITH .T.
      ENDIF
      SKIP -1
      DO VendSay                     && Redisplay screen
      SET COLOR TO &ColStand
      DO VendGet                     && Redisplay data for previous vendor
      CLEAR GETS
      SKIP 1
      DO VendGet
      CLEAR GETS                     && Redisplay data for current vendor
      KEY = F2Key
      KEYBOARD CHR(F2Key)
      RETURN
ENDCASE
FirstTime = .F.
KEY       = INKEY(0)                 && Get key to determine what to do next.
HereIAm   = RECNO()
DO CASE
   CASE KEY = CurDn .AND. SUBSTR(B->VendNum,1,9) = RecKey .AND. .NOT. EOF()
      SKIP                           && Get next insurance record
   CASE KEY = CurUp .AND. SUBSTR(B->VendNum,1,9) = RecKey .AND. .NOT. BOF()
      SKIP -1                        && Get previous insurance record
   CASE KEY = ESCAPE .OR. KEY = F2Key .OR. KEY = F4Key
      EXIT                           && Get out of the insurance area
ENDCASE
DO CASE
   CASE (SUBSTR(B->VendNum,1,9) <> RecKey .OR. BOF() .OR. EOF()) .AND.;
      (Action = 3 .OR. Action = 5)  && Change or Add and
      DO NoMore WITH Action          && No more insurance for vendor
      GOTO HereIAm
   CASE (SUBSTR(B->VendNum,1,9) <> RecKey .OR. BOF() .OR. EOF()) .AND.;
      (Action = 1 .OR. Action = 7)  && View or delete and
      SAVE SCREEN TO Temp            && No more insurance for vendor
      Dummy = MESSBOX(12, "There are no additional records " +;
                      "for this vendor",.T., "D", ColHelp)
      Dummy = INKEY(3)
      RESTORE SCREEN FROM Temp
      GOTO HereIAm
ENDCASE
IF KEY = ESCAPE .OR. KEY = F2Key .OR. KEY = F4Key
                                     && Get out of the insurance area
   EXIT                              && if key indicates it
ENDIF
```

```
   FirstTime = .F.
ENDDO
IF B->VendNum <> A->VendNum .AND. A->Certif && No Insurance Record
   REPLACE A->ConInsCom WITH .F.
ENDIF
RETURN
*END:INSPROF


*_______________
PROCEDURE FIXFLAG                    && Fix all the flags depending on
*_______________                     && all the insurance and
PARAMETERS DBInUse                   && confidentiality records
DO CASE
   CASE DBInUse = "B" .AND. (B->Amount < B->ContAmt .OR. B->ContAmt = 0)
      REPLACE A->ConInsCom WITH .F.   && Below contract amount current
   CASE DBInUse = "B" .AND. .NOT. A->ConInsCom
      HereIam = RECNO()               && Out of contract compliance
      SET NEAR ON
      SEEK A->VendNum + "  "          && now - Check all records
      DO WHILE A->VendNum = B->VendNum .AND. .NOT. EOF()
         IF B->ContAmt > B->Amount ;
            .OR. B->ContAmt = 0       && If any contract is out of
            Ans = .F.                 && compliance set ans to false
            EXIT                      && and do NOT check any more
         ELSE
            Ans = .T.
         ENDIF
         SKIP
      ENDDO
      GOTO HereIam                    && Go to initial record
      REPLACE A->ConInsCom WITH Ans   && Reset compliance flag
      SET NEAR OFF
   CASE DBInUse = "C" .AND. EMPTY(C->ConfRecvd) .AND.;
      A->Confident .AND. .NOT. C->SignOff
      REPLACE A->ConConfCom WITH .F.  && Bad confidentiality
   CASE DBInUse = "C" .AND. A->Confident
      HereIam = RECNO()               && Good confidentiality - may be
      SET NEAR ON
      SEEK A->VendNum + "1"
      DO WHILE C->VendNum = A->VendNum .AND. .NOT. EOF()
         IF .NOT. EMPTY(C->ConfRecvd) .AND. C->SignOff
            Ans = .T.
         ELSE
            Ans = .F.                 && If any one is bad set Ans to
            EXIT                      && false and stop checking
         ENDIF
         SKIP
      ENDDO
      GOTO HereIam                    && Go back to where you started
      SET NEAR OFF
      SELECT A
      REPLACE A->ConConfCom WITH Ans  && Reset confidentiality flag
      SELECT C
   CASE DBInUse = "A" .AND. .NOT. A->Confident
      REPLACE A->ConConfCom WITH .T.  && Must be true in this case
   CASE DBInUse = "A" .AND. A->Confident
      SELECT C                        && Is true - may be false
      HereIam = RECNO()
      SET NEAR ON
      SEEK A->VendNum + "  "
      DO WHILE .NOT. EOF() .AND. C->VendNum = A->VendNum
         IF EMPTY(C->ConfRecvd) .AND. .NOT. C->SignOff
            SELECT A
```

```
            REPLACE A->ConConfCom WITH .F.  && Ooh Ooh - false
            EXIT
         ENDIF
         SELECT C
         SKIP
      ENDDO
      SELECT C
      GOTO HereIAm
      SELECT A
      SET NEAR OFF
ENDCASE
RETURN
*END:FIXPLAG

*_______________
PROCEDURE NOMORE                        && No more insurance records
*_______________                        && may be you want to add one?
PARAMETERS Action
SAVE SCREEN TO Temp
Dummy = BOXES(10,5,14,73,.T., "D", ColHelp)
Dummy = CENT(11,80, "There are no additional records for this vendor")
Dummy = CENT(13,80, 'Press "F8" to add a new record or "F2" ' +;
                    'to return to Vendors')
KEY = INKEY(0)
SET COLOR TO &ColStand
RESTORE SCREEN FROM Temp
RETURN
*END:NOMORE


*_________________
PROCEDURE CONFPROF                      && Update confidentiality
*_________________
PARAMETERS Action
DO Adc WITH Action, "C"                 && Redraw bottom of the screen
SET COLOR TO &ColStand
SELECT A
SET ORDER TO TAG Vendor                 && Set order to relation order
RecKey = A->VendNum
SELECT C
IF (Action = 1 .OR. Action = 7) .AND. RecKey <> SUBSTR(C->VendNum,1,9)
   SAVE SCREEN TO DScreen
   Dummy = MESSBOX(12, "There are no confidentiality records " +;
                   "for this vendor",.T., "D", ColHelp)
   Dummy = INKEY(3)
   RESTORE SCREEN FROM DScreen
   KEY = F2Key
   SELECT A
   SEEK RecKey
   SET ORDER TO TAG (COrder)
   RETURN
ENDIF
DO WHILE .T.
   DO DoConf WITH RecKey                && Display confidentiality screen
   CLEAR GETS
   IF (Action = 3 .AND. KEY = F9Key) .OR.;
      (Action = 3 .AND. KEY = F8Key) .OR.;
      (Action = 5 .AND. KEY = F8Key) .OR.;
      (Action = 7 .AND. KEY = Del)
      DO WHILE .T.
         ATitle  = IIF(Action=3, "change", IIF(Action=5, "add", "delete"))
         ATitle  = IIF(LASTKEY()=F8Key, "add", ATitle)
         AHead1  = "Select the Number of the"
         AHead2  = "arrangement to " + ATitle
```

```
      SAVE SCREEN TO DScreen
      Dummy = BOXES(2,26,11,54,.F., "D", ColMenu)
      Dummy = CENT(3, 80, AHead1)
      Dummy = CENT(4, 80, AHead2)
      @ 5,27 TO 5,53                && Use Clipper like AChoice to
      @ 5,26 SAY "├"                && select record to alter
      @ 5,54 SAY "┤"
      JJ = 0
      Dummy = ZeroM()
      DO WHILE JJ <= 5
         JJ = JJ + 1
         AMenu[JJ] = STR(JJ,1,0)
      ENDDO
      APick = JJ
      SET MESSAGE TO
      SET COLOT TO &ColMenu
      DO ACHOICE WITH APick, " ", 5, 27, 11, 53
      SET COLOT TO &ColStand
      SET MESSAGE TO " " AT 23,0
      SAPick = STR(APick,1,0)
      SAPick = IIF(EMPTY(SAPick), "1", SAPick)
      RESTORE SCREEN FROM DScreen
      IF LASTKEY() = ESCAPE         && Leave if requested
         KEY = F2Key                && But reset key first to know
         EXIT                       && what to do next
      ENDIF
      SELECT C
      SEEK RecKey + SAPick          && Look for record
      DO CASE
         CASE (Action = 3 .OR. Action = 7) .AND. KEY <> F8Key
            IF FOUND()
               EXIT
            ELSE
               Dummy = MyError(7, "D")        && Can't fix what isn't there
            ENDIF
         CASE Action = 5 .OR. KEY = F8Key     && Add or Add
            IF .NOT. FOUND()                  && OK
               EXIT
            ELSE                              && Can't add if there already
               Dummy = MyError(8, "D")
            ENDIF
      ENDCASE
      SELECT A
      SET ORDER TO TAG Vendor                 && Set order to relation order
      SEEK RecKey
      SELECT C
   ENDDO
ENDIF
DO CASE
   CASE Action = 1                            && View
      CLEAR GETS
   CASE Action = 3 .AND. KEY = F9Key          && Change and change
      DO ConfAC                               && Do it
   CASE Action = 5 .OR. KEY = F8Key           && Add or add
      APPEND BLANK
      REPLACE C->VendNum WITH RecKey, C->ConfCode WITH SAPick
      DO ConfAC                               && Do it
      IF LASTKEY() = ESCAPE
         DELETE
         KEY = ESCAPE
      ENDIF
```

```
      CASE Action = 7 .AND. KEY = Del              && Delete
         Dummy = DelRec("Confidentiality " + VendNum + ConfCode)
         SET COLOR TO &ColStand
         @ 16,7 CLEAR TO 21,73
         SEEK RecKey                               && Redisplay
         DO DoConf WITH RecKey                     && new confidentiality
         CLEAR GETS                                && screen
   ENDCASE
   KEY  = INKEY(0)                        && Get a key
   IF KEY = ESCAPE .OR. KEY = F2Key .OR. KEY = F3Key
      EXIT                                && Leave if not wanted
   ENDIF
ENDDO
IF C->VendNum <> A->VendNum .AND. A->Confident     && No Confidentiality Record
   REPLACE A->ConConfCom WITH .F.
ENDIF
RETURN
*END:CONPROF


*_______________
PROCEDURE GETNEXT                         && Process keystroke and
*_______________                          && do what is expected
PARAMETERS KEY
DO WHILE .T.
   KEY  = INKEY(0)                        && Get keystroke
   FKey = CHR(KEY)                        && Convert to character
   DO CASE
      CASE KEY = CurDn .AND. .NOT. EOF()
         SKIP
         EXIT
      CASE KEY = CurUp .AND. .NOT. BOF()
         SKIP -1
         EXIT
      CASE (FKey >= "A" .AND. FKey <= "Z") .OR.;
           (FKey >= "0" .AND. FKey <= "9") .OR.;
           (FKey >= "a" .AND. FKey <= "z")
         SEEK FKey
         EXIT
      CASE KEY = F5Key .OR. KEY = F6Key            && Popup correct
         DO F5F6Key WITH KEY                       && screen
         EXIT
      CASE KEY = Del .OR. KEY = F9Key .OR. KEY = ESCAPE .OR.;
         KEY = F3Key .OR. KEY = F4Key .OR. KEY = F8Key
         EXIT                             && By By
   ENDCASE
ENDDO
IF EOF()                                  && Wrap database if at either end
   GOTO TOP
ENDIF
IF BOF()
   GOTO BOTTOM
ENDIF
RETURN
*END:GETNEXT


*________________
PROCEDURE VENDSAY                         && Display a vendor record
*________________
SELECT A
```

```
SET ORDER TO TAG Vendor                  && Set order to relation order
SET COLOR TO &ColStand
@ 0,0 CLEAR TO 1,79
SET COLOR TO &ColOther
Dummy = CENT(0,80, "INSURANCE COMPLIANCE SYSTEM") && Top heading
SET COLOR TO &ColData
DO CASE
   CASE MastC = 1
      @ 1,27 SAY " VIEW"
      IC = 33
   CASE MastC = 3
      @ 1,27 SAY "CHANGE"
      IC = 34
   CASE MastC = 5
      @ 1,27 SAY "  ADD"
      IC = 33
   CASE MastC = 7
      @ 1,27 SAY "DELETE"
      IC = 34
ENDCASE
SET COLOR TO &ColOther
@ 1,IC SAY "VENDOR INFORMATION"          && Complete top heading
SET COLOR TO &ColStand                   && Display fixed screen
@  2,5  TO 22,74 DOUBLE                  && information like borders
@  9,6  TO  9,74                         && and headings
@ 15,6  TO 15,74
@ 16,39 TO 21,39
@ 15, 5 SAY "╟"
@ 15,74 SAY "╢"
@  9, 5 SAY "╟"
@  9,74 SAY "╢"
@ 15,39 SAY "┬"
@ 22,39 SAY "╧"
@  3,10 SAY "Number"
@  3,37 SAY "Name"
@  3,62 SAY "Short Name"
@  7,66 SAY "Status"
@  8,44 SAY "Telephone:"
@ 10,16 SAY "Type of Vendor"
@ 10,54 SAY "Arrangement"
@ 12,34 SAY "Cancellation"
@ 13,13 SAY "Primary Business"
@ 13,37 SAY "Terms"
@ 13,55 SAY "COS Unit"
@ 16,18 SAY "Input Date:"
@ 17, 8 SAY "Initial Cert. Letter:"
@ 18,10 SAY "Certificate Letter:"
@ 19, 8 SAY "Cancel. Terms Letter:"
@ 20,13 SAY "Sign Off Letter:"
@ 21, 7 SAY "Attn:"
@ 16,61 SAY "Original:"
@ 17,58 SAY "On Premises:"
@ 18,58 SAY "Certificate:"
@ 19,54 SAY "Confidentiality:"
@ 20,45 SAY "Contract Ins. Compliance:"
@ 21,44 SAY "Contract Conf. Compliance:"
SET ORDER TO TAG (COrder)
RETURN
*END:VENDSAY
```

```
*______________
PROCEDURE VENDGET                              && Display data for vendor screen
*______________
SET ORDER TO TAG Vendor                        && Set order to relation order
SET COLOR TO &ColStand
@  4, 8 GET A->VendNum   VALID NEWV(A->VendNum) COLOR &ColEntry
@  4,24 GET A->VendName  COLOR &ColEntry
@  4,62 GET A->VenShortN COLOR &ColEntry
@  6, 8 GET A->Address1  COLOR &ColEntry
@  6,42 GET A->Address2  COLOR &ColEntry
@  8, 8 GET A->City      COLOR &ColEntry
@  8,29 GET A->State     COLOR &ColEntry
@  8,33 GET A->Zip       COLOR &ColEntry
@  8,55 GET A->Telephone COLOR &ColEntry
@  8,68 GET A->STATUS    COLOR &ColEntry
@ 11, 8 GET A->TypeCode  VALID VAIE(A->TypeCode,"V") COLOR &ColEntry
IF VAL(A->TypeCode) = 0
   REPLACE A->TypeCode WITH "  "
   @ 11, 8 SAY A->TypeCode
ENDIF
@ 11,11 SAY SPACE(25)                         && Display vendor type
@ 11,11 SAY IIF(VAL(A->TypeCode)=0, SPACE(25), Ven[VAL(A->TypeCode)]);
            PICTURE "!!!!!!!!!!!!!!!!!!!!!!!!!"
@ 11,44 GET A->ArrangCod   VALID VAIE(A->ArrangCod,"A") COLOR &ColEntry
IF VAL(A->ArrangCod) = 0
   REPLACE A->ArrangCod WITH "  "
   @ 11,44 SAY A->ArrangCod
ENDIF
@ 11,47 SAY SPACE(25)                         && Display arrangement type
@ 11,47 SAY IIF(VAL(A->ArrangCod)=0, SPACE(25), Arr[VAL(A->ArrangCod)]);
            PICTURE "!!!!!!!!!!!!!!!!!!!!!!!!!"
@ 14, 8 GET A->PrimeBu                                   COLOR &ColEntry
@ 14,38 GET A->CancelTerm  VALID CT(A->CancelTerm)       COLOR &ColEntry
@ 14,44 GET A->ExpenseCd   VALID VAIE(A->ExpenseCd,"E") COLOR &ColEntry
IF VAL(A->ExpenseCd) = 0
   REPLACE A->ExpenseCd WITH "  "
   @ 14,44 SAY A->ExpenseCd
ENDIF
@ 14,47 SAY SPACE(25)                         && Display expense code
@ 14,47 SAY IIF(VAL(A->ExpenseCd)=0, SPACE(25), Exp[VAL(A->ExpenseCd)]);
            PICTURE "!!!!!!!!!!!!!!!!!!!!!!!!!"
@ 16,30 SAY A->VenInput
@ 17,30 SAY A->InCertLet
@ 18,30 SAY A->CertLet
@ 19,30 SAY A->TermLet
@ 20,30 SAY A->SignLet
@ 21,13 GET A->AttnName  COLOR &ColEntry
@ 16,71 GET A->Original  COLOR &ColEntry
@ 17,71 GET A->OnPremise COLOR &ColEntry
@ 18,71 GET A->Certif    COLOR &ColEntry
@ 19,71 GET A->Confident COLOR &ColEntry
@ 20,71 SAY A->ConInsCom
@ 21,71 SAY A->ConConfCom
SET ORDER TO TAG (COrder)
RETURN
*END:VENDGET


*__________
FUNCTION NEWV
*__________                                   && When adding or changing a vendor
PARAMETERS mVendNum
PRIVATE    mVendNum
```

```
IF LASTKEY() = ESCAPE
   KEYBOARD CHR(PgDn)
   RETURN(.T.)
ENDIF
HereIAm = RECNO()
SEEK mVendNum
SKIP
IF A->VendNum = mVendNum                              && Can't add a duplicate vendor
   Dummy = MyError(2, "D")
   SET COLOR TO &ColStand
   GOTO HereIAm
   RETURN(.F.)
ELSE
   IF A->VendNum <> mVendNum .AND. .NOT. EMPTY(A->VendNum)
      IF B->VendNum = A->VendNum .OR. C->VendNum = A->VendNum
         Dummy = MyError(13, "D")
         SET COLOR TO &ColStand
         GOTO HereIAm
         RETURN(.T.)
      ELSE
         GOTO HereIAm
         RETURN(.T.)
      ENDIF
   ENDIF
   GOTO HereIAm
   RETURN(.T.)
ENDIF
IF EMPTY(mVendNum)                                    && Can't add a blank vendor number
   Dummy = MyError(10, "D")
   SET COLOR TO &ColStand
   GOTO HereIAm
   RETURN(.F.)
ENDIF
GOTO HereIAm
RETURN(.T.)
*END:NEWV


*__________
FUNCTION NV                                           && Make sure there really is
*__________                                           && a valid ConfCode
PARAMETERS mConfCode                                  && 1 through 6 are valid
PRIVATE NFld
NFld = VAL(mConfCode)
RETURN(IIF(NFld>0 .AND. NFld<6, .T., .F.))
*END:NV


*____________
FUNCTION VAIE                                         && Check for valid code and return
*____________                                         && alphabetic description based
PARAMETERS Code, CodeType                             && upon code in popup box
VCode = VAL(Code)                                     && Use AChoice to select
IF Code = " 0" .OR. Code = "  " .OR. Code = "0 " .OR. Code = "00" .OR.;
   VCode = 0
   KEYBOARD " 1" + CHR(Enter)                         && Zero and blanks are not valid
   Code = " 1"                                        && return a one and False
   RETURN(.F.)
ENDIF
IF VCode > MaxNum .OR. VCode < 1                      && Can't be greater than the max
   Dummy = MyError(5, "D")                            && or negative
   SET COLOR TO &ColStand                             && Return False
   RETURN(.F.)
```

```
ENDIF
SAVE SCREEN TO Temp
SET COLOR TO &ColMenu
DO CASE                                            && Valid code - Process
   CASE CodeType = "V"
      Pre = "Ven"                                  && Set box location based upon
      DBVar = "TypeCode"                           && CodeType
      DBX   = 11                                   && Also tell rest of routine
      DBY   = 8                                    && which array to use for list
      DBZ   = 11                                   && of choices
      Top   = 1
      Lft   = 41
      Rgt   = 71
   CASE CodeType = "A"
      Pre   = "Arr"
      DBVar = "ArrangCod"
      DBX   = 11
      DBY   = 44
      DBZ   = 47
      Top   = 1
      Lft   = 1
      Rgt   = 31
   CASE CodeType = "E"
      Pre   = "Exp"
      DBVar = "ExpenseCd"
      DBX   =  14
      DBY   =  44
      DBZ   =  47
      Top   = 1
      Lft   = 41
      Rgt   = 71
   CASE CodeType = "I"
      Pre   = "Ins"
      DBVar = "InsurType"
      DBX   =  16
      DBY   =  8
      DBZ   =  11
      Top   = 1
      Lft   = 1
      Rgt   = 31
ENDCASE
NLast = 0
DO WHILE NLast < 23
   NLast = NLast + 1
   IF LEN(ALLTRIM(&Pre[NLast])) = 0
      EXIT
   ENDIF
ENDDO

SELECT A
Dummy = BOXES(Top,Lft,NLast+1,Rgt,.T.,"D",ColMenu)
Dummy = ZeroM()
KEYBOARD REPLICATE(CHR(CurDn), VCode-1) && Go to old choice
J = 1
DO WHILE J <= NLast + 1
   AMenu[J] = &Pre[J]
   J        = J + 1
ENDDO
VCode = NLast
SET MESSAGE TO
SET COLOR   TO &ColMenu
```

```
DO ACHOICE WITH VCode, " ",Top, Lft, NLast+1, Rgt
SET COLOR   TO &ColStand
SET MESSAGE TO " " AT 23,0


IF CodeType = "I"                                && For Insurance record
   SET NEAR OFF
   SELECT B
   HereIAm = RECNO()
   GOTO TOP
   SEEK A->VendNum + STR(VCode,2,0)
   DO CASE
      CASE FOUND() .AND. RECNO() = HereIAm          && If current NOT Duplicate
         SKIP                                        && get next
         IF VAL(B->InsurType) = VCode .AND. A->VendNum = B->VendNum
            Dummy = MyError(9, "D")                  && Ooh Ooh - Duplicate
            RESTORE SCREEN FROM Temp
            GOTO HereIAm
            RETURN(.F.)                              && Go back to where you were
         ENDIF
      CASE FOUND() .AND. RECNO() <> HereIAm         && Duplicate
         Dummy = MyError(9, "D")                     && NOT allowed
         RESTORE SCREEN FROM Temp
         GOTO HereIAm
         RETURN(.F.)
   ENDCASE
   GOTO HereIAm
ENDIF
SET COLOR TO &ColStand
RESTORE SCREEN FROM Temp
REPLACE &DBVar WITH STR(VCode,2,0)     && Put new choice in database
@ DBX,DBY SAY &DBVar                   && and display on screen
@ DBX,DBZ SAY SPACE(25)
@ DBX,DBZ SAY IIF(VCode=0, SPACE(25), &Pre[VCode]);
              PICTURE "!!!!!!!!!!!!!!!!!!!!!!!!!"
SET COLOR TO &ColStand
RETURN(.T.)
*END:VAIE


*__________
FUNCTION CT                            && Check for term of insurance
*__________                            && Must be a number between
PARAMETERS CTerm                       && 1 and 99 or blank
VCTerm = VAL(CTerm)
IF EMPTY(CTerm) .OR. (VCTerm > 0 .AND. VCTerm < 100)
   RETURN(.T.)
ELSE                                   && Bad entry - disallow
   Dummy = MyError(6, "D")
   SET COLOR TO &ColStand
   RETURN(.F.)
ENDIF
*END:CT


*______________
PROCEDURE DOINS                        && Display insurance part of screen
*______________
SET COLOR TO &ColStand
@ 1,0
```

```
SET COLOR TO &ColData
DO CASE
   CASE MastC = 1
      @ 1,25 SAY " VIEW"
      IC = 31
   CASE MastC = 2
      @ 1,25 SAY "CHANGE"
      IC = 32
   CASE MastC = 3
      @ 1,25 SAY "  ADD"
      IC = 31
   CASE MastC = 4
      @ 1,25 SAY "DELETE"
      IC = 32
ENDCASE
SET COLOR TO &ColOther
@ 1,IC SAY "INSURANCE INFORMATION"     && Say what you are processing
SET COLOR TO &ColStand                 && Display fixed info and headings
CLEAR GETS
@ 16,7 CLEAR TO 21,73
@ 15,6  TO 15,74
@ 16,39 TO 21,39
@ 19,9  TO 19,34
@ 15, 5 SAY "├"
@ 15,74 SAY "┤"
@ 15,39 SAY "┬"
@ 22,39 SAY "┴"
@ 16,52 SAY "Input Date:"
@ 17,48 SAY "Effective Date:"
@ 18,12 SAY "Dollars in Thousands"
@ 18,47 SAY "Expiration Date:"
@ 19,43 SAY "Expiration Letter 1:"
@ 20, 9 SAY "Insurance in Effect:"
@ 20,43 SAY "Expiration Letter 2:"
@ 21,13 SAY "Contract Amount:"
@ 21,43 SAY "Expiration Letter 3:"
@ 16,8  SAY "  "
@ 16,11 SAY SPACE(25)
@ 20,30 SAY "$      "
@ 21,30 SAY "$      "
@ 16,64 SAY CTOD("  /  /  ")
@ 17,64 SAY B->Effective
@ 18,64 SAY B->Expiration
@ 19,64 SAY CTOD("  /  /  ")
@ 20,64 SAY CTOD("  /  /  ")
@ 21,64 SAY CTOD("  /  /  ")
** Display data **
@ 16,8  GET B->InsurType VALID VAIE(InsurType,"I") COLOR &ColEntry
@ 16,11 SAY SPACE(25)                    && Display type of insurance
@ 16,11 SAY IIF(VAL(B->InsurType)=0, SPACE(25), Ins[VAL(B->InsurType)]);
            PICTURE "!!!!!!!!!!!!!!!!!!!!!!!!!"
@ 20,30 SAY "$"
@ 21,30 SAY "$"
@ 20,31 GET B->Amount   PICTURE "99,999" COLOR &ColEntry
@ 21,31 GET B->ContAmt  PICTURE "99,999" COLOR &ColEntry
REPLACE B->INPUT WITH IIF(EMPTY(B->INPUT), CurrentDate, B->INPUT)
@ 16,64 SAY IIF(EMPTY(B->INPUT), CurrentDate, B->INPUT)
@ 17,64 GET B->Effective  COLOR &ColEntry
@ 18,64 GET B->Expiration COLOR &ColEntry
IF B->Expiration > CurrentDate + 60    && Turn off letters if dates OK
   REPLACE;
      B->ExpLet1 WITH CTOD("  /  /  "),;
      B->ExpLet2 WITH CTOD("  /  /  "),;
```

```
         B->ExpLet3 WITH CTOD("  /  /  ")
 ENDIF
 IF B->Expiration > CurrentDate + 31
    REPLACE;
       B->ExpLet2 WITH CTOD("  /  /  "),;
       B->ExpLet3 WITH CTOD("  /  /  ")
 ENDIF
 IF B->Expiration > CurrentDate
    REPLACE B->ExpLet3 WITH CTOD("  /  /  ")
 ENDIF
 @ 19,64 SAY B->ExpLet1
 @ 20,64 SAY B->ExpLet2
 @ 21,64 SAY B->ExpLet3

 RETURN
 *END:DOINS


 *_______________
 PROCEDURE DOCONF                                && Display confidentiality screen
 *_______________
 PARAMETERS VendCheck
 SET COLOR TO &ColStand
 @ 1,0
 SET COLOR TO &ColData
 DO CASE
    CASE MastC = 1
       @ 1,22 SAY " VIEW"
       CI = 28
    CASE MastC = 2
       @ 1,22 SAY "CHANGE"
       CI = 29
    CASE MastC = 3
       @ 1,22 SAY "  ADD"
       CI = 28
    CASE MastC = 4
       @ 1,22 SAY "DELETE"
       CI = 29
 ENDCASE
 SET COLOR TO &ColOther                          && Tell what you are processing
 @ 1,CI SAY "CONFIDENTIALITY INFORMATION"
 SET COLOR TO &ColStand                          && Display fixed part of screen
 CLEAR GETS
 @ 16,7 CLEAR TO 21,73
 @ 15,39 SAY "-"
 @ 22,39 SAY "—"
 @ 16, 8 SAY "#"
 @ 16,11 SAY "Arrangement "
 @ 16,26 SAY "Input"
 @ 16,36 SAY "Received"
 @ 16,47 SAY "Effective"
 @ 16,57 SAY "Expiration"
 @ 16,68 SAY "Sign"
 @ 17,10 SAY SUBSTR(Con[1],1,13)
 @ 18,10 SAY SUBSTR(Con[2],1,13)
 @ 19,10 SAY SUBSTR(Con[3],1,13)
 @ 20,10 SAY SUBSTR(Con[4],1,13)
 @ 21,10 SAY SUBSTR(Con[5],1,13)

 SET COLOR TO &ColStand                          && Display up to 5 data lines
 CCode = 1
 DO WHILE CCode <= 5 .AND. .NOT. EOF()
    IF C->VendNum = VendCheck
       LineNum = VAL(C->ConfCode) + 16
```

```
         @ LineNum, 8 GET C->ConfCode COLOR &ColEntry
         REPLACE C->ConfInput WITH;
               IIF(EMPTY(C->ConfInput), CurrentDate, C->ConfInput)
         @ LineNum,25 SAY IIF(EMPTY(C->ConfInput), CurrentDate, C->ConfInput)
         @ LineNum,36 GET C->ConfRecvd  COLOR &ColEntry
         @ LineNum,47 GET C->ConfEffect COLOR &ColEntry
         @ LineNum,58 GET C->ConfExpire COLOR &ColEntry
         @ LineNum,70 GET C->Signoff    COLOR &ColEntry
      ENDIF
      SKIP
      CCode = CCode + 1
   ENDDO
   SEEK VendCheck
   RETURN
   *END:DOCONF
   *_______________
   PROCEDURE CONFAC                                      && Change on line of
   *_______________                                      && confidentiality data
   SET COLOR TO W+/G                                     && Redisplay bottom of screen
   @ 23,32 SAY "  Pg Dn "
   SET COLOR TO N/G
   @ 24,32 SAY "  done  "
   SET COLOR TO &ColStand
   SET CURSOR ON
   LineNum = VAL(C->ConfCode) + 16
   @ LineNum, 8 GET C->ConfCode    VALID NV(C->ConfCode) COLOR &ColEntry
   REPLACE C->ConfInput WITH IIF(EMPTY(C->ConfInput), CurrentDate, C->ConfInput)
   @ LineNum,25 SAY IIF(EMPTY(C->ConfInput), CurrentDate, C->ConfInput)
   @ LineNum,36 GET C->ConfRecvd  COLOR &ColEntry
   @ LineNum,47 GET C->ConfEffect COLOR &ColEntry
   @ LineNum,58 GET C->ConfExpire COLOR &ColEntry
   @ LineNum,70 GET C->Signoff    COLOR &ColEntry
   READ
   REPLACE C->ConfInput WITH CurrentDate  && Change date
   @ LineNum,25 SAY C->ConfInput
   DO FixFlag WITH "C"                    && FIx the flags
   SET CURSOR OFF
   SET COLOR TO &ColStand
   @ 23,32 CLEAR TO 24,39
   SET AUTOSAVE ON
   SKIP 0
   SET AUTOSAVE OFF
   RETURN
   *END:CONFAC
   *_______________
   PROCEDURE F5F6KEY                                      && Process F5 and F6 Key
   *_______________                                       && DIsplays the popup to
   PARAMETERS LK                                          && find a Vendor number (F5)
   F5F6Hold = SPACE(4096)                                 && of Vendor Name (F6) and
   SAVE SCREEN TO F5F6Hold                                && set searching order to either
   SET COLOR TO &ColStand                                 && Vendor number sequence or
   @ 23,0 CLEAR TO 24,79                                  && Vendor Name sequence.
   Dummy = FKEYS(5)
   SELECT A                                               && to select search key
   HoldRec = RECNO()
   SET NEAR ON
   SET COLOR TO &ColMenu
   IF LK = F5Key                                          && Set variables for either
      SET ORDER TO TAG Vendor                             && Set order to relation order
      COrder       = "Vendor"                             && VENDOR NUMBERS
```

```
   Rep           = 11
   DO DbEdit WITH 2, 35, 20, 45, "VendNum", "VendorNum"
ELSE                                                  && or
   SET ORDER TO TAG VendName
   COrder        = "VendName"
   Rep           = 33
   DO DbEdit WITH 2, 24, 20, 55, "VendName", "VendorName"
ENDIF
SET COLOR TO &ColStand
RESTORE SCREEN FROM F5F6Hold
SET NEAR OFF
RETURN
*END:F5F6KEY


*_______________
PROCEDURE DBEDIT
*_______________
PARAMETERS T, L, B, R, FName, New
ON KEY LABEL CTRL-M KEYBOARD CHR(ESCAPE) && Enter acts as Escape
DEFINE WINDOW Temp FROM T, L TO B, R
BROWSE WINDOW Temp NOMENU COMPRESS NOEDIT NOAPPEND NODELETE;
     FIELD &New=DISP(&FName)
RELEASE WINDOW Temp
ON KEY
RETURN
*END:DBEDIT


*____________
FUNCTION DISP
*____________
PARAMETERS FName
New = FName
RETURN(New)
*END:DISP


*___________
FUNCTION ADC                               && Figure out what to display
*___________                               && on the bottom of the screen
PARAMETERS Action, IC
SET COLOR TO &ColStand                     && (Valid function keys) based
@ 23,0 CLEAR TO 24,79                      && upon where you are
SET COLOR TO W+/G
@ 23,3  SAY "  F2  "
@ 23,59 SAY "   Esc  "
@ 23,71 SAY IIF(IC= "C", "  F3   ", "  F4  ")
DO CASE
   CASE Action = 3
      @ 23,13 SAY "  F8 "
      @ 23,22 SAY "  F9  "
   CASE Action = 5
      @ 23,13 SAY "  F8 "
   CASE Action = 7
      @ 23,32 SAY "   del  "
ENDCASE
IF IC = "I"
   @ 23,44 SAY "          "
ENDIF
SET COLOR TO N/G
@ 24,3  SAY " vend "
@ 24,59 SAY " return "
@ 24,71 SAY IIF(IC= "C", " insur ", " conf ")
```

```
DO CASE
   CASE Action = 3
      @ 24,13 SAY " add "
      @ 24,22 SAY " edit "
   CASE Action = 5
      @ 24,13 SAY " add "
   CASE Action = 7
      @ 24,32 SAY " delete "
ENDCASE
IF IC = "I"
   @ 24,44 SAY " prev-next "
ENDIF
RETURN(.T.)
*END:ADC


*______________
PROCEDURE DRPTS                                  && Main Report Menu
*______________
SubHead = " "                                    && Set printer codes depending
SubSel  = .F.                                    && on laser or dot matrix
Laser   = .T.                                    && Default is laser
InitP   = IIF(Laser, Esc+ "E"+Esc+ "&l8d00"+Esc+"&k2S"+Esc+"(10U", "15")
InitL   = IIF(Laser, Esc+ "E"+Esc+ "&l8d10"+Esc+"&k2S"+Esc +;
                     "(10U"+Esc+"&l8D", "15")
Side    = IIF(Laser, "|", "|")
Under   = IIF(Laser, "-", "-")
BTop    = IIF(Laser, "┌──────────────────────────────────┐",;
                     ":==================================:")
BBot    = IIF(Laser, "└──────────────────────────────────┘",;
                     ":==================================:")
FSW     = .F.

DO WHILE .T.
   SET PRINT OFF
   SET DEVICE TO SCREEN
   Dummy = START()
   Dummy = FKEYS(2)
   Dummy = MBOX(30,7,17,.T., "D", ColMenu, "REPORT  MENU")
   @ 23,0
   SET BORDER TO NONE
   DEFINE POPUP POPUP1 FROM 9, 25
   DEFINE BAR 1 OF POPUP1 PROMPT " 1. Vendor Reports              ";
      MESSAGE MESSCENT("Select Vendor Reports.")
   DEFINE BAR 2 OF POPUP1 PROMPT " 2. Confidentiality Reports     ";
      MESSAGE MESSCENT("Select Confidentiality Reports.")
   DEFINE BAR 3 OF POPUP1 PROMPT " 3. Summary Reports             ";
      MESSAGE MESSCENT("Select Summary Reports.")
   DEFINE BAR 4 OF POPUP1 PROMPT " 4. Control Reports             ";
      MESSAGE MESSCENT("Select Control Reports.")
   DEFINE BAR 5 OF POPUP1 PROMPT " 5. Form Letters                ";
      MESSAGE MESSCENT("Select Form Letter Reports.")
   DEFINE BAR 6 OF POPUP1 PROMPT IIF(Laser, " 6. Use Laser Printer        ",;
                                   " 6. Use Dot Matrix Printer   ");
      MESSAGE MESSCENT("Select Printer to Use - " +;
                       "Press Enter to Change Printer Type.")
   DEFINE BAR 7 OF POPUP1 PROMPT " 7. Return to Main Menu ";
      MESSAGE MESSCENT("Return to the Main Menu.")
   RptChoice = 0
   ON SELECTION POPUP POPUP1 DO POPSEL WITH RptChoice
   SET BORDER TO SINGLE
   ACTIVATE POPUP POPUP1
   DO CASE
      CASE RptChoice = 1                    && Vendor
```

```
            DO RptVend
         CASE RptChoice = 2                     && Confidentiality
            DO RptConf
         CASE RptChoice = 3                     && Summary
            DO RptSum
         CASE RptChoice = 4                     && Control
            DO RptCon
         CASE RptChoice = 5                     && Letters
            DO RptLet
         CASE RptChoice = 6                     && Printer Selection - flip/flop
            Laser = IIF(Laser, .F., .T.)
            InitP = IIF(Laser, Esc+"E"+Esc+"&l8d0O"+Esc+"&k2S"+Esc+"(10U", "15")
            InitL = IIF(Laser, Esc+"E"+Esc+"&l8d1O"+Esc+"&k2S"+Esc+;
                               "(10U"+Esc+"&l8D", "15")
         CASE RptChoice = 0 .OR. RptChoice = 7   && RETURN
            EXIT
      ENDCASE
   ENDDO
   SET PRINT OFF
   SET DEVICE TO SCREEN
   IF FILE ("TEMPDBA.DBF")
      DELETE FILE TEMPDBA.DBF
   ENDIF
   IF FILE ("TEMPDBB.DBF")
      DELETE FILE TEMPDBB.DBF
   ENDIF
   IF FILE ("TEMPDBC.DBF")
      DELETE FILE TEMPDBC.DBF
   ENDIF
   RETURN
   *END:DRPTS


   * ______________
   PROCEDURE RPTLET                             && Form letter menu
   * ______________
   DO WHILE .T.
      Dummy = START()
      Dummy = FKEYS(2)
      Dummy = MBOX(28,2,20,.T., "D", ColMenu, "PRINT LETTERS")
      @ 23,0
      SET BORDER TO NONE
      DEFINE POPUP POPUP2 FROM 4, 25
      DEFINE BAR 1  OF POPUP2 PROMPT " 1. Expiration Letter One   ";
         MESSAGE MESSCENT ("Print Expiration Letter One.")
      DEFINE BAR 3  OF POPUP2 PROMPT " 2. Expiration Letter Two   ";
         MESSAGE MESSCENT ("Print Second Expiration Letter Two.")
      DEFINE BAR 5  OF POPUP2 PROMPT " 3. Expiration Letter Three ";
         MESSAGE MESSCENT ("Print Third Expiration Letter Three.")
      DEFINE BAR 7  OF POPUP2 PROMPT " 4. Certification Letter    ";
         MESSAGE MESSCENT ("Print the Certification Letter.")
      DEFINE BAR 9  OF POPUP2 PROMPT " 5. Terms Letter            ";
         MESSAGE MESSCENT ("Print the Terms Letter.")
      DEFINE BAR 11 OF POPUP2 PROMPT " 6. No Insurance Letter     ";
         MESSAGE MESSCENT ("Print the No Insurance Letter.")
      DEFINE BAR 13 OF POPUP2 PROMPT " 7. Sign Off Letter         ";
         MESSAGE MESSCENT ("Print the Sign Off Letter.")
      DEFINE BAR 15 OF POPUP2 PROMPT " 8. Return to Report Menu   ";
         MESSAGE MESSCENT ("Return to the Report Menu.")
      LetChoice = 0
      ON SELECTION POPUP POPUP2 DO POPSEL WITH LetChoice
      SET BORDER TO SINGLE
      ACTIVATE POPUP POPUP2

```

```
   IF LetChoice = 0 .OR. LetChoice = 15
      EXIT
   ELSE
      DO NotYet
*     mLetChoice = (LetChoice + 1) / 2
*     DO VenRpt1 WITH STR(mLetChoice,1,0)
   ENDIF
ENDDO
RETURN
*END:RPTLET


* _______________
PROCEDURE RPTVEND                              && Vendor Report Menu
* _______________
DO WHILE .T.
   Dummy = START()
   Dummy = FKEYS(2)
   Dummy = MBOX(36,5,17,.T., "D", ColMenu, "VENDOR  REPORTS")
   SET BORDER TO NONE
   DEFINE POPUP POPUP3 FROM 7, 21
   DEFINE BAR 1 OF POPUP3 PROMPT " 1. 31 - 60 Day Expiration            "
   DEFINE BAR 2 OF POPUP3 PROMPT " 2.  0 - 30 Day Expiration            "
   DEFINE BAR 3 OF POPUP3 PROMPT " 3. Past Due Expiration               "
   DEFINE BAR 4 OF POPUP3 PROMPT " 4. Vendor Termination                "
   DEFINE BAR 5 OF POPUP3 PROMPT " 5. Insurance Deficiency              "
   DEFINE BAR 6 OF POPUP3 PROMPT " 6. Contract Noncompliance            "
   DEFINE BAR 7 OF POPUP3 PROMPT " 7. Cancellation Term Deficiency      "
   DEFINE BAR 8 OF POPUP3 PROMPT " 8. Original Certificate Exceptions "
   DEFINE BAR 9 OF POPUP3 PROMPT " 9. Return to the Report Menu         "
   VenChoice = 0
   ON SELECTION POPUP POPUP3 DO POPSEL WITH VenChoice
   SET BORDER TO SINGLE
   ACTIVATE POPUP POPUP3
   DO CASE                                     && Choose report to run
      CASE VenChoice = 1                       && Choice 1 through 4 and the
         DO NotYet
*        DO VenRpt1 WITH "31"                  && form letters are run from
      CASE VenChoice = 2                       && the same procedure (VenRpt1)
         DO NotYet
*        DO VenRpt1 WITH "00"
      CASE VenChoice = 3
         DO NotYet
*        DO VenRpt1 WITH "PD"
      CASE VenChoice = 4
         DO NotYet
*        DO VenRpt1 WITH "TR"
      CASE VenChoice = 5
         DO NotYet
*        DO VenRpt2 WITH "I"
      CASE VenChoice = 6
         DO NotYet
*        DO VenRpt2 WITH "N"
      CASE VenChoice = 7
         DO NotYet
*        DO VenRpt3 WITH "3"
      CASE VenChoice = 8
         DO NotYet
*        DO VenRpt3 WITH "4"
      CASE VenChoice = 0 .OR. VenChoice = 9
         EXIT
   ENDCASE
ENDDO
RETURN
```

```
*END:RPTVEND


* ______________
PROCEDURE RPTSUM                                      && Summary report menu
* ______________
DO WHILE .T.
   Dummy = START()
   Dummy = FKEYS(2)
   Dummy = MBOX(31,3,17,.T., "D", ColMenu, "SUMMARY  REPORTS")
   SET BORDER TO NONE
   DEFINE POPUP POPUP4 FROM 5, 23
   DEFINE BAR 1  OF POPUP4 PROMPT "  1. Summary Compliance          "
   DEFINE BAR 3  OF POPUP4 PROMPT "  2. Summary Vendor Type         "
   DEFINE BAR 5  OF POPUP4 PROMPT "  3. Detail Profile              "
   DEFINE BAR 7  OF POPUP4 PROMPT "  4. Vendor Contact              "
   DEFINE BAR 9  OF POPUP4 PROMPT "  5. Contract Detail             "
   DEFINE BAR 11 OF POPUP4 PROMPT "  6. Return to the Report Menu "
   SumChoice = 0
   ON SELECTION POPUP POPUP4 DO POPSEL WITH SumChoice
   SET BORDER TO SINGLE
   ACTIVATE POPUP POPUP4
   DO CASE
      CASE SumChoice = 1
         DO NotYet
*        DO SumComp
      CASE SumChoice = 3
         DO NotYet
*        DO SumType
      CASE SumChoice = 5
         DO NotYet
*        DO SumVP
      CASE SumChoice = 7
         DO NotYet
*        DO SumVC
      CASE SumChoice = 9
         DO NotYet
*        DO SumCD
      CASE SumChoice = 0 .OR. SumChoice = 11
         EXIT
   ENDCASE
ENDDO
RETURN
*END:RPTSUM


* ______________
PROCEDURE RPTCONF                                     && Confidentiality Report Menu
* ______________
DO WHILE .T.
   Dummy = START()
   Dummy = FKEYS(2)
   Dummy = MBOX(35,5,17,.T., "D", ColMenu, "CONFIDENTIALITY REPORTS")
   * SET MESSAGE TO
   SET BORDER TO NONE
   DEFINE POPUP POPUP5 FROM 7, 21
   DEFINE BAR 1 OF POPUP5 PROMPT " 1. Vendor Non-compliance           "
   DEFINE BAR 3 OF POPUP5 PROMPT " 2. Vendor Employee Non-compliance "
   DEFINE BAR 5 OF POPUP5 PROMPT " 3. Contract Expiration  0 - 30    "
   DEFINE BAR 7 OF POPUP5 PROMPT " 4. Contract Expiration  Past Due  "
   DEFINE BAR 9 OF POPUP5 PROMPT " 5. Return to the Report Menu       "
   ConfChoice = 0
   ON SELECTION POPUP POPUP5 DO POPSEL WITH ConfChoice
   SET BORDER TO SINGLE
```

```
   ACTIVATE POPUP POPUP5
   DO CASE
      CASE ConfChoice = 1
         DO NotYet
*        DO ConfNC WITH "R"
      CASE ConfChoice = 3
         DO NotYet
*        DO ConfNC WITH "E"
      CASE ConfChoice = 5 .OR. ConfChoice = 7
         DO NotYet
*        DO ConfNC WITH "X"
      CASE ConfChoice = 0 .OR. ConfChoice = 9
         EXIT
   ENDCASE
ENDDO
RETURN
*END:RPTCONF


* ______________
PROCEDURE RPTCON                               && Control Report Menu
* ______________
DO WHILE .T.
   Dummy = START()
   Dummy = FKEYS(2)
   Dummy = MBOX(32,5,17,.T., "D", ColMenu, "CONTROL  REPORTS")
   * SET MESSAGE TO
   SET BORDER TO NONE
   DEFINE POPUP POPUP6 FROM 7, 23
   DEFINE BAR 1 OF POPUP6 PROMPT " 1. Input Control                "
   DEFINE BAR 3 OF POPUP6 PROMPT " 2. Outstanding Insurance        "
   DEFINE BAR 5 OF POPUP6 PROMPT " 3. Outstanding Confidentiality "
   DEFINE BAR 7 OF POPUP6 PROMPT " 4. No Insurance Coverage        "
   DEFINE BAR 9 OF POPUP6 PROMPT " 5. Return to the Report Menu    "
   ContChoice = 0
   ON SELECTION POPUP POPUP6 DO POPSEL WITH ContChoice
   SET BORDER TO SINGLE
   ACTIVATE POPUP POPUP6
   DO CASE
      CASE ContChoice = 1
         DO NotYet
*        DO ContIn
      CASE ContChoice = 3
         DO NotYet
*        DO ContOut WITH "I"
      CASE ContChoice = 5
         DO NotYet
*        DO ContOut WITH "C"
      CASE ContChoice = 7
         DO NotYet
*        DO ContNo
      CASE ContChoice = 0 .OR. ContChoice = 9
         EXIT
   ENDCASE
ENDDO
RETURN
*END:RPTCON


* ______________
PROCEDURE RPTSTART                             && Standard screen display
* ______________                               && for all reports
IF .NOT. ByPass
   SET DEVICE TO PRINT
```

```
   SET PRINT ON
   Dummy = TESTPRNT()                           && Check if printer is ready
   IF .NOT. PrntOK
      RETURN
   ENDIF
ENDIF
SET DEVICE TO SCREEN                            && Put bar graph display
SET COLOR TO &ColStand                          && on screen
CLEAR
@ 14,10 TO 19,69 DOUBLE
@ 17,11 TO 17,68 DOUBLE
@ 17,10 SAY "╟"
@ 17,69 SAY "╢"
@ 15,24 SAY "P E R C E N T   C O M P L E T E"
@ 16,14 SAY "0    10   20   30   40   50"
@ 16,44 SAY "60   70   80   90   100"
Dummy = MESSBOX(10, "P R O C E S S I N G",.T., "D", ColMenu)
SET COLOR TO R/B                                && Bar graph bar is always Red
Dummy = XYBar(1)                                && Put first box in graph
RETURN
*END:RPTSTART


* ________________
PROCEDURE CONFHEAD
* ________________
PARAMETERS HeadInfo, PageNumber, LineNumber, RptType
IF RptType <> 3 .AND. RptType <> 4
   @ 0,0 SAY InitP
ELSE
   @ 0,0 SAY InitL
ENDIF
PageNumber = PageNumber + 1
@ 1,0 SAY CMONTH(CurrentDate) + " " + ALLTRIM(STR(DAY(CurrentDate),2,0))+;
         "," + STR(YEAR(CurrentDate),4,0)
Dummy = CENT(1,MaxWidth,BTop)
@ 1,MaxWidth-9 SAY "Page: " + ALTRIM(STR(PageNumber,4,0))
Dummy = CENT(2,MaxWidth, Side + "     Insurance Compliance System    " + Side)
Dummy = CENT(3,MaxWidth, Side + "    Vendor Confidentiality Report   " + Side)
Dummy = CENT(4,MaxWidth,HeadInfo)
Dummy = CENT(5,MaxWidth,BBot)
DO CASE
   CASE RptType = 1 .OR. RptType = 5
      Line7 = "         VENDOR NAME             VEND NUMBER   ORIGINATING " +;
          "DEPARTMENT       TYPE OF ARRANGEMENT              VENDOR TYPE"
      IF Laser
         Line8 = REPLICATE("─",30) + "  ─────────  " + REPLICATE("─",25) +;
                 REPLICATE("─",25) + "  " + REPLICATE("─",25)
      ELSE
         Line8 = REPLICATE("=",30) + "  =========  " + REPLICATE("=",25) +;
                 REPLICATE("=",25) + "  " + REPLICATE("=",25)
      ENDIF
   CASE RptType = 3
      @ 7,125 SAY "CLAUSE    SIGNOFF"
      Line8 = "         VENDOR NAME             VEND NUMBER   ORIGINATING " +;
          "DEPARTMENT       TYPE OF ARRANGEMENT              VENDOR TYPE" +;
          "          RECEIVED    SENT"
      IF Laser
         Line9 = REPLICATE("─",30) + "  ─────────  " + REPLICATE("─",25) +;
                 REPLICATE("─",25) + "  " + REPLICATE("─",25) +;
                 "  ────────  ────────"
      ELSE
         Line9 = REPLICATE("=",30) + "  =========  " + REPLICATE("=",25) +;
                 REPLICATE("=",25) + "  " + REPLICATE("=",25) +;
```

```
                      "  ========  ========"
      ENDIF
      @ 8,1 SAY Line8
      @ 9,1 SAY Line9
      LineNumber = 10
   CASE RptType = 4
      @ 7,125 SAY "CLAUSE    SIGNOFF"
      Line8 = "  ORIGINATING DEPARTMENT                 VENDOR NAME           " +;
               "VEND NUMBER    TYPE OF ARRANGEMENT                 VENDOR TYPE" +;
               "              RECEIVED    SENT"
      IF Laser
         Line9 = REPLICATE("—",25) + "  " + REPLICATE("—",30) +;
                 "  ————————  " + REPLICATE("—",25) + "  " +;
                 REPLICATE("—",25) + "  ————————  ————————"
      ELSE
         Line9 = REPLICATE("=",25) + "  " + REPLICATE("=",30) +;
                 "  =========  " + REPLICATE("=",25) + "  " +;
                 REPLICATE("=",25) + "  ========  ========"
      ENDIF
      @ 8,1 SAY Line8
      @ 9,1 SAY Line9
      LineNumber = 10
   CASE RptType = 2 .OR. RptType = 6
      Line7 = "  ORIGINATING DEPARTMENT                 VENDOR NAME" +;
              "              VEND NUMBER    TYPE OF ARRANGEMENT" +;
              "               VENDOR TYPE"
      IF Laser
         Line8 = REPLICATE("—",25) + "  " + REPLICATE("—",30) +;
                 "  —————————  " + REPLICATE("—",25) + "  " +;
                 REPLICATE("—",25)
      ELSE
         Line8 = REPLICATE("=",25) + "  " + REPLICATE("=",30) +;
                 "  =========  " + REPLICATE("=",25) + "  " +;
                 REPLICATE("=",25)
      ENDIF
ENDCASE
IF RptType = 5 .OR. RptType = 6
   Line7 = Line7 + "           EXPIRES"
   Line8 = Line8 + IIF(Laser, "  ————————", "  ========")
ENDIF
IF RptType <> 3 .AND. RptType <> 4
   @ 7,1 SAY Line7
   @ 8,1 SAY Line8
   LineNumber = 9
ENDIF
RETURN
*END:CONFHEAD


* _________________
PROCEDURE CONHEAD                              && Confidentiality Headings
* _________________
PARAMETERS HeadInfo, PageNumber, LineNumber, RptType
IF PageNumber = 0
   @ 0,0 SAY InitL
ENDIF
PageNumber = PageNumber + 1
@ 1,0 SAY CMONTH(CurrentDate) + " " + ALLTRIM(STR(DAY(CurrentDate),2,0)) +;
          "," + STR(YEAR(CurrentDate),4,0)
Dummy = CENT(1,MaxWidth,BTop)
@ 1,MaxWidth-9 SAY "Page: " + ALLTRIM(STR(PageNumber,4,0))
Dummy = CENT(2,MaxWidth, Side + "      Insurance Compliance System    " + Side)
Dummy = CENT(3,MaxWidth, Side + "          System Control Report        " + Side)
Dummy = CENT(4,MaxWidth,HeadInfo)
```

```
Dummy = CENT(5,MaxWidth,BBot)
Dummy = CENT(6,MaxWidth,SubHead)
DO CASE
   CASE RptType = 1
      @ 7,1   SAY    "                                                    S"
      @ 7,170 SAY    "O P C C"
      @ 8,1   SAY    "                                                    T"
      @ 8,170 SAY    "R R E O"
      @ 9,1   SAY    "           VENDOR                       VENDOR  A"
      @ 9,52  SAY    "ORIGINATING"
      @ 9,170 SAY    "I E R N"
      @ 10,1  SAY    "            NAME                        NUMBER  T"
      @ 10,53 SAY    "DEPARTMENT            TYPE OF VENDOR"
      @ 10,98 SAY    "TYPE OF ARRANGEMENT      PRIMARY BUSINESS"
      @ 10,152 SAY   "ATTENTION          G M T F"
      IF Laser
         @ 11,1 SAY REPLICATE("—",30) + " ————————— — " +;
                    REPLICATE("—",25) + " " + REPLICATE("—",25) + " " +;
                    REPLICATE("—",20) + " " + REPLICATE("—",25) + " " +;
                    REPLICATE("—",25) + " — — — —"
      ELSE
         @ 11,1 SAY REPLICATE("=",30) + " ========= = " +;
                    REPLICATE("=",25) + " " + REPLICATE("=",25) + " " +;
                    REPLICATE("=",20) + " " + REPLICATE("=",25) + " " +;
                    REPLICATE("=",25) + " = = = ="
      ENDIF
      @ 12,1 SAY " "
      LineNumber = 13
   CASE RptType = 2
      @ 7,44   SAY "S"
      @ 8,44   SAY "T"
      @ 9,13   SAY "VENDOR                    VENDOR   A"
      @ 9,75   SAY "CERTIFICATE  CONTRACT  EFFECTIVE  EXPIRATION  CANCELLATION"
      @ 10,14  SAY "NAME                      NUMBER   T"
      @ 10,50  SAY "TYPE OF INSURANCE         AMOUNT     AMOUNT      DATE"
      @ 10,110 SAY "DATE         TERMS"
      IF Laser
         @ 11,1 SAY REPLICATE("—",30) + "  —————————  - " +;
                    REPLICATE("—",25) + "  ——————    ——————    ————————" +;
                    "   ————————    —————"
      ELSE
         @ 11,1 SAY REPLICATE("=",30) + "  =========  = " +;
                    REPLICATE("=",25) + "  ======    ======    ========" +;
                    "   ========    ====="
      ENDIF
      @ 12,1 SAY " "
      LineNumber = 13
   CASE RptType = 3
      @ 7,44   SAY "S"
      @ 8,44   SAY "T"
      @ 9,1    SAY "A"
      @ 9,13   SAY "VENDOR                    VENDOR   A"
      @ 9,72   SAY "ARRANGEMENT   RECEIVED   EFFECTIVE   EXPIRATION"
      @ 9,121  SAY "INDIVIDUAL"
      @ 10,14  SAY "NAME                      NUMBER   T    ORIGINATING"
      @ 10,61  SAY "DEPARTMENT   NUMBER          DATE        DATE"
      @ 10,112 SAY "DATE      SIGNOFF"
      IF Laser
         @ 11,1 SAY REPLICATE("—",30) + "  —————————  -  " +;
                    REPLICATE("—",25) + "  —       ————————  ————————" +;
                    "    ————————        -"
      ELSE
         @ 11,1 SAY REPLICATE("=",30) + "  =========  =  " +;
                    REPLICATE("=",25) + "  ==      ========  ========" +;
                    "    ========        ="
```

```
      ENDIF
      @ 12,1 SAY " "
      LineNumber = 13
   CASE RptType = 4
      @ 7,10  SAY "VENDOR NAME           VEND NUMBER  IN DATE"
      @ 7,62  SAY "ADDRESS LINE 1                  ADDRESS LINE 2"
      @ 7,126 SAY "CITY          STATE    ZIP CODE"
      IF Laser
         @ 8,1 SAY REPLICATE("—",30) + "  ─────────  ────────  " +;
                   REPLICATE("—",30) + "  " + REPLICATE("—",30) + "  " +;
                   REPLICATE("—",20) + "  ─────   ────────"
      ELSE
         @ 8,1 SAY REPLICATE("=",30) + "  =========  ========  " +;
                   REPLICATE("=",30) + "  " + REPLICATE("=",30) + "  " +;
                   REPLICATE("=",20) + "  =====   ========="
      ENDIF
      LineNumber = 10
   CASE RptType = 5
      @ 7,10  SAY "VENDOR NAME           VEND NUMBER  IN DATE"
      @ 7,56  SAY "ORIGINATING DEPARTMENT          TYPE OF VENDOR"
      @ 7,111 SAY "TYPE OF ARRANGEMENT      LETTER"
      IF Laser
         @ 8,1 SAY REPLICATE("—",30) + "  ─────────  ────────  " +;
                   REPLICATE("—",25) + "  " + REPLICATE("—",25) + "  " +;
                   REPLICATE("—",25) + "  ────────"
      ELSE
         @ 8,1 SAY REPLICATE("=",30) + "  =========  ========  " +;
                   REPLICATE("=",25) + "  " + REPLICATE("—",25) + "  " +;
                   REPLICATE("=",25) + "  ========"
      ENDIF
      LineNumber = 10
   CASE RptType = 6
      @ 7,3   SAY "ORIGINATING DEPARTMENT             VENDOR NAME"
      @ 7,59  SAY "VEND NUMBER  IN DATE        TYPE OF VENDOR"
      @ 7,111 SAY "TYPE OF ARRANGEMENT      LETTER"
      IF Laser
         @ 8,1 SAY REPLICATE("—",25) + "  " + REPLICATE("—",30) + "  " +;
                   "─────────  ────────  "+ REPLICATE("—",25) + "  " +;
                    REPLICATE("—",25) + "  ────────"
      ELSE
         @ 8,1 SAY REPLICATE("=",25) + "  " + REPLICATE("=",30) + "  " +;
                   "─────────  ========  "+ REPLICATE("=",25) + "  " +;
                    REPLICATE("=",25) + "  ========"
      ENDIF
ENDCASE
RETURN
*END:CONHEAD


* ──────────────
PROCEDURE VENHEAD                          && General heading routine for
* ──────────────                           && Vendor reports
PARAMETERS HeadInfo, PageNumber, LineNumber, RptType
DO CASE                                    && Select landscape or portrait
   CASE PageNumber = 0 .AND. RptType <> 2
      @ 0,0 SAY InitP
   CASE PageNumber = 0 .AND.  RptType = 2
      @ 0,0 SAY InitL
ENDCASE
PageNumber = PageNumber + 1
@ 1,0 SAY CMONTH(CurrentDate) + " " + ALLTRIM(STR(DAY(CurrentDate),2,0)) +;
          "," + STR(YEAR(CurrentDate),4,0)
Dummy = CENT(1,MaxWidth,BTop)
@ 1,MaxWidth-9 SAY "Page: " + ALLTRIM(STR(PageNumber,4,0))
Dummy = CENT(2,MaxWidth, Side + "     Insurance Compliance System   " + Side)
```

```
Dummy = CENT(3,MaxWidth, Side + "        Vendor Insurance Report     " + Side)
Dummy = CENT(4,MaxWidth,HeadInfo)
Dummy = CENT(5,MaxWidth,BBot)
Dummy = CENT(6,MaxWidth,SubHead)
DO CASE                                    && Use correct heading
   CASE RptType = 1
      @ 7,13 SAY "VENDOR                    VENDOR          ORIGINATING"
      @ 7,97 SAY "EXPIRATION  AMOUNT   LETTER"
      @ 8,14 SAY "NAME                     NUMBER              DEPARTMENT"
      @ 8,76 SAY "TYPE OF INSURANCE      DATE   (Thousand)  DATE "
      IF Laser
         @ 8,1 SAY REPLICATE("—",30) + "  _________  " +;
                   REPLICATE("—",25) + "  " + REPLICATE("—",25) + "  " +;
                   "  ________  _______  ________"
      ELSE
         @ 8,1 SAY REPLICATE("=",30) + "  =========  " +;
                   REPLICATE("=",25) + "  " + REPLICATE("=",25) + "  " +;
                   "  ========  =======  ========"
      ENDIF
   CASE RptType = 2
      @ 7,13  SAY "VENDOR                             VENDOR"
      @ 7,61  SAY "ORIGINATING"
      @ 7,152 SAY "AMOUNTS (Thousands)"
      @ 8,14  SAY "NAME                              NUMBER"
      @ 8,62  SAY "DEPARTMENT                         TYPE OF ARRANGEMENT"
      @ 8,122 SAY "TYPE OF INSURANCE                  VENDOR      DEFICIENCY"
      IF Laser
         @ 8,1 SAY REPLICATE("—",30) + "         _________          " +;
                   REPLICATE("—",25) + SPACE(7) + REPLICATE("—",25) +;
                   SPACE(7) + REPLICATE("—",25) + SPACE(7) +;
                   REPLICATE("—",7) + SPACE(7)  + REPLICATE("—",7)
      ELSE
         @ 8,1 SAY REPLICATE("=",30) + "         =========          " +;
                   REPLICATE("=",25) + SPACE(7) + REPLICATE("=",25) +;
                   SPACE(7) + REPLICATE("=",25) + SPACE(7) +;
                   REPLICATE("=",7) + SPACE(7)  + REPLICATE("=",7)
      ENDIF
   CASE RptType = 3
      @ 7,13  SAY "VENDOR                    VENDOR              ORIGINATING"
      @ 7,104 SAY "VENDOR    DAYS         LETTER"
      @ 8,14  SAY "NAME                     NUMBER              DEPARTMENT"
      @ 8,80  SAY "TYPE OF ARRANGEMENT     TERMS   DEFICIENT    DATE"
      IF Laser
         @ 9,1 SAY REPLICATE("—",30) + "    _________    " +;
                   REPLICATE("—",25) + "    " + REPLICATE("—",25) + ;
                   "   __    _________    ________"
      ELSE
         @ 9,1 SAY REPLICATE("=",30) + "    =========    " +;
                   REPLICATE("=",25) + "    " + REPLICATE("=",25) + ;
                   "   ==    =========    ========"
      ENDIF
   CASE RptType = 4
      @ 7,13  SAY "VENDOR                             VENDOR"
      @ 7,64  SAY "ORIGINATING"
      @ 7,126 SAY "LETTER"
      @ 8,14  SAY "NAME                              NUMBER"
      @ 8,65  SAY "DEPARTMENT                         TYPE OF ARRANGEMENT"
      @ 8,127 SAY "DATE"
      IF Laser
         @ 9,1 SAY REPLICATE("—",30) + "         _________      " +;
                   REPLICATE("—",25) + "         " + REPLICATE("—",25) + ;
                   "         ________"
      ELSE
         @ 9,1 SAY REPLICATE("=",30) + "         =========      " +;
                   REPLICATE("=",25) + "         " + REPLICATE("=",25) + ;
                   "         ========"
```

```
      ENDIF
ENDCASE
LineNumber = 10
RETURN
*END:VENHEAD


* ________________
PROCEDURE VENHEAD1                              && Headings for part2 of vendor reports
* ________________
PARAMETERS HeadInfo, PageNumber, LineNumber, RptType
IF PageNumber = 0
   @ 0,0 SAY InitP
ENDIF
PageNumber = PageNumber + 1
@ 1,0 SAY CMONTH(CurrentDate) + " " + ALLTRIM(STR(DAY(CurrentDate),2,0)) +;
         "," + STR(YEAR(CurrentDate),4,0)
Dummy = CENT(1,MaxWidth,BTop)
@ 1,MaxWidth-9 SAY "Page: " + ALLTRIM(STR(PageNumber,4,0))
Dummy = CENT(2,MaxWidth, Side + "      Insurance Compliance System   " + Side)
Dummy = CENT(3,MaxWidth, Side + "       Vendor Insurance Report      " + Side)
Dummy = CENT(4,MaxWidth,HeadInfo)
Dummy = CENT(5,MaxWidth,BBot)
Dummy = CENT(6,MaxWidth,SubHead)
DO CASE
   CASE RptType = 1
      @ 7,7   SAY "ORIGINATING                VENDOR            VENDOR"
      @ 7,97  SAY "EXPIRATION  AMOUNT   LETTER"
      @ 8,8   SAY "DEPARTMENT                 NUMBER                NAME"
      @ 8,76  SAY "TYPE OF INSURANCE        DATE   (Thousand)  DATE"
      IF Laser
         @ 9,1 SAY REPLICATE("─",25) + "  ─────────  " +;
                   REPLICATE("─",30) + "  " + REPLICATE("─",25) + ;
                   "  ────────  ───────  ────────"
      ELSE
         @ 9,1 SAY REPLICATE("=",25) + "  =========  " +;
                   REPLICATE("=",30) + "  " + REPLICATE("=",25) + ;
                   "  ========  =======  ========"
      ENDIF
   CASE RptType = 2
      @ 7,7   SAY "ORIGINATING                     VENDOR"
      @ 7,69  SAY "VENDOR"
      @ 7,160 SAY "AMOUNTS (Thousands)"
      @ 8,8   SAY "DEPARTMENT                      NUMBER"
      @ 8,61  SAY "NAME                               TYPE OF INSURANCE"
      @ 8,122 SAY "TYPE OF ARRANGEMENT          VENDOR      DEFICIENCY"
      IF Laser
         @ 9,1 SAY REPLICATE("─",25) + "       ─────────       " +;
                   REPLICATE("─",30) + "      " + REPLICATE("─",25) +;
                   "      " + REPLICATE("─",25) + "       ───────" +;
                   "      ───────"
      ELSE
         @ 9,1 SAY REPLICATE("=",25) + "       =========       " +;
                   REPLICATE("=",30) + "      " + REPLICATE("=",25) +;
                   "      " + REPLICATE("=",25) + "       =======" +;
                   "      ======="
      ENDIF
   CASE RptType = 3
      @ 7,7   SAY "ORIGINATING                            VENDOR"
      @ 7,65  SAY "VENDOR"
      @ 7,103 SAY "VENDOR    DAYS          LETTER"
      @ 8,8   SAY "DEPARTMENT                             NAME"
      @ 8,65  SAY "NUMBER         TYPE OF ARRANGEMENT     TERMS"
      @ 8,111 SAY "DEFICIENT      DATE"
      IF Laser
         @ 9,1 SAY REPLICATE("─",25) + "    " + REPLICATE("─",30) + ;
```

```
                     "     ─────────      " + REPLICATE("─",25) + ;
                     "     ──    ─────────    ────────"
        ELSE
           @ 9,1 SAY REPLICATE("=",25) + "     " + REPLICATE("=",30) + ;
                     "     =========      " + REPLICATE("=",25) + ;
                     "     ==    =========    ========"
        ENDIF
     CASE RptType = 4
        @ 7,7   SAY "ORIGINATING                                  VENDOR"
        @ 7,73  SAY "VENDOR"
        @ 7,125 SAY "LETTER"
        @ 8,8   SAY "DEPARTMENT                                    NAME"
        @ 8,73  SAY "NUMBER              TYPE OF ARRANGEMENT"
        @ 8,126 SAY "DATE"
        IF Laser
           @ 9,1 SAY REPLICATE("─",25) + "          " + REPLICATE("─",30) + ;
                     "       ─────────          " +;
                     REPLICATE("─",25) + "          ────────"
        ELSE
           @ 9,1 SAY REPLICATE("=",25) + "          " + REPLICATE("=",30) + ;
                     "       =========          " +;
                     REPLICATE("=",25) + "          ========"
        ENDIF
ENDCASE
LineNumber = 10
RETURN
*END:VENHEAD1


* ────────────────
PROCEDURE SUMHEAD                                  && Summary reports standard heading
* ────────────────
PARAMETERS HeadInfo, PageNumber, LineNumber, RptType
IF PageNumber = 0
   @ 0,0 SAY InitL                         && Always landscape mode
ENDIF
PageNumber = PageNumber + 1
@ 1,0 SAY CMONTH(CurrentDate) + " " + ALLTRIM(STR(DAY(CurrentDate),2,0)) +;
         "," + STR(YEAR(CurrentDate),4,0)
Dummy = CENT(1,MaxWidth,BTop)
@ 1,MaxWidth-9 SAY "Page: " + ALLTRIM(STR(PageNumber,4,0))
Dummy = CENT(2,MaxWidth, Side + "    Insurance Compliance System    " + Side)
Dummy = CENT(3,MaxWidth, Side + "       Vendor Profile Report       " + Side)
Dummy = CENT(4,MaxWidth,HeadInfo)
Dummy = CENT(5,MaxWidth,BBot)
Dummy = CENT(6,MaxWidth,SubHead)
DO CASE                                          && Pick the correct heading
   CASE RptType = 1
      @  7,21  SAY "V E N D O R"
      @  7,78  SAY "I N S U R A N C E"
      @  7,130 SAY "C O N F I D E N T I A L I T Y"
      IF Laser
         @  8,1 SAY REPLICATE("─",52) + "┬" + REPLICATE("─",66) + "┬" +;
                    REPLICATE("─",46)
      ELSE
         @  8,1 SAY REPLICATE("=",52) + "|" + REPLICATE("=",66) + "|" +;
                    REPLICATE("=",46)
      ENDIF
      @  9,53  SAY "|"
      @  9,94  SAY "VENDORS NOT    VENDORS   |   VENDORS"
      @  9,158 SAY "EMPLOYEE"
      @ 10,35  SAY "VENDORS   PERCENT |  VENDORS  VENDORS PERCENT  VENDORS"
      @ 10,93  SAY "IN COMPLIANCE    WITHOUT   |  REQUIRING  VENDORS PERCENT"
      @ 10,150 SAY "VENDORS  SIGNOFF "
      @ 11,8   SAY "ORIGINATING           TOTAL     ON       ON    |"
      @ 11,55  SAY "REQUIRING WITHOUT WITHOUT   WITH           WITH"
```

```
        @ 11,110 SAY "ORIGINAL  |  CONFIDENT  WITHOUT WITHOUT  WITH       NOT"
        @ 12,9   SAY "DEPARTMENT         VENDORS PREMISES PREMISES |"
        @ 12,55  SAY "INSURANCE  CERTIF  CERTIF  CERTIF  CONTRACT  STANDARD"
        @ 12,110 SAY "EVIDENCE  |   CLAUSE    CLAUSE  CLAUSE  CLAUSE  REQUESTED"
        IF Laser
           @ 13,1 SAY REPLICATE("─",25) + " ─────── ──────── ──────── | " +;
                      "───────── ────── ────── ────── ────────  " +;
                      "──────── ──────── |  ──────    ────── ──────  " +;
                      "────── ─────────"
        ELSE
           @ 13,1 SAY REPLICATE("=",25) + " ======= ======== ======== | " +;
                      "========= ====== ====== ====== ========  " +;
                      "======== ======== |  ======    ====== ======  " +;
                      "======  ========="
        ENDIF
        LineNumber = 14
     CASE RptType = 2
        @ 7,8    SAY "ORIGINATING                                MAINTENANCE"
        @ 7,58   SAY "ON-GOING"
        @ 7,114  SAY "SERVICE                                     TOTAL"
        @ 8,9    SAY "DEPARTMENT        CONSTRUCTION   CONTRACTOR"
        @ 8,57   SAY "SUPPLIERS    DESIGN FIRM      TENANT       FURNITURE"
        @ 8,112  SAY "CONTRACTOR    CONSULTANT        OTHER       VENDORS"
        IF Laser
           @ 9,1 SAY REPLICATE("─",25) + " ────────────  ────────────  " +;
                     "────────────  ────────────  ────────────  " +;
                     "────────────  ────────────  ────────────  " +;
                     "────────────  ────────────"
        ELSE
           @ 9,1 SAY REPLICATE("=",25) + " ============  ============  " +;
                     "============  ============  ============  " +;
                     "============  ============  ============  " +;
                     "============  ============"
        ENDIF
        LineNumber = 10
     CASE RptType = 3
        @ 7,13   SAY "VENDOR                        VENDOR              ORIGINATING"
        @ 7,144  SAY "INSURANCE AMOUNTS IN THOUSANDS"
        @ 8,14   SAY "NAME                          NUMBER              DEPARTMENT"
        @ 8,82   SAY "TYPE OF ARRANGEMENT           TYPE OF INSURANCE"
        @ 8,141  SAY "BTCO       CONTRACT    CERTIFICATE"
        IF Laser
           @ 9,1 SAY REPLICATE("─",30) + "     ─────────     " +;
                     REPLICATE("─",25) + "     " + REPLICATE("─",25) +;
                     REPLICATE("─",25) + "     " + REPLICATE("─",25) +;
                     "     " + REPLICATE("─",25) + ;
                     "     ────────   ────────    ────────"
        ELSE
           @ 9,1 SAY REPLICATE("=",30) + "     =========     " +;
                     REPLICATE("=",25) + "     " + REPLICATE("=",25) +;
                     REPLICATE("=",25) + "     " + REPLICATE("=",25) +;
                     "     " + REPLICATE("=",25) + ;
                     "     ========   ========    ========"
        ENDIF
        LineNumber = 10
     CASE RptType = 4
        @ 7,8    SAY "ORIGINATING                                  VENDOR"
        @ 7,68   SAY "VENDOR"
        @ 7,144  SAY "INSURANCE AMOUNTS IN THOUSANDS"
        @ 8,9    SAY "DEPARTMENT                                   NAME"
        @ 8,68   SAY "NUMBER        TYPE OF ARRANGEMENT"
        @ 8,114  SAY "TYPE OF INSURANCE            BTCO        CONTRACT"
        @ 8,165  SAY "CERTIFICATE"
        IF Laser
```

```
4219          @ 9,1 SAY REPLICATE("─",25) + "        " + REPLICATE("─",30) + ;
4220                    "  ─────────          " + REPLICATE("─",25) + ;
4221                    "   " + REPLICATE("─",25) + ;
4222                    "  ─────────   ─────────      ─────────"
4223          ELSE
4224          @ 9,1 SAY REPLICATE("=",25) + "        " + REPLICATE("=",30) + ;
4225                    "  =========          " + REPLICATE("=",25) + ;
4226                    "   " + REPLICATE("=",25) + ;
4227                    "  ========    ========       ========"
4228          ENDIF
4229          LineNumber = 10
4230       CASE RptType = 5
4231          @ 7,13  SAY "VENDOR                    VENDOR    NO INSURANCE     SIGNOFF"
4232          @ 7,76  SAY "CERTIFICATE      CANCELLATION"
4233          @ 7,137 SAY "INSURANCE      EXPIRATION LETTERS"
4234          @ 8,14  SAY "NAME                    NUMBER        LETTER     CODE  LETTER"
4235          @ 8,75  SAY "ORIG. LETTER     TERMS  LETTER         TYPE OF INSURANCE"
4236          @ 8,136 SAY "EXPIRATION    ONE          TWO       THREE"
4237          IF Laser
4238             @ 9,1 SAY REPLICATE("─",30) + "  ─────────     ─────────      " +;
4239                   "──────────────   ──────────────   ──────────────       " +;
4240                   REPLICATE("─",25) + "  ─────────    " + REPLICATE("─",26)
4241          ELSE
4242             @ 9,1 SAY REPLICATE("=",30) + "  =========     ========       " +;
4243                   "==============   =============    ==============       " +;
4244                   REPLICATE("=",25) + "  ========    " + REPLICATE("=",26)
4245          ENDIF
4246          LineNumber = 9
4247    ENDCASE
4248    RETURN
4249    *END:SUMHEAD
4250
4251
4252    * ──────────────
4253    FUNCTION FINISHED                             && Delete temporary files
4254    * ──────────────                              && and restore original
4255    CLOSE DATA                                    && databases
4256    IF FILE ("TEMPA.DBF")
4257       DELETE FILE ("TEMPA.DBF")
4258    ENDIF
4259    IF FILE ("TEMPB.DBF")
4260       DELETE FILE ("TEMPB.DBF")
4261    ENDIF
4262    IF FILE ("TEMPC.DBF")
4263       DELETE FILE ("TEMPC.DBF")
4264    ENDIF
4265    DO OpenData
4266    RETURN(.T.)
4267    *END:FINISHED
```

The Phillips Memorial Hospital Example

We finished the entire Phillips Memorial Hospital insurance compliance system in slightly over 4200 lines of code (without any hard-copy reports). As far as systems go, this one is rather small. A 30,000-line system could take up to 1400 hours to complete.

Let us look at the code in detail. Many of the user-defined functions (UDFs) are documented in the code. In these cases, the functionality discussion is omitted.

LINES 1–14 STARTUP

This standard information box contains the copyright notice and the programmer's name, address, and telephone number so that the reader will know where to obtain additional programming services. It also has the dates of the system so that the programmer can tell when it was written and which version it is.

LINES 15–33 PREAMBLE

First, old memory values, windows, and procedures are cleared from memory. Then STEP, ECHO, TALK, and the BELL are turned off. (You have not experienced confusion until you have worked in a large room with many systems running, all with the BELL turned on.) Next, PRINT is turned off and deleted records ignored (DELETED is set ON). SAFETY and ESCAPE are turned off to prevent unnecessary user confusion (only necessary user confusion is allowed). CONFIRM is turned on to present a consistent user interface to the data entry operator. By setting CONFIRM on, all fields require you to press enter after you have entered data; thus, there is *no* jumping of the cursor from one field to the next on some occasions and not on others. This is very important in a professional application. All unnecessary screen displays, such as STATUS, HEADING, and SCOREBOARD, are turned off. Since this is a complete application, there is no reason to leave these areas on the screen, and the space they are occupying can be used to better advantage. Finally, the screen is set to the 25-line mode and turned on without a cursor. Most users do not have a screen capable of displaying more than 25 lines, and most applications have to run on existing equipment at the user's premises. Thus, you write to the lowest common denominator—25-line screens. As for the cursor, should be on *only* for data entry functions.

LINES 34–54 STANDARD COLORS

Since even minor changes in color as requested by the client can take hours to accomplish, it is advisable to write the code in such a manner that the user can choose the colors, and all the major portions will reflect any changes made by the user. To effect this, all colors must be used in macro form. Instead of setting the color of the screen to high-intensity white on blue (SET COLOR TO W+/B), you have to set the color to a variable that is set to high-intensity white on blue (ColStand = "W+/B,N/W,B" SET COLOR TO &ColStand). In this manner, you can change the system colors by updating the value of a group of memory variables. If you save these memory variables to a file and RESTORE them, you never even have to change the code to change the colors, just change them in the memory file. You can even write a routine to permit the user to change the system colors. The commented code in this section can be used to generate the initial memory file needed to use this technique. Copy the code, remove the comments, and run it.

LINES 55–107 MISCELLANEOUS CONSTANTS

These are constants used to make code more readable, and thus easier to debug. Would you rather see IF Key = 3 or (preferably) IF Key = PgDn? You may add or delete from this list for your own applications.

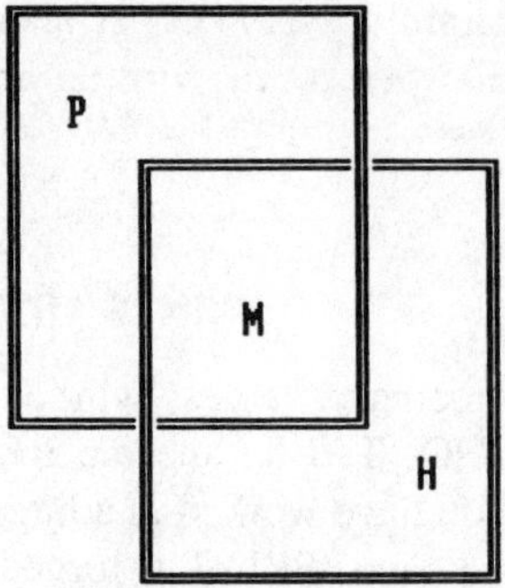

Figure 15-1

LINES 108–131 STARTUP CODE

First place a corporate logo on the screen and make it move in some way (Figure 15-1). Next, place the system or company initials on the screen, weaving them from both sides to the center of the screen (Figure 15-2). Finally, place an exploding box on the screen (Figure 15-3) containing the name of the system, the release number, and the copyright notice (Figure 15-4). The data bases then can be opened, arrays filled, and other housekeeping tasks, such as getting the date, performed (Figure 15-5). These are all prewritten functions that are called from this area.

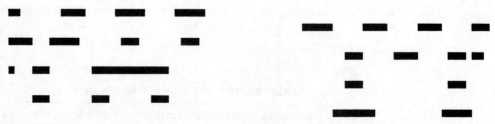

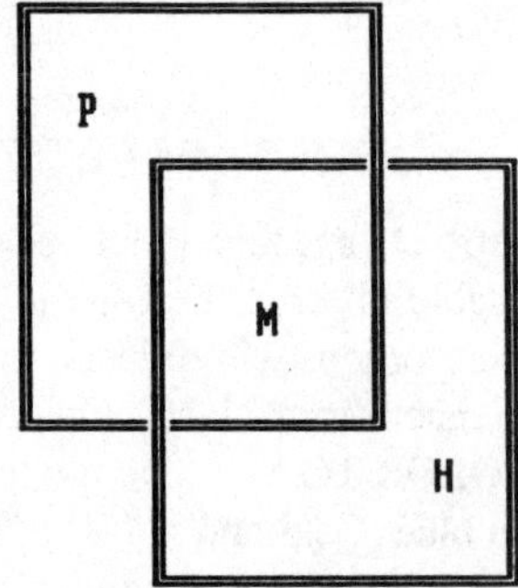

Figure 15-2

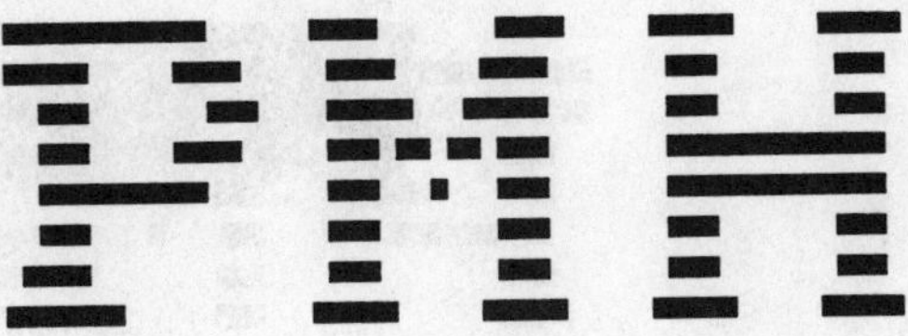

Figure 15-3

LINES 132–175 MAIN MENU

Many systems start with a main menu containing the same four choices (Figure 15-6), permitting the user to select additional menus or exit from the system. These choices are (1) Inquiry and Update Menu, (2) Report Menu, (3) Utility Menu, and (4) exit from the system. Since this is a small menu of only four items, they are placed on every other line. Before the menu is displayed, clear the screen and then place a heading on the top of it (UDF Start). Next place a prompt containing operational keys that can be used in conjunction with the menu on the bottom of the screen (UDF Fkeys). Finally, place a box on the screen for the menu that also contains an area for the menu heading. After the menu is activated, the result is a CASE construct with calls to the other menus that can be selected and to the exit procedure (Fini). All of this is contained in a DO WHILE .T. loop that can only be left by selecting choice 4—exit from the system (Figure 15-7).

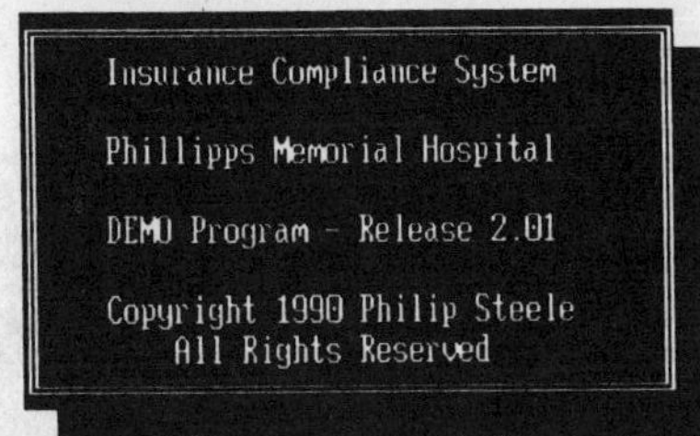

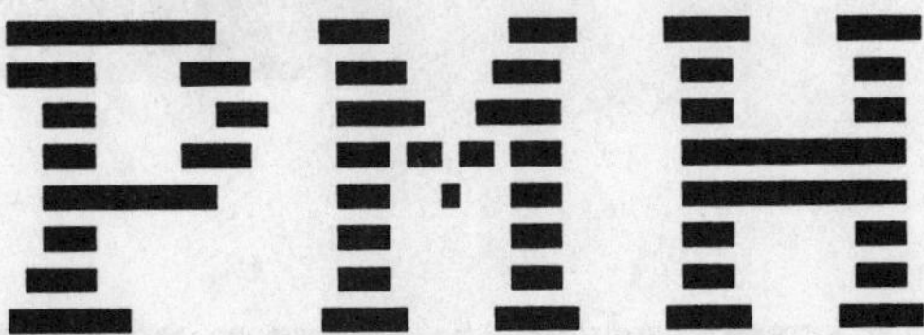

Figure 15-4

Figure 15-5

LINES 176–179 USER DEFINED FUNCTIONS (UDFs)

This section contains all the programmers special UDFs. A professional programmer's job is made much easier by having a large library of UDFs. Many of these functions are contained in the book *85 dBASE IV User Defined Functions and Procedures* (Windcrest book no. 3236.).

LINES 180–203 FINI

This procedure asks if the user really wishes to exit. The user may have pressed the wrong key. If the answer is "Yes," the screen is cleared, temporary files are deleted,

Insurance Compliance System

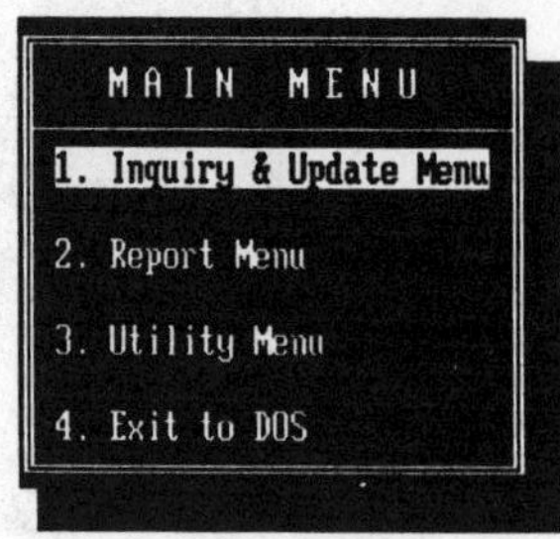

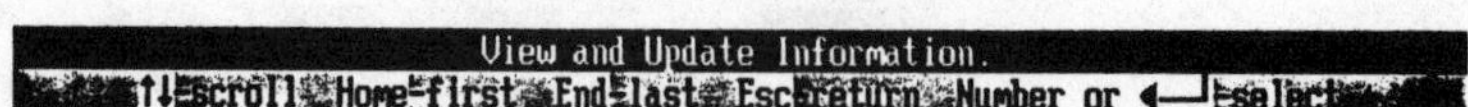

Figure 15-6

Figure 15-7

and the cursor is turned on and placed at the top left of the screen, before exiting to DOS.

LINES 204–233 INTRO

This function presents an exploding box with a drop shadow that is used at the beginning of the system to show the system name, author, and release number. It uses a *hard* color choice of yellow on red because of restrictions in using macros in UDF in release 1.0 of dBASE IV. This should be changed to SET COLOR TO &ColMenu for the current release of dBASE IV. A DO WHILE loop is used to draw five different boxes, each slightly larger than the next. You may notice that J (the loop control counter) is being incremented by 0.2. This is not a misprint. It slows down the exploding effect so that it is visible.

LINES 234–261 OPENDATA

It is best to check to see if an index exists and only to use the INDEX command if there is no index. In this application, the user wanted to make sure that the indexes were not corrupted, and so insisted that all files be indexed when the system started. After the files are opened and indexed, the relations are established. In this application, there can be between zero and 11 insurance records for each vendor, and between zero and four confidentiality records for each vendor. The SELECT statements could have been eliminated by USING the files in an AREA. However, this construct makes it easier to convert the code to another language for product evaluation and benchmarking purposes.

LINES 262–299 FILLARRY

This procedure uses the CODE data base and places its data into arrays that are used to speed up processing in various other parts of the system.

LINES 300–311 ZEROM

The array AMENU is used in a UDF and its elements must be set to zero at various times in the code. Instead of repeating this operation in many different places, it was converted to a UDF and called.

LINES 312–322 CENT

This function centers a line of text on either the screen or a printed page. It accepts the row on which the message will appear, the maximum length of the area where the message will be placed (usually 80 for the screen), and the message. It computes the amount of space needed in front of the message and SAYs the message at the appropriate spot.

LINES 323–335 MESSCENT

This function centers a line of text by placing blanks on either side of the message. It is usually used in the message portion of a menu (lines 149–159, for example). The advantage of this UDF over the previous one is that characters other than blanks can be placed in the returned string. If you have a double-line box surrounding the area in which the message line will appear, you can replace the first and last characters in the string with a CHR(186) and still maintain the box around your message.

LINES 336–381 ASCAN

Many functions available in other dBASE-like languages (such as Clipper) are not available in dBASE IV but can be simulated. This UDF uses a double DO loop to check the elements in an array for a specific STRING value, making use of the SUBSTR function. The AT function also could have been used instead of the second DO loop.

LINES 383–441 YESORN

How many times do you ask whether a user wants to proceed with an application or cancel it? For example; "Do you wish to print the report (Yes or No)?" This UDF uses a horizontal menu, in the requested color, to ask the passed question, which can be answered by Yes or No. After the user selects Yes or No, the last passed parameter is set to true for yes or false for no. The original screen is restored before returning to the calling code by using a window box UDF called in line 414.

LINES 442–483 WBOX

This is a general-purpose box drawing UDF that uses a window. To create a drop shadow effect around a box, an initial window consisting of a black box is drawn one position down and one position to the right of the top left of the "*real*" window box, and ending one line down and two characters to the right of the "*real*" window box. The border is controlled using the @ x,y TO x1,y1 construct with the additional parameter of DOUBLE or NONE.

LINES 484–507 BOXES

This is a general-purpose box drawing UDF that does not use a window. To create a drop shadow effect around a box, an initial window consisting of a black box is drawn one position down and one position to the right of the top left of the "*real*" box, and ending one line down and two characters to the right of the "*real*" box. The border is controlled using the @ x,y TO x1,y1 construct with the additional parameter of DOUBLE or NONE.

LINES 508–530 MBOX

This is yet another type of box, (Figures 15-6, 15-8, 15-9, 15-10, and 15-14). Depending on the passed parameters, it will be a double-line box with a single line area for the heading or the reverse - A single line box and a double line for the heading area. Drop shadows are created in the BOXES UDF, which is called in line 515.

LINES 531–549 MESSBOX

Another type of box—one that is used to dress up a message. This UDF accepts a one line message and parameters for the box, including the line number on which to put the message, the message to be displayed, a drop shadow indicator, a single or double indicator, and the color for the box and message. The message is displayed centered in the chosen style of box. This UDF also calls the BOXES UDF at line 543.

LINES 550–650 FKEYS

Most of the useable function keys for a specific screen can be placed at the bottom of the screen, a technique that is preferred by most users. This UDF clears the bottom two lines of the screen and places the appropriate key descriptions there.

LINES 651–675 DELREC

This UDF addresses the common need to delete data. A message is given to the user by calling the YESORN UDF at line 661 and the user is informed of the deletion through the use of calls to BOXES and CENT on lines 666 and 667. However, most of the calls in lines 662–670 can be replaced with one call to MESSBOX.

LINES 676–685 LR

This UDF is used in the DELREC UDF and has been replaced with the MESSCENT UDF. This is a leftover from another system and was never changed. If it isn't broken—Don't fix it!

LINES 686–695 XYBAR

This UDF is used to draw a bar graph on the screen to depict the progress of a long operation, such as printing a report. It works by drawing a bar equal to the progress of the operation, with each position on the screen equal to 2 percent completion of the operation.

LINES 696–708 START

Before new data is placed on the screen, the screen must be cleared and a centered heading placed at the top. This UDF performs these operations.

LINES 709–768 MYERROR

We all make errors—This UDF displays them in a unique manner, namely, in an "exploding" error box. Using the technique described in the INTRO UDF, an error box appears to explode on the bottom three lines of the screen, and the appropriate message is centered in the box and displayed for five seconds. If you like bells, you can sound a tone at this point; however, the exploding box gets the user's attention without noise.

LINES 769–801 TESTPRNT

Before trying to print a report, you have to be sure the printer is turned on and one-line to the computer. This UDF accomplishes this function using the PRINTSTATUS() function in dBASE IV. If the printer is not ready, the user is asked to turn it on or abort the operation.

LINES 802–902 LOGO

One item separating a "professional" system from an amateurish one is the initial startup screens. Most professional systems have a unique starting screen. This UDF will show you how to add movement and excitement to a normally dull system. Usually, the user likes to see a unique presentation of the initial menu. For example, one can use moving logos, exploding logos, slowly appearing logos, and logos written in other languages and "RUN" from the dBASE system. This UDF comes in two parts. The first part assigns the Phillipps Memorial Hospital logo to an array (lines 810–821). The MOVE WINDOW feature of dBASE IV is used to move the logo up the screen. The second part of the UDF defines and fills the array LOGO1 with the initials "PMH" in striped form. Next a double DO loop is set up and the leading portions of the even rows and trailing portions of the odd rows filled with blanks. These new strings are placed on the screen in order, thus presenting a unique animation effect (Figures 15-1, 15-2, and 15-3).

LINES 903–914 KILLTIME

Many screen displays are too fast to obtain a particular effect, but call to this UDF slows things down just enough to obtain that effect. All it does is generate two random numbers and divide one by the other.

LINES 915–941 EMPTY

Another Clipper replacement, this UDF checks the variable type and removes blanks where appropriate, or sets up a test to determine if no value exists, such as a month of zero in a date field. It returns a true if the computed value of the field is zero (no data in the field) or false if there is data present. This function is very useful and may be included in future releases of dBASE IV based upon recommendations from dLAB.

LINES 942–954 ALLTRIM

This UDF removes both leading and trailing blanks from a string using the dBASE IV LTRIM and TRIM functions.

LINES 955–996 ACHOICE

Another Clipper replacement UDF, it pops up array elements and permits the user to select one. In this version, the passed field "TITLE" is not used, but is included so that the reader can modify it to more closely resemble the Clipper function.

LINES 997–1006 POPSEL

In dBASE IV you cannot easily assign a variable to a menu selection item. This procedure returns the selected bar from a menu in a variable name. This makes the code more readable and faster because you can use a variable in place of the function BAR() in the CASE statement following a menu selection.

LINES 1007–1015 PADSEL

In dBASE IV you cannot easily assign a variable to a horizontal menu item. This procedure returns the selected horizontal menu pad in a numeric variable. This makes the code more readable and faster because you can use a variable in place of the function PAD() in the CASE statement following a horizontal menu selection.

LINES 1016–1027 NOTYET

When writing complex systems, you can just write the shell with call to the procedures you feel will be needed. To test functioning portions of the system before the entire system is complete, call the NOTYET UDF from the shell routines as follows:

```
PROCEDURE NEWINPUT
Dummy = NotYet
RETURN
```

All NOTYET does is display the message "This function is NOT available yet" on the screen by calling BOXES and CENT, which can be replaced by a single call to MESSBOX.

LINES 1028–1069 DUTIL

This menu (Figure 15-8) permits the user to choose utility functions such as Download data, DOS utilities, changing of system, and special restricted utilities that require a password to use.

LINES 1070–1122 DUTIL1

This menu (Figure 15-9) permits the user to make changes to the system, such as changing the popup choices or the Letters. In addition, you can display the amount of remaining free memory and make distribution copies of the system and data. The password needed to access this menu is restricted to supervisory personnel.

Insurance Compliance System

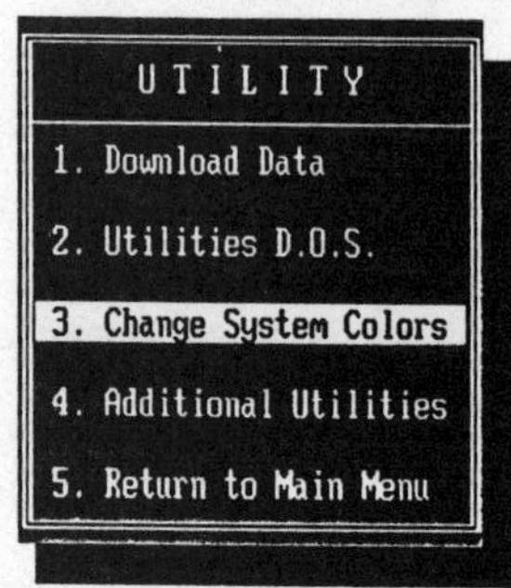

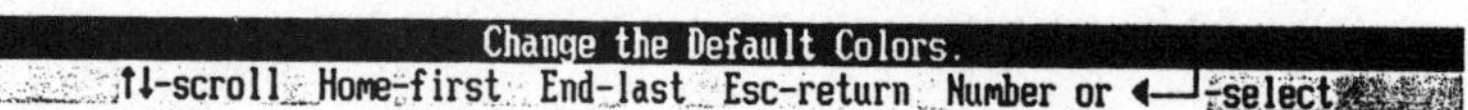

Figure 15-8

LINES 1123–1183 DIST

This procedure copies the system files, data files, memo files, indexes, and memory files, as well as the programs needed to download the fonts and the fonts needed to print the form letters, to floppy disks using the RUN command in conjunction with the DOS COPY command.

Insurance Compliance System

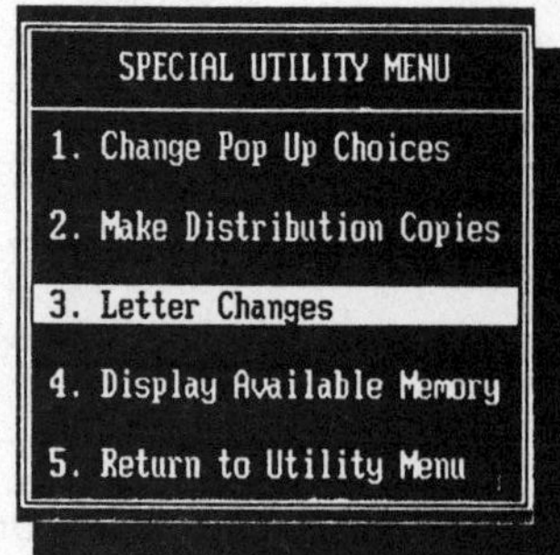

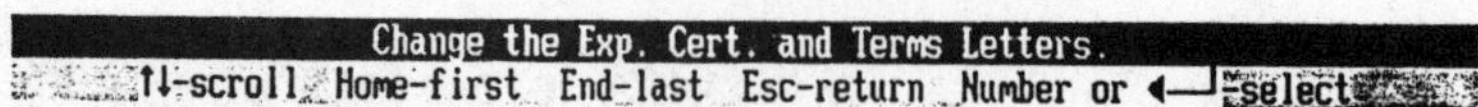

Figure 15-9

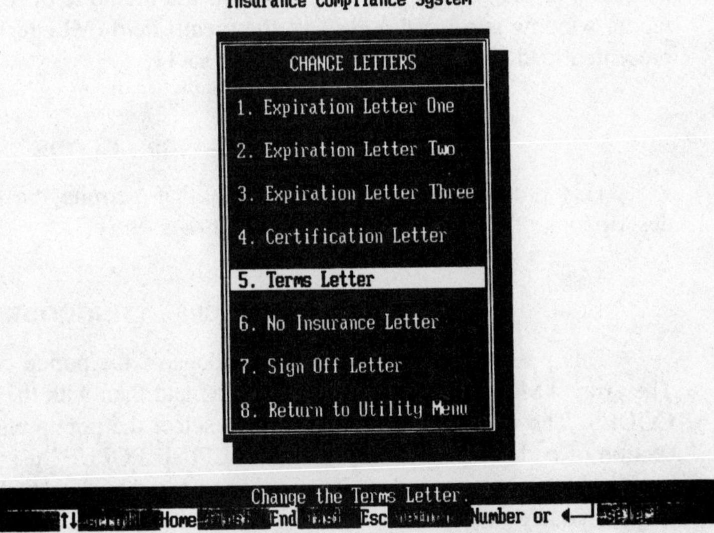

Figure 15-10

LINES 1184–1222 LETTERS

This procedure produces the "CHANGE LETTERS" menu (Figure 15-10), using a standard menu format.

LINES 1223–1252 LETFIX

This procedure permits the user to change the form letters. The letters are contained in the Memo file (MLET.DBT). A memo window "NewMemo" is defined and the

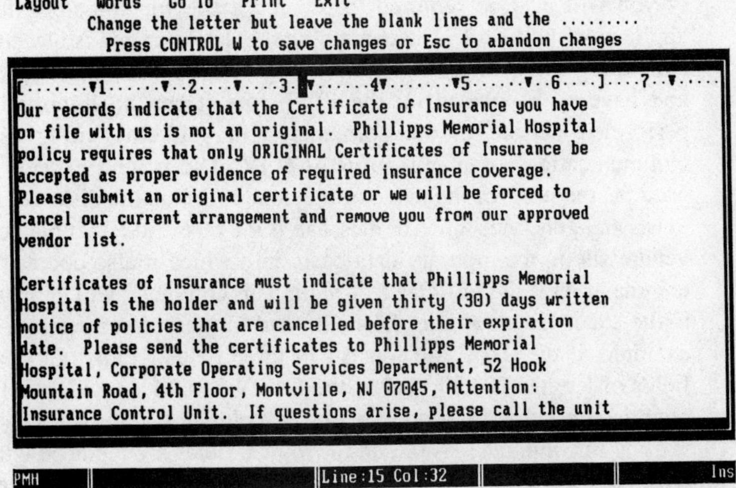

Figure 15-11

MEMOWIDTH is set to 78, which permits the memo to occupy the entire window. The memo window is set and a GET of the memo field (MLetter) is performed. The screen presented to the user is shown in Figure 15-11.

LINES 1253–1289 CCODE

This procedure produces the menu that permits the supervisor to change the descriptions of the popup choices used in data entry.

LINES 1290–1396 CHNGCODE

This procedure changes the descriptions of the popup choices used in data entry. The array AMenu is first filled with blanks, and then with the entries from the data base CODES. The UDF ACHOICE is used to select the popup choices to be changed. This section of code can be rewritten as a "DEFINE POPUP" using the "PROMPT FIELD" option to present a popup list similar to that created by the "ACHOICE" UDF. If you have Clipper code that you are converting to dBASE IV, the ACHOICE is the construct you will probably use. If you are coding a new application from scratch, you would probably use the DEFINE POPUP with the PROMPT FIELD construct. After the selection has been made, it is displayed at the bottom of the screen with trailing blanks and a GET - READ construct is use to effect the change. The changed value is stored back to the data base and the temporary memory variable being used to display the popup choices in the data entry portion of the code.

LINES 1397–1580 DOWNLOAD

This procedure accepts data from the mainframe computer and places it in the vendor file. In many professional systems that you will write, data will often be on the mainframe computer. You will have to import this data into your application. Occasionally you will also be required to prepare a file for uploading to the mainframe. In this application, a "FLAT" file containing the data we need is placed on diskette by corporate computing and given to us to import. In other applications, this data may be on a network and have to be placed on the PC before it can be imported. This operation is best performed outside of the normal system you are writing as there currently are no communication commands in dBASE IV. The system expects the data on diskette and prompts the user for the name of the vendor file on the diskette. It checks to see if the file exists and generates an error message if it cannot find it. It then copies the structure of the vendor file to a temporary data base, into which it also copies the diskette file using the command APPEND FROM . . . SDF. This command will copy a flat file where each field is the exact length as the .DBF file and in the correct position as in the .DBF file. For example, if the .DBF file consists of three fields (Name, City, and State) with character fields of lengths 20, 20, and 2, the COPY FROM . . . SDF will work if the flat file has records consisting of Name starting in column 1, City starting in column 21, and State starting in column 41. Next, all the logical fields are replaced with true, Status is replaced with "A" for active, and AttnName is replaced with Insurance Department. The main vendor file is updated on the basis of the data in the file that was downloaded in lines 1492–1524. The temporary file is deleted and the logical fields updated depending on data

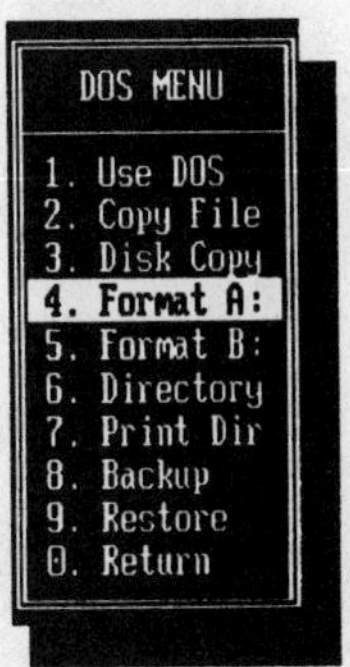

Figure 15-12

in the insurance and confidentiality files. The user is kept informed as to the progress of the update using the XYBar UDF.

LINES 1581–1734 DODOS

This procedure permits the user to access DOS functions. Since many users need to access DOS from inside almost any system, this general purpose DOS procedure and it should be included in any code you might write. First the menu shown in Figure 15-12 is displayed. A DO CASE . . . ENDCASE construct is used to process the user's selection. To access DOS, save the current directory and path and invoke a secondary command process using the command "RUN COMMAND" in line 1635. When "EXIT" is entered in DOS, the program resumes at line 1636. The drive and subdirectory are changed to those in effect before DOS was entered, the screen and memory variables are restored, and the temporary files created for this procedure are removed. If "copy files" is chosen, the user is prompted for the "from" and "to" file names. Then the DOS copy command is run. No file checking is included. The other DOS routines are straightforward and will not be explained here; all you have to do is look at the code to see how they work. To copy the .DBF, .MEM, and index files, backup and restore use the COPY command of DOS rather than the DOS backup and restore commands. No space checking of the diskette or hard disk is performed.

LINES 1735–2182 COLORS

The purpose of COLORS is to popup a replicate of a typical screen showing all the possible color combinations that the user is allowed to change and instantaneously to update to reflect the user's preferences. *Note:* Using this program, the user *cannot* change:

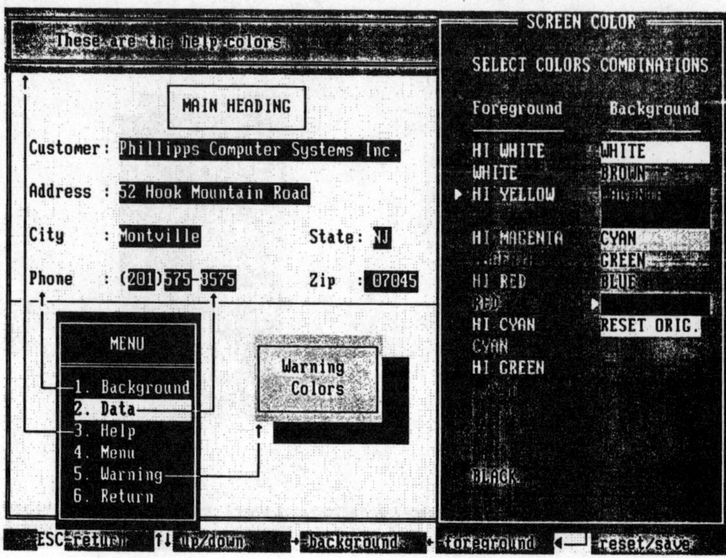

Figure 15-13

The error colors
The black borders on the drop shadow menus
The data entry colors (black on white)
The function key colors

The user can change the following foreground and background colors:

BACKGROUND	**Fixed screen items such as borders and headings.**
DATA	**Data colors.**
HELP	**Colors for help screens and the function key background**
MENU	**Menu and popup colors.**
WARNING	**Colors of warning messages.**

However, you can modify the code to permit as many or as few color changes as make sense for your application. The simulated screen that is produced by COLORS is shown in Figure 15-13. You can change the code in lines 1964–2068 to duplicate a typical screen from your application if you wish. This is easier than it looks. The technique is to run a program that lets you take a snapshot of your screen in color. If you do not have such a program, you can use Sidekick® and obtain a black-and-white text file to which you can add color. If all else fails, use the code you used to generate the screen in the first place. After you have the screen image in your editor, change all the TEXT/ENDTEXT statements to @SAY statements. Then group all the similar color functions together. For example, put all the data statements in one place, all the menu/pop-up statements in another place, and so on. This should give you some unreadable code equivalent to that in lines 1964–2068. Now let us look at all the code. First we place the selection menu on the screen (lines 1752–1781) and call the CLRS procedure with the user's selection. CLRS places the default colors into an array (mColArray). Next the screen is displayed in COLDISP. Lines 1815–1947 control the changing of the screen colors. Each time the down arrow key is pressed, a blank is drawn over the spot where a '''' is pointing (A is character 16), and '''' is redrawn one row lower. The inverse occurs when the up arrow key is pressed. When a left or right arrow key is pressed, the current '''' is rewritten in normal intensity and the opposite '''' is changed to high intensity. After the '''' is written, the color update to correspond to the arrow position is performed. The array and COLOR.MEM file are updated depending on the user's selections. The procedure NOARROW is used to remove the "arrows" from the screen display, regardless of their positions on the screen.

LINES 2183–2228 PASSWORD

This procedure prompts the user for the password needed to access the additional utility menu. As the password does not appear in the code directly, anyone looking at the code could not determine the password without analyzing the code. You can set up a string of all the letters in the alphabet in line 2191 and use the SUBSTR function in dBASE IV to see if the entered password is correct. If the choice does not match, the user is returned to the initial menu—which should discourage the user from trying too many times.

LINES 2229–2264 DVEND

This procedure displays the Inquiry and update menu (Figure 15-14), which permits the user to view, change, add, or delete data.

Insurance Compliance System

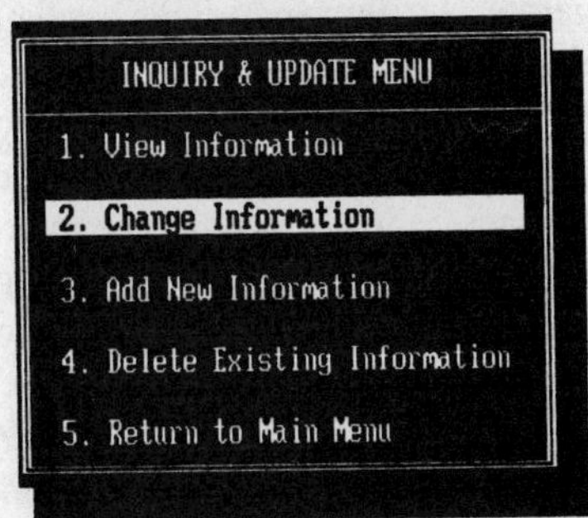

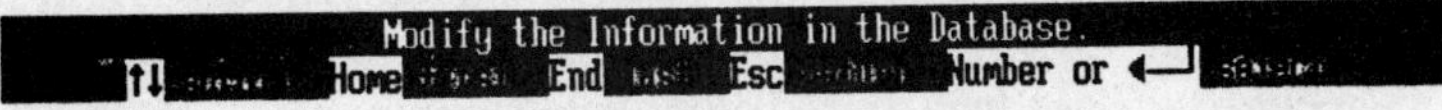

Figure 15-14

LINES 2265–2301 MASTCONT

This procedure contains the DO CASE . . . ENDCASE construct to implement the Inquiry and update menu. After the user-defined action occurs, the functions keys F2, F3, and F4 are checked and the appropriate procedure executed if any of these function keys were pressed. The Esc key exits from this procedure.

LINES 2302–2431 VENDPROF

This procedure performs the view, addition, change, or delete function requested by the user and contained in the "Action" parameter. Lines 2309–2318 place the proper action function keys on the bottom of the screen. Action function keys are keys that will result in some action when they are pressed. The action taken and the valid keys change depending on the current state of the screen. After these actions are shown, the procedure displays the screen by calling the "VendSay" procedure. The DO CASE . . . ENDCASE construct at lines 2324–2355 finishes executing the desired action. If the F3 or F4 function key is pressed, the procedure ends the DO WHILE loop and awaits the next key press. If the "Action" requested was "View," the data portion of the screen is displayed using the "VendGET" procedure followed by the "CLEAR GETS" command (Figure 15-15). This technique for displaying data has several advantages. First, you do not need a separate section of code to display data and another to get the same data in the same position on the screen. Next, the GET colors are used to display the data, which differentiates it from the prompt fields. Finally, it is easier to code and maintain than two separate but different procedures. Notice that both the View data and Change data issue the "CLEAR GETS" command. This permits paging through the records until the user finds the record to be changed. At this point, the F9 function key is pressed and the update started. To add a new record, a blank is appended to the data base, VendGet is executed, and the GETs read. If the Esc key is pressed, the record just added is deleted to prevent invalid records from cluttering up the data base; otherwise an Escape is placed in the keyboard buffer to exit the procedure after the data base is updated. Notice the code in lines 2349–2351. This code flushes the memory buffers and forces the data to be written to disk. Sometimes operators turn off the computer when they are finished, thus causing most of their work to be lost. These three instructions save all work as it is completed, and so prevent data loss resulting from operator error. The delete "Action" just displays the data and waits for the delete key to be pressed. Lines 2356–2425 continue to process the data. If an F3 or F4 function key is pressed, the procedure is exited and control is returned to the loop that called this procedure. If F9 was pressed and the "Action" was "change", the color of the data is changed to bright white on black, various actions are displayed, and the VendGet procedure is called again, followed by a READ to update the data base (Figure 15-16). Various procedures save the user's changes in temporary memory variables and ask if the user really wants to update the data base after finishing the entry of the data. This technique is not necessary unless the system is being used by more than one person at a time, because most individual users are intelligent enough to perform their jobs without such hand-holding. The reason for using the technique on a network is that the record or records are not locked until the update occurs. For example, if an insurance record is associated with the vendor record, update the ContAmt (Contract Amount) field with the "New" information, even if the ContAmt did not change (it takes longer to check than to update the data). Then update the appropriate flags, depending on logical conditions (lines

```
INSURANCE COMPLIANCE SYSTEM
CHANGE VENDOR INFORMATION

Number                    Name                          Short Name
065505204    Phillipps Computer Systems Inc             Phillipps

52 Hook Mountain Road
                                                            Status
Montville            NJ  07045     Telephone: 2015758575     A

        Type of Vendor                        Arrangement
  8 CONSULTANT                          1 PURCHASE ORDER
                              Cancellation
      Primary Business           Terms          COS Unit
 Computer Services                30     10 REAL ESTATE MGNT ACCNTNG

           Input Date: 10/07/89                       Original: T
 Initial Cert. Letter:   / /                       On Premises: T
   Certificate Letter:   / /                       Certificate: T
 Cancel. Terms Letter:   / /                   Confidentiality: T
      Sign Off Letter:   / /       Contract Ins. Compliance: F
 Attn: Insurance Department        Contract Conf. Compliance:

F3     ↑↓          F9     F5 find F6    Esc      F4
insur  prev-next   edit   numb  name    return   conf
```

Figure 15-15

2389–2394). Once again, update the "Action" function keys, fix other flags by calling the FixFlag procedure, and force the system to write the records to the disk. If delete was selected and the delete key pressed, check to see if there are any associated insurance or confidentiality records. If there are, display an error message. In a related data base you cannot remove the parent record without first deleting the children. If you do, you will create orphan children records. If there are no children records, the record is deleted by

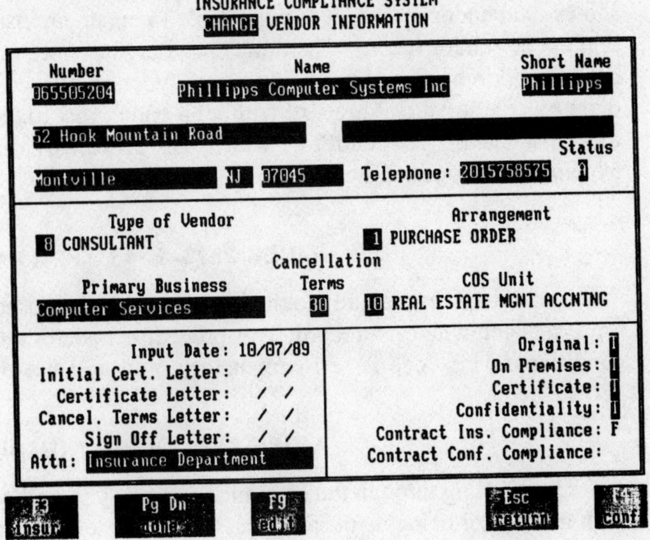

```
INSURANCE COMPLIANCE SYSTEM
CHANGE VENDOR INFORMATION

Number                    Name                          Short Name
065505204    Phillipps Computer Systems Inc             Phillipps

52 Hook Mountain Road
                                                            Status
Montville            NJ  07045     Telephone: 2015758575     A

        Type of Vendor                        Arrangement
  8 CONSULTANT                          1 PURCHASE ORDER
                              Cancellation
      Primary Business           Terms          COS Unit
 Computer Services                30     10 REAL ESTATE MGNT ACCNTNG

           Input Date: 10/07/89                       Original: T
 Initial Cert. Letter:   / /                       On Premises: T
   Certificate Letter:   / /                       Certificate: T
 Cancel. Terms Letter:   / /                   Confidentiality: T
      Sign Off Letter:   / /       Contract Ins. Compliance: F
 Attn: Insurance Department        Contract Conf. Compliance:

F3     Pg Dn   F9                       Esc      F4
insur  done    edit                     return   conf
```

Figure 15-16

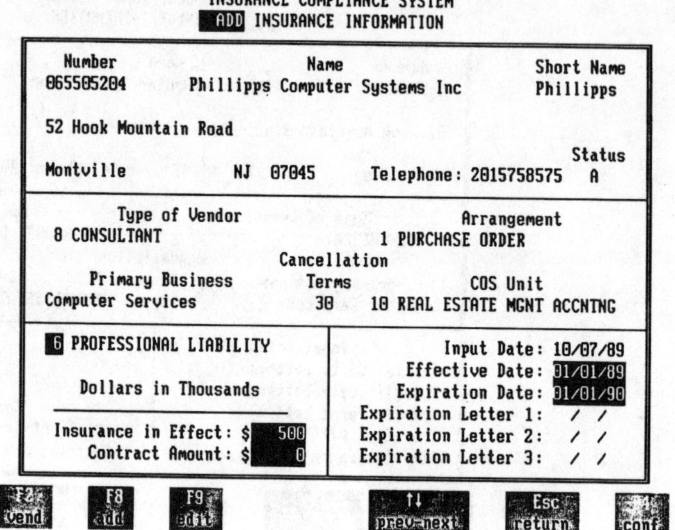

Figure 15-17

calling DelRec in line 2420. This is repeated until the user elects to leave the procedure in. In other words, you can view many different records, change many different records, or delete many different records.

LINES 2432–2574 INSPROF

This procedure works in a manner similar to that in VendProf, except that it works with the insurance record rather than the vendor record and it uses the lower portion of the screen to display the insurance record (Figures 15-16 and 15-17). Since the screen always shows the vendor record, it is impossible to create an insurance or confidentiality record without a Vendor record. Therefore, not only have we prevented the user from creating orphan children records using the delete function but we also prevented this from being done by creating a child record without a parent record. Since this procedure operates in the same manner as VendProf, which was previously discussed in great detail, further explanation is omitted here.

LINES 2575–2643 FIXFLAG

Various flags (actually logical fields), which are used to generate exception reports, are associated with each record. This procedure updates these flags, depending on various conditions. This code is self-explanatory, and will not be further explained here.

LINES 2644–2659 NOMORE

In scrolling through the insurance records, you will come to the end of those records with the vendor being displayed. This procedure tells you when you have reached the last of the insurance records, and how to add a new record or return to the vendor search procedure.

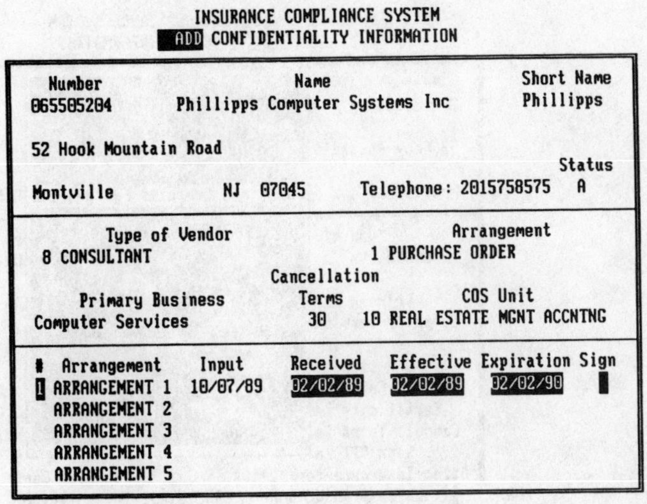

```
                    INSURANCE COMPLIANCE SYSTEM
                ADD CONFIDENTIALITY INFORMATION

  Number                  Name                        Short Name
 065505204     Phillipps Computer Systems Inc         Phillipps

 52 Hook Mountain Road
                                                          Status
 Montville            NJ  07045     Telephone: 2015758575   A

        Type of Vendor                      Arrangement
 8 CONSULTANT                       1 PURCHASE ORDER
                               Cancellation
     Primary Business             Terms          COS Unit
 Computer Services                 30    10 REAL ESTATE MGNT ACCNTNG

 # Arrangement      Input      Received  Effective Expiration Sign
 1 ARRANGEMENT 1  10/07/89    02/02/89  02/02/89   02/02/90
   ARRANGEMENT 2
   ARRANGEMENT 3
   ARRANGEMENT 4
   ARRANGEMENT 5
```

Figure 15-18

LINES 2660–2774 CONFPROF

This procedure works in a manner similar to that in VendProf, except that it works with the confidentiality record rather than the vendor record and it uses the lower portion of the screen to display the confidentiality record (Figure 15-18). Since the screen always shows the vendor record, it is impossible to create an insurance or confidentiality record without a Vendor record. Therefore, not only have we prevented the user from creating orphan children records using the delete function, but we also prevented this from being done by creating a child record without a parent record. Since this procedure operates in the same manner as VendProf, which was previously discussed in great detail, further explanation is omitted here.

LINES 2775–2811 GETNEXT

This procedure obtains a key from the user by using the dBASE IV INKEY() function. It then checks to see which key was pressed. If a Cursor up or down key was pressed, it moves the pointer in the active data base (SKIP or SKIP -1) and returns. If a letter or number key was pressed, a SEEK is issued to find the records nearest to the key that was pressed and then returns. If an F5 or F6 key was pressed, the popup procedure F5F6Key is executed. Figure 15-19 shows one of the available popups. If another valid key was pressed, the loop is exited and control passed back to the calling procedure. If no valid key was pressed, this procedure waits for another key press and continues until a valid key is pressed.

LINES 2812–2876 VENDSAY

This procedure displays the appropriate prompts for each of the fields in the vendor data base that are displayed or updated.

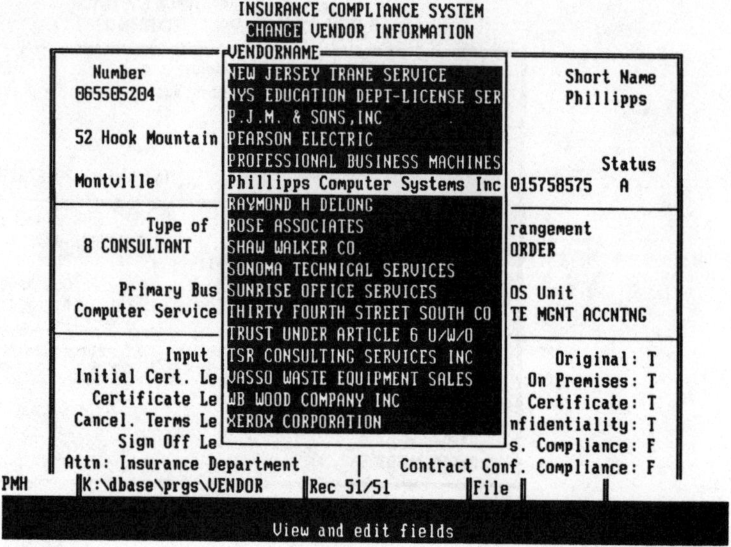

Figure 15-19

LINES 2877–2934 VENDGET

This procedure displays the appropriate data for each of the fields in the vendor data base that are displayed or updated. It calls the UDF VAIE to display the popups for the *V*endor code, *A*rrangement type, *I*nsurance type, and *E*xpense code. See Figure 15-17 for a screen with a popup display on it.

LINES 2935–2977 NEWV

This procedure checks for and prevents duplicate vendor numbers during an add operation. It SEEKs for the entered vendor number and returns an error message if it finds it or a blank vendor number.

LINES 2978–2987 NV

This procedure checks for a valid ConfCode (Confidentiality code) that is between 1 and 5. It returns a false if an incorrect code is entered.

LINES 2988–3103 VAIE

This function places the popup choices on the screen. First it checks for a zero or blank, and if and is found, replaces it with a 1, since zero is a nonpermitted code. It also returns a false so the user can enter the correct code. It next checks to see if the entered code is within the valid range of numbers, and not negative, for the popup. It also returns false if a code does not match the editing parameters. Next it saves the screen and popsup the appropriate choices for the field. The use of a window would have avoided the saving and restoring of the screen; however, what was being sought in this case was compatibility with other data base languages, such as FoxPro and Clipper. The parameters for the window location are set, depending on the field in use, and the last nonblank entry in the

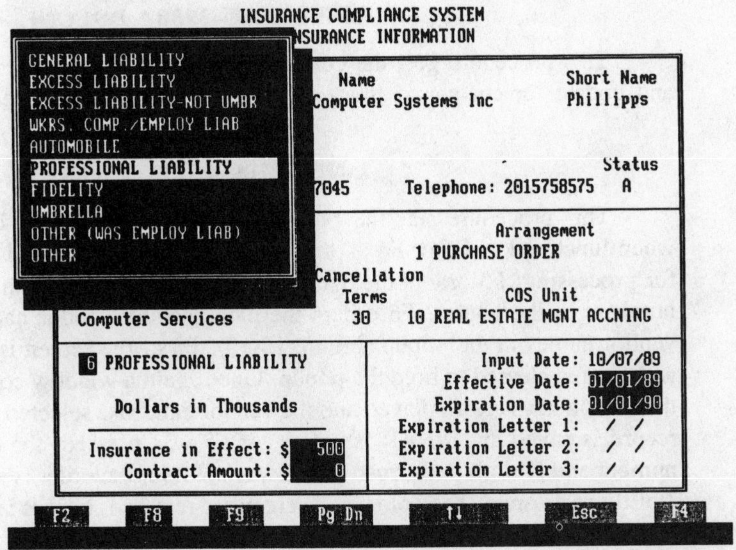

Figure 15-20

popup is determined. A box is drawn using the BOXES UDF and the AMenu array is zeroed using the ZeroM UDF. AMenu is then filled from the correct array and the UDF AChoice is used to select the field entry. Notice that the keyboard is stuffed with the appropriate number of cursor downs to position the lightbar on the current selection in the popup, line 3055. In Figure 15-20, the lightbar is on entry 6 and the data base contains a size for the entry being processed. If the code type is insurance, a check is made to prevent a duplicate entry, and a germane error message is displayed. The selected choice is placed on the screen at the position provided, and a true is returned to the calling GET.

LINES 3104–3118 CT

This procedure checks for a valid insurance term (between 1 and 99) and returns a false if the entry is not within this range. Note that the field contains character data and we are checking for a numeric range. This is why a UDF is being used rather than a RANGE parameter in the GET statement.

LINES 3119–3204 DOINS

This procedure changes the lower portion of the screen and processes the insurance children records, depending on the passed desired action—View, Change, Add, or Delete. The lower portion of the screen is cleared and filled with the prompts and data in the suitable colors. The actual processing is done in the InsProf procedure.

LINES 3205–3267 DOCONF

This procedure changes the lower portion of the screen and processes the confidentiality children records, depending on the passed desired action—View, Change, Add, or Delete. The lower portion of the screen is cleared and filled with the prompts and data in the suitable colors. The actual processing is done in the ConfProf procedure.

LINES 3268–3298 DOCONF

This procedure gets the correct confidentiality child record and performs the GET and update for changes to the confidentiality child data base.

LINES 3299–3327 F5F6KEY

This procedure sets the proper parameters so that the correct popup will appear when function key F5 or F6 is pressed. This procedure is used to select the proper record for processing. F5 orders the data base by vendor number and displays available vendor numbers in the popup. F6 orders the data base by vendor name and displays available vendor names in the popup (Figure 15-19). First, the screen is saved, the color changed and an area cleared to hold the popup. Once again a window could have been used. Next, the Action keys are displayed and the vendor data base selected (data base A). The current record is saved and NEAR is set on. If F5 was pressed, the order is set to the vendor number and DbEdit performed. If F6 was pressed, the order is set to the vendor name and DbEdit performed. The colors and screen are restored, NEAR is set off, and the procedure returns control to the calling procedure.

LINES 3330–3343 DBEDIT

This procedure uses the BROWSE command inside of a window to permit the user to select a vendor on basis of the vendor's name or number. Note that the enter key (Control M) is set to act as the escape key is pressed (line 3334). This is essential if this procedure is to work. It also calls a UDF DISP inside the FIELD option, which is also necessary for this procedure to operate correctly.

LINES 3344–3352 DISP

This is the UDF called by DbEdit. All it does is return the selected field to the calling procedure (DbEdit). These two procedures operate in a manner similar to Clipper's dbedit function. They are much better than the one supplied by StepIVward, which enables you to convert from other languages to dBASE IV.

LINES 3353–3394 ADC

This procedure changes the Action keys displayed on the bottom of the screen during the changes from Vendor to Insurance to Confidentiality. It bases its display on the action requested by the user and the portion of the screen that is being displayed.

LINES 3395–3475 DRPTS

Although no reports are included in this system (for legal and ethical reasons), the menus and headings for most of the reports are included in the code. You can produce almost any report you can think of using dBASE IV's report generator, a procedure that produced the main report menu (Figure 15-21). This code for a menu is unique in that the prompt of one of the bars changes depending on the value of a memory variable (lines 3431–3434). This is accomplished by using the immediate if function (IIF) after the PROMPT verb. The technique is useful in any situation in which you need a different prompt, depending on the values of various memory variables or data values.

Insurance Compliance System

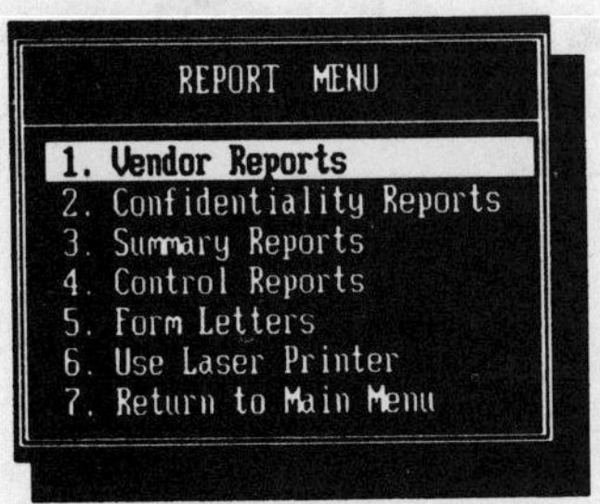

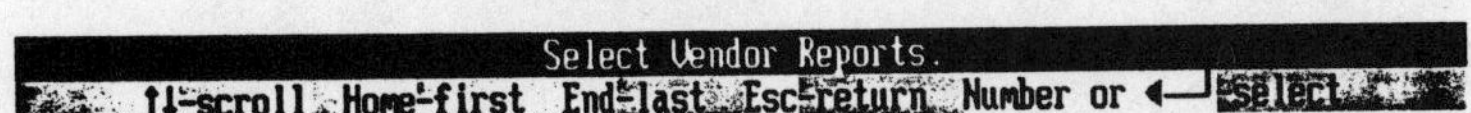

Figure 15-21

LINES 3476–4267 Miscellaneous

The rest of the code displays the various report menus and headers. We will not go into detail at this point because we will do the reports in the next chapter using the built-in report generator of dBASE IV rather than hard-coding them.

CHAPTER 16

Report Generation

Most professional systems contain a large number of reports, and most professional programmers dislike writing reports as they are usually quite mundane and present no programming challenge. Here is where dBASE IV comes to the rescue. By using the ASSIST, QBE, and REPORT writer features of dBASE IV, the time, effort, and drudgery

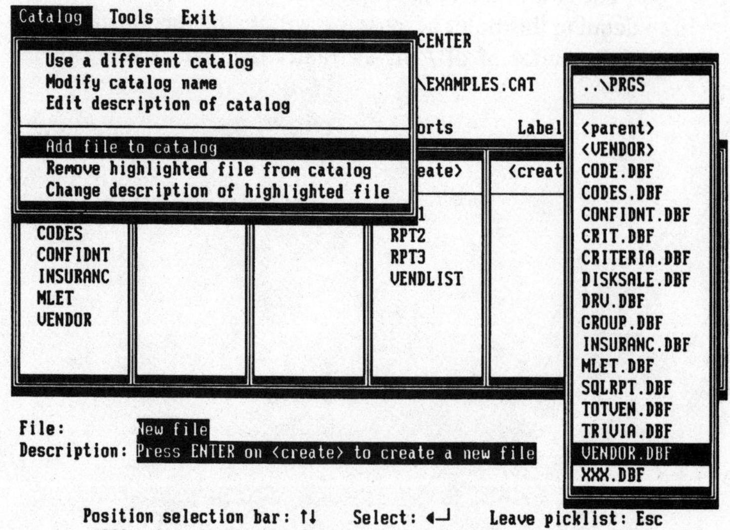

Figure 16-1

of report writing are banished. Most reports are nothing more than simple listings that can be produced quite easily.

Let us say you need a list of all vendors in the system, along with their complete addresses, and telephone numbers. Start dBASE IV by entering DBASE /T ←. Now enter the command ASSIST. The standard assist screen will be seen. Press F10 and select the "Use a different catalog" option. Give the catalog a name (such as Examples) and add the vendor file to the catalog (Figure 16-1). Next make the vendor file active and select Reports (Figure 16-2). The screen shown in Figure 16-3 will appear. Select the Quick layout and Column layout options and screen 16-4 will appear. Since all the fields in the data base will be included in the quick layout, select the fields you do not want and delete them one by one by using the delete key. In Figure 16-4, the VENDNUM field description is highlighted. Pressing the delete key on the keyboard removes it. Continue using the F6 and delete keys to remove fields. By using the F6 and F7 keys, you can move fields around. By pressing enter in the Report Detail band, you can "open" it up and move the second address line to beneath the first. If you do not like the way page numbers are displayed, you can select the page number field "999" on the screen, press F10, and select the Modify field. Next, the Picture function are selected, the Blanks changed for zero values and it is turned ON. Left align is also selected and turned on (Figure 16-5). To obtain a column report with all the columns starting in the same position, each field in the report is selected and the Trim option is changed from ON to OFF (Figure 16-6). By selecting the Box Double option, the title box is added to the report. After testing the report by printing it to the screen, it is saved. The final report is shown on page 492.

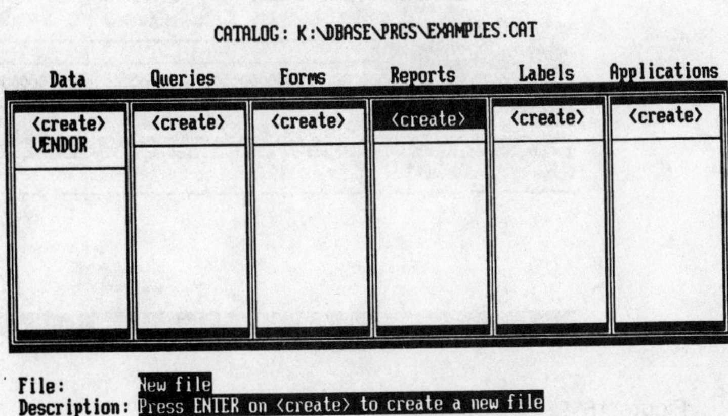

Figure 16-2

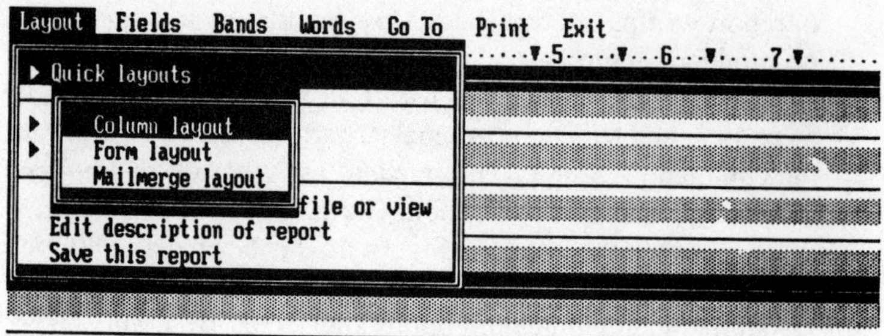


```
Report  K:\dbase\prgs\<NEW>   Band 1/5   File:Vendor   Num
        Position selection bar: ↑↓   Select: ◄┘   Leave menu: Esc
   Place all fields in the current view horizontally across the layout surface
```

Figure 16-3

```
Layout  Fields  Bands  Words  Go To  Print  Exit
[······▼·1·····▼···2···▼·····3·▼·······▼·······▼·5·····▼···6···▼·····7·▼·······
Page      Header  Band

Page No. 999
MM/DD/YY

VENDNUM   VENDNAME                          VENSHORTN   ADDRESS1

Report    Intro   Band
Detail            Band
XXXXXXXX  XXXXXXXXXXXXXXXXXXXXXXXXXXXXXXXXXX XXXXXXXXX XXXXXXXXXXXXXXXXXXXXXXXXX
Report    Summary Band

Page      Footer  Band



Report  K:\dbase\prgs\<NEW>   Line:4 Col:7   File:Vendor   Num   Ins
                    Complete selection with ENTER
```

Figure 16-4

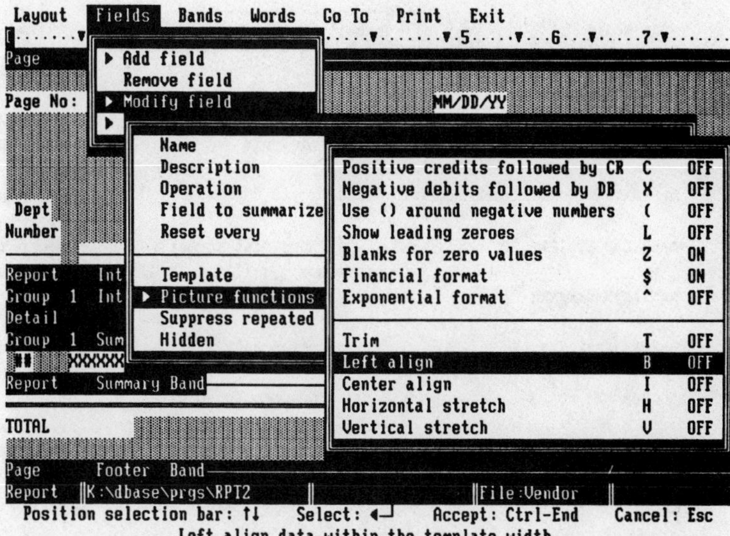

Figure 16-5

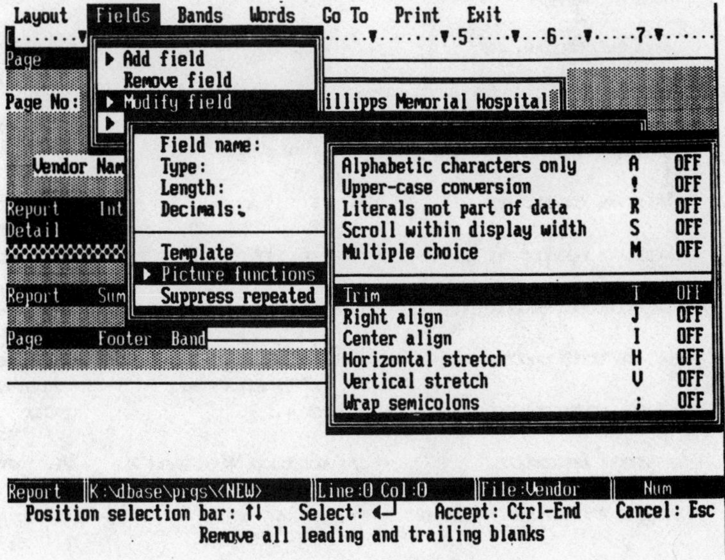

Figure 16-6

Page No: 1	Phillipps Memorial Hospital			09/02/89
Vendor Name	Address	City Telephone	State	Zip
ADVANCED XXXXXXXXX INC	1111 BROADWAY	NEW YORK	NY	10036
ALL-XXXXXXXX XXXXXXXXXXXXXXXX	111 111 AVENUE	NEW YORK (212)555-1111	NY	10017
AMERICAN SOCIETY FOR XXXXXXXXX	FOR INDUSTRIAL SECURITY P O BOX 11111	BALTIMORE (702)555-5555	MD	21274
AXXXXX XXXXXXXXX	CONSUMER PRODUCTS DIV PO BOX 111	NEWARK	NJ	07101-0239
BXX XXXXXXXXXX,INC	111 YORK ROAD	HINSDALE (312)555-5555	IL	60521
BONDED XXX CO	11 RIDGEWOOD AVE WEST AT ROUTE 11	PARAMUS (212)555-5555	NJ	07652
BURXXX XXXXXXX ASSOC INC	11 EXCHANGE PLACE	NEW YORK (212)555-5555	NY	10005
XXXX ACME SYSTEMS XXXXXXXXXXX	111 PATERSON AVENUE	LITTLE FALLS	NJ	07424
CITY XXXXXXXXX	BOX 1111	NEW YORK	NY	10008
COLXXXXXXX XXXXX INC	1 11111 STREET PO BOX 111	E RUTHERFORD (212)555-1111	NJ	07073
CXXXXXX XXXXXXXXXX & CO	111 WEST 11TH ST	NEW YORK	NY	10019
DAVXX ELEXXXXXXXX CORP	111 MAIN ST	HEMPSTEAD (516)555-5555	NY	11550
DIXXXXX INC	P.O. BOX 111	AKRON (216)555-5555	OH	44309
EASTERN XXXXXXXXXX XXXX INC	1-11 11TH AVENUE	LONG ISLAND CITY	NY	11101
EMERXXXXX XXXXXX, INC	111 EAST 11TH ST	NEW YORK (212)555-5555	NY	10016
EXECXXXXX XXXXXXXXXXX INC	11 WEST 1ST STREET	NEW YORK	NY	10010
FIRE XXXXXXXX XXXXXXX INC	11 DEER RUN	EAST ISLIP	NY	11730
FOLIAGE XXXXX XXXXXXX INC	P O BOX 111 111 CHANGE BRIDGE ROAD	PINE BROOK (201)555-5555	NJ	07058
GEORGE XXXXXXXXXXXE	P O BOX 111	BRONX	NY	10471
GRENXXXXX ASSOCXXXXX	C/O XXXXXXXXX MANAGEMENT 111 EAST 111TH STREET	NEW YORK	NY	10017
HERBERT XXXXXXXXXXXXX XXXX INC	11 WEST 11TH STREET	NEW YORK (212)555-5555	NY	10010

Now let us create a more complex report. However, before we go any further, add the rest of the data base files to the catalog by pressing F10 and selecting the add files option (Figure 16-1). For this report, we want a listing of the department codes and department names and a total of the number of vendors assigned to each department, as well as a grand total. This report requires a file we do not have. We need to create a file consisting of the department numbers and codes. First, we need to return to the dot prompt. Select the "Exit to dot prompt" option by pressing F10 and selecting exit. Next

"USE CODES" and "COPY STRUCTURE TO TEMP". and now "USE TEMP" and "APPEND FROM Codes FOR Code = 'Exp'".

We next need to change the CodeType to department numbers. By using the command "REPLACE ALL CodeType WITH LTRIM(STR(RECNO()))", we have number strings in place of "Exp". We then will modify the structure of this file by entering the command "MODIFY STRUCTURE". First change the field name Code to CodeDesc and then the field CodeType to Code. Press Control–End and permit dBASE IV to update the fields. This changes the field type from character to numeric. Now use DOS commands to rename the existing CODES.DBF to CODES.OLD (RUN REN CODES.DBF *.OLD), and rename TEMP to CODES.DBF. Close the data base using the command USE. Rename the file (RUN REN TEMP.DBF CODES.*), and then edit the Vendor data base to change the ExpenseCd field to numeric.

We are ready to create our report. Get back into "ASSIST" and select Queries (Figure 16-7). Now we will create a Query to use as input for our report. Select Layout and add the files Codes and Vendor. Next create a link between Code in the Code data base and ExpenseCd in the Vendor data base. This is done by placing the cursor on the field to be included in the link, pressing F10, and selecting the Create link by pointing option (Figure 16-8). Next we need to sort the Vendor data base by expense code. Place the cursor on the ExpenseCd field of the Vendor data base and press F10. Select the fields option and sort on this field (Figure 16-9). We now need to add fields to the view for the report. We need the ExpenseCd, Code, and CodeDesc fields. Place the cursor on the ExpenseCd field, press F10, and select the Add field to view option. Continue for the Code and CodeDesc fields (Figure 16-10). After you have completed these operations, the screen should look like Figure 16-11. Select exit and save. Select the Reports option from "ASSIST" and quick layout. Remove the Detail band and create a Group Summary band. Place the Expense code and code description in the group band and total on code.

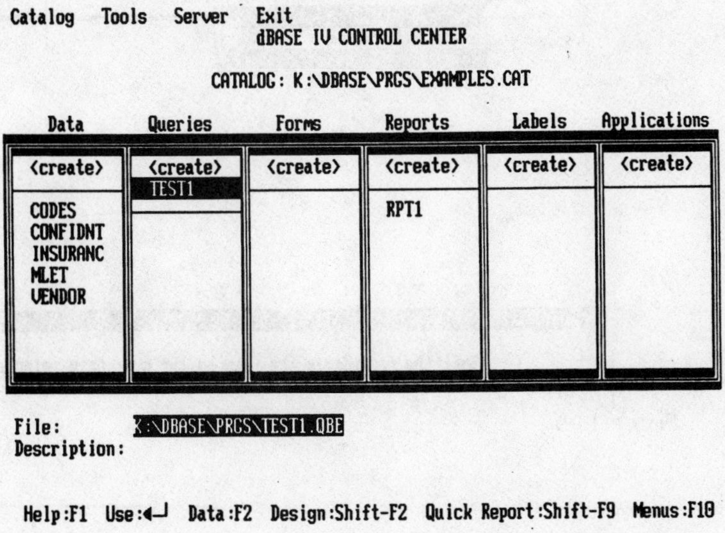

```
Catalog   Tools   Server   Exit
                           dBASE IV CONTROL CENTER

                      CATALOG: K:\DBASE\PRCS\EXAMPLES.CAT

    Data       Queries      Forms      Reports      Labels    Applications
  <create>    <create>    <create>    <create>    <create>    <create>
              TEST1
  CODES                               RPT1
  CONFIDNT
  INSURANC
  MLET
  VENDOR

File:          K:\DBASE\PRCS\TEST1.QBE
Description:

Help:F1  Use:◄┘  Data:F2  Design:Shift-F2  Quick Report:Shift-F9  Menus:F10
```

Figure 16-7

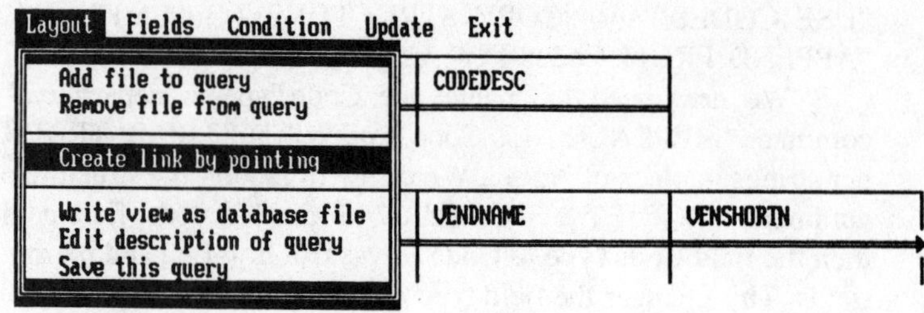

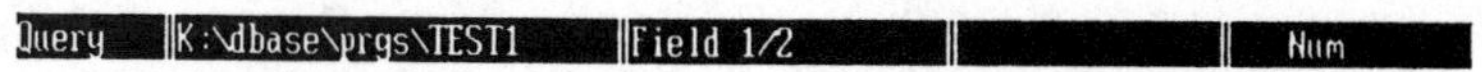

Link the currently selected field to a field in another file skeleton

Figure 16-8

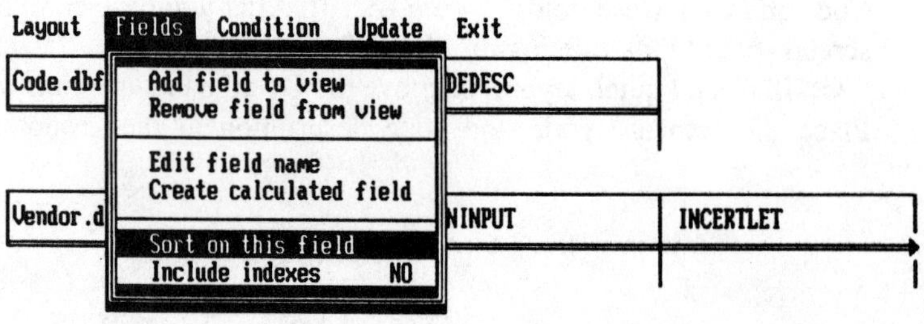

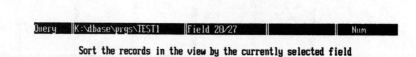

Sort the records in the view by the currently selected field

Figure 16-9

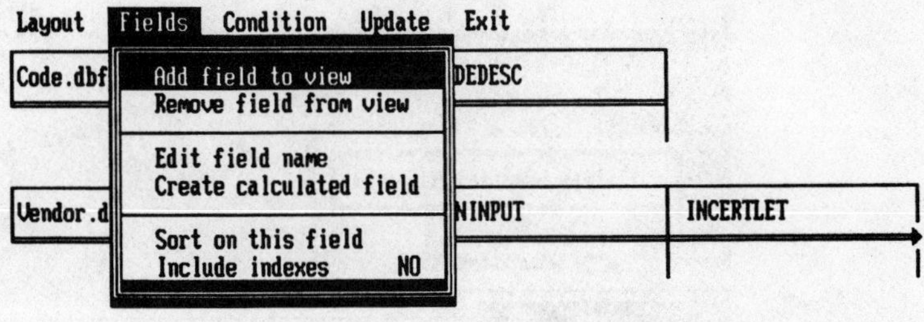

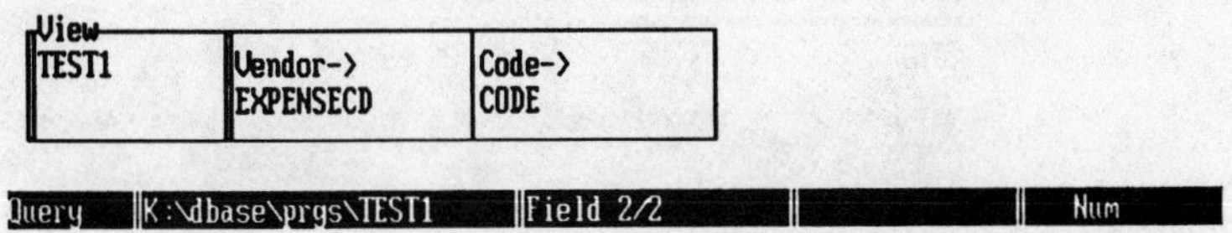

Figure 16-10

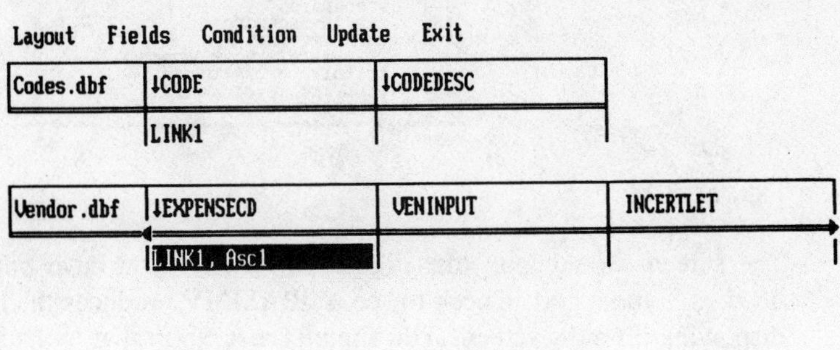

Figure 16-11

```
Layout  Fields  Bands  Words  Go To  Print  Exit
[·······▼·1·····▼···2···▼·····3·▼·······▼·······▼·5·····▼···6···▼·····7·▼·······
Page      Header  Band
Page No: 999                          MM/DD/YY

  Phillipps Memorial Hospital

Dept                                 TOTAL
Number        Department             Vendors

Report   Intro   Band
Group  1  Intro  Band
Detail           Band
Group  1  Summary Band
##   XXXXXXXXXXXXXXXXXXXXXXXXX 9,999
Report   Summary Band

TOTAL                         99,999

Page      Footer  Band
Report  ||K:\dbase\prgs\RPT1     ||Band 1/7        ||View:TEST1    ||   Num   Ins
         Add field:F5  Select:F6  Move:F7  Copy:F8  Size:Shift-F7
```

Figure 16-12

```
Page No: 1                                    08/29/89

          Phillipps Memorial Hospital

 Dept                                          TOTAL
Number            Department                  Vendors

   3     PURCHASING                              6
   4     OFFICE TECHNOLOGY                       2
   8     SECURITY SERVICES                       1
  10     REAL ESTATE MGNT ACCNTNG                1
  11     BUILDING OPERATIONS                    19
  12     REAL ESTATE FINANCE                     4
  15     ADMINISTRATION                          4

TOTAL                                           37
```

Figure 16-13

The screen should look like Figure 16-12 after you have put "nice" field names and headers in the report. Check to see if dBASE IV produces the report you think it will by displaying it on the screen. You should see a report that looks like Figure 16-13. If all is well, save it to RPT1 and exit.

Let us look at what dBASE IV generates in both the QBE and Report sections of "ASSIST".

```
* dBASE IV .QBE file
SET FIELDS TO
SELECT 2
USE CODE.DBF AGAIN NOUPDATE
USE VENDOR.DBF AGAIN NOUPDATE IN 1 ORDER EXPENSECD
SET EXACT ON
SET FILTER TO FOUND(1)
SET RELATION TO B->CODE INTO A
SET SKIP TO A
QBE__SAFE = SET("SAFETY")
```

```
QBE___CATA = SET("CATALOG")
SET SAFETY OFF
SET CATALOG OFF
GO TOP
SET FIELDS TO A->EXPENSECD,B->CODEDESC,B->CODE
QBE___21 = STR(RAND(-1)*100000000,8)
COPY TO &QBE___21
USE &QBE___21 NOSAVE NOUPDATE
IF RECCOUNT() > 1
QBE___22 = STR(RAND(-1)*100000000,8)
SORT TO &QBE___22 ON EXPENSECD/A
USE &QBE___22 NOSAVE NOUPDATE
ENDIF
SET SAFETY &QBE___SAFE
SET CATALOG &QBE___CATA
SET FIELDS TO
SET FIELDS TO EXPENSECD,CODEDESC,CODE
GO TOP

* Program............: D:\DBASE\RPT1.FRG
* Date...............: 8-22-89
* Versions...........: dBASE IV, Report 1
*
* Notes:
* ------
* Prior to running this procedure with the DO command
* it is necessary use LOCATE because the CONTINUE
* statement is in the main loop.
*
*-- Parameters
PARAMETERS gl_noeject, gl_plain, gl_summary, gc_heading, gc_extra
** The first three parameters are of type Logical.
** The fourth parameter is a string.  The fifth is extra.
PRIVATE _peject, _wrap

*-- Test for no records found
IF EOF() .OR. .NOT. FOUND()
   RETURN
ENDIF

*-- turn word wrap mode off
_wrap=.F.

IF _plength < 12
   SET DEVICE TO SCREEN
   DEFINE WINDOW gw_report FROM 7,17 TO 11,62 DOUBLE
```

```
   ACTIVATE WINDOW gw_report
   @ 0,1 SAY "Increase the page length for this report."
   @ 2,1 SAY "Press any key ..."
   x=INKEY(0)
   DEACTIVATE WINDOW gw_report
   RELEASE WINDOW gw_report
   RETURN
ENDIF

_plineno=0          && set lines to zero
*-- NOEJECT parameter
IF gl_noeject
   IF _peject="BEFORE"
      _peject="NONE"
   ENDIF
   IF _peject="BOTH"
      _peject="AFTER"
   ENDIF
ENDIF

*-- Set-up environment
ON ESCAPE DO prnabort
IF SET("TALK")="ON"
   SET TALK OFF
   gc_talk="ON"
ELSE
   gc_talk="OFF"
ENDIF
gc_space=SET("SPACE")
SET SPACE OFF
gc_time=TIME()      && system time for predefined field
gd_date=DATE()      && system date  "     "    "     "
gl_fandl=.F.        && first and last page flag
gl_prntflg=.T.      && Continue printing flag
gl_widow=.T.        && flag for checking widow bands
gn_length=LEN(gc_heading)  && store length of the HEADING
gn_level=2          && current band being processed
gn_page=_pageno     && grab current page number
gn_pspace=_pspacing && get current print spacing

*-- Initialize group footer field variables
r_foot1=.F.
r_foot2=.F.


*-- Set up procedure for page break
```

```
gn_atline=_plength - (_pspacing + 1)
ON PAGE AT LINE gn_atline EJECT PAGE

*-- Print Report

PRINTJOB

*-- Initialize group break vars.
r_mvar4=CODE

*-- Initialize summary variables.
r_msum1=0
r_msum2=0

IF gl_plain
   ON PAGE AT LINE gn_atline DO Pgplain
ELSE
   ON PAGE AT LINE gn_atline DO Pgfoot
ENDIF

DO Pghead

gl_fandl=.T.          && first physical page started

*-- File Loop
DO WHILE FOUND() .AND. .NOT. EOF() .AND. gl_prntflg
   DO CASE
   CASE .NOT. (CODE = r_mvar4)
      gn_level=4
   OTHERWISE
      gn_level=0
   ENDCASE
   *-- test whether an expression didn't match
   IF gn_level <> 0
      DO Grpfoot WITH 100-gn_level
      DO Grpinit
   ENDIF
   DO Upd_Vars
   r_foot1=EXPENSECD
   r_foot2=CODEDESC
   CONTINUE
ENDDO

IF gl_prntflg
   gn_level=3
   DO Grpfoot WITH 97
```

```
      DO Rsumm
      IF _plineno <= gn_atline
         EJECT PAGE
      ENDIF
   ELSE
      gn_level=3
      DO Rsumm
      DO Reset
      RETURN
   ENDIF

   ON PAGE

   ENDPRINTJOB

   DO Reset
   RETURN
   * EOP: D:\DBASE\RPT1.FRG

   *-- Determine height of group bands and detail band for widow checking
   FUNCTION Gheight
   PARAMETER Group_Band
   retval=0                  && return value
   IF Group_Band <= 4
      retval = retval + gn_pspace
   ENDIF
   RETURN retval
   * EOP: Gheight

   *-- Update summary fields and/or calculated fields in the detail band.
   PROCEDURE Upd_Vars
   *-- Count
   r_msum1=r_msum1+1
   *-- Count
   r_msum2=r_msum2+1
   RETURN
   * EOP: Upd_Vars

   *-- Set flag to get out of DO WHILE loop when escape is pressed.
   PROCEDURE prnabort
   gl_prntflg=.F.
   RETURN
   * EOP: prnabort

   *-- Reset group break variables.  Reinit summary
   *-- fields with reset set to a particular group band.
```

```
PROCEDURE Grpinit
IF gn_level <= 4
   r_msum1=0
ENDIF
IF gn_level <= 4
   r_mvar4=CODE
ENDIF
RETURN
* EOP: Grpinit

*-- Process Group Summary bands during group breaks.
PROCEDURE Grpfoot
PARAMETER ln_level
IF ln_level >= 96
   DO Foot96
ENDIF
RETURN
* EOP: Grpfoot.PRG

PROCEDURE Pghead
?
?? IIF(gl_plain,'' , "Page No: " ) AT 0,
?? IIF(gl_plain,'',_pageno) FUNCTION "TB" PICTURE "999" ,
?? IIF(gl_plain,'',gd_date) AT 34
?
?
*-- Print HEADING  REPORT FORM <name> HEADING <expC>
IF .NOT. gl_plain .AND. gn_length > 0
   ?? gc_heading FUNCTION "I;V"+LTRIM(STR(_rmargin-_lmargin))
   ?
ENDIF
DEFINE BOX FROM 4 TO 34 HEIGHT 3 DOUBLE
?
?? " Phillipps Momorial Hospital " AT 5
?
?
?? " Dept" AT 0,
?? "TOTAL" AT 36
?
?? "Number" AT 0,
?? "Department" AT 16,
?? "Vendors" AT 35
?
?? "──────" AT 0,
?? "────────────────────────" AT 8,
?? "───────" AT 34
```

```
?
RETURN
* EOP: Pghead



PROCEDURE Foot96
?? r_foot1 PICTURE "99" AT 0,
?? r_foot2 AT 7,
?? r_msum1 FUNCTION "Z" PICTURE "9,999" AT 34
?
RETURN

PROCEDURE Rsumm
IF SET("PRINT") = "ON" .AND. _ppitch <> "ELITE"
   PRIVATE _ppitch
   _ppitch = "ELITE"
ENDIF
?? "————————————————————————————————————————" AT 0
?
?? "TOTAL          " AT 0,
?? r_msum2 FUNCTION "Z" PICTURE "99,999" AT 33
?
gl_fandl=.F.          && last page finished
?
RETURN
* EOP: Rsumm

PROCEDURE Pgfoot
PRIVATE _box, _pspacing
gl_widow=.F.          && disable widow checking
_pspacing=1
?
IF .NOT. gl_plain
ENDIF
EJECT PAGE
*-- is the page number greater than the ending page
IF _pageno > _pepage
   GOTO BOTTOM
   SKIP
   gn_level=0
ENDIF
IF .NOT. gl_plain .AND. gl_fandl
   _pspacing=gn_pspace
   DO Pghead
```

```
ENDIF
gl_widow=.T.          && enable widow checking
RETURN
* EOP: Pgfoot

*-- Process page break when PLAIN option is used.
PROCEDURE Pgplain
PRIVATE _box
EJECT PAGE
RETURN
* EOP: Pgplain
*-- Reset dBASE environment prior to calling report
PROCEDURE Reset
SET SPACE &gc_space.
SET TALK &gc_talk.
ON ESCAPE
ON PAGE
RETURN
* EOP: Reset
```

Although the code produced is good, we cannot use it directly in a program. Changing both files and incorporating them into a program to print report 1 produces the following:

```
*
*  Program.: RPT1
*  Author..: Phil Steele - President Phillipps Computer Systems Inc.
*  Address.: 52 Hook Mountain Road,  Montville NJ 07045
*  Phone...: (201) 575-8575
*  Date....: 01/02/90
*  Notice..: Copyright 1990  Philip Steele, All Rights Reserved
*  Version.: dBASE IV   Rel 1.1
*  Notes...: An example showing how to turn a QBE and report .FRG
*            into code which you can put into your applications
*
*
*_________________
* STANDARD PREAMBLE
*_________________
SET STEP OFF
SET ECHO OFF
SET TALK OFF
SET BELL OFF
SET PRINT   OFF
SET DELETE  ON
SET STATUS  OFF
SET SAFETY  OFF
SET ESCAPE  OFF
```

```
SET CONFIRM ON
SET HEADING OFF
SET SCOREBOARD OFF
SET DISPLAY TO EGA25
SET DEVICE  TO SCREEN
SET CURSOR OFF

SET COLOR TO W+/B
CLEAR
@ 12,19 SAY "P R I N T I N G   -   P L E A S E   W A I T"

*____________________________________________________________
* This next section is the QBE generated file - cleaned up
*____________________________________________________________
* Reset fields to ALL
SET FIELDS TO

* Make sure there is a corresponding record in area 1 for
* each occurrence in area 2 and set the relationship
SELECT 2
USE CODE.DBF AGAIN
USE VENDOR.DBF AGAIN IN 1 ORDER EXPENSECD
SET EXACT ON
SET FILTER TO FOUND(1)
SET RELATION TO B->CODE INTO A
SET SKIP TO A

* Housekeeping
QBE___SAFE = SET("SAFETY")
QBE___CATA = SET("CATALOG")
SET SAFETY  OFF
SET CATALOG OFF

* Save records to a temporary file
GO TOP
SET FIELDS TO A->EXPENSECD, B->CODEDESC, B->CODE
QBE___21 = STR(RAND(-1)*100000000,8)
COPY TO &QBE___21

* Use the temporary file and sort as requested
USE &QBE___21 NOSAVE NOUPDATE
IF RECCOUNT() > 1
   QBE___22 = STR(RAND(-1)*100000000,8)
   SORT TO &QBE___22 ON EXPENSECD/A
   USE &QBE___22 NOSAVE NOUPDATE
ENDIF
```

```
* Restore environment
SET SAFETY  &QBE___SAFE
SET CATALOG &QBE___CATA

* Select fields to use.
SET FIELDS TO
SET FIELDS TO EXPENSECD, CODEDESC, CODE
GO TOP
*END:QBE PORTION
*_______________


*______________
* Code I added
*______________
* Prior to running the report generator code it is necessary use
* LOCATE because of the CONTINUE statement in the main loop.
LOCATE FOR RECNO() <= RECCOUNT()
SET DEVICE TO PRINT           && Turn on the printer
SET PRINT   ON
SET CONSOLE OFF               && Turn off the screen
DO MainRpt WITH .T., .T., .T., " ", " "
SET DEVICE TO SCREEN          && Turn the screen back on
SET PRINT   OFF
SET CONSOLE ON                && Now really turn it on
SET CURSOR  ON
CLEAR
RETURN                        && Return to the calling code
*END:MYCODE
*__________


*________________
PROCEDURE MAINRPT
*________________
PARAMETERS gl_noeject, gl_plain, gl_summary, gc_heading, gc_extra
** The first three parameters are of type Logical.
** The fourth parameter is a string.  The fifth is extra.

PRIVATE _peject, _wrap
IF EOF() .OR. .NOT. FOUND()  && Test for no records found
   RETURN
ENDIF

_wrap = .F.                   && turn word wrap mode off
IF _plength < 12              && Increase page length if necessary (<12)
```

```
      SET DEVICE TO SCREEN
      DEFINE   WINDOW gw_report FROM 7,17 TO 11,62 DOUBLE
      ACTIVATE WINDOW gw_report
      @ 0,1 SAY "Increase the page length for this report."
      @ 2,1 SAY "Press any key ..."
      x = INKEY(0)
      DEACTIVATE WINDOW gw_report
      RELEASE    WINDOW gw_report
      RETURN
   ENDIF

   _plineno = 0                     && set lines to zero
   IF gl_noeject                    && NOEJECT parameter
      IF _peject = "BEFORE"         && Set to BEFORE, AFTER or NONE
         _peject = "NONE"
      ENDIF
      IF _peject = "BOTH"
         _peject = "AFTER"
      ENDIF
   ENDIF

   ON ESCAPE DO prnabort            && Set-up environment
   IF SET("TALK") = "ON"
      SET TALK OFF
      gc_talk = "ON"
   ELSE
      gc_talk = "OFF"
   ENDIF
   gc_space   = SET("SPACE")
   SET SPACE OFF
   gc_time    = TIME()              && System time for predefined field
   gd_date    = DATE()              && System date for predefined field
   gl_fandl   = .F.                 && First and last page flag
   gl_prntflg = .T.                 && Continue printing flag
   gl_widow   = .T.                 && Flag for checking widow bands
   gn_length  = LEN(gc_heading) && Store length of the HEADING
   gn_level   = 2                   && Current band being processed
   gn_page    = _pageno             && Grab current page number
   gn_pspace  = _pspacing           && Get current print spacing
   r_foot1    = .F.                 && Initialize group footer field variables
   r_foot2    = .F.

   *-- Set up procedure for page break
   gn_atline = _plength - (_pspacing + 1)
   ON PAGE AT LINE gn_atline EJECT PAGE
```

```
PRINTJOB                      && Start print job


   r_mvar4 = CODE             && Initialize group break vars.
   r_msum1 = 0                && Initialize summary variables.
   r_msum2 = 0
   IF gl_plain
      ON PAGE AT LINE gn_atline DO PgPlain
   ELSE
      ON PAGE AT LINE gn_atline DO PgFoot
   ENDIF
   DO PgHead
   gl_fandl = .T.             && First physical page started

   * MAIN LOOP FOR REPORTS *
   DO WHILE FOUND() .AND. .NOT. EOF() .AND. gl_prntflg
      IF .NOT. (CODE = r_mvar4)
         gn_level = 4
      ELSE
         gn_level = 0
      ENDIF
      IF gn_level <> 0        && test whether an expression didn't match
         DO GrpFoot WITH 100-gn_level
         DO GrpInit
      ENDIF
      DO Upd_Vars
      r_foot1 = EXPENSECD
      r_foot2 = CODEDESC
      CONTINUE                && Get next record
   ENDDO

   IF gl_prntflg
      gn_level = 3
      DO GrpFoot WITH 97
      DO RSumm
      IF _plineno <= gn_atline
         EJECT PAGE
      ENDIF
   ELSE
      gn_level = 3
      DO RSumm
      DO Reset
      RETURN
   ENDIF

   ON PAGE
ENDPRINTJOB
```

```
DO Reset
RETURN
*END:MAINRPT
*___________
*_______________
FUNCTION GHEIGHT
*_______________
PARAMETER Group_Band
*-- Determine height of group bands and detail band for widow checking
RetVal = 0                    && return value
IF Group_Band <= 4
   RetVal = RetVal + gn_pspace
ENDIF
RETURN retval
*END:GHEIGHT
*___________


*________________
PROCEDURE UPD_VARS
*________________
*-- Update summary fields and/or calculated fields in the detail band.
r_msum1 = r_msum1 + 1
r_msum2 = r_msum2 + 1
RETURN
*END:UPD_VARS
*___________


*________________
PROCEDURE PRNABORT
*________________
*-- Set flag to get out of DO WHILE loop when escape is pressed.
gl_prntflg = .F.
RETURN
*END:PRNABORT
*___________


*_______________
PROCEDURE GRPINIT
*_______________
*-- Reset group break variables.  Reinit summary
*-- fields with reset set to a particular group band.
IF gn_level <= 4
   r_msum1 = 0
```

```
   r_mvar4 = CODE
ENDIF
RETURN
*END:GRPINIT
*____________


*________________
PROCEDURE GRPFOOT
*________________
*-- Process Group Summary bands during group breaks
PARAMETER ln_level
IF ln_level >= 96
   DO Foot96
ENDIF
RETURN
*END:GRPFOOT
*____________


*________________
PROCEDURE PGHEAD
*________________
?
?? IIF(gl_plain, '', "Page No: " ) AT 0,
?? IIF(gl_plain, '', _pageno) FUNCTION "TB" PICTURE "999" ,
?? IIF(gl_plain, '', gd_date) AT 34
?
?
*-- Print HEADING parameter ie. REPORT FORM <name> HEADING <expC>
IF .NOT. gl_plain .AND. gn_length > 0
   ?? gc_heading FUNCTION "I;V" + LTRIM(STR(_rmargin-_lmargin))
   ?
ENDIF
DEFINE BOX FROM 4 TO 34 HEIGHT 3 DOUBLE
?
?? " Phillipps Memorial Hospital " AT 5
?
?
?? " Dept" AT 0, .
?? "TOTAL" AT 36
?
?? "Number" AT 0,
?? "Department" AT 16,
?? "Vendors" AT 35
?
```

```
?? "————" AT 0,
?? "——————————————————————" AT 8,
?? "——————" AT 34
?
RETURN
*END:PGHEAD
*————————


*——————————
PROCEDURE FOOT96
*——————————
?? r_foot1 PICTURE "99" AT 0,
?? r_foot2 AT 7,
?? r_msum1 FUNCTION "Z" PICTURE "9,999" AT 34
?
RETURN
*END:FOOT96
*————————


*——————————
PROCEDURE RSUMM
*——————————
IF SET("PRINT") = "ON" .AND. _ppitch <> "ELITE"
   PRIVATE _ppitch
   _ppitch = "ELITE"
ENDIF

?? "══════════════════════════════════════" AT 0
?
?? "TOTAL            " AT 0,
?? r_msum2 FUNCTION "Z" PICTURE "99,999" AT 33
?
gl_fandl = .F.                  && last page finished
?
RETURN
*END:RSUMM
*————————


*——————————
PROCEDURE PGFOOT
*——————————
PRIVATE _box, _pspacing
gl_widow = .F.                  && disable widow checking
```

```
_pspacing = 1
?
EJECT PAGE
IF _pageno > _pepage              && is the page number greater
  GOTO BOTTOM                     && than the ending page
  SKIP
  gn_level = 0
ENDIF
IF .NOT. gl_plain .AND. gl_fandl
  _pspacing = gn_pspace
  DO PgHead
ENDIF
gl_widow = .T.                    && enable widow checking
RETURN
*END:PGFOOT
*__________


*_______________
PROCEDURE PGPLAIN
*_______________
*-- Process page break when PLAIN option is used.
PRIVATE _box
EJECT PAGE
RETURN
*END:PGPLAIN
*__________


*_____________
PROCEDURE RESET
*_____________
*-- Reset dBASE environment prior to calling report
SET SPACE &gc_space.
SET TALK &gc_talk.
ON ESCAPE
ON PAGE
RETURN
*END:RESET
```

The QBE generated by dBASE IV does not indent any code, which makes reading very difficult. It also uses many underlines for field names, also making reading difficult. In this example, most of the code produced by the dBASE IV QBE generator was used, but was indented to make it easier to read. Let us look at this code. First, the usual information block was added at the start, as well as a preamble. If this code were to be part of a larger system, these sections would be omitted. Next, a "Main Program" was needed to call the QBE and Report writer code. After writing three lines of code, the QBE-generated code was placed after them. Comments were then added to the code to make it easier to understand. Next, a dozen lines were included to use the report-generated code and return to the calling procedure. By adding a locate-all statement "LOCATE FOR RECNO() <- RECCOUNT()," the entire data base would be used. The printer was turned on, but no check was made to see whether it was ready. This code could be added from the main portion of the system code with a simple call to the TESTPRNT function at line 769. The screen then was turned off using the "SET CONSOLE OFF" statement. This prevents distracting displays from appearing on the screen while the report is printing, and you can add a progress bar graph and not have to worry about print appearing on the screen. Of course, you would have to turn the screen on and printer off to use it. Next, "DO" the generated code "DO MainRpt", passing three trues and two blanks to the generated code as required. After control is returned to the user, the printer is set to off and the screen to on. The console and cursor are reset, the screen is cleared, and you return to the calling procedure. The main report program is basically unchanged from the generated code, except for some formatting to make it easier to read. As you can see, dBASE IV does a good job of producing a fairly complex report.

Our final example of report generation will be to produce the same report using QBE that was produced in the SQL section using SQL. This report will be of the total insurance in effect by department, with a count of the total number of vendors in each department. In other words, it is the previous report updated to include the total insurance in effect. The last report looks like this:

```
Page No: 1                                 09/02/89

              Phillipps Memorial Hospital

Dept                                        TOTAL
Number          Department                 Vendors
------   ----------------------------     --------
  3    PURCHASING                              6
  4    OFFICE TECHNOLOGY                       2
  8    SECURITY SERVICES                       1
 10    REAL ESTATE MGNT ACCNTNG                1
 11    BUILDING OPERATIONS                    19
 12    REAL ESTATE FINANCE                     4
 15    ADMINISTRATION                          4
==================================================
TOTAL                                         37
```

The next report should look like this:

Page No: 1 09/02/89

Phillipps Memorial Hospital

Dept Number	Department	Total Ins in effect	TOTAL Vendors
3	PURCHASING	$X,XXX	6
4	OFFICE TECHNOLOGY	$X,XXX	2
8	SECURITY SERVICES	$X,XXX	1
10	REAL ESTATE MGNT ACCNTNG	$X,XXX	1
11	BUILDING OPERATIONS	$X,XXX	19
12	REAL ESTATE FINANCE	$X,XXX	4
15	ADMINISTRATION	$X,XXX	4
TOTAL		$184,583	37

To produce this report, we will copy Test1.QBE to Test2.QBE and RPT1.FRG to RPT2.FRG using the DOS COPY command. Next we bring up dBASE IV and, using "ASSIST," we select TEST2 from the Query choices and modify the QBE. Add a new file "Insuranc" and add a link between VendNum of Vendor and VendNum in Insuranc. Add the Amount field from the Insuranc data base to the View and save the changes. Select the report writer RPT2 and modify the report to include the amount field. When you are finished, you should have created the following report:

Page No: 1 09/02/89

Phillipps Memorial Hospital

Dept Number	Department	Total Ins in effect	TOTAL Vendors
3	PURCHASING	$9,000	6
4	OFFICE TECHNOLOGY	$5,739	2
8	SECURITY SERVICES	$19,500	1
10	REAL ESTATE MGNT ACCNTNG	$5,000	1
11	BUILDING OPERATIONS	$132,344	19
12	REAL ESTATE FINANCE	$9,000	4
15	ADMINISTRATION	$4,000	4
TOTAL		$184,583	37

Summary

You have seen how a complex professional system is developed and coded in dBASE IV using a series of user-defined functions (UDFs) and general-purpose routines that are coded and tested and then modified slightly to fit the current problem. You have also seen how to use SQL for various complex relationships and reporting needs. And you have learned how to save time and to produce usable programs incorporating automatically generated code by utilizing various aspects of the "ASSIST" feature of dBASE IV.

Most important of all, you now have a complete reference book incorporating all the COMMANDS, FUNCTIONS, SET COMMANDS, SQL COMMANDS, and SYSTEM MEMORY VARIABLES available in dBASE IV release 1.1.

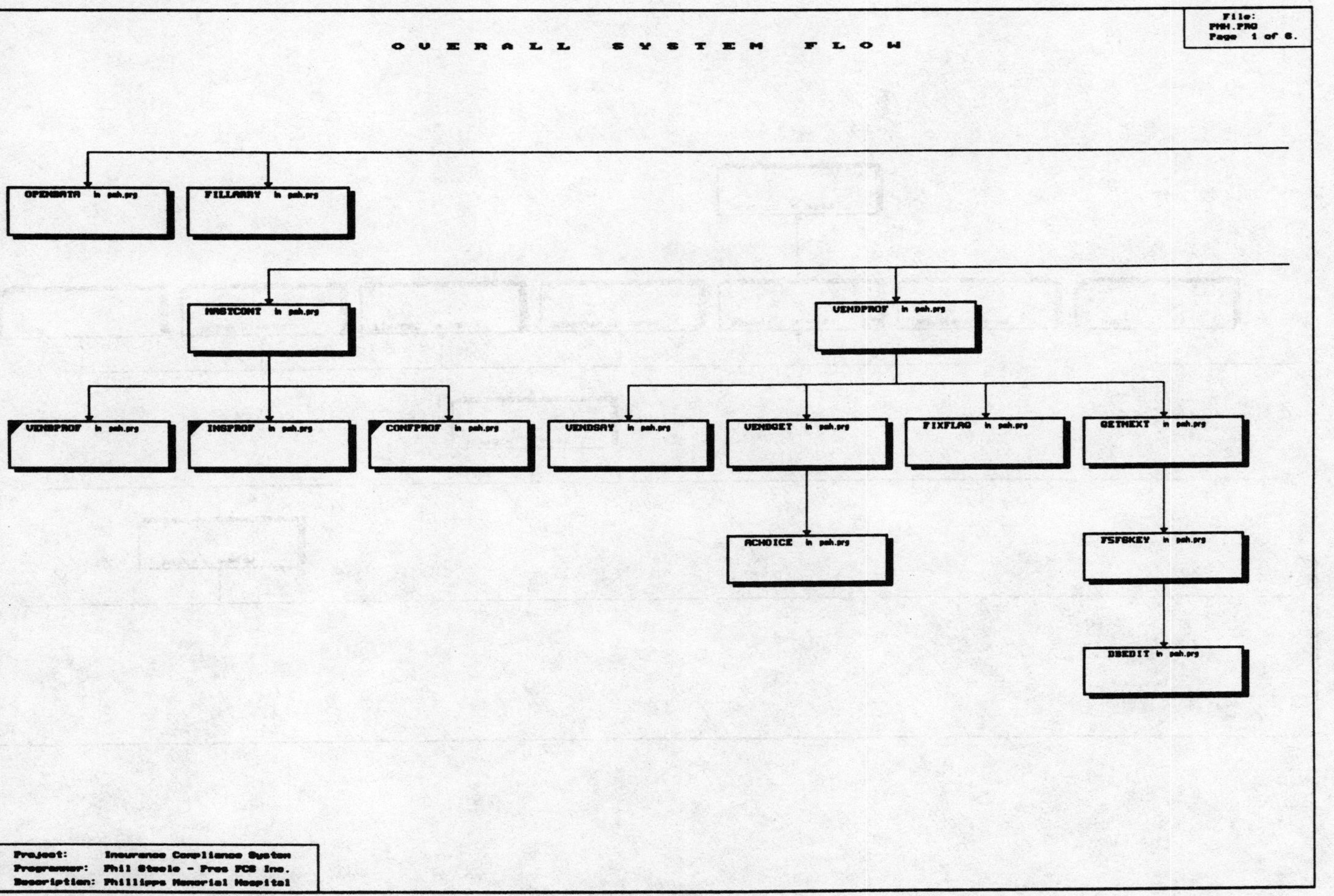

OVERALL SYSTEM FLOW
File:
PHM.PRO
Page 1 of 6.
OPENDATA in pah.prg
FILLARRY in pah.prg
MASTCONT in pah.prg
VENDPROF in pah.prg
VENDPROF in pah.prg
INSPROF in pah.prg
CONFPROF in pah.prg
VENDSAV in pah.prg
VENDGET in pah.prg
FIXFLAG in pah.prg
GETNEXT in pah.prg
ACHOICE in pah.prg
F5F6KEY in pah.prg
DBEDIT in pah.prg
Project: Insurance Compliance System
Programmer: Phil Steele - Pros PCS Inc.
Description: Phillips Memorial Hospital

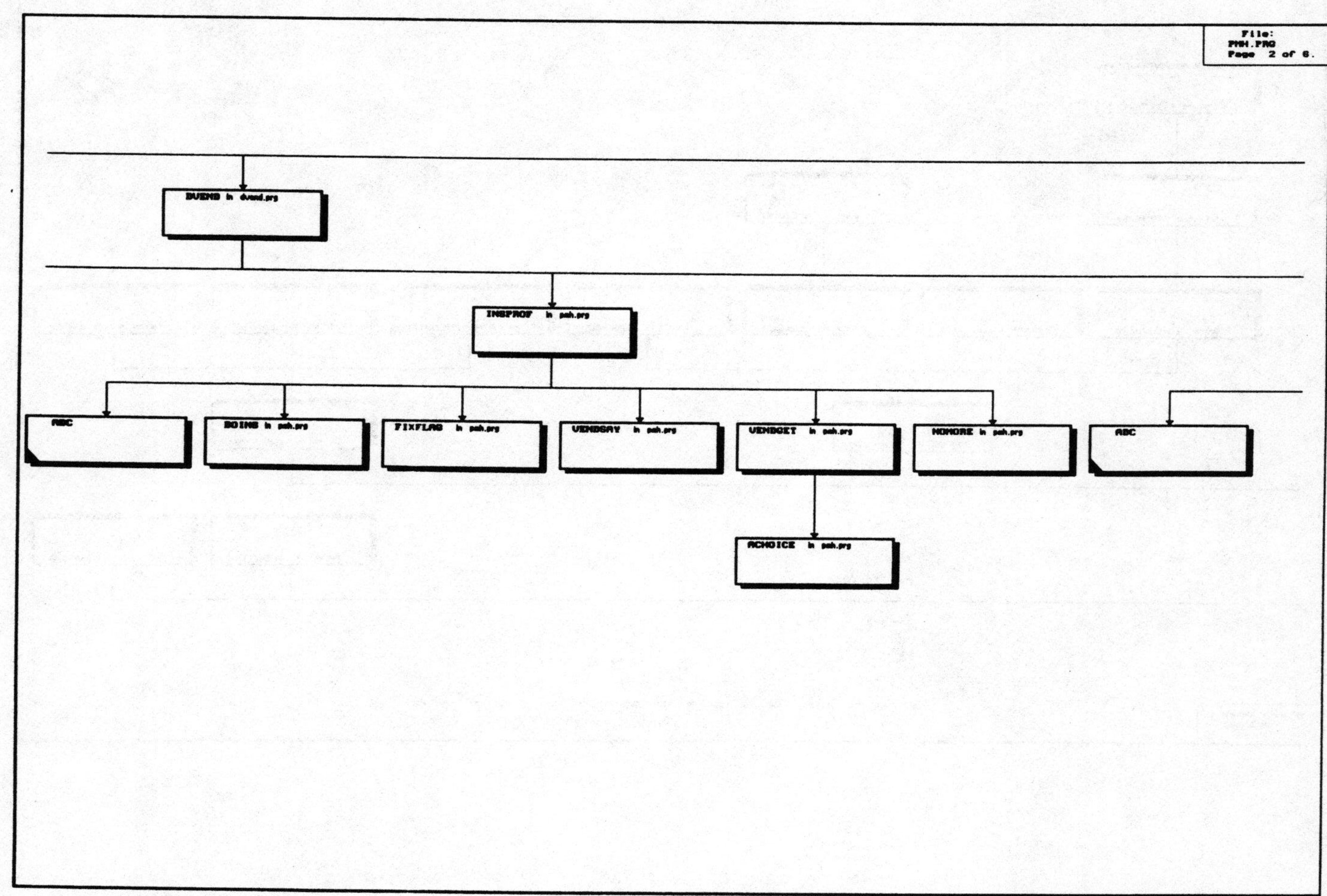
File:
PMH.PRG
Page 2 of 6.
DVEND in dvend.prg
INSPROF in pah.prg
ABC
BOINS in pah.prg
FIXFLAG in pah.prg
VENDSAY in pah.prg
VENDGET in pah.prg
NOMORE in pah.prg
ABC
ACHOICE in pah.prg

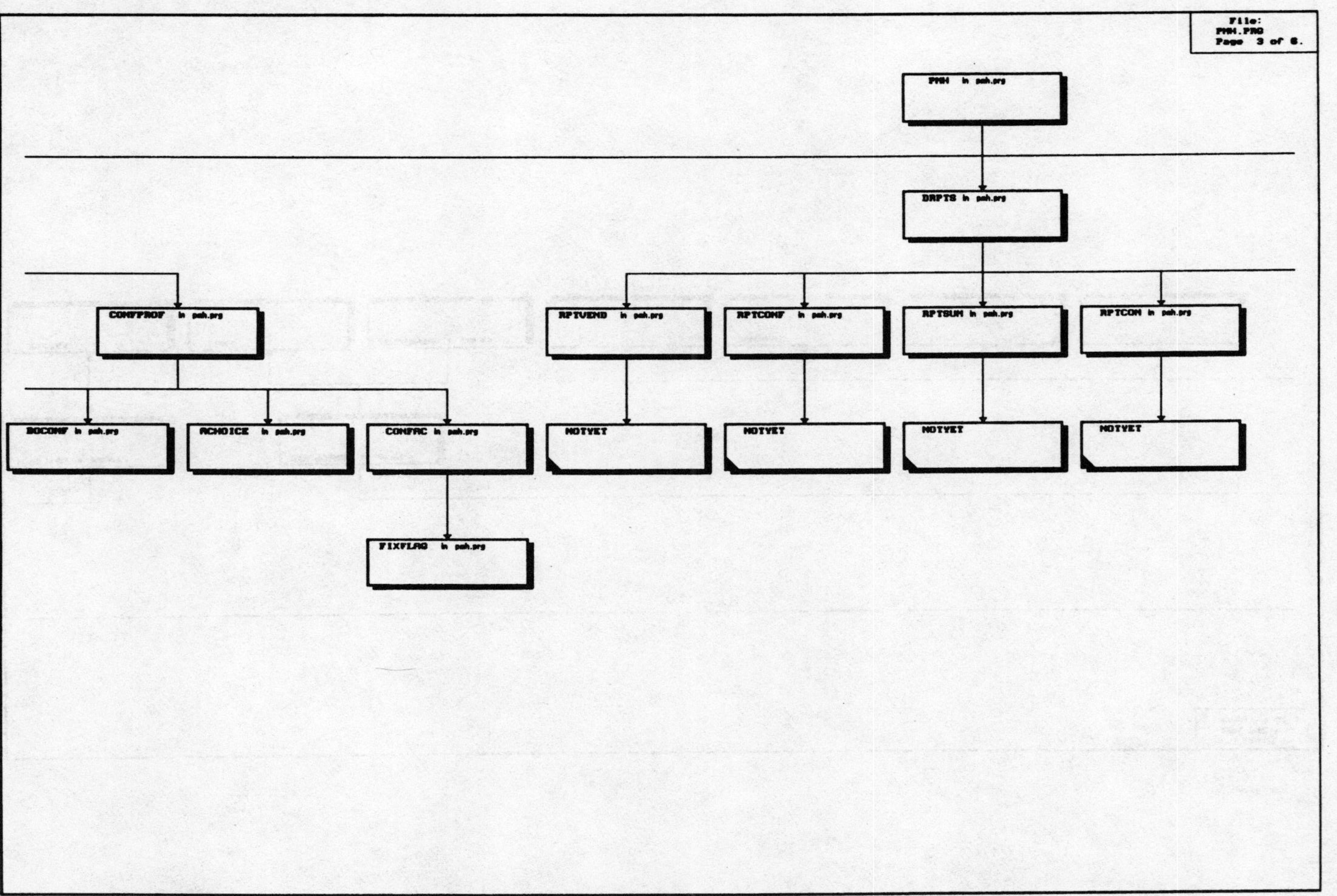
File:
PMH.PRG
Page 3 of 6.
PMH in pmh.prg
DRPTS in pmh.prg
CONFPROF in pmh.prg
RPTVEND in pmh.prg
RPTCONF in pmh.prg
RPTSUM in pmh.prg
RPTCON in pmh.prg
BOCONF in pmh.prg
ACHOICE in pmh.prg
CONFRC in pmh.prg
NOTYET
NOTYET
NOTYET
NOTYET
FIXFLAG in pmh.prg

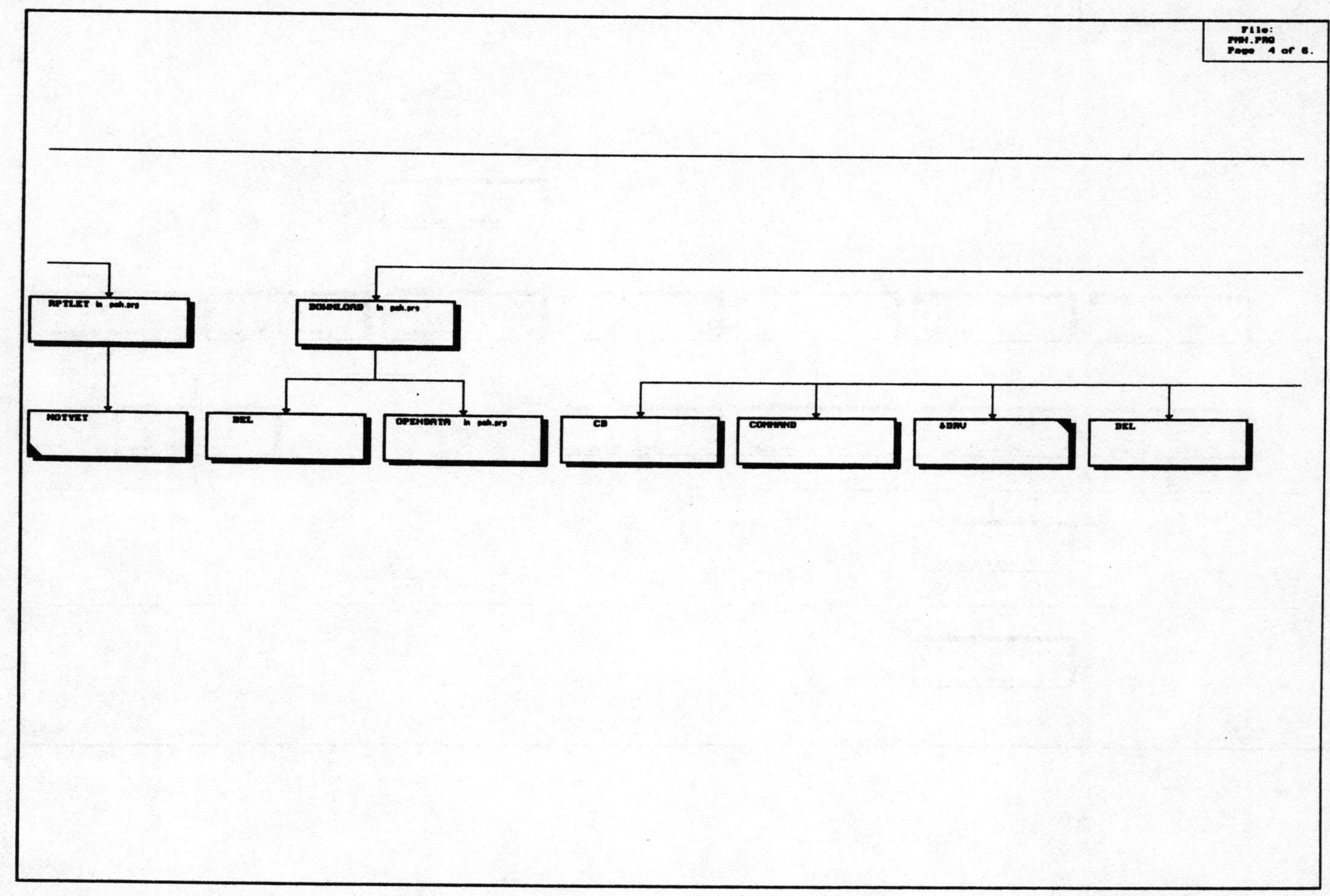
File:
PMM.PRG
Page 4 of 6.
RPTLET in pah.prg
DOWNLOAD in pah.prg
NOTYET
DEL
OPENDATA in pah.prg
CD
COMMAND
&DRV
DEL

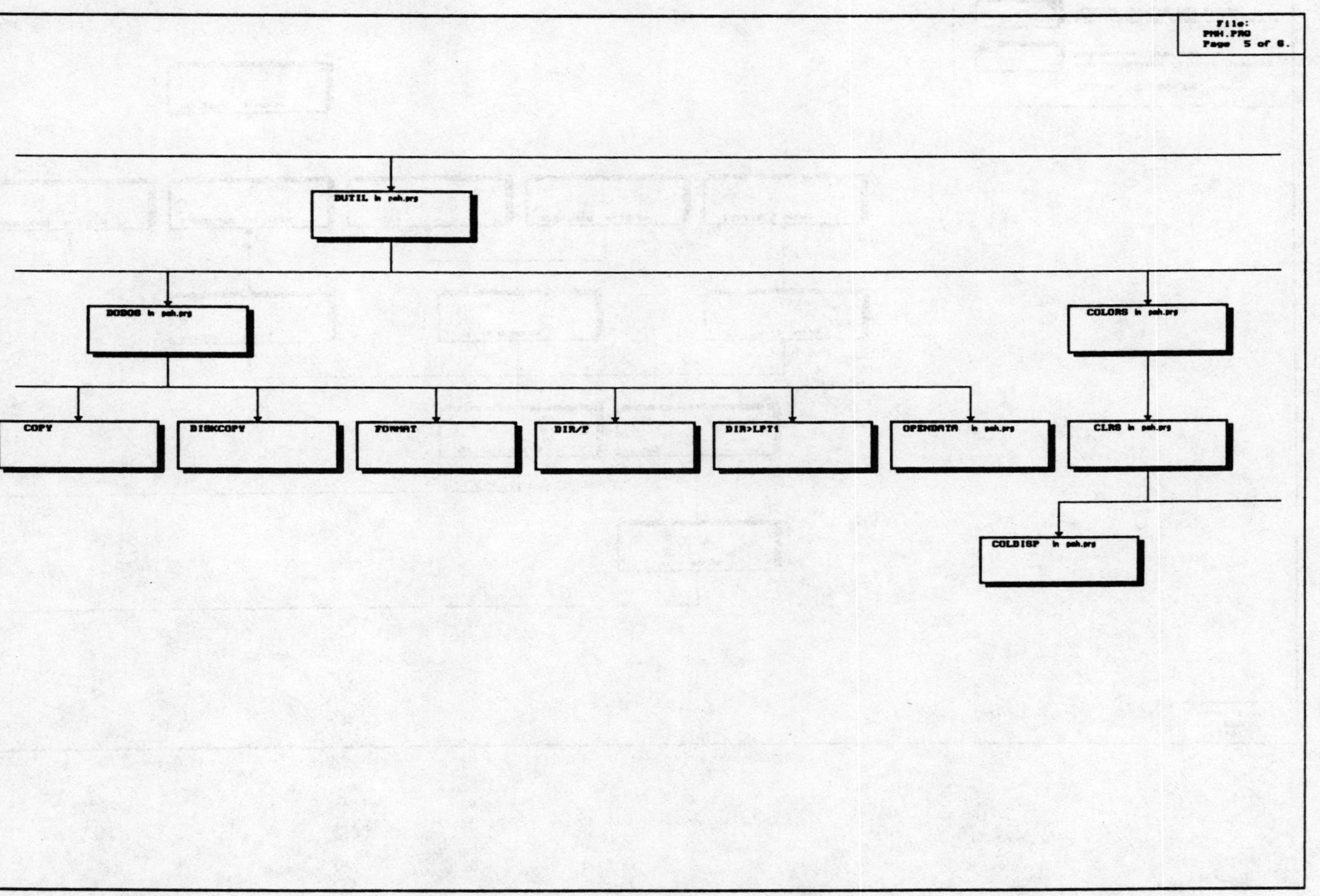
File:
PMH.PRG
Page 5 of 6.
BUTIL in pmh.prg
DOSOS in pmh.prg
COLORS in pmh.prg
COPY
DISKCOPY
FORMAT
DIR/P
DIR>LPT1
OPENDATA in pmh.prg
CLRS in pmh.prg
COLDISP in pmh.prg

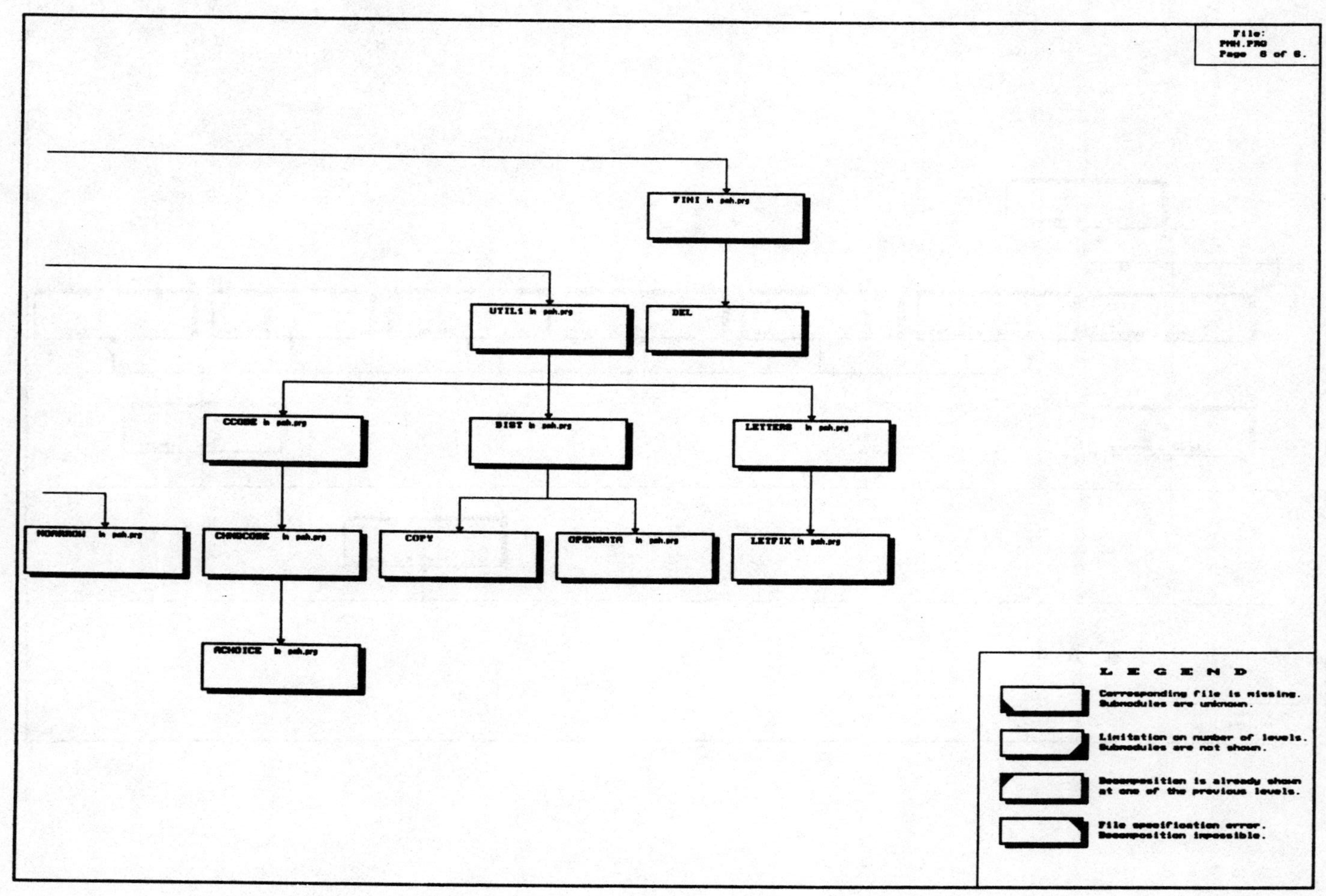
File:
PMH.PRG
Page 8 of 8.
FINI in pmh.prg
UTIL1 in pmh.prg
DEL
CCODE in pmh.prg
DIST in pmh.prg
LETTERS in pmh.prg
NOARROW in pmh.prg
CHNGCODE in pmh.prg
COPY
OPENDATA in pmh.prg
LETFIX in pmh.prg
ACHOICE in pmh.prg
L E G E N D
Corresponding file is missing.
Submodules are unknown.
Limitation on number of levels.
Submodules are not shown.
Decomposition is already shown
at one of the previous levels.
File specification error.
Decomposition impossible.

Index

E

F

T

U

Send all orders to:

Phillipps Computer Systems Inc.
52 Hook Mountain Road
Montville, New Jersey 07045
Attn: Book division

....

Please send me ______ copies of dBASE IV Code
Please send me ______ copies of dBASE IV SQL Code
I am enclosing a check or money order for $49.95 each copy or $80.00 for both. (Shipping & handling *IS* included). Outside of North America—Add $2.00 to offset postage costs.
Enclosed is $____________
Please charge my credit card number (Visa or Mastercard):

____

Expiration date ____________
Signature (Order invalid unless signed):

____

Name (please print): ______________________________
Title: ______________________________________
Company: ___________________________________
Address: ____________________________________
____
City: ______________________ State: _____ Zip:_____

U.S. dollars only accepted.
Prices and terms subject to change without notice.